# THE BIBLE AND THE LATTER-DAY SAINT TRADITION

# The Bible and the Latter-day Saint Tradition

*edited by*
TAYLOR G. PETREY, CORY CRAWFORD,
AND ERIC A. ELIASON

The University of Utah Press | Salt Lake City

The Defiance House Man colophon is a registered trademark of the University of Utah Press. It is based on a four-foot-tall Ancient Puebloan pictograph (late PIII) near Glen Canyon, Utah.

Library of Congress Cataloging-in-Publication Data
Names: Petrey, Taylor G., editor. | Crawford, Cory, editor. | Eliason, Eric A., editor.
Title: The Bible and the Latter-day Saint Tradition / Taylor G. Petrey, Cory Crawford, Eric A. Eliason.
Description: Salt Lake City : University of Utah Press, [2023] | Includes bibliographical references and index.
Identifiers: LCCN 2022950979 | ISBN 9781647690977 (hardback) | ISBN 9781647690984 (paperback) | ISBN 9781647690991 (ebk)
LC record available at https://lccn.loc.gov/2022950979

Errata and further information on this and other titles available online at UofUpress.com

Printed and bound in the United States of America.

## CONTENTS

## PART III. A VARIETY OF CRITICAL BIBLICAL APPROACHES AND THEIR RELEVANCE TO MORMON STUDIES



## PART IV. INHERITANCE AND DIVERGENCE: LATTER-DAY SAINTS READ OTHERS READING THE BIBLE



## PART V. LATTER-DAY SAINT APPROACHES TO THE BIBLE'S MAJOR GENRES AND DIVISIONS

# Introduction

# Latter-day Saints and Biblical Scholarship

TAYLOR G. PETREY

Latter-day Saints have a complex relationship with the Bible and with biblical scholarship.[1] They are interpreters of the Bible, but also emerged during a particular historical moment that produced critical approaches to the Bible. In this way, Latter-day Saints have developed their tradition in the context of both a biblical culture and biblical criticism's impact on that culture.[2] The roots of Mormonism are inseparable from biblical influence, but also represent a distinctive relationship to biblical authority. According to his 1838 account of the First Vision, during the Second Great Awakening, Joseph Smith Jr. (1805–1844) was seeking for answers about which church he should join when he came across a passage in the New Testament Epistle of James: "If any of you lack wisdom, let him ask of God" (1:5, KJV). This inspired him to take his question to prayer and receive an answer that launched his prophetic career. This foundational narrative curiously mixes the authority of the Bible with divine visions and revelations and eventually led to newly revealed scripture. His subsequent experiences, revelations, and translations both relativize biblical

1. Philip L. Barlow, *Mormons and the Bible: The Place of Latter-day Saints in American Religion* (New York: Oxford University Press, 1991, 2013); Laurie Maffly-Kipp, "Mormons and the Bible," in *The Oxford Handbook of Mormonism*, edited by Terryl Givens and Philip Barlow (New York: Oxford University Press, 2015), 121–33; David Holland, "The Bible and Mormonism," in *The Oxford Handbook of the Bible in America*, edited by Paul C. Gutjahr (New York: Oxford University Press, 2017), 611–26. See also, David Rolph Seely, "'We Believe the Bible to Be the Word of God as Far as It Is Translated Correctly': Latter-day Saints and Historical Biblical Criticism," *Studies in the Bible and Antiquity* 8 (2016): 64–88.

2. Seth Perry, *Bible Culture and Authority in the Early United States* (Princeton, NJ: Princeton University Press, 2018); Robert N. Hullinger, *Joseph Smith's Response to Skepticism* (Salt Lake City, UT: Signature Books, 1980, 1992), 121–65; Samuel M. Brown, *Joseph Smith's Translations: The Words and Worlds of Early Mormonism* (New York: Oxford University Press, 2020), 127–61; Grant Adamson, "Joseph Smith, Thomas Paine, and Matthew 27:51b–53," *Dialogue: A Journal of Mormon Thought* 54, no. 4 (Winter 2021): 1–33.

authority and at the same time affirm the Bible's centrality and reliability by adding supplemental testimony.[3] Historian Samuel Brown has suggested that Joseph Smith attempted to "save the Bible" by "killing it."[4]



Latter-day Saints trace their beginnings back to these early experiences of Joseph Smith, the founding prophet of the tradition. His peregrinations from New York, to Ohio, Missouri, and Illinois attracted followers and trouble. After his assassination at the hands of an anti-Mormon mob in 1844, the bulk of the faithful made their way to what is now Utah under the direction of Brigham Young (1801–1877). Young reaffirmed Smith's robust system of church governance for the Church of Jesus Christ of Latter-day Saints. That included an authoritative, hierarchical set of church leaders with a President at the top and a collection of Apostles responsible for defining the teachings, practices, and direction for the church. This body of "General Authorities" represents the "official" position of the church on doctrinal matters, including biblical interpretation. However, this authority to interpret the Bible has been wielded unevenly. Not only have they expressed a variety of opinions over the past two centuries, but the general membership of the church has engaged with biblical scholarship beyond the borders of the Latter-day Saint tradition. The result has been a flourishing of competing perspectives and possibilities among scholars and lay members of the church.

At the same time, it is possible to discern some common threads among this variety. The tensions between belief and skepticism that Joseph Smith navigated impacted other nineteenth-century LDS leaders as well. Brigham Young responded to a Christian minister, "As I read the Bible it contains the words of the Father and Son, angels, good and bad, Lucifer, the devil, of wicked men and good men, and some are lying and some . . . are telling the truth; and if you believe it all to be the word of God you can go beyond me. I cannot believe it all to be the word of God, but I believe it as it is."[5] Rather than emphasizing the harmony between Mormonism and the Bible, Young questioned biblical authority by suggesting that there were competing perspectives within the text and therefore not a singular book with a unified message. Smith and Young's relativization of biblical authority—supplemented with, and sometimes supplanted by, prophetic authority—was a unique response to the emerging critical assessment of the Bible. Philip Barlow suggests that critical Latter-day Saint

3. See Grant Hardy, "How the Book of Mormon Responds to the Bible," in this volume.

4. Brown, *Joseph Smith's Translations*, 127–61.

5. Brigham Young, "The Gospel—The Spirit of the Lord—Revelation," August 13, 1871, *Journal of Discourses* 14: 209.

approaches to the Bible worked "to create a potential buffer against the coming onslaught of modern critical biblical studies."[6]

## MODERNISM AND FUNDAMENTALISM



The idea that critical biblical studies resulted in an "onslaught" against Latter-day Saint understandings may be an exaggeration. Perhaps it is still coming, but most LDS members today have not been much exposed to this scholarship. The study of the Bible has taken many forms, but among the most challenging to a traditional reception has sometimes been called "higher criticism." This approach, developed in Enlightenment-era Europe and brought to the United States, suggested that historical and literary context should guide biblical interpretation rather than theological presuppositions. In scholarship, "criticism" was not (necessarily) about a negative attitude toward the text, but referred to the reasoned use of evidence. And "higher" did not mean morally better, or more intellectually lofty, just distinct from "lower criticism." Today these methods would more likely be called "historical criticism" and "textual criticism" respectively. Bible scholarship's results were often controversial on matters of traditional belief. In both Catholic and Protestant communities, different factions developed responses to these new challenges to traditional biblical interpretation. In broad outline, the "modernists" sought to reconcile their religious faith with scientific and historical discoveries. The "conservatives" and "fundamentalists" prioritized what they saw as the traditional understanding and framed certain scientific and historical approaches as wrong, or even diabolical.[7]

In broad outline, these orientations framed how Latter-day Saints responded as well. Some LDS thinkers were optimistic about new academic achievements and saw potential compatibility with LDS teachings. Though many LDS students were exposed to these ideas in their university studies outside of Utah, William H. Chamberlin (1870–1921) was the first LDS scholar to take biblical

6. Barlow, *Mormons and the Bible*, 111.

7. In LDS contexts, *fundamentalism* refers to Mormons who accept polygamy and break away from the LDS Church. In broader context, the term refers to a mode of religion that is an extreme reaction against modernity. George M. Marsden, *Fundamentalism and American Culture: The Shaping of Twentieth-Century Evangelicalism, 1870–1925* (New York: Oxford University Press, 1980); Marvin Richard O'Connell, *Critics on Trial: An Introduction to the Catholic Modernist Crisis* (Washington, DC: Catholic University of America Press, 1994).

studies seriously.[8] He researched Hebrew, Greek, and biblical criticism at the University of Chicago and philosophy at Harvard and the University of California, Berkeley. Bringing his training back to Brigham Young University (BYU), he wrote two books and developed his courses based on his scholarly training. However, senior administrators at BYU and some church officials treated him and other professors who shared his ideas with skepticism and even hostility. Chamberlin and others left BYU under pressure in 1911.[9]

The century following Chamberlin's censure did not resolve the issue of the place of biblical studies among the Latter-day Saints. Numerous new approaches and waves emerged, and it is useful to briefly consider a few that have shaped the present. Significantly, the shape of LDS engagement with modern biblical studies has taken a distinctive path in part because of the additional canon, especially Joseph Smith's translation of the Book of Mormon. This record principally describes an ancient Israelite family who leaves Jerusalem shortly before the Babylonian destruction of the temple and exile of several Judeans in the sixth century BC. With divine guidance, this family makes their way to the Americas, where they establish a civilization. They kept with them a record of scripture from Israel but wrote their own account as well, abridged by one prophet named Mormon. Most importantly, this record reports knowledge about Jesus Christ prophesied before his birth, as well as a post-resurrection visit of Jesus Christ to the Americas. Smith's other scriptural projects, a "New Translation" of the Bible and the Book of Abraham, further supplement the biblical narrative with added stories about Adam and Eve, Enoch, Moses, Abraham, and more.

These other texts granted Latter-day Saints some freedom to question to the historical accuracy of some parts of the Bible but also required them to accept the miraculous historicity of other parts to buttress the claims of these new scriptural texts. Part of the tradition allowed Latter-day Saints to adopt a skeptical orientation toward the Bible within limits. For instance, B.H. Roberts (1857–1933), a General Authority and leading intellectual expounder of Mormonism, was neither a professional scholar nor conversant with the primary languages of biblical scholarship. Yet, he wrote, "[the] methods of higher criticism are legitimate."[10] But he did not always accept its rationalist objection to

8. James M. McLachlan, "W.H. Chamberlin and the Quest for a Mormon Theology," *Dialogue: A Journal of Mormon Thought* 29, no. 4 (Winter 1996): 151–67.

9. Thomas Simpson, *American Universities and the Birth of Modern Mormonism, 1867–1940* (Chapel Hill: University of North Carolina Press, 2016), 72–76.

10. B.H. Roberts, "Higher Criticism and the Book of Mormon," *Improvement Era* 14 (June 1911): 667–68.

miracles and prophecy. To Roberts, this objection seemed more like an underlying beginning premise of the method's practitioners rather than the process's necessary conclusion.[11] He also saw biblical criticism as a potential threat to the Book of Mormon. In an early assessment, he responded to the claim that "higher criticism shoots to pieces the Book of Mormon" with "Pardon me, my brother . . . you have misstated the matter; you mean that the Book of Mormon shoots holes into higher criticism!"[12]

The controversies that Chamberlin, Roberts, and others found themselves in are just a few examples of how LDS thinkers were already entangled with the modernist theology and biblical studies project in the early twentieth century. Other efforts continued this trend. In the 1930s, LDS leaders "called" a group of promising young men to study theology at University of Chicago Divinity School.[13] Chicago's liberal Protestant ecumenical attitude created space for Latter-day Saints.[14] Their task was to return with knowledge for the growing cadre of church educators.[15] This group of students were thus thrust into the heart of the contemporary debates between, on one hand, the theological modernists who sought to make room for faith in the intellectual world and, on the other hand, the traditionalists, conservatives, and fundamentalists who were suspicious of academic conclusions.[16]

Some LDS leaders were aligning themselves with more conservative perspectives on biblical interpretation. J. Reuben Clark (1871–1961), then the first counselor in the First Presidency of the church, saw biblical scholarship as heresy and made opposing higher criticism in the Church Educational System one of his main commitments.[17] Referencing modernists like the Chicago scholars, Clark explained, "[O]n more than one occasion our church members have gone to other places for special training in particular lines; they have had

11. Barlow, *Mormons and the Bible*, 126–8.

12. Roberts, "Higher Criticism and the Book of Mormon," 781. Later, Roberts's studies left him with unanswered historical questions about the origins of the Book of Mormon. B.H. Roberts, *Studies of the Book of Mormon*, edited by Brigham D. Madsen (Salt Lake City, UT: Signature Books, with University of Illinois Press, 1985, 1992).

13. Russel B. Swensen, "Mormons at the University of Chicago Divinity School: A Personal Reminiscence," *Dialogue: A Journal of Mormon Thought* 7, no. 2 (Summer 1972): 37–47.

14. Simpson, *American Universities*, 100.

15. Casey Paul Griffiths, "The Chicago Experiment: Finding the Voice and Charting the Course of Religious Education in the Church," *BYU Studies* 49, no. 4 (2010): 91–130.

16. Swensen, "Mormons at the University of Chicago," 45–6; Simpson, *American Universities*, 111–12, 116–20. Terryl Givens, *People of Paradox: A History of Mormon Culture* (New York: Oxford University Press, 2007), 195–240.

17. D. Michael Quinn, *Elder Statesman: A Biography of J. Reuben Clark* (Salt Lake City, UT: Signature Books, 2002), 229–37.

the training which was supposedly the last word, the most modern view . . . then they have brought it back and dosed it upon us without any thought as to whether we needed it or not."[18] Some years later, he was even more adamant: "[P]aganistic theories and tenets of so-called 'higher criticism' . . . should be wholly eliminated from our literature."[19] Unlike Protestant fundamentalists, Clark was not necessarily attached to traditional authorship of the biblical books.[20] Yet, he reliably echoed fundamentalist views throughout his church leadership, including rejecting 1950s biblical translation projects that were updating the 1611 King James Version with more accurate manuscripts and better linguistic knowledge.[21] Clark's message undercut the modernist scholars in church education and beyond.[22]

Joseph Fielding Smith (1876–1972) and his son-in-law Bruce R. McConkie (1915–1985) were allied with Clark in opposing the modernists. Smith, a grand-nephew to Joseph Smith and the son of a former church president, took on the role of an expert who could answer all doctrinal questions from the scriptures. He gave maximal authority to the near inerrancy of scripture as God's own autograph.[23] Similarly, McConkie found little to no value in learning biblical languages and believed that scholarly dictionaries and commentaries could be harmful.[24] In his influential encyclopedic handbook *Mormon Doctrine,* the entry under "Higher Criticism" read "See Apostasy" and denounced its "theories" as "speculative," as his father-in-law had done.[25] For Smith and McConkie, a modernist faith different from their own was little or no faith at all. Their writings eventually came to dominate church-produced handbooks and

18. J. Reuben Clark, "The Charted Course of the Church in Education," address to seminary and institute of religion leaders at the BYU summer school in Aspen Grove, Utah, on August 8, 1938, available at https://www.lds.org/bc/content/shared/content/english/pdf/language-materials/32709_eng.pdf?lang=eng.

19. Heber J. Grant, J. Reuben Clark, and David O. McKay, address to Committee on Publications, August 9, 1944. Quoted in Quinn, *Elder Statesman,* 232.

20. J. Reuben Clark, *On the Way to Immortality and Eternal Life* (Salt Lake City, UT: Deseret Book, 1950), 210.

21. J. Reuben Clark, *Why the King James Version* (Salt Lake City, UT: Deseret Book, 1956); Philip Barlow, "Why the King James Version? From the Common to the Official Bible of Mormonism," *Dialogue: A Journal of Mormon Thought* 22, no. 2 (Summer 1989): 19–42. See also Thomas A. Wayment, "The King James Version and Modern Translations of the Bible," in this volume.

22. Barlow, *Mormons and the Bible,* 173–90; *By Study and Also by Faith: One Hundred Years of Seminaries and Institutes of Religion* (Salt Lake City, UT: The Church of Jesus Christ of Latter-day Saints, 2015), especially 93–138.

23. Barlow, *Mormons and the Bible,* 133–41.

24. Bruce R. McConkie, "The Bible: A Sealed Book," CES Symposium on the New Testament, BYU (August 17, 1984).

25. Bruce R. McConkie, *Mormon Doctrine* (Salt Lake City, UT: Deseret Book, 1966), 251–52.

manuals for scriptural instruction from the 1970s to the 2000s, completing Clark's project of eliminating higher criticism entirely from church curricula.

In some respects, LDS suspicion about biblical studies was concerned with the historicity of many key events and characters. The interest in protecting the Bible has been connected to its shared fate with historicity of the Book of Mormon, Book of Abraham, and the prophetic authority of Joseph Smith and his successors.[26] If the stories of the Tower of Babel, Abraham, and Moses are relegated to myth, how then does that affect the claims in LDS scriptures that depend on these stories? Modernist Jews and Christians have been able to maintain biblical authority in light of these critiques by appealing to a deeper meaning.[27] Modernist Latter-day Saints had less clearly laid out the case for how historical-critical conclusions may be compatible with the historical and theological claims of the LDS scriptural and prophetic tradition. Latter-day Saints tend to share beliefs about historicity, literalism, and supernaturalism with non-LDS traditionalists, but never fully accepted the biblical inerrancy held by fundamentalists. Rather, in principle if not always in practice, they went even further than most mainline denominations in questioning the Bible's inerrancy, and certainly its sufficiency and sole authority. All through the twentieth century, the same LDS leaders who were vocally suspicious of "higher criticism" would have also affirmed that the Bible contained errors, omissions, and instances of "tampering" by people with theological agendas. This made for some distinctive sympathies among Latter-day Saints for some kinds of biblical scholarship. While findings that undercut belief in the perfect integrity of the Bible text might even be celebrated, Latter-day Saints did not so positively react to scholarship suggesting miracles did not happen, angels did not literally appear, or that Bible figures were fictional characters.



## BEYOND FUNDAMENTALISM AND MODERNISM

By the 1970s, the broader field of biblical studies increasingly fractured as new theological and methodological approaches gained ascendency. Sometimes these were in competition with historical-critical approaches, and sometimes

26. Paul Y. Hoskisson, ed., *Historicity and the Latter-day Saint Scriptures* (Provo, UT: Religious Studies Center, BYU, 2001).

27. Marc Brettler, Peter Enns, and Daniel J. Harrington, *The Bible and the Believer: How to Read the Bible Critically and Religiously* (New York: Oxford University Press, 2012); Christopher M. Hays and Christopher B. Ansberry, eds., *Evangelical Faith and the Challenge of Historical Criticism* (Grand Rapids, MI: Baker Academic, 2013).

they were building on that scholarship. These included new literary approaches, the introduction of anthropological and sociological methods, feminist and liberationist approaches, ethics, a resurgent biblical theology, and archeological discoveries, including texts previously unknown to scholars.[28] Experts in this era paid greater attention to newly discovered historical contexts of the Bible and brought new questions to the material—such as reexamining the anti-Jewish or androcentric biases of earlier scholarship—and other cultural shifts in the second half of the twentieth century.[29]

In this period, a new round of LDS scholars were receiving graduate training in biblical studies and related fields—now, however, without the official sponsorship of the church.[30] A cohort of apologists, often inspired by LDS scholar Hugh Nibley, engaged biblical scholarship primarily for the purposes of locating the Book of Mormon and Book of Abraham in ancient contexts. Rather than defending against historical-critical authorship or dating questions, Nibley had looked for literary themes about ancient temples, Enoch, and Egyptian parallels that might validate Joseph Smith's translations as authentically ancient.[31] Nibley gained the trust of many church leaders and inspired other scholars to follow his lead.[32] This new wave of scholars came of age as new ancient texts were being published, including the Dead Sea Scrolls and the Nag Hammadi Codices. Many of these LDS scholars looked to apocryphal literature as their focus and bonded in their common project to vindicate the alternative history offered by Joseph Smith's novel scripture. In 1979, John W. Welch started the Foundation for Ancient Research and Mormon Studies (FARMS), which flourished as a host for many of these scholars from the 1980s to early 2000s. Rather than tending toward modernism or fundamentalism, these apologetic approaches promoted distinctive LDS theological views. Framing these teachings as a "restoration" of ancient Israelite, Jewish, and Christian religion, these writers looked to biblical scholarship to support LDS belief in anthropomorphic deities; deification; a divine council; a divine feminine;

28. J.W. Rogerson, "Old Testament," in *Oxford Handbook of Biblical Studies,* edited by J.W. Rogerson and Judith M. Lieu (New York: Oxford University Press, 2006), 15–21.

29. Robert Morgan, "New Testament," *Oxford Handbook of Biblical Studies,* 42–49.

30. Scott Kenney, "Saints in Divinity Schools," *Sunstone* (May/June 1978): 22–24.

31. See, for instance, Hugh Nibley, *Lehi in the Desert and the World of the Jaredites* (Salt Lake City, UT: Bookcraft, 1952); *An Approach to the Book of Mormon* (Salt Lake City, UT: Council of the Twelve Apostles of the Church of Jesus Christ of Latter-day Saint, 1957); *The Myth Makers* (Salt Lake City, UT: Bookcraft, 1961); "What Is a Temple? The Idea of the Temple in History" (Pamphlet, 1963); *Since Cumorah: The Book of Mormon in the Modern World* (Salt Lake City, UT: Deseret Book, 1970).

32. Boyd Jay Petersen, *Hugh Nibley: A Consecrated Life* (Salt Lake City, UT: Greg Kofford Books, 2002), especially Ch. 19.

opposition to creation *ex nihilo*; the unreliability of the biblical text; parallels of temple, priesthood, and ritual; and so on.[33] These developments accepted some historical-critical ideas of dating and authorship, finding parallels with LDS teachings and mapping different stages of Israelite and early Christian ideas onto a narrative of apostasy and restoration. Often using postmodern theories, apologists offered new perspectives about biblical and Book of Mormon historicity.[34] Their efforts became well-known to well-read LDS members and leaders and even earned praise from Evangelicals for their sophistication.[35]

Other LDS scholars of the Bible from this era resisted these new apologetic approaches, seeking different foundations for faith through a historical-critical lens. Anthony Hutchinson, a doctoral student in biblical studies at the Catholic University of America, explained LDS scripture as a type of *midrash*.[36] David P. Wright completed a PhD in biblical studies at the University of California, Berkeley and taught at BYU (Department of Asian and Near Eastern Languages) for a time. He was a vigorous defender of historical criticism as a necessary aspect of faith.[37] Nevertheless, Wright has described himself in conflict with others at BYU, especially in Religious Education, over his understanding of historical critical matters. He eventually landed as a faculty member at Brandeis University's Near Eastern and Judaic Studies department. Wright was excommunicated in February 1994 for what he believed were concerns

33. The bibliography on these topics is vast, but the following are a few representative examples: Jordan Vajda, *"Partakers of the Divine Nature": A Comparative Analysis of Patristic and Mormon Doctrines of Divinization* Occasional Papers 3 (Provo: FARMS, 2002); Daniel C. Peterson, "Nephi and His Asherah," *Journal of Book of Mormon Studies* 9, no. 2 (2000): 16–81; John Gee, "The Corruption of Scripture in Early Christianity," in *Early Christians in Disarray: Contemporary LDS Perspectives on the Christian Apostasy*, edited by Noel B. Reynolds (Provo: FARMS and BYU Press, 2005); Stephen D. Ricks, "Ancient Views of Creation and the Doctrine of Creation ex Nihilo" in *Revelation, Reason, and Faith: Essays in Honor of Truman G. Madsen*, edited by Donald W. Parry, Daniel C. Peterson, and Stephen D. Ricks (Provo: FARMS, 2002); Donald W. Parry, ed., *Temples of the Ancient World: Ritual and Symbolism* (Salt Lake City, UT: Deseret Book and FARMS, 1994); Kevin Christensen, *"Paradigms Regained": A Survey of Margaret Barker's Scholarship and its Significance for Mormon Studies* Occasional Papers 2 (Provo: FARMS, 2001). For a critique of this methodology, see Taylor G. Petrey, "Purity and Parallels: Constructing the Apostasy Narrative of Early Christianity," in *Standing Apart: Mormon Historical Consciousness and the Concept of Apostasy*, edited by Miranda Wilcox and John D. Young (New York: Oxford University Press, 2014), 174–95.

34. Massimo Introvigne, "The Book of Mormon Wars: A Non-Mormon Perspective," *Journal of Book of Mormon Studies* 5, no. 2 (1996): 1–25; John-Charles Duffy, "Can Deconstruction Save the Day? 'Faithful Scholarship' and the Uses of Postmodernism," *Dialogue: A Journal of Mormon Thought* 41, no. 1 (Spring 2008): 1–33; Joseph M. Spencer, "Mormonism in the Enlightenment: A Response to John-Charles Duffy," *SquareTwo* 3, no. 3 (Fall 2010), available at http://squaretwo.org/Sq2ArticleSpencerPostmodernism.html.

35. Paul Owen and Carl Mosser, "Mormon Scholarship, Apologetics, and Evangelical Neglect: Losing the Battle and Not Knowing It?," *Trinity Journal* 19, no. 2 (1998): 179–205.

36. Anthony A. Hutchinson, "A Mormon Midrash?," *Dialogue: A Journal of Mormon Thought* 21, no. 4 (Winter 1988): 11–74.

37. David P. Wright, "Historical Criticism: A Necessary Element in the Search for Religious Truth," *Sunstone* 16, no. 3 (September 1992), 28–38.

about his publications about the Bible and Book of Mormon, a few months after a series of excommunications of other LDS scholars in September 1993.[38] Hutchinson and Wright, among others, had challenged the traditional historicity of the Book of Mormon and Book of Abraham, revealing how disputes about the value of historical critical biblical studies were often proxy wars for other LDS scripture.[39]

For the most part, LDS biblical conservatism and modernism, as well as the new breed of apologists, were white, male-dominated enterprises. Yet, LDS women were also going to graduate school to study in the Bible in the 1970s and 1980s during a period of resurgent feminist analysis in Mormonism and in biblical studies. Mormon feminists like Jolene Edmunds Rockwood and Melodie Moench Charles studied the Old Testament at Harvard Divinity School.[40] Other LDS women like Lynn Matthews Anderson engaged feminist biblical scholarship on their own and produced important articles that built on these insights.[41] LDS feminist biblical scholars from this period did not, however, develop careers in the field, and these approaches have often remained marginal. The shortage of LDS women—feminist or otherwise—involved in critical biblical studies may reflect the legacy of the male-centered field in the academy and in LDS priesthood culture. The racial makeup of LDS biblical scholars may similarly explain why they have largely ignored various liberatory and post-colonial hermeneutical movements, including those arising in Mormon studies more broadly.[42] Numerous cultural and structural issues have created these conditions, both in and out of the faith; yet no institution has yet arisen to address the problems. Indeed, this volume reflects the skewed

38. David P. Wright, letter to Bishop Reeder, February 17, 1994; Dianne T. Wright, letter to Bishop Reeder, February 17, 1994; David P. Wright, letter to Bishop Reeder, February 20, 1994, available at http://www.lds-mormon.com/dpw.shtml.

39. Dan Vogel, ed., *The Word of God: Essays on Mormon Scripture* (Salt Lake City, UT: Signature Books, 1990); John W. Welch, ed. *Reexploring the Book of Mormon* (Salt Lake City, UT: Deseret Book, 1992); Brent Lee Metcalfe, ed., *New Approaches to the Book of Mormon: Explorations in Critical Methodology* (Salt Lake City, UT: Signature Books, 1993); Noel Reynolds, ed., *Book of Mormon Authorship Revisited: The Evidence for Ancient Origins* (Provo, UT: FARMS, 1997); John W. Welch and Melvin J. Thorne, eds., *Pressing Forward With the Book of Mormon: The FARMS Updates of the 1990s* (Provo, UT: FARMS, 1999).

40. See, for instance, Jolene Edmunds Rockwood, "The Redemption of Eve" and Melodie Moench Charles, "Precedents for Mormon Women from Scriptures," in *Sisters in Spirit: Mormon Women in Historical and Cultural Perspective,* edited by Maureen Ursenbach Beecher and Lavina Fielding Anderson (Urbana: University of Illinois Press, 1987), 3–63.

41. Lynn Matthews Anderson, "Toward a Feminist Interpretation of Latter-day Saint Scripture," *Dialogue: A Journal of Mormon Thought* 27, no. 2 (Summer 1995): 185–203.

42. For example, Hokulani K. Aikau, *A Chosen People, A Promised Land: Mormonism and Race in Hawai'i* (Minneapolis: University of Minnesota Press, 2012); Gina Colvin and Joanna Brooks, eds., *Decolonizing Mormonism: Approaching a Postcolonial Zion* (Salt Lake City: University of Utah Press, 2018).

makeup of the field, which requires support and investment in a new generation of scholars who can offer more diverse perspectives.

## CONTEMPORARY STATE



In the early twenty-first century, biblical studies is still undergoing radical transformation. Postmodern approaches have upended the split between fundamentalists and modernists by challenging the totalizing interpretations that both approaches offered.[43] Such approaches bring new perspectives on history, ethics, hermeneutics, ideology, and politics. They challenge the supposedly objective presuppositions of historical-critical analysis and revealed the ideological frameworks behind much of these studies. Calling into question both the singularity of meaning and the privileging of the "original" authorial intention, postmodern critics seek out multidimensional interpretation. Reception history has emerged and grown within the field causing the question, "What has this text meant to various communities over time?" to stand alongside, and perhaps even eclipse, the venerable, "What was the original text and what was its original meaning?" Despite these challenges, historical-criticism remains influential, though for many there can be a reconciliation between the two approaches.[44]

Where do Latter-day Saints fit into this landscape of the broader field? How do the historical and contemporary concerns of modern biblical studies in all of its diversity inform LDS interests? Do historical approaches, whether critical or apologetic, provide the best path forward for LDS scripture studies?[45] The essays that follow provide more in-depth discussions of numerous topics related to these and other questions. The present volume focuses on Latter-day Saint reception and scholarly engagement with the Bible. Latter-day Saints have engaged biblical studies in ways that are distinct from other American churches. Besides new texts, such differences include an active prophetic tradition that takes on the same (or greater) authority than the biblical text and distinctive religious practices and institutions inspired by biblical precedent. These differences set Latter-day Saint approaches to the Bible's authority on

43. The Bible and Culture Collective, *The Postmodern Bible* (New Haven, CT: Yale University Press, 1995); A.K.M. Adam, ed., *The Handbook of Postmodern Biblical Interpretation* (St. Louis, MO: Chalice Press, 2000).

44. John J. Collins, *The Bible After Babel: Historical Criticism in a Postmodern Age* (Grand Rapids, MI: Eerdmans, 2005).

45. James E. Faulconer and Joseph M. Spencer, eds., *Perspectives on Mormon Theology: Scriptural Theology* (Salt Lake City, UT: Greg Kofford Books, 2015).

different terms that require explanation and analysis as distinct from Jewish, Catholic, and Protestant reception tradition.

This volume seeks to set a new standard as an accessible single resource for LDS biblical studies. The audiences for these essays are diverse, including biblical studies scholars interested in LDS reception history, scholars of American religion interested in the impact of biblical studies as a discipline on specific religious communities, and Latter-day Saints interested in how biblical studies intersects with their tradition. For each of these audiences, some of the information here will be rather new and other treatments feel more introductory depending on one's familiarity with the topics. A volume such as this then seeks to advance the field of LDS biblical studies, broadly defined, by offering both an introductory survey of the major issues and topics as well as providing new, more sophisticated analysis and clarity to the most important issues. Readers should approach these essays with some awareness of the basics of LDS history with the Bible and biblical studies as outlined in this introduction. At the same time, many of these issues are covered in more depth and analysis in later chapters.

This volume divides the field into five main areas. Each essay can be read independently from the others, and as a result there is some overlap, but the authors often take different perspectives on the same set of problems. As editors, we encourage readers to engage with multiple essays in multiple sections to gain a clear sense of the variety of options that LDS scholars have offered. Part I includes scholarship that examines the "The Ancient World of the Bible as Understood by Latter-day Saints: From Joseph Smith to Contemporary Scholarship." This includes how modern biblical scholarship has been received, how and why the King James Version has influenced the English-speaking church, and how Joseph Smith's "New Translation" treats the Bible. There are also essays engaging some of the most important topics in LDS approaches to the Bible, such as temple and priesthood. Essays on LDS approaches to the Dead Sea Scrolls as well as a discussion of critical eras in biblical history also help to explain and situate LDS understandings of the ancient world and historical engagement with these materials.

Part II includes scholarship that covers "Conceptions of Canon and Not Canon: The Bible(s) and Restoration Scripture." Essays in this section explore the concept of "canon" historically and in the LDS tradition. They consider canon formation, as well as influential non- and semi-canonical literature. Importantly, these essays also consider the entanglement of the Bible in LDS canonical texts like the Book of Mormon and the Pearl of Great Price. How does the Book of Mormon use the Bible? How does the Book of Mormon imagine the biblical world? How do Joseph Smith's other translation projects in the Book of Moses and Book of Abraham engage with the Bible? These essays offer clarifying treatment of these vexed issues.



The next set of essays tackle another important topic about how Latter-day Saints think about biblical interpretation. In Part III, "A Variety of Critical Biblical Approaches and Their Relevance to Mormon Studies," the authors examine some important methods of biblical scholarship. Some consider the rise of "historical criticism," biblical scholarship that emphasizes historical contextualization to understand the Bible. Others look at biblical theology as a discipline and reflect on its relevance to Latter-day Saints. Other methods such as archeology, the study of oral culture, and feminist biblical criticism are also particularly relevant.

Throughout the present volume, the double treatment of the critical scholarship alongside LDS interpretation helps to see more clearly the points of contact, conflict, and possibility in LDS biblical interpretation. The methods analyzed in this section are not exhaustive of the many approaches in the broader field of biblical studies but have found particular purchase among Latter-day Saints. We also hope to see more treatment of an even larger set of approaches.

In Part IV, "Inheritance and Divergence: Latter-day Saints Read Others Reading the Bible," the essays consider how Latter-day Saints fit into other historical interpretive traditions. Modernism and fundamentalism are not the only ways that the Bible has been approached in Christian contexts. From the use of scripture in the New Testament, to early Christian, medieval, and Reformation and early modern biblical interpretation, these essays offer a brief glimpse into some of the diverse ways that Christians have thought about scripture in different historical and cultural contexts and invite Latter-day Saints to consider such approaches.

In the final section, "Latter-day Saint Approaches to the Bible's Major Genres and Divisions," these scholars discuss how Latter-day Saints have engaged specific parts of the Bible. Short of a complete commentary on each book of the Bible, these essays at least discuss dominant themes in historical LDS interpretation and the relevance of modern biblical studies to those traditions. The Bible of course covers several different periods and types of literature, and scholarship on these areas has grown increasingly specialized. The essays here offer basic introductions to those genres and divisions of the Bible and offer key insights into the history of LDS interpretation and critical issues that remain.

As previously noted, these various movements in biblical studies and LDS scholarship have had little effect on those in the pews. The general skepticism toward biblical scholarship of some church leaders in earlier generations contributed to the conditions that prevented LDS readers from engaging in this scholarship, a "buffer" that has delayed serious conversations. While the LDS Church History Department in Salt Lake City employs many professionally trained historians, the Scripture department there does not. Neither does it meaningfully engage with biblical scholarship in church publications or curricula, despite a handful of current apostles inclined to occasionally cite Bible scholars in their public addresses.[46] Scholars Matthew Grey and Cory Crawford have suggested that in the wake of broader and more mature LDS engagement with the church's own history, "a sobering encounter between Latter-day Saints and modern biblical scholarship does not loom far on the horizon."[47]

The contributors to this volume can all be read in the light of this "sobering encounter." While the unique LDS scriptures' historical claims are not the primary subject of this volume, the scholars writing here examine the implications of critical biblical scholarship on these texts and describe how previous scholars have attempted to resolve or reconcile these problems. When the contributors of this volume describe such approaches, or describe the characters in LDS scripture, such descriptions should not be taken as uncritical assessment but rather reflective of how the text presents itself. While implications of modern biblical scholarship do not support pre-critical acceptance of historical claims in LDS scripture as much as many members might like, the approach adopted in the following essays is neither apologetic nor antagonistic, but explanatory and analytical.

The reception of biblical scholarship among Latter-day Saints may be entering a new phase. Professional historians' work on the Mormon experience has, beginning in the 1950s, become a largely nonpartisan enterprise following the same methods and publishing with mostly the same university presses and in the same academic journals.[48] In comparison, for the reasons discussed, scholarship on LDS scripture has had a more difficult time emerging. However, this

46. *Old Testament Seminary Teacher Material* (Salt Lake City, UT: Church of Jesus Christ of Latter-day Saints, 2019) for high school students states bluntly, "Moses is the author of Genesis." *New Testament Seminary Teacher Manual* (Salt Lake City, UT: Church of Jesus Christ of Latter-day Saints, 2016) affirms the traditional attribution of all New Testament texts to their reported authors, leaving doubt only on Hebrews.

47. Matthew J. Grey and Cory Crawford, "Introduction: Forum on Faith and Biblical Scholarship," *Studies in the Bible and Antiquity* 8 (2016): 5.

48. Patrick Q. Mason, ed., *Directions for Mormon Studies in the Twenty-first Century* (Salt Lake City: University of Utah Press, 2016).

situation is beginning to change with the recent appearance of new scholarship on LDS scripture and a new scholarly vocabulary.[49] The present volume adds to the new conversations by consolidating what has come before and advancing the field by clarifying key issues and clearing out the underbrush. It is exciting to imagine what lies ahead.



49. Terryl L. Givens, *By The Hand of Mormon: The American Scripture that Launched a New World Religion* (New York: Oxford University Press, 2002) and *The Book of Mormon: A Very Short Introduction* (New York: Oxford University Press, 2009); Grant Hardy, *Understanding the Book of Mormon: A Reader's Guide* (New York: Oxford University Press, 2010); William L. Davis, *Visions in a Seer Stone: Joseph Smith and the Making of the Book of Mormon* (Chapel Hill: University of North Carolina Press, 2020); Royal Skousen, ed., *The Book of Mormon: The Earliest Text* (New Haven, CT: Yale University Press, 2009); Paul C. Gutjahr, *The Book of Mormon: A Biography* (Princeton, NJ: Princeton University Press, 2012). Laurie Maffly-Kipp, *American Scripture: An Anthology of Sacred Writing* (New York: Penguin, 2010). Michael Hubbard MacKay, Mark Ashurst-McGee, and Brian M. Hauglid, *Producing Ancient Scripture: Joseph Smith's Translation Projects in the Development of Mormon Christianity* (Salt Lake City: University of Utah Press, 2020); Terryl L. Givens with Brian Hauglid, *The Pearl of Greatest Price: Mormonism's Most Controversial Scripture* (New York: Oxford University Press, 2019).

PART I

# The Ancient World of the Bible as Understood by Latter-day Saints

*From Joseph Smith to Contemporary Scholarship*

1

# The Place of the Bible and Biblical Scholarship among Latter-day Saints in the Twentieth and Twenty-First Centuries

PHILIP L. BARLOW AND STEPHEN T. BETTS

In developing countries, each generation during the past 150 years seems less biblically literate. Yet few books rival the Bible's influence in the development of western civilization and the Holy Book remains vital for a sizeable portion of today's global population.[1] The Bible is, however, a complex assemblage. The Hebrew Bible is not the same as the Christian Bible and the composition of the Christian Bible varies among Eastern Orthodox, Roman Catholic, and Protestant traditions. The nature of purported revelation is not self-evident, to say nothing of the relation of inspiration to recorded scripture, the evolution of the texts, the meaning of texts, the connection of scripture to culture or history or "truth," and the differing perspectives within even single denominations about such matters. In the case of the Church of Jesus Christ of Latter-day Saints, of smaller related denominations, and of the wider Mormon culture, biblical belief and usage is yet more complex. These complexities derive from an expanded canon, intertextuality within this canon, belief in living prophets, and a history including oral scripture, private scripture, noncanonized scripture, temporary scripture, and shifting dynamics among these disparate authorities in relation to the Bible.

1. A classic assessment of biblical influence in law, politics, art, music, literature, common speech, education, social welfare, and religion may be found in Gabriel Sivan, *The Bible and Civilization* 1st ed. (New York: Quadrangle/New York Times Book Co., 1974). See also Nathan Hatch and Mark Noll, eds., *The Bible in America: Essays in Cultural History* (New York: Oxford University Press, 1982). In recent decades the Pew Research Center has published periodic glimpses of Americans' religious and biblical literacy; examples include "US Religious Knowledge Survey," Sept. 28, 2010, available at http://www.pewforum.org/U-S-Religious-Knowledge-Survey-Who-Knows-What-About-Religion.aspx and "What Americans Know About Religion," available at https://www.pewforum.org/2019/07/23/what-americans-know-about-religion/.

The volume you are encountering offers informed views on much of this terrain and is itself a marker of the state of biblical scholarship within and about "Mormonism."[2] The collection offers treatments probing feminist biblical criticism, textual and historical criticism, the relation of the Bible to modern scripture, and much else. Given this context, we restrict the focus of this chapter to two interrelated developments unfolding since the advent of the twentieth century and helping to define the present. The first is the Church's conflicted, muted, yet consequential response to modern biblical scholarship—a reconsideration of scripture's origins and character that fractured Judaism and Christianity. This topic prompts particular attention to the Church's hierarchical and educational leaders, dominated by men, who by commission and omission largely shaped official and public Latter-day Saint perspectives. The second development traces an inversion in the Bible's relative stature among the Saints during the past century.

## THE EARLY TWENTIETH CENTURY

The first half of the twentieth century built on the decades preceding it to ripen an intellectual shift. In western civilization the shift was a veritable revolution, splintering synagogues and churches more than at any time since the Reformation. Behind it all lay a sense of *change* erratically displacing *stationary fact* as key to understanding the world we live in. Even before the Civil War, geology was revealing a world that was many millions, not several thousands, of years in age. What did this mean for the accounts of creation recorded in Genesis? The most famous expression of this contested reconfiguration of the perceived changing world was Darwin's compelling paradigm of the evolution and connectedness of all life. Whether or not one bothered to understand the argument and evidence for evolution, opinions smoldered and charred the religious landscape. It was not lost on many that Darwin's insight bore implications for interpreting not only Genesis, but the place of human beings—and God—in the world.

Equally startling to traditional orthodoxies, though less readily popularized, was the rise of "higher criticism," a label for new critical methods developed to better understand the sources, authorship, audiences, literary

2. The contemporary Church of Jesus Christ of Latter-day Saints prefers use of its formal name rather than historically accepted nicknames [especially Mormon(ism)] to stress its Christian devotion. Derivatives of "Mormon" occurring in this chapter refer to something broader than the institutional church: a movement and a culture.

traits, historical contexts, form, formation, and evolution of ancient texts. As with biological evolution, apprehension of these tools complicated traditional notions of divine-human communication, because the new tools revealed aspects of the apparently human part of the equation. Scriptural texts were shown not to have arrived *ex nihilo*; they possessed instead a more or less discernible history. At issue for believers was the extent to which inspiration entailed a vague divine assistance to those who produced scripture as opposed to a warranty that human writers had stenographically penned the mind of God. Should the human-forged tools of scholars critique the nature of holy writ? Or should divine scripture judge human culture, including its scholarship? Or was a dialectic required?

Sorting such issues was fraught: sectors of Judaism discerned anti-Semitism lurking in scholarship that, for example, suggested that not Moses, but anonymous and much later writers composed the internally and historically conflicting accounts of Israel's exodus from Egypt and formation as a people. New Testament scholarship raised questions concerning the historical Jesus. In the United States, where the critical mass of Latter-day Saints lived, most major Christian denominations during the decades surrounding the turn of the twentieth century endured a series of widely publicized heresy trials, schisms, or papal condemnations of leading clergy and scholars who employed higher critical tools.[3] One result was the partial reconfiguration of Christianity into conservative-fundamentalist versus liberal-modernist camps. Orientation to either group hinged in part on how far any group might go to challenge or defend scriptural inerrancy and its implications.

Joseph Smith's "restoration"[4] harbored in its DNA the capacity to respond variously to these fissures. On one hand, the church from its beginnings had spurned a professional and educated ministry in favor of prophets and

3. Among the most famous manifestos in reaction new biblical approaches was a 1903 speech by Solomon Schechter, a founder of Conservative Judaism: "Address: In Honor of Kaufmann Kohler—Higher Criticism—Higher Anti-Semitism," *The American Hebrew* 72, no. 20 (April 3, 1903): 654–55. Pope Leo XIII's 1893 encyclical, *Providentissimus Deus,* and subsequent decrees of the Holy Office quashed the use of historical-literary methods in Catholic biblical studies during the first half of the twentieth century. For Protestant clashes, see William Hutchison, *The Modernist Impulse in America Protestantism* (Durham, NC: Duke University Press, 1992) and George Marsden, *Fundamentalism and American Culture,* 2nd ed. (New York: Oxford University Press, 2006).

4. Joseph Smith's enactment of "restoration" was rich and varied, sometimes attaching to the restoration of primitive Christianity and/or the restoration of ancient Israel, sometimes to "the restoration of all things," including esoterica and primordial Eden, and sometimes to "hidden things" never previously revealed to humankind. Smith's usage everywhere knits with his relationship to the Bible. In the twenty-first-century Church, "restoration" has expanded to include even relatively commonplace evolutions in policy: "the restoration is ongoing."

a priesthood-bearing laity. This lay leadership was not inclined to replace a "learned clergy" with professional scholars. As among conservative Baptists or Methodists, many Saints scorned "the philosophies of men" as an intrusion to "the plain sense" of scripture and the teachings of the Holy Spirit. In addition, a legacy of biblical literalism ran deep in the Mormon tradition, extended beyond even that of most Protestants by modern Bible-patterned scripture that, for example, describes an apparently literal Satan in face-to-face conversation with Moses and another ancient prophet who by faith moved an actual rather than a poetic mountain.[5] Healings, miracles, and current-day prophets whom one might meet in the street were live realities for believing Saints. Theirs was not a disenchanted world. Hence scholarship bent on understanding what it could of human influence on sacred texts might understandably put off a people for whom correctly translated scripture was the word of God. Furthermore, the Church's theology had posited a gospel once delivered in purity to Adam and Eve, followed by a series of apostasies and restorations over centuries, the latest and most complete restoration being itself. This model of recurrent revelation-devolution-restoration seemed alien to the notions of progressive scriptural, theological, and religious evolution disclosed by modern approaches.

On the other hand, several elements in Joseph Smith's movement ran counter to an orientation that in the early twentieth century would become known as fundamentalism, a Protestant-based insistence on biblical inerrancy and related principles.[6] Joseph Smith's restoration had been launched by the appearance of the Book of Mormon, which, even while reinforcing the Bible, showed it open to correction and addition. While Smith insisted on the reality of his revelations, many of which were cast in the first-person singular as though God himself were speaking, his revelations and remarks also alluded to the weakness inherent in human language and the "mistakes of men" in

5. Moses 1:12–24; 7:13; Ether 12:30. Cf. Matthew 17:20, wherein Jesus urges that nothing, including moving a mountain, shall be impossible to those possessing even a tiny grain of faith. The fundamentalist Protestants alluded to here had analogues among Catholics and Orthodox Jews or, selectively, Muslims and others. For a fuller sense of selective "literalism" among the Saints, see the index entry in Barlow, *Mormons and the Bible* (New York: Oxford University Press, 2013), 275.

6. The widespread movement derived its popular name from *The Fundamentals,* ninety essays authored by scholarly or ecclesiastical luminaries from most major Protestant denominations (1910–1915, originally twelve volumes). Some three million copies were distributed without charge throughout the United States and beyond. The collection defended the inerrancy of the (non-extant) "original autographs" of the biblical texts along with such traditional tenets of Christianity as the Virgin Birth and Christ's physical resurrection. It criticized biological evolution and allegedly Christian expressions that deviated from its own premises, including Roman Catholicism and "Mormonism."

scripture. Moreover, half a century before theories about the multiple authorship and redaction of biblical books were widely known in America even among scholars, Smith had offered the world a dramatic instance of higher criticism's Documentary Hypothesis at work: the entire structure of the Book of Mormon portrays the fifth-century prophet-historian, Mormon, freely abridging, appropriating, conflating, and commenting on the records of earlier writers in his account of the rise and fall of ancient peoples. This forthright redaction resembled the very theory of the construction of the Pentateuch that would later scandalize Orthodox Jews and Protestant Fundamentalists. In addition, the notion and practice of open-ended new revelation prompted Smith sometimes to amend, expand, or reinterpret previous revelations (whether his own or the Bible's) "line upon line, precept on precept," thus undermining concepts of a flawless and self-sufficient scripture. Beyond this, Joseph Smith had taught adherents to value truth, beauty, wisdom, and virtue no matter their source. All such strands theoretically opened the tradition to the historical and literary insights of the higher critics that came upon the Church's horizons a century after its founding.[7]



Latter-day Saint church leaders, honored as inspired, held far more sway than scholars, and a handful of these leaders, such as John Widtsoe and James Talmage, did acquaint themselves modestly with historical-literary tools. The accomplished and moderate autodidact, B.H. Roberts, went beyond most. Like some higher critics among themselves, Roberts disagreed selectively with the conclusions of some scholars but was comparatively open to weighing them. He advocated that the Book of Mormon must submit to them as one among many tests of its authenticity.[8] Like conservative and professionally trained contemporaneous Protestant defenders of the Bible, such as A.A. Hodge and B.B. Warfield, Roberts attributed whatever seemed worthy in scripture to inspiration, whatever seemed flawed to limited human vision. All three men

7. Barlow, *Mormons and the Bible*, 119–20. For Mormon's ancient redaction of the Book of Mormon, see the "Words of Mormon," the book "Mormon" within the Book of Mormon, and *passim*. Joseph Smith's injunction to embrace truth, virtue, and beauty no matter their source was eventually codified in the thirteenth article of faith (the Pearl of Great Price).

8. B.H. Roberts, "The Translation of the Book of Mormon," *Improvement Era* 9 (April 1906): 435–36. Unlike most Latter-day Saint leaders who were also amateur scholars (persons who, whether or not trained in some other field, were untrained in religion, biblical studies, or their cognates), Roberts did read a range of liberal or radical scholars such as David Strauss, Ernest Renan, Charles Briggs, Lyman Abbott, and S.R. Driver, as well as conservative sources like J.R. Dummelow, George Rawlinson, and Alfred Edersheim. Despite diligence and exceptional native ability, however, Roberts was not burdened with the requisite languages for professional-grade study and was dependent on secondary syntheses such as Bible dictionaries and commentaries.

allowed that biblical writers drew from natural sources when writing and gave evidence of their varying knowledge and intellect. The scriptures were written upon specific historical occasions coloring their production; yet, the three men sensed a divine spirit presiding over the human elements, yielding truth and wisdom that transcended mere human productions. Literal dictation from God was not the general rule in scripture and allowance should be made for degrees of inspiration.

A few Latter-day Saint educators were conversant with the new trends and did attempt to bring the church's knowledge of the Bible into the modern world. The first to do so with full competence was William Chamberlin, who for his labors was, in the second decade of the century, squeezed from his position at BYU. The effective dismissal of Chamberlin brought the private displeasure of, among others, apostle and eventual church president David O. McKay: "That a lofty, sincere soul like W.H. Chamberlin should have been compelled to struggle in our community and to have been misunderstood by those who should have known him best, seems to me to be nothing short of a tragedy."[9] The slightly earlier (1911) forced resignations of Chamberlin's brother and two sympathetic colleagues, who grappled with both the Bible and biological evolution, provoked a petition of protest signed by more than 80 percent of the BYU student body.

The condemnation of the professors' positions by the Church's Board of Education captures predominating perceptions and fears toward the new scholarship. These fears were often manifest through complaints to general church and university authorities from students' parents. The board found the group guilty of teaching biological evolution as if it were an established law; "following the higher criticism of [Congregationalist theologian] Lyman Abbot"; treating the Bible as a "collection of myths, folklore, dramas, literary productions, history, and some inspiration"; and rejecting Noah's Flood, Babel's confusion of tongues, and Christ's temptation in the desert as objectively real phenomena.

There was substance to these charges, though the Board's summary of William Chamberlin's views also distorted them. While he felt duty-bound to acknowledge the insights of modern scholarship so as not to leave his students unprepared for demonstrable facts, Chamberlin retained a genuine Latter-day Saint faith in a real God who revealed himself, among other ways, to prophets and in Christ. The tangible resurrection of Jesus and of all God's children was

9. McKay to Ralph Chamberlin, February 17, 1926 (David C. Chamberlin private collection).

a reality for him; personal life extended beyond death. Western civilization was right to honor the spirit of Greek intellectual striving, he believed, but amiss in neglecting the yearning of the Hebrew prophets to know God and to become righteous. Yet it is true that Chamberlin, like Brigham Young, believed the Bible incorporated lore. Even inspired biblical authors wrote according to the best understanding of their times, and the Bible itself proved that cultural views and doctrines, including conceptions of God, had evolved across time. The episode dismissing Chamberlin and his colleagues from BYU roiled the university, incited the Utah press, and, for at least a generation, depressed the school's reputation.[10] But the need for college-level competence in teaching the Bible did not disappear with the purge.

Two decades later, the Church sent several young religious educators to the University of Chicago Divinity School for formal training in biblical studies.[11] Upon their return, some church leaders, who felt the mantle of protecting the Church, were dismayed to find several of the returning men converted to the value of historical-literary approaches. Joseph Fielding Smith, influential son of a church president and ultimately church president himself, believed that if even a single passage of the original form of Genesis was not historically accurate, Christianity would fall. Joined by Apostles Mark E. Petersen and J. Reuben Clark and others, Smith saw modern scholarship as blasphemy. His son-in-law Bruce R. McConkie, the most widely cited church leader on doctrinal and scriptural matters in the second half of the twentieth century, gauged that if worldly, uninspired scholars (those lacking faith and knowledge in the restored gospel he championed) "get anything right, it is an accident." Although not official and opposed by a minority of other leaders, these perspectives descended to the general church membership explicitly in the form of books and speeches, and implicitly through approved curricula for the Church's Sunday Schools, Seminaries, and Institutes of Religion, which showed little concern with modern scholarship. Elder McConkie's perspectives in particular are woven in the chapter headings and various reference notes of the official LDS edition of the Bible, which he had a hand in preparing.[12]

Despite these predominant views, a more neutral attitude toward modern scholarship was not without ecclesiastical influence in the twentieth century. In

10. Barlow, *Mormons and the Bible,* 146–47, 152.

11. Casey Griffiths, "The Chicago Experiment: Finding the Voice and Charting the Course of Religious Education in the Church," *BYU Studies* 49, no. 4 (2010): 91–130.

12. 1979; still the official Bible for English-speaking adherents. Many of the headings and notes were subsequently transposed to Spanish and Portuguese editions.

1921, Charles Penrose, writing for the First Presidency of the Church, indicated the presidency's unwillingness to commit the Church to a particular position on higher criticism, just as they were unwilling to pronounce the final word on evolution. Officially to "answer yes or no" to the higher critics was "unwise and should not be undertaken by one representing the Church."[13] William Chamberlin himself was rehired as a professor of philosophy at the Church's Brigham Young College in Logan, Utah, four years after his dismissal from BYU. Shortly after Chamberlin's death, the new superintendent of the Church's education system, future Apostle Adam S. Bennion, volunteered his office as a distribution center for a new book about Chamberlin's life and philosophy and desired every church schoolteacher to read it.[14] Overall, the Church greeted the higher criticism either by inattention or with more disapproval than approval, but it published no official stance and tolerated a range of understandings without endorsing any. Unlike broad swaths of the wider Judeo-Christian world, this muted response perhaps spared it any major rupture.

## INTO THE TWENTY-FIRST CENTURY

The subdued response also meant, however, that the issues remained unresolved into the twenty-first century. One expression of this lack of resolution may be sampled through the teaching in (the de facto college of) Religious Education[15] at BYU. In the Department of Ancient Scripture, faculty differ in their capacity and perspective on higher critical tools. The current century witnessed the hiring of a growing cadre of trained scholars equipped to use historical-literary tools in their work. Some other faculty spurn or leave unmentioned the historical-literary dimensions of scripture because the teachers are innocent or wary of them or because they do not aid the teachers' objectives. Some believe the introduction of modern approaches might unsettle students, parents, colleagues, administrators, or donors.[16] This means that many students, who must take approximately seven religion courses to graduate, may

13. Charles W. Penrose ("with the support of [fellow First Presidency counselor] Anthony Ivins"), letter to Joseph W. McMurrin, October 31, 1921, in *Minutes of the Apostles of the Church of Jesus Christ of Latter-day Saints* (Salt Lake City, UT: privately published, 2010).

14. Barlow, *Mormons and the Bible*, 150–4.

15. Religion as a subject and as a practical faith dimension appears in many disciplines at BYU. Allusions to "Religious Education" in this context, however, reference the large, specific academic unit labelled Religious Education, which grants the fourteen credit hours in religion required of all undergraduates. It functions as a college, but for unspecified reasons declines the label of "college" or "school," unlike its analogues at BYU, such the "College of Humanities" or "School of Business."

16. Discussions between the author and colleagues in Religious Education over many years.

leave the University without ever hearing of higher criticism, which is perhaps analogous to a music major graduating without having worked through the principles of music theory.

This becomes more plausible by noting that scholarly pedagogy in matters of religion is emphatically secondary to the University's concern to build faith and spirituality.[17] This pastoral primacy has historically meant that a portion of the Religious Education faculty are, and another portion are not, trained in academic fields elsewhere judged pertinent to a department of religion. Many faculty in Religious Education have been equipped with advanced degrees in law, technology, educational leadership, business, or botany rather than in Bible, religious studies, or Near Eastern languages and culture. The implied point in the faculty's composition and the explicit point in Religious Education's mission statement is that content mastery in religion is helpful in some respects, but it is manifest faith, practical thought, institutional loyalty, the ability to engage students, pastoral commitment, doctrinal soundness, and virtuous lives that are essential for building precisely those desirable qualities in students.



In practice this means that in some classrooms effort is less weighted to understanding scripture itself and more weighted to building faith and everyday life skills while marshalling a scriptural pretext, as per this student's report of a representative class period in her accredited ancient scripture course at BYU:

> 2 Samuel 20 tells the story of Joab, David's general, who pursued his enemy Sheba to a walled city. He attacked the city to intimidate Sheba, who was inside. An old woman came out and asked Joab why he was attacking, and Joab explained that his enemy Sheba was hiding inside her city walls. She returned to her city, and presently Sheba's decapitated head was tossed over the city walls to Joab. The lesson we were taught from this violent story is that when we communicate clearly with one another, we can avoid a lot of conflict. Joab and the people of the city avoided further violence because Joab and the old woman communicated.[18]

17. Religious Education website, accessed February 8, 2022, at https://religion.byu.edu/about-us. "Gospel scholarship" in this context might or might not require professional-grade background and capacity such as would be expected in the university's other colleges and programs.

18. This not untypical, contemporary account is one of many that has come to the author during years of studying and participating in the Church, its system of education, and its biblical connections. Barlow, private files.

While this sort of engagement with the biblical text betrays little concern for scholarship, neither is it alien to the lived religious experience of many devout Christians. Evangelical philosopher and theologian Richard Mouw noted four primary tendencies among Bible-believing Protestants in the twentieth century: doctrinalism (intellectual submission to correct beliefs), pietism (devotional emphasis), culturalism (the Bible as stimulus for cultural transformation), and moralism (the Bible as a source book for personal ethics).[19] To the extent that it was accurately conveyed, the BYU professor's use of Joab and Sheba seems related to the last of these, if we replace "moralism" with "every day pragmatism."

The pragmatic and devotional roles of scriptural study are, then, elemental in the church's practice, as in many faiths. But decoupling these usages from college-level academic study carries potential consequences. One is a comparative biblical illiteracy,[20] which may attach eventually and ironically to common faith struggles, leaving some Saints unprepared when their learning in other fields jars with their unevolved lens of scripture's and religion's nature. Another is neglect of various key portions of the Bible that do not lend themselves readily to moral or practical lessons and familiar concepts.

## THE DECLINE OF THE BIBLE'S STATURE

Latter-day Saints in the nineteenth century cited the Bible more often by far than the Book of Mormon and other modern scriptures during public worship.[21] For example, Lorenzo Snow, the Church's Prophet-President at the turn of the twentieth century, called on the Book of Mormon only nineteen times in his publicly recorded sermons, while citing the Doctrine and Covenants 160 times and the Bible nearly thrice as often as that (422 times). As sampled in similar settings from the last five years of his life, Snow's successor, Joseph F. Smith, cited the Bible fifteen times, but the Book of Mormon only once.

Like these before him, James E. Talmage, a disproportionately influential apostle from 1911 to 1933, held the Bible, the Book of Mormon, and

19. Mouw, "The Bible in Twentieth-Century Protestantism: A Preliminary Taxonomy," in *The Bible in America: Essays in Cultural History*, edited by Nathan Hatch and Mark Noll (New York: Oxford University Press, 1982), 139–62.

20. A Pew survey on biblical and religious literacy (see note 1) showed Latter-day Saints compared favorably to other Christians, although literacy in the study was construed as rudimentary, asking respondents, for example, to name three of the four Gospels in the New Testament.

21. The work of Janiece Johnson, as yet unpublished in book form, is revising the notion that Book of Mormon usage in the early church was slight and not textually probing. See Johnson, "Becoming a People of the Books: Toward an Understanding of Early Mormon Converts and the New Word of the Lord," *Journal of Book of Mormon Studies* 27 (2018): 1–43.

contemporary prophets to be "a unit in their testimony of the everlasting gospel." Also like many predecessors, he stressed approvingly that his fellow believers excelled in reading the Bible "literally." This did not, of course, signal that his people were incapable of figurative interpretation; when Revelation 5:5 called Christ the "lion of the tribe of Judah," the Saints did not imagine he bore fangs and claws. Rather, Talmage meant that the substance of the Bible's narrative and proclamation were historical and real. Visiting angels were real beings, God inscribed the Ten Commandments on tangible tablets of stone, Christ indeed walked on water and was physically resurrected. A geologist by training, Talmage espoused the "simplicity" and "plain sense" of the Bible and praised the Book of Mormon effusively on grounds of its exceeding clarity. Nonetheless, in 1899, in what became one of the most influential Latter-day Saint volumes of the twentieth century, the future apostle allowed that "the Bible is the foremost of [the Church's] standard works, first among the books which have been proclaimed as her written guides in faith and doctrine."[22]



It is possible that Talmage's prioritization of the Bible was influenced by the situation of the church at the turn of the twentieth century, then a decade into its attempted rapprochement with federal authority and American culture, over which a civil-Protestant establishment reigned. The Saints wanted to be accepted. This speculation notwithstanding, Talmage's formulation articulated a long and widely held Latter-day Saint sentiment. Moreover, his perspectives, specified in *The Articles of Faith* and *Jesus the Christ*, attained semi-canonical status in the decades following their publication. Both works were among volumes most likely to be in Latter-day Saint homes in the twentieth century. Both were long-time anchors in the Church's "missionary library," the few non-scriptural books approved by the church for study by active missionaries, thus informing the gospel heard by prospective converts and the gospel taught by the Church's future local and general authorities.

Despite this, the Bible's ambiguous place as "first among equals" in the Church's canon began subtly to erode as the twentieth century unfolded. One sign of the change is revealed through a simple statistical word analysis. At the pulpit during semiannual general conferences of the faithful, the term *Bible* was pronounced by the Church's central authorities more frequently than "Book of Mormon" in each decade from the 1850s through the end of the

22. James E. Talmage, *Articles of Faith*, rev. ed. (Salt Lake City, UT: Deseret Book, 1990, [1st ed. 1899]): 5, 18, 240. James P. Harris, ed., *The Essential James E. Talmage* (Salt Lake City, UT: Signature Books, 1997), 122–27,

century, but the reverse was true for each decade from 1900 onward.[23] By the 1990s, the Book of Mormon was cited almost four times more often than the considerably longer Bible; by the next decade, more than four times as often; by the 2010s, nearly six times more often.



A more textured sketch of this shift may be sensed by sampling the weighting of the relative import of the Bible and the Book of Mormon given by a series of key leaders over time. There has always been a diversity of views in the hierarchy, but preponderant sentiment has also changed across the decades. For example, B.H. Roberts (d. 1933) and John A. Widtsoe (d. 1952), influential intellectuals and theological moderates within the Mormon spectrum, joined James Talmage in giving the Bible pride of place among the Church's four canonized volumes. Roberts and Widtsoe, however, increased their attention to the Book of Mormon, particularly as witness for and defense of the reliability of the Bible, which they understood to be under assault by the "new" biblical criticism that had seeped down to popular audiences during previous decades.

Like these men, the far more conservative Joseph Fielding Smith (d. 1972), apostle and future church president, stressed that all scripture acts in concert. However, in his hands the Bible began to feel more ancillary to restoration scriptures. Rather than the Book of Mormon seen as verification of the Bible, Smith cast the besieged Bible as bulwark for the Book of Mormon. His theological heir, the oft-cited Bruce R. McConkie (d. 1985), lent a juridical tone to his similar but more forcefully stated conclusions. His 1985 book, *A New Witness for the Articles of Faith*, marshalled an apparent corrective to James Talmage's classic *Articles of Faith.* McConkie paraphrases Talmage in noting that the Bible is the "foremost of the standard works," but sheers "foremost" of meaning except as "the first to be accepted" in the canon, whose ancient formation was, he notes, problematic. McConkie proceeded to dismantle the priority of the Bible: While "there is no way to overstate the worth and blessing of the Bible for mankind," yet "when the eternal ledgers are finally balanced, more souls will have been saved in the celestial kingdom—ten thousand times over—because of the Book of Mormon than have so obtained because of the Bible." This is to say that, once we transcend rhetorical homage, there is indeed a way to overstate the worth and blessing of the Bible. "As the law was a schoolmaster to prepare backsliding Israel to receive Christ and his gospel … so the Bible prepares men for the endless outpouring of eternal truth that is to be showered

23. Data is taken from Mark Davies, *LDS General Conference Corpus (2018),* accessed August 1, 2018 at https://www.lds-general-conference.org/.

upon the faithful in the last days" through new revelation. "The Bible shines with a dim and reflected light, showing forth portions of what holy men of old believed and taught"; by contrast the modern word "blazes forth in all the brilliance of the noonday sun." [24] Elder McConkie's influence, unsurpassed in the second half of the twentieth century among ordinary church members, was diffused through his voluminous books (including a multivolume doctrinal New Testament commentary), over the pulpit, in content and citations in official church manuals, and in interpretive reference guides woven into the now-ubiquitous 1979/1981 edition of the Church's standard scriptural works. All this both reflected and abetted the dwindling of the Bible's stature among church members.

This relative decline of the Bible was accompanied by the proportionate ascent of the Book of Mormon. In the early 1950s, lawyer Thomas Ferguson launched the New World Archeological Foundation[25] in hopes of finding archeological evidence for the Book of Mormon in Central America. Although unsuccessful, his efforts both reflected and contributed to the growing interest in Book of Mormon study, manifest a decade later, for example, when BYU began to offer a required Book of Mormon course for BYU freshmen.[26] Church leaders also showed increased attention to the Book of Mormon, supported by the work of scholars, especially prodigy Hugh Nibley (d. 2005) and the establishment in 1979 of the independent FARMS (later absorbed into BYU), whose prolific apologetic labors centered especially on the Book of Mormon.

Such contributions as these prepared the way for the decisive turning point in the Book of Mormon's conquest of church members' attention: the presidency of Ezra Taft Benson (d. 1994). Beginning earlier but particularly by the mid-1980s as he became president of the Church, Benson preached numerous sermons in General Conference and in local settings extolling the virtues of the Book of Mormon and warning of divine censure to be visited upon church members who took it lightly: "When we are called upon to study or teach other scriptures," he said, "we need to strengthen that undertaking by frequent reference to the additional insights which the Book of Mormon may provide on the subject." His aspiration for the book and the Church of the

24. Bruce R. McConkie, *A New Witness for the Articles of Faith* (Salt Lake City, UT: Deseret Book, 1985), 390–91, 394, 397–98, 405–6, 411.

25. Paul Gutjahr, *The Book of Mormon: a Biography* (Princeton, NJ: Princeton University Press, 2012), 102–04.

26. Gutjahr, 106. This was mirrored in a similar and contemporaneous rise in the Book of Mormon's visibility in other materials produced by the church's education system.

future could even assume rhetorical patterns akin to those Martin Luther King passionately applied to the cause of racial and civil justice. "I have a vision," Benson proclaimed,



> of homes alerted, of classes alive, and of pulpits aflame with the spirit of Book of Mormon messages.... I have a vision of artists putting into film, drama, literature, music, and paintings great themes and great characters from the Book of Mormon.... I have a vision of thousands of missionaries going into the mission field with hundreds of passages memorized from the Book of Mormon so that they might feed the needs of a spiritually famished world.[27]

The Church responded to this call; the consequent change endured. A generation later, it remains common for church families and congregations jointly to read the entire book in the course of a year or a more compressed season. This rarely occurs with the Bible. Over the pulpit, church members pronounce their testimonies of the truthfulness of the Book of Mormon in monthly "fast and testimony" meetings. They believe in the other revelations, but the scripture to which they most frequently attach their expressions of faith is the Book of Mormon. The heroes they cite in their sermons and church classes are not typically Joshua, David, or Paul, but Nephi, King Benjamin, and Moroni. Plays, stories, films, and music on Book of Mormon themes did in fact emerge. It is not too much to say that President Benson inaugurated the Book of Mormon era in the restoration's scriptural engagement. Relative to this thrust, the Bible is less prominent in the minds of the Latter-day Saints today than at any time in their past.

One could inflate or distort this change in the scriptural awareness of adherents of the Church of Jesus Christ of Latter-day Saints. To them, the Bible remains holy writ that, despite its flaws, conveys the word of God; its two testaments are occasionally given homage as a single, independent entity in itself.[28] Nonetheless, the century-long decline in the Bible's relative stature and usage in the Saints' canon is documentable.

27. Ezra Taft Benson, "Flooding the Earth with the Book of Mormon," *Ensign* (November 1988), accessed September 5, 2018, at https://www.lds.org/ensign/1988/11/flooding-the-earth-with-the-book-of-mormon?lang=eng.

28. For example, M. Russell Ballard, "The Miracle of the Holy Bible," *Ensign* (April 2007), accessed September 5, 2018, at https://www.lds.org/general-conference/2007/04/the-miracle-of-the-holy-bible?lang=eng. A contemporary official perspective on the Bible's value appears on the Church's website, accessed February 12, 2022, at https://www.churchofjesuschrist.org/comeuntochrist/believe/bible/what-is-the-holy-bible.

It is also apt to be consequential. Along with the absence of theological seminaries and a comparative disinterest in modern biblical scholarship, we have noted that the pronounced but selective literalism characteristic of approaches to scripture among the earliest Latter-day Saints was extended by traits of their additional new Bible-patterned scriptures. It may be that the later eclipse of the Bible by the Book of Mormon and additional new scriptures, with their heightened literalism, have nourished a sense of interpretive assurance among church members so strong that, in circular fashion, it further erodes the perceived need for the Bible.[29]

In any case, a minimal response to modern scholarship and a dilution of biblical influence seems likely to be consequential in other ways. The Book of Mormon, the Doctrine and Covenants, and the Pearl of Great Price augment, amend, and complement the Bible, but are themselves poorly comprehended apart from the Bible. They are premised upon the Bible even where they reinterpret it. One example of the impact of a diminished biblical consciousness among this Christian people might be an evolving sense of the Christ they worship. For what scriptures convey is not Christ himself, but distinct *portraits* of Christ. "The map is not the territory."[30] John's portrait of Christ is not the same as Mark's nor Luke's nor the portrayal in 3 Nephi. Whether or not one is a believer, the range of portraits offers distinct perspectives and aspects of the figure of Christ. The deliberate or unconscious effort to homogenize these portraits may not inevitably yield the best historical, visual, or theological insight into the figure of Christ any more than would a computerized composite of you or me, made from a yearbook photo, an older crayon self-portrait, an interpretive professional painter, and photographs of us in contrasting moods.[31]

The Son of God whom Latter-day Saints have come to have in mind when they preach and pray and worship is not principally the biblical suffering servant who hangs impaled on a cross or who is represented by the cross alone—a

29. A related, speculative suggestion was offered by an anonymous critic of an earlier draft of this essay.

30. The Polish-American philosopher and scientist, Alfred Korzybski, did not originate but did probe the saying, pointing out in 1933 the conceptual dangers of confusing some real thing with one's abstraction of, or reaction to, it. He acknowledged his imagery's debt to mathematician Eric Bell: *Numerology* (Baltimore: Williams and Wilkins), 138.

31. The problematic but natural impulse to "harmonize" the various gospel accounts enjoys a long tradition in Christianity, going back at least as early as the second-century writer Tatian, whose synthetic *Diatesseron* temporarily supplanted the four canonized (or canonizing) gospels in the ancient Syriac church. Among the Latter-day Saints the impulse may be seen in James Talmage, Bruce McConkie, and a number of lesser lights.

cruciform that has presided over the consciousness of more traditional forms of Christianity for the last millennium.[32]

Instead, the Latter-day Saint image of Christ is better disclosed in the *Christus*: Bertel Thorvaldsen's magisterial early nineteenth-century sculpture, eleven feet in height, located in the Church of Our Lady in Copenhagen. A replica of this piece is installed since 1966 at Temple Square in Salt Lake City, subsequently at temple visitor centers internationally, in miniature at LDS bookstores and on the mantles of Latter-day Saint homes, and displayed increasingly in church literature for the past half-century. While replicas are also found in cemeteries, churches, and related spaces outside of Mormondom, such as in the Johns Hopkins Hospital in Baltimore, the Latter-day Saint attachment to this image seems unexcelled elsewhere in contemporary Christendom. In 2020, the Christus became the center point of the movement's new official logo. The Church has adopted the Christus, and the Christus has adopted the Church.

Although the original statue was created by a Danish Lutheran, the image's resonance in Latter-day Saint culture seems derived less from the early New Testament Gospels of Mark, Matthew, and Luke than from the later, more theologized Gospel of John, which sees Christ in cosmic terms. In the Latter-day Saint mind this vantage is further amplified in 3 Nephi in the Book of Mormon.[33] This is not the suffering Christ, but the having-already-conquered Christ. This is Christ in Majesty, the towering and resurrected Ruler. This is the inviting Christ whose arms are outstretched, ready to embrace the world, who is available to every believer in the present moment. He is remote from Gethsemane and Golgotha, this Christus. He is the Lord God of all creation.[34]

32. Charles Taylor analyzes Christianity's historical tilt toward the passion and death of Christ as beginning near the commencement of the second millennium CE, intensifying in the twelfth and thirteenth centuries, and coming to full fruition during the Reformation and Renaissance. Charles Taylor, *A Secular Age*, 1st ed. (Cambridge, MA: The Belknap Press of Harvard University Press, 2007), 64, 93–94.

33. 3 Nephi 11–28.

34. Although sharing a sense of awe and reverence for their magisterial Lord as depicted by the Christus, Latter-day Saint church members have only a vestigial bond to verbal images developed in earlier Christendom. They do not use terms such as "Christ in Majesty" (early Christian west) or "Pantokrator" ("all-powerful ruler," Byzantine).

## 2

# The King James Version and Modern Translations of the Bible

THOMAS WAYMENT

In 1820, a young Joseph Smith read, pondered, and sought for insight regarding a passage from his King James Bible (hereafter KJV; James 1:5). The story of his heavenly vision is a familiar topic for Mormons, one that connects scriptural hope with religious enlightenment, but it also points to the underlying tensions in the Latter-day Saint (hereafter LDS) approach to the Bible. The Bible directed Smith's quest to ask God, and Joseph seems to have expected a liberal answer. Smith's was a plain sense reading of James, "If any of you lack wisdom, let him ask of God, that giveth to all men liberally." The gateway to God was the word of God, and as with so many of Smith's contemporaries, the KJV Bible represented the word of God itself, the very words of God that he spoke to all believers. This "Word of God in English" commanded people in a new day, it spoke across generations, and for "the men who wanted the Word of God in English," the KJV was the source for it.[1] Smith found his own prophetic voice through the KJV, and his own revelations—his "thus saith the Lord" directives—would later compete for authority with the very words that brought him to ask God for an answer. This remains one of the primary tensions for LDS believers: does the modern or ancient word of God take precedence? The history of LDS use of the KJV Bible is one that is defined by a complex relationship of acceptance and tension, of trying to make sacred the work of seventeenth-century scholars.

Since their organization on April 6, 1830, English-speaking Latter-day Saints have overwhelmingly favored the KJV. The process by which LDS



1. Melvyn Bragg, *Book of Books: The Radical Impact of the King James Bible, 1611–2011* (London: Hodder & Stoughton, 2011), 8.

leaders formally adopted the KJV as the official Bible of the church is itself a fascinatingly complex story.[2] To understand the LDS approach to the Bible, particularly the KJV, this chapter will begin with a brief outline of the history of KJV and modern translations highlighting the Mormon participation in the discussion. The paper will then move on to explore intersections between the LDS experience and the wider academic conversation regarding the KJV and modern Bible translations.

## HISTORY OF BIBLE TRANSLATIONS

For nineteenth-century American Protestants, there were realistically few options when choosing a Bible, and the KJV was more readily available for purchase than other Bibles such as the Geneva, Coverdale, or Bishop's Bibles.[3] Mormons used the KJV because they were part of the wider Bible culture of their day, and not because of an overt theologically informed decision to do so. No single denomination owned the KJV, but in America it was *the* Protestant Bible, and therefore in the twentieth century, when academics began to call for a retranslation of the Bible, many American churches did not have a unique sense of ownership of a single translation. As a result, many faith traditions were able to welcome the calls for a new translation, in part because their clergy who were trained in biblical studies were able to explain the benefits of the newer translations.

Already at the beginning of the nineteenth century, New Testament scholars were drawing attention to deficiencies in the Greek text used for the major translations, but such calls faced strong headwinds by those who declared the KJV to be "the most beautiful piece of writing in any language."[4] Similar calls for a new translation were made for the Old Testament as well.[5] For new translations to succeed, better Hebrew and Greek texts were needed to replace Erasmus' eclectic *textus receptus* and the Masoretic text used for the KJV Old Testament. Tischendorf (1846), Westcott-Hort (1881), Nestle (1898), Von Soden (1902–1910), and others led the way in the nineteenth and early

2. The most thorough and thoughtful study of this topic is Philip L. Barlow, *Mormons and the Bible: The Place of the Latter-day Saints in American Religion* (Oxford, UK: Oxford University Press, 2013).

3. Harry M. Orlinsky and Robert G. Bratcher, *A History of Bible Translation and the North American Contribution* (Atlanta: Scholars Press, 1991), xii.

4. Bragg, *Book of Books*, 8.

5. Jonathan Sheehan, *The Enlightenment Bible: Translation, Scholarship, Culture* (Princeton, NJ: Princeton University Press, 2005), 20–25. See also Eldon J. Epp, "The Multivalence of the Term 'Original Text' in New Testament Textual Criticism," *HTR* 92.3 (1999): 245–81.

twentieth centuries through the creation of a Greek text that was based on the scientific study of New Testament Greek manuscripts. The academic publication of the Hebrew Bible began with Kittel's 1906 edition of the *Biblia Hebraica* and then later through the *Biblia Hebraica Stuttgartensia* editions. Despite the fact that these scholars did not produce modern language translations, their texts drew attention to one of the reasons modern translations were deemed necessary: the KJV clearly departed in places from the Greek and Hebrew manuscript evidence.

Modern translations began in earnest in 1885 with the publication of the Revised Version, which explicitly promoted the ideal of improving the KJV. In 1946, a committee formed under the directorship of the National Council of Churches published a new translation of the New Testament—the Revised Standard Version (RSV)—that was based on a better Greek text. In 1952, they followed with a new translation of the Old Testament that was based on the Masoretic text, the same textual basis for the KJV, but they supplemented their text with new readings from the recently discovered Dead Sea Scrolls and the Septuagint. The number of new translations based on improved Greek and Hebrew texts has now reached well over one thousand.[6] However, some denominations continue to hold to the KJV, and some Baptists, Pentecostals, Presbyterians, and Mormons lead the way in this regard. Catholics continue to favor translations based on Jerome's Vulgate, while Evangelicals tend to favor the New International Version (NIV).[7] Two of the most popular translations of the Bible today, the NRSV (a 1989 update of the RSV) and the NIV (1978), tell an interesting story of the success of modern translations. The NRSV and NIV were both translated by teams of academics, who worked independently of the *textus receptus*. They communicated an atmosphere of transparency in their approach, and they published their goals and expected outcomes of the new translations.[8]

Despite the success of the NIV and NRSV, however, a 2014 national study commissioned by the Center for the Study of Religion and American Culture

6. David Daniell, *The Bible in English: Its History and Influence* (New Haven, CT: Yale University Press, 2003), 764–69; Bruce Metzger, *The Bible in Translation, Ancient and English Versions* (Grand Rapids, MI: Baker, 2001).

7. For a discussion of usage of the RSV and NIV, see Peter J. Thuesen, *In Discordance with the Scriptures: American Protestant Battles over Translating the Bible* (New York: Oxford University Press, 1999), 67–144.

8. Bruce M. Metzger, "The Revised Standard Version of the Bible: Its Making and Character," *Proceedings of the American Philosophical Society* 135.3 (1991): 368–81; John H. Stek, "The New International Version: How it Came to Be," in *The Challenge of Bible Translation: Communicating God's Word to the World: Essays in Honor of Ronald F. Youngblood*, edited by Glen G. Scorgie, Mark L. Strauss, and Steven M. Voth (Grand Rapids, MI: Zondervan, 2003), 235–63.

(CSRAC), notes that even though there has been an uptick in the number of copies of modern translations sold such as the NIV and NRSV, the KJV is still the top choice for Bible readers "by a wide margin."[9] A surprising 55 percent of Bible readers prefer the KJV to other modern translations even though the NIV significantly outsells the KJV.[10] The CSRAC study confirms some of the underlying tensions among Bible readers, who continue to prefer a translation that was familiar to past generations despite frequently hearing the NIV and NRSV read over the pulpit.[11] Mormons read and hear the KJV almost exclusively, and church curricular materials in English use the KJV.

Facing the challenges of familiarity and widespread cultural usage, Mormon academics have called for change in the churchwide acceptance of the KJV, telling readers that "the KJV suffocates scriptural understanding."[12] In a May 22, 1992 statement affirming the official status of the KJV, the church appeared to recognize that there are legitimate concerns regarding the KJV when it noted that "other Bible versions may be easier to read than the King James Version." The same statement also made it clear that change was unlikely.[13]

Simply put, English-speaking LDS readers continue to use the KJV for many of the same reasons that early Americans used it: it is familiar, eloquent, and still broadly used. The factors contributing to continued LDS acceptance of the KJV despite growing recognition that it may not be the most accurate translation are multifaceted, and Philip Barlow sees the major factors for retaining it as (1) the publication of Joseph Smith's Bible revision in 1867, (2) the nineteenth-century Protestant-Catholic conflict over a government-sponsored Bible version for use in American schools, (3) twentieth-century concerns about biblical or higher criticism, (4) the rise of modern translations, and (5) "a modern popular misunderstanding of the nature of Joseph Smith's

9. Philip Goff, Arthur E. Farnsley II, and Peter J. Thueson, "The Bible in American Life," (March 6, 2014), 7, accessed March 6, 2017, at http://www.raac.iupui.edu/files/2713/9413/8354/Bible_in_American_Life_Report_March_6_2014.pdf.

10. Of respondents, 19 percent prefer the NIV, the next closest to the KJV. The number of KJV readers increases significantly among Black communities (77 percent) but decreases significantly in conjunction with income (69 percent for those who make less than $25,000 but 44 percent for those who earn above $75,000). Those with graduate degrees report using the KJV 33 percent of the time, while those with a high school education prefer it only 72 percent of the time. Paul C. Gutjahr, "From Monarchy to Democracy: The Dethroning of the King James Bible in the United States," in *The King James Bible after 400 Years: Literary, Linguistic, and Cultural Influences,* edited by H. Hamlin and Norman Jones (Cambridge, UK: Cambridge University Press, 2010), 164.

11. Goff, Farnsley II, and Thueson, "The Bible in American Life," 12–14.

12. Philip Barlow, "Why the King James Version? From the Common to the Official Bible of Mormonism," *Dialogue* 22, no. 2 (Summer 1989) 19.

13. Ezra Taft Benson, Gordon B. Hinckley, and Thomas S. Monson, "First Presidency Statement on the King James Version of the Bible," *Ensign* (August 1992): 80.

recorded revelations."[14] Additional factors include the 1979 (revised again in 2013) publication of an LDS edition of the KJV that incorporated many passages from Joseph Smith's Bible revision into the footnotes, and the fact that the Book of Mormon and Doctrine and Covenants rely heavily upon KJV language and style. In 1979–1981, the LDS Church invested significantly in the printing of an official version of the KJV that would be used by all English-speaking members, and the church followed up with official publications of Spanish (2009) and Portuguese (2015) Bibles.[15]



Although the publication of the Spanish and Portuguese Bibles have created challenges to maintaining the KJV as the official Bible of the English-speaking church, the official nature of those publications and the imprimatur given to the church's English edition effectively closes the discussion for English, Spanish, and Portuguese speaking members of the church. As Jonathan Sheehan has proposed, an authoritative translation, one that settles the issue of the quality of the underlying text and related academic issues effectively closes the canon of inspiration.[16] As Gordon Campbell has observed, "The Mormon Version of the KJV has not exercised significant influence beyond adherents of its various branches, but it has served to maintain the centrality of the KJV in a strand of the Christian faith that has millions of adherents."[17]

## ORIGIN OF THE LDS USE OF THE KJV

The great paradox regarding LDS usage of the KJV was captured succinctly by Barlow who noted, "Nineteenth-century Latter-day Saints shared much with their contemporaries but reacted creatively against a confining orthodoxy; early twentieth-century Saints shared much with their non-Mormon peers but reacted conservatively against a changing, secular world."[18] Joseph Smith, like

14. Barlow, "Why the King James Version?," 19. Here, Barlow seems to be referring to a fundamental misunderstanding about the way Joseph Smith's own language shaped the revelations he received. Compare J. Reuben Clark, *Why the King James Version* (Salt Lake City, UT: Deseret Book, 1956); Bruce R. McConkie, *A New Witness for the Articles of Faith* (Salt Lake City, UT: Deseret Book, 1985).

15. See Robert J. Matthews, "The New Publications of the Standard Works—1979, 1981," *BYU Studies* 22, no. 4 (1982): 387–424; Fred E. Woods, "The Latter-day Saint Edition of the King James Bible," in *The King James Bible and the Restoration*, edited by Kent P. Jackson (Provo, UT: BYU Religious Studies Center, 2011), 260–80. Lavina Fielding Anderson, "Church Publishes First LDS Edition of the Bible," *Ensign* (October 1979).

16. Sheehan, *The Enlightenment Bible*, 17.

17. Gordon Campbell, *Bible: The Story of the King James Version: 1611–2011* (Oxford, UK: Oxford University Press, 2010), 157. Campbell's reference to "various branches" would include the Church of Jesus Christ of Latter-day Saints, the Community of Christ, FLDS, and a number of smaller splinter groups.

18. Barlow, "Why the King James Version?," 24.

his contemporaries, probably thought little about what Bible would become the official text of the church, and when he and Oliver Cowdery purchased a Bible at the Grandin printing shop in 1829, they did so to prepare for a massive revision of the Bible and not in an effort to establish the KJV as the church's official Bible. Interestingly, their effort to revise the Bible was broadly antagonistic toward the American canonical consciousness because it subjected the Bible of faith to revelatory revision, and thus potentially raised the possibility that the Bible itself could be significantly expanded. What was initially antagonistic turned out to almost guarantee continued usage of the KJV in LDS congregations despite the KJV's recognized flaws. This is in part, because, Smith's revisions of the Bible make little sense when read outside of a KJV Bible-reading environment. The passages that do make sense independently have largely been excerpted and placed in the church's Pearl of Great Price as standalone revelations.

Smith at one time declared Luther's German Bible to be the best modern language translation, probably referring to the Luther translation of the *textus receptus*, and the official church newspaper, the *Times and Seasons*, quoted several modern translations, but at times was also critical of modern translations.[19] These early editorials do not promote the KJV as superior, and an anonymous editor equally condemns all of the translations, including the KJV, saying, "The first four translations came from the same Hebrew, but not by inspiration."[20]

Such an open approach to modern translations of the Bible reflects the nineteenth-century attitudes of Latter-day Saints and Smith's attempt to revise the KJV Bible, but the twentieth century witnessed a shift toward a single translation that near the end of the century evolved into an official recognition that the KJV was the Bible of English-speaking Mormons. The origins of this process probably began in Brigham Young's school of the prophets—the title used to designate a gathering of LDS leaders to discuss issues related to church beliefs and practices. During a meeting where the issue of the publication of Joseph Smith's revised version of the Bible was under consideration, Young asserted, "The King James translation is good enough."[21]

19. History, 1838–1856, vol. E-1 [July 1, 1843–April 30, 1844], 1972, available at http://www.josephsmithpapers.org/paper-summary/history-1838-1856-volume-e-1-1-july-1843-30-april-1844/344?highlight=-german%20bible. The Coverdale and Michaelis translations were cited in *Times and Seasons* 5, no. 14 (August 1, 1844): 600–1. The Bishop's Bible, an unnamed Polyglot Bible (probably Bagster's), and the Douay-Rheim's translation were cited in *Times and Seasons* 6, no. 2 (February 4, 1845): 791.

20. *Times and Seasons* 6, no. 2 (February 4, 1845): 791. The four translations were the Bishop's Bible, the KJV, a Polyglot, and the Hebrew text of Michaelis.

21. Reed C. Durham, "A History of Joseph Smith's Revision of the Bible" (PhD diss., BYU, 1965), 245–75. Barlow, "Why the King James Version?", 21, also sees this school of the prophets meeting as the

Brigham's "good enough" quickly developed along traditional lines with respect to the KJV, where the KJV became the best, most eloquent, and even an inspired translation.[22] The critical turning point came as the result of J. Reuben Clark's publication of an impassioned defense of the KJV.[23] According to David O. McKay's biographer, the president of the LDS Church was resistant to Clark's ideas, and rightly so given Clark's lack of training in Hebrew or Greek.[24] Clark's reasoning for promoting the KJV was not based on awareness of historical sources and linguistic arguments he had originated, but instead it promoted the scholarship of the anti-RSV movement into the LDS conversation. Today, LDS acceptance of the KJV for English speakers is almost unquestioned, and its legacy has transitioned from being a good Bible to being "probably the best Bible ever prepared and preserved by the scholars among men."[25] More cautious LDS voices describe the situation differently, "We clearly prefer the King James Version of the New Testament, but we are not adamant about that."[26]

## WHY LATTER-DAY SAINTS CONTINUE TO USE THE KJV

Despite modern advances in textual criticism, archaeological discoveries, and the evolution of English since the seventeenth century, Latter-day Saints continue to publish, circulate, and use the KJV exclusively in English-speaking areas of the church. There are perhaps three fundamental reasons, among other less significant reasons, for doing so. KJV wording, grammar, and phraseology are intricately interwoven into LDS scripture—the Book of Mormon and the Doctrine and Covenants—and adopting a modern translation would perhaps push restoration scriptures to the periphery of the Mormon canon because they would likely become part of an older, archaic language tradition of the

beginning point for the LDS church officially recognizing the KJV. See also Gary James Bergera, "The Orson Pratt–Brigham Young Controversies: Conflict within the Quorums, 1853 to 1868," *Dialogue* 13, no. 2 (Summer 1980): 39–40. On another occasion, Young challenged those who criticized the KJV to produce a better translation.

22. Joseph Fielding Smith, *Doctrines of Salvation*, three vols. (Salt Lake City, UT: Bookcraft, 1954–1956), 3:191; John A. Widtsoe, *Gospel Interpretations* (Salt Lake City, UT: Bookcraft, 1947), 257–60. Russell M. Ballard, "The Miracle of the Holy Bible," *Ensign* (May 2007): 80, "I believe even the scholars of King James had spiritual promptings in their translation work."

23. J. Reuben Clark, *Why the King James Version* (Salt Lake City, UT: Deseret Book, 1956); D. Michael Quinn, *J. Reuben Clark: The Church Years* (Provo, UT: BYU Press, 1983), 133.

24. Quinn, *J. Reuben Clark*, 177.

25. Bruce R. McConkie, *A New Witness for the Articles of Faith* (Salt Lake City, UT: Deseret Book, 1985), 391, 393.

26. John K. Carmack, "The New Testament and the Latter-day Saints," in *The New Testament and the Latter-day Saints* (Orem, UT: Randall Book, 1987), 2. Compare Franklin S. Gonzalez, "I Have a Question," *Ensign* 17 (June 1987): 23–5.

church. The KJV already feels archaic to many Mormons, and by taking away that point of comparison, the Book of Mormon and Doctrine and Covenants would quickly become archaic with no clear pathway toward modernizing their language. Second, the KJV is the language of Mormon liturgy and hymns, and third, LDS theology, particularly from the Smith period, is tightly connected to the language of the KJV.[27]

For example, the LDS canon adds two additional creation accounts to those found in the Bible: one from the Book of Moses (Joseph Smith's revision of the Bible) and one from the Book of Abraham. Because the LDS accounts arose directly through Smith's revision of Genesis, the four creation accounts placed in historical order present an interesting case study: Genesis 1:1 ("In the beginning God created the heaven and the earth)," Genesis 2:4 ("These are the generations of the heavens and of the earth when they were created, in the day that the Lord God made the earth and the heavens."), Moses 2:1 ("I am the Beginning and the End, the Almighty God; by mine Only Begotten I created these things; yea, in the beginning I created the heaven, and the earth upon which thou standest"), Abraham 4:1 ("And then the Lord said: Let us go down. And they went down at the beginning, and they, that is the Gods, organized and formed the heavens and the earth").[28]

Unique Mormon theological tenets, such as Satan's commanding the serpent in Eden to tempt and deceive Adam and Eve (Moses 4:6–7), are built on the KJV text using seventeenth-century Jacobean English, and the obvious intertextual connections would be difficult to recognize if the underlying KJV language was removed. For example, the Book of Mormon's use of New Testament language would be difficult to recognize when it states, "this corruption shall put on incorruption," which is nearly verbatim to KJV 1 Corinthians 15:53, but which is rendered in the NRSV, "this perishable body must put on imperishability." Additionally, modern LDS commentators have promoted the idea that God speaks in KJV-influenced language, so that when one hears the voice of God in English, God speaks like the KJV translators.[29]

For English-speaking Latter-day Saints, the language of the KJV is also the language of prayer, sacrament, and baptism. As recently as 1993, LDS leaders called on members to continue praying in KJV language:

27. Grant Underwood, "Joseph Smith and the King James Bible," in *The King James Bible and the Restoration,* edited by Kent P. Jackson (Provo, UT: Religious Studies Center, 2011), 215–33.

28. Anthony A. Hutchison, "A Mormon Midrash? LDS Creation Narratives Reconsidered," *Dialogue* 21, no. 4 (Winter 1988) 18–74, and Barlow, "Why the King James Version?," 20.

29. Joseph Fielding McConkie, "Modern Revelation," in *To Be Learned Is Good if*... edited by Robert Millet (Salt Lake City, UT: Bookcraft, 1987), 126.

> When we address prayers to our Heavenly Father in English, our only available alternatives are the common words of speech like *you* and *your* or the dignified but uncommon words like *thee, thou,* and *thy* which were used in the King James Version of the Bible almost five hundred years ago. Latter-day Saints, of course, prefer the latter. In our prayers we use language that is dignified and different, even archaic.[30]

Finally, the Book of Mormon is replete with KJV language. The Book of Mormon king Benjamin speaks in clear KJV style when he says, "how much more just will be your condemnation for withholding your substance, which doth not belong to you but to God, to whom also your life belongeth; and yet ye put up no petition, nor repent of the thing which thou hast done" (Mosiah 4:22). Modern translations of the Book of Mormon into Spanish, German, French, and other languages have not been able to reproduce the affected KJV style. Modern language translations adopted by the LDS Church tend to favor translations that render the text in a word-for-word fashion using modern language. This pattern of using a word-for-word literal translation tends to result in a modernizing of the text rather than archaicizing the translation. This is because the word choices are almost wholly modern, and without recourse to an ancient text like the Greek New Testament or Hebrew, the translators are not able to approach the translation process the KJV or NRSV that tend to avoid word-for-word correspondence but often follow the original language word order.

## INTERSECTIONS

Academic discussion of the KJV in the twenty-first century has shifted to considering its intent as a translation, with N.T. Wright calling it an endeavor to support the monarchy and political ideals of England.[31] Others have sought to discover reasons for its American success, and Campbell has argued, "[T]he rhythms of the KJV made it ideally suited to such environments," referring to its popularity as a preacher's Bible during the Second Great Awakening.[32]

30. Dallin H. Oaks, "The Language of Prayer," *Ensign* (May 1993): 16.

31. N.T. Wright, "The Monarchs and the Message: Reflection on Bible Translation from the Sixteenth to the Twenty-First Century," in *Biblical Scholarship in North America: The King James Version at 400: Assessing its Genius as Bible Translation and its Literary Influence*, edited by David G. Burke, John F. Kutsko, and Philip H. Towner (Atlanta: Society of Biblical Literature, 2013), 312–16.

32. Campbell, *The Story of the King James Version*, 195–96.

If such contexts really did lay the foundation for the KJV becoming part of the religious fabric of nineteenth-century America, then such contexts shape the meaning of the text. Those contexts may depart significantly from LDS usage and interest in the Bible. However, LDS scholars have not pursued these questions, possibly because they imply that the KJV has become a historical artifact. The KJV is anything but an artifact for LDS readers.



The LDS discussion, instead, exhibits two clear avenues of engagement with questions about the quality of the KJV. At the turn of the century, LDS scholar and church leader B.H. Roberts appeared open to engaging biblical criticism with the understanding that it could result in a better Bible.[33] He was followed by others who were equally willing to employ terminology suggesting the KJV is a flawed translation.[34] Another part of the LDS tradition has pushed back against these efforts by demonizing "higher criticism" of the Bible and attempting to promote counter-academic arguments developed by the KJV-only movement.[35] Regardless of the counterarguments against those who have promoted a more open discussion about the KJV, the LDS Church has recently published Spanish and Portuguese editions of the Bible, and it endorses other translations in dozens of other languages with none of them using the same Greek and Hebrew textual base as the KJV.[36] Without publicly acknowledging the efforts, the LDS Church is functionally marginalizing the dominance of the KJV among its now global membership, and unique KJV-isms will continue to make sense to a smaller and smaller swath of the LDS population.

An additional challenge is that in non-English speaking-areas of the world, the LDS Church has subtly corrected and updated the language of the Book of Mormon. Without implying a direct causal connection, research into the development of the translation of the Book of Mormon demonstrates that ambiguous and difficult passages resulting from the book's reliance on the KJV are being adjusted, clarified, and corrected in foreign language translations.[37]

33. B. H. Roberts, *The Seventy's Course in Theology*. 5 vols. (Salt Lake City, UT: Deseret Book, 1907–1912), 31.

34. James E. Talmage, *Articles of Faith* (Salt Lake City, UT: Deseret News, 1899), 236–37; Frederick Clift, "The Bible: The King James Translation—A Compromise," *Improvement Era* (July 1904): 655, 663; Frederick Clift, "The Bible, English Revision, 1881—American Standard Revision, 1901," *Improvement Era* 7 (August 1904): 774–78.

35. Joseph Fielding Smith, *Seek Ye Earnestly* (Salt Lake City, UT: Deseret Book, 1970), 364; J. Reuben Clark, *Why the King James Version* (Salt Lake City, UT: Deseret Book, 1956), 6–7, passim. James R. White, *The King James Only Controversy: Can You Trust the Modern Translations?* (Minneapolis, MN: Bethany House, 1995) cited in Goff, Farnsley II, and Thueson, "The Bible in American Life," 13, no. 3.

36. Josh Sears, "Santa Biblia: The Latter-day Saint Bible in Spanish," *BYU Studies* 54, no. 1 (2015): 45–52.

37. My own survey of the Danish, German, Swedish, Italian, and French editions of the Book of Mormon demonstrates that a more literal translation of the Book of Mormon was done in the mid-nineteenth century, but that errors were subsequently corrected when the Book of Mormon was retranslated in those

It may be that a shift in the usage of a modern translation of the Bible would permit similar adjustments to be made in the English Book of Mormon.

The last foothold that the KJV is able to consistently maintain is its perceived elegance and moving prose, a position that betrays the obvious reality that the text is based on poor manuscript evidence and is difficult to understand in the modern era. The idea that the KJV is regarded as the "high-water mark of the English language" elevates the text into a perceived sacred space, one that makes arguments against it seem imprudent and even heretical.[38] As long as the language of God and the language of printed scripture are perceived to be the same or to exist in the same sacred space, it will be difficult for Latter-day Saints to adopt a modern translation of the Bible.

## LATTER-DAY SAINTS AND THE CHALLENGE OF CONTINUING WITH THE KING JAMES VERSION

Strong headwinds face those denominations that continue to use the KJV exclusively as a religiously alert readership confronts the increasingly difficult task of reading the Bible in a dialect that is quickly becoming foreign. In one of the stronger criticisms of the effort to maintain the KJV, R.S. Sugirtharajah writes, "Commentators work on the assumption that only seventeenth-century English is capable of bringing out the complex and multiple meanings of the original Hebrew and Greek texts. It is not clear why the Bible could be transmitted only through the English of the Jacobeans."[39] But the issue may run deeper than simple assumption, and if the KJV's intent was truly the promotion of the British Empire, to engage the suggestion of N.T. Wright, then the interest in promoting empire might ironically topple it as a religious text for those grappling with the problems of colonialism in a postmodern era.

Theoretically, the production of a scholarly KJV—called the New King James Version—could soften the criticisms of the KJV's flawed textual base. David Norton's critical edition attempted something similar, namely a critical

languages in the twentieth century. I looked at misuse of the adverb *goodly* in 1 Nephi 1:1, shifts from singular to plural pronouns in Mosiah 4:22; 1 Nephi 11:7; confusing nouns in 2 Nephi 13:18–23; and an incorrect verb conjugation in 1 Nephi 12:9. Compare Marcellus Snow, "The Challenge of Theological Translation: New German Versions of the Standard Works," *Dialogue* 17, no. 2 (Summer 1984): 136.

38. Campbell, *The Story of the King James Version*, 170.

39. R.S. Sugirtharajah, "The Master Copy: Postcolonial Notes on the King James Bible," in *The King James Version at 400: Assessing its Genius as Bible Translation and its Literary Influence*, edited by David G. Burke, John F. Kutsko, and Philip H. Towner (Atlanta: Society of Biblical Literature, 2013), 511.

edition based on the manuscripts used by the KJV translators.[40] But such an effort would need to expand to include all of the available textual evidence, which is precisely the goal of modern translations like the NRSV. The problems of revising the KJV to conform to modern academic standards are many and insurmountable. Among the most significant of these is the fact that a revised KJV will result in places where the older 1611 text is corrected or found to be in error. Such a result would lead to the troubling conversation that the KJV was not, indeed, a perfect translation and claims about its inspiration, to which the Joseph Smith translation of the Bible is closely aligned, will come into question. One only need look at the longer ending of the Gospel of Mark, which is included in the KJV (Mark 16:9–20), which is based on a questionable manuscript evidence and which was also retained and revised slightly in Smith's Bible revision. Removal of the questionable verses would trigger hard questions about the inspiration behind the KJV and Smith's Bible revision.

40. David Norton, *A Textual History of the King James Bible* (Cambridge, UK: Cambridge University Press, 2005).

3

# Joseph Smith's "New Translation" of the Bible

GRANT UNDERWOOD

Historian Mark Noll commenced his recent monograph on the place of the Bible in the public life of colonial America with this remark: "The Bible in American history defines a subject of extraordinary depth and vast complexity."[1] Part of that complexity is a particular paradox with which 7 Americans lived in the early nineteenth century. On one hand, the Bible was regarded as the supreme authority and pattern for everything from ecclesiology to ethics. On the other hand, Americans lived in the shadow of more than a century of especially intense debate about the validity of the Bible. Attacks on biblical inconsistencies and improbabilities were met with an outpouring of apologetic "evidences" literature. And between Deistic rejection of the Bible as divine revelation and traditionalist support for scripture as the unerring word of God lay the incipient realm of biblical criticism that critiqued and qualified but did not discard Holy Writ.[2] Whether or not one considered the Bible sacrosanct, it would have been nearly impossible to be unaware of the assault on the Holy Scriptures. Joseph Smith's grandfather, for instance, who was far from belonging to the eastern intelligentsia, upon learning that his son (Joseph's father) was taking an interest in Methodism, "came to the door one day and threw

1. Mark A. Noll, *In the Beginning Was the Word: The Bible in American Public Life, 1492–1783* (New York: Oxford University Press, 2015), 1.

2. The literature on this contest over the Bible is extensive. Still useful as an accessible starting place is Nathan O. Hatch and Mark A. Noll, eds., *The Bible in America: Essays in Cultural History* (New York: Oxford University Press, 1982). Also helpful is E. Brooks Holifield, *Theology in America: Christian Thought from the Age of the Puritans to the Civil War* (New Haven, CT: Yale University Press, 2005), 5–8, 31–34, 159–96.

Tom Pains age of reason into the house and angrily bade him read that until he believed it."[3]

An alternative to substantial disparagement of the scriptures (like Paine's) was the effort to produce a refined Bible, a better translation. Historian Paul Gutjahr has documented the publication of hundreds of different American editions of the Bible in the century after the American Revolution, including a number of new translations.[4] To a significant degree, this was driven by nineteenth-century efforts to purge the Bible of perceived textual and translational impurities in search of an "authentic" text. The irony was that, in an effort to preserve the Bible, God's supposedly immutable Word mutated. This is the milieu out of which emerged Joseph Smith's "New Translation" of the Bible—what Mormons today call the "Joseph Smith Translation" or, simply, the "JST." Like others before and after him, Smith hoped to save the proverbial scriptural baby by dealing with the problematic bath water. As expressed by Smith contemporary Alexander Campbell, who produced his own translation of the New Testament in 1826, the problem was that "the tenets of [previous] translators, whether designedly or undesignedly, did, on many occasions, give a wrong turn to words and sentences bearing upon their favorite dogmas."[5]

By the time Joseph Smith laid aside his New Translation manuscripts (large folio gatherings of stitched-together foolscap sheets usually producing more than forty numbered pages per folio), three years after beginning the project, he had revised more than three thousand of the approximately 31,000 verses in the King James Version of the Bible (KJV), or about 10 percent of its content. In addition to what was "in the air" about the infelicities and shortcomings of the Bible, Joseph Smith's first and longest revelation, the Book of Mormon, explicitly confirmed that the Good Book had arrived on the shores of the Americas bereft of certain "plain and precious" truths and covenants.[6] Smith later added, "[F]rom sundry revelations which had been received, it

3. Lavina Fielding Anderson, ed., *Lucy's Book: A Critical Edition of Lucy Mack Smith's Family Memoir* (Salt Lake City, UT: Signature Books, 2001), 291.

4. Paul C. Gutjahr, *An American Bible: A History of the Good Book in the United States, 1777–1880* (Stanford, CA: Stanford University Press, 1999). For instance, see the detailed study of Alexander Campbell's "New Version" of the New Testament in Cecil K. Thomas, *Alexander Campbell and His New Version* (St. Louis, MO: Bethany Press, 1958). A popular study that ranges widely is Harry Freedman, *The Murderous History of Bible Translations: Power, Conflict, and the Quest for Meaning* (New York: Bloomsbury, 2016).

5. Alexander Campbell, *The Sacred Writings of the Apostles and Evangelists of Jesus Christ, Commonly Styled The New Testament* (Buffalo, VA: Alexander Campbell, 1826), v. Campbell singled out the Genevan reformers as ones who "willfully and knowingly interpolate[d] the scriptures, and torture[d] many passages to favor their system" (vi).

6. 1 Nephi 13:26, 28–29, 32, 34–35, 40; 14:23.

was apparent that many important points, touching the salvation of man, had been taken from the Bible, or lost before it was compiled."[7] If some of the words of ancient prophets and apostles had been lost before they were recorded, or garbled over time after they were written down, or even expurgated from the Bible, then the Mormon prophet envisioned his role as that of restoring the Scriptures to their original fullness and purity. Indeed, he sometimes referred to his revision of the Bible as reclaiming the "fulness of the scriptures."[8] And that fullness was to be restored, not through a knowledge of ancient languages and text-critical skills, but by the same divine inspiration and direct revelation that Smith believed had produced the Bible in the first place.

## HISTORY OF THE NEW TRANSLATION

In early October 1829, Oliver Cowdery, Joseph Smith's close associate and amanuensis for the Book of Mormon, purchased a copy of the King James Bible that would later serve as the basis for the New Translation. In June 1830, some three months after the publication of the Book of Mormon and the formal organization of the "Church of Christ," Smith dictated the revelation that set the stage for his revision of Genesis. The revelation is described as "the words of God which he spake unto Moses at a time when Moses was caught up into an exceeding high Mountain & he saw God face to face & he talked with him," and is chronologically situated after the "burning-bush" incident but before Moses's return to Egypt.[9] At the conclusion of the revelation, God tells Moses that in the future "when the children of men shall esteem my words as naught & take many of them from the Book which thou shalt write," God will "raise up another like unto thee & they shall be had again among the Children of men."[10]

7. "History, 1838–1856, volume A-1," *The Joseph Smith Papers*, 183, accessed February 22, 2018, at http://www.josephsmithpapers.org/paper-summary/history-1838-1856-volume-a-1-23-december-1805-30-august-1834/189.

8. Michael Hubbard MacKay et al., eds., *Documents Volume 1: July 1828–June 1831, The Joseph Smith Papers* (Salt Lake City, UT: Church Historian's Press, 2013), 251; and Matthew C. Godfrey et al., eds., *Documents Volume 2: July 1831–January 1833, The Joseph Smith Papers* (Salt Lake City, UT: Church Historian's Press, 2013), 85, 123. Hereafter cited as JSP D1 and JSP D2.

9. The scholarly critical edition of the New Translation manuscripts is Scott H. Faulring, Kent P. Jackson, and Robert J. Matthews, eds., *Joseph Smith's New Translation of the Bible: Original Manuscripts* (Provo, UT: BYU Religious Studies Center, 2004). Hereafter, this volume will be cited with the abbreviation *NTOB*. The words quoted are found in *NTOB*, 83. They also happen to be among those included in the LDS canonical volume, the Pearl of Great Price, where the entire June 1830 revelation is reproduced and designated "Moses 1." For ease of reading in this essay, *NTOB*'s strikethroughs, angle brackets, and other critical editorial apparatus are not reproduced here. However, original spelling and punctuation are preserved.

10. *NTOB*, 86.

Although Smith's New Translation may have been contemplated from the time he dictated the Book of Mormon's description of an incomplete Bible, the June 1830 revelation served to propel this modern Moses forward with the project.

Because Smith intended his New Translation to be comprehensive, he started out by dictating every verse of the Bible, including those he left unaltered (which was the majority). In early March 1831, while Smith was working on Genesis 24, he reported being directed by God to switch to the New Testament. Over the next year, Smith completed work on the New Testament through John 5. By that time, he had been dictating the New Translation off and on for almost two years and had only worked through approximately 12 percent of the Bible (the first 600 or so verses out of more than 23,000 in the Old Testament and the first 3,000 plus verses of the New Testament's nearly 8,000). Smith must have realized that to continue in this manner would require another decade or more to complete his New Translation. So, from the end of John 5 through Revelation, and later from Genesis 24 to the end of the Old Testament, once he completed the New Testament, for the most part Smith only dictated (and had his scribes record) changes or additions to the biblical text. With this abbreviated procedure, Joseph Smith and his associates were able to complete the New Translation by July 1833, just over a year after they made the procedural change.[11]

Some have wondered if Smith considered the work he completed in 1833 only as a "first draft" that he intended to revisit and revise before publication. The evidence, however, suggests otherwise. To be sure, in later years Smith occasionally made additional Bible emendations in the course of his sermons. Moreover, it is clear from an examination of the manuscripts that much editorial work remained to be accomplished before the New Translation of the Bible could be printed in its entirety. Still, Smith authorized publication in early church periodicals of several key portions of the New Translation. That, and the fact that to the end of his short life he referred to the New Translation as a discrete project has convinced most scholars that Smith considered his formal, textual work of revising and amplifying the Bible to be complete.[12]

11. On July 2, 1833, Smith wrote to his associates in Missouri, "[W]e this day finished the translating of the Scriptures for which we returned gratitude to our heavenly father" (JSP, D3:166). The full details of dictation and inscription procedures, the number and size of the various folio manuscripts that together constitute the New Translation, the overall chronology of the project, and a whole range of editorial minutia are exhaustively discussed in *NTOB*. See also Robert J. Matthews, *"A Plainer Translation:" Joseph Smiths Translation of the Bible—A History and Commentary* (Provo, UT: BYU Press, 1975).

12. "A misconception that survived among Latter-day Saints for over a century and a half is that Joseph Smith never finished his Bible translation. A more recent misconception is that he continued to make modifications to it until the end of his life. Neither of these ideas is true. The evidence is clear that, in July

After his death, the New Translation manuscripts remained with his wife, Emma, who several decades later made them available to the Reorganized Church of Jesus Christ of Latter Day Saints (RLDS) with which she was then affiliated. In 1867, after painstaking transcriptional, editorial, and printing efforts, the RLDS Church published as their official Bible the *Holy Scriptures*, later sometimes referred to among believers as the "Inspired Version," which integrated the New Translation with the 90 percent of the KJV that remained untouched by Smith's revisions.[13] A century later, when relations between the RLDS and LDS churches improved and LDS scholars demonstrated to fellow Mormons the fidelity of the *Holy Scriptures* to the original New Translation manuscripts, the LDS Church decided to include excerpts from the New Translation in the footnotes and appendices of its new 1979 study edition of the Bible. The church had already (since 1880) accepted as canonical two key, previously published portions of the New Translation that were included in the original, pre-canonical Pearl of Great Price (1851). Today, these Pearl of Great Price excerpts are titled "Selections from the Book of Moses" (the New Translation through Genesis 6:13), and "Joseph Smith-Matthew," (the New Translation of Matthew 24).

It is important to stress that the New Translation was not a Bible translation in the conventional sense of the word. Joseph Smith never explained why he chose to call it a "new translation" when at the time he had no knowledge of biblical languages. In the 1830s, "translate" could also mean "to interpret" and "to explain," which certainly is what is taking place in parts of the New Translation.[14] Smith believed he was making the Bible read as it really should read, which is what justifies many a new translation. In a sense, calling his project a "translation" was his way of saying "version," although he never would have considered it just one more among many Bible versions. Joseph Smith considered his "translation" to be authoritative, accomplished by revelation and superior to ordinary linguistic decipherment. To be sure, from the standpoint of modern scholarship, many of Smith's revisions appear to draw on human wisdom, ranging from common sense or popular religious notions about what should be corrected in the KJV to guidance from more scholarly sources such

---

1833, Joseph Smith finished his revision of the entire Bible, and he considered it ready to go to press either then or shortly thereafter ... But he was never able to publish the work because of lack of funds and because other priorities, persecutions, and circumstances took precedence." Kent Jackson, "Joseph Smith Translating Genesis," *BYU Studies* 56, no. 4 (2017): 24.

13. *The Holy Scriptures, Translated and Corrected by the Spirit of Revelation by Joseph Smith, Jr., the Seer* (Church of Jesus Christ of Latter-Day Saints, 1867).

14. Noah Webster, *American Dictionary of the English Language* (1828), s.v. "translate."

as the widely popular multivolume commentary of Adam Clarke or Smith's biblically astute scribe and collaborator, Sidney Rigdon.[15]

Yet, this was consistent with how one of Joseph Smith's earliest revelations described the revelatory process itself:



> Behold I say unto you, that you must study it out in your mind; then you must ask me if it be right, and if it is right, I will cause that your bosom shall burn within you: therefore, you shall feel that it is right; but if it be not right, you shall have no such feelings, but you shall have a stupor of thought, that shall cause you to forget the thing which is wrong: therefore, you cannot write that which is sacred, save it be given you from me.[16]

Whatever the initiating stimuli to Joseph Smith's emendations and expansions, whether common sense or Adam Clarke or Sidney Rigdon, it was the perceived divine stamp of approval on Smith's revisions, not their originality, that constituted them as revelatory in Smith's mind. At the same time, some of his most extensive textual amplifications, generally of a narrative nature, seem to reflect his own imaginative "genius" (in the historical sense of the term), what Smith and his associates would have considered direct, rather than merely confirmatory revelation.

## SCOPE AND CONTENT OF THE NEW TRANSLATION

Broadly characterized, Smith's revisions and expansions may be classified into one or more of three categories: theological clarification, narrative enrichment, and stylistic refinement.[17] Before considering specific examples, a few big picture observations on the extent of Smith's revisions are in order. First, it is worth noting that the number and nature of Smith's changes and

15. Thomas A. Wayment and Haley Wilson-Lemmon, "A Recovered Resource: The Use of Adam Clarke's Bible Commentary in Joseph Smith's Bible Translation," in *Producing Ancient Scripture: Joseph Smith's Translation Projects in the Development of Mormon Christianity*, edited by Michael Hubbard MacKay, Mark Ashurst-McGee, and Brian M. Hauglid (Salt Lake City: University of Utah Press, 2020), 262–84.

16. Revelation, April 1829–D [D&C 9], in JSP, D1:50.

17. Similar categorizations can be found in Matthews, *A Plainer Translation*; Philip L. Barlow, *Mormons and the Bible: The Place of the Latter-day Saints in American Religion* (New York: Oxford University, 1991); and the introductory essays of *NTOB*.

additions vary considerably between Old and New Testaments and from book to book.[18] In some books—Ruth, Ezra, Esther, Ecclesiastes, Song of Solomon, Lamentations, Obadiah, Micah, Nahum, Habakkuk, Zephaniah, Haggai, and Malachi, 2 John, and 3 John—Smith made no alterations or additions at all. Although the Old Testament is more than three times the length of the New Testament, the number of verses Joseph Smith emended or added to in the New Testament is more than half again as many as he revised in the entire Old Testament.[19] In the Old Testament, Genesis is by far the most extensively revised book, particularly in the early chapters. Alone, it accounts for half of all Smith's Old Testament revisions. When Isaiah and Psalms are factored in, the three books, which represent just over 20 percent of the total Old Testament text, account for nearly 80 percent of Smith's revisionary work in the Old Testament. A similar concentration is discernible in the New Testament where the three Synoptic Gospels, which constitute just over a third of the total word count of the New Testament, are the site of nearly 70 percent of Smith's New Testament revisions. Although Joseph Smith's Genesis contains approximately 50 percent of all his Old Testament revisions, the disproportionality is even more pronounced when one focuses on the first nine chapters. By the time Joseph Smith finished his work of editing and amplifying the first nine chapters of Genesis, the New Translation version contained well over twice as many words as in the original KJV of the same chapters (13,219 versus 5,662). In the process, Smith emended or expanded four-fifths of the 235 verses in Genesis 1–9. It is hardly surprising, then, that a leading scholar of the New Translation opined, "I believe it can be stated safely that Joseph Smith's Genesis text is the most important part of his New Translation of the Bible."[20]

Because the narrative expansions in Genesis are more extensive than anywhere else in the New Translation, they provide an excellent example of this type of revision. The longest and one of the most significant expansions pertains to Enoch, son of Jared, who is mentioned only briefly in the Bible.

18. The *NTOB* contains all revisions as they appear in the original manuscripts. Also useful are two volumes that present the revisions in parallel columns next to the KJV verses that have been modified: Thomas A. Wayment, ed., *The Complete Joseph Smith Translation of the New Testament: A Side-by-Side Comparison with the King James Version* (Salt Lake, UT: Deseret Book, 2005); and Thomas A. Wayment, ed., *The Complete Joseph Smith Translation of the New Testament: A Side-by-Side Comparison with the King James Version* (Salt Lake, UT: Deseret Book, 2009).

19. This statistic and the ones that follow reflect the tabulation in Matthews, *"A Plainer Translation,"* 424–5.

20. Jackson, "Joseph Smith Translating Genesis," 27.

Genesis 5:24 notes, "Enoch walked with God: and he was not; for God took him."[21] Biblical coverage of Enoch amounts to just over one hundred words, but the New Translation expands it to over 4,500 words. It is worth reviewing in detail. The expansion begins by depicting Enoch's hesitant acceptance of a divine call to preach repentance to the wicked, antediluvian world and by noting Enoch's reception of visionary sight as a "seer." The narrative then presents a lengthy speech by Enoch in which he details Adam's knowledge of the "plan of salvation," including the fall, the atonement of the Son of God, and the salvific need for individuals to be "born again of water & the spirit."[22] This is followed by an equally lengthy recounting of Enoch's seeric vision of the future. God shows him how he will lead the righteous in battle against their enemies and how his followers will build "a City that was called the City of holyness, even Zion." Zion is portrayed as an idyllic society where people "were of one heart and one mind and dwelt in righteousness and there was no poor among them." In time, Enoch sees Zion (and himself) being "taken up into heaven."

Following Enoch's "translation" (Heb 11:5), he sees Noah's day, the building of the Ark, and how God will send the Flood upon the earth. Before this, though, Enoch witnesses God lament and "weep" over the wayward "workmanship of [his] hands." Enoch then "cried unto the Lord saying when shall the day of the Lord come[,] when shall the blood of the righteous be shed that all they that mourn may be sanctyfied and have eternal life[?]" The vision then skips intervening history to answer Enoch's queries by portraying the life, death, and ascension of God's Only Begotten Son. Moved by the miracle of salvation, Enoch speaks to the Lord: "[T]hou hast made me and given me a right to thy throne and not of myself but through thine own grace wherefore I ask thee if thou wilt not come again on the earth." The vision again passes over intervening years and describes the time of Christ's Second Coming. It is a day of apocalyptic judgment on the wicked, but it brings the returning Lord to "dwell on the earth in righteousness for the space of a thousand years." In that latter day, Enoch sees another "holy city," also called "Zion," where the

21. Hebrews 11:5 elaborates, "[B]y faith Enoch was translated that he should not see death; and was not found, because God had translated him: for before his translation he had this testimony, that he pleased God."

22. *NTOB*, 101–3; (compare 612–15). The New Translation of the Old Testament occupies two manuscripts. Scholars label them OT1 and OT2. OT1 contains only Smith's dictation through the middle of Genesis 24. OT2 is a scribal copy of OT1 that later served as the principal manuscript for the remainder of the New Translation of the Old Testament. OT2 also contains some additional editorial revisions to the initial dictation. In this and subsequent notes that reference material from the overlapping Genesis 1-24 portion of OT1 and OT2, the first pages listed are OT1 references, and the comparison pages are from OT2. Unless the wording of OT2 varies significantly due to editorial revisions, quotations are taken from OT1.

righteous are gathered as in his own lifetime. The vision account then climaxes with a depiction of Enoch's Zion descending from heaven to join with the latter-day Zion and together constitute a realm of holiness which, the Lord says, "shall be mine abode."[23]



Embedded in the Enoch expansion are many of the theological claims characteristic of the New Translation (and Mormonism) as a whole. First and foremost is its robust portrayal of pre-Christian knowledge of the Christian message. From Adam and Eve onward, the name and identity of Jesus Christ, as well as the gospel plan of salvation, are depicted as being fully revealed to, and consistently taught by, the ancient patriarchs and prophets. Enoch, for instance, is given a commandment to perform Christian baptisms and to do so using a perfectly Trinitarian formula: "[The Lord] gave me a commandment that I should baptise in the name of the father and of the Son which is full of grace and truth and of the Holy Ghost, which beareth record of the father and the Son."[24] Moral agency is another cardinal principle that is accentuated in the revisions. Enoch reports God's voice as saying of all human beings: "[I]t is given unto them to know good from eavel [evil] wherefore they are agents unto themselves." Elsewhere, God declares that he gave "unto man his agency" and a commandment "that they should chose me their Father." And Enoch is instructed to "say unto this people: choose ye this day to serve the Lord God who made you."[25] A third example among many that could be chosen is the text's interest in the end times. Some four hundred words in the Enoch expansion deal with the "last days" and give voice to such prominent Mormon themes as the physical gathering of God's people, dramatic "signs of the [end] times," and a plainly premillennialist eschatology in which the wicked are destroyed at the personal return of Jesus Christ and a literal thousand years of peace and harmony are inaugurated.[26]

Joseph Smith's interest in, and particular perspective on, the end times is also prominent in his New Testament revisions. The most notable example is his extensive revision of the Synoptic accounts of the "Olivet Discourse" (Matt 24, Mark 13, Luke 21). In each account, Smith clearly distinguishes between the imminent tribulations the Jews would experience at the time of the Roman assault on Palestine and the tribulations of the last days that would foreshadow

23. *NTOB*, 103–9; (compare 610–22).

24. *NTOB*, 104; (compare 616).

25. *NTOB*, 101, 106, 611 (OT2); (compare 613, 618, 99). The latter phrase is from OT2. OT1—"say unto this people choose ye this day a God who made you"—is less clear.

26. *NTOB*, 109–10; (compare 621–22).

the Second Coming. Elsewhere, Smith corrects texts that seems to imply belief in an imminent Parousia, as for instance in 1 Thessalonians 4. Verse 15 reads: "For this we say unto you by the word of the Lord, that we which are alive and remain unto the coming of the Lord shall not prevent [precede] them which are asleep." Joseph Smith renders the passage in this manner: "For this we say unto you by the word of the Lord, that *they* who are alive *at* the coming of the Lord, shall not prevent them who remain unto the coming of the Lord, who are asleep." Similarly, in verse 17, he changes "we which are alive and remain shall be caught up" to "*they who are alive*, shall be caught up."[27] And Paul's marital counsel to the Corinthians in light of his expectation of an imminent end—"this I say, brethren, the time is short" (1 Cor 7:29ff)—is de-eschatologized in the New Translation to read: "*I speak unto you, who are called unto the ministry*, For this I say, brethren, The time that remaineth is but short, *that ye shall be sent forth unto the ministry*."[28]

Along with these prominent perspectives in the New Translation, Joseph Smith's sensibilities on a range of other theological matters are also discernible. Only a few may be sampled here: his views on God, his high Christology, and his soteriological concern that faith not be separated from concomitant works. In light of his own claims to have seen God, it is not surprising that Smith corrects passages that deny such a possibility. Thus, he changes John 4:24—"no man hath seen God at any time"—to read: "no man hath seen God at any time, *except he hath born record of the son*."[29] And Exodus 33:20—"there shall no man see me, and live"—is emended to "no *sinful* man hath at any time, neither shall there be any *sinful* man at any time that shall see my face and live."[30] Smith also corrects what he considers unseemly or unlikely behavior in God. Thus, he cannot countenance the idea that God "repents," as for instance in Gen 6:6 ("it repented the Lord that he made man") or Ex 32:14 ("the Lord repented of the evil which he thought to do unto his people"). Although in Elizabethan English, "repent" had connotations of "regret" or

27. *NTOB*, 527, emphasis added. As with the Old Testament, there are two dictation manuscripts for the Smith's New Testament—NT1 and NT2. NT1 was the original dictation manuscript and covers through Matthew 26. NT2 began as a copy of NT1 but became the working manuscript for Smith's further revision of the New Testament. The quotations here and in subsequent notes are taken from NT2. with any significant wording variation in NT1 identified in the notes.

28. *NTOB*, 503, emphasis added.

29. *NTOB*, 443, emphasis added.

30. *NTOB*, 701, emphasis added. Similarly, 1 Timothy 6:16 speaks of the glorified Lord "who only hath immortality, dwelling in the light which no man can approach unto; whom no man hath seen, nor can see." Smith emends it to read "whom no man hath seen, nor can see, unto whom no man can approach, only he who hath the light, and the hope of immortality dwelling in him" (*NTOB*, 531).

"rue," and so was an appropriate translation of the underlying *nacham*, Joseph Smith understood the word in a soteriological sense and considered it inappropriate for God. Thus, he rendered the first passage "it repented *Noah*," and the second "the Lord said unto Moses, *If they will repent* of the evil which they have done, I will spare them."[31]



Smith's high Christology is apparent in a number of New Testament revisions and additions. When considering the young Jesus, Joseph Smith adds these words to the end of Matthew 2: "And it came to pass that Jesus grew up with his brethren and waxed strong and waited upon the Lord for the time of his ministry to come and he served under his father and he spake not as other men neither could he be taught for he needed not that any man should teach him and after many years the hour of his ministry drew nigh."[32] Smith also revises passages to emphasize Christ's earthly omniscience. For example, he emends the account of young Jesus "sitting in the midst of the doctors [in the temple], both hearing them, and asking them questions" (Luke 2:46) to read "sitting in the midst of the Doctors, and *they were hearing him, and asking him questions*."[33] Even so minor a matter as the account of Jesus "seeing a fig tree afar off" on his way from Bethany to Jerusalem and approaching it "if haply he might find any thing thereon" (Mark 11:13), was modified to preserve Jesus' omniscience: Jesus "came to [the tree] with his disciples; and *as they supposed*, he came to it to see if he might find any thing thereon."[34]

In LDS theology, salvation in an eschatological sense requires that works of Christian discipleship not be separated from Christian faith, and Smith emended the New Testament accordingly where this seemed to be in question. Thus, Romans 4:16—"Therefore it is of faith, that it might be by grace"—is modified to read: "Therefore ye are justified of faith and works, through grace."[35] Earlier in Romans 4, Smith believed Paul had Jewish law (*halakhah*) rather than Christian discipleship in mind when he wrote of "works" and their salvific insufficiency. He replaced each instance of "works" or its cognates in verses 2–6 with "the law of works."[36] This coincides with the soteriological contrast between the "law of Moses" and faith in Christ set forth in Romans 3:28 where Paul avers that "a man is justified by faith without the deeds of the law," or, as the NRSV renders it, "apart from works prescribed by the law." On

31. *NTOB*, 625, 699, emphasis added.
32. *NTOB*, 162–63; (compare 239).
33. *NTOB*, 371–72, emphasis added.
34. *NTOB*, 342, emphasis added.
35. *NTOB*, 483, emphasis added.
36. *NTOB*, 483.

the other hand, Smith made quite clear his view that Christ-prescribed works, as fruits of the Spirit, were inextricable from saving faith. He even intensified this affirmation in the book of James. To the famous line "faith without works is dead," Smith added "and cannot save you." Then, he reinforced the idea by an additional sentence addressed to James's imagined interlocutor who considered belief sufficient for salvation: "Thou hast made thyself like unto them [the devils], not being justified."[37] These changes suggest that Joseph Smith believed that an unadulterated Bible would have taught justification by faith, but not by faith *alone*.

## REFLECTIONS ON THE NATURE OF THE NEW TRANSLATION

Scholars have sometimes been interested in identifying possible analogues to the New Translation. In this final section, a number of such comparisons will be reviewed, but with the clear (and presumably obvious) understanding that the New Translation has no exact analogue. Comparisons are always approximations. No matter how similar certain ideas or practices may seem, they originate in different contexts and carry different connotations. Still, comparisons can be instructive. They can make aspects and tendencies in a piece of literature like the New Translation stand out that otherwise might go unnoticed. Moreover, human comprehension requires some degree of generalization and comparison. In the words of cognitive scientist Douglas Hofstadter, "analogy [is] the core of cognition."[38] With these caveats in mind, probing suggestive parallels should prove illuminating.

One early and persistent comparison has been made to the "Rabbinical Midrash."[39] The Hebrew term *midrash* broadly refers to "study," "exegesis," or "interpretation." More specifically, the *Midrash Rabbah* (Great Midrash) is an extensive collection of midrashim on the Torah and other books of the Hebrew Bible generated by the classical Jewish Rabbis of the early centuries CE. Both the Midrash Rabbah and its contemporary, the Mishnah, offer rabbinic reflection

37. *NTOB*, 549.

38. Douglas R. Hofstadter, "Analogy as the Core of Cognition," in *The Analogical Mind: Perspectives from Cognitive Science*, edited by Dedre Gentner, Keith J. Holyoak, and Boicho N. Kokinov (Cambridge, MA: MIT Press, 2001), 499–538.

39. Anthony A. Hutchinson, "A Mormon Midrash? LDS Creation Narratives Reconsidered," *Dialogue: A Journal of Mormon Thought* 21, no. 4 (1988): 11–72; and Avram R. Shannon, "Mormons and Midrash: On the Composition of Expansive Interpretation in *Genesis Rabbah* and the Book of Moses," *BYU Studies* 54, no. 2 (2015), 18 (15–34).

on *halakhah* and *aggadah* (nonlegal matters), but what most commentators have in mind when drawing a Midrashic parallel with the New Translation is its aggadic material. Aggadic midrashim contain homiletic commentary on, and extra-biblical stories about, scriptural personalities and events designed to teach moral and religious values. Just as with New Translation revisions and amplifications, these aggadic midrashim add layers of interpretation to the "plain" meaning of the text and sometimes run counter to that meaning when the stakes are high enough. For instance, "when Scripture attributes a sinful act to an otherwise righteous character, or one whose reputation was considered ... sacrosanct, the Rabbis did not hesitate to reinterpret the relevant v[erse] or v[erses]."[40] The same is occasionally true of Joseph Smith's revisions. Patriarchal and prophetic behaviors, from Abraham asking Sarah to prevaricate to Lot's handling of matters in Sodom, called for ethical refinement in both the Midrash and New Translation.

Because such homiletic intentions and interpretive approaches were on full display in Jewish literature earlier than the Midrash, another source of comparison is the Second Temple period writings known as the Apocrypha and Pseudepigrapha. Regarded by some at the time as *sacra scriptura*, these "books" never found their way into the Masoretic Text. Still, some were highly regarded. The book of Jubilees, for example, "is arguably the most important and influential of all the books written by Jews in the closing centuries BCE."[41] In ways that resemble Joseph Smith's expansions of the biblical narrative, Jubilees and other works such as the *Genesis Apocryphon* revise and retell biblical narratives to resolve scriptural inconsistencies, answer questions that arise from the text, and make the material morally and religiously relevant to their communities. All of which was done without editorial comment. Explains James Kugel, in words that could just as readily describe the New Translation, the authors would not "cite a verse and then offer an explanation, but rather ... explain via *retelling*. Commentators would rewrite a text in their own words, inserting into it their own understanding ... of how something happened, or what motivated this or that biblical figure to act as he or she did. Sometimes these insertions went on for pages."[42] Some have tellingly labeled Second Temple literature of

40. Yaacov Elman, "Classical Rabbinic Interpretation," in *The Jewish Study Bible*, 2nd ed., (New York: Oxford University Press, 2014), 1875.

41. James L. Kugel, "Jubilees," in *Outside the Bible: Ancient Jewish Writings Related to Scripture*, three vols., edited by Louis H. Feldman, James L. Kugel, and Lawrence H. Schiffman (Philadelphia: Jewish Publication Society, 2013), 1:272.

42. James L. Kugel, "The Apocrypha and Pseudepigrapha," in *Outside the Bible*, three vols., edited by Louis H. Feldman, James L. Kugel, and Lawrence H. Schiffman (Philadelphia: Jewish Publication Society, 2013), 1:8.

this kind the "Rewritten Bible," and similarities with the New Translation are noteworthy.[43]



Nonetheless, although similar in spirit and intent to the New Translation, the pseudepigrapha were separate compositions. In this way, their closer LDS parallel would be the Book of Abraham, a separate revelation to Smith recounting episodes from the patriarch's life. Closer to the New Translation in form because they present biblical texts in their entirety are ancient Jewish translations from Hebrew into Greek (the Septuagint) and Aramaic (the Targumim). Differences large and small with what would become the Masoretic Text appear in the Septuagint and reflect the cultural environment and exegetical traditions of the translators, much as New Translation renderings reflect Smith's theological and exegetical background. This is even more true of the Aramaic Targumim whose translations (*targum* means "translation") often incorporate interpretive glosses and midrashic expansions in their renderings of the Hebrew text. Like the Pseudepigrapha and New Translation, the Targumim offer textual variations and additions that resolve discrepancies, rehabilitate biblical heroes, and provide contemporary halakhic guidance.[44]

Yet another parallel to the New Translation is the developmental evolution of the Hebrew Bible itself. It is widely recognized that between initial composition and final redaction, changes occurred that reflected the thought and perspectives of the transmitters and redactors. Ancient scribes were as intent on communicating what they considered correct understandings as they were with transmitting a faithful copy of the text. As one scholar summarized it,

> The formal separation of "text" and "commentary" with which moderns are familiar does not readily apply to the period before both canon and text were fixed. Before this act of "freezing" the canon's form and

43. The term "Rewritten Bible" was coined by Geza Vermes in 1961. A half-century later, the state of the field is summarized in Jozsef Zsengeller, ed., Rewritten Bible *after Fifty Years: Texts, Terms, or Techniques?* (Leiden, Netherlands: Brill, 2014). An accessible overview is Sidnie Crawford White, *Rewriting Scripture in Second Temple Times* (Grand Rapids, MI: Eerdmans, 2008). Although focused on Joseph Smith's other biblically related scriptural productions, several Mormon scholars in *Producing Ancient Scripture* have also noticed structural and rhetorical similarities with the "Rewritten Bible." See Nicholas J. Frederick, "Translation, Revelation, and the Hermeneutics of Theological Innovation: Joseph Smith and the Record of John," 308–31; and David W. Grua and William V. Smith, "The Tarrying of the Beloved Disciple: The Textual Formation of the Account of John," 232n, 255–6.

44. Pseudepigraphical and targumic efforts to make the biblical text relevant to their times are consistent with how some contemporary Latter-day Saint thought-leaders view the New Translation. One Mormon Apostle remarked that a primary purpose of the New Translation is "to help us know what the Lord would have us understand from the scriptures today." Dallin H. Oaks "Scripture Reading, Revelation, and Joseph Smith's Translation of the Bible," in *Plain and Precious Truths Restored*, edited by Robert L. Millet and Robert J. Matthews (Salt Lake City, UT: Deseret Book, 1995), 13.

content, biblical texts were not merely copied and recopied, but in the copying process were also adapted, enlarged, and edited, as a kind of ongoing interpretative exercise.[45]



## CONCLUSION

As illustrated previously, comparisons between the New Translation and ancient biblical and biblically related texts and their development can be both interesting and suggestive. Yet, the New Translation in the sum of its parts, in its self-conception, in its internal reworking of a fixed, canonical text, and in its own various textual distinctives is something different. And parallels from Joseph Smith's own day are even less promising. Despite being birthed in the milieu of a flurry of new nineteenth-century publications of the Bible, Smith's New Translation has little in common with any of them.

It remains, therefore, to ask what Joseph Smith himself thought he was doing in the New Translation. Restoring pure, original biblical text is certainly a prominent part of it, but something more fundamental seems to have been at work in his mind. Perhaps the best way to get at this is to characterize the New Translation as the product of a self-understood prophet who, perceiving himself on par with his predecessors, felt free to edit and expand the biblical text (just as he did his own previously recorded revelations).[46] As a prophet, Smith believed he was entitled to interpretive as well as declarative inspiration and insight. Early in his ministry, Smith reported, "our minds being now enlightened, we began to have the Scriptures laid open to our understandings, and the true meaning and intention of their more mysterious passages revealed unto us, in a manner which we never could attain to previously, nor ever before (had) thought of."[47] From the beginning, Joseph Smith believed that through divine inspiration he had access to something beyond and behind the written text, original or otherwise. That something was the "true meaning" and "intention" of difficult passages in the Bible. As the Mormon prophet once

45. Philip Davies, "Qumran Studies," in *The Oxford Handbook of Biblical Studies*, edited by J.W. Rogerson and Judith M. Lieu (New York: Oxford University Press, 2006), 104. See also, Molly M. Zahn, *Genres of Rewriting in Second Temple Judaism: Scribal Composition and Transmission* (New York: Cambridge University Press, 2020). The Mormon authors cited in footnote 43 employ other though similar scholarly assessments of the composition of the Hebrew Bible to suggest parallels with Smith's scriptural productions.

46. Grant Underwood, "The Dictation, Compilation, and Canonization of Joseph Smith's Revelations," in *Foundational Texts of Mormonism: Examining Major Early Sources*, edited by Mark Ashurst-McGee, Robin Scott Jensen, and Sharalyn D. Howcroft (New York: Oxford University Press, 2018), 101–23.

47. JSP, H1: 294, 296.

explained about a passage in 2 Peter 1, "These are but hints of those things that were revealed to Peter and … are not Known neither can be except by direct Revelation."[48]

As a prophet and seer, Smith seemed to feel he could step into his predecessors' own revelatory encounters with God, reporting on what he saw and heard and felt to disclose of that ancient encounter. This moved the New Translation beyond a restoration of pure, original text. It allowed that portions of the New Translation had never been written, perhaps never even grasped, by earlier oracles. "Could you gaze in heaven five minutes," declared the Mormon seer, "you would know more than you possibly can know by read[ing] all that ever was written on the subject."[49] Near the beginning of his work on the New Translation, Joseph Smith said that God told him "the scriptures shall be given, even as they are in mine own bosom."[50] Smith seemed to believe that God would enable him as a Latter-day seer to peer into the infinite realm of truth that was in the very bosom of God and thereby enrich the extant biblical text. To the believer, this is an inspiring gift from Heaven. To the nonbeliever, it is the height of human hubris. To both, it is a fascinating glimpse at the moral, ethical, and theological mind of Joseph Smith and its concomitant exegetical and interpretive engagement with the Bible.

48. Andrew F. Ehat and Lyndon W. Cook, eds., *The Words of Joseph Smith: The Contemporary Accounts of the Nauvoo Discourses of the Prophet Joseph* (Provo, UT: Religious Studies Center, BYU, 1980), 206.

49. *Words of Joseph Smith*, 254.

50. JSP, D1:223 (D&C 35:20).

# 4

# Temple and Priesthood in the Bible and in Mormonism

CORY CRAWFORD

The Latter-day Saint institutions of priesthood and temple are among the most distinctive, visible, and central characteristics of the tradition, representing a unique constellation of antebellum American conceptions of restoration and authority. Far from marginal forces that play only a narrow role in sporadic religious observance, temple and priesthood are the engine that drive modern mainline LDS behavior and are the means by which understandings of gender, sexuality, and race are reinforced, challenged, and revised. Since they represent the gateway to vital rites of passage in this life and salvation in the next, these structures, both metaphorical and physical, ensure Latter-day Saints adhere to behavioral and even theological norms, such as the dietary restrictions of the "Word of Wisdom" and the surrender of 10 percent of their annual income as tithing to the church.

What distinguishes Mormonism's holy personnel and sacred space is in the ways they are yoked to concepts derived from biblical narrative at the same time they depart radically from it. Prominent among these differences is the way the LDS notion of priesthood came to be divorced from the idea of a narrow lineage of males, as many biblical texts have it, distributed instead to any males who meet the proper age and behavior requirements. Mormonism thus adopted a unique take on the Protestant "priesthood of all believers," opting for, as Kathleen Flake put it, an "*ordained* priesthood of all believers."[1] This broad distribution of priesthood, now reconceived as a "power" that men can "hold," would become integrated in the temple experience of space and ritual,



1. Kathleen Flake, "Ordering Antinomy: An Analysis of Early Mormonism's Priestly Offices, Councils, and Kinship," *Religion and American Culture* 26, no. 2 (2016): 140; emphasis mine. This priesthood, of course, does not include *all* LDS believers, as it is only open to men and boys.

and it would have decisive effects on the way gender is currently constructed in the Mormon cosmos. As in the Bible, these conceptions are entwined with temple ritual and space, with men performing and managing the most important rituals, including those that allow women's access to the holiest spaces.[2]

Temples in Mormonism similarly show radical departures from biblical tradition even while they preserve the general notion that they are a locus of special encounter with the divine, in which rituals are performed and authoritative hierarchies are constituted. Even a cursory visual comparison of (reconstructions of) ancient Israelite and Jewish temples with any Mormon temple will leave the viewer straining to discern similarities. Rather, these latter are a visual monument to the eclectic forces—which included the Bible, among many others—that produced sacred architectural forms in the Mormon tradition.

Although both priesthood and temple in the LDS tradition are marked far more by differences from the biblical precedent they claim than they are by similarities, they proved to be foundational in Joseph Smith's ability to navigate the paradoxes of democratizing authority and religion. Even though the ways in which Mormonism attempts to reconstruct biblical architecture and authority are fairly thin, their presence at the core of Mormon belief and practice make the connection all the more vital and productive within the tradition. Even more interesting from a phenomenological perspective is the way in which this relatively recent religious tradition makes visible the interconnectedness of power and space. Joseph Smith can be seen working out both in a mutually constitutive pattern. It is no accident that both temple and priesthood end up an amalgam of influences operative in the early United States that are virtually unrecognizable when compared with biblical tradition, but far more interesting is the study of the dialectic process that involved a welter of socioreligious forces (including the Bible, but also Freemasonry and others) and that galvanized these institutions at the heart of Latter-day Saint life. Because of this configuration, it is perhaps best to study the relationship between these Latter-day Saint institutions and the Bible as one of the many "afterlives" of Christian canon, discourse, and practice, one unique strand in the tapestry made by an ongoing engagement with the Judeo-Christian foundational texts.[3] My purpose here is to lay out the groundwork required to tell

2. To women is delegated the authority to administer to other women in sensitive contexts, a feature that has given some hope that priesthood authority would be granted to women in a more general sense.

3. A proper history of this kind would account for multiple traditions within the larger canopy of Mormonism as well, since the LDS tree ramified many times. Most of my comments here focus on the biblical narrative, but they also reflect my experience in and study of only one of those branches, the one headquartered in Salt Lake City. For examples of work on temples and priesthood in other Mormon traditions, see, e.g., Richard Brown, "The Temple in Zion: A Reorganized Perspective on a Latter Day Saint

such a story—namely, to understand the range of Biblical notions of sacred space and personnel, so as to facilitate comparison with the claims Mormonism makes to its authority.

Any investigation of the nexus of the ancient world and modern Mormonism should acknowledge up front the more recent history of LDS scholarship on temples and priesthood. In the second half of the twentieth century, after the scientific study of the ancient world was well established in North American and European universities and archaeological ground truthing of Judeo-Christian texts was both robust and epistemologically disruptive, Latter-day Saint academics and amateurs began attempting to address the readily apparent discontinuity between biblical and Mormon texts and practices. This rise of apologetics was pioneered in large measure by Hugh Nibley, whose work generally sought to prove the antiquity of LDS notions of temple and ritual, and inspired others in the LDS tradition to seek doctoral training, often with the (implicit if not explicit) goal of using tools of the academy to shore up LDS truth claims about these subjects. Thus, the latter half of the twentieth century saw a proliferation of LDS studies designed to locate the nonbiblical particularities of the LDS temple in ancient tradition.[4] Although this apologetic trend appears to be on the decline among LDS scholars actively pursuing graduate degrees, temple and priesthood remain of active interest to students of LDS culture, belief, and practice, and active loci of argument for structural continuity and change within Mormonism. As I hope will become obvious if not already, in investigating the nexus of Bible and Mormonism on the matter of temple(s) and priesthood(s), I have no apologetic aims, but rather approach the question under the assumption that the development of these institutions can be explained and understood as the result of creative recombination and dialectics in the nineteenth-century United States.

## TEMPLE IN THE HEBREW BIBLE

According to the Hebrew Bible, Israelite sacred sites and sanctuaries, or loci of contact with the divine, were eventually funneled to the single temple at

Institution" *Dialogue: A Journal of Mormon Thought* 24, no. 1 (1991): 86–98, available at https://www.dialoguejournal.com/articles/the-temple-in-zion-a-reorganized-perspective-on-a-latter-day-saint-institution/; Roger D. Launius, "An Ambivalent Rejection: Baptism for the Dead and the Reorganized Church Experience" *Dialogue: A Journal of Mormon Thought,* 23, no. 2 (1990): 61–83, available at https://www.dialoguejournal.com/articles/an-ambivalent-rejection-baptism-for-the-dead-and-the-reorganized-church-experience/.

4. For one example relevant to the present topic, see Donald W. Parry, ed., *Temples of the Ancient World* (Provo, UT: Foundation for Ancient Research and Mormon Studies, 1994).

Jerusalem during the reign of Solomon in the middle of the tenth century BCE (1 Kings 6–7). In biblical texts describing earlier times, many authors were comfortable describing shrines existing in a variety of places during the narratives of the patriarchs, exodus, conquest, and rise of the monarchy. Several of these sites devoted to YHWH seem at one point to have been open-air sanctuaries associated with trees or other natural features, as with the Palm of Deborah (Judg 4:5) and the Oak of Moreh at Shechem (Gen 12:6) or the great "high place" at Dan.[5]

The two most prominent shrines in the Bible are the wilderness tabernacle (described in Exod 25–31; 35–44) and Jerusalem temple (described in 1 Kgs 6–7). Although the wilderness tabernacle is described as having been revealed by YHWH and built by Moses at Sinai, many scholars have concluded that the tabernacle description was written much later and was modeled on the layout and furnishings of the Jerusalem temple.[6] This brought together what were probably two originally separate streams of Israelite tradition, one that remembered worship primarily in a tent-shrine in Shiloh, and the other a brick-and-mortar building. The construction of the Jerusalem temple also prompted the coalescence of another wilderness tradition, that of Sinai, with the Jerusalem Zion traditions. The work required to integrate these traditions eventually produced some of the most distinctive features of Israelite religion, such as covenant and a centralized cult.[7]

The described plan of the Jerusalem temple was relatively straightforward, even if its lack of precision leaves ambiguities in our ability to reconstruct a model. It consisted of a basic rectangular box with its main door set in a porch in one of the short sides. This opened into a main hall and a shrine at the back—which was closed off by another set of doors—in the same axis as the entry. The doors were said to be gilded and, like the windows, recessed in rabbeted frames. Running around the sides and back of this rectangular building was another structure of three stories that did not communicate with the main hall (its entrance was on one side). The functions of these rooms are unknown; they may have served administrative purposes given their separation from the

5. "Dan," in the *New Encyclopedia of Archaeological Excavations in the Holy Land,* edited by E. Stern, A. Gilboa, and J. Aviram (Jerusalem: Israel Exploration Society, Simon & Schuster, 1993), 1:323–332.

6. For discussion and bibliography see Cory Crawford, "Between Shadow and Substance: The Historical Relationship between Tabernacle and Temple in Light of Architecture and Iconography," in *Levites and Priests in Biblical History and Tradition,* edited by M. Leuchter and J. Hutton (Ancient Israel and its Literature 9; Atlanta: Society of Biblical Literature, 2011), 117–33.

7. Jon D. Levenson, *Sinai & Zion: An Entry into the Jewish Bible* (San Francisco: Harper & Row, 1987).

main hall (1 Kgs 6:6). The temple space was bounded by at least one courtyard and was probably further subsumed in the palace complex.[8]

The temple structures were outfitted with furnishings that enhanced the space and marked it as divine. The outer courtyard boasted a gigantic lotus-shaped bronze tank, called the "molten (or cast) sea," with twelve bovine statues underneath oriented toward the cardinal directions in sets of three (1 Kgs 7:23–26). No contemporary text indicates its use. Related to this water installation were ten basins, arranged in fives on either of the long sides of the temple, set on square wheeled stands that were decorated on their four sides (7:27–38). Although not mentioned in the building description, subsequent texts make reference to a bronze altar, the function of which changed after King Ahaz copied one he had seen in Damascus (2 Kings 16:10–15).



The building itself had a main doorway, with a separate entrance for the surrounding three-story structure, and windows in unspecified locations. The doorways were rabbeted with recessed frames—a common element of monumental passageways in the Bronze and Iron Ages—and the doors themselves were decorated with composite creatures (*cherubim*) and palm trees, and they were also gilded. The interior was furnished with ten lampstands (or menorahs), a table for bread offerings, and an incense altar. The innermost shrine also had gilded, carved doors, which opened into the *debir*, the innermost shrine (called the "holy of holies" in the tabernacle analogue). The text of Kings describes this as decorated with two massive, gilded cherubim, ten cubits high, under which the ark of the covenant came to rest.

Over the course of the existence of the temple, changes were made to this apparently original plan. These changes could be motivated by natural need for repair (2 Kgs 12:4–17; 22:3–7), by evolving standards (2 Kgs 16:17–18; 18:4), and by the need to pay tribute owed to foreign kings (2 Kgs 18:16). The most prominent elements to be removed were the gilded doors (2 Kgs 18:16), the frames of basin stands, and the bovine under the molten sea (16:17). Some biblical texts refer obliquely to the installation of foreign cultic items at various points (23:4).

Nothing in the building, furnishing, or artistic plan of the temple as described is uniquely Israelite, with the possible exception of the absence of a divine statue, and even this is not unheard of in the ancient Near East.[9] The

8. André Lemaire, "The Evolution of the 8th-Century BCE Jerusalem Temple," in *The Fire Signals of Lachish: Studies in the Archaeology and History of Israel in the Late Bronze Age, Iron Age, and Persian Period in Honor of David Ussishkin*, edited by Israel Finkelstein and Nadav Na'aman (Winona Lake, IN: Eisenbrauns, 2011), 195–202.

9. See Tryggve Mettinger, *No Graven Image? Israelite Aniconism in its Ancient Near Eastern Context* (Stockholm, Sweden: Almqvist & Wiksell International, 1995).

building footprint appears to have come from traditions whose origins lie to the north of Israel, probably in northern Syria or southeastern Turkey, where dozens of temples of this type have been found stretching back into the bronze age.[10] The Bible itself nods at the interregional derivation of the temple and its decoration in naming Phoenician (Canaanite) craftsmen and suppliers for the temple construction (1 Kgs 5; 7:13).

After Solomon's Temple was destroyed by the Babylonians in 586 BCE, eventually another, "second" temple was constructed in Jerusalem after the return of Babylonian exiles (dedicated 515 BCE), presumably on the site of the first, under Persian oversight (Haggai; Zech 1–8; Ezra 3:1–6:22). Centuries later, Herod's extensive remodeling would far exceed it in grandeur.[11]

The fundamental practice of temple worship, we reason from Leviticus, was daily slaughter of animals for various cultic purposes.[12] Analyses of Leviticus have attempted to draw out its symbolic logic of impurity that is purged through sacrifice.[13] Other texts, especially Psalms, indicate rituals of entry, including the requirement that the moral state of the worshipper be beyond reproach (Ps 24; cf. Jer 7); processions (Exod 15; Ps 132); covenant making (2 Kgs 23); coronation (2 Kgs 11), and, of course, festival celebration (Deut 16; 2 Kgs 23).

Beyond the texts that imply temple rituals, we also find texts in which the temple plays a central role in narrative and theology. Most obvious, perhaps, is in Psalms, where scholars see the temple as the primary setting for many, if not most, of these compositions, which are not limited to the theology of sacrifice and hint at a wide range of theological and mythological ideas wrapped up in the temple. Scholars have pointed to familiar stories, creation and Noah's ark, for example, as having been influenced by temple imagery, architecture, and ideals.[14] These probably arose from the sense that this was a

10. Jens Kamlah, "Temples of the Levant—Comparative Aspects," in *Temple Building and Temple Cult: Architecture and Cultic Paraphernalia of Temples in the Levant (2.–1. Mill.* BCE*): Proceedings of a Conference on the Occasion of the 50th Anniversary of the Institute of Biblical Archaeology at the University of Tübingen (May 28–30, 2010;* Abhandlungen des Deutschen Palästina Vereins 41; Wiesbaden, Germany: Harrassowitz, 2012), 507–34.

11. Josephus, *War* I.401; *Antiquities* XV.380–402, 410–423; cf. John 2:20. C.T.R. Hayward, *The Jewish Temple: A Non-Biblical Sourcebook* (London: Routledge, 1996), 1–17; Elias J. Bickerman, *The Jews in the Greek Age* (Cambridge, MA: Harvard University Press, 1988), 133–47.

12. Menahem Haran, *Temples and Temple-Service in Ancient Israel: An Inquiry into the Character of Cult Phenomena and the Historical Setting of the Priestly School* (Oxford, UK: Clarendon Press, 1978).

13. Jonathan Klawans, *Impurity and Sin in Ancient Judaism* (Oxford, UK: Oxford University Press, 2000); Jonathan Klawans, *Purity, Sacrifice, and the Temple: Symbolism and Supersessionism in the Study of Ancient Judaism* (Oxford, UK: Oxford University Press, 2006).

14. Important for the discussion of temple "ideology" has been the work of John Lundquist, especially his "temple typology," found among a wealth of collected essays by various scholars on related topics in L. Michael Morales, ed., *Cult and Cosmos: Tilting Toward a Temple-Centered Theology*, Biblical Tools and

place of divine encounter and abode, as we see in Isaiah 6, in which the prophet sees YHWH and his winged divine attendants (*seraphim*), while he is in the Jerusalem temple. This prophetic tradition of temple-influenced theophany became more elaborate even in the absence of the temple, as the growth of apocalyptic texts depended heavily on temple features and cosmic symbolism to characterize the ornate visions (e.g., Ezek 1–3; Zech 1–8; Revelation). The dwelling of God, unsurprisingly, reflected the architecture and ornamentation of the temple of Jerusalem, as much as the earthly temple would come to take on cosmic significance.[15]



## PRIESTHOOD IN THE HEBREW BIBLE

The concept of "priesthood" (Heb. *kehunâ*) in the Hebrew Bible most immediately refers to performing the social role of a priest, including the care for the various sacred shrines and altars, usually within a designated familial lineage.[16] The Hebrew Bible tacitly acknowledges the existence of legitimate non-Israelite and non-Levitical priests. For example, Melchizedek, to whom we will return later, is depicted as a priest-king of Canaanite Salem (probably Jerusalem) in Genesis 14, and Joshua 9 attempts to make sense of how Hivites ended up in Israelite cultic service. Moses' father-in-law is portrayed as a leading Midianite priest (Exod 3:1; 18; Num 10:29–32).

Eventually the preeminent priestly identity coalesced under the tribal banner of Levi, to which Moses, Aaron, and Miriam are connected in the final form of the Pentateuch. Stories such as the appointment of Aaron as Moses' spokesman (Exod 4:10–16, 27–29), the Golden Calf (Exod 32), and the complaint of Aaron and Miriam (Num 12:1–15) suggest later attempts to sort out competing priesthood lines (Mushite, Aaronid, Miriamite), each of which traced their authority to a different figure from Israel's past.[17] The inclusion of Miriam, also called a prophetess (Exod 15:20), suggests the possibility of a line of female

Studies 18 (Leuven, Belgium: Peeters, 2014); Mark S. Smith, *The Priestly Vision of Genesis I* (Minneapolis, MN: Fortress Press, 2009); John H. Walton, *Genesis 1 as Ancient Cosmology* (Winona Lake, IN: Eisenbrauns, 2011); and Cory Crawford, "Noah's Architecture: The Role of Sacred Space in Ancient Near Eastern Flood Myths," in *Constructions of Space IV: Further Developments in Examining Ancient Israel's Social Space*, edited by Mark K. George (New York: Bloomsbury, 2013), 1–22.

15. Paul D. Hanson, *The Dawn of Apocalyptic: The Historical and Sociological Roots of Jewish Apocalyptic Eschatology*, rev. ed. (Philadelphia: Fortress Press, 1979); John J. Collins, *The Apocalyptic Imagination: An Introduction to Jewish Apocalyptic Literature*, 3rd ed. (Grand Rapids, MI: Eerdmans, 2016); Hayward, *The Jewish Temple*, 8–13.

16. Mark Leuchter, "The Priesthood in Ancient Israel," *Biblical Theology Bulletin* 40, no. 2 (2010): 100–10.

17. Mark Leuchter, "The Fightin' Mushites," *Vetus Testamentum* 62, no. 4 (2012): 479–500.

priests whose power was eventually usurped by the male lineages since there is evidence in these stories of male anxiety over Miriam's power and special attempts to punish her exercise of it.[18]



It is important to note that while many biblical texts assume priesthood to be the sole prerogative of males, no text articulates an explicit rationale or even clear declaration of such. Exclusive male priestly authority was not a given in the broader ancient Near East, and several important biblical texts point to an underlying struggle that suggests women at an earlier point, like the non-Levites above, could serve as priests.[19]

The priestly struggle between Aaronids and other Levites is expressed in the different ways different authors conceive of the duties and access of Levites. The Aaronid texts of the Pentateuch (including portions of Exodus, Leviticus, and Numbers) envision little role for the average Levite male at the Temple. Deuteronomy, however, collapses at some level the notion of Levite and priest, such that any Levite could potentially serve at the temple. Ezekiel's particular views of the priesthood, like the (Aaronid) Priestly pentateuchal texts, left little room for priests outside of the Zadokite (Aaronid) line. According to Ezekiel, the Zadokites were the only ones allowed to serve at the altar, while the Levites were relegated to lesser duties. The second century BCE Hasmonean revolt disrupted this line when the Hasmoneans took control of the high priesthood for themselves. The end of Zadokite high priesthood in Jerusalem during the Hasmonean period was likely what motivated the retreat and reformation of

18. Rita J. Burns, *Has the Lord Indeed only Spoken Through Moses? A Study of the Biblical Portrait of Miriam*, (SBLDS 84; Atlanta: Scholars Press, 1987); Susan Ackerman, *Warrior, Dancer, Seductress, Queen: Women in Judges and Biblical Israel*, Anchor Yale Bible Reference Library (New Haven, CT: Yale University Press, 2009); Susan Ackerman, "Why Is Miriam Also among the Prophets? (And Is Zipporah Among the Priests?)," *Journal of Biblical Literature* 121, no. 1 (2002): 47–80.

19. Susan Ackerman, "Who Is Sacrificing at Shiloh?: The Priesthoods of Ancient Israel's Regional Sanctuaries," in *Levites and Priests in Biblical History and Tradition*, edited by Mark Leuchter and Jeremy Hutton (Ancient Israel and Its Literature 9; Atlanta: Society of Biblical Literature, 2012), 25–43; Susan Ackerman, "Women and the Religious Culture of the State Temples of the Ancient Levant, or: Priestesses, Purity, and Parturition," in *Temple Building and Temple Cult: Architecture and Cultic Paraphernalia of Temples in the Levant*, edited by Jens Kamlah (Abhandlungen Des Deutschen Palästina Vereins 41; Wiesbaden, Germany: Harrassowitz, 2012), 259–89; Phyllis A. Bird, "The Place of Women in the Israelite Cultus," in *Ancient Israelite Religion: Essays in Honor of Frank Moore Cross*, edited by Patrick D. Miller, Paul D. Hanson, and S. Dean McBride (Philadelphia: Fortress, 1987), 397–419. Of note here also is the study of LDS scholar Donald Parry, who has shown through recensional evidence the way Hannah's ritual activity in 1 Sam 1 was removed or downplayed by scribes; see Donald W. Parry, "Hannah in the Presence of the Lord," in *Archaeology of the Books of Samuel*, edited by P. Hugo and A. Schenker (Leiden, Netherlands: Brill, 2010), 53–73. For treatment in an LDS context, see Cory Crawford, "The Struggle for Female Authority in Biblical and Mormon Theology," *Dialogue: A Journal of Mormon Thought* 48, no. 2 (2015): 1–66.

the Qumran community and the production of many of the sectarian Dead Sea Scrolls, including a text that envisioned a New Jerusalem and a New Temple.[20]

## TEMPLE AND PRIESTHOOD IN THE NEW TESTAMENT



The Gospels report limited interaction between Jesus and the temple and its priesthood, including both participation with and perhaps hostility toward it. The Gospel of Luke uniquely recounts Mary and Joseph offering a sacrifice at the Jerusalem temple upon presentation of the infant Jesus (2:22–23), as well as the prophecies of Simeon and Anna, apparently in the temple precinct. In the same chapter (2:41–52) the third Gospel reports that Jesus' family went regularly to the Jerusalem temple to observe Passover, during one instance of which he was found impressing the teachers in the temple courts with his knowledge. Jesus' prediction in the Gospels of the temple's destruction is a motif that calls out references to the destruction of the first temple by the Babylonians.[21] All four Gospels report a moment in which Jesus disrupted temple commerce in Jerusalem, which apparently led directly to his death sentence.[22] Some scholars have noted that the Gospel of John stands apart from the synoptics also in its view of the temple and related festivals.[23] The fourth Gospel moves Jesus' conflict at the temple to the beginning of his ministry (John 2:13–22) and also portrays Jesus teaching in the temple (here as an adult) multiple times (7:14, 28; 8:20; 18:20).

The destruction of the Temple in 70 CE at the hands of the Romans did not prompt the same sort of institutional reorganization among Christians that it did for other Jews, who witnessed the growth of rabbinic authority in the wake of this event. It was, still, a loss that needed to be processed. The letter to the Hebrews, a sermon produced by an unknown author possibly in the early second century, is the most sustained meditation on temple and priesthood in the New Testament. Hebrews casts Jesus as the sacrifice and even the tabernacle itself, his death and resurrection enabling entrance into the holy of holies.[24]

20. Frank Moore Cross, *The Ancient Library of Qumran*, 3rd ed., (Sheffield, UK: Sheffield Academic Press, 1995), 127–60; Frank Moore Cross, *Canaanite Myth and Hebrew Epic: Essays in the History of the Religion of Israel* (Cambridge, MA: Harvard University Press, 1973), 334–42.

21. For example, Mark 13:1–2; 14:58; 15:29 (and parallels); John 2:19; Acts 6:14; Gos. Thom. 71.

22. Matt 21:12–13; Mark 11:15–17; Luke 19:45–46; John 2:14–17.

23. Bruce G. Schuchard, "Temple, Festivals, and Scripture in the Gospel of John," in *Oxford Handbook of Johannine Studies*, edited by Judith M. Lieu and Martinus C. de Boer (Oxford, UK: Oxford University Press, 2018), 380–95. For a skeptical view, see Judith Lieu, "Temple and Synagogue in John," *New Testament Studies* 45 (1999): 51–69.

24. Some traditions contemporary with Hebrews saw the death of the high priest as triggering a release of unintentional manslaughterers from the cities of refuge (cf. Num 35:25).

In doing so, according to Hebrews, Jesus obviated the need for the continued existence of the temple and its priesthood, thus solving the problem of the temple's destruction for Christians and arguing for Christian superiority over Judaism, a primary concern of many Christian authors of this time.

Hebrews had one other major problem to solve, however, in clothing Jesus's salvation in priestly garb: his non-priestly lineage, since tradition had Jesus born in the tribe of Judah, not Levi. To reconcile the issue, the author seized on the two lone enigmatic references to the figure of Melchizedek in the Hebrew scriptures (Gen 14; Psalm 110). It is by virtue of Melchizedek that Hebrews finds precedent for an eternal, non-hereditary priesthood, of which Jesus was the sole successor. Jesus' existence as the "great high priest" canceled the need for any further priesthood or sacred space since he had entered the holy of holies once and for all (Heb 9:12).

Alternatively, in 1 Peter 2:4–10, believers are compared to the "kingdom of priests" of Exodus 19:6. The most likely significance of these texts lies in the metaphorization of the Israelites (à la Exodus) or believers (1 Peter) as set apart or elected from the world. They were to the nations as the Levites were to the other tribes of Israel—set apart for special divine attention. Although this means that neither the Hebrew Bible nor the New Testament envisioned a democratized priesthood, it did not stop Christian commentators from reading it as a general reference to all Christians. This can be seen as early as the second century in the patristic writings, where early church fathers blended the line between priests and laity on the basis of 1 Peter's reading of Exodus 19:6.[25]

The book of Revelation borrows imagery from the Jerusalem temple cult and texts related to it (e.g., Isaiah 6, Ezekiel 1–3, 8–10) in depicting the residence of God, from which the disasters break forth leading up to the final imprisonment of the beast and the descent of the New Jerusalem. The latter is a moment in which the heavenly abode comes down to overlay the old Jerusalem in what has been compared to the form of a "holy of holies" (Rev 21:15–16; cf. 1 Kgs 6:19–20).[26] Yet in this situation the text says explicitly that there was no temple in this city because the Lord himself would be there (21:22); the city itself had become the temple. This, like Hebrews, was a means to solve the major theological problem confronting Jews as well as Christians in the wake of the Roman destruction of the temple.

25. John H. Elliott, *1 Peter: A New Translation with Introduction and Commentary*, Anchor Bible 37B (New York: Doubleday, 2000), 449–55.

26. J. Massyngberde Ford, *Revelation*, Anchor Bible 38 (Garden City, NY: Doubleday, 1975), 333–46.

The Jerusalem temple also appears in writing of and about Paul, whose letters constitute the earliest texts of Christianity. It provides the backdrop for Paul's arrest in Acts 21:27–36, where, not long after he had returned to Jerusalem, a group of Jews from Asia were said to have incited a crowd against him on the charge that he was "teaching everyone everywhere against our people, our law, and this place" (21:28). Further, they accused him of having "brought Greeks into the temple and ... defiled this holy place," recalling both the prohibition on non-Jews' access to the temple beyond the court of the Gentiles and the pervasive threat of foreign influence that was sometimes the flashpoint for armed revolt. Perhaps most important for understanding Paul's view of the temple was the way he appealed to it as a metaphor for the body and the church (1 Cor 3:16).[27]



## TEMPLES IN THE LATTER-DAY SAINT TRADITION

Among the variety of influences bearing on early Mormonism, biblical narratives are entangled with temple and priesthood in the Church of Jesus Christ of Latter-day Saints. Even before any particular Mormon building was built, Latter-day Saints could find reference to biblical temples toward the beginning of the Book of Mormon (published 1830), where one of the prophets recounts having built a temple in the Americas "after the manner of the temple of Solomon save it were not built of so many precious things" (2 Ne 5:16). The thread of temple building is woven throughout the Book of Mormon and provided a kind of conceptual, if not practical, grounding and precedent for later LDS temple building practices. Already by 1832 Joseph Smith's revelations included plans to build a "city of New Jerusalem" in Missouri, "beginning at the temple lot" (D&C 84:2–3), a plan which, though never realized in Missouri, ultimately would inform city planning in the Utah territory.[28]

Latter-day Saint notions of temple exhibit considerable evolution, with the core ideal being the construction of a hallowed space through which power could be channeled toward its visitors. The first LDS temple, in Kirtland, Ohio, was envisioned and dedicated in words that reverberated with the Bible.[29] It was generally used for rituals of "washing and anointing" that took their

27. Calvin Roetzel, *Paul: The Man and the Myth* (Minneapolis: Fortress, 1999), 34–38; David A. Renwick, *Paul, the Temple, and the Presence of God* (Brown Judaic Studies 224; Atlanta: Scholars Press, 1991).

28. Matthew Bowman, *The Mormon People: The Making of an American Faith* (New York: Random House, 2012), 47.

29. Cf. D&C 94:4–8; 109; 110; Bowman, *Mormon People*, 49–52.

inspiration from the priestly initiations described in Leviticus (e.g., Lev 8) and the New Testament references to anointing and washing the feet (e.g., Mark 6:13; John 13).[30] The next major turning point for temple practice came after the church had left Kirtland and fled Missouri, retreating to Illinois and building the city of Nauvoo on the banks of the Mississippi. The arrival of Freemasons and a Masonic lodge there led Smith to adapt and incorporate Masonic rites, which claimed to have a lineage of esoteric knowledge from the builders of the Solomonic temple, for use in the Mormon temple.[31] Smith adjusted the Masonic ritual drama into one that drew on the biblical creation narratives, in which participants envision themselves as Adam and Eve and make covenants in exchange for blessings upon them and their offspring.[32] The initiation moved through an idealized life cycle situated in Mormon cosmology, from the creation of the universe to human life on earth and on to a progression through the LDS three-tiered heavenly kingdoms (telestial, terrestrial, and celestial). This ritual drama came to be known as the endowment, which now took a central place among other rituals such as washings and sealings. Smith also found inspiration in 1 Corinthians 15:29, an enigmatic verse that mentions "baptism for the dead," for an extension of these "saving ordinances" through proxy rituals, whereby living individuals would perform the rites of salvation on behalf of a deceased person. Temples eventually became the sole venue for the performance of these rituals in Mormonism.

The architecture of the typical LDS temple illustrates the syncretism of its conceptual development. No effort was made to replicate the ornate biblical building descriptions of temple or tabernacle. The driving forces were rather located in Anglo-American Protestant expectations of sacred architecture (perhaps most visible in the now-characteristic steeples topped with a statue of the angel Moroni, the final prophet of the Book of Mormon). Some of the biblical structures in the temple are evoked, such as with the baptismal fonts, which present twelve "oxen" underneath a water tank, a clear reference to the bronze "sea" (1 Kgs 7:23–26), and in the use of fabric veils to partition differentiated zones of holiness (e.g., Exod 26:31–35; 2 Chr 3:14). To these we might

30. David John Buerger, *The Mysteries of Godliness: A History of Mormon Temple Worship* (San Francisco: Smith Research Associates, 1994), 11–34; see also Benjamin Park, *Kingdom of Nauvoo: The Rise and Fall of a Religious Empire on the American Frontier*, (New York: Norton, 2020).

31. Bowman, *Mormon People*, 75–84; detailed in Buerger, *Mysteries of Godliness*, 35–68. See also Edward Ashment, "The Temple: Historical Origins and Religious Value" *Dialogue: A Journal of Mormon Thought* 27, no. 3 (1994): 289–98, available at https://www.dialoguejournal.com/articles/the-temple-historical-origins-and-religious-value/.

32. Bowman, *Mormon People*, 77.

also add the garments, white robes, sashes, and aprons worn by participants, designed as a representation of priestly clothing described in Exodus and features of the biblical narratives dramatized in the ritual. This particular mélange of symbols, drawn from biblical precedent as well as from American religious culture, is part of what makes LDS temple worship a most distinctive feature of the tradition. And despite the lack of robust formal parallels or meticulous reconstruction, biblical and LDS temples overlap at basic levels: they are spaces of divine encounter, graded holiness, and ritual performance and are overseen by priesthood functionaries, to which we now turn.



## PRIESTHOOD IN THE LATTER-DAY SAINT TRADITION[33]

The impetus toward temples, biblical and LDS, both required and reinforced the priesthood structure that claimed divine mandate. In the church today, "priesthood" is used in two basic ways: (1) to describe the power of God used to order and run both church and cosmos and (2) to encompass the ecclesiastical structure consisting of two orders (Melchizedek and Aaronic) and several offices within each order.[34] All LDS males who meet age and behavior requirements (determined through personal "worthiness" interviews with local leadership) are "ordained" to the appropriate order and "set apart" to an office within the priesthood. These offices are largely defined by the scope of the ritual activities allowed for each.

Most informed members of the church today could relate what has become the standard narrative of the means by which priesthood authority was conferred on Joseph Smith: it was delivered by angelic messengers who possessed authority in their earthly sojourn. Few, however, would be able to recount the development of these ideas. In the early months and years of the church, Smith spoke of his authority to baptize, for example, but it was not described in terms of priesthood. It instead followed the pattern in the New Testament and Book of Mormon, where Jesus commissioned individuals to baptize and preach, but this authority is not labeled as "priesthood" (see 3 Ne 11–12). This comes into higher relief in light of Alma 13, which describes a "high priesthood" after the

33. On the development of authority in early Mormonism, see Kathleen Flake, "Ordering Antinomy," 139–83; Michael H. MacKay, *Prophetic Authority: Democratic Hierarchy and the Mormon Priesthood* (Urbana: University of Illinois Press, 2020), especially ch. 5, "The Development of Mormon Priesthood."

34. Jonathan Stapley argues that there is a third and almost entirely overlooked notion of priesthood, which he calls the "cosmological" priesthood (*The Power of Godliness: Mormon Liturgy and Cosmology* [New York: Oxford University Press, 2018], 17–23). He argues that this priesthood was understood in the Nauvoo period as the materialization of heaven through a social network of sealings performed in the temples (26).

order of the Son and connected to Melchizedek, but this seems an effort to establish and explain a pre-Christian authority that was nevertheless esoterically connected to Jesus. In any case, these terms were not used in either the Book of Mormon or in the first three years of the church to describe the ritual authority bestowed on Joseph Smith and his associates. This indirectly follows biblical narrative, too, since, as we have seen, biblical tradition understands priesthood not as an inherent power or authority removed from particular social structures, but as a social role filled by a particular segment of society. Aaron, on the biblical picture, did not *hold* the priesthood—he *was* a priest.

Over the course of the 1830s Smith systematized notions of ecclesiastical authority, which coalesced in dialogue with biblical narratives. This systematization drew most heavily on the Pentateuchal stories of priestly struggles over authority and on Hebrews in the New Testament, which is fixated on the superior relationship of Jesus (who was not of a priestly lineage) to Jewish priesthood, appealing to the enigmatic figure of Melchizedek in Genesis 14 as precedent for non-Levitical priesthood. These threads come together in Doctrine and Covenants 84, recorded in 1832 in Ohio as the church looked to expand to westward. There Smith articulated a genealogy of a "Holy Priesthood" from Moses backward through Jethro, Abraham, Melchizedek, and others, all the way to Adam.[35] This continuity was broken by the Exodus generation in the wilderness, when "they hardened their hearts and could not endure his presence.… Therefore, he took Moses out of their midst, and the Holy Priesthood also, and the lesser priesthood continued, which priesthood holdeth the … preparatory gospel" (D&C 84:24–26). Section 84 relates that this "lower" priesthood continued until John the Baptist, which would lay the groundwork to the *post-facto* identification of the angelic messenger of 1829 as John.

This hierarchical systematization of "greater" and "lesser" priesthoods was likely motivated by Smith's revision of Exodus 34, which reports Moses' acquisition of an apparently new set of tablets to replace the ones he had destroyed upon discovering the Israelites reveling at the feet of the golden calf.[36] In his revision, Smith indicates that this is the moment in which the higher priesthood, which had sufficient authority to conduct one into the presence of God,

35. D&C 107 also evidences the development of priesthood, especially in its textual growth. The earliest portion of the text, which describes offices and duties within church administration, was later fronted with an explanation about the higher priesthood that was used to assign a relative hierarchy to those offices.

36. Crawford, "Struggle for Female Authority," 40; n. 171.

was taken from the Israelites (JST Exod 34:1–2). Doctrine and Covenants 84, produced some few weeks or months after the revision of Exodus, reproduces key phrases from the revision, all indicating a heavy influence of biblical interpretation in the creation of LDS priesthood orders.[37] Like the author of Hebrews (quoted not by accident here), Smith appropriates the power of priesthood discourse while relegating its Jewish expression to secondary status.



This structure of higher and lower priesthoods would be imposed on the existing offices, as the multistage composition of Doctrine and Covenants 107 shows. Section 107:60–100, written on November 11, 1831, introduces a "high priesthood" that governs all the offices in place at that point (deacon, teacher, priest, elder, bishop) below it. There is no connection yet to higher and lower priesthoods as defined by Doctrine and Covenants 84. In spring 1835, a revelation that was later added in front of the 1831 verses drew together concepts from Alma 13, Doctrine and Covenants 84, and other sources to organize the offices into their higher and lower priesthood orders, now called "Melchizedek" and "Aaronic." These interpretative developments allowed Smith to simultaneously claim (1) the greater antiquity of the higher priesthood, (2) the superiority of it to Judaism, and (3) and its restoration to him and his nascent church. It came to mean that the priesthood progression in the life cycle of a Mormon male enacts an embodied supersession as he rises through the ranks of the lower Aaronic priesthood as an adolescent, receiving only the higher Melchizedek priesthood as an adult.

Although this structure clearly drew inspiration from biblical precedent, its extension of "priesthood" to roles not considered part of priestly duties in the Bible—such as deacon, elder, and even prophet—has also created some interpretative conundrums for LDS readers of the Bible. The LDS move to extract priesthood from social hierarchies and make it a disembodied authority sidelines, for example, the understanding of competing priestly lineages as determinative of the scope of priestly activity—that different kin-based structures vied with each other for control of sanctuary space and ritual efficacy.[38] This disembodiment allowed for the extension of the concept of priesthood broadly to include a maximal range of roles linked to the Bible but not necessarily

37. For a fuller discussion, see Cory Crawford, "Competing Histories in the Bible and Latter-day Saint Tradition," in *Standing Apart: Mormon Historical Consciousness and the Concept of Apostasy* (New York: Oxford University Press, 2014), 129–46, especially 131–32.

38. See Leuchter, "Priesthood," for examples. For biblical examples of this struggle for competing lines, see Num 12:1–16; 25:6–13; 1 Kgs 2:26–27.

associated with priesthood there. This would have implications for gendered access to leadership in LDS contexts, since Smith's widening net of priesthood offices scooped up relatively unambiguous biblical references to female judges, prophets, deacons, and apostles, and brought them within the orbit of priesthood.[39] Perhaps, in fact, it is because of this widening definition that Smith appeared to make moves before his death to extend priesthood authority to the nascent female organizations in the church.[40] This, of course, was never realized, and the vast majority of administrative authority and ritual performance remain in the hands of LDS males, beginning with their ordination to the "Aaronic" Priesthood at age eleven or twelve. With the LDS extension of priesthood far beyond the biblical bounds of a relative handful of men from particular lineages to include potentially every male, priesthood becomes a concept that is key to the production of gendered hierarchy and ideology in Mormonism. Recent struggles over the ordination of women have all but confirmed this as the church has attempted to justify the male hierarchy and control while maintaining that it is a distinction without a difference.[41]



We have seen that although in the Church of Jesus Christ of Latter-day Saints temple and priesthood authority are produced through discourses tied to the Hebrew and Christian scriptures, they also differ in fundamental ways—conceptual, practical, and material—and these differences have crucial effects on basic Mormon worldviews, especially when it comes to gender. These discourses are responsive also to a variety of other stimuli that draw on Christian tradition, voluntary associations, and unique Latter-day Saint scripture, and their meaning continues to be shaped by shifting social atmospheres.

What should remain fascinating and worthy for further exploration, especially for religious and even architectural historians, is the entanglement of

39. For example, Exod 15:20; Judg 4:4; 2 Kgs 23:14; Romans 16:1, 7. The hermeneutical conundrum this produces is visible in the lengths LDS interpreters feel forced to go to in explaining how, for example, Phoebe's status as "deacon" is, *in only her case*, to be understood generically as a "servant" instead of "deacon" (Gk. *diaconos*). See, for example, Richard Holzapfel, Eric Huntsman, and Thomas Wayment, *Jesus Christ and the World of the New Testament* (Salt Lake City, UT: Deseret Book, 2006), 250–51.

40. Stapley, *Power of Godliness*, 26–32; Jonathan A. Stapley, "Women and Mormon Authority," in *Women and Mormonism: Historical and Contemporary Perspectives*, edited by Kate Holbrook and Matthew Bowman (Salt Lake City: University of Utah Press, 2016), 101–17; Jonathan A. Stapley and Kristine Wright, "Female Ritual Healing in Mormonism," *Journal of Mormon History* 37, no. 1 (2011): 1–85; Bowman, *Mormon People*, 72–74.

41. See discussion in Crawford, "Struggle for Female Authority" 1–5; see also recent General Conference talks, including Dallin H. Oaks, "The Melchizedek Priesthood and the Keys," *Ensign* (May 2020): 69–71. For a case study charting the role of the temple in the social struggle over race, priesthood, and temple in Mormonism, see Mark Grover, "The Mormon Priesthood Revelation and the São Paulo, Brazil Temple" *Dialogue: A Journal of Mormon Thought* 23.2 (1990): 39-55.

practice, space, and theology, which is concentrated in a tradition whose history is relatively well documented and continues to be the subject of analysis in the academy. Although LDS temple worship reveals nothing specific about biblical religion, it remains an instructive and overlooked case study in the way religious thought, space, text, and practice are fused in a reciprocally influential cycle.

# 5

# Dead Sea Scrolls

DANA M. PIKE

Discovered between 1947 and 1956, the Dead Sea Scrolls from the caves around Qumran have had an invaluable impact on biblical and early Jewish studies and have repeatedly been described as one of the greatest discoveries of ancient texts during the twentieth century.[1] These several scrolls and thousands of scroll fragments from the area along the northwestern Dead Sea generated a great deal of excitement among scholars and the general public. It is no surprise, therefore, that Latter-day Saints, too, were and still are interested in the Qumran scrolls.

During the past nearly seventy-five years a great deal of time and energy have gone into sorting, identifying, studying, and publishing the scrolls and scroll fragments. This ongoing effort has led to many responsible publications, such as those cited in the footnotes of this essay, and, sadly, to many sensational and misleading ones.[2] This essay provides an introduction to the basics of the

1. For example, Professor William Foxwell Albright declared in a letter dated March 15, 1948 that the Dead Sea Scrolls constituted "the greatest [manuscript] discovery of modern times!" This statement has been cited by many authors, including Peter W. Flint, *The Dead Sea Scrolls* (Nashville, TN: Abingdon, 2013), 5. Joe Uziel, the recently appointed Director of the Israeli Antiquity Authority's Dead Sea Scrolls Unit, in speaking of the scrolls in an interview with the *Jerusalem Post,* observed, "[W]e are dealing with the most important archaeological finding in Israel in the twentieth century" (July 14, 2020; available at https://www.jpost.com/israel-news/what-is-the-future-of-the-2000-year-old-dead-sea-scrolls-635040). For details of the discovery and early work on the scrolls, see Weston W. Fields, *The Dead Sea Scrolls: A Full History*, vol. 1 (Boston: Brill, 2009). For a more concise overview, see George J. Brooke, Lawrence H. Schiffman, and James C. VanderKam, "Scrolls Research," in *Encyclopedia of the Dead Sea Scrolls*, two vols., edited by Lawrence H. Schiffman and James C. VanderKam (New York: Oxford University Press, 2000), 2: 844–851.

2. Several reputable books for general readers have been recently published. English translations of the DSS include Geza Vermes, *The Complete Dead Sea Scrolls in English*, rev. ed. (New York: Penguin Putnam, 2004); and Martin G. Abegg, Peter W. Flint, and Eugene C. Ulrich, *The Dead Sea Scrolls Bible: The Oldest Known Bible* (San Francisco: HarperSanFrancisco, 1999). With introductory overviews of the DSS, newer works are generally preferable since their authors have had access to more up-to-date information.

Dead Sea Scrolls (DSS) and then overviews seven decades of Latter-day Saint interest in and involvement with the DSS.

## OVERVIEW OF THE DEAD SEA SCROLLS AND QUMRAN[3]



*What.* The DSS are Jewish religious documents. The remains of about 930 manuscripts (c. 350 distinct documents) survive, most of which are written on leather, with some on papyrus, and one on copper sheets.[4] The vast majority of these documents are written in Hebrew, although some are written in Aramaic, and a few in Greek. Although a few of them date as early as about 250 BCE, most date from about 150 BCE–65 CE.

These documents divide mainly into three broad categories:

1. Copies of texts that eventually became known as biblical (meaning the Hebrew Bible, the Christian Old Testament).[5] At least fragmentary remains of all the books of the Hebrew Bible except Esther have been identified. Some books, such as Psalms, Deuteronomy, Isaiah, Genesis, and Exodus are represented by many more remains than others, which are scarcely represented, such as Proverbs, Chronicles, and Ezra-Nehemiah.
2. Copies of texts that were widely read by many Jews at the turn of the era (meaning the last century BC to the first century AD, or BCE to

Examples include John J. Collins, *The Dead Sea Scrolls, A Biography* (Princeton, NJ: Princeton University Press, 2013); Peter W. Flint, *The Dead Sea Scrolls*; and James C. VanderKam and Peter W. Flint, *The Meaning of the Dead Sea Scrolls: Their Significance for Understanding the Bible, Judaism, Jesus, and Christianity* (San Francisco: HarperSanFrancisco, 2002). For Latter-day Saint approaches to the DSS, see, for example, Dana M. Pike, "The Dead Sea Scrolls and Latter-day Saints: Where Do We Go from Here?," *Studies in the Bible and Antiquity* 2 (2010): 29–48; Donald W. Parry and Stephen D. Ricks, *The Dead Sea Scrolls: Questions and Responses for Latter-Day Saints* (Provo, UT: FARMS, 2000); and Donald W. Parry and Dana M. Pike, eds., *LDS Perspectives on the Dead Sea Scrolls* (Provo, UT: FARMS, 1997). Additionally, pictures of many DSS fragments, along with introductory comments, are now available online through the Israel Antiquities Authority at http://www.deadseascrolls.org.il/home.

3. Unless otherwise noted, greater detail on all the points mentioned in this overview can be found in publications such as those cited previously.

4. The "Copper Scroll" (3Q15), as the one metal scroll is called, lists sixty-five locations of buried treasure. The origins and even the reality of this treasure is debated. None has been found. It is possible (likely) that the Copper Scroll was not even part of the Qumran community's documents, even though it was found in a cave with documents that apparently were.

5. Since the final formation of the biblical canon had not completely occurred by this point in time, and since it appears that all Jews of that period did not share exactly the same view of what was authoritative scripture, referring here and in what follows to certain texts as "biblical" is convenient but anachronistic. The Hebrew scriptures were not completely delimited beyond the traditional core of the Law, the Prophets, and the Psalms (Luke 24:44) to the Hebrew Bible/Old Testament canon as we now have it until about 100–150 CE. The Jews at Qumran, for example, appear to have accepted books such as Jubilees, 1 Enoch, and the Temple Scroll as authoritative, although these compositions never became part of the traditional biblical canon.

CE), such as 1 Enoch and Jubilees, but which were not admitted into what became the traditional biblical canon.

3. Copies of previously unknown texts that are distinctive to the Jewish sect who lived at Qumran and their associates who lived elsewhere in Palestine.[6] These so-called sectarian texts include, for example, the Rule of the Community (1QS), which primarily focuses on the purpose and organization of the community, and rules for admittance into it; the Thanksgiving Hymns (1QH[a]), which contains about two dozen non-biblical psalms expressing gratitude in the first person for God's assistance in difficult circumstances; the War Scroll (1QM), which foretells the eschatological conflict that would culminate in the destruction of the evil forces that opposed God's rule; and 4QMMT (4Q394–399), which was originally thought to be a personal letter, but is now commonly judged to be a legal treatise in which certain calendrical and other religious rulings are explicated from what appears to be the more strict point of view of the Qumran community.[7]

Because of the number and variety of texts found in the Qumran caves, and because these copies of manuscripts date to over two centuries and were produced by a variety of scribes, many of these texts were undoubtedly *brought to* the Dead Sea region from elsewhere, while others, especially the sectarian ones, were *copied at* the Dead Sea site called Qumran.

These texts—some scrolls, many scroll fragments—were discovered in eleven caves proximate to the small archaeological site named Qumran. The largest number of fragments was found in cave 4, but caves 1 and 11 held the best-preserved documents.

Following the Qumran discoveries, other Jewish texts from the last century BCE and the first two centuries CE were also discovered in sites and caves along the western side of the Dead Sea, including Masada, Wadi Murabbaat, and Nahal Hever. These latter texts were sometimes also referred to collectively as "Dead Sea Scrolls," but now more broadly as "Judean Desert scrolls." As important as they are, due to limited space the primary focus here is on the textual remains found in the eleven Qumran caves.

6. The term *sect*, when used for ancient religious groups, designates a small subset of a larger religious tradition. Individuals associated with a particular sect or faction typically had distinctive beliefs and practices and considered themselves to be legitimate successors to the larger tradition from which they separated.

7. Abbreviations for the DSS need some decoding. The "Q" indicates Qumran, the number preceding it indicates in which of the eleven caves the document was found, and the letter or number following the "Q" signifies the particular text from that cave).

*Where.* Qumran is situated on a terrace in the northwest region of the Dead Sea, with the rugged rocky cliffs of the Judean Wilderness to the west and the Dead Sea to the east. Not much remains at this small site, mainly the lower portions of the walls of several rooms and of a tower, water channels, and several cisterns and ritual bathing pools. The main excavation of the site occurred in 1951–1956, after and because of the discovery of scrolls in nearby caves.[8] Only pottery, coins, and other generally small-scale finds turned up in the excavations. No scroll fragments were found "in" Qumran; they all came from nearby caves.

The site itself most likely functioned as a community center (not a town), with members of the religious community entering daily for ritual purification, worship, instruction, study, and group meals. The number of Jews living at Qumran likely consisted of only about 150 people at any given time. Most if not all of them would have slept in caves and tents in the surrounding area, not in the site itself. Other proposals have been made for Qumran's function, including a trading center, a fortress, and a country villa, but none of these have gained much popularity, and the available evidence best supports understanding Qumran as a religious community center.

*When.* Earlier publications suggested habitation by the Jewish group at Qumran began about 150 or 130 BCE, but the current assessment is that an initial date of about 80 BCE is more likely.[9] Habitation seems to have continued at Qumran, with a few short interruptions due to an earthquake and other factors, until 68 CE. Jewish habitation ceased at that time, because Roman soldiers encamped at Qumran during their successful suppression of the First Jewish Revolt.

*Who.* What the DSS provide is an important but incomplete introduction to a separatist and reforming movement under the umbrella of ancient Jewish religion at the turn of the era. The Qumran sectarian texts provide much of the information about the community's particular organization, views, and identity. Scholars continue to debate and refine the majority view that the Qumran community or group was comprised of Jews who *in some ways* appear similar to the Essenes, a Jewish faction that appears to have developed in the

8. Jodi Magness, *The Archaeology of Qumran and the Dead Sea Scrolls*, 2nd ed. (Grand Rapids, MI: Eerdmans, 2021). See also, Dennis Mizzi, "Archaeology of Qumran," in *T&T Clark Companion to the Dead Sea Scrolls*, edited by George J. Brooke and Charlotte Hempel (New York: T&T Clark, 2018), 2.

9. This is based on the recent analysis presented in Magness, *The Archaeology of Qumran* 2nd ed., 64–78, particularly 66.

mid-to-late second century BCE (about the same time the better-known Pharisees and Sadducees also emerged). The proposed connection between the Qumran inhabitants and the Essenes draws on the writings of three first-century CE authors—Josephus, Philo, and Pliny. Their collective depiction of Jewish Essenes living along the western shore of the Dead Sea and elsewhere in Palestine who believed, for example, in divine determinism, and who had particular initiation and communal practices, display certain similarities with some of the beliefs and practices of the Qumran community. However, there appears to have been variety even among Essenes, since some are described as ascetic and some had families. And there were likely other separatist-oriented communities of Jews of which we lack knowledge. Therefore, the Essenes and the Qumran group are no longer viewed by some scholars as *exactly* the same, although there appears to have been significant overlap between them.[10]

The Qumran inhabitants moved to the wilderness to separate themselves from the Jerusalem temple and what they viewed as the corrupt priestly hierarchy who controlled it. Those who joined the Qumran group believed that they embodied the true remnant of Israel with whom God had renewed his covenant, that they lived at the end of times (the last days), and that ancient (biblical) prophecies would be fulfilled with and through them in their time. They also believed they were destined by God as his chosen "sons of light" who would fight to victory with their soon-to-return messiah(s) over all the "sons of darkness" (Jews not aligned with their views, and all non-Jews).

The majority of scholars have long assumed that no women were part of the Qumran community. This presumed celibacy of Qumran males is generally based on (1) the claims of the authors Josephus, Philo, and Pliny (mentioned just previously) that Jewish Essene men were celibate, (2) the presumed connection between Essenes and the Qumran inhabitants, (3) the lack of regulations regarding women, marriage, or families in the significant Qumran sectarian regulatory document, the Community Rule (1QS), and (4) the heightened focus

10. For comments on the parallels, see, for example, John Bergsma, *Jesus and the Dead Sea Scrolls: Revealing the Jewish Roots of Christianity* (New York: Image, 2019), 7–9; and Magness, *The Archaeology of Qumran* 2nd ed., 40–44. Both scholars think the Qumran community consisted of Essenes. John J. Collins, *Beyond the Qumran Community: The Sectarian Movement of the Dead Sea Scrolls* (Grand Rapids, MI: Eerdmans, 2010), considers the Qumran settlers were likely Essenes (10, 150–51, 209), but emphasizes that the Qumran group "was at most one of many settlements of the sect" (10; cf. 209). For a recent claim that the Qumran community should *not* be directly equated with the Essenes, see Maxine Grossman's presentation, "Why NOT the Essenes: How to Talk about the Dead Sea Sectarians," May 19, 2020, in "The Dead Sea Scrolls in Recent Scholarship: A Public Conference," sponsored by New York University and the Friends of the Israel Antiquities Authority (streamed via Zoom due to the COVID-19 pandemic), in which she concluded, "it's really time to let the word Essene go" when discussing Qumran's inhabitants.

on ritual purity, like that required of temple-officiating priests, exhibited in Qumran sectarian texts.

However, by the 1990s several DSS scholars, many of them women, began to question this assumption.[11] After all, the brief descriptions by Josephus, Philo, and Pliny indicate that some Essenes living throughout the land of Israel were married and had families. And although absent from the Community Rule, the Damascus Document and some other sectarian documents found in the Qumran caves do reference marriage and families (e.g., CD 5.7–11, 7.6–9; 4Q270).



Given this interpretive dilemma, recourse has been sought in the human skeletal remains from the Qumran cemetery. However, only 40-some of an approximately 1,200 graves have actually been excavated. This very small dataset, along with "the poor state of preservation of the [very few excavated] Qumran skeletons,"[12] has brought little clarity to the question of women at Qumran 2,000 years ago. The excavated skeletal remains of a few females are often considered to be the remains of more recent Bedouin. However, the skeletal remains of a few other females suggest a limited number of women *died* at Qumran at the turn of the era.[13] Likewise, gendered remains from Qumran that would indicate a female presence are extremely scant. Thus, "the archaeological evidence suggests only minimal female presence at Qumran and an absence of families with children."[14] Even if the presence of a minimal number of females at Qumran is granted, it is still not possible to determine if they were long-term residents there (as opposed to visitors) nor if they ever became part of that particular covenant community. The available evidence still supports a predominately if not exclusively male presence and role among Qumran inhabitants.

Aaronide priests (also called Aaronite or Aaronic; priests claiming descent from Aaron) constituted the hierarchy of the Qumran community, but the group also included Levites and non-Levitical Jews (mostly if not all males). They had strict rules regarding obedience and purity, and emphasized repentance and regular ritual self-immersion, holiness, and spiritual preparation

11. See, for example, Maxine L. Grossman, "Women and Men in the Rule of the Congregation: A Feminist Critical Assessment," in *Rediscovering the Dead Sea Scrolls, An Assessment of Old and New Approaches and Methods*, edited by Maxine L. Grossman (Grand Rapids, MI: Eerdmans, 2010), 229–45; and more recently, Esther Chazon's presentation "Women in the Sectarian Texts from Qumran," May 19, 2020 in "The Dead Sea Scrolls in Recent Scholarship: A Public Conference," sponsored by New York University and the Friends of the Israel Antiquities Authority (streamed via Zoom due to the COVID-19 pandemic). See also the comment by Magness, *The Archaeology of Qumran*, 2nd ed., 196.

12. Magness, *The Archaeology of Qumran*, 2nd ed., 205.

13. For a summary of the various details involved in the discussion of the cemetery—various sectors of the cemetery, burial orientation, grave goods, etc.—see Magness, *The Archaeology of Qumran*, 2nd ed., 200–11.

14. Magness, *The Archaeology of Qumran*, 2nd ed., 222; also stated on 211 and 220; plus see her summary of female-gendered artifacts, 211–15, and her conclusions on the question of women at Qumran, 219–22.

for the imminent arrival of their messiah(s), and the great last battle with the evil forces of the world.

Despite occasional claims to the contrary, *no* New Testament passages occur in the DSS, and the Jews who settled at Qumran were not Christian.[15] The DSS are Jewish texts collected, copied, and studied by one portion of the Jewish population at the turn of the era who did not as a group embrace Jesus of Nazareth as their messiah.



*Value.* The DSS have great value for studying the various beliefs and practices among some of the Jews in Palestine at the turn of the era. They are also essential for studying the text and transmission of the Hebrew scriptures, the Christian Old Testament, because they preserve the oldest known copies of these biblical texts. Furthermore, they demonstrate the variety that existed then between different text "families" of Hebrew scriptures prior to the domination of what became the traditional text of the Hebrew scriptures after about 100 CE (the Masoretic Text). The DSS are also important for studying the Hebrew and Aramaic languages at the turn of the era and analyzing the scribal practices of making scrolls and of copying texts.

## EXAMPLES OF LATTER-DAY SAINT INTEREST IN THE DSS

As is likely the case in other faith traditions, many Latter-day Saints probably know only a small to moderate amount about the DSS and have only a passing interest in them. Speaking in generalities, some church members adopted and adapted the perspective preserved in scripture passages such as Psalm 85:11, "Truth shall spring out of the earth; and righteousness shall look down from heaven" (see also Moses 7:62). Latter-day Saints believe the Book of Mormon came forth on golden plates from the earth to Joseph Smith with angelic assistance in 1827 (JS-History 1:27–62). Some church members wondered if the DSS—which also come "out of the earth"—were part of a divine "restoration" by God of ancient texts that would corroborate distinctive Latter-day Saint teachings and practices.[16] This perspective meshes with the Latter-day Saint belief that Jesus Christ restored through Joseph Smith doctrinal knowledge

15. Flint, *The Dead Sea Scrolls*, 184–5.

16. A few Latter-day Saints have specifically published this claim. See, for example, Einar C. Erickson, mentioned hereafter. For more on this Latter-day Saint restoration perspective in general, see Dana M. Pike, "Recovering the World of the Bible," in *Prelude to the Restoration: From Apostasy to the Restored Church*, edited by Stephen C. Harper et al. (Provo, UT: Religious Studies Center, BYU, and Deseret Book, 2004), 159–84.

and practices that had been lost in the years following the early Christian period. While Psalm 85:11 does not explicitly foretell the discovery and modern dissemination of the DSS, it was not too difficult for some Latter-day Saints to see the scrolls' discovery as part of deity's restoration of knowledge about the Bible, its text, and the world from which it came (see also D&C 27:13).[17]



Interest in the DSS for at least some Latter-day Saints in the past seventy years has arisen, in part, from not fully appreciating what the DSS are. Given a broad Latter-day Saint interest in finding support for their distinctive organization, beliefs, and practices, certain passages in the sectarian DSS have attracted more attention than others. Proposed connections generally represent superficial similarities between the Qumran community and Latter-day Saints.[18] For example, for the governing structure of the Qumran community, "there shall be twelve men and three priests who are blameless in all that has been revealed from all the Law" (1QS 8, 1–2; my translation). Some Latter-day Saints have seen this as foreshadowing their church's chief governing organizations, a three-member Quorum of the First Presidency plus a Quorum of the Twelve Apostles, all who, according to Latter-day Saints, have Melchizedek priesthood authority and "priesthood keys" to direct the church.[19] However, the Qumran community was governed by Aaronide priests, and the "twelve men" were no doubt Israelites who had no priesthood lineage at all. With the significance of the numbers three and twelve in the Old Testament, and the non-mention of Melchizedek priesthood authority and keys at Qumran, it is difficult to see how the content of this passage in 1QS provides specific support for a modern Latter-day Saint organizational structure.[20]

A second example involves the claim in the Community Rule (1QS 3.16–25) that God created the Prince of Lights and the Angel of Darkness to influence

17. Eric F. Mason, "The Saints and the Scrolls: LDS Engagement with Mainstream Dead Sea Scrolls Scholarship and its Implications," in Quincy D. Newell and Eric F. Mason, eds., *New Perspectives in Mormon Studies: Creating and Crossing Boundaries* (Norman: University of Oklahoma Press, 2013), 172–73, suggests additional underlying passages in Latter-day Saint scriptures that provided support for this perspective, including 1 Nephi 13:39–40 and D&C 91.

18. The examples that follow can be found, with fuller discussion, in Pike, "The Dead Sea Scrolls and Latter-day Saints: Where Do We Go from Here?," 34–37.

19. For example, after quoting this passage in 1QS 8, O. Preston Robinson, *The Dead Sea Scrolls and Original Christianity* (Salt Lake City, UT: Deseret Book, 1958), 76, refers to these Qumran leaders as "General Authorities," the Latter-day Saint designation for their highest church officials. See similarly page 79. Robinson also claims that 1QS "further outlines ... a regular system of bishops, priests, teachers, and deacons" (76). Despite some interesting and not unexpected similarities between these two religious groups, this claim cannot be substantiated.

20. Additionally, in the New Testament, Peter, James, and John are depicted *among* the twelve apostles Jesus chose. There is no indication that they constituted a separate three-member "First Presidency," distinct from the twelve apostles, as is the case in the Church of Jesus Christ of Latter-day Saints.

people on earth to follow "truth" or "deceit." This vaguely echoes what Latter-day Saints call the "war in heaven" (see e.g., Revelation 12:3–13; Moses 4:1–4; D&C 29:36–38). In their view, Lucifer/Satan rebelled against God, resulting in him being cast out of heaven along with the one-third of God's premortal spirit children who followed Satan. However, the Qumran texts do not mention a "war" in heaven, nor the Angel of Darkness being cast out, nor are premortal beings identified as God's spirit children therein. True, there is a vaguely defined notion of premortal existence in some of the sectarian DSS, and similar notions also appear in certain other early Jewish and Christian writings. However, none of these demonstrate close alignment with Latter-day Saint belief nor provide them with further doctrinal insight.[21]

A third example involves claims of the practice of "baptism" at Qumran. For example, a 1968 article in the church's monthly publication *Improvement Era* claimed, "The Dead Sea Scroll covenanters ... practiced baptism by immersion for remission of sins after full repentance. A baptismal font has been uncovered in the Qumran community ruins."[22] Although it is true that there were several *miqva'ot*, or ritual immersion pools at Qumran, and that some passages in the Community Rule (1QS) refer to the practice of self-immersion as an external sign of inner repentance and purification (e.g., 1QS 3.4–10), to claim "baptism" was practiced at Qumran extrapolates well beyond the actual evidence.[23] For many Christians, and for Latter-day Saints in particular, baptism involves an authorized person (e.g., priest, elder, minister) performing a (usually) one-time ritual act for a recipient. Latter-day Saints baptize *only* by immersion and require (as some other Christians do) a set prayer or statement, uttered by the one performing the baptism. The evidence from Qumran, and from elsewhere in the land of Israel at the turn of the era, indicates that many Jewish people regularly participated in the normative practice of self-immersion as an act of

21. For more on this concept in the DSS, see Dana M. Pike, "Is the 'Plan of Salvation' Attested in the Dead Sea Scrolls?," in *LDS Perspectives on the Dead Sea Scrolls*, edited by Donald W. Parry and Dana M. Pike (Provo, UT: FARMS, 1997), 73–94, especially 76–81. For more on the general idea of premortality in antiquity, see Terryl Givens, *When Souls Had Wings: Pre-Mortal Existence in Western Thought* (New York: Oxford University Press, 2012), especially 39–70. For the Latter-day Saint doctrine of premortality, see, for example, Gayle O. Brown, "Premortal Life," in *Encyclopedia of Mormonism*, edited by Daniel H. Ludlow (New York: Macmillan, 1992), 1123–25.

22. O. Preston and C.H. Robinson, "The Antiquity of Christ's Gospel," *Improvement Era* (December 1968), 7. This claim had also been published earlier by O. Preston Robinson in his 1958 volume, *The Dead Sea Scrolls and Original Christianity*, 81–82.

23. For more information on the Qumran *miqva'ot* and related matters (singular *miqvah, miqveh, mikvah*), see, for example, Magness, *The Archaeology of Qumran*, 2nd ed., 168–90.

worship and ritual cleansing.[24] This is not surprising given the injunctions in the Hebrew Bible/Christian Old Testament about self-washings as part of the process of removing ritual impurity from oneself (e.g., Lev 14:8–9; 22:4–6). However, there is no evidence for priestly performance or authorized statements as part of this self-immersive practice at Qumran. Therefore, although there are conceptual similarities between the self-immersion that the Qumranites (and other Jews) practiced and the Christian ordinance or sacrament of baptism, there are distinct differences between self-immersion at Qumran and what Latter-day Saints think of when they hear the term *baptism*.[25]

Certainly, there are interesting similarities between several Qumran and early Christian texts and practices (after all, the first Christians were Jewish), as well as interesting echoes between Qumran and Latter-day Saint practices. But in all these instances, first examining each belief or practice on its own terms and in its own context leads to a more accurate assessment.

A last example illustrates an unfulfilled hope. The Latter-day Saint Book of Mormon maintains that there were prophets and prophetic writings in ancient Israel that were not included in what became the canonical Old Testament (e.g., Zenos, mentioned 1 Nephi 19:10; Jacob 5:1). Early hopes were that some of these prophecies would be found in the DSS. However, none of the Qumran or other texts from the Judean Desert preserve any of what Latter-day Saints consider lost writings of prophets unknown in the Bible but named in Latter-day Saint tradition or even the lost writings of known biblical prophets.

More problematic, the zeal of a few Latter-day Saints to popularize the DSS during the past seven decades has led to false claims about the scrolls and their supposed value for "proving" uniquely Latter-day Saints practices and beliefs. This is because, in part, these individuals have lacked the knowledge and skill to effectively use the DSS as primary sources, have relied on outdated and sometimes inaccurate secondary sources (especially during the initial stages of claims being made about the DSS in the 1950s and 1960s), and have sometimes blended information about the DSS with other ancient but decidedly different manuscripts, such as those discovered at Nag Hammadi, Egypt. Although this has all been presumably unintentional, it has still been harmful.

24. In addition to Magness, cited in the previous note, see, for example, J.D. Lawrence, *Washing in Water: Trajectories of Ritual Bathing in the Hebrew Bible and Second Temple Literature* (Atlanta: Society of Biblical Literature, 2006); and Stephen J. Pfann, "The Essene Yearly Renewal Ceremony and the Baptism of Repentance," in *The Provo International Conference on the Dead Sea Scrolls: Technological Innovations, New Texts, and Reformulated Issues, edited by D. Parry and E. Ulrich* (Leiden, Netherlands: Brill, 1999), 336–52.

25. For thoughts on the overlap between Qumranite self-immersion and Christian baptism, see, for example, Bergsma, *Jesus and the Dead Sea Scrolls*, 70–5.

For example, large numbers of Latter-day Saint "firesides" on the DSS and Mormonism have been presented over the years, especially in the 1960s and 1970s. These typically evening gatherings usually focused on interesting church-related topics and were intended to help church members know their religion better. Likely the best-known presenter on the DSS at such "firesides" was Einar C. Erickson, whose professional training was in geology and mining engineering. His lectures and audiotapes were popular in some circles as early as the 1950s and were heard by thousands of Latter-day Saints. In 1957 Erickson claimed, "There is a close similarity between the LDS Church of 1957 and the Qumran church of 5 AD. While no new doctrines are added to the knowledge of the Latter-day Saints, all their unique doctrines are corroborated."[26] His current approach is essentially unchanged, as evident from this statement on his website in 2022: "[T]he Dead Sea Scrolls, Nag Hammadi, and other ancient documents confirm LDS doctrine."[27] However, this is a position that simply cannot be sustained.

A corollary to these "firesides" and related materials was the appearance in the late 1950s and the ensuing decades of publications on the DSS *for* Latter-day Saints *by* enthusiastic Latter-day Saint authors who were *not* trained in biblical and related ancient studies. One example is the book by O. Preston Robinson entitled *The Dead Sea Scrolls and Original Christianity*, published in 1958.[28] Robinson had a PhD in and had been a professor of marketing and retailing, and worked as the editor of the *Deseret News* newspaper in Salt Lake City in 1958. Although more responsible than some Latter-day Saint authors who have written about the DSS, Robinson's encounter with the scrolls led him to conclude that they preserved "beliefs and practices," which were very similar to "the concepts of original Christianity." Robinson's book intended to highlight these similarities and "to explain how the [Qumran] Covenanters may have obtained these concepts even before the birth of the Savior."[29]

Consideration must be given here to the fact that during the 1950s and 1960s there was (relatively) great excitement about the DSS in the media, as

26. Einar Erickson, "Pre-Christian Christianity," *U.A.S. Newsletter*, November 7, 1957. Erickson, who was trained and worked in geology and mining engineering, has presented himself as "Dr. Erickson," but as his website states, "He received his PhD in A. S. Near Eastern Studies from George Wythe College," a very small, unaccredited institution in Utah (https://www.einarerickson.com/biography).

27. See https://www.einarerickson.com for this quote. As indicated on his still-active website, Einar Erickson passed away in March 2021.

28. O. Preston Robinson, *The Dead Sea Scrolls and Original Christianity* (Salt Lake City, UT: Deseret Book, 1958). He later published *Christ's Eternal Gospel: Do the Dead Sea Scrolls, the Pseudepigrapha and Other Ancient Records Challenge or Support the Bible?* (Salt Lake City, UT: Deseret Book, 1976).

29. Robinson, *The Dead Sea Scrolls and Original Christianity*, v.

well as among scholars. This was not something specific to Latter-day Saints. As Professor Theodor Gaster claimed in the introduction to his book *The Dead Sea Scrolls in English Translation* (1956), "The archaeologists tell us that the Dead Sea caves are hot and dark. The same might be said of the controversy which has raged around their contents."[30] And more recently (2005), Lawrence H. Schiffman, a noted Jewish scholar of the Dead Sea Scrolls and early Judaism, insisted, "[T]here *still remains* a large gap between the realities of scrolls research and public perception.... These misconceptions, as well as a host of related false information, result from the nature of the press coverage of the scrolls, their discovery, their contents and publication history, *from the very beginning* of the story *until today*.... This inversion of reality is of course to be expected in sensationalist articles or videos. More surprising is the fact that supposedly responsible journalists often use these misconceptions as a come-on."[31] In his critique of "responsible journalists," Schiffman acknowledges that there have been, and probably always will be, "sensationalist articles and videos" about the DSS (as well as other biblically related discoveries). Uniquely Latter-day Saint perspectives on the DSS that were popularized in the first few decades following the discovery of the scrolls must therefore be seen and evaluated against this larger backdrop of worldwide claims and counterclaims being made about the scrolls in many popular media venues.

Early controversy and sensationalism relating to the DSS were, at least in part, fueled by claims made about how the content of the scrolls would undermine many of the claims of traditional Christianity.[32] However, unlike the traditional Christian perspective that Christianity began with Jesus' ministry and the subsequent growth of the Christian church, Latter-day Saints accept that the basics of Christ's "gospel" were known and taught from the beginning of time (e.g., Moses 5:6–9; 6:51–62), and that this knowledge was passed down in one form or another, with many disruptions and corruptions, through the pre-Christian millennia. So O. Preston Robinson and others brought their own Latter-day Saint angle to the discussion of features in the DSS that were used to claim the existence of Christian practices in what were regarded as pre-Christian Jewish religious texts. For them, the DSS offered support for the

30. Theodor H. Gaster, *The Dead Sea Scriptures in English Translation* (Garden City, NY: Doubleday, 1956). Subsequent revised editions appeared in 1964 and 1976.

31. Lawrence H. Schiffman, "Inverting Reality: The Dead Sea Scrolls in the Popular Media," *Dead Sea Discoveries* 12, no. 1 (2005): 24–37, emphasis added.

32. See, for example, Schiffman, "Inverting Reality," 27–9, with references to the publications of Wilson, Allegro, Eisenman, and others.

Latter-day Saint view that Jesus' gospel and aspects of the Christian church had been on the earth before Jesus' mortal ministry.[33]

Beyond this issue of Christian origins, many other lay Latter-day Saint presenters borrowed heavily from Einar Erickson's materials, teaching, for example, that the DSS contain items that are uniquely Latter-day Saint, such as their temple "endowment" ceremony, their doctrine of eternal marriage, and the Latter-day Saint prayers used in blessing the Sacrament (the Lord's Supper).[34] In reality, *none* of these specific beliefs or ceremonies is attested in the DSS. Thus, sadly, many inaccurate and false claims have been propagated among interested but misinformed Latter-day Saints.

These "fireside" ventures and other publications by well-intentioned but less-informed Latter-day Saints, summarized above, have required an ongoing rectification to help other less-informed Latter-day Saints more accurately understand and appreciate the real value and contributions of the DSS.[35] To be fair, only a small number of Latter-day Saints have been involved in this type of enthusiastic and unintended misrepresentation, and "sensational and fanciful interpretations of the scrolls certainly are not the exclusive prerogatives of Mormons."[36] Thus, such rectification has been and is still required among the general non-Latter-day Saint public as well.[37]

33. Robinson, *The Dead Sea Scrolls and Original Christianity*, 60–69. In this context, the question is not whether this Latter-day Saint perspective of pre-Jesus Christianity is legitimate, but only whether the claim that the DSS support or prove this view is accurate.

34. These claimed DSS contents are all included, for example, in the transcript of a presentation given at an LDS "fireside" in California in the late 1990s, and is in the author's possession. The presenter indicates Erickson was his first and main source of information. Even though instructions in Community Rule on a ritual community meal that included bread and wine (1QS 7:1–8) as well as other evidence leads Bergsma, *Jesus and the Dead Sea Scrolls*, 92, to enthusiastically claim, "[T]his Essene practice sheds considerable light on the Gospel narratives about the Last Supper, and the early Christian celebration of the Eucharist"; he also states, "[W]e are not, at this point, arguing that Jesus modelled the Last Supper *directly* on Essene practice" (87). And to repeat, the Latter-day Saint sacrament prayers are not in the DSS.

35. As a last example of well-intentioned but inaccurate publications, see Keith Terry and Stephen Biddulph, *Dead Sea Scrolls and the Mormon Connection* (Maasai, 1996). Because of its large number of inaccuracies, my review of this book concluded with the statement, "I cannot recommend this book to anyone in its present form. Reader beware!" See Dana M. Pike, "Review of Keith Terry and Stephen Biddulph, *Dead Sea Scrolls and the Mormon Connection*," in *FARMS Review of Books* 9, no. 2 (1997): 88–98.

36. Eric F. Mason, "The Saints and the Scrolls," 174. There is likely a complex number of reasons for this phenomenon as exhibited among some Latter-day Saints. It is *my* opinion that one significant reason for this situation is that *some* Latter-day Saints seem to place great value on external verification for what are uniquely Latter-day Saint beliefs and practices. However, exploring this topic further ventures way beyond the parameters of this essay.

37. As observed in 2005 by Schiffman, "Inverting Reality," 36: "[I]n the case of the scrolls, certain formative concepts began a process of scroll imaging in the media that will not so easily be reversed."

It is regrettable that counterbalancing statements such as this one from former BYU Professor Sidney B. Sperry, also published in 1957, carried so little weight in popular circles: "After reading the Scrolls very carefully, I come to the conclusion that there is not a line in them that suggests that their writers knew the Gospel [of Jesus Christ] as understood by Latter-day Saints."[38]

## EXAMPLES OF FORMAL LATTER-DAY SAINT INVOLVEMENT WITH THE DSS

Early examples of responsible Latter-day Saint publications on the DSS for a Latter-day Saint audience include Lewis M. Rogers, "The Dead Sea Scrolls–Qumran Calmly Revisited," (1960; Rogers had had some formal biblical training and taught religion at BYU for a few years).[39] In 1975, BYU professor Hugh Nibley became the first Latter-day Saint scholar with significant training in ancient studies to publish about the DSS for Latter-day Saint readers. Additional publications aimed at a Latter-day Saint audience by trained scholars such as Nibley and BYU professors S. Kent Brown, Stephen D. Ricks, Stephen E. Robinson, and others followed in the 1970s and have continued to the present.[40]

Several major developments occurred in the 1990s involving Latter-day Saints and the DSS. For example, BYU religion and philosophy professor Truman G. Madsen, while serving as the director of BYU's Jerusalem Center for Near Eastern Studies, was invited in Fall 1991 to serve on the advisory board of the newly formed Dead Sea Scrolls Foundation (DSSF). Dr. Weston W. Fields was the founder, and is still the executive director of the DSSF, the primary purpose of which, as explained on its website, is "the financial support of publications of the scrolls and related projects. From 1991–2010 the Foundation supported the series *Discoveries in the Judaean Desert*."[41] *Discoveries*

38. "The Special Meaning of the Dead Sea Scrolls to Latter-day Saints," *U.A.S. Newsletter*, November 7, 1957. Sperry made a few claims in this article that I do not fully accept, but this particular one I do.

39. Lewis M. Rogers, "The Dead Sea Scrolls–Qumran Calmly Revisited," *BYU Studies* 2, no. 2 (1960): 109–28.

40. For a convenient listing of publications by Latter-day Saints on the DSS, by authors too numerous to list here, see Daniel B. McKinlay and Steven W. Booras, "The Dead Sea Scrolls: Select Publications by Latter-day Saint Scholars," *Studies in the Bible and Antiquity* 2 (2010): 105–16.

41. Additionally, "The Foundation also supported the production of the *Dead Sea Scrolls Concordance* (three vols., Brill). The Foundation also serves as a clearing house and information center for many other matters relating to scrolls research and scholarship," accessed June 5, 2020, at https://www.deadseascrolls-foundation.com. For further information on Weston Fields, see http://www.westonfields.com.

*in the Judaean Desert* (*DJD*) is the official scholarly publication series for the DSS, published by Oxford University Press. Conceived in 1951, the first volume appeared in 1955. The forty-volume series was completed in 2010.



Through further relationships cultivated by Dr. Fields, several Latter-day Saints contributed very generously to help publish *DJD* volumes.[42] Furthermore, as of this writing, BYU Professors Donald W. Parry and Andrew C. Skinner have served on the DSSF Board of Advisors and currently serve on the DSSF Board of Directors.[43]

Growing out of these relationships and contributions, the opportunity developed for the first significant involvement with the DSS themselves by academically trained Latter-day Saints. This occurred in the mid-1990s, when BYU professor Donald W. Parry and subsequently BYU professors David R. Seely, Dana M. Pike, and Andrew C. Skinner, were invited by then *DJD* Editor-in-Chief Emanuel Tov to participate on the expanded team of "international editors" of the official publication of the DSS.[44] Their contributions are found in *DJD* volumes 17, 29, 33, and 36.

Although several trained Latter-day Saint scholars have presented at many academic DSS conferences in the past three decades, such involvement is conveniently illustrated by three particular conferences. First, BYU's Jerusalem Center for Near Eastern Studies hosted a small international conference on the DSS in Israel in April 1995.[45] BYU then hosted a large international conference of DSS scholars in Provo, Utah, in July 1996.[46] Both of these "scholars talking to scholars" conferences received financial and logistical support from the

42. The names of donors, Latter-day Saints and others, whose contributions made through the DSSF supported the publication of particular *DJD* volumes are usually mentioned in the "Dedication" for each volume, and they are sometimes also mentioned in the "Foreword" remarks from Editor-in-Chief Emanuel Tov. As one example of many, see Tov's comments in the Foreword to *DJD* 19 (1995): "This volume is dedicated to Alan and Karen Ashton of Orem, Utah, in profound gratitude for their support of the research leading to the publication of the texts and of the preparation of this volume, as well as for their commitment to the publication of the Qumran scrolls in general." For further general comments on Latter-day Saint donors, see Mason, "The Saints and the Scrolls," 178, 191n.31.

43. Other Latter-day Saints who previously served on the DSSF's Board of Advisors include Truman Madsen, Grant Cannon, and Alan Ashton.

44. Greater background and details on these activities than can be recounted here are available in Noel B. Reynolds, "From the Caves of Qumran to CD-ROM," *BYU Magazine* 50, no. 4 (Nov 1996): 44–52; and more recently (by non-Latter-day Saint) Mason, "The Saints and the Scrolls," 169–95.

45. See the resulting conference volume: Donald W. Parry and Stephen D. Ricks, eds., *Current Research and Technological Developments on the Dead Sea* Scrolls (New York: Brill, 1996), which includes contributions by BYU professors Donald W. Parry, David Rolph Seely, Dana M. Pike, and Andrew C. Skinner.

46. See the resulting conference volume: Donald W. Parry and Eugene C. Ulrich, eds. *The Provo International Conference on the Dead Sea Scrolls: Technological Innovations, New Texts, and Reformulated Issues* (New York: Brill, 1999), which includes contributions by BYU professors Donald W. Parry, Dana M. Pike, David Rolph Seely, and Scott R. Woodward.

Foundation for Ancient Research and Mormon Studies (FARMS), whose president, Noel B. Reynolds, was a BYU political science professor and passionate proponent of scripture-related studies.[47] And third, BYU professors co-organized a smaller conference with international scholars on the DSS in Salt Lake City, Utah, in 2014.[48] This conference was held in conjunction with the exhibit "Dead Sea Scrolls: Life and Faith in Biblical Times," hosted at Salt Lake City's Leonardo Museum from November 2013 to April 2014.[49] Additionally, several public lectures were presented in association with this exhibit, some of which were given by Latter-day Saint scroll scholars.



Latter-day Saint scroll scholars' involvement in other public-focused events include the March 1996 one-day FARMS-sponsored conference at BYU titled "LDS Perspectives on the Dead Sea Scrolls" and the 1997 exhibit "Qumran and the Dead Sea Scrolls" at BYU's Museum of Art.[50] "The Story of Masada: Discoveries from the Excavations" ran as a concurrent exhibit at the same venue. Several scrolls and fragments, from both Israel and Jordan, as well as replicas and photographs were on display in Provo, Utah, for six months, and attracted well-over one hundred thousand visitors.[51] A much larger-scale DSS exhibit was planned at the Latter-day Saint Church History Museum in conjunction with the 2002 Olympics, hosted in Salt Lake City, but was cancelled due to repercussions from the major terrorist attacks in the United States on September 11, 2001 ("9/11"). In addition to such public presentations and academic publications and presentations on the DSS, BYU professors, FARMS associates, and other Latter-day Saints have also written responsibly in the past few decades about the DSS for Latter-day Saints.[52]

Finally, several Latter-day Saint scholars are contributing to *Dead Sea Scrolls Editions*, a current effort (begun in 2018) to republish the DSS in order

47. In addition to Reynolds, two professionals who worked for FARMS in relation to DSS projects, Steven W. Booras and E. Jan Wilson, presented or co-presented at the two conferences just mentioned as well as elsewhere.

48. See the resulting conference volume: Donald W. Parry, Stephen D. Ricks, and Andrew C. Skinner, eds., *The Prophetic Voice at Qumran: The Leonardo Museum Conference on the Dead Sea Scrolls, 11–12 April 2014* (New York: Brill, 2017), which includes contributions by BYU professors Matthew J. Grey, Donald W. Parry, Dana M. Pike, and Joshua M. Sears (a graduate student at the time of the conference).

49. This exhibit, produced by the Israel Antiquities Authority and Discovery Times Square, was hosted in seven major cities in the United States from 2011 to 2018.

50. For the one-day event, see the resulting conference volume: Donald W. Parry and Dana M. Pike, eds., *LDS Perspectives on the Dead Sea Scrolls* (Provo, UT: FARMS, 1997).

51. See, conveniently, Miles Gerald Bradford, "Ancient Scrolls from the Dead Sea: Photographs and Commentary on a Unique Collection of Scrolls," *Maxwell Institute Publications* 9 (1997), available at https://scholarsarchive.byu.edu/mi/9; and Mason, "The Saints and the Scrolls," 182, 193.

52. Again, see McKinlay and Booras, "The Dead Sea Scrolls: Select Publications by Latter-day Saint Scholars," as well as the items listed in several previous notes.

to take better advantage of what has been learned from and about them since their original publication in the *DJD* series.[53]

Of all the Latter-Saint scholars who have been academically engaged with DSS research, BYU professor Donald W. Parry (who has a PhD in Hebrew Literature and Language), has been the most involved and prolific, authoring and co-editing a large body of work. His numerous publications on the DSS include the recent volume, *Exploring the Isaiah Scrolls and Their Textual Variants* (Brill, 2019).[54] There is no particular focus or trend to the work on the DSS that Latter-day Saint scholars have pursued, although much of their work, as exemplified by Parry's recent volume, is Bible and scrolls related.



Along with Latter-day Saint scholars' involvement with the DSS texts themselves, Latter-day Saint technologically-oriented contributions to scroll study have included Scott R. Woodward's early DNA studies on the leather of some of the scrolls,[55] and especially the initiative begun by FARMS, now BYU's Neal A. Maxwell Institute for Religious Scholarship, to produce a searchable database of all published DSS texts with pictures. This latter effort eventuated in *The Dead Sea Scrolls Electronic Library CD-ROM*, co-published by Brill and BYU in 1999. Revised editions of this valuable resource have been available online since 2015 as *Dead Sea Scrolls Electronic Library Non-Biblical Texts* (Emanuel Tov, editor) and *Dead Sea Scrolls Electronic Library Biblical Texts* (Donald W. Parry and Andrew C. Skinner, editors).[56]

## FUTURE PROSPECTS

Given the formal, professional involvement with the DSS by a relatively small number of Latter-day Saint scholars during the past three decades, and given the small but steady number of Latter-day Saints who continue to engage in graduate studies on the Hebrew Bible, early Judaism, and the DSS, it can confidently be

53. Sponsored by the DSSF, E.J. Brill will publish this new series, with Martin G. Abegg Jr., Daniel K. Falk, and Alison Schofield as general editors. *Dead Sea Scrolls Editions* is an updated scholarly edition of the Dead Sea scrolls and fragments, with new transcriptions, translations, and critical notes.

54. See also, for example, Donald W. Parry and Emanuel Tov, eds., *The Dead Sea Scrolls Reader*, 2nd expanded ed., two vols. (Boston: Brill, 2014).

55. See, for example, Scott R. Woodward, "Putting the Pieces Together: DNA and the Dead Sea Scrolls," in *LDS Perspectives on the Dead Sea Scrolls*, edited by Parry and Pike, 191–205. See now the DNA work of Israeli and other scholars in Sarit Anava, et al., "Illuminating Genetic Mysteries of the Dead Sea Scrolls," *Cell* 181 (June 11, 2020): 1218–31 (https://doi.org/10.1016/j.cell.2020.04.046).

56. See https://cpart.mi.byu.edu/home/dss/. For interesting background information on this project, as well as other technology-based efforts, see Reynolds, "From The Caves of Qumran to CD-ROM," in *Y Magazine* (Fall 1996), available without page numbers at https://magazine.byu.edu/article/from-the-caves-of-qumran-to-cd-rom/.

asserted that Latter-day Saint involvement with the DSS, at BYU and elsewhere, will no doubt continue onwards. This activity is not what some would call Mormon apologetics. Such academic involvement focuses on the scrolls themselves, for the sake of studying their content in their own historical and religious context. There is still much work to be done in analyzing the DSS, and Latter-day Saint scholars can and will participate with other scholars in this productive effort to better explore, synthesize, and refine knowledge about Qumran, the DSS, and how they fit into the larger religious landscape at the turn of the era.



Going forward, many Latter-day Saints, speaking broadly, will no doubt retain some level of interest in how their own beliefs and practices—including the concept of an open and expanding canon, modern-day temple worship, the role of living prophets, the significance of covenants with deity, and the belief in the premortal existence of all human souls—are echoed to one extent or another in ancient documents, especially those like the DSS that are associated with the Jewish and Christian traditions. Therefore, on one hand, it would not be at all surprising for future Latter-day Saint scholars, who are particularly attuned to such concepts, to make scholarly contributions on such topics.[57] On the other hand, it is very likely that some Latter-day Saints will continue to be drawn to the DSS and additional new discoveries because of their hope that these finds will somehow complement Latter-day Saint beliefs and practices.

Therefore, in a more popular context, Latter-day Saints, as well as the public at large, can maximize their understanding of the DSS in a number of productive ways. One is to access more recently published, responsible treatments of the DSS. As respected as Hugh Nibley and his publications have been in the eyes of some Latter-day Saints, he and each non-Latter-day Saint scholar in the early decades of scroll research was working with incomplete data when producing their publications fifty to sixty years ago. Many of the scroll fragments were not even published until the 1990s and early 2000s. So for Latter-day Saints interested in the DSS, reading *just* Nibley on the DSS is not ever enough.

Publications on the DSS by Latter-day Saint scholars for a Latter-day Saint audience have helped tamp down and will likely continue to help offset lingering sensational and unsubstantiated claims among Latter-day Saints about the scrolls and their contents.[58] So hopefully an increasing number of Lat-

57. This is not to suggest that non-Latter-day Saint scholars are not interested in nor capable of producing quality scholarship on such topics.

58. Past examples include Parry and Pike, eds., *LDS Perspectives on the Dead Sea Scrolls* (1997), and Parry and Ricks, *The Dead Sea Scrolls: Questions and Responses for Latter-day Saints* (2000), both cited previously.

ter-day Saints will better realize what the DSS are and what they are *not*. This will include the correct idea that the Qumran community was not a divinely authorized restoration group, as a few Latter-day Saints have claimed.[59] More Latter-day Saints will hopefully realize they will not find a catalog of Latter-day Saint-oriented gospel truths preserved in the DSS. No matter what one's religious inclinations, the DSS and all ancient texts must be first evaluated in their own historical and cultural context and not pressed as proof texts for later religious beliefs and practices that exist in different contexts.

One major value of the DSS, for Latter-day Saints and all Bible-reading people, is that they include the oldest surviving copies, typically incomplete, of the Hebrew scriptures. None of the "original" biblical texts survive, and there is a gap, often of many centuries, between when the Hebrew scriptures were authored or redacted and when the Qumran copies of them were produced at the turn of the era. But these copies get us many centuries closer to the time of their original composition than was previously the case. Translators of the Hebrew Bible/Old Testament since the mid-twentieth century have, to varying degrees, taken advantage of what are deemed "preferred" readings in certain biblical passages. These are variant readings judged by scholars to be more accurate than the traditional Masoretic Text of the Hebrew Bible. The textual variants in the biblical DSS manuscripts do impact the meaning of certain passages and are worth considering, although the differences they make can be described as relatively minor (the degree of their significance is, of course, a matter of opinion; some alternative readings are similar to those already known from the Greek Septuagint). Examples of passages for which some modern translation committees have chosen readings attested in the DSS include Deuteronomy 32:8–9; 32:43; 1 Samuel 10:27–11:1; 17:4; Psalm 22:16–17; and several passages in the books of Isaiah and Jeremiah.[60]

Since English-speaking Latter-day Saints continue to institutionally use the Authorized (King James) Version of the Bible, they are often unaware of, and thus lack the benefit of, these different readings, although some Latter-day Saint publications have begun discussing them.[61] This may be viewed as ironic,

---

59. This view has been repeated a number of times. See Andrew C. Skinner's corrective remark that the Qumran community is *not* a previously "unknown group of pre-Christian 'Latter-day Saints' living down by the Dead Sea," in "The Dead Sea Scrolls and Latter-day Truth," *Ensign* (February 2006): 44.

60. For a concise overview of these and other examples, see, for example, Flint, *The Dead Sea Scrolls*, 52–81.

61. See, for example, Donald W. Parry, "The Dead Sea Scrolls Bible," *Studies in the Bible and Antiquity* 2 (2010): 1–27; and Parry and Ricks, *The Dead Sea Scrolls: Questions and Responses for Latter-day Saints*, question 37.

since according to the Latter-day Saint Articles of Faith, penned by Joseph Smith, "We believe the Bible to be the word of God as far as it is translated correctly; we also believe the Book of Mormon to be the word of God" (A of F 8; "translated" here is generally understood to mean transmitted as well as translated). But many Latter-day Saints have yet to tap into this biblical DSS resource. Perhaps someday Latter-day Saint editions of the Bible will take advantage of such variant readings, either in the text of scripture or at least in annotations. Although opinions may differ on the importance of many of these variant readings, awareness of their existence is important for appreciating the history of the biblical text and the inherent challenges in studying its transmission, as well as the value these texts can have for Latter-day Saints and others in their own personal scripture study. Thus, helping Latter-day Saints and other students of the Bible better understand the nature and significance of the biblical texts found at Qumran and elsewhere in the Judean desert is a worthwhile endeavor that deserves ongoing attention.

A final consideration: Joseph Smith said the Lord told him and Latter-day Saints generally to "study and learn, and become acquainted with all good books, and with languages, tongues, and people" (D&C 90:15) and to "obtain a knowledge of history, and of countries, and of kingdoms" (D&C 93:53; see also 88:77–80). Responsibly studying the DSS assists in better understanding Jews and Jewish thought at the turn of the era and assists students of the New Testament in better understanding certain aspects of its content in its originally Jewish context.[62]

The DSS are thus one example of religious literature that can stimulate productive religious insight and discussion. They do not "prove" that the Latter-day Saint view of things is true. They do, however, preserve the thoughts and beliefs of certain ancient Jewish males who were dissatisfied with the religious authorities of their day, who separated themselves from Jerusalem and attempted to worship their God in a somewhat different way with somewhat different beliefs (while still accepting their broad Jewish religious heritage). Their struggles, their hopes for God to deliver them from their personal trials,

62. For more on this latter topic, see, written for a Latter-day Saint audience, Dana M. Pike, "The Dead Sea Scrolls and the New Testament," in *New Testament History, Culture, and Society: A Background to the Texts of the New Testament*, edited by Lincoln H. Blumell (Provo, UT: Religious Studies Center and Deseret Book, 2019), 109–21. See additional discussions on this topic in chapters in the introductory volumes on the DSS cited, as well as books that specifically address possible connections between the Dead Sea Scrolls and the New Testament and early Christianity, including, for example, Bergsma, *Jesus and the Dead Sea Scrolls* (2019), Joseph A. Fitzmyer, *The Dead Sea Scrolls and Christian Origins* (Grand Rapids, MI: Eerdmans, 2000); and James Charlesworth, *Jesus and the Dead Sea Scrolls* (New Haven, CT: Yale University Press, 1992).

their eschatological expectations for divine intervention in their world to overcome the wickedness and injustices they encountered—these are human dimensions with which many modern people can resonate, Latter-day Saints and non-Latter-day Saints alike. Greater awareness of these elements can provide a richer experience for all who choose to encounter the Dead Sea Scrolls.

# 6

# The Persian, Hellenistic, and Roman Periods

MATTHEW J. GREY

The nearly six centuries that spanned the Judean return from Babylonian exile and the events of the New Testament, an era commonly referred to as the Second Temple or "intertestamental" period, produced a series of historical developments that had a transformative impact on the world of the Bible and western religious thought. Ranging from the sixth century BCE to the first century CE, the periods of Persian, Greek, and Roman rule in Judea saw, among other things, the completion and canonization of the Hebrew Bible, the transition from ancient Israelite religion to early Judaism (with its central ritual practices, social institutions, and theological concepts), and the formation of a religious landscape that gave rise to the Jesus movement, early Christianity, and the early rabbinic movement. Despite these salient developments, however, the Latter-day Saint community (like many modern readers of the Bible) has traditionally had only limited engagement with this period and its importance for Jewish and Christian origins.

In an effort to provide the historical background to these issues, to highlight their relevance to biblical literacy, and to contextualize their potential significance to Latter-day Saint thought, this essay will summarize the Persian, Hellenistic, and Roman periods of Jewish history–outlining the main historical events and socioreligious developments of each period—and will briefly consider the varying approaches to Second Temple Judaism that have appeared in Latter-day Saint historiography since the nineteenth century. Although spatial constraints will not allow for a detailed or comprehensive treatment of these complex topics, it is hoped that this survey will introduce readers to the historical world of the Second Temple period and will contribute to a fuller understanding of Latter-day Saint interaction with the Bible.

## THE PERSIAN PERIOD: THE RETURN TO JUDEA, THE REBUILDING OF THE JERUSALEM TEMPLE, AND THE BEGINNINGS OF EARLY JUDAISM



Events that shaped biblical history "between the testaments" began with the transition from the Babylonian exile to the Persian rule of the Near East in the sixth century BCE. The Babylonian destruction of Jerusalem and Solomon's Temple in 586 resulted in the deportation of Judah's upper classes (including members of the royal court and priestly families) and their forced resettlement in Mesopotamia. Although many Judahite families would remain in Babylonia for several centuries—eventually leading to the establishment of influential rabbinic academies and other Jewish intellectual circles in the region—for biblical purposes the era of "the exile" came to an end with the fall of Babylon and the rise of the Persian Empire.[1]

Babylon's decline began with the political instability that followed the death of Nebuchadnezzar II (ca. 562 BCE) when a usurper named Nabonidus seized the Babylonian throne and appointed his son Belshazzar as co-regent (an episode reflected in the legendary account of "Belshazzar's Feast" in Daniel 5). Around this time (ca. 550) Cyrus the Great became ruler of the neighboring Persian kingdom, and by 539, he had succeeded in conquering Babylon and incorporating all of its former land holdings into his own empire, which by then had included most of the ancient Near East. Contemporary documents indicate that shortly after the formation of the Persian Empire, Cyrus initiated one of the earliest policies of religious toleration in the ancient world by allowing the foreign peoples who had been conquered by Babylon to return to their ancestral homelands and rebuild the temples of their native deities, a policy of repatriation at least partially motivated by Cyrus's desire to earn the support of local gods.[2]

With Cyrus's edict, a relatively small group of elite Judean families began the process of leaving Babylon and returning to the province of Yahud (Judah), resettling Jerusalem as its capital, and rebuilding the temple dedicated to the God of Israel.[3] Several biblical authors looked to these developments as a divine

1. Accessible overviews of this historical period can be found in Lester Grabbe, *A History of the Jews and Judaism in the Second Temple Period, Vol. I: The Persian Period (539–331 BCE)* (New York: T&T Clark, 2004) and Jodi Magness, *The Archaeology of the Holy Land: From the Destruction of Solomon's Temple to the Muslim Conquest* (New York: Cambridge University Press, 2012), 46–62.

2. For example, see the text and commentary on the Cyrus Cylinder in William W. Hallo, ed., *The Context of Scripture* (Leiden, Netherlands: Brill, 2003), 2:314–16.

3. Ezra 1:1–4 and 6:1–5 record Cyrus' edict of liberation as applied to Yahud and as interpreted by the author, who was likely a member of Jerusalem's priestly or scribal class in the early fourth century BCE.

restoration of Israel's past glory; for example, the anonymous exilic writer of Second Isaiah (Isaiah 40–55) viewed Cyrus as a messiah ("anointed one") sent by God to lead the return of his people in a new exodus,[4] and visionary material in the book of Zechariah portrayed Zerubbabel (the Davidic governor appointed over Yahud) and Joshua (the first High Priest of the new Jerusalem temple) as a divinely commissioned diarchy of prince and priest that would preside over the renewal of Israel's sociopolitical institutions.[5] However, a close reading of the biblical text and contemporary sources shows that—for various political, social, and religious reasons—the resettlement of Yahud was actually a long, complex, and tumultuous process that was often interrupted by external threats from neighboring provinces,[6] as well as by competing internal visions for the implementation of the restoration program.[7]



Nevertheless, under a new Persian king (Darius I; r. 521–476) and at the behest of local prophetic figures (such as Haggai and Zechariah), the imperial initiative to restore Yahud persisted as Zerubbabel coordinated the resettlement of returning Judean clans, oversaw the return of the temple treasures from Babylon and, in 516, completed the rebuilding of the Jerusalem temple.[8] Although various prophetic writers had greatly anticipated the completion of this project and its accompanying restoration of the divine presence among God's people, the consecration of the second Jerusalem temple (the "Temple of Zerubbabel") caused divisions within the Judean community, with some of the younger generation rejoicing that a temple again stood in Jerusalem and some of the older generation contrasting it with the past grandeur of Solomon's

4. Isaiah 44:24–45:7. Josephus, *Antiquities* 11.1–7 contains a later legend of Cyrus being inspired in his actions by reading the prophetic writings of Isaiah concerning his role in leading the restoration of Jerusalem.

5. Zechariah 3:1–4:14 (cf. Haggai 1:1; 2:20–23).

6. According to Ezra-Nehemiah, these included the ethnic tensions between the inhabitants of Yahud and the inhabitants in the provinces of Samaria to the north, Idumea to the south, and Ammon to the east, each of which had its own Persian-appointed governor but also its own competing political interests. For example, interference by the Samaritans—whose assistance to rebuild the Jerusalem temple was refused by Judean authorities—delayed the reconstruction of the temple for almost two decades (Ezra 4:1–23).

7. Competing ideologies among Judeans in the early Persian period are reflected in the social tensions that existed between the influential families who—with political and economic support from the Persian government—were returning to Yahud and who viewed themselves as the preserved "remnant" prophesied to restore Israel (Isaiah 11:11–16 and Jeremiah 29:10–14; cf. Ezra 9:8, 13 and Zechariah 8:6, 11–12), and those lower class families ("the people of the land") who had remained in the region throughout the Babylonian exile and whose interests were threatened by the returnees (Ezra 4:5–5:2; Haggai 1:1–12). For recent studies on these tensions and the different prophetic voices that contributed to the visions for Yahud's restoration, see Kenneth A. Ristau, *Reconstructing Jerusalem: Persian-Period Prophetic Perspective* (Winona Lake, IN: Eisenbrauns, 2016) and John Robert Barker, *Disputed Temple: A Rhetorical Analysis of the Book of Haggai* (Minneapolis, MN: Fortress Press, 2017).

8. See Ezra 1:7–11; 5:1–2; Haggai 2:1–23; and Zechariah 1–8.

temple.[9] Furthermore, criticisms of the lifestyles and ritual practices performed by the newly reinstalled priests would lead some circles to question the legitimacy of the temple's priestly administrators for generations to come.[10]



Another major event in this period occurred around 458 BCE when the Persian king Artaxerxes I (r. 464–424) commissioned Ezra—a Judean priest and scribe who had been living in Babylon—to return to Yahud with imperial authority to establish the Torah as official law of the province. This process seems to have included efforts to edit, collate, and codify the writings of the Pentateuch, to implement it as the civic legal code of Yahud, and to enforce a strict application of its genealogical purity laws (such as imposing a ban on marriages to non-Israelites) among local Judeans who were not adhering to the standards promoted by the families who had returned from exile.[11] These latter efforts led to contentious debates among different groups over the nature of God's covenant with Israel; while some enthusiastically endorsed Ezra's requirements for Judeans to divorce their foreign wives and to exclude "unclean" individuals from the community as a stipulation of the covenant,[12] others envisioned a community in which foreigners and other marginalized peoples could fully participate in the worship of the God of Israel.[13] Nevertheless, Ezra's success in implementing the Torah as the official law of Yahud—as well as the various interpretations of it that followed—helped shape Judean national identity and laid the foundation for subsequent conceptions of holiness (or being "set apart") within early Judaism.

9. Ezra 3:10–13.

10. Such criticisms began as early as the fifth century BCE (e.g., Malachi 1.6–2:9) and continued among some groups (such as the authors of the Enochic literature and Dead Sea Scrolls corpus) until the end of the Second Temple period.

11. Ezra promoted this legal system through a series of covenant renewal festivals and by instructing priests to teach the correct application of the law throughout the province (Ezra 9; Nehemiah 8–10). According to some scholars, these state-sponsored efforts to teach and interpret Torah in public settings may have established a framework for the eventual development of local synagogues; see Anders Runesson, *The Origins of the Synagogue: A Socio-Historical Study* (Stockholm, Sweden: Almqvist & Wiksell International, 2001).

12. Prohibitions on mixed marriages of Jewish men and foreign women, as well as on the presence of "unclean" individuals in the community (based on Deuteronomy 23:1–7), can be seen in Ezra 10; Nehemiah 13; Ezekiel 44:6–9 (a passage that, during the Persian period, seems to have been inserted into the earlier writings of Ezekiel); and Malachi 2:10–17.

13. For example, the post-exilic author of Third Isaiah (Isaiah 56–66) proclaimed that the renewed covenant would extend to the very foreigners and unclean individuals (such as eunuchs) excluded from the community by Ezra's reforms (see Isaiah 56:1–8). Similarly, the book of Ruth—a story about a non-Israelite woman remaining loyal to her Israelite in-laws after the death of her spouse—may have been written around the same time as a counter-narrative to Ezra's removal of foreign women from the community. This latter strand of thought which envisioned a place for outsiders within God's covenant would later be promoted by the early Jesus movement in its efforts to fellowship gentiles and those deemed ritually unclean by the Torah (see fn. 36).

Other significant developments over the two centuries of the Persian period include the appointment of Nehemiah as a governor of Yahud (ca. 445–424) and his rebuilding the walls of Jerusalem (an initiative opposed by neighboring provinces);[14] a remarkable amount of literary and scriptural production by Jerusalem's priestly and scribal classes;[15] and the early beginnings of Jewish social movements (such as proto-sectarian groups debating Judean law and Diaspora communities finding ways to maintain their religious identity apart from the Jerusalem temple), institutions (such as local synagogue gatherings for learning Torah), cultural shifts (such as using Aramaic in place of Hebrew), literary forms (such as *targums*, or "translations," of Hebrew scripture), and theological developments (such as more defined notions of monotheism and what it means to be God's chosen people) that would eventually have a significant impact on the formation of Judaism and the world of the New Testament.

## THE HELLENISTIC PERIOD: CULTURAL CHANGE, JUDEAN STRUGGLES FOR INDEPENDENCE, AND THE FORMATION OF JEWISH SECTARIANISM

The Persian era in Yahud—which was viewed by many Jews as a golden age in which the Judean law, temple, priesthood, and cultural standards of holiness could flourish in a semiautonomous political environment—came to an end with the fall of the Persian Empire resulting from the conquests of Alexander the Great (ca. 336–323 BCE).[16] Persia and Greece had been warring over their mutually encroaching borders for over a century when Alexander carried out his vision for an invasion of Persia and an expansion of Greek presence in the Near East. Alexander's victory over Persian forces at the battle of Issus in 333 allowed him to march down the eastern Mediterranean coast and gain control over the provinces of Samaria, Judea, and Idumea before getting as far as

14. Nehemiah 1–7.

15. In addition to the writings of the Pentateuch being edited and collated in this period, other biblical books that were composed between the sixth and fourth century BCE include 1–2 Chronicles, Ezra-Nehemiah, Haggai, Zechariah, Malachi, Third Isaiah, some psalms, and possibly Job, some proverbs, Ecclesiastes, and Esther.

16. Classic (if somewhat dated) treatments of the Hellenistic period and its impact on Jewish history can be found in Victor Tcherikover, *Hellenistic Civilization and the Jews* (Philadelphia: Jewish Publication Society, 1959) and Elias Bickerman, *The Jews in the Greek Age* (Cambridge, MA: Harvard University Press, 1988). For an updated survey of Judean material culture during this period, see Magness, *Archaeology of the Holy Land*, 63–107.

Egypt, after which he proceeded eastward and dismantled the remainder of the Persian Empire before his campaigns ended with his early death in 323.[17]

In addition to the vast political changes Alexander brought to the Near East, his conquest of the Persian Empire resulted in a major cultural shift that would dramatically alter the historical landscape of the biblical world. This shift came with Alexander's introduction of a new syncretistic culture ("Hellenism") that fused Greek and local Near Eastern customs, and that transformed the social dynamics of the region. The Hellenistic cultural innovations that followed Alexander's conquest of the Near East included the widespread use of *koine* Greek, the establishment of Greek civic, educational, and religious institutions (such as cities, theaters, gymnasia, and temples), and the introduction of Greek philosophy, art, literature, and forms of government. Although Hellenism was not forcibly imposed on Judeans by Alexander and his immediate successors, these new cultural elements gradually began to fragment Judean society as different groups debated the extent to which Jews could interact with Hellenism and still maintain their covenantal commitment to "holiness" as God's people. Over time, Judean responses to this issue would show varying degrees of resistance, tolerance, adaption, and adoption of Hellenistic culture along a spectrum that included some families (often conservative traditionalists in rural settings) that rejected many aspects of Hellenism as being incompatible with Jewish holiness, and others (often elite families in urban settings) that embraced Hellenistic lifestyles while still identifying as Torah-observant Jews.[18]

Following the death of Alexander the Great, his vast territory was divided among his generals and their descendants, with the Ptolemies gaining control of Egypt (and Judea until 198 BCE), and the Seleucids governing Syria, Asia Minor, and Mesopotamia (as well as controlling Judea from 198 to 141). Because Judea was located on the border between rival kingdoms, many Jews in this period became divided politically as well as culturally, with loyalties split between the Ptolemies to the south and the Seleucids to the north.[19] The rulers of both regimes, however, afforded Judeans a significant degree of religious

17. Accounts and legends of Alexander the Great gaining control of Samaria and Judea can be found in Josephus, *Antiquities* 11.313–47. For the most part, Alexander left the existing Persian political organization of these regions in place, but appointed his own governors to administer the provinces on his behalf.

18. For more detailed discussion of the complex cultural encounters between Judaism and Hellenism, see Erich Gruen, *Heritage and Hellenism: The Reinvention of Jewish Tradition* (Berkeley: University of California Press, 1992) and John J. Collins, *Between Athens and Jerusalem: Jewish Identity in the Hellenistic Diaspora*, 2nd ed. (Grand Rapids, MI: Eerdmans, 1999).

19. Daniel 7–12 contains a series of symbolic visions that describe the wars between Persia and Greece, the rise of Alexander the Great, and the conflicts between the Ptolemies and Seleucids over Judea leading up to the reign of Antiochus IV.

autonomy by allowing the traditional High Priestly families to retain administrative control over the Jerusalem temple. This arrangement was challenged—and the socioreligious world of Judea was destabilized—under the reign of the Seleucid king Antiochus IV Epiphanes (r. 175–163), who accepted bribes from individuals seeking to be appointed to the High Priesthood, attempted to convert Jerusalem into a Greek *polis* (with the Jerusalem temple being rededicated to the Olympian Zeus), and rescinded the Torah as the law of Judea.[20]

Although some Hellenized and pro-Seleucid Judeans supported these policies, conservative factions viewed them as fatal to their covenant with the God of Israel and responded with a violent uprising. The Maccabean Revolt (ca. 167–164/142) was led by a traditionalist priestly family who assembled a coalition of like-minded Judeans, fought against the Seleucids and their local supporters (making the revolt, to some extent, a Judean civil war), rededicated the Jerusalem temple, and—over the next two decades—gained political independence in the form of an autonomous Jewish state known as the Hasmonean kingdom (ca. 142–63).[21] Initially these developments encouraged among some Judeans a messianic hope for a restoration of Israel's past glory, however, such hopes were soon dashed as the Hasmoneans themselves adopted Hellenistic lifestyles, appropriated the High Priesthood in violation of Jewish law, often ruled through corruption and brutality, and expanded the borders of Judea (as far north as Galilee and as far south as Idumea) through military conquest, colonization, and the forced conversion of other ethnic peoples to Judaism.[22]

Naturally this sociopolitical turmoil had a significant impact on Judean religious developments; as a result of different responses to Hellenism, questions of legitimacy with regard to the Jerusalem temple priesthood, unrealized messianic hopes, and divergent interpretations of the Torah, Judaism in the late Hellenistic period began to fracture into various groups with their own beliefs and practices. For example, while most Jews maintained a shared loyalty to the temple and Torah (with its Sabbath, circumcision, and kosher laws), some circles in this era began to intensify their application of purity rituals, establish regulations on table fellowship, debate the perimeters of the scriptural canon, and express alternative views on the nature of religious authority, all of which

20. For contemporary descriptions of these events from the perspective of those opposed to the decrees of Antiochus and the actions of his Hellenized Judean supporters, see 1 Maccabees 1–2 and 2 Maccabees 3–6.

21. For pro-Maccabean accounts of the revolt and its aftermath, see 1 Maccabees 3–16 and 2 Maccabees 8–15.

22. For a fuller treatment of the Hasmonean dynasty and the socioreligious dynamics of this period, see Eyal Regev, *The Hasmoneans: Ideology, Archaeology, Identity* (Göttingen, Germany: Vandenhoeck and Ruprecht, 2013).

contributed to the emergence of Jewish sectarianism in the Hasmonean era. This would eventually include groups known from the New Testament period such as the Sadducees (priestly aristocrats associated with the Jerusalem temple who exclusively adhered to the laws of the Torah), Pharisees (lay Torah scholars who gave religious weight to non-Pentateuchal writings and ancestral tradition), and Essenes (a community of exiled priests awaiting God's purification of Jerusalem),[23] along with smaller movements of ascetic holy men, mystics, philosophers, and nationalists.[24] Other theological developments included the formation among some groups of apocalyptic thought with its emphasis on a cosmic war between good and evil, angelology, a messianic end times, a resurrection, and an eternal judgment.[25] Although most of the literature from this era would not be canonized by later rabbinic and Christian circles, a wide array of genres and texts produced between the fourth and first centuries BCE (including various apocryphal and pseudepigraphic writings) reflects the vibrant debates and diverse Jewish worldviews of the Second Temple period.

## THE ROMAN PERIOD: HERODIANS, THE DESTRUCTION OF JERUSALEM, AND THE EMERGENCE OF THE JESUS MOVEMENT

By the mid-60s BCE, the Hasmonean dynasty had become embroiled in a civil war. At the same time, the Roman Republic was expanding eastward in its efforts to dismantle the Seleucid kingdom in Syria. Seeing an opportunity to further increase Rome's influence in the region, the Roman general Pompey led his legions to Jerusalem, intervened in the Hasmonean civil war, and (beginning in 63) asserted Roman control over Judea, thus bringing to an end the brief era of Jewish political independence.[26] The Romans initially controlled Judea through local families who were loyal to Rome and who

23. Josephus, *War* 2.119–166; *Antiquities* 13.288–300 and 18.11–25.

24. For more on the development of Jewish sectarianism in this period, see E.P. Sanders, *Judaism: Practice and Belief 63 BCE–66 CE* (London: SCM Press, 1992); Albert I. Baumgarten, *The Flourishing of Jewish Sects in the Maccabean Era* (New York: Brill, 1997); and Anthony J. Saldarini, *Pharisees, Scribes, and Sadducees in Palestinian Society* (Grand Rapids, MI: Eerdmans, 2001).

25. A classic treatment of apocalyptic thought and literature from this period is John J. Collins, *The Apocalyptic Imagination: An Introduction to Jewish Apocalyptic Literature* 3rd ed. (Grand Rapids, MI: Eerdmans, 2016).

26. Detailed surveys of the history of Judea during the early Roman period can be found in Emil Schürer, *The History of the Jewish People in the Age of Jesus Christ (175 BC–AD 135)*, vols. 1–3, rev., Geza Vermes, Fergus Millar, and Martin Goodman (Edinburgh, UK: T&T Clark, 1986) and Martin Goodman, *Rome and Jerusalem: The Clash of Ancient Civilizations* (New York: Knopf, 2007).

governed the area on its behalf, but in 40—as a response to increasing threats made to Roman borders by the Parthians—the Roman senate appointed the young Herod the Great (an ethnic Idumean whose grandfather was forcibly converted to Judaism by the Hasmoneans) to rule Judea as a client king with the title "King of the Jews."[27]



Herod the Great (r. 37–4 BCE) was one of the most complex and controversial rulers of Judea during the Roman period. Throughout his reign, Herod sought to demonstrate loyalty to his Roman patrons (such as Marc Antony and Caesar Augustus) on one hand, and yet placate the Jewish population of his kingdom (much of which viewed him as an illegitimate ruler) on the other. This political balancing effort was shown by Herod's Romanization of Judea—including his building of Roman-style cities, displays of personal affinity to Roman culture, and cultivation of a Romanized Jewish aristocracy in Jerusalem—along with his extensive renovations of the Jerusalem temple and public adherence to Jewish law.[28] Herod's popular title "the Great" reflects not only the unprecedented scale of his building projects and his success in integrating Judea into the larger Roman Empire, but also his violent attempts to suppress potential rivals to the throne, including the murder of several members of his own family.[29]

Following the death of Herod the Great in 4 BCE, Rome decided to not appoint a single successor to rule Herod's client kingdom, but instead divided Herod's territory among three of his surviving sons: Herod Archelaus (r. 4 BCE–6 CE) was appointed ethnarch over Judea, Idumea, and Samaria; Herod Antipas (r. 4 BCE–39 CE) was appointed tetrarch over Galilee and Perea; and Herod Philip (r. 4 BCE–34 CE) was appointed tetrarch over the mostly gentile regions to the northeast of Galilee.[30] The two tetrarchs (Antipas and Philip) proved to be relatively stable rulers who effectively administered their respective territories for several decades (including during the life and ministry of Jesus). Archelaus, however, was deposed by the Romans after only ten years as a result of his excessive cruelty and ineffectual governance. After

27. For detailed biographical information on Herod the Great, see Peter Richardson, *Herod: King of the Jews and Friend of the Romans* (Columbia: University of South Carolina Press, 1996).

28. Overviews of Herod's Romanization of Judea and monumental building projects can be found in Ehud Netzer, *The Architecture of Herod the Great Builder* (Grand Rapids, MI: Baker, 2006) and Magness, *Archaeology of the Holy Land*, 133–229.

29. Josephus, *Antiquities* 15.50–61; 15.161–86; 15.218–46; 15.364–69; 16.150–59; 16.387–94; 17.146–48; 17.168–81; and Matthew 2:1–18.

30. For more on the history and politics of Galilee in this period, see Morten H. Jensen, *Herod Antipas in Galilee: The Literary and Archaeological Sources on the Reign of Herod Antipas and its Socio-Economic Impact on Galilee* (Tübingen, Germany: Mohr Siebeck, 2010).

removing Archelaus, Rome annexed Judea (making it a formal province) and asserted its direct control by appointing its own prefects (who ruled 6–41 CE), the most famous of which was Pontius Pilate.[31] Roman prefects of Judea were responsible to administer, defend, and keep order in the province, supervise the collection of Roman taxes, and adjudicate court cases involving Roman citizens or interests. Although they did not impose a military occupation on the province and they often left local civic bodies (such as Jerusalem's priestly aristocracy) to manage daily affairs, the prefects were known for their corruption and lack of sympathy for local religious sensitivities.

In the 40s CE, the Herodians experienced a brief resurgence of prominence and authority with the Roman appointment of Herod Agrippa I (r. 37–44; a grandson of Herod the Great) as king over the entirety of Judea and Galilee,[32] followed by the appointment of Herod Agrippa II (r. ca. 48–100) as ruler of a much smaller territory in Lebanon.[33] With the death of Agrippa I, the Romans again annexed Judea and directly governed the province through appointed procurators (a position similar to the earlier prefects) from 44 to 66. During those decades a number of political, social, economic, and religious factors combined to gradually drive Judea toward armed rebellion against Roman occupation. These included the increasing corruption, oppression, incompetence, and religious insensitivities of the procurators, as well as the increasing feelings of Judean nationalism, messianic claimants, apocalyptic anticipation, and banditry resulting from a growing economic gap between the upper and lower classes. Together, these factors led to the outbreak of the First Jewish Revolt against Rome (66–74), a bloody conflict that resulted in the destruction of the Jerusalem temple in 70 and thus brought the Second Temple period to a close.[34]

Of the many religious developments that occurred within Judaism during the Early Roman period (such as the continuing evolution of synagogue liturgy,

31. Non-biblical references to Pontius Pilate's term as prefect of Judea include Josephus, *War* 2.169–77; *Antiquities* 18.55–64, 85–89; and Philo, *Legatio ad Gaium* 299–305.

32. Agrippa I was remembered in the New Testament as a persecutor of early Christians (see Acts 12:1–11). Despite his local popularity, he appears to have experienced an ignominious death on account of his impiety (see Acts 12:19–24; cf. Josephus, *Antiquities* 19.343–61).

33. Even though he was not able to rule the entire kingdom of Judea, Agrippa II retained oversight of the Jerusalem temple and the right to appoint High Priests. He is also remembered in the New Testament for being present at the hearing of Paul in Caesarea Maritima (see Acts 26).

34. For more on the origins, events, and impact of this revolt, see Martin Goodman, *The Ruling Class of Judea: The Origins of the Jewish Revolt against Rome AD 66–70* (Cambridge, UK: Cambridge University Press, 1987) and Andrea M. Berlin and J. Andrew Overman, eds., *The First Jewish Revolt: Archaeology, History, and Ideology* (New York: Routledge, 2002).

forms of Jewish mysticism, and the early beginnings of rabbinic thought), one of the most prominent was the emergence of a group of Jews who followed Jesus of Nazareth as the messiah sent by God to usher in the eschatological kingdom. Following Jesus's traumatic execution in Jerusalem as an enemy of the state for challenging the social, economic, and political status quo, his followers attempted to find theological meaning in his death as an atonement for human sin, to perpetuate his teachings throughout the eastern Mediterranean world, and to establish the kingdom he anticipated (which eventually included the welcoming of non-Jews into the community, understood by proponents as the fulfillment of Third Isaiah's vision for the restoration of Israel).[35] Over time the Jesus movement began diverging from its Jewish roots and became a predominantly gentile religion that provided the framework of belief and practice for modern Christianity.[36]



## LATTER-DAY SAINTS AND THE HISTORY OF THE SECOND TEMPLE PERIOD

This survey of the nearly six centuries spanning the Persian, Greek, and Roman rule of Judea has highlighted the historical, sociopolitical, and theological developments of the Second Temple period that were critical for the formation of both early Judaism and early Christianity. As noted previously, these developments had a significant impact on the world, texts, and interpretation of the Bible, and are essential for understanding religious belief and practice within the subsequent Jewish and Christian traditions. However, like many modern readers of the Bible, the Latter-day Saint community has traditionally had only minimal engagement with the history of this period and, despite having an inherent appreciation for Jewish thought, has commonly held overtly negative views regarding the nature of Second Temple Judaism.[37] At times these views

35. For examples of the latter, see Isaiah 56:1–8 (cf. Acts 8:26–40); Isaiah 60:1–18 (cf. Matthew 2:1–12); Isaiah 61:1–4 (cf. Luke 4:16–30); and Isaiah 65:17–25, 66:18–23 (cf. Revelation 21:1–5). Additional insights into the use of Isaiah's prophetic writings by the early Jesus movement can be found in Sean Freyne, *Jesus, A Jewish Galilean: A New Reading of the Jesus Story* (London: T&T Clark, 2004), 92–121.

36. For detailed discussions of this complex development, see the essays in James D.G. Dunn, ed., *Jews and Christians: The Parting of the Ways AD 70 to 135* (Grand Rapids, MI: Eerdmans, 1992) and Adam H. Becker and Annette Yoshiko Reed, eds., *The Ways that Never Parted: Jews and Christians in Late Antiquity and the Early Middle Ages* (Minneapolis, MN: Fortress Press, 2007).

37. Latter-day Saint interest in Judaism began in the 1830s as early leaders of the movement interacted with Jewish contemporaries and made passing references in church periodicals to ancient Jewish writings such as Josephus, apocryphal books, and kabbalistic texts; for examples of these interactions, see the various essays in Lincoln H. Blumell, Matthew J. Grey, and Andrew H. Hedges, eds., *Approaching Antiquity: Joseph Smith and the Ancient World* (Provo, UT: BYU Religious Studies Center, 2015). By the late nineteenth and

have even been reflected in claims by Latter-day Saint writers that the intertestamental period was one of the darkest periods of apostasy in human history.[38]

While it is likely rooted to some extent in New Testament polemics, this negative assessment seems to have derived less from Latter-day Saint doctrine and scripture and more from an uncritical reliance upon older Protestant scholarship with its unsympathetic approach to early Judaism. For instance, Protestant scholars of previous generations often implied that nothing of scriptural relevance or theological inspiration occurred in the centuries between the Old and New Testaments, a view possibly related to the exclusion of the Apocrypha from the Protestant canon. Latter-day Saint scripture, on the other hand, contains an openness to there being divine truth within apocryphal writings from this period (D&C 91:1–5), affirms a continuous legitimacy of Levitical priesthood lineage from Sinai to the end times (D&C 84:24; Joseph Smith–History 1:69), draws heavily on the apocalyptic worldview that began to emerge in the second century BCE (e.g., 1 Nephi 11–14; D&C 45, 133), and at times resembles the pseudepigraphical expansions of biblical texts common to the late Second Temple period (e.g., Moses 1, 6–7; Abraham 1–3). Therefore, it would seem that Latter-day Saint thought has an inherent potential to engage more meaningfully with intertestamental historical and religious developments than did the approach taken by earlier generations of Protestant writers.[39]

Nevertheless, Latter-day Saint writers have long based their historical information and perceptions of Judaism in the time of Jesus (i.e., the era of the Second Temple) on conservative Protestant scholarship, particularly as it was expressed in the mid- to late nineteenth century. Although many valuable and theologically compatible insights may have been gleaned from this historiographic foundation, this use of source material has also proved to be problematic in several ways, among which is the observation that the Protestant historians from this period who most heavily influenced subsequent generations of Latter-day Saints often showed an anti-Judaic bias in their treatments of ancient Jewish history. This is seen, for example, in the writings of Victorian

early twentieth centuries, some Latter-day Saint writers had developed a deeper interest in Jewish history as it related to the world of the New Testament but, as will be seen hereinafter, their efforts tended to adopt the negative attitudes toward early Judaism found in contemporary Protestant scholarship.

38. See, for example, Victor L. Ludlow, *Principles and Practices of the Restored Gospel* (Salt Lake City, UT: Deseret Book, 1992), 501–19.

39. For a fuller consideration of the complex relationship between Latter-day Saint thought and Second Temple Judaism discussed in this section, see Matthew J. Grey, "Latter-day Saint Perceptions of Jewish Apostasy in the Time of Jesus," in *Standing Apart: Mormon Historical Consciousness and the Concept of Apostasy,* edited by Miranda Wilcox and John D. Young (New York: Oxford University Press, 2014), 147–73.

scholars such as Frederic W. Farrar, J. Cunningham Geikie, and Alfred Edersheim who, in their biographies of Jesus, describe early Judaism as a monolithic entity (with derisive references to "the Jews"), as a corruption of the divinely revealed religion of ancient Israel (with its meaningless rituals replacing the inspired prophetic voice), and as a spiritually stagnant religious system. In short, these writers often used Second Temple Judaism as a foil to the charismatic teachings of Jesus who—in supposed contrast to his allegedly legalistic Jewish contemporaries—taught principles of ethics, love, faith, and grace.[40]



More recent scholarship has shown this traditional approach to be overly simplistic at best, and inaccurate or even harmful at worst. Instead, most scholars since the mid-twentieth century have recognized that Judaism in the intertestamental period was complex in its socioreligious diversity, prolific in its literary production, rich in its ongoing manifestations of spiritual gifts (such as visions, prophecy, and mystical experience), and innovative in its theological developments (such as the emergence of apocalyptic thought). As a result, most scholars now acknowledge that Second Temple Judaism did not stand in sharp contrast to the teachings of Jesus, but rather provided a formative context for Jesus's ministry, the growth of the Jesus movement, and the central theological views of Christianity.[41]

Yet, despite these important advances in scholarship, Latter-day Saint treatments of the Second Temple period throughout the twentieth century—including by such prominent ecclesiastical writers as James E. Talmage and Bruce R. McConkie, as well as the institutional and popular literature influenced by them—drew heavily on long outdated Protestant resources, which naturally (if inadvertently) perpetuated their problematic assumptions and approaches within the modern Latter-day Saint community.[42] In recent decades, though,

40. Frederic W. Farrar, *The Life of Christ* (1874); J. Cunningham Geikie, *The Life and Words of Christ* (1877); and Alfred Edersheim, *The Life and Times of Jesus the Messiah* (1883). For fuller context on these works and their negative views of ancient Judaism, see Daniel L. Pals, *The Victorian "Lives" of Jesus* (San Antonio, TX: Trinity University Press, 1982) and Grey, "Latter-day Saint Perceptions," 149–52.

41. For modern research that situates Jesus within the context of early Judaism, rather than pitting him against it as was common in earlier scholarship, see John P. Meier, *A Marginal Jew: Rethinking the Historical Jesus*, five vols. (New Haven, CT: Yale University Press, 1991–2016), and the essays and commentary in Amy-Jill Levine and Marc Zvi Brettler, eds., *The Jewish Annotated New Testament* (New York: Oxford University Press, 2011).

42. For example, James E. Talmage's *Jesus the Christ* (1915) and Bruce R. McConkie's *Messiah* series (1978–1982)—both of which came to define LDS readings of the New Testament in the twentieth century—almost exclusively derived their historical information on (and attitudes toward) early Judaism from the nineteenth century Protestant writings of Farrar, Geikie, and Edersheim mentioned in fn. 40; see Grey, "Latter-day Saint Perceptions," 152–54.

an increasing number of Latter-day Saint scholars have received formal academic training in biblical and cognate studies, such as the Dead Sea Scrolls, Jewish pseudepigraphical writings, the archaeology of Roman Palestine, the history of early Judaism, and Christian origins, and have begun to make valuable contributions in these fields of research. While this newer research has not yet been integrated into church educational programs or widely circulated among non-specialists, accessible summaries of the Second Temple period in popular literature increasingly contain greater historical precision, nuance, and awareness of current scholarship than the writings of previous generations, and therefore have the potential to continue refining Latter-day Saint understandings and perceptions of this critical era of biblical history.[43]

43. See, for example, the evolving writings of Latter-day Saint scholars pertaining to the Second Temple period in volumes such as David B. Galbraith, D. Kelly Ogden, and Andrew C. Skinner, *Jerusalem: The Eternal City* (Salt Lake City, UT: Deseret Book, 1996); S. Kent Brown and Richard Neitzel Holzapfel, *The Lost 500 Years: What Happened between the Old and New Testaments* (Salt Lake City, UT: Deseret Book, 2006); Richard Neitzel Holzapfel, Eric D. Huntsman, and Thomas A. Wayment, *Jesus Christ and the World of the New Testament* (Salt Lake City, UT: Deseret Book, 2006); Kent P. Jackson, ed., *A Bible Reader's History of the Ancient World* (Provo, UT: Jerusalem Center for Near Eastern Studies, BYU, 2016); and Lincoln H. Blumell, ed., *New Testament History, Culture, and Society: A Background to the Texts of the New Testament* (Provo, UT: Religious Studies Center, BYU, 2019).

PART II

# Conceptions of Canon and Not Canon

*The Bible(s) and Restoration Scripture*

7

# The Biblical Canon

DANIEL BECERRA

The study of the biblical canon may be understood broadly as an exploration into the origins, transmission, acceptance, and continuing viability of the collection of sacred books that comprise the Jewish and Christian bibles. The complex issues associated with these topics have demanded that scholars draw on work from numerous fields of inquiry including but not limited to biblical studies, theology, early church history, and rabbinics. Several broad and interrelated topics govern most canon scholarship on both the New Testament and Hebrew Bible. The most prominent of these include (1) defining and dating the canon, (2) influences on its formation and closure, and (3) the status of the canon today. These topics, therefore, will provide the basis for a brief introduction to scholarly discourse on the biblical canon as well as guide my treatment of Latter-day Saint engagement with this subject.

To orient the reader to the following discussion, it will be helpful at the outset to provide four general observations regarding Latter-day Saint attitudes toward the biblical canon and its development. First, while Latter-day Saints accept the Protestant canon of the Old and New Testaments as scripture, they do not consider the Bible to be perfect, complete, or sufficient for religious life.[1] Second, Latter-day Saint scholarly engagement with issues of canon is limited and pertains primarily to the New Testament. Accordingly, the bulk of the following discussion will center on this collection of scripture. Third, most literature on the canon produced by Latter-day Saints seems to be intended for

1. See "Bible" in the "Topics" section of the Church of Jesus Christ of Latter-day Saints' official website, accessed May 9, 2018 at https://www.lds.org/topics/bible?lang=eng. For Joseph Smith's attitudes toward the Bible, see Philip Barlow, *Mormons and the Bible: The Place of the Latter-day Saints in American Religion* (New York: Oxford University Press, 1991), 71–73.

a non-specialist Latter-day Saint audience. Authors therefore seldom engage in contemporary scholarly debates in great detail or publish in venues outside the auspices of the Church of Jesus Christ of Latter-day Saints. Finally, what typically distinguishes traditional Latter-day Saint approaches to the biblical canon is their reliance on the church's scriptural and prophetic traditions. I will therefore focus chiefly on how these interpretive tools inform Latter-day Saint attitudes toward the biblical canon and its development as well as on what is at stake in these discussions.

## DEFINING AND DATING THE CANON

Since the turn of the twentieth century considerable efforts have been made to clarify the notion of "canon" (from the Greek *kanon*, meaning "measuring rod") and its relationship to scripture. Traditionally, two positions regarding the proper sense of "canon" predominate in modern scholarship, one which highlights the exclusive sense of the word and the other, the inclusive. Employed in the *exclusive* sense, canon has been applied to a fixed standard or collection of scripture to which nothing can be added or removed. So defined, canon is largely coterminous with "list" and thus assumes a sharp semantic distinction from "scripture."[2] Scholars who conceptualize canon in this way tend to see evidence of its creation and closure predominantly in the form of canon lists, manuscript collections, and ecclesiastical councils. Accordingly, the finalization of the canon tends to be dated comparatively late, when the majority of such lists were created and councils were convened—circa the second to fifth centuries CE for the Hebrew Bible and the fourth to fifth centuries CE for the New Testament.

Many scholars reject exclusive characterizations of canon on the grounds that they fail to recognize a text's popularity and authority within a religious community before its formal acknowledgement as part of a larger "orthodox" scriptural corpus. Applied in a more *inclusive* sense, canon denotes a norm rather than a list and overlaps considerably with the concept of "scripture," in that all scriptural texts were normative before being collected together.[3]

2. For examples of positions which insist on a sharp distinction between canon and scripture see: John Barton, "Canonical Approaches Ancient and Modern, in *The Biblical Canons*, edited by Jean-Marie Auwers and H. J. de Jonge (BETL 163; Leuven, Belgium: Leuven University Press, 2003), 202; Albert Sundberg, *The Old Testament of the Early Church* (HTS 20; Cambridge, MA: Harvard University, 1964); Theodore Swanson, *The Closing of the Collection of Holy Scripture* (PhD diss., Vanderbilt University, 1970), 7.

3. For examples of positions which assume a substantial overlap between canon and scripture, see Richard Campbell Leonard, *The Origin of Canonicity in the Old Testament* (PhD diss., Boston University, 1972), 43; Gerald Sheppard, "Canon," in *Encyclopedia of Religion*, 2nd ed., fifteen vols., edited by Lindsay Jones (Detroit: Thomson Gale, 2005), 3:1405–11; Theodore Zahn, *Geschichte des neutestamentlichen Kanons,*

Canonization within this framework, thus, implies not the conferral of authority but the gradual recognition of an already authoritative standard. Canon understood as "norm," as opposed to "list," is arguably truer to how ancient Jews and Christians conceptualized the term. The earliest clear use of *canon* to refer to a literary corpus does not appear until the middle of the fourth century CE. Before this point, the term was understood more broadly to refer to the principles that govern belief and practice: a tradition of teaching or "rule of faith" based in but not limited to written documents.[4] Scholars who espouse the more inclusive view of canon characteristically posit the existence of an inchoate "core canon" and different degrees and stages of canonicity,[5] and thus place the canon's formation at an earlier date than those who adopt a more exclusive view—the first century CE for the Hebrew Bible and the second century CE for the New Testament.



Latter-day Saint scholars tend to favor a more inclusive definition of canon and share several assumptions with non-Latter-day Saint scholars in reaching this conclusion. With respect to the documents that would become the New Testament for example, these scholars cite their broad dissemination and high rate of incidence in the writings of early Christian authors, as well as explicit statements from antiquity regarding their value, as evidence for the existence of a core collection of authoritative writings by the early second century.[6] Latter-day Saint scholars also typically accept the existence of authoritative oral traditions and the customary second-century dating of a significant text known as the Muratorian fragment.[7] Not unlike other Protestants, some Latter-day

two vols. (Erlanger Deichert, 1888–1892); Theodore Zahn, *Grundriss der Geschichte des neutestamentlichen Kanons* (Leipzig, Germany: A Deichert: 1904).

4. Eugene Ulrich, "The Notion and Definition of Canon," in *The Canon Debate*, edited by Lee McDonald and James Sanders (Peabody: Hendrickson, 2002), 21–35.

5. Stephen B. Chapman, "Second Temple Jewish Hermeneutics: How Canon Is Not an Anachronism," in *Invention, Rewriting, Usurpation: Discursive Fights over Religious Traditions in Antiquity*, edited by Jörg Ulrich, Anders-Christian Jacobsen, David Brakke (Early Christianity in the Context of Antiquity, 11; Frankfurt am Main, Germany: Peter Lang, 2011), 281–96; Michael Holmes, "The Biblical Canon," in *The Oxford Handbook of Early Christian Studies*, edited by Susan Ashbrook Harvey and David G. Hunter (New York: Oxford University Press, 2008), 414–5; Bruce Metzger, *The Bible in Translation: Ancient and English Versions* (Grand Rapids, MI: Baker Academic, 2001); David Trobisch, *The First Edition of the New Testament* (New York: Oxford University Press, 2000).

6. Richard Draper, "The Earliest 'New Testament,'" in *How the New Testament Came to Be*, edited by Kent P. Jackson and Frank Judd, (Provo, UT: Religious Studies Center, BYU, and Deseret Book 2006), 260–91; Thomas Wayment, "The Historical Context of the New Testament," *Ensign* (January 2011): 50–61; Thomas Wayment, "The Story of the New Testament," in *The Life and Teachings of Jesus Christ: From Bethlehem to the Sermon on the Mount*, edited by Richard Neitzel Holzapfel and Thomas Wayment (Salt Lake City, UT: Deseret Book, 2005), 21–47

7. Alexander Morrison, "Plain and Precious Things: The Writing of the New Testament," in *How the New Testament Came to Be*, 1–26; Daniel C. Peterson and Stephen D. Ricks, "Comparing LDS Beliefs with

Saint scholars and church authorities likewise assume the self-evident value of many of the texts that would become the New Testament, viewing their authority as largely independent of the ecclesiastical traditions of the fourth and fifth centuries.[8]



Uniquely, however, Latter-day Saint scholars sometimes come to these conclusions based on claims made in the Book of Mormon. One frequently cited chapter is 1 Nephi 13—a prophet-historian said to live in the sixth century BCE named Nephi is shown a vision of the future in which a book proceeds "out of the mouth of a Jew" and is supplemented with "records of the twelve apostles of the lamb" (1 Ne 13:23, 41). The contents of these oral and literary traditions are ostensibly portrayed as converging sometime in the late first to early second century CE (1 Ne 13:21–26), which many believing Latter-day Saints interpret as evidence for a codified volume of Christian teachings that predates the councils and canon lists of later centuries. The Book of Mormon also lauds these writings for their inherent worth, describing them as "plain and pure, and most precious and easy to the understanding of all" and as containing the "fullness of the gospel of the Lord" and "covenants of the Lord" with the house of Israel (1 Ne 13:23–24).

On a similar basis, many Latter-day Saints depart from popular scholarly arguments regarding when the Hebrew Bible's components were first gathered into a collection. Whereas many scholars hypothesize that significant portions of the book were first assembled after the Babylonian captivity (ca. fifth century BCE),[9] the Book of Mormon suggests that at least one collection of Hebrew Scriptures existed as early as the late seventh century BCE.[10] In 1 Nephi, Nephi mentions a collection of brass plates in the possession of a wealthy man living in Jerusalem years prior to the Babylonian invasion. On these plates were engraved "five books of Moses … a record of the Jews from the beginning,

First-Century Christianity," *Ensign* (March 1988): 7–11; Thomas Wayment, "False Gospels: An Approach to Studying the New Testament Apocrypha," in *How the New Testament Came to Be*, 292–303; Thomas Wayment, "First-Century Sources on the Life of Jesus," in *How the New Testament Came to Be*, 109–122.

8. The inspired, plain, and precious content of the text itself, for example, is sometimes cited as a locus of its value and authority. See Morrison, "Plain and Precious Things," 18–24; and M. Russell Ballard, "The Miracle of the Holy Bible," *Ensign* (May 2007), 80–82.

9. The canonical acceptance of the Torah is traditionally dated ca. 400 BCE and of the Prophets, to ca. 200 BCE. This consensus view was championed in H. E. Ryle, *The Canon of the Old Testament* (New York: Macmillan, 1892). It has been recently challenged on the grounds that the various literary elements within Israel's scriptures were not always strictly demarcated in tripartite terms but were fluid, interrelated, and developed mutually. See Stephen Chapman, "The Canon Debate," *Journal of Theological Interpretation* 4, no. 2 (2010): 273–94.

10. See Richard Holzapfel, Dana Pike, and David Seely, eds., *Jehovah and the World of the Old Testament* (Salt Lake City, UT: Deseret Book, 2009), 378; Lenet H. Read, "How the Bible Came to Be: Part 1, A Testament Is Established," *Ensign* (January 1982).

even down to the commencement of the reign of Zedekiah, king of Judah; And also the prophecies of the holy prophets [Isaiah and Jeremiah are named specifically], from the beginning ... down to the commencement of the reign of Zedekiah" (1 Ne 5:11–12). Nephi also records that the plates contained a genealogy of his ancestors—he being from the tribe of Manasseh—as well as some writings of additional prophets named Zenos, Zenock, and Neum (1 Ne 19:10; Alma 33:3–17). In addition to its mention of a pre-exilic collection of Jewish scripture, this passage has also been levied in the past by some conservative Latter-day Saint scholars as evidence for Mosaic authorship of the Pentateuch,[11] a claim that is generally nuanced or rejected in both mainstream Latter-day Saint and non-Latter-day Saint scholarly circles.[12]



Very few Latter-day Saint works of scholarship deal directly with the closure of the Jewish canon. However, several Latter-day Saint authors as well as some official pedagogical materials of the church assert that the Jewish canon was officially closed at the council of Jamnia ca. 90 CE or earlier.[13] This view has been challenged by scholars who contend, among other things, that Rabbis continued to discuss the status of books like Ecclesiastes, Song of Songs, Esther, Ruth, and Ben Sira after the first century, suggesting that the Hebrew Bible did not likely reach its final form until sometime between the second and fifth centuries CE.[14]

## INFLUENCES ON THE FORMATION AND CLOSURE OF THE CANON

Scholarship regarding what factors influenced the formation and closure of the canon has historically assumed a distinction between internal and external influences.[15] Internal influences refer to those dynamics present within the

11. Sidney Sperry, "Some Problems of Interest Relating to the Brass Plates," *Journal of Book of Mormon Studies* 4, no. 1 (1995), 185–87. See also Moses 1:40–2:1, which implies Mosaic authorship of Genesis.

12. David Bokovoy, *Authoring the Old Testament: Genesis—Deuteronomy* (Draper, UT: Greg Kofford Books, 2014); Holzapfel, Pike, and Seely, eds., *Jehovah and the World*, 144–45. For a brief history of non-LDS views on the authorship of the Pentateuch, see Cory Crawford, "Pentateuch," in this volume. See also "Pentateuch" in LDS Bible Dictionary (accessed online).

13. See "Canon" in LDS Bible Dictionary (accessed online); Robert J. Matthews, "Whose Apocrypha? Viewing Ancient Apocrypha from the Vantage of Events in the Present Dispensation," in *Apocryphal Writings and the Latter-day Saints*, edited by C. Wilfred Griggs (Provo, UT: Religious Studies Center, BYU, 1986), 1–18; Holzapfel, Pike, and Seely, eds., *Jehovah and the World*, 378.

14. Lee McDonald, *Forgotten Scriptures: The Selection and Rejection of Early Religious Writings* (Louisville, KY: Westminster/John Knox, 2009), especially 65–84, 137.

15. Michael Kruger refers to "intrinsic" and "extrinsic" models of canon-formation: *The Question of Canon: Challenging the Status Quo in the New Testament Debate* (Downer's Grove, IL: IVP Academic Press,

boundaries of a religious group. These include the frequency and manner of citation of different texts; the terminology used to refer to them (e.g., "Law," "Prophets," "Gospels," etc.); their authorship, transmission, and circulation; the creation of canon lists and book collections; liturgical formulae, ritual instructions, and confessional statements; statements made by individual authors and ecclesial authorities (in councils or otherwise) regarding the status of various writings; and discourses relating to scripture, hermeneutics, and orthodoxy. External influences, on the other hand, refer to those factors arguably located outside of the boundaries of a religious group. These include evolving technologies of literary production, such as the transition from the use of papyrus and parchment scrolls to codices; the dynamics of political governance; persecution (which sometimes involved the confiscation and destruction of sacred books) and other social conflicts; heterodox movements and figures; and supernatural intervention.

Latter-day Saints tend to see the creation of a scriptural canon as a semi-organic development, both true to the spirit of the Jewish and Christian traditions,[16] while at the same time a necessary response to theological, technological, social, and political pressures. The aforementioned influences, therefore, are understood collectively to motivate, facilitate, and hasten the canon's delimitation and recognition. There is however, a discernable emphasis in Latter-day Saint scholarship on the role of heretical movements and figures during the formative years of the canon's development.[17] While it is certainly not uncommon in modern scholarship to highlight these polemics and controversies, at least two unique reasons may account for this focus in Latter-day Saint literature. On one hand, much of Latter-day Saint scholarship and official church publications are informed by the traditional Latter-day Saint narrative of the "Great Apostasy."[18] According to this narrative, the authority, revelatory inspiration, and doctrinal purity of the early Christian church were lost following the deaths of Jesus and

---

2013). See also Everett Ferguson, "Factors Leading to the Selection and Closure of the New Testament Canon: A Survey of Some Recent Studies," in *Canon Debate*, 295–320. Some scholars, however, have challenged the utility of this dichotomy on the grounds that the boundaries of both Christianity and Judaism were still being negotiated—and thus there was no clear internal/external demarcation—during the formative years of the biblical canon. See David Brakke, "Scriptural Practices in Early Christianity: Towards a New History of the New Testament Canon," in *Invention, Rewriting, Usurpation*, 263–80.

16. The "Canon" entry in the LDS Bible Dictionary (accessed online) asserts that a pattern of record keeping was established by Adam and continued by succeeding patriarchs and leaders.

17. See Draper, "The Earliest 'New Testament'"; Morrison, "Plain and Precious Things"; Wayment, "Story of the New Testament," 21–47.

18. For a treatment of this narrative see Miranda Wilcox and John Young, eds., *Standing Apart: Mormon Historical Consciousness and the Concept of Apostasy* (New York: Oxford University Press, 2014).

the apostles. One reason for this gradual decline is understood to be the introduction of heretical teachings and practices into the church, evinced especially by the heterodox movements of Marcion, so-called Gnostics, and Montanus.[19] A further consequence of the Great Apostasy was that the church became liable to make erroneous judgments regarding the scope of its scriptures. Thus, some texts of value were not included in the canon while some of lesser value were.[20]

Another likely reason for the Latter-day Saint focus on the early church's polemical encounters is the Book of Mormon's presentation of the early transmission—or more accurately, corruption—of the biblical texts. In the same chapter discussed above, Nephi records that beginning sometime in the late first century CE, "many parts which are plain and most precious; and also many covenants of the Lord" were removed from the texts that would become part of the scriptural canon (1 Ne 13:36).[21] Joseph Smith similarly taught that "many important points, touching the salvation of man, had been taken from the Bible or lost before it was compiled."[22] Nephi identifies the culprit as a "great and abominable church," whose founder is the devil and whose formation is concurrent with the spread of Christianity to the gentiles (1 Ne 13:4–6, 20–29). Modern Latter-day Saint authorities have interpreted the "great and abominable church" to refer to any individual, organization, or ideology that leads one away from God, truth, and salvation, including but not limited to heretical figures and movements in the early church (1 Ne 13:4–6, 20–29).[23] While Joseph Smith understood the corruption of the biblical texts to have occurred with some degree of malignity,[24] he also placed responsibility on "ignorant translators [and] careless transcribers," whose motives were likely not malicious.[25]

19. Consistent with some Protestant historiographical currents, Latter-day Saints have customarily assumed firm boundaries between orthodoxy and heterodoxy in the early church. See Matthew Bowman, "James Talmage, B.H. Roberts, and Confessional History in a Secular Age," in *Standing Apart*, 77–92; Eric Dursteler, "Historical Periodization in the LDS Great Apostasy Narrative" in *Standing Apart*, 22–54. This assumption has been challenged by Taylor Petrey in "Purity and Parallels: Constructing the Apostasy Narrative of Early Christianity," in *Standing Apart*, 174–82.

20. "Canon," LDS Bible Dictionary (accessed online).

21. Kent P. Jackson, "Asking Restoration Questions in New Testament Scholarship," in *How the New Testament Came to Be*, 27–42.

22. Joseph Fielding Smith, comp., *Teachings of the Prophet Joseph Smith* (Salt Lake City, UT: Deseret Book, 1976), 9–10.

23. Bruce R. McConkie, *Mormon Doctrine* (Salt Lake City, UT: Deseret Book, 1966), 137–8; Stephen E. Robinson, "Warring against the Saints of God," *Ensign* (January 1988): 38.

24. Joseph Fielding Smith, *Teachings of the Prophet Joseph Smith*, 327.

25. Numerous Latter-day Saint scholars, following Bart Ehrman, ascribe these changes to both "orthodox" and "heretical" scribes. See Morrison, "Plain and Precious Things," 13; Wayment, "Story of the New Testament," 31–40. See also Bart D. Ehrman, *The Orthodox Corruption of Scripture: The Effect of Early Christological Controversies on the Text of the New Testament, 2nd ed.*(New York: Oxford University Press, 2011).

At stake in traditional Latter-day Saint portraits of the canon's formation, are two related theological claims. The first relates to the legitimacy of the church as the "only true and living church" of Jesus Christ on the earth (D&C 1:30). Many Latter-day Saints believe that the Great Apostasy lasted until God appeared to Joseph Smith in 1820 and through him, initiated the restoration of the church to its pristine, pre-apostasy state. Depicting the canon's formation as response to heterodox pollutions both legitimizes this apostasy narrative and suggests the need for a restoration. The second claim relates to the validity of the Book of Mormon and other Latter-day Saint canonical works. The Book of Mormon asserts that following the corruption of the biblical texts, additional texts would come forth at a future time, as Nephi says, to "make known the plain and precious things which have been taken away" (1 Ne 13:40). Latter-day Saints often understand this passage as a prophecy foreshadowing and substantiating the expanded scriptural canon of the church, which includes the Bible as well as three additional books of scripture: the Book of Mormon, Doctrine and Covenants, and the Pearl of Great Price.[26] These four books are collectively referred to as "the standard works [i.e., of scripture]."

## THE CANON TODAY

No single biblical canon is currently accepted by all Christian denominations. The Syrian Orthodox and Chaldean Syrian churches for example, reject 2 Peter, 2–3 John, Jude, and Revelation. The canon of the Roman Catholic Church contains books sometimes called "Apocryphal" or "Deuterocanonical," while Ethiopian Christians include the Shepherd of Hermas, two letters of Clement, and a collection of church law called the *Apostolic Constitutions*. All these biblical canons, however, while distinct, are also essentially closed.[27]

In the last fifty years, some scholars, such as Bruce Metzger and Lee McDonald, have raised questions regarding the continuing viability of the biblical canon as a fixed collection.[28] This may be attributed in part to the recent discovery and recovery of ancient documents like the Dead Sea Scrolls, Nag

26. For more on early American debates, including among Latter-day Saints, on the authority of the biblical canon, see David Holland, *Sacred Borders: Continuing Revelation and Canonical Restraint* (Religion in America; New York: Oxford University Press, 2011).

27. For Jonathan Z. Smith's view of supposedly closed canons, see, *Imagining Religion: From Babylon to Jonestown* (Chicago: University of Chicago, 1982), 36–52; "Canons, Catalogues, and Classics" in *Canonization and Decanonization*, edited by A. van der Kooij and K. van der Toorn (Leiden, Netherlands: Brill, 1998), 295–312.

28. McDonald, *Formation of the Christian Biblical Canon*, 254–57; Bruce Metzger, *The Canon of the New Testament: Its Origin, Development, and Significance* (New York: Oxford University Press, 1997), 267–75.

Hammadi library, and many New Testament papyri, as well as a renewed interest in apocryphal and pseudepigraphic writings. Other reasons may include (1) the notion of a closed canon does not seem to cohere with how many ancient Jews and Christians understood their scripture, (2) there exists no scriptural evidence for adjudicating the precise limits of the canon, (3) numerous non-canonical documents are perhaps "as reliable" as canonical ones in their portrayal of the teaching and preaching of early Jews and Christians, (4) questions regarding the appropriateness of committing the modern church to a canon that emerged out of ancient historical circumstances, and (5) the belief held by some that God continually speaks to the church through the Holy Spirit on issues of contemporary significance.[29]



Consequently, some scholarly discourse explores what might be excluded from or added to the current canon, as well as which books might take precedence within it. Such discussions, however, certainly do not constitute a majority of canon scholarship. Some scholars motivated by pastoral concerns have advocated for the removal of books understood to hinder Christian unity and compound anxieties over diversity in the Bible, such as 2 Peter and Revelation.[30] Others have proposed expanding the canon to include apocryphal and pseudepigraphic writings, including the Gospel of Thomas, the Gospel of Mary, the "Unknown Gospel" of the Egerton Papyri, and other such documents.[31] Still others argue that the canon might profitably be expanded to include the "best of critical scholarship" in addition to ancient texts.[32] In terms of hierarchical discourse, one argument is that the earliest extant, as opposed to the most commonly used form of a biblical text, should be more authoritative for the church.[33] The earliest available forms of Mark and John, for instance, contain significant differences from their traditional canonized forms. Additionally,

29. McDonald, *Formation of the Christian Biblical Canon*, 254–57; Metzger, *The Canon of the New Testament*, 267–75.

30. Kurt Aland, *The Problem of the New Testament Canon* (London: Mowbray, 1962), 28–33; Ernst Kasemann, "The Canon of the New Testament Church and the Unity of the Church," in *Essays on New Testament Themes* (London: SCM, 1968), 95–107. Some reasons cited, often by Protestant scholars, for removing such texts include: their theological inconsistency, apocalyptic content, and disputed authorship.

31. Jeffrey L. Sheler, "Cutting Loose the Holy Canon: A Controversial Re-examination of the Bible," *U.S. News & World Report* 15, no. 18 (November 8, 1993): 75; Kim Sue Lia Perkes, "Scripture Revision Won't Be a Bible," *Arizona Republic*, October 24, 1993, B1 and B4. See also Jacob Milgrom, "An Amputated Bible, Peradventure?" *Bible Review* 10, no. 4 (August 1994): 17.

32. Robert Funk, "The Once Future New Testament," in *Canon Debate*, 557.

33. See the following chapters in *Canon Debate*: Eldon Epp, "Issues in the Interrelation of New Testament Textual Criticism and Canon," 485–515; James Sanders, "The Issue of Closure in the Canonical Process," 252–66; Emanuel Tov, "The Status of the Masoretic Text in Modern Text Editions of the Hebrew Bible: The Relevance of Canon," 234–51.

it has been noted that, whether consciously or unconsciously, many religious persons gravitate to certain portions of scripture and largely ignore the rest, creating what is functionally a "canon within a canon."[34] The significance of discourses relating to the canon's fixity is that the scope of the biblical canon holds important hermeneutical consequences for the documents within it: new meanings emerge from texts by their placement in new canonical contexts and hierarchies.[35]

For different reasons, Latter-day Saints reject the notion of a fixed canon and thus do not regard the Bible as perfect, complete, or sufficient. Two reasons may account for this: (1) the aforementioned corruption of the Bible's component parts in the course of their transmission and (2) the belief that God currently does and "will yet reveal many great and important things pertaining to the kingdom of God" to the church (Article of Faith 9). Accordingly, Latter-day Saints accept three additional books of canonical scripture and expect more to come forth at a future point.[36] They also rely on two additional sources of revelation (personal inspiration and prophetic leadership) as normative. Because these foundations of authority mutually inform one another, the Latter-day Saint canon cannot be properly limited to a literary collection. Rather, as one scholar wrote, it must encompass

> the entire portrait of the faith, with all its historical, personal, and institutional brushstrokes . . . every glint of revelation reflecting off the pages of church magazines, every breath of inspired counsel whispered by a mother at the bedside of her child, every glimpse of heaven—however fleeting—received in an act of prayerful yearning.[37]

34. James Dunn, "Has the Canon a Continuing Function," in *Canon Debate*, 560.

35. Interest in the relevance of the canon's scope for modern theological exegesis catalyzed in the early 1970s, when James Sanders and Brevard Childs introduced "canonical criticism" to the study of the biblical canon. Canonical criticism respects the Bible's traditional role as a vehicle for religious faith and worship. It assumes the final canonical form of the Bible to be the foundation for exegesis and highlights the complementary relationship of canonical documents. Such an approach, therefore, tends to subordinate historical and sociological analysis to the theologically normative meaning of the text. See James Sanders, *Torah and Canon* (Eugene, OR: Cascade Books, 1972) and Brevard Childs, *Biblical Theology in Crisis* (Philadelphia: Westminster Press, 1972).

36. The most recent additions to the "standard works" were D&C 137 and 138, which were made in 1976. The Book of Mormon makes several prophecies regarding the coming forth of future books of scripture. See 1 Nephi 14:20–26; 29:1–14; Ether 4:4––5.

37. David Holland, "Revelation and the Open Canon in Mormonism," in *The Oxford Handbook of Mormonism*, ed. Philip L. Barlow and Terryl Givens (New York: Oxford University Press, 2015), 161.

With respect to the hierarchy of these sources of revelation, a statement attributed to Joseph Smith arguably establishes the supremacy of the Book of Mormon over other canonical literature: "I told the brethren that the Book of Mormon was the most correct of any book on earth, and the keystone of our religion, and a man would get nearer to God by abiding by its precepts, than by any other book" (Introduction to the Book of Mormon). Rather than supplanting the Bible, however, the Book of Mormon frames itself as a tool for establishing the Bible's truth, in order that these two records might be "established in one; for there is one God and one Shepherd over all the earth" (1 Ne. 13:40–41).[38] Following the Book of Mormon in importance are the other modern books of Latter-day Saint scripture: the Doctrine and Covenants and the Pearl of Great Price. The preeminence of these texts notwithstanding, Latter-day Saint discourse persists in seeing prophetic authority—especially of living persons—as superseding scriptural authority.[39] Modern prophets, therefore, add a significant layer of canonical validation absent in other traditions, in that prophets may adjudicate the relative authority of different sources of revelation from God. For this reason, some Latter-day Saints may judge the relative value of different scriptural texts based on how well those texts conform to contemporary prophetic teachings.[40]

Belief in an open canon and continuing revelation has naturally stimulated discourse regarding what additional texts and teachings might inform Latter-day Saint religious life. Brigham Young, for example, taught that such a life "embraces all truth, wherever found, in all the works of God and man."[41] True to the spirit of this statement, Latter-day Saints are encouraged to "seek out of the best books words of wisdom ... even by study and also by faith" and heavy importance is placed on cultivating the capacity to discern truth, wherever its source, with the aid of the Holy Spirit (D&C 88:118). For example, commenting on the utility of the Apocrypha, Joseph Smith taught in 1833: "There are many things contained therein that are true ... And whoso is enlightened by the

38. For one Latter-day Saint authority's view of other highly regarded biblical books, see *Teaching Seminary Preservice Readings Religion 370, 471, and 475* (2004), 123–32

39. Terryl Givens, *Feeding the Flock: The Foundations of Mormon Thought— Church and Praxis* (New York: Oxford University Press, 2015), 278; Wilford Woodruff, *Sixty-Eighth Semi-Annual Conference of the Church of Jesus Christ of Latter-day Saints*, 22; Dallin Oaks, "Scripture Reading, Revelation, and Joseph Smith's Translation of the Bible," in *Plain and Precious Truths Restored: The Doctrinal and Historical Significance of the Joseph Smith Translation*, edited by Robert L. Millet and Robert J. Matthews (Salt Lake City, UT: Bookcraft, 1995), 2.

40. I am grateful to my colleague Luke Drake for this insight.

41. Brigham Young, *Journal of Discourses* 10:50.

Spirit shall obtain benefit therefrom; And whoso receiveth not by the Spirit, cannot be benefited" (D&C 91:1–6).

No official statement made by a Latter-day Saint authority or scholar, to my knowledge, explicitly advocates the removal of books from the biblical canon. A marginal note in Joseph Smith's revision of the Bible—although it is unclear if Smith wrote it—states, however, "[T]he Songs of Solomon are not inspired writings [*sic*]."[42] Latter-day Saints have made similarly detractive statements about books whose utility for Christian life seems questionable (e.g., Leviticus).[43] Such rhetoric, in addition to these books' relative absence from official church curriculum, have essentially relegated some texts to an unofficial, sub-canonical status. One possible reason for the reluctance in the Latter-day Saint tradition to exscind books entirely from the canon may be the expectation that new hermeneutical contexts, resulting from ongoing revelation and the ever-changing circumstance of life, will illuminate a significance in these texts, which has hitherto remained occluded.



42. Faulring, Jackson, and Matthews, *Joseph Smith's New Translation of the Bible*, 785. For a discussion of the Song of Songs in the Latter-day Saint tradition, see Dana M. Pike, "Reading the Song of Solomon as a Latter-day Saint," *Religious Educator* 15, no. 2 (2014): 91–113. See also Grant Underwood, "Joseph Smith's 'New Translation' of the Bible," in this volume.

43. *Teaching Seminary 370, 471, and 475* (2004), 123–32.

# 8

# The Apocrypha and Pseudepigrapha

JARED W. LUDLOW

The Apocrypha and Pseudepigrapha are two collections of ancient religious texts mostly associated with Hebrew Bible figures and settings even though they come from later periods, primarily the Second Temple period (ca. 400 BCE–200 CE). While none of these texts are included in the canon of the Church of Jesus Christ of Latter-day Saints, they have had some influence on members of the church. Latter-day Saints have been particularly interested in possible parallels with their own additional canonical accounts of figures such as Enoch, Melchizedek, Moses, and Abraham found in the Pearl of Great Price. This chapter will review what the Apocrypha and Pseudepigrapha are, Latter-day Saint interpretation of them, and the benefit these texts provide to the study of the ancient world.

## CONTENT OF THE APOCRYPHA

The Apocrypha has long been recognized as a collection of texts, although their canonical status varies among denominations. The term itself, Greek for things hidden or covered, can be seen positively—texts hidden from the general public because of their sacred character—or negatively—texts that should be buried and hidden away because they are dangerous. The Apocrypha (capital *A* as opposed to the more general term *apocryphal writings* of which there are many Jewish and Christian examples) as a title for these texts is more common among Protestants who exclude these texts from their scriptural canon and do not grant them authority to determine doctrine or practice. For Roman Catholics and Orthodox Christians, these texts are scripture, and rather than place them at the end of their Old Testament as a separate collection such as the Protestants usually do, they usually intersperse them among the other Old Testament books. They often refer to these texts as "deuterocanonical," not because of a secondary status, but because they entered the canon later such as finally ratified by the Roman Catholics in the Council of Trent in the sixteenth century.



The origins of the texts in the Apocrypha vary, but they were originally written by Jewish authors, later preserved by early Christians and then eventually excluded from the Jewish canon. All except one of them were included among the Septuagint manuscripts, the Greek translation of the Hebrew Bible. But Hebrew-speaking Jews did not accept them into their canon because they were written in Greek and not Hebrew, and in later rabbinic claims, they came after the time of prophecy had ended with Malachi.[1]

The texts of the Apocrypha fit into three categories: Biblical Expansions, Heroic Stories, and Wisdom Literature. The Biblical Expansions include additional stories about Daniel (Susanna, Bel and the Dragon, and the Song of the Three Young Men) and a different version of Esther recounting her challenges with living in her Gentile environment. 1 and 2 Esdras are related to Ezra as either a different version of Ezra and Nehemiah or presenting new revelations he experienced. The Prayer of Manasseh is the repentant petition of King Manasseh, one of the most wicked kings according to 2 Kings 20–24. Baruch and the Letter of Jeremiah are both set in the time of Jeremiah and the Babylonian Exile warning the Jews against succumbing to their polytheistic environment.

The Heroic Stories include historical texts like 1 Maccabees (and its adaption in 2 Maccabees), which recounts the Maccabean Revolt against the Greek Seleucid overlords. The other two exemplars from this category are more like historical fiction or didactic tales. The book of Tobit is placed in the Assyrian exile recounting a family's efforts to remain faithful to the law there, while the book of Judith recounts the defeat of an Assyrian army by a shrewd, beautiful woman.

Two examples of Wisdom Literature are included in the Apocrypha. The Wisdom of Solomon purports to relate more wisdom sayings from Solomon. Ecclesiasticus or the Wisdom of Jesus ben Sirach is a collection of sayings from

1. The single text that was found in old Latin manuscripts and not the Septuagint is variously named 2 Esdras, 4 Esdras, or the Latin Apocalypse. Some rabbinic texts discuss the view that prophecy had ceased in Israel (e.g., *t. Soṭah* 13.2: "When the last of the prophets [i.e., Haggai, Zechariah, and Malachi] died, the holy spirit ceased in Israel. Despite this they were informed by means of oracles (*bat qôl*)." See also *Seder Olam Rabbah 30*. From *The Eerdmans Dictionary of Early Judaism*, ed. John J. Collins and Daniel C. Harlow (Grand Rapids, MI: William B. Eerdmans Publishing Company, 2010), 1101.

a scribal school in Jerusalem that preserves wisdom sayings and perspectives from around 100 BCE.

## THE APOCRYPHA IN THE LATTER-DAY SAINT COMMUNITY



Joseph Smith approached the Apocrypha in a variety of ways. As he was completing his inspired version of the Bible (usually known as the Joseph Smith Translation, or "New Translation"), he asked the Lord if he should translate the Apocrypha, which his copy of the Bible contained, as part of that project. The response is recorded in Doctrine and Covenants 91, where the Lord states that there are things in the Apocrypha that are true and it is mostly translated correctly, but there are also untrue things in it that are interpolations by men.[2] Smith is further told it is not needful that he include the Apocrypha in his New Translation, but that one can receive benefit from reading it when enlightened by the Spirit. This revelation confirmed the non-canonical status of the Apocrypha in Latter-day Saint tradition even though that was not the primary focus of Smith's inquiry. Yet despite its non-canonical status, Smith felt that the Apocrypha should be included physically with the Bible, such as when he placed a Bible with an Apocrypha section from another Bible within the cornerstone of the Nauvoo Temple.[3]

There are no recorded instances of Joseph Smith preaching from the Apocrypha, but he likely approved some quotations from the Apocrypha found in early church periodicals, such as *The Evening and the Morning Star* and *Times and Seasons.* In one article connecting Esdras with Ezra of the Old Testament and outlining several prophecies of the last days, the author says of the book of Esdras: "We advise all to read it, and then judge its merits."[4] For many, the Apocrypha's prophecies were seen as fulfilled by the restoration of the Church of Jesus Christ of Latter-day Saints, especially through Smith's bringing forth of additional scripture.[5]

2. Bruce R. McConkie was of the opinion that the interpolations came in the later transmission of these texts, but that they were originally written in purer, truthful form. "From the answer [Doctrine and Covenants 91] it is clear that the books of the Apocrypha were inspired writings in the first instance, but that subsequent interpolations and changes had perverted and twisted their original contexts so as to leave them with doubtful value." See *Mormon Doctrine,* 2nd ed. (Salt Lake City, UT: Bookcraft, 1966), 41–42.

3. As related in "Recollections of the Prophet Joseph Smith," *Juvenile Instructor*, (March 15, 1892): 174.

4. "The Beauty of the Writings of the Prophet Esdras," *Times and Seasons* 2, no. 17 (July 1, 1841): 466.

5. For example, "Hosea Chapter III," *The Evening and the Morning Star* 1, no. 2 (July 1832): 14.

Since the time of Joseph Smith, some discussion of the Apocrypha has showed up in a few Latter-day Saint sermons or writings. These cases turn to the Apocrypha mostly to provide historical context to the period preceding the New Testament, for the concept of the restoration of lost scriptures, and for wisdom sayings.[6] They often introduce these quotations with some discussion on their disputed canonical status. These citations demonstrate some familiarity with the content of the Apocrypha, but do not grant it authoritative status.

More recent Latter-day Saint interest in these texts is part of a larger scholarly turn to ancient materials to shed light on historical Judaism and early Christianity. In 1983, BYU held a symposium on non-canonical writings.[7] The collection of essays from this symposium only cursorily discussed the Apocrypha, with one exception being an essay on the book of Susanna. Other papers looked at the broader category of apocryphal writings including the Dead Sea Scrolls, Nag Hammadi manuscripts, and other early Christian apocryphal texts.[8] At the conference, Stephen Robinson warned Latter-day Saints against accepting ancient documents at face value without considering their possible spurious origin, and against citing proof-texted passages for doctrinal support from these texts without properly acknowledging their context that could include doctrines and practices far different from Latter-day Saint theology.[9] More recently, a general overview of the books of the Apocrypha

6. For example, "Some of these books illustrate the progress of knowledge among the Jews, their religious character, and their government during the time between the Prophet Malachi and John the Baptist. In some of them, we see the fulfilment of prophecy, and in most of them there are found exalted sentiments and principles." From Hyrum M. Smith and Janne M. Sjodahl, *The Doctrine and Covenants Commentary*, rev. ed. (Salt Lake City, UT: Deseret Book, 1957), 585.

7. See C. Wilfred Griggs, ed., *Apocryphal Writings and the Latter-day Saints* (Provo, UT: Religious Studies Center, BYU, 1986).

8. In this volume, Gary Gillum makes the claim that Latter-day Saint scholar Hugh Nibley "has probably quoted from apocryphal writings more than anyone else in the world. Nibley's apocryphal, classical, and patristic sources include 105 different apocryphal and pseudepigraphical books, from the Acts of John to the Wisdom of Solomon." "Apocryphal Literature—Those 'Hidden' Books in the Stacks: A Selected Bibliography," *Apocryphal Writings and the Latter-day Saints*, 127.

9. "Lying for God: The Uses of Apocrypha," *Apocryphal Writings and the Latter-day Saints*, 133–54. Robinson sees these ancient writers as taking not only the *name* of earlier figures, but their whole *persona*. In this way, it is a deception usually to draw on the authority of the earlier figure for the presentation of teachings by the later writer.

> The degree to which the apocryphal literature proves that the Latter-day Saints are right or supports our beliefs has been greatly exaggerated in the unofficial literature of the church, and I believe that those who make these exaggerated claims either do so in ignorance or else perpetrate a 'pious fraud.' Some of the tapes and other material that circulate in the church on the subject are very misleading. The apocrypha *do* often prove that ideas peculiar to the Latter-day Saints in modern times were widely known and widely believed anciently, but this is not the same as proving that the ideas themselves are true, or that those who believed them were right in doing so, or that they would have had anything else in common with the Latter-day Saints" (148).

from a Latter-day Saint perspective came out in 2018.[10] This volume reviews early Latter-day Saint interaction with the Apocrypha, discusses each book in its own literary and historical context, and suggests points of connection Latter-day Saints may have with each book.



## PSEUDEPIGRAPHA

The Pseudepigrapha is a modern collection of dozens of texts that primarily give additional stories about Old Testament figures. The Greek term *Pseudepigrapha* literally means "falsely ascribed" and refers to the fact that these stories were most likely written by later authors using the name of earlier figures—not so much in an effort to create a hoax or as literary forgery, but to put forth teachings and effect religious changes under the authority of the earlier, more well-known figure. There is some possibility that certain stories may contain actual oral or written accounts of biblical figures passed down until found in these later texts without ever having become part of the canonical Old Testament. Another possible avenue for the production of these texts came from later readers of the Hebrew Bible who saw gaps in the text or felt uncomfortable with something in a story so they would create additional stories or alter existing stories about Old Testament figures.

Like the texts in the Apocrypha, the Pseudepigrapha texts likely originated among Jewish communities from the Second Temple period.[11] This is the time period of great copying and translating of the Hebrew Bible, which produced the Septuagint, Targums (Aramaic translations of the Hebrew Bible), and the Dead Sea Scrolls. The Pseudepigrapha texts were eventually deemed non-canonical; yet their non-canonical status was not always shared by ancient readers. Some of these texts were read and copied by many ancient Jewish and Christian readers who probably accepted them as either part of their authoritative canon or at least as having some teachings worthy of their attention.

10. Jared W. Ludlow, *Exploring the Apocrypha from a Latter-day Saint Perspective* (Springville, UT: CFI, 2018).

11. Since many of these texts are found in manuscripts of Christian production, there is scholarly debate about how many of them go back to Jewish roots or whether they originated with Christians. (See, for example, Robert A. Kraft, "The Pseudepigrapha and Christianity Revisited: Setting the Stage and Framing Some Central Questions," *Journal for the Study of Judaism* 32 [2001]: 371–95.) With the exception of some overtly Christian texts, it is this author's view that most Pseudepigrapha texts originated among Jewish communities and then subsequently were transmitted among Christians whereby Christian interpolations were introduced.

Some of these texts became influential on early Christian writings and some were even quoted or alluded to in the New Testament.[12]

The term Pseudepigrapha can be found in ancient sources talking about the spurious authorship of certain texts,[13] yet the actual grouping of these texts into a collection, particularly related to the Old Testament, is a modern phenomenon beginning in the 1700s, and in fact, today even more texts have been added to this corpus.[14] The earliest of such collections that used the term *Pseudepigrapha* as scholars do today was done entirely in Latin by Johann Albert Fabricius in 1713 (vol. 1) and 1723 (vol. 2).[15] His volumes were forerunners for later collections such as the English volume by W.J. Deane: *Pseudepigrapha: An Account of Certain Apocryphal Sacred Writings of the Jews and Early Christians* (Edinburgh, UK, 1891); E. Kautzsch's collection of German translations (*Die Apocryphen und Pseudepigraphen des Alten Testaments*, two vols., Tübingen, Germany: Mohr, 1900); R.H. Charles's influential collection of English translations (*The Apocrypha and Pseudepigrapha of the Old Testament*, two vols., Oxford, UK: Clarendon, 1913); and the standard collection used today: J.H. Charlesworth, *The Old Testament Pseudepigrapha*, two vols. (Garden City, NJ: Doubleday, 1983).



Through time this collection has progressively become larger as more newly discovered texts have been added to the corpus by editors. In addition, the access to English translations of these manuscripts, most of which were originally written in Greek, Latin, and eastern languages such as Slavonic, Ethiopic, Syriac, etc., has increased in time. Before the middle of the nineteenth century, very few of them were available in English, some in Latin, while the majority of manuscripts were still untranslated in their original languages.

12. For example, Jude 1:14–15 quotes from 1 Enoch 1:9. 2 Timothy 3:8 alludes to the legend of the magicians Jannes and Jambres, who opposed Moses. Jude 1:9 preserves a tradition early Christian writers equated with *The Assumption of Moses*.

13. For example, Serapion used it to refer to New Testament Pseudepigrapha, specifically *The So-Called Gospel of Peter*, an example of what scholars today would call the New Testament apocrypha. Cf. Eusebius, *The History of the Church*, 6.12.

14. See *Old Testament Pseudepigrapha: More Noncanonical Scriptures*. This is a two-volume series meant to add many previously unpublished or newly translated texts. With these volumes, it is hoped that all known pre-Islamic period pseudepigrapha related to the Old Testament will be accounted for either here or in previously published collections. For an in-depth study on the development of the term and corpus of Pseudepigrapha see Annette Yoshiko Reed, "The Modern Invention of 'Old Testament Pseudepigrapha,'" *Journal of Theological Studies, ns* 60, no. 2 (October 2009): 403–36. For another brief discussion on the problematic term *Pseudepigrapha*, see James R. Davila, "Pseudepigrapha, Old Testament," in *Dictionary of Early Judaism*, edited by John J. Collins and Daniel C. Harlow (Grand Rapids, MI: William B. Eerdmans Publishing Company, 2010), 1110– 1114.

15. *Codex pseudepigraphus Veteris Testamenti* (Hamburg and Leipzig, 1713). *Codicis pseudepigraphi Veteris Testamenti, Volumen alterum accedit Josephi veteris Christiani auctorial Hypomnesticon* (Hamburg, 1723).

## THE PSEUDEPIGRAPHA IN THE LATTER-DAY SAINT COMMUNITY

There was not a collection of Pseudepigrapha texts in English at the time of Joseph Smith, but some individual texts were available in English translations. Still, there is some question whether Joseph Smith accessed any of these individual texts and was influenced by them in his creation of additional scripture (particularly in the Pearl of Great Price).

One figure who garnered a lot of attention in the Pseudepigrapha and who influenced later texts is Enoch.[16] From very early on, it was recognized that a passage in Jude (verse 9) came from a text about Enoch. Joseph Smith made allusion to this fact as early as the end of 1830 when he stated,

> Much conjecture and conversation frequently occurred among the Saints, concerning the books mentioned, and referred to, in various places in the Old and New Testaments, which were now nowhere to be found. The common remark was, 'They are *lost books*'; but it seems the Apostolic Church had some of these writings, as Jude mentions or quotes the Prophecy of Enoch, the seventh from Adam.[17]

Besides accessing some of this information from New Testament commentaries of the day, some material from early Enoch texts could have been available to Joseph Smith and early Latter-day Saints in various sources and literature of the day. As Colby Townsend, an early American literature and religion scholar, has argued, aspects of the Enoch stories were part of the literary culture of the late 1700s and early 1800s.[18] Most of these texts focus on the story in Genesis 6 of the sons of God (the "Watchers" in Enochic terminology), coming down and having relations with the daughters of men. These references witness to the existence of Enoch texts, and even include some translations of sections of them, but they are scattered throughout English sources in various newspapers, books, and academic collections and never include the complete text, thereby still raising the question of how likely Joseph Smith or other members

16. In fact, R. H. Charles argued, "[T]he influence of Enoch in the New Testament has been greater than that of all the other apocryphal and pseudepigraphical books taken together." from *The Apocrypha and Pseudepigrapha of the Old Testament*, 2:180.

17. B. H. Roberts, ed., *History of The Church of Jesus Christ of Latter-day Saints*, seven vols. (Salt Lake City, UT: Church of Jesus Christ of Latter-day Saints, 1907), 1:132.

18. Colby Townsend, "Revisiting Joseph Smith and the Availability of the *Book of Enoch*," *Dialogue: A Journal of Mormon Thought* 53, no. 3 (2020): 41–72.

of the church had actually read any of the pseudepigraphic works of Enoch especially since the story of the Watchers does not appear in Latter-day Saint sources. There is considerable debate on the issue of whether Joseph Smith had access to the Pseudepigraphic text of 1 Enoch before he wrote the Enoch passages now found in the Book of Moses.[19] While it is true there was an English translation of 1 Enoch done in 1821 by Richard Laurence (*The Book of Enoch, the Prophet: An Apocryphal Production, Supposed to Have Been Lost for Ages* [Oxford, UK: Oxford University Press, 1821]), it is not until 1840 when Latter-day Saint missionaries in England come across an English version of 1 Enoch that explicit mention of this published text is found. They could hardly contain their excitement about finding a possible lost text related to the Enoch material in the Pearl of Great Price. It would seem the same excitement would have been present if earlier sections of the Enoch story were uncovered in the previous decade, but the only earlier connection Joseph Smith specifically made to other sources of Enoch was when he quoted some extracts from *his* prophecy of Enoch as found in the Book of Moses (which does not contain the passage quoted in Jude). Joseph Smith introduced it by saying the Lord revealed "the following doings of olden times, from the prophecy of Enoch."[20]

19. For a full discussion of the differences between "Laurence's Enoch" and the Enoch in the Book of Moses, see Jed L. Woodworth, "Extra-Biblical Enoch Texts in Early American Culture," in *Archive of Restoration Culture: Summer Fellows' Papers 1997–1999*, edited by Richard L. Bushman (Provo, UT: Joseph Fielding Smith Institute for Latter-day Saint History, 2000), 185–93. As part of his project, Woodworth lays out the two opposing views on Joseph Smith's acquaintance with Laurence's Enoch text: the "parallelist" that argues Joseph Smith did not know Laurence's Enoch text but included remarkable parallels with Enoch texts in his writings (represented by Hugh Nibley, *Enoch the Prophet*, Collected Works of Hugh Nibley, vol. 2 [Salt Lake City, UT: Deseret Book and FARMS, 1986]; and the "derivativist" position that argues Joseph Smith knew Laurence's text and was influenced by it in his writings (represented by D. Michael Quinn, *Early Mormonism and the Magic World View*, rev. ed. [Salt Lake City, UT: Signature Books, 1998]. A master's thesis on this issue was done by Salvatore Cirillo at the University of Durham ("Joseph Smith, Mormonism, and Enochic Tradition," 2010). Cirillo was heavily influenced by Quinn's work and argues against Nibley's conclusions and thinks Joseph Smith or his scribes were familiar with Enochic texts, and this influence led to the production of the Enoch account in the Book of Moses. He points out that there were other English translations done before Laurence's; however, these were not complete translations of the entire text of 1 Enoch but mostly on the story of the Watchers at the beginning. Another perspective posits that Joseph Smith could have become acquainted with Enoch traditions via Freemasonry where Enoch is a significant figure. Cheryl Bruno argues for a trajectory of mystical themes (such as theophany, grand assembly, and heavenly ascent), that originated in non-canonical Enoch traditions were then adopted in Freemasonry and then adapted by Joseph Smith. She stated, "Though access to the Enoch pseudepigrapha was possible from several places, it seems more plausible that Smith utilized Masonic tradition rather than other sources for inspiration in his Enoch writings." "Congruence and Concatenation in Jewish Mystical Literature, American Freemasonry, and Mormon Enoch Writings," *Journal of Religion and Society* 16 (2014): 5 [1–19]. A weakness of this claim is that Joseph Smith did not become a Freemason until 1842, long after the creation of the Enoch material in the Book of Moses in the early 1830s. Bruno asserts that this is still possible due to cultural familiarity of Masonic ritual and legend and the prevelance of anti-Masonic literature in the region which would have included the Enoch material.

20. *History of the Church of Jesus Christ of Latter-day Saints*, 1:133.

The first Latter-day Saint source that specifically mentions the book of Enoch is the 1840 issue of *Times and Seasons* in an advertisement reprinted from the *New York Star* about the forthcoming publication of the Book of Jasher.[21] As part of early members' eagerness for lost books of the Bible, the advertisement also mentioned that "recently the Book of Enoch has been discovered, translated from the Ethiopic, and published in England." The following month's issue of the *Millennial Star*, published in England, gave a description of this apocryphal book of Enoch:

> We have now in our possession a book, the title page of which reads as follows: "The Book of Enoch the Prophet; an Apocryphal Production, supposed for ages to have been lost, but discovered at the close of the last century in Abyssinia; now first translated from an Ethiopic MS. [manuscript] in the Bodleian Library, by Richard Laurence, LLD, Archbishop of Cashel, late Professor of Hebrew in the University of Oxford."
>
> This book carries with it indisputable evidence of being an ancient production. It steers clear of modern sectarianism, and savours much of the doctrine of the ancients, especially in regard to the things of the latter day. Notwithstanding it was translated and published in England, and that, too, by an English Bishop, who stands entirely unconnected with the church of Latter-Day Saints, yet it seems plainly to predict the coming forth of the Book of Mormon, and the mission of our Elders, which they are now performing among the nations, together with the late persecution which has befallen our people in America, with the conduct of the rulers of that Republic, in refusing to give us redress; yes, in fact, it predicts the final result of that matter, and the complete triumph of the saints.
>
> We give the following extract, commencing at page 156, without further comment, and leave our readers to form their own judgment in regard to this *remarkable Book.*[22]

The article then proceeds to quote from the book of 1 Enoch. (In today's numbering of 1 Enoch, the quoted passages cover 103:1–2, 10–15; 104; and 105.) It is not hard to see how a Latter-day Saint reader could see a parallel between the struggles against persecution recounted in 1 Enoch and the experiences of

21. "The Book of Jasher," *Times and Seasons* 1, no. 8 (June 1840): 127.

22. "The Apocryphal Book of Enoch," *The Latter-day Saints' Millennial Star* 1, no. 3 (July 1840): 61–62, emphasis in the original text.

the early Latter-day Saints, particularly the lack of government action to stop the persecution and, in fact, the government's participation in it. A few passages also foretell the coming forth of books that will bring the reader great joy (a newer translation even uses the word *scripture* for these future texts). Some early Latter-day Saints saw their books of scripture, like the Book of Mormon, foretold in these prophesies.

Similarly, a Latter-day Saint book published in 1841 shared the same enthusiasm for access to Enoch texts and gave further interpretation of Enoch's prophecies. It asserted that the Book of Enoch had prophecies of the coming forth of the Book of Mormon, Latter-day Saint missionaries teaching throughout the world, and the persecution the church was currently facing.[23] It then goes on to quote the same introduction and passage from 1 Enoch as the *Millennial Star*.

The book then interprets Enoch's intention when he said he would point out a "mystery." For the author, the mystery was an apostasy of the church from the apostolic faith that included some people writing their own books without inspiration.[24] The last section addresses Enoch's prophecy of "books of joy," over which the righteous will rejoice, which Thompson interprets as future books of truth that will come forth as well as the Book of Mormon's collection of fourteen books. "Thus the truth of the Book of Mormon is established, proved and confirmed by this prophesy of Enoch, the seventh from Adam."[25]

Unlike the Apocrypha, there do not seem to be any sermons or writings by church leaders referencing the texts later included in the Pseudepigrapha. Yet the fact that the first English translation in America of the Apocalypse of Abraham was published in a Latter-day Saint periodical, the *Improvement Era*, in 1898 demonstrates a continued interest in this early material. The editor gave his reasoning for this publication in his initial introduction and in subsequent issues: there were accounts in these Slavic manuscripts that ran parallel to doctrines and episodes in the Book of Abraham of the Pearl of Great Price,[26] and they believed Abraham likely left behind written records, which, though may have been tampered with or lost, may be compared with these existing texts about Abraham. They then go on to discuss six points of comparison with the Book of Abraham, especially highlighting the doctrine of preexistence of spirits.[27] In the next century, Latter-day Saint scholars like Hugh Nibley, Michael

23. Charles Blancher Thompson, *Evidences in Proof of the Book of Mormon* (Batavia, NY: D.D. Waite, 1841), 125.

24. *Evidences in Proof of the Book of Mormon*, 130–1.

25. *Evidences in Proof of the Book of Mormon*, 131–2.

26. From "The Book of the Revelation of Abraham," *The Improvement Era* 1/10 (August 1898): 705–6.

27. See "Comments on the Book of the Revelation of Abraham," *The Improvement Era* 1, no. 12 (October 1898): 896–901.

Rhodes, Jeffrey M. Bradshaw, and David L. Larsen combed Pseudepigrapha texts for support of the stories in the Pearl of Great Price, particularly about Enoch and Abraham.[28] Beyond this apologetic work in the Pseudepigrapha, some Latter-day Saint scholars have focused on the Pseudepigrapha in their historical research. Stephen Robinson did significant English translations of the Testament of Adam and the Apocryphon of Ezekiel (cowritten with J. R. Mueller) included in Charlesworth's collection, and Jared Ludlow wrote his dissertation on a Pseudepigrapha text, the Testament of Abraham, subsequently published as *Abraham Meets Death: Narrative Humor in the Testament of Abraham.*[29]

## CONCLUSION

Modern scholarship has debated the appropriateness of the terms Apocrypha and Pseudepigrapha for these early Jewish and Christian texts, since some are considered canonical by some groups and not all are falsely attributed to their ancient authors (e.g., Jesus ben Sira), but suitable replacements have not been found so they continue to define these significant texts that tell us more about early Judaism and Christianity. As these texts have become more widely translated and known, they have become important building blocks on which to reconstruct our understanding of the variety of thought and religious expression from the Second Temple period. While they may not exactly reveal one dimension of Judaism, like popular Judaism or apocalyptic Judaism, as some scholars in the past have argued, they certainly tell us that the communities who produced these texts had diverse ideas and approaches to earlier biblical material. Their appropriation and rearticulation of Old Testament figures and events created new perspectives, trajectories, and understandings for their religious communities. Concerns such as the end of days, resurrection, survival amidst Gentile imperialism, revelation, religious law, ethics, and many others run through these texts. Modern scholars thus use these texts to better understand the concerns and aspirations of these ancient communities in the transmission of their traditions. Scholars today could not adequately represent

28. For an annotated Bibliography on Pseudepigrapha sources related to Enoch and the Flood, see Jeffrey M Bradshaw and David J. Larsen, *In God's Image and Likeness 2 Enoch, Noah, and the Tower of Babel* (Salt Lake City, UT: Eborn Books, 2014), 467–79.

29. James H. Charlesworth, ed., *The Old Testament Pseudepigrapha, Vol. 1. Apocalyptic Literature and Testaments* (Garden City, NY: Doubleday & Company, Inc., 1983), 487–95, 989–95. Jared W. Ludlow, *Abraham Meets Death: Narrative Humor in the Testament of Abraham* (New York: Sheffield Academic Press/ Continuum, 2002).

early Judaism and Christianity by ignoring these texts and relying only on canonical literature.

When looking at the few references to the Apocrypha and Pseudepigrapha in the writings of Joseph Smith and his contemporaries, we see great interest in only a few of these texts and very little acquaintance with the vast majority of the corpus (as constituted today). There was certainly an interest by early saints for "lost books" of scripture, and some equated the Pseudepigrapha texts with these lost books. The early saints read and interpreted the Apocrypha and Pseudepigrapha for their own time and age (the "end of days"). These texts depicted an eschatological period of severe persecution, and certainly this is what the saints were experiencing at its worst in Missouri without any protection or redress from the government. These texts also foresaw a time for bringing forth additional scripture reserved for the last days, sometimes out of lost books from the past, but certainly heralding in a new era of joyful preaching of new messages. Thus the early saints eagerly explored them to find messages for their day and corroboration for the latter-day events unfolding around them.



Latter-day Saint interest in these texts continued, particularly as Pseudepigrapha texts became more available in English, mostly as efforts to find parallels with the additional scriptural accounts of biblical figures in the Pearl of Great Price and as support for unique Latter-day Saint doctrines. While Latter-day Saint readers have often combed these Pseudepigrapha texts for remnants of true stories and teachings from these Old Testament figures, holding out the notion of these texts passing down oral traditions or written stories from the time period of these individuals, there is no way to prove this transmission or lack of it. We should approach these texts with healthy skepticism since many later authors likely created stories around these earlier figures to boost the authority of their own writings.

What is more certain, is that the Apocrypha and Pseudepigrapha can be fruitfully studied to better understand the ancient world. They record the concerns, questions, perspectives, influences, and thoughts of groups of people from the first centuries BC and AD. They give us a glimpse into the variety of early Judaism and emerging Christianity. Their preservation and transmission by early Christians showed their reverence for the authority of these earlier Old Testament figures, and carried on the legacy of their Jewish roots. They are a fascinating cornucopia of religious literature that helps us understand the Bible better because of the texts' interactions with and beyond biblical themes, figures, and concerns.

# 9

# How the Book of Mormon Responds to the Bible

GRANT HARDY

When the Book of Mormon was first published in 1830, it was clearly meant to be a companion volume to the Bible. It was written in an archaic diction reminiscent of the King James Version and was filled with biblical phrases, along with several entire chapters quoted nearly verbatim from Isaiah, Matthew, Micah, and Malachi. Like the Bible, it was divided into books that were generally named for prophets, and its contents included historical accounts, stories of miracles and divine interventions, sermons, letters, and prophecies—many of which were fulfilled at the coming of the resurrected Christ to the Americas.[1] The main narrative presents the history of a family that left Jerusalem a few years before the Babylonian conquest of 586 BCE. God led them across the sea to the New World, where they founded a civilization that lasted for about a thousand years before being destroyed by internecine warfare between two hostile lineages, the Nephites and the Lamanites. Several centuries into the story, the Nephites encountered and merged with another group that God had also brought from Jerusalem to the New World, the Mulekites (who included a scion of the Davidic monarchy), and they learned of yet a third party of refugees from Mesopotamia, the Jaredites, who had preceded them to the Americas many centuries earlier but had destroyed themselves.

The book sees itself in continuity with the Bible—describing the same God, the same covenants, the same prophetic impulse and hope of redemption—and the basic story can be regarded as a sequel to the Deuteronomistic History.[2]

1. Surprisingly, the first edition was not divided into verses, as had been standard for Bibles since the sixteenth century; verses were added to the Book of Mormon in 1879.

2. The term *Deuteronomistic History* refers to a widely accepted hypothesis, first proposed by Martin Noth in 1943, that the books of Joshua, Judges, 1–2 Samuel, and 1–2 Kings were written by a single historian,

Picking up where 2 Kings ends, with the reign of Zedekiah, a small group of Israelite refugees reach the western hemisphere, where they reenact much of the biblical narrative. They receive a new promised land and another chance to live the law of Moses, augmented by an additional covenant in which God tells Lehi, "Inasmuch as ye shall keep my commandments ye shall prosper in the land; but inasmuch as ye will not keep my commandments ye shall be cut off from my presence" (2 Ne. 1:20)—a promise that is repeated some twenty times throughout the text. This moral framework is reminiscent of the list of blessings and curses that Moses sets before the Israelites in Deuteronomy 30, as they are about to enter the promised land of Canaan. The Deuteronomistic History in the Bible correlates Israel's successes and failures in the promised land with their obedience or disobedience to Mosaic legislation, specifically that of Deuteronomy; Book of Mormon narrators take a very similar approach in their own records. For instance, the level of Nephite faithfulness determines the ebb and flow of conflicts with the Lamanites, there is a parallel transition in government structure (though the Nephites move from kings to judges, rather than vice versa), and the "pride cycle" of the book of Helaman is analogous to the recurring cycles of sin and deliverance in the book of Judges.[3]

As historians in the Bible tried to make sense of the conquests of Israel and Judah (why had the Lord allowed his people to fall?), the classic prophets also responded to the devastation, sometimes with justifications for God's fierce anger, but also with promises that the exiles would someday return and the Lord himself would establish his kingdom among them. The events recounted in Ezra-Nehemiah were only a partial fulfillment of those prophecies, but in the Book of Mormon, the God of Israel, identified as Jesus Christ, quite literally comes to his temple in the city Bountiful and sets up a kingdom among the righteous Nephites and Lamanites (3–4 Nephi). Though this political situation lasts for only four generations, it is nevertheless the culmination of a pattern in which Old Testament concepts of historical development are conjoined with New Testament understandings of God and salvation. The Nephites are portrayed as having received remarkably clear prophecies of Jesus's ministry, atonement, and resurrection, and they established a church, complete with

---

or a school of historians, reflecting the themes, language, and concerns of the book of Deuteronomy, which was probably the "book of the law" discovered in the temple in 622 BCE, during the reign of King Josiah. The Deuteronomistic History went through several redactions, both before and after the fall of Judah to the Babylonians in 586 BCE. The same biblical books are referred to as "the Former Prophets" in Judaism.

3. The "pride cycle" is often described in LDS writings as a sequence beginning with righteousness and prosperity, which gives rise to pride and wickedness, then destruction and suffering, and finally humility and repentance, which leads back to prosperity.

baptismal rituals, more than a century before his birth, in anticipation of his coming. In this way, the Book of Mormon blurs the division between the Old and New Testaments.



It also views itself as having a significant role to play in the events of the last days. In several passages a scenario is laid out in which the new Mormon scripture will herald and facilitate the fulfilling of God's promises to Israel—gathering their scattered remnants a second time, as prophesied in Isaiah 11:11 (cited five times in the Book of Mormon), and restoring them to their lands of inheritance. This includes bringing the Lamanites, whom Latter-day Saints understand to be among the ancestors of the native peoples of the Americas, to a knowledge of their Israelite ancestry and restoring them to preeminence in the New World. The book would also be instrumental in converting the Gentiles, who would then assist the Jews and Lamanites in their restoration and be numbered themselves among the people of the covenant.

The Christian Bible, which Nephite prophets saw in vision, is mentioned a few times, with the Book of Mormon affirming its authority but also offering something more. The language can be somewhat oblique, though the message is clear:

- "These last records [primarily the Book of Mormon], which thou hast seen among the Gentiles, shall establish the truth of the first [the Bible], which are of the twelve apostles of the Lamb, and shall make known the plain and precious things which have been taken away from them." (1 Ne. 13:40)
- "Wherefore, the fruit of thy loins shall write [i.e., the Book of Mormon]; and the fruit of the loins of Judah shall write [i.e., the Bible]" and they "shall grow together, unto the confounding of false doctrines and laying down of contentions." (2 Ne. 3:12)
- "For behold, this [the Book of Mormon] is written for the intent that ye may believe that [the Bible]; and if ye believe that, ye will believe this also." (Morm. 7:9)

While there will always be debates about the nature of Joseph Smith's revelations, the historicity of early migrations from west Asia to the Americas, and the canonical authority of Mormon scripture, all readers can agree that the Book of Mormon was written, at least in part, as a response to the Bible. From one perspective, Smith composed his book to remedy what he perceived as deficiencies in the Old and New Testaments (he famously lamented that "the teachers of religion of the different sects understood the same passages of scripture so differently as to destroy all confidence in settling the question by an appeal to the Bible"; JS–History 1:12). Alternatively, God himself inspired ancient American prophets—who apparently had access to some early Old Testament texts through the Brass Plates—and preserved their words, providing for their translation and publication at a time when biblically based Christianity was adrift. Either way, it is fair to ask how the Book of Mormon supports, or even improves on, the witness of the Bible. Possible answers can be arranged into three categories: provenance, narrative, and theology.

## PROVENANCE

In the late eighteenth and early nineteenth centuries, Americans became increasingly aware of arguments, mostly derived from European scholarship, that seemed to undermine traditional understandings of the Bible and its authority. There were questions about the authorship of the Pentateuch and the Gospels, the authenticity of miracles, the inspiration behind the canonization process, the reliability of the Hebrew and Greek manuscripts that were the foundation for translations, and the accuracy of translations themselves.[4] For each of these concerns, Joseph Smith presented the Book of Mormon to the world as comparable to the Bible, but with superior credentials.[5] According to Latter-day Saints, their scripture had been translated from autographs written on gold plates by the original author/editors (who were prophets themselves) and then transmitted intact to Joseph Smith. The major narrators wrote openly of their own lives and ambitions, they were told by God what to include or exclude in their accounts, and they spoke directly to their readers in the latter-days, whom they had seen in vision.[6] The translation was produced by divine, supernatural means rather than by human scholarship, and the Book of Mormon was a complete, integrated whole that was canonical from the

4. See Paul C. Gutjahr, *An American Bible* (Stanford, CA: Stanford University Press, 1999), 89–105; Jonathan Sheehan, *The Enlightenment Bible* (Princeton, NJ: Princeton University Press, 2005); David F. Holland, *Sacred Borders* (New York: Oxford University Press, 2011); Michael J. Lee, *The Erosion of Biblical Certainty* (New York: Palgrave Macmillan, 2013).

5. Robert N. Hullinger, *Joseph Smith's Answer to Skepticism* (Salt Lake City, UT: Signature Books, 1992), particularly 128–29, where Hullinger lists nine criticisms from *The Age of Reason* for which the Book of Mormon provides a tangible rebuttal. Terryl L. Givens, in *By the Hand of Mormon* (New York: Oxford University Press, 2002), offers a cogent analysis of the impact the Book of Mormon had simply by virtue of its existence as supposed new revelation (62–88), as well as a comparison of some of its teachings with those of the Bible (185–208).

6. 1 Ne. 6, 9, 14:24–27; 2 Ne. 33; W of M 1; 3 Ne. 5, 26, 29, 30; Morm. 8–9; Moro. 10.

moment Smith dictated it to his scribes. For Americans wondering about the possibility of miracles, especially in modern times, the book was introduced as a miracle in itself. Of course, all this had to be taken on faith, especially given the inaccessibility of the gold plates that had been returned to the angel, but such claims sparked curiosity among some Americans.[7]



## NARRATIVE

The narrative and literary style was similar enough to the King James Bible to feel familiar, including accounts of kings and prophets, angels and visions, missionaries and martyrs, and disasters and deliverances, with God as the leading character. While some of the stories mirrored biblical precedents closely (Lehi, like Moses, led his people to a new promised land; Alma, like Paul, was confronted by an angel as he went about persecuting believers), most were fresh incidents that nevertheless took place within the parameters of a biblical worldview.[8] Readers who may have harbored suspicions about the reliability of Old and New Testament stories could have their faith shored up by new examples of revelations, miracles, and prophecies fulfilled, and the Book of Mormon demonstrated that dramatic instances of divine intervention were not confined to a single nation or region. Instead, the God of the Nephites proclaimed, "I am a God of miracles; and I will show unto the world that I am the same yesterday, today, and forever" (2 Ne. 27:23, with phrasing from Heb. 13:8). Or as Mormon asked, "Have miracles ceased? Behold I say unto you, Nay; neither have angels ceased to minister unto the children of men . . . showing themselves unto them of strong faith and a firm mind" (Moro. 7:29–31).

The Book of Mormon depicts a world in which God is regularly and directly involved in human affairs, much like the Bible, but in a manner that seems to have been updated to better fit nineteenth-century sensibilities. While supernatural elements are still very much present, the book contains many fewer of the sorts of puzzling, irrational, or morally problematic episodes that so agitated skeptics like Thomas Paine (Nephi's killing of Laban in 1 Nephi 4 and God's destruction of entire cities at 3 Nephi 8 are rare exceptions). The Lord never commands the Nephites to exterminate their enemies. Prophets do not attempt to kill their children, marry prostitutes, challenge God's justice,

7. For more on these ideas, see Grant Hardy, "The Book of Mormon and the Bible," in *Americanist Approaches to the Book of Mormon*, edited by Elizabeth Fenton and Jared Hickman (New York: Oxford University Press, 2019), 107–35.

8. For example, compare Mosiah 27:8–37 and Acts 9:1–22.

or rationalize slavery. Animal sacrifices, idolatry, exorcisms, and speaking in tongues are mentioned in passing but without detailed accounts (perhaps unexpectedly, there are no highlighted stories of miraculous healings, aside from Zeezrom). Predictions of future events are communicated in plain language, without the sort of cryptic symbolism found in the books of Daniel and Revelation. Because Jesus came to the Nephites as a divine being, the Christology in the Book of Mormon is high, with little need to explain perplexing actions of a mortal Jesus. A few miracles outdo those in the Bible, as when Jesus produces sacramental bread and water from thin air (3 Ne. 20:1–8), as opposed to multiplying loaves and fishes, yet the narrative remains for the most part history-like, rarely reaching fantastical extremes.[9] And since there are so few instances of otherwise unknown cultural beliefs and practices, the world of the Book of Mormon undoubtedly seemed less strange to its American readers than Iron Age Canaan or the Roman Empire.

Nephite writers are obsessed with records, much more so than in the Bible, where anonymous authors and editors often compiled oral traditions and then revised and augmented texts over time (as would become increasingly clear in the century after Joseph Smith). By contrast, the most extraordinary events in the Book of Mormon are presented as having been written down at the time by eyewitnesses, and subsequent narrator/editors are explicit about how they used those sources. In this manner, the credibility of accounts of miracles is heightened in ways that might appeal to readers in an age of widespread literacy who valued the identity and intentions of authors, when the authorship of canonical texts was starting to be challenged. The narration is also more unified and deliberate than in the Bible. Although its contents are somewhat heterogeneous, incorporating history, preaching, memoirs, letters, political documents, allegories, an apocalypse, prayers, and poetry, there is a single narrative arc, and most of the book is attributed to just three narrators: Nephi, who comes at the beginning of the Nephite story, and Mormon and Moroni, who write at its cataclysmic conclusion a thousand years later. While it is possible to draw distinctions between their characteristic styles and concerns, they nevertheless share a common theological perspective, and as a result, there are many fewer voices, tensions, and contradictions than in the Old and New Testaments (though this is also what one would expect if the book was authored by Joseph

9. Examples of rationalizing moderation include the allusion at Hel. 12:14–16 to the sun standing still at Josh 10:12–15, with an explanation affirming the heliocentric solar system, as well as the allegorizing of the flames of hell as psychological anguish at Morm. 9:4–5.

Smith).[10] Biblically savvy readers in the nineteenth century may have found the Book of Mormon more rational, more moral, and more cohesive than the Bible itself, especially since the Mormon scripture generally shows good things happening to good people, and bad things happening to evildoers, with few examples of unmerited suffering—and in such cases the narrators are quick to offer faithful interpretations.[11]



## THEOLOGY

Book of Mormon theology is more straightforward and consistent than what readers often encounter in the Bible, where the words of even a single influential figure, such as Paul, can be fraught with convoluted arguments, difficult allusions, and odd metaphors. By contrast, in two key passages, 2 Nephi 31:1–32:6 and 3 Nephi 27:13–22, the "doctrine of Christ," or "the gospel," is concisely and rather simply defined as faith in Christ, repentance, baptism, reception of the Holy Ghost, enduring to the end, and eternal life.[12] In addition, the spiritual implications of political events are quite often made explicit in "thus we see" comments from the narrators. What the Book of Mormon loses in literary and theological richness (there is nothing in the Nephite record quite like the Joseph narrative, or Job, or Hebrews, or even Ruth) may be made up for in its utility. The New Testament, as a collection of historical narratives, occasional letters, and an apocalypse, has proven itself somewhat limited as the foundational text for a religion, in the sense that Christians of various sects and denominations have been arguing over theology and church organization for two thousand years. Of course, this is a challenge for most religions with a strong scriptural tradition, but it is particularly a problem for Protestants who adhere to the principle of *sola scriptura*.

The Book of Mormon clarifies ambiguities and fills in gaps in the Bible with regard to a number of key doctrinal issues such as the restoration of Israel (1 Ne. 22; 2 Ne. 10; 3 Ne. 16; 20–21); the fall and the atonement (2 Ne. 2; Mosiah 3); the resurrection and judgment (2 Ne. 9; Alma 12; 34; 40–41); the purpose of the law of Moses (2 Ne. 25; Mosiah 12–13; 3 Ne. 15); church regulation (Mosiah 26; 3 Ne. 18); the nature of faith (Alma 32; Ether 12; Moro. 7); the reconciliation of God's justice and mercy (Alma 42); and proper procedures and liturgical

10. Grant Hardy, *Understanding the Book of Mormon* (New York: Oxford University Press, 2010).

11. As at Mosiah 23:19–24, Alma 14:9–11, 24:23–27.

12. Noel B. Reynolds, "The Gospel of Jesus Christ as Taught by the Nephite Prophets," *BYU Studies* 31, no. 3 (1991): 31–50.

wording for baptism, the Eucharist, and ordination (3 Ne. 11; Moro. 2–6; 8). Strikingly, several Nephite prophets insist that God's covenants with Israel will remain in force even after the establishment of the Christian Church (1 Ne 19:13–16; 2 Ne 29:5; 3 Ne 29; Moro 10:31), and that salvation for Gentiles will come as they are adopted into the house of Israel.[13]

And while the Mormon scripture is characterized by broad continuities with the Bible, there are also a few instances of theological innovation. For example, the covenant made between God and King Benjamin's people at Mosiah 5 seems distinct from the Abrahamic and Mosaic Covenants of the Old Testament, both of which are regularly cited by Nephite prophets (with nary a mention of the Davidic Covenant), as well as the New Covenant of the New Testament. The transfiguration of the Nephite Twelve (3 Ne. 19:24–36) and the commissioning of the Three Nephites who were promised immortality (3 Ne. 28; cf. John 21:21–23) extend biblical precedents in intriguing ways. However, the most striking and pervasive theological contribution of the Book of Mormon is the way it merges the Old and New Testaments, particularly with regard to salvation.

At the beginning of the book, set in Jerusalem in the years just before the Babylonian Exile, God tells Lehi of a coming Messiah (1 Ne. 1:19), later identified as "a Savior of the World" or "the Son of God" (1 Ne. 10:4, 17). Through a series of dreams and visions, Lehi and Nephi come to realize that in addition to the collective salvation offered to Israel in terms of land, posterity, prosperity, and political security, with God intervening in human history, there was also a possibility of individual salvation in the next life, as a consequence of Christ's atoning sacrifice.[14] (Within the framework of the narrative, such ideas would have been comforting given the national humiliation, indiscriminate suffering,

13. There are also notable omissions in Book of Mormon theology. For instance, there are no legal codes, there is virtually no discussion of the second coming of Christ or the millennium (though these events are assumed), and there is nothing like the missionary outreach to Gentiles in the New Testament, with its consequent reformulating of Second Temple Judaism, though it certainly would have been interesting if the Nephites had taken their religious message to the non-Israelite, Indigenous inhabitants of the ancient Americas.

14. These two modes of salvation are exemplified in Lehi's two allegories, both of which center on trees. The olive tree mentioned at 1 Ne 10:12-14 (and later greatly expanded on in Jacob 5) embodies God's dealings with collective entities in history: Gentiles, Jews, and other branches of the house of Israel. His dream in 1 Nephi 8 of an iron rod leading to a tree with sweet fruit, on the other hand, illustrates the invitation to individuals to come to Christ and be saved in the eternities, regardless of the worldly conditions in which they may find themselves. Borrowing a term from academic theology, we might label the communal, this-worldly mode of redemption "salvation history," which will eventually remedy the fall of Jerusalem and the Exile. The Book of Mormon refers to individual salvation in the afterlife as the "plan of salvation," which rectifies the fall of Adam. See Heather Hardy, "The Double Nature of God's Saving Work: The Plan of Salvation and Salvation History," in *The Things Which My Father Saw: Approaches to Lehi's Dream and Nephi's*

and religious dislocation of the Exile.) The phrasing is often derived from the New Testament, with talk of "faith," "the Holy Ghost," "hell," "the devil," and "the kingdom of God," and it takes Nephi most of 1–2 Nephi to work out the implications of Christian salvation, which apparently does not preclude God continuing to deal with humanity in terms of lineages, ethnicities, and religious communities into the latter days. There is considerable resistance to these new revelations on the part of other members of their family, and indeed, serious opposition lasts for several centuries, until the coming of the resurrected Jesus to the Nephites and Lamanites vindicates the prophecies of Lehi and Nephi. In addition, Nephite pre-Christian Christianity allows the Book of Mormon to integrate concepts of God's justice and mercy that are often characterized (or caricatured) as primarily manifest in the Old and New Testaments respectively.

Nephite prophets occasionally cite the same prooftexts as New Testament authors (e.g., Gen. 22:18; Deut. 18:15; Ps. 95:7–11; Isa. 52–53); yet the Book of Mormon also draws deeply on Old Testament verses that were not regularly employed in early Christianity. For instance, Isaiah's promise of "a marvelous work" at Isaiah 29:14 is cited eight times by Nephite writers (usually with regard to the Book of Mormon itself), and in Lehi's counsel to his sons, his enlarged conception of salvation is expressed through an expansion of Moses's last words to the community of Israel:

> I have **set before you life and death**, blessing and cursing: therefore **choose life**, that both thou and thy seed shall live (Deut. 30:19)
>
> And they are **free to choose** liberty and **eternal life** through the great mediation of all men, or to choose captivity **and death**, according to the captivity and power of the devil . . . Now my sons, I would that ye should . . . **choose eternal life** (2 Ne. 2:27–28)

More typical are passages where the Book of Mormon incorporates multiple, distinct phrases from the King James Bible. This happens with great regularity, as at Mosiah 5:15:

> Therefore, I would that ye should be **steadfast and immovable, always abounding in** good **works**, that Christ, the **Lord God Omnipotent**, may seal you his, that you may be brought to heaven, that ye may have

*Vision*, edited by Daniel L. Belnap, Gaye Strathearn, and Stanley A. Johnson (Salt Lake City, UT: Deseret Book and BYU Religious Studies Center, 2011), 14–36.

**everlasting salvation** and eternal life, through the wisdom, and power, and justice, and mercy of him **created all things, in heaven and in earth, who is God above all**. Amen.

be ye **stedfast, unmoveable, always abounding in the work** of the Lord—1 Cor. 15:58; cf. 2 Cor. 9:8

**Lord God omnipotent**—Rev. 19:6

**everlasting salvation**—Isa. 45:17

by him were **all things created**, that are **in heaven, and** that are **in earth**—Col. 1:16

One **God . . . who is above all**—Eph. 4.6

Sometimes the original context of the shared wording seems irrelevant, as if the author had simply borrowed a familiar phrase, though there are many cases in which the biblical context enriches the meaning of the Book of Mormon or where the language has been modified, juxtaposed, repurposed, or appropriated in ways that shed new light on the Biblical usage.[15] But just as the Book of Mormon merges the Old and New Testaments, so also it collapses differences between biblical authors, since the Mormon scripture anachronistically and unapologetically quotes and alludes to verses from throughout the Bible—not just the pre-exilic writings that might have been available to ancient Nephites, according to the narrative (see 2 Ne. 29:8). This means that if the English Book of Mormon is thought of as a translation, as most Latter-day Saints do, it must be a rather free rendering, and it further suggests that the God of the Nephites (and of Joseph Smith) is a being who delights in intertextuality, wordplay, and creative reinterpretations of scripture.

It is important, however, to recognize that the Book of Mormon is not organized as a series of doctrinal treatises. It takes the form of an extended, integrated narrative, and a great deal of the theological work is done through stories. Conversion, faithfulness, seeking after God and receiving revelation, repentance, self-sacrifice, compassion, and proper and improper modes of worship are usually shown through action rather than discussed in the abstract. And in contrast to the New Testament, where expectations of Jesus's triumphant return go unrealized, in the Book of Mormon Christ comes in glory at

15. See David P. Wright, "'In Plain Terms that We May Understand': Joseph Smith's Transformation of Hebrews in Alma 12–13," in *New Approaches to the Book of Mormon*, edited by Brent Lee Metcalfe (Salt Lake City, UT: Signature Books, 1993), 165–229; Mark D. Thomas, "A Mosaic for a Religious Counterculture: The Bible in the Book of Mormon," *Dialogue: A Journal of Mormon Thought* 29, no. 4 (1996): 47–68; and Nicholas J. Frederick, *The Bible, Mormon Scripture, and the Rhetoric of Allusivity* (Madison, NJ: Fairleigh Dickinson University Press, 2016).

3 Nephi.[16] The sermons and passages of scriptural exegesis are always placed within thick narrative contexts. For instance, the first blocked quote above is part of Lehi's last words to his sons, which readers can assess after fifty pages of observing personalities and relationships. And the second blocked quote occurs within an extraordinary farewell address made by King Benjamin to his people—a speech with its own backstory, structure, and literary integrity, which constitutes a pivotal moment in the history of Nephite and Mulekite relations (and which draws on genre conventions from Deuteronomy and the Deuteronomistic History).[17]

## UPDATING THE BIBLE FOR A MODERN WORLD

The Book of Mormon may have a limited religious and aesthetic appeal; yet it has been one of the most successful additions to the library of world scriptures in the last several centuries.[18] Clearly, a number of its early readers appreciated its affirmation and extension of the biblical witness, as well as the way it reduced dissonances in the Old and New Testaments that threatened to undermine their authority.[19] It may be that the Mormon scripture appeared at an opportune moment, in the aftermath of the American Enlightenment, when many people knew the King James Bible well but were somewhat open to skeptical, rationalist perspectives, and before the cascade of critical biblical scholarship later in the century.[20] This was also an era when American biblicism transitioned from political discourse focused on the Old Testament and the fate of nations to evangelical revivals that promised New Testament salvation

16. Nevertheless, Latter-day Saints, like earlier generations of Nephites, are still waiting for the fulfillment of Book of Mormon prophecies concerning the last days; verses like 3 Ne. 29:1–3 offer reassurance.

17. John W. Welch and Stephen D. Ricks, eds., *King Benjamin's Speech* (Provo, UT: Foundation for Ancient Research and Mormon Studies, 1998), especially 89–117, 233–75.

18. For a brief survey of recent attempts to integrate the Book of Mormon into college courses in American literature, see Grant Shreve, "The Book of Mormon Gets the Literary Treatment," *Religion and Politics* (May 23, 2017), available at http://religionandpolitics.org/2017/05/23/the-book-of-mormon-gets-the-literary-treatment/.

19. Timothy Smith identified five ways in which the Book of Mormon "served to strengthen the authority of scripture." These included its integration of the Old and New Testaments, its insistence that salvation was open to all, an emphasis on ethical uprightness, demonstrations of the Holy Spirit working in the lives of believers, and the literal fulfillment of prophecies concerning the last days. See Timothy L. Smith, "The Book of Mormon in a Biblical Culture," *Journal of Mormon History* 7 (1980): 3–21; the quotation is from 10.

20. Steven C. Harper has written of the appeal of the Book of Mormon to those "acculturated by the twin influences of the Bible and the democratization of rationalism," pointing out that "those who became Mormons were almost always first contemplative Bible believers who were skeptical of false prophets. They considered it reasonable that signs would follow true believers, and they held out for empirical confirmation." See his "Infallible Proofs, Both Human and Divine: The Persuasiveness of Mormonism for Early Converts," *Religion and American Culture* 10, no. 1 (2000): 99–118 (quotations from 101, 104).

to individuals who were newly emboldened by the freedoms of democratization and the market economy.[21] In an age of denominational division, when theology mattered, the Book of Mormon simplified and harmonized divergent doctrines of the Bible, infusing New Testament concepts into an historical account whose narrative conventions and rhetorical patterns are more like the Deuteronomistic History than the Gospels.[22] And the prospect of biblicizing the American story by discovering the ancestry of the native Americans in ancient Israel was exhilarating to at least a few citizens of the new Republic. In short, the Book of Mormon's provenance, narrative, and theology not only supplemented the Bible, but also updated its balancing of divine sovereignty versus human agency, communal versus individual salvation, regional versus global revelation, and faith versus reason in ways that found an audience in the nineteenth century.

Given the strength of the text that anchors Mormonism, Latter-day Saints may well be forever tied to a nineteenth-century religious sensibility that is on the cusp of rational skepticism—a worldview that values education, science, and historical criticism, but which at the same time is deeply committed to the supernaturalism of angels, miracles, and prophecy, and which continues to read scripture in premodern ways (Mormons have long resisted both contemporary translations of the Bible and academic biblical scholarship). It is an open question as to whether the relationship of the Book of Mormon and the Bible holds a similar attraction nearly two hundred years later. Some may feel an increasing gap from the book's original audience. For instance, swooning conversions, militarism, the association of curses with skin color, and the virtual absence of women or family relationships aside from fathers and sons do not sit comfortably in the twenty-first century. Stories of gold plates and seer stones, as well as claims of lost civilizations and Israelite origins for Native Americans, are less persuasive in a culture that values independent scientific verification over the type of affidavits provided by the Three and Eight Witnesses. The literalism of the Book of Mormon with regard to traditions such

21. See Harry S. Stout, "Word and Order in Colonial New England" and Mark A. Noll, "The Image of the United States as a Biblical Nation, 1776–1865," both in *The Bible in America: Essays in Cultural History*, edited by Nathan O. Hatch and Mark A. Noll (New York: Oxford University Press, 1982), 19–38, 39–58; and Eran Shalev, *American Zion: The Old Testament as a Political Text from the Revolution to the Civil War* (New Haven, CT: Yale University Press, 2013).

22. Mark Noll is fond of quoting Perry Miller's 1955 observation that "the Old Testament is truly so omnipresent in the American culture of 1800 or 1820 that historians have as much difficulty taking cognizance of it as of the air the people breathed." See Mark A. Noll, *In the Beginning Was the Word: The Bible in American Public Life, 1492–1783* (New York: Oxford University Press, 2016), 19.

as the garden of Eden and the tower of Babel can also be an obstacle.[23] And yet for people who are interested in the Bible and its reception, either as literature or as scripture, purported Nephite explorations of revelation, covenants, commandments, the nature of salvation, the role of scripture, divine deliverances both physical and spiritual, exile and restoration, and the loss and recovery of sacred truths can still be of value. Whether one reads the Book of Mormon as a fantasia on biblical themes or as a new scripture sent by God to reform Christianity and convert the world, it is impossible to understand the Book of Mormon, or even to read it well, without a thorough grasp of how it is both similar to and different from the book that inspired it.

23. Whatever else he might have been, Joseph Smith was hardly a fundamentalist. For a discussion of "selective literalism" in LDS scriptural interpretation, see Philip L. Barlow, *Mormons and the Bible: The Place of the Latter-day Saints in American Religion* (New York: Oxford University Press, 1991), 32–38.

# 10

# The Biblical World in the Book of Mormon

DAVID CALABRO

The Book of Mormon occupies "the interstices of biblical narrative" by introducing a new story that takes place within the biblical world.[1] As an addition to the Bible, it is analogous to parabiblical narrative and to midrashic literature.[2] However, while parabiblical narrative generally takes as its point of departure a biblical personage, and midrash the words of the biblical text, the Book of Mormon's point of departure is the biblical world itself. This essay focuses on this setting and its contribution to the book's message.

The Book of Mormon presents two Old World horizons, which form the backdrops for the first eighteen chapters of 1 Nephi and for the first six chapters of the book of Ether.[3] The first horizon is that of ancient Israel and the Arabian Peninsula around 600 BCE. God commands a prophet named Lehi, a resident of Jerusalem during the reign of Zedekiah, to take his family and depart southward into the wilderness. Guided by miraculous means, they travel along the Red Sea coast of Arabia and across the desert eastward to a fertile coast, whence they are commanded to journey by sea to a new promised land. The

1. Christopher N. Phillips, *Epic in American Culture: Settlement to Reconstruction* (Baltimore: Johns Hopkins University Press, 2012), 69, uses the quoted phrase in reference to Milton's *Paradise Lost*, in contrast to biblical retelling in the work of the eighteenth-century American poet Thomas Brockway.

2. Some of Joseph Smith's other revelations, including his Inspired Version of the Bible and the Book of Abraham, are more straightforwardly comparable to ancient parabiblical narratives. These other revelations have also been compared with Jewish midrashic literature; see Anthony A. Hutchinson, "A Mormon Midrash? LDS Creation Narratives Reconsidered," *Dialogue* 21 (1988): 11–73; Avram R. Shannon, "Mormons and Midrash: On the Composition of Expansive Interpretation in Genesis Rabbah and the Book of Moses," *BYU Studies* 54, no. 2 (2015): 15–34.

3. These Old World origins are referenced throughout the Book of Mormon; nevertheless, the scope of the present contribution is limited to those portions of the narrative geographically set in the Old World, with reference to other portions only where especially relevant to the points being made.

second horizon is that of southern Mesopotamia in the more remote past, at the time of the confusion of tongues at the tower of Babel. The family and friends of a prophet known as the Brother of Jared are spared the confusion of tongues and are led in a mass migration across land and sea, ultimately arriving in the distant promised land centuries before Lehi and his family.



Descriptions of the setting in both 1 Nephi and Ether are limited and deal mostly with aspects that relate directly to the narrative. In general, the text eschews lengthy description, except for unusual or miraculous things, such as the "round ball of curious workmanship" whose two spindles point the way Lehi's family should travel in the wilderness (1 Nephi 16:10). Even so, the explicit descriptions that do feature in the narrative, combined with extensive reliance on the implicit, are enough to give the impression of fully developed ancient contexts.

Both the style of the English-language text of the Book of Mormon and the elements of the Old World settings as described in the book are closely related to the King James version of the Bible. The strong resemblance between the two enabled the Book of Mormon to resonate with a nineteenth-century American readership steeped in Bible-based discourse. However, just as important as the book's invocation of the familiar are the ways in which the book leads its readers into unfamiliar territory. Indeed, the book's geographical progression is paradigmatic of the conceptual work it performs as new scripture. The records of Nephi and Ether both begin in settings which receive some degree of focus in the Bible (Jerusalem and Babylon), but the bulk of the narrative takes place in locales that are scarcely mentioned in the Bible: the Arabian Peninsula in the case of 1 Nephi and undefined regions north of Mesopotamia in the case of Ether. The Book of Mormon also develops some cultural aspects beyond the information in the Bible (1 Nephi 3–4, for instance, includes details on the private life of a military commander), as well as some completely new elements (such as writing on metal plates). These nonbiblical elements contribute to the freshness of the narrative and ultimately support the book's function as a complementary witness, closely related to the Bible and yet by no means identical.

The majority of studies on the Book of Mormon's relationship to the biblical world are concerned with issues of historicity. Among these studies is a plethora of apologetic works, produced by Latter-day Saint scholars, seeking to show that the book's descriptions agree with the results of archaeology and ancient history. The thrust of these studies is that the Book of Mormon accurately portrays details that were unknown to Joseph Smith (since they could be found only in obscure sources or were not discovered until after Joseph Smith's time), and therefore the book must be a revealed ancient text.[4] However, since this approach presupposes a confessional commitment to the book's historicity, the approach does not lend itself to scholarly dialogue.

A more promising direction of inquiry, as far as the book's relationship to the biblical world is concerned, is to study the ways in which the Book of Mormon *performs* the past—how the book creates a sense of place in the past that is both coherent and, for millions of Latter-day Saints from all walks of life, believable. The Book of Mormon accomplishes this performance of the past through multiple means, including the sparing use of direct description, extensive reliance on the implicit, the use of "translation English" based on the language and style of the King James Bible, and a Christology situated in the context of prophetic revelation. An understanding of these techniques can contribute to a broader understanding of religious literature that performs the past, such as the Quran, pseudepigraphal narratives, the biblical book of Genesis, and Homeric epics.

## RETICENCE

The Book of Mormon generally lacks detailed description of common elements of the cultural and material environment. In contrast to texts that adopt a descriptive style to present realistic portrayals of the past, the Book of Mormon delivers the impression of a native account through its very brevity, by omitting details that would be obvious from an insider's standpoint. In the fifteen chapters recounting the family's journeys in the wilderness, for instance, there is not a single mention of their means of transportation. Nibley argues that the use of camels is implicit and that this detail is omitted "for the very reason that [camels] receive no notice in many an Arabic poem which describes travel in the desert, simply because they are taken for granted."[5] Whether or not Nibley is correct about camels in 1 Nephi, his point illustrates how the text's style

4. Foremost among those taking this apologetic approach is the late Hugh Nibley, whose books and articles on this subject charted a path, which many later studies have followed. Especially important are Nibley's extended essays *Lehi in the Desert*, *The World of the Jaredites*, and *There Were Jaredites* (originally published in the periodical *Improvement Era* between 1950 and 1957, the first two essays being published in book form in 1952), and his books *An Approach to the Book of Mormon* (Salt Lake City, UT: Deseret Book, 1988, first published 1957) and *Since Cumorah* (Salt Lake City, UT: Deseret Book, 1988, first published 1967). Studies following in the same vein have appeared under the auspices of the Neal A. Maxwell Institute for Religious Scholarship, formerly called the Foundation for Ancient Research and Mormon Studies. See, for example, the essays in Donald W. Parry, Daniel C. Peterson, and John W. Welch, eds., *Echoes and Evidences of the Book of Mormon* (Provo, UT: Foundation for Ancient Research and Mormon Studies, 2002).

5. Nibley, *Lehi in the Desert*, 56.

supports its self-presentation as an ancient record. Similarly, when Nephi and his brothers return to their home to retrieve precious objects to trade at the house of Laban (1 Nephi 3:22, 24), instead of going into detail about the objects, the text refers to "our gold, and our silver, and our precious things"—terms that could belong to almost any civilization. The sparing description of Ishmael's burial in 1 Nephi 16:34–35 gives us the name of the place where he was interred (Nahom) but mentions none of the rites associated with his burial.[6] The narrative of Lehi's journey does contain some detailed description, but it is reserved for exceptional things, such as Laban's ornate sword (1 Nephi 4:9) and the miraculous compass-like instrument that points the way for Lehi's family in the wilderness (1 Nephi 16:10).

These observations are even more applicable to the narrative of the Jaredite migration in the book of Ether. The brevity and lack of detail in Ether correspond to the larger scale of the migration, as well as to the greater chronological remoteness of the events. It is as if the narrator zooms out to give the reader a sense both of distance and of epic scale.[7] The third-person narrative voice of Ether, in contrast with the first-person voice of 1 Nephi, reinforces this sense of increased distance. Similarly to 1 Nephi, detailed description is reserved for miraculous things, namely the Jaredite barges built "according to the instructions of the Lord" (Ether 2:16–17), and the luminous stones placed in the barges to provide light (Ether 3:1, 4–6).

The terse descriptive style of the Book of Mormon aligns with the book's performance of the biblical world, including its use of "translation English" based on the King James Bible (on which see hereinafter). Robert Alter has called attention to the Hebrew Bible's "technique of studied reticences" in characterization. According to Alter, this technique involves heavy reliance on the implicit; further, the omission of detail is often meaningful in the narrative.[8] Similarly, the Book of Mormon relies heavily on the implicit to portray the setting, and the choice to use implicit description can carry significance. For example, references to "hunger, thirst, and fatigue" (1 Nephi 16:35) and living "upon raw meat in the wilderness" (1 Nephi 17:2) are enough to convey the impression of travel through a barren environment, even though the desert is nowhere explicitly described in the text. The mention of "hunger, thirst, and fatigue" is placed in the mouths of Ishmael's daughters as they murmur about their afflictions; this contrasts with Nephi, whose narrative does not dwell on

6. Contrast the more elaborate description of a burial in Homer's *Odyssey*, 12:9–19.
7. On the difference in scale between 1 Nephi and Ether, see Nibley, *The World of the Jaredites*, 185–58.
8. Robert Alter, *The Art of Biblical Narrative* (New York: Basic Books, 1981), 17, 114–15, 126.

the harshness of the environment. Nephi does briefly mention that his group "did travel and wade through much affliction in the wilderness," but he then immediately extols the Lord's blessings in strengthening the women while they lived on raw meat (see also 1 Nephi 17:12–13). The omission of details about the environment thus subtly underscores Nephi's piety. Therefore, the use of the implicit in the Book of Mormon follows a biblical pattern.

## CONSTRUCTION OF THE ANCIENT SETTING

Despite the text's reticence in matters of detail, references to features of the book's Old World settings are informative enough to permit analysis. The text constructs its environment through direct description and through the implicit. The features often align closely with the Bible. Some features, however, are nonbiblical. The settings which the book invokes have two important characteristics: (1) they are internally consistent, and (2) they are far removed from the culture of the Book of Mormon's earliest readers (the northeastern United States around 1830), as well as from most modern cultures. These characteristics help to provide a sense of place in the past. We can begin with the 600 BCE setting of 1 Nephi 1–18, which is more extensively developed in the text than the Mesopotamian setting of the book of Ether.[9]

### *Geography*

The Jerusalem of Lehi has walls and gates (1 Nephi 4:4–5). Laban, a military leader, has a house and a treasury within the walls of the city (1 Nephi 4:5, 20). The text consistently refers to going "up" to the city and "down" from the city to other locations (1 Nephi 3:9–10, 16, 22–23; 4:1–4). The same is true of the city of Nephi in the Book of Mormon's New World setting; in both cases, there is likely both a physical implication of the city being on high ground and an ideological implication of the city being highly revered.[10] The area outside of Jerusalem is rocky and has caves, in one of which Nephi and his brothers hide after fleeing the city (1 Nephi 1:6; 3:27). Within the framework of the narrative, Nephi is aware of certain other locations in ancient Palestine and

9. In the following overview, elements that are rare in the Hebrew Bible or nonbiblical are provided with references to the King James Bible. Common elements, however, are left without biblical references.

10. See Jeffrey R. Chadwick, "Lehi's House at Jerusalem and the Land of His Inheritance," in *Glimpses of Lehi's Jerusalem*, edited by John W. Welch, David Rolph Seely, and Jo Ann H. Seely (Provo, UT: Foundation for Ancient Research and Mormon Studies, 2004), 84–85; John L. Sorenson, *An Ancient American Setting for the Book of Mormon* (Salt Lake City, UT: Deseret Book, 1985), 23–25.

the Near East mentioned in the Bible, including "Bethabara beyond Jordan" (1 Nephi 10:9; cf. John 1:28), Nazareth (1 Nephi 11:13), the Red Sea (1 Nephi 2:5), and Babylon (1 Nephi 1:13; 10:3); beyond these, he knows vaguely of "the nations of the Gentiles" (1 Nephi 13:1–4). In their journey through the southern Levant and across Arabia, Lehi and his family encounter a valley and river, which Lehi names after his two eldest sons, and large stretches of "wilderness" in which the primary food source is meat from "wild beasts" (1 Nephi 2:4–10; 8:2; 16:9–16, 20, 30–31, 35; 17:1–2, 4). The party finally reaches a fertile shore of Arabia which they name Bountiful, where there is fruit, wild honey, a mountain, timber adequate for building a ship, and ore suitable for making tools (1 Nephi 17:5–10).



### *Material Culture*

Nephi mentions several weapons and other objects of metal, including a sword with a golden hilt and a blade of "the most precious steel" (1 Nephi 4:9), a book written on "plates of brass" (1 Nephi 4:24), and a bow of "fine steel" used in hunting (1 Nephi 16:18; cf. 2 Samuel 22:35; Job 20:24). 1 Nephi 4:19 refers to armor that one "gird[s] on . . . about [the] loins," but the material of the armor is not specified. Other than the bow and arrow, the main hunting weapon is the stone and sling (1 Nephi 16:15). There is no mention of coins, only of bartering with gold, silver, and other property (1 Nephi 3:16, 22, 24). Laban's servant possesses keys to Laban's treasury (1 Nephi 4:20). Lehi has a house and a bed, but these are not described in any detail (1 Nephi 1:7). Lehi and his family dwell in tents in the wilderness (1 Nephi 2:4, 15; 17:6). Clothing is mentioned in some places (1 Nephi 4:19; 8:5, 27; 13:7–8), but the only specific article of clothing that receives notice is the "robe" (1 Nephi 8:5). Fabrics for "exceedingly fine" and "precious" clothing include "silks, and scarlets, and fine-twined linen" (1 Nephi 8:27; 13:7–8; cf. "silk" in Proverbs 31:22; Ezekiel 16:10, 13; "fine-twined linen" in Exodus 26:1, etc.). The foods mentioned include varieties of grain and of fruit (1 Nephi 8:1). Jacob 5, a text found on the plates of brass, contains extensive discussion of olive cultivation. Meat, eaten cooked or (in extreme circumstances) raw, is mentioned only in the context of wilderness travel (1 Nephi 16:14; 17:2, 12). The only drink that receives mention is wine (1 Nephi 4:7), and the only sweetener honey (1 Nephi 17:5; 18:6).

The main writing support mentioned in both 1 Nephi and Ether is metal (1 Nephi 3:3; 9:1–5; Ether 1:2). The writing of religious narratives on metal plates is nonbiblical (although writing on bronze tablets is mentioned in

1 Maccabees 8:22; 14:18, 27, 48). In any case, this very salient feature of the Book of Mormon's ancient settings is far removed from the material culture of nineteenth-century America.



### *Institutions and Social Structure*

While the Book of Mormon mentions many prophets (1 Nephi 1:4), there are not many details about the place of prophets in society. Prophethood involves visionary experiences and challenging the political and moral status quo, which entails some danger (1 Nephi 1:18–20). Lehi's relative Laban is a military man; as Nephi mentions that Laban "can command fifty," his occupation seems to be that of the "captain of fifty" mentioned in the Hebrew Bible (1 Nephi 3:31; 2 Kings 1:9–11, 13; Isaiah 3:3). Slavery is also a feature of Lehi's world; Laban has multiple male "servants," among whom is Zoram, who eventually joins Lehi's party when Nephi promises him his freedom (1 Nephi 4:30–35). There are also "elders of the Jews" with whom Laban is out meeting late at night and getting drunk, perhaps implying some form of conspiracy among influential people in the city (1 Nephi 4:7–8, 22).

Kinship is important in Lehi's world. When Lehi discovers the genealogy of his ancestors on the plates of brass, he is overcome with joy and begins to prophesy concerning his descendants (1 Nephi 5:14–22); yet this also suggests that the tradition of genealogical knowledge in Lehi's line has been disrupted. Filial piety is compelling enough that even Lehi's rebellious sons obey his commands at great self-sacrifice, although they murmur (1 Nephi 2:4, 11; 3:5, 9; 7:2–3). Family organization is apparently patriarchal and patrilocal (note the phrase "the land of our father's inheritance," 1 Nephi 2:4; 4:16), and the right of the oldest sons to rule is assumed, although this is a troubled issue in Lehi's family (1 Nephi 16:37; 18:10; 2 Nephi 1:25, 28–29). Indeed, the prophetic gift and leadership of Nephi, the favored younger son, in opposition to his older brothers is strongly evocative of the biblical story of Joseph (Genesis 37–49).

The only woman named in Nephi's narrative is his mother, Sariah. She is also the only woman quoted in the narrative (1 Nephi 5:2, 8), except for the murmuring of the daughters of Ishmael (1 Nephi 16:34–35). Nephi's wife, however, is neither named nor quoted, even though she appears in his narrative (1 Nephi 18:19), and his sisters are hardly mentioned (2 Nephi 5:6).[11] It is

11. On the women in Nephi's narrative, see John Sorenson, "The Composition of Lehi's Family," in *By Study and also by Faith: Essays in Honor of Hugh W. Nibley*, Vol. 2, edited by John M. Lundquist and Stephen D. Ricks (Provo, UT: FARMS, 1990), 174–96; Camille Fronk, "Desert Epiphany: Sariah and the Women in 1 Nephi," *Journal of Book of Mormon Studies* 9, no. 2 (2000): 4–15, 80; Camille S. Williams, "Women in the

possible that this reflects special honor associated with motherhood in contrast to other female kin relationships.[12] In all these aspects relating to kinship, the Book of Mormon fits well with the biblical world.[13]

Although Nephi's record lacks any explicit statement about educational institutions, his statement at the beginning of his record is intriguing: "I, Nephi, having been born of goodly parents, therefore I was taught in all the learning of my father ... therefore I make a record of my proceedings in my days. Yea, I make a record in the language of my father, which consists of the learning of the Jews and the language of the Egyptians" (1 Nephi 1:1). This may imply father-son instruction or a scribal school available to elite families. Both of these scenarios might fit with the scant biblical evidence; the Book of Mormon's lack of detail again mirrors the Bible.[14]

## *Social Practices*

Upon arriving at a valley in the wilderness, Lehi builds an altar of stones, on which he makes offerings and gives thanks to the Lord on three occasions (1 Nephi 2:7; 5:9; 7:22). This is reminiscent of the biblical patriarchal narratives (Genesis 12:7–8; 13:18; 33:20; 35:7). Nephi and his brothers cast lots to determine which of them will confront Laban to ask for the plates of brass; the idiom used for the result is that the lot "fell upon" the one who should go (1 Nephi 3:11; cf. Jonah 1:7). Twice Nephi swears an oath, using the formula "As the Lord liveth, and as I/we live" (1 Nephi 3:15; 4:32). In one part of the narrative, Lehi's family intermarries with the family of one Ishmael; the initiative appears to be primarily on the part of the fathers and the young men in the two families (1 Nephi 7:1–2; 16:7–8). The marriages are described using the idiom "X took Y to wife." There is no hint of romantic courting anywhere in the text, which aligns with biblical norms against those of early nineteenth-century literature and society.[15]

---

Book of Mormon: Inclusion, Exclusion, and Interpretation," *Journal of Book of Mormon Studies* 11, no. 1 (2002): 66–79.

12. Camille S. Williams, "Women in the Book of Mormon: Inclusion, Exclusion, and Interpretation," *Journal of Book of Mormon Studies* 11, no. 1 (2002): 71–72, challenges the assumption that naming a woman in a narrative indicates "the importance of the name or the named person." Quoting can likewise be ambiguous; however, the quoting of Sariah's testimony in 1 Nephi 5:8 seems to convey respect for her words.

13. On kinship in the biblical world, see Philip J. King and Lawrence E. Stager, *Life in Biblical Israel* (Louisville, KY: Westminster John Knox Press, 2001), 36–40.

14. See James L. Crenshaw, *Education in Ancient Israel: Across the Deadening Silence* (New York: Doubleday, 1998), 85–113.

15. John Gee, "The Wrong Type of Book," in *Echoes and Evidences of the Book of Mormon*, edited by Donald W. Parry, Daniel C. Peterson, and John W. Welch (Provo, UT: FARMS, 2002), 310–12, takes this up as evidence of authenticity. The more appropriate conclusion, however, is that this contributes to a world both foreign to that of nineteenth-century America and reminiscent of the Bible.

## *Names*

Several of the personal and geographical names in 1 Nephi are biblical.[16] Some are also not found in the Bible, most of which sound Hebraic, and all of which sound exotic from a nineteenth-century American standpoint (see Table 1).

TABLE 10.1. Names in 1 Nephi

| Name | Explanation | First occurrence | Biblical parallel |
|---|---|---|---|
| **Personal names** | | | |
| Ishmael | Friend of Lehi's family | 1 Nephi 7:2 | Genesis 16:11 |
| Jacob | Nephi's younger brother | 1 Nephi 18:7 | Genesis 25:26 |
| Joseph | Nephi's younger brother | 1 Nephi 18:7 | Genesis 30:24 |
| Laban | Military leader who possesses the biblical record on the plates of brass | 1 Nephi 3:3 | Genesis 24:29 |
| Laman | Nephi's oldest brother | 1 Nephi 2:5 | — |
| Lehi | Nephi's father | 1 Nephi 1:4 | Judges 15:9, 14, 19 (geographical name) |
| Lemuel | Nephi's older brother | 1 Nephi 2:5 | Proverbs 31:1, 4 |
| Nephi | Son of Lehi, author and main protagonist of the narrative | 1 Nephi 1:1 | — |
| Sam | Nephi's older brother | 1 Nephi 2:5 | — |
| Sariah | Nephi's mother | 1 Nephi 2:5 | (Compare Sarai/Sarah, Genesis 11:29; 17:15) |
| Zoram | Servant of Laban | 1 Nephi 4:35 | — |
| **Geographical names** | | | |
| Irreantum | Name given to the sea, said to mean "many waters" | 1 Nephi 17:5 | — |
| Nahom | Place where Ishmael dies | 1 Nephi 16:34 | (Compare Nahum, Nahum 1:1) |
| Shazer | Place where Lehi's family pitches its tents | 1 Nephi 16:13–14 | — |

## *Technical Knowledge*

Being a scribe in Lehi's world apparently entails knowledge of Egyptian characters and possibly Egyptian language as well.[17] While it is clear that both Lehi

16. Names and other non-English words belonging to the New World portions of the narrative are excluded from this discussion, since their relationship to the book's Old World setting is not straightforward.

17. This detail is nonbiblical. There is substantial archaeological evidence that scribes in the kingdom of Judah learned Egyptian hieratic signs for limited purposes; however, there is no evidence that this was

and his son Nephi can read and write, there is no indication at all of the level of literacy among others in the society. Given the number of precious metal objects mentioned in Nephi's record, it is not surprising that he also reports information about metallurgy: "And it came to pass that I, Nephi, did make a bellows wherewith to blow the fire, of the skins of beasts; and after I had made a bellows, that I might have wherewith to blow the fire, I did smite two stones together that I might make fire ... And it came to pass that I did make tools of the ore which I did molten out of the rock" (1 Nephi 17:11, 16; for bellows, cf. Jeremiah 6:29). The allegory of the olive trees, attributed to a prophet Zenos whose record is found on the plates of brass (Jacob 5), contains extensive descriptions of olive tree cultivation, including grafting, digging about, pruning, dunging, long periods of "nourishing" and waiting, and gathering the fruits. The verbs for these agricultural activities connect this allegory with biblical passages such as Isaiah 5:3–6, Luke 13:6–9, and Romans 11:17–24. Many of the horticultural practices described in this chapter are unlike those of the northeastern United States, again evoking a foreign setting.[18]



### Historical Knowledge

At several points, Nephi connects the experience of his family's journey to the Exodus, either explicitly or through allusion (1 Nephi 4:2–3; 5:15; 17:4–5, 23–44; also the notion of being led to a "land of promise," 1 Nephi 2:20; 5:5; 7:13; 10:13). Other events of salvation history are invoked sporadically throughout 1 Nephi, often based on the plates of brass; these events include the creation, Adam and Eve in the garden of Eden, and Joseph in Egypt (1 Nephi 5:10–14; 7:16; 11:25; 15:22; on Joseph, see also Lehi's long quote from the brass plates in 2 Nephi 3). Lehi's conception of the garden of Eden is significantly different from the version in Genesis, including such concepts as the sweetness and bitterness of the fruit of the tree of life and of knowledge, the inability of Adam and Eve to have children until partaking of the forbidden fruit, and the identity of the serpent as a fallen angel and as the devil (2 Nephi 2:17–25). His conception includes the characteristically Christian concepts of the fall, a probationary

---

used for extended religious narratives. See Stefan Wimmer, *Palästinisches Hieratisch: Die Zahl- und Sonderzeichen in der althebräischen Schrift* (Wiesbaden, Germany: Harrassowitz, 2008); David Calabro, "The Hieratic Scribal Tradition in Preexilic Judah," in *Evolving Egypt: Innovation, Appropriation, and Reinterpretation in Ancient Egypt*, edited by Kerry Muhlestein and John Gee (Oxford, UK: Archaeopress, 2012), 77–85. See also Hugh Nibley, *Lehi in the Desert*, 13–19.

18. Arthur Wallace, "The Allegory of the Tame and Wild Olive Trees Horticulturally Considered," in *Scriptures for the Modern World*, edited by Paul R. Cheesman and C. Wilfred Griggs (Provo, UT: Religious Studies Center, 1984), 113–20.

state (although it is the period after the expulsion rather than the time in the garden that is "probationary"), and redemption through the Messiah (2 Nephi 2:21, 25–29; on the Book of Mormon's anticipation of New Testament Christology, see hereinafter).



### *Visionary Motifs*

The visions of Lehi and Nephi are full of biblical motifs: a pillar of fire (1 Nephi 1:6; Exodus 13:21–22), an angelic guide (1 Nephi 8:5–7; Ezekiel 40:3–4), a tree of life (1 Nephi 8:10–12; 11:25; Genesis 2:9), a fountain of living waters (1 Nephi 11:25; Jeremiah 2:13), cataclysmic destructions (1 Nephi 12:4; Isaiah 13:9–13), and so on.

The review of physical and cultural features up to this point applies to 1 Nephi. The first chapters of the book of Ether are sparser in detail than 1 Nephi, but they reveal enough to get a general picture. Jared and his people migrate from the location of the great tower "down into the valley which was northward," taking with them their flocks "of every kind" (Ether 2:1). This could indicate that the Jaredites are transhumance pastoralists.[19] Other than this valley, which is named Nimrod "after the mighty hunter" (Ether 2:1; compare Genesis 10:8–10), and a mount that the Jaredites name Shelem "because of its exceeding height" (Ether 3:1), the geographical features are not named. The Jaredites travel through a quarter of wilderness "where there never had man been," a wilderness clearly different from that through which Lehi's party travels, since it includes "many waters" that the Jaredites have to cross in barges (Ether 2:5–6). As in 1 Nephi, some Jaredite names are biblical, while others are not, and the nonbiblical names tend to sound ancient and exotic (see Table 2). Other than their flocks, the only indication of domesticated animals, and a major component of the Jaredites' livelihood, is apiculture (Ether 2:3). The brother of Jared melts rock to produce stones that are "white and clear, even as transparent glass" (Ether 3:1); however, in stark contrast to 1 Nephi, there is no mention at all of metal in the Old World chapters of Ether. It is not until several generations have passed in the New World that swords of "steel" are mentioned (Ether 7:9).

It is evident from this overview that the Book of Mormon's two Old World settings are different from each other, yet each is internally consistent and each is far removed from the environment of the book's earliest audience. At

19. Nibley, *The World of the Jaredites*, 185–88.

TABLE 10.2. Names in Ether 1–3

| Name | Explanation | First occurrence | Biblical parallel |
|---|---|---|---|
| Deseret | Word for "a honey bee" | Ether 2:3 | — |
| Jared | Leader of the Jaredites | Ether 1:33 | Genesis 5:15 |
| Nimrod | Valley (named "after the mighty hunter" in the Bible) | Ether 2:1 | Genesis 10:8–9 |
| Shelem | Mountain (named "because of its exceeding height") | Ether 3:1 | (Compare the personal name Shelemiah, Jeremiah 36:14) |

many points, these settings connect with the Bible, even in minute matters that might escape the notice of a casual reader. Those features that do not directly connect with the Bible are nevertheless equally distant from the culture of nineteenth-century America.

## TRANSLATION ENGLISH

Given that 1 Nephi and Ether purport to be eyewitness accounts by people within the respective settings (or in the case of Ether, a redaction of such an account), the language of each text is itself part of the construction of the ancient setting and is thus an important part of the text's performance of the past. Sidney B. Sperry has described the Book of Mormon's characteristic "translation English" style.[20] Grammatical features such as the extensive use of phrases with the genitive exponent *of* in preference to adjective-noun phrases (e.g., "mist of darkness" instead of "dark mist"), the overabundant use of the phrase "it came to pass," the extensive use of the conjunction *and*, and strung-out syntax give the impression of an ancient text in wooden translation. This is evident, for example, in the following text from 1 Nephi:

> And it came to pass that we had gathered together all manner of seeds of every kind, both of grain of every kind, and also of the seeds of fruit of every kind. And it came to pass that while my father tarried in the wilderness he spake unto us, saying: Behold, I have dreamed a dream; or, in other words, I have seen a vision. And behold, because of the thing which I have seen, I have reason to rejoice in the Lord because of Nephi

20. Sidney B. Sperry, "The Book of Mormon as Translation English," reprinted, *Journal of Book of Mormon Studies* 4, no. 1 (1995): 209–17. On the text's translation-like style, see hereinafter.

> and also of Sam; for I have reason to suppose that they, and also many of their seed, will be saved. (1 Nephi 8:1–3)



Note in this example the two occurrences of the phrase "it came to pass" and the extensive conjunctive repetition.

In these grammatical features as well as in vocabulary, the Book of Mormon draws heavily on the idiom of the King James Bible, an idiom that was firmly established in the culture of the eastern United States around 1830. This accounts for many of the features that have been described as "Hebraisms" in the Book of Mormon, including the cognate accusative "dreamed a dream" in the quote from 1 Nephi 8:1–3 (cf. Genesis 37:5, etc.).[21] Some Book of Mormon terms that appear anachronistic to modern readers may simply be adopted from the King James Old Testament, such as the words *brass* (1 Nephi 3:3; cf. Genesis 4:22; Exodus 25:3, etc., where the word translates Hebrew *nəḥōšet* "bronze"), *steel* (1 Nephi 4:9; 16:18; cf. 2 Samuel 22:35; Job 20:24, where the word translates Hebrew *nəḥûšâ*, another word for "bronze"), and *Jews* (1 Nephi 1:19–20; 2:13, etc.; cf. 2 Kings 16:6; 25:25; Jeremiah 32:12, etc., where the word translates Hebrew *yəhûdîm* "people of Judah"). Poetic portions of Nephi's narrative are also reminiscent of the parallelistic style of biblical poetry (1 Nephi 1:14; 2:9–10; 2 Nephi 4:16–35). The use of the language of the King James Bible supports the book's self-presentation as ancient scripture according to the expectations of its nineteenth-century audience. This also helps to evoke the biblical world in the imagination of a reader familiar with the Bible, so the construction of the biblical setting does not have to rely on description alone.

## HIGH CHRISTOLOGY BEFORE CHRIST

The aspect of the biblical world that is most central to the Book of Mormon's message, and perhaps most challenging to modern sensibilities, is the assertion that ancient prophets living long before the birth of Christ had a complete knowledge of the future Messiah's life according precisely with the New Testament Gospels, as well as a developed Christology anticipating Johannine and Pauline doctrines. Lehi, Nephi, and the Brother of Jared learn of the Messiah through direct revelation (1 Nephi 1:9–10, 19; 10:4–11, 17; 11:6–7, 13–36; Ether 3:9, 13–16). The prophets teach this knowledge to their contemporaries as if

21. The literature on Hebraisms in the Book of Mormon is extensive; for a useful overview, see Donald W. Parry's article "Hebraisms and Other Peculiarities," in *Echoes and Evidences of the Book of Mormon*, 155–89.

it is new—or in the case of the Brother of Jared, are commanded to seal it up for future generations. Along with this revelation, the prophets learn that all previous prophets knew and prophesied of the Messiah (1 Nephi 10:5; 19:8–23; 22:20–21; 2 Nephi 11:2–4, 6–7; 25:12–30; 31:2–21; Jacob 4:4–5; 7:10–11). The Book of Mormon thus invokes a historical paradigm in which the Christ of the New Testament is unambiguously known in the ancient world of the Hebrew Bible, a paradigm that fulfills Christian expectations based ultimately on the New Testament itself (Matthew 22:42–45; John 5:39–47; 8:56; Acts 3:24; Romans 1:1–6; 1 Peter 1:10–12).

Latter-day Saint scholars have addressed this aspect of the religious worldview of the Book of Mormon in different ways. Daniel Peterson argues that the revelation to Nephi may be brought into line with ancient Canaanite religious motifs; thus Book of Mormon Christology could be not so different from received knowledge of the pre-exilic biblical world.[22] Teachings about Christ in the earlier portions of the Book of Mormon could also be regarded as later interpolations.[23]

However, the Christological portions of these earlier chapters are part of the book's performance of the past, and theories that minimize their stark nature do nothing to explain the book's power for believers in the text as ancient scripture. In fact, the starkness of the Christological portions against the backdrop of the book's ancient settings is crucial. Readers of the Book of Mormon are introduced to unfamiliar worlds long before the birth of Christ and find there something familiar: testimonies of the birth, ministry, crucifixion, and resurrection of Jesus Christ.[24]

In view of the fact that the Book of Mormon presents itself as a complement to the Bible (2 Nephi 3:12; 29:7–14; Mormon 7:8–10), the developed Christology of the Book of Mormon can also be seen as a reconciliation of Hebrew Bible and New Testament theology. According to the Book of Mormon, the Hebrew Bible itself once contained "the fulness of the gospel of the Lord" but was modified by hostile hands during the time of the Apostles (1 Nephi 13:20–29). The Book of Mormon restores some of these "plain and precious things" (1 Nephi 13:34–41), thus establishing a three-part scriptural canon (the re-envisioned Hebrew Bible, the New Testament, and the Book of Mormon) that is consistent

22. Daniel C. Peterson, "Nephi and His Asherah," *Journal of Book of Mormon Studies* 9, no. 2 (2000): 16–25, 80–81.

23. David Rolph Seely, "'We Believe the Bible to Be the Word of God as Far as It Is Translated Correctly': Latter-day Saints and Historical Biblical Criticism," *Studies in the Bible and Antiquity* 8 (2016): 81–85.

24. Terryl L. Givens, "Joseph Smith's American Bible: Radicalizing the Familiar," *Journal of Book of Mormon Studies* 18, no. 2 (2009): 10–12.

in its witness of Christ. Scriptures that Joseph Smith produced subsequent to the Book of Mormon, including the Inspired Version of the Bible, the Book of Abraham, and the Doctrine and Covenants, continued this program of attributing a fully developed Christology to the ancient prophets. This ultimately creates a radical image not only of the prophets, but also of the Hebrew Bible as a background to the New Testament. This would imply, for instance, that those who knew the scriptures during Jesus' ministry had access to very clear prophecies about him, so the reception of Jesus as the Messiah was not based solely on esoteric interpretation.

## CONCLUSION

The ways in which the Book of Mormon performs the past contribute to dialogue on revealed pasts in religious texts, in line with a focus on the Book of Mormon as world scripture.[25] In this respect, the Book of Mormon bears comparison with the Quran, the book of Jubilees, the biblical book of Genesis, Greek epics, and so on. How the Book of Mormon's performance of the past compares with these other texts remains to be fully studied, but some initial thoughts may be offered here, concluding the analysis by way of comparison.

The Book of Mormon establishes as its settings essentially realistic ancient worlds that interlock with the Bible on many levels: the use of reticence, the specific details of the setting, and the King James English style and vocabulary. The realistic elements of the setting function as a backdrop for the miraculous elements, such as the compass-like ball or director and especially the highly developed Christology, elements that appear in stark contrast to the otherwise realistic Old Testament-like setting. On one hand, this differs from books like 1 Enoch, in which miraculous elements pervade the setting, such that the performance of the past becomes a creation of mythic space. On the other hand, it also contrasts with performances of the past that tend to minimize the cultural distance between the contemporary world and the ancient setting, such as the story of Joseph as recounted in the Quran.[26]

The Book of Mormon's essentially realistic portrayal of the biblical world suggests a possible comparison with fiction set in the biblical world (one classic example being Lew Wallace's 1880 novel *Ben-Hur: A Tale of the Christ*), and

25. Grant Hardy, "Introduction," in *The Book of Mormon: The Earliest Text*, edited by Royal Skousen (New Haven, CT: Yale University Press, 2009), vii–viii, xxv–xxviii.

26. In this account, Joseph wears a shirt (*qamīṣ*) and is sold for a handful of dirhams; instead of traveling with donkeys as in the biblical account, his brothers use camels (Quran 12:18, 20, 25–29, 65, 70, 72).

more broadly with world-building in fiction. While a characterization of the Book of Mormon as fiction would run contrary to the book's claim of being authentic ancient scripture, the comparison is nevertheless informative; the Book of Mormon shares with fiction novels the need to convey its setting through textual description.[27] From this standpoint, the Book of Mormon is notable for its Bible-like reticence and its use of "translation English," which support the book's claim regarding its origins. These features set the Book of Mormon apart from at least the majority of modern fiction. In short, the Book of Mormon's setting is constructed in such a way that believers can easily understand the book as a companion to the Bible.



27. Wolf describes a continuum of literary genres employing different degrees of creativity in world-building, from autobiography to modern fantasy and science fiction. See Mark J.P. Wolf, *Building Imaginary Worlds: The Theory and History of Subcreation* (New York: Routledge, 2012), 28; on the Bible specifically, see 191.

11

# The Bible in the Pearl of Great Price

BRIAN M. HAUGLID

In 1851, twenty-one years after the Book of Mormon first appeared in print (1830), Franklin D. Richards, a Mormon apostle supervising missionary activities in England, compiled and published a miscellaneous collection of Joseph Smith's revelations for Mormon members in England.[1] Richards titled this collection the Pearl of Great Price (PGP) based on Jesus's parable in Matthew 13:45–46 in which "the kingdom of heaven is like unto a merchant man, seeking goodly pearls: Who, when he had found one pearl of great price, went and sold all that he had, and bought it" (KJV). In 1878, Orson Pratt revised the 1851 edition and produced the first American edition of the PGP, which was canonized in October 1880.[2] Its canonization marks the first occurrence of adding a new book of scripture to the Mormon canon in the post-Joseph Smith period (1805–1844).

Although the PGP has been somewhat overlooked because of its more popular predecessor, the Book of Mormon, it has also become beloved by many Mormons because it contains unique contributions to Mormon doctrines such as Enoch's account of the building of a utopian community (Zion), the nature of God, the eternal nature of existence, a covenantal priesthood, premortality, foreordination, two variant creation accounts, as well as three enigmatic vignettes. At present, the PGP (1981 ed.) contains the Book of Moses, which Smith produced between 1830 and 1831 while engaged in his "New Translation"



1. Terryl Givens with Brian M. Hauglid, *The Pearl of Greatest Price: Mormonism's Most Controversial Scripture* (Oxford, UK: Oxford University Press, 2019), 1–26. See also H. Donl Peterson, *The Pearl of Great Price: A History and Commentary* (Salt Lake City, UT: Deseret Book, 1987), 6–15.

2. Givens, *The Pearl of Greatest Price*, 21–2. In preparing the 1878 American edition of the PGP, Pratt removed outdated or duplicate materials (Peterson, *The Pearl of Great Price*, 21–23).

project;[3] the Book of Abraham, translated after Smith purchased four mummies and several rolls of papyri in 1835;[4] Joseph Smith-Matthew (JS-M), an expansion of Matthew 24, another product of Smith's "New Translation" project; Joseph Smith-History (JS-H), an 1838 autobiographical account of Smith's first visionary experiences that led to his acquisition and translation of the Book of Mormon; and the Articles of Faith (AoF), a list of thirteen creedal statements of belief Smith wrote in a letter to a Chicago newspaper editor.[5] To the faithful, these are clear evidences of Smith's divine, prophetic mission.

Yet, one text in the PGP, the Book of Abraham, has received severe criticism primarily due to the fact that Smith never overtly detailed his process of translating the Book of Abraham, thus leaving open many questions surrounding its origins. From the historical record and surviving physical evidence, we know that Smith purchased four Egyptian mummies and several rolls of papyrus in early July 1835. After his initial inspection, Smith declared that Abraham's writings were contained on one of the rolls and the writings of Joseph Egypt on another.[6] From there the historical record and manuscript evidence shows that Smith translated the first part of the Book of Abraham during the second half of 1835 and the rest of what we have in early 1842.[7] At the same time Smith was translating the Book of Abraham in 1835 he and his scribes also created a corpus of miscellaneous Egyptian alphabet and grammar materials (see more on these materials hereinafter). Though these documents were not related to the actual Egyptian language, they were related to certain parts of the Book of Abraham.[8]

3. See Grant Underwood, "Joseph Smith's 'New Translation' of the Bible," in this volume. Givens, *Pearl of Greatest Price*, 27–108. Kent P. Jackson, *The Book of Moses and the Joseph Smith Translation Manuscripts* (Provo, UT: Religious Studies Center, BYU, 2005).

4. Givens, *The Pearl of Greatest Price*, 109–222. H. Donl Peterson, *The Story of the Book of Abraham: Mummies, Manuscripts, and Mormonism* (Salt Lake City, UT: Deseret Book, 1995).

5. For a historical review of Matthew 24, see Givens, *The Pearl of Greatest Price*, 60–67. For the Joseph Smith-History see Givens, *The Pearl of Greatest Price*, 223–40. For the Articles of Faith see Givens, *The Pearl of Greatest Price*, 241–70. See also Peterson, *The Pearl of Great Price*, 6–65.

6. Joseph Smith, History, 1838–1856, 6 July 1835, vol. B-1, 596, accessible in the *Histories* series of the online edition of the *Joseph Smith Papers*, www.josephsmithpapers.org.

7. *The Joseph Smith Papers, Revelations and Translations, vol. 4, The Book of Abraham and Related Manuscripts*, edited by Robin Scott Jensen and Brian M. Hauglid (Salt Lake City, UT: Church Historians Press, 2018), xxvi–xxviii.

8. See Brian M. Hauglid, "'Translating an Alphabet to the Book of Abraham' Joseph Smith's Study of the Egyptian Language and His Translation of the Book of Abraham," in *Producing Ancient Scripture: Joseph Smith's Translation Projects in the Development of Mormon Christianity*, edited by Michael Hubbard MacKay, Mark Ashurst-McGee, and Brian M. Hauglid (Salt Lake City: University of Utah Press, 2020), 363–89.

Criticisms against the Book of Abraham began to arise not long after the text was published in 1842. These were leveled specifically at three Egyptian illustrations (Facsimiles 1, 2, and 3 respectively) copied from the original papyri. Smith published these illustrations as part of the Book of Abraham and he provided his own interpretations of the figures and some of the hieroglyphs. However, as the Egyptian language began to be understood during the second half of the nineteenth century, scholars could see that Smith's interpretations did not match their understanding of the language or the illustrations.[9] More fuel was added to the controversy in 1967 when the New York Metropolitan of Art returned about a dozen papyri fragments that once belonged to Joseph Smith to the Church of Jesus Christ of Latter-day Saints. Characters from one of the fragments matched the characters in the left margin of three 1835 Abraham manuscripts with paragraphs from the Abraham narrative juxtaposed to the right of the character. When Egyptologists deciphered the characters on the fragment it was quickly determined that the Abraham text did not at all correspond to the Egyptian characters but was instead a common Egyptian funerary document. Since 1967, many books and articles from both critics and Mormon defenders have engaged in a banter that ranges from friendly to hostile.[10]

As far as Mormon scholarship related to the PGP, scholars have focused on studying it historically, doctrinally, and devotionally in commentaries[11] and apologia;[12] with fewer published materials on theological,[13] literary, or

9. For a more detailed discussion of the controversy with the three facsimiles, see Givens, *The Pearl of Greatest Price,* 142–53.

10. For a sampling, see Klaus Baer, "The Breathing Permit of Hôr: A Translation of the Apparent Source of the Book of Abraham," *Dialogue: A Journal of Mormon Thought* 3, no. 3 (1968): 109–34; Edward H. Ashment, "Reducing Dissonance: The Book of Abraham as a Case Study," in *The Word of God: Essays on Mormon Scripture*, edited by Dan Vogel (Salt Lake City, UT: Signature Books, 1990), 221–35; Robert K. Ritner, "The 'Breathing Permit of Hôr' Thirty Four Years Later," *Dialogue: A Journal of Mormon Thought* 33, no. 4 (2000): 97–119. For responses to these criticisms see John Gee, *An Introduction to the Book of Abraham* (Salt Lake City, UT: Deseret Book, 2017), 26–33; Kerry Muhlestein, "The Explanation-Defying Book of Abraham," in *A Reason for Faith: Navigating LDS Doctrine & Church History*, edited by Laura Harris Hales (Provo, UT: Religious Studies Center, BYU, 2016), 79–91.

11. A few examples include James R. Clark, *The Story of the Pearl of Great Price* (Salt Lake City, UT: Bookcraft, 1955). George Reynolds and Janne M. Sjodahl, *Commentary on the Pearl of Great Price* (Salt Lake City, UT: Deseret Book, 1980); Peterson, *The Pearl of Great Price: A History and Commentary:* Richard D. Draper, S. Kent Brown, and Michael D. Rhodes, *The Pearl of Great Price: A Verse-by-Verse Commentary* (Salt Lake City, UT: Deseret Book, 2005).

12. For critical sources see Edward H. Ashment, "Reducing Dissonance," 221–35; Robert K. Ritner, *The Joseph Smith Egyptian Papyri: A Complete Edition* (Salt Lake City, UT: Smith-Pettit Foundation, 2011). For apologetic sources see Hugh Nibley, *An Approach to the Book of Abraham*, Collected Works of Hugh Nibley 19 (Salt Lake City, UT: Deseret Book and Neal A. Maxwell Institute for Religious Scholarship, 2009); John Gee, *A Guide to the Joseph Smith Papyri* (Provo, UT: Foundation for Ancient Research and Mormon Studies, BYU, 2000); Kerry Muhlestein and John Gee, "An Egyptian Context for the Sacrifice of Abraham," *Journal of the Book of Mormon and Other Restoration Scripture* 20, no. 2 (2011): 70–77. Muhlestein, "The Explanation-Defying Book of Abraham," 79–91.

13. Terryl L. Givens and Fiona Givens, *The God Who Weeps* (Salt Lake City, UT: Ensign Peak, 2012).

intertextual subjects.[14] Interestingly, PGP commentaries and apologetics have tended to focus on PGP distinctness from the Bible (or even a corrective to the Bible) while theological, literary, and intertextual studies have leaned toward showing a more holistic relationship between the PGP and the Bible. Thus, a significant question addressed here concerns how Smith's views of the Bible may have helped shape these revelatory texts in both their direct and subtle interactions with the Bible. And by extension, how PGP and biblical interplay in Smith's scriptural revelations led to his Egyptian project that many read as being concerned with recapturing the pure Adamic language and later how Smith's biblical views influenced the development of priesthood and temple endowment, especially as evidenced within the books of Moses and Abraham. Finally, this essay will briefly examine the insertion and elaboration of the biblical Hamitic/black curse in the PGP (particularly in the books of Moses and Abraham), which became justification for a nineteenth-century priesthood/temple ban for Black Mormon women and men.



## DIRECT AND SUBTLE INTERACTIONS WITH THE BIBLE

From a textual, historical perspective, Joseph Smith's views of the Bible played a prominent role in his creation of these texts. We see in the PGP a high reliance on biblical materials that look much like Smith's 1833–1835 work on the Bible, something akin to a Midrashic commentary (e.g., Moses 2-4).[15] But, at the same time, we occasionally find whole chapters that are not found in the Bible at all (e.g., Moses 1; Abraham 1). According to Seth Perry, over the course of his translation pursuits Smith developed the ability "to synthesize, compile, rearrange, allude to, and play with biblical texts" as an integral part of his revelatory process, whether consciously or unconsciously.[16]

In terms of the creation account, Smith imported the two version of the creation in Genesis 1–3 (sources J and P)[17] into the Moses and Abraham creation accounts, recasting one as a spiritual creation and the other as a temporal creation. One source-critical scholar has identified that Genesis 1:1–2:4a (P) "is an ancient Israelite story about the creation of the world, while 2:4b–3:24

14. Nicholas J. Frederick, *The Bible, Mormon Scripture, and the Rhetoric of Allusivity* (Madison, NJ: Fairleigh Dickinson University Press, 2016); Kathleen Flake, "Translating Time: The Nature and Function of Joseph Smith's Narrative Canon," *Journal of Religion* 87, no. 4 (2007): 497–527.

15. Anthony A. Hutchinson, "A Mormon Midrash? LDS Creation Narratives Reconsidered," *Dialogue: A Journal of Mormon Thought* 21, no. 4 (Winter 1988): 11–74.

16. Seth Perry, "The Many Bibles of Joseph Smith: Textual, Prophetic, and Scholarly Authority in Early-National Bible Culture," *Journal of the American Academy of Religion* 84, no. 3 (September 2016): 752.

17. Marc Zvi Brettler, *How to Read the Bible* (Philadelphia: Jewish Publication Society, 2005), 34–35.

(J) is a different story, by a different Israelite author with different ideas, and its focus is the creation of humankind."[18] These two stories also appear, albeit with variant revisions, in the Moses 2:1–3:4a and 3:4b–4:31; and the Abraham 4:1–5:4a and 5:4b–21 (Abraham 5:21; Genesis 2:20), at which point the Abraham account ends. Smith's new versions of Genesis creation account are not just repackaging, but express his desire to resolve problems in these texts. According to David Bokovoy, "his revelations provide order to biblical chaos, as he adds to and develops earlier religious constructs. Joseph's own pseudepigraphic books of Abraham and Moses can be seen as a crucial part of this process."[19]

Thus, Smith's narrations in the Book of Moses, the Book of Abraham, and JS-Matthew exhibit both a corrective impulse for the biblical narrative as well as a reimagining of the biblical account in expansive and novel ways. Indeed, this reimagining likely stemmed from Smith's notion of restoring lost text and reinterpreting the narrative to create new meanings in distinctly fresh religious contexts. In the Book of Moses, for example, the biblical notion of Zion as Jerusalem (including its people)[20] emerges in the Enoch narrative in an expanded and newly contextualized form, giving rise to an impassioned desire among Mormons in the Missouri period to gather together as a holy community in preparation for the Second Coming of Christ.[21]

In addition to the many direct and subtle interactions with the Bible, the PGP signals significant theological developments in Smith's thinking about pure language, priesthood, and the temple theology.

## THE BIBLE, PURE LANGUAGE, PRIESTHOOD, AND THE TEMPLE ENDOWMENT

Immersed in the biblical culture of his day, Smith's "language and thought patterns had been colored by" the Bible, so "when Deity did come, Smith heard him speak in both biblical and Bible-like language," in Philip Barlow's analysis.[22] Yet Smith struggled to put prose to the revelations, lamenting, "Oh Lord God deliver us in thy due time from the little narrow prison almost as it

18. Brettler, *How to Read the Bible*, 33.

19. David Bokovoy, *Authoring the Old Testament: Genesis to Deuteronomy* (Draper, UT: Greg Kofford Books, 2014), 171.

20. Cf. James Wood, *A Dictionary of the Holy Bible* (Liverpool, UK: J. Nuttall, 1804), 600.

21. Cf. Moses 7:18–21, 62–63. Kathleen Flake examines how early Mormons viewed themselves as new Israelites for whom Zion becomes at once an ever-present reality. Cf. Flake, "Translating Time."

22. Philip L. Barlow, *Mormons and the Bible: The Place of the Latter-day Saints in American Religion*, rev. ed. (New York: Oxford University Press, 2013), 15.

were totel [*sic*] darkness of paper pen and ink and a crooked broken scattered and imperfect language."[23] To compensate for this, Smith may have employed the pseudo-biblical language used in many political and secular texts of his day, which has been described as an "ontologically privileged language" for lending "authority and legitimacy in public discourse."[24]



Advancing the argument that the Bible had an enormous influence on the language of Smith's textual revelations may seem rather straightforward, but when analyzing his larger narratives (Moses and Abraham), it becomes clearer that Smith's revelations show a reimagining of what the biblical text looked like in its original state, not just in terms of content, but in terms of its language as well. Significantly, the Book of Mormon itself states that "many plain and precious things" had been taken from the Bible or were lost.[25] In Smith's view, the original, pure language of the Bible had become corrupted. This may have generated in Smith an intense passion for studying ancient languages, especially Hebrew and Egyptian, probably going all the way back to 1829, when he reported that "reformed Egyptian" was the primary language in the Book of Mormon.[26] Even later, in 1836, Smith's language interests led him to create a formal Hebrew class in which a Jewish teacher instructed him and others in reading the book of Genesis in Hebrew.[27]

Among Smith's early interest in ancient languages and his search for an "original," he imagined what the original language spoken by Adam and Eve may have been. Notably, in late fall 1830, John Whitmer scribed Moses 5:43–6:18, which introduced the concept of a "language which was pure and undefiled" that Adam and Eve used for speaking and teaching their children to read and write.[28] Here, Smith's concern for ancient languages seems to have

23. To W.W. Phelps 27 November 1832 in *Joseph Smith Papers* D2: 320.

24. Eran Shalev, "'Written in the Style of Antiquity': Pseudo-Biblicism and the Early American Republic, 1770–1830," *Church History* 79, no. 4 (2010): 801.

25. 1 Nephi 13:28. The "plain and precious" parts are also promised to be restored (1 Nephi 13:40).

26. Mormon 9:32. Smith's interest in Hebrew led to a formal study of the Hebrew language in early 1836. Cf. Matthew J. Grey, "'The Word of the Lord in the Original': Joseph Smith's Study of Hebrew in Kirtland," in *Approaching Antiquity: Joseph Smith and the Ancient World,* edited by Lincoln H. Blumell, Matthew J. Grey, and Andrew H. Hedges (Provo, UT: Religious Studies Center, BYU, 2015), 249–302. However, Joseph Smith could not take any formal training in Egyptian since the teaching of Egyptian would be many years after Smith's death.

27. Kevin Barney, "Joseph Smith's Emendation of Hebrew Genesis 1:1," *Dialogue: A Journal of Mormon Thought* 30, no. 4 (Winter 1997): 103–35. Louis C. Zucker, "Joseph Smith as a Student of Hebrew," *Dialogue: A Journal of Mormon Thought* 3, no. 2 (Summer 1968): 41–55; D. Kelly Ogden, "The Kirtland Hebrew School (1835–1836)," in *Regional Studies in Latter-Day Saint History: Ohio,* edited by Milton V. Backman Jr. (Provo, UT: Department of Church History and Doctrine, BYU, 1990).

28. Moses 6:5–6.

further evolved to include the notion of a pure Adamic language that was in the beginning of the world and "shall be in the end of the world also."[29]

This reference to a pure language proved to be a novel idea within the body of Smith's textual work and prompted a flurry of discussions that ultimately built an evolving theology around the notion. The main idea centered on a pristine, pure language that existed in the time of Adam but was corrupted at the tower of Babel.[30] This notion of a corrupted language (via the tower of Babel) was not new to the early nineteenth century,[31] but Smith refocused on a restoration of the pure language in an eschatological context broadly based on Zephaniah 3:9, "For then I will turn to the people a pure language, that they may all call upon the name of the LORD, to serve him with one consent."[32] Smith taught that this verse points to the pure language of Adam that would return at the end of the world ushering in a thousand-year millennium.[33] Early on, Smith and others believed the pure language to be biblical Hebrew. In 1832, just four years before the Kirtland Hebrew School, it was thought "the Hebrew, in which they [i.e., poets of sacred poetry] wrote, was nearer the pure language, with which Adam gave names, than any other since used by man."[34]

For Smith, language was important because it was connected to power. Interestingly, Smith's 1830 revelation on the pure language in Moses 6:6–7 also becomes associated with the power of the priesthood: "And by them [scriptures] their children were taught to read and write, having a language which was pure and undefiled. Now this same Priesthood, which was in the beginning, shall be in the end of the world also." Later in the Enoch account we find that "so great was the faith of Enoch that … he spake the word of the Lord, and the earth trembled, and the mountains fled … so powerful was the word

29. Moses 6: 6–7.

30. March–June 1833 saw a concentration of articles mentioning the tower of Babel. Cf. *The Evening and the Morning Star*, "Reflections," 1, no. 10 (March 1833), 75; "Lamentable Facts," 1, no. 11 (April 1833), 85; "Children," 1, no. 12 (May 1833), 94; "All Flesh" and "Great Events," 1, no. 13 (June 1833), 102.

31. Samuel Morris Brown, "Joseph (Smith) in Egypt: Babel, Hieroglyphs, and the Pure Language of Eden," *Church History* 78, no. 1 (March 2009): 36–40.

32. Instances when Zephaniah 3:9 is cited or paraphrased in early church periodicals. *Evening and the Morning Star*, "Writing Letters," 1, no. 4 (September 1832), 25; "Sacred Poetry," 1, no. 6 (November 1832), 45; "To the Patrons of the Evening and the Morning Star," 2, no. 15 (December 1833), 113; "The Prophecy of Zephaniah," 2, no. 18 (March 1834), 141–42; *Latter-day Saints' Messenger and Advocate*, "Dear Friends and Neighbors," 1, no. 4 (January 1834), 60; "The Indians," 2, no. 4 (January 1836), 245; *Times and Seasons*, "The Millennium," 3, no. 8 (February 15, 1842), 688–89; "To the Editor of the Times and Seasons," 3, no. 21 (September 1, 1842), 907; "History of Joseph Smith," 5, no. 19 (October 15, 1844), 672 (extracted from *Evening and the Morning Star* September 1832).

33. Samuel Morris Brown, *In Heaven as It Is on Earth: Joseph Smith and the Early Mormon Conquest of Death* (New York: Oxford University Press, 2012), 139.

34. *The Evening and the Morning Star*, "Sacred Poetry," 1, no. 6 (November 1832), 45.

of Enoch, and so great was the power of the language which God had given him" (Moses 7:13). Thus, in this pericope, the power of the language and the power of the priesthood appear to be one and the same thing.

The quest for the pure language continued to influence Smith's prophetic activity. Later, in March 1832, Smith produced a document titled, "A Sample of pure language given by Joseph the Seer," recorded in the recently discovered *Kirtland Revelation Book*, in which Adamic terms from the pure language for God, Christ, and angels were given English meanings.[35] About three years later (May 1835), on the back of a letter written to his wife Sally, W.W. Phelps included what he titled, "a specimen of some of the 'pure language,'" using the same pure language terms and meanings found on the "Sample,"[36] but newly incorporated into vertical columns with the apparent function of a lexical aid.



Transitioning from Hebrew, to an unknown script, and then to Egyptian, Smith's efforts to discover the pure language shaped the Book of Abraham as well. After Smith acquired four Egyptian mummies and several papyri rolls in late June or early July 1835, he and several others built on their previous pure language work by pursuing an Egyptian language project[37] assuming, like many in antebellum America, that the ancient Hebrew and Egyptian languages were closely related and a gateway for recovering the pure language of Adam.[38] This Egyptian project was a serious, albeit naïve, heuristic study that appears to have been instrumental in producing at least portions of two non-biblical chapters in the Book of Abraham (i.e., Chapters 1 and 3).[39] Further, the Egyptian project produced a number of manuscripts that appear to follow the lexical format Phelps had put in his 1835 letter to Sally noted previously.

35. Robin Scott Jensen, Robert J. Woodford, and Steven C. Harper, eds., *Manuscript Revelation Books*, facsimile edition, first volume of the Revelations and Translations series of *The Joseph Smith Papers*, edited by Dean C. Jessee, Ronald K. Esplin, and Richard Lyman Bushman (Salt Lake City, UT: Church Historian's Press, 2009), 264–65. A few pure-language words made their way into two revelations contained in the Doctrine and Covenants; see D&C 78:20 and 95:17.

36. MSS 810 Box 2, folder 1 is in the Church History Library, Salt Lake City, Utah.

37. Brian M Hauglid, "The Book of Abraham and the Egyptian Project: 'A Knowledge of Hidden Languages,'" in *Approaching Antiquity: Joseph Smith and the Ancient World*, edited by Lincoln H. Blumell, Matthew J. Grey, and Andrew H. Hedges (Provo, UT: Religious Studies Center, BYU, 2015), 476.

38. For the view that Hebrew and Egyptian were intimately related, see J.G.H. Greppo, *Essay on the Hieroglyphic System of M. Champollion, Jun. and the Advantages Which It Offers to Sacred Criticism* (Boston: Perkins and Marvin, 1830), 66–82. Samuel Morris Brown, "Joseph (Smith) in Egypt: Babel, Hieroglyphs, and the Pure Language of Eden," *Church History* 78, no. 1 (2009): 26–65. Brown, *In Heaven as It Is on Earth*, 135–37. See also Matthew J. Grey, "'The Word of the Lord in the Original': Joseph Smith's Study of Hebrew in Kirtland," in *Approaching Antiquity*, 249–302.

39. Christopher C. Smith, "The Dependence of Abraham 1:1–3 on the Egyptian Alphabet and Grammar," *John Whitmer Historical Association Journal* 29 (2009): 38–54.

Smith's 1835 Egyptian documents contain potent connections to the Bible in both their pseudo-biblical prose and their dealings with biblical figures, most notably Noah, Ham, and Abraham. Yet non-biblical figures such as Pharaoh (pre-Abrahamic and Abrahamic), Egyptus, Katumin, and Onitas, also show up in these manuscripts and go well beyond the biblical Abrahamic narrative. These new characters in the Book of Abraham address new narratives and concerns (i.e., the near sacrifice of Abraham, the founding of Egypt, and priesthood restriction to the descendants of Ham, etc.).[40]

Smith's later theological reflections on the patriarchal period are also connected to the Book of Abraham. While some of the Book of Abraham dates to the 1835–1836 context, evidence also seems to suggest that Smith produced material in the Book of Abraham while in Nauvoo, Illinois, in early 1842 (Abraham 2:19–5:21).[41] Abraham 1 and 3 incorporate priesthood, masonry, and temple theology, new developments in the Nauvoo context. For instance, Smith's interest in recapturing the original biblical text and the purity and power of language/priesthood presaged his ultimate aim in reinstituting what he viewed as the ancient temple "endowment," which Smith believed also originated in the time of Adam.[42] Smith's Nauvoo-era temple endowment is directly related to the Book of Abraham.[43] Indeed, two months after the second installment of the Book of Abraham (Abraham 2:19–5:21) was published in the *Times and Seasons* on 15 March 1842, Smith introduced a more elaborate form of the temple endowment.[44] To make this even more interesting, on the same day

40. If these Egyptian materials were produced after the current narrative of the Book of Abraham had already originated, as some argue, then the Egyptian manuscripts would be of little or no significance to the origins of the Abrahamic narrative. Among them is John Gee, *A Guide to the Joseph Smith Papyri*, 4–5. Cf. also Kerry Muhlestein and Megan Hansen, "The Work of Translating: The Book of Abraham's Translation Chronology," in *Let Us Reason Together: Essays in Honor of the Life's Work of Robert L. Millet*, edited by J. Spencer Fluhman and Brent L. Top (Provo, UT: Religious Studies Center and the Neal A. Maxwell Institute for Religious Scholarship at BYU, 2016), 139–62. However, if the Egyptian documents were produced prior to, concurrently, or even after the Abraham text, new dimensions of Smith's translation process could be addressed and a space for both human and divine interaction under the rubric of translation could be posited. Hauglid, "The Book of Abraham and the Egyptian Project: 'A Knowledge of Hidden Languages.'"

41. Two translation sessions (which produced Abr 2:19–5:21) are recorded in Smith's journal for March 8–9, specifically designated for the tenth number of the *Times and Seasons*. *JSP* J2: 42. See also Brian M Hauglid, "The Book of Abraham and Translating the Sacred," *BYU Religious Education Review* 10, no. 1 (Winter 2017): 13. For more discussion relating to translation activity in 1842, see note 7 above..

42. According to the Book of Moses, "all things were confirmed unto Adam, by an holy ordinance" (Moses 5:59), which may refer to the temple.

43. Cf. Facsimile 2, Figure 3 ("Key-words of the Holy Priesthood"); Figure 7 (note vignette and "Key-words of the Priesthood); Figure 8 ("Contains writings that cannot be revealed unto the world; but is to be had in the Holy Temple of God").

44. *JSP* J2:53–54 (entry on 4 May 1842).

(March 15), Smith and Sidney Rigdon "were initiated as Entered Apprentice Masons."[45] All this is to say that Smith seemed intent on recovering what he saw as taking place in the ancient biblical world in terms of priesthood, masonry, and ultimately, temple theology.[46]

## BIBLICAL AND PGP RACIAL ISSUES IN THE MODERN PERIOD

For over a century and a half, the PGP has held an uneasy relationship with subsequent prophetic leadership in an ever-changing theological landscape. A good example of this emerges when considering Mormon racial theology wherein early church leaders relied on the Bible, the Book of Moses, and the Book of Abraham (especially) to advocate the curse of Ham as theological justification for banning the priesthood to Black Mormon males and, which also consequently banned temple ordinance for Black women and men.[47] The most explicit verse in the Book of Abraham, to justify this ban, declares that Pharaoh, of the lineage of Ham, was "cursed . . . as pertaining to the priesthood" (Abraham 1:26), which, of course, also connects the overwrought Hamitic/black curse so prevalent in the nineteenth century that was used to justify slavery in America.[48]

It seems clear that although Brigham Young may have officially implemented the priesthood ban in the 1850s, and Joseph Smith may have ordained several men of African descent, it was also Smith who should be credited with receiving a revelation in the Book of Abraham that created justification for the

45. *JSP* J2:45, note 158.

46. On the Nauvoo "Abrahamic Project" that brings all these aspects together see Benjamin E. Park, *Kingdom of Nauvoo: The Rise and Fall of a Religious Empire on the American Frontier*, (New York: Liveright Publishing Corporation, 2020), 104–18.

47. Moses 7:8, 21; Abraham 1:21–22, 24, 26. Orson Hyde, *Speech of Elder Orson Hyde* (Liverpool, UK: James and Woodburn, 1845), 30. Parley P. Pratt, General Minutes, April 25, 1847, Brigham Young Papers, CHL. First Presidency Minutes of 1900 and 1912 also refer to the Book of Abraham as justification for the priesthood ban. August 18, 1900; Journal History; First Presidency Office Journal, Minutes of the Twelve. See also, January 13, 1912, First Presidency, Letter to Milton H. Knudson; "Statement of Judson Tolman," in Minutes of the Twelve. See May 1, 1912; First Presidency, Letter to Ben E. Rich, Minutes of the Twelve as one of several additional examples. I thank Terryl Givens for these sources. The Book of Mormon also refers derogatorily to black skin. See, for example, 2 Nephi 5:21. See also Lester E. Bush Jr., "Mormonism's Negro Doctrine: An Historical View," *Dialogue: A Journal of Mormon Thought* 8, no. 1 (Spring 1973): 11–68; Ryan Stuart Bingham, "Curses and Marks: Racial Dispensations and Dispensations of Race in Joseph Smith's Bible Revision and the Book of Abraham," *Journal of Mormon History* 41, no. 3 (July 2015): 22–57.

48. See Stephen R. Haynes, *Noah's Curse: The Biblical Justification of American Slavery* (New York: Oxford University Press, 2002).

priesthood/temple ban in the first place. Successive church leaders followed suit for the next 125 years.[49]

Notably, when the LDS Church reversed this teaching in June 1978, it (perhaps unwittingly) produced a disconnect with past PGP scriptural and prophetic justification for priesthood/temple restriction that has been difficult to square for some Mormons. If the ban was rooted in scripture, on what basis could it be overturned? Was the ban's origins divine or human? Over three decades later, it appears church leadership has come to recognize this problem and has recently issued an official essay discussing the ban.[50] Yet, questions concerning past scriptural justification still remain: if scriptural and prophetic justification for the ban was right in the nineteenth century and most of the twentieth century, how can it now be wrong in the twenty-first century? What does this mean in terms of the nature of Mormon scripture, continuing revelation, and prophetic leadership? Can a view of scriptural and prophetic fallibility be a positive way to address these questions? It remains to be seen how the church will deal with the paradox of its post-1978 policy of reversing the priesthood/temple ban with the scriptural justification of the ban.

Engaging the Pearl of Great Price as a biblically infused text demonstrates that it holds both an explicit and implicit relationship to the Bible. Although, at present, the distinct biblical influence contained in the PGP remains relatively unstudied by intertextual specialists, the analysis of Joseph Smith's biblical views in the PGP, shown here, can be most fruitful. We can see from this examination that Smith relies on excerpts from the Bible, such as what is found from the Genesis creation account in the books of Moses and Abraham, as well as its biblical prose. Later, while "re-translating" the Bible (1830–1833), however, Smith's use of the Bible employed biblical themes from the PGP that reinforced his authority and legitimacy as a prophetic voice in the early nineteenth-century religious landscape. Smith's interest in an ancient pure language/priesthood also developed early on but developed with his translation of the Moses and Abraham texts. During 1835 and after Smith's quest for the pure language included a biblically inspired Egyptian language project that shortly thereafter led to a formal Hebrew class from a Jewish teacher. These language projects later evolved into a priesthood-masonic-patterned temple theology during the Nauvoo period (1840–1844).

49. Givens, *Pearl of Greatest Price*, 134–37.

50. See the Gospel Topics essay "Race and the Priesthood" at https://www.lds.org/topics/race-and-the-priesthood?lang=eng

Examining Smith's views of the Bible through the Moses and Abraham narratives and the other texts in the PGP reveals in a somewhat diachronic fashion his evolving thinking on revelation, translation, language, priesthood, and temples. Significantly, his Nauvoo temple theology (1841–1844) crowns all of the work, study, and preparation that had gone on over the years prior. Of course, some hard issues still remain, especially in terms of the PGP retaining the biblical Hamitic/black curse, but, it can at least be said that Smith's detailed reworking of the Moses and Abraham narratives, as well as the other contents of the PGP, demonstrates his approach to what he viewed as his divine injunction to restore a biblical purity.

PART III

# A Variety of Critical Biblical Approaches and Their Relevance to Mormon Studies

12

# Nineteenth-Century Biblical Interpretation in the Church of Jesus Christ of Latter-day Saints

AMY EASTON-FLAKE

> *I said in my heart that there was not then upon earth the religion which I sought. I therefore determined to examine my Bible, and taking Jesus and the disciples as my guide, to endeavor to obtain from God that which man could neither give nor take away.... The Bible I intended should be my guide to life and salvation.*
>
> —Lucy Smith, *History of the Prophet Joseph Smith*

These words penned by Lucy Mack Smith, mother of the prophet Joseph Smith, about a decision she came to in the early nineteenth century after a disheartening experience at a Presbyterian church, capture in part the feelings of many earnest Christians in nineteenth-century America. The Bible's preeminence in Smith's religious life, her belief in her ability to read the Bible and gain truth unaided by others, and her distrust of church intermediaries place her in the mainstream of nineteenth-century Protestant thought. Smith's conclusion, however, "that there was not upon the earth the religion which I sought," moves her out of the mainstream and likely alludes to the establishment of a church by her son in 1830. Although Joseph Smith would introduce new books of scripture to The Church of Jesus Christ of Latter-day Saints canon, the Bible remained the primary religious text for nineteenth-century members of the faith. Given the Bible's status as "the most imported, most printed, most distributed, and most read text in North America up through the nineteenth century,"[1] the Bible's preeminent status in religious sermons and written documents produced by members of the Church of Jesus Christ is not surprising.



1. Paul C. Gutjahr, *An American Bible: A History of the Good Book in the United States, 1777–1880* (Palo Alto, CA: Stanford University Press, 1990), 1.

As Philip Barlow writes, nineteenth-century members of the Church of Jesus Christ were "Bible-believing Christians with a difference."[2]



This chapter examines their similarities to and differences from Protestants' use of the Bible and provides a highly contextualized look at how members of the Church of Jesus Christ of Latter-day Saints interpreted the Bible from the founding of the church (1830) until the end of the nineteenth century when higher criticism had made significant inroads into how Americans interpreted the Bible. In general, members of the Church of Jesus Christ of Latter-day Saints remained in the mainstream of nineteenth-century American Christianity Bible usage as they continued to see the Bible as the inspired word of God and to turn to it for guidance and comfort. What most separated church members' understanding and interpretation of the Bible from their Protestant contemporaries was their emphasis on acquiring knowledge through revelation in addition to scripture and the way they interpreted and selected certain portions of the Bible to support their faith practices and theology.

## BIBLICAL CULTURE IN AMERICA: 1820S–1840S

Scholar Mark Noll writes, "[M]odern historians have recognized the nearly ubiquitous bearing of Scripture on American consciousness in the half century before the Civil War."[3] In particular, Old Testament narratives and images became the common dialogue for early Americans as white Protestant Americans saw their country as "God's new Israel,"[4] Blacks found hope in the stories of deliverance, and "leaders as diverse as Nat Turner, Stonewall Jackson, and Abraham Lincoln seemed almost to speak naturally in biblical cadences."[5] While a profusion of competing sects characterized the American religious scene, a broadly based and widely shared biblicism that superseded racial, gender, and class divisions united the American people. Prior to the Civil War, the Bible held the preeminent position of authority as individuals and the nation as a whole believed it provided not only a blueprint for living a Christian life

2. Philip L. Barlow, *Mormons and the Bible: The Place of the Latter-day Saints in American Religion*, rev. ed. (New York: Oxford University Press, 2013), 111.

3. Mark A. Noll, *America's God: From Jonathan Edwards to Abraham Lincoln* (New York: Oxford University Press, 2002), 371.

4. Eran Shalev, *American Zion: The Old Testament as a Political Text from the Revolution to the Civil War* (New Haven, CT: Yale University Press, 2013), 85, 102.

5. George M. Marsden, "Everyone One's Own Interpreter?: The Bible, Science, and Authority in Mid-Nineteenth-Century America," in *The Bible in America: Essays in Cultural History*, edited by Nathan O. Hatch and Mark A. Noll (New York: Oxford University Press, 1982), 79.

but also the answers to religious, social, and political issues.[6] Adding to our understanding of this phenomena, Seth Perry writes, "the scripturalized environment of early America meant that biblical usage—citation of and creating from the Bible—served as the terms for earning and accounting for authority as institutional and traditional means faltered."[7] The Bible's authority was not static, but something that individuals continuously established.[8]

*Sola scriptura*—the belief in the Bible as the primary and absolute source for all faith and practice—defined Protestant understanding of the Bible in nineteenth-century America. While Protestant Christians since the sixteenth-century Reformation claimed scripture alone as the supreme authority in all religious matters, America's populist emphasis on the sovereignty of the people and disregard for elites and tradition gave this belief new intensity and a new twist.[9] As Nathan O. Hatch notes, "What strikes one in studying the use of the Bible in the early years of the American Republic, is how much weight becomes placed on private judgment and how little on the role of history, theology, and the collective will of the church."[10] A statement by Alexander Campbell, well-known Restorationist preacher, encapsulates well the populist hermeneutic: "I have endeavored to read the Scriptures as though no one had read them before me."[11]

The populist, literal (e.g., Eve was created from Adam's rib) hermeneutic that dominated nineteenth-century American understanding of the Bible was informed by the most influential epistemologies in early nineteenth-century America—Scottish Common Sense Realism and Baconian Science.[12] In nineteenth-century America, Scottish Common Sense Realism and Baconian Science essentially equated to observing, collecting, and carefully studying evidence to determine "facts" and then carefully classifying these facts—what is often known today as inductive scientific reasoning. These epistemologies emphasized that individuals' senses could provide direct and uncomplicated

6. Noll, *America's God*, 375–79.

7. Seth Perry, *Bible Culture and Authority in the Early United States* (Princeton, NJ: Princeton University Press, 2018), 9.

8. Perry, *Bible Culture and Authority*, 1–9, 76

9. Nathan O. Hatch, *The Democratization of American Christianity* (New Haven, CT: Yale University Press, 1989), 70–73, 81. For a fuller discussion, see Hatch, "Sola Scriptura and Novus Ordo Seclorum," in *Bible in America*, 59–79.

10. Hatch, "Sola Scriptura," 70.

11. Alexander Campbell, "Reply," *Christian Baptist* 3 (April 3, 1826), 204. Quoted in Noll, *America's God*, 380.

12. For the best discussion of this reformed, literal hermeneutic, see Noll, *America's God*, 376–85.

knowledge of the world that was available and comprehensible to all.[13] Nineteenth-century readers of the Bible applied this same logic to the Bible. Pervasive assumptions undergirding this hermeneutic were the convictions that the Bible spoke without ambiguity, that the Bible truly revealed God, that the Bible contained the very words God caused to be written, and that truth was unchanging. Consequently, readers privileged common-sense or "literal" readings of the Bible that were thought to be apparent to anyone, believed that the truths contained in the Bible were applicable to all individuals at all times, and felt confident that their Bible knowledge enabled them to find answers to religious and social questions.[14]

The problem with this democratized theory of biblical interpretation and understanding of truth came when individuals reached different conclusions. How were people to resolve their belief in the "immutable truths of the Bible" with their right to judge for themselves the meaning of scripture? The result was a proliferation of new denominations and answers to pressing social questions. Standing out among these many sects was the Church of Jesus Christ of Latter-day Saints.

## JOSEPH SMITH AND THE EARLY CHURCH'S BIBLICAL INTERPRETATIONS: 1830S–1840S

The deep commitment early members of the Church of Jesus Christ of Latter-day Saints had to the Bible is underscored by the frequency and nature of biblical references in their writings. A study of early periodicals published by the church from 1832 to 1846 revealed that "the Bible was cited nearly twenty times more frequently than the Book of Mormon."[15] Individuals cited passages from the New Testament more often than the Old Testament (63 percent versus 37 percent), and similar to other Bible-believing Christians of the time, they were highly selective in their use of the Bible.[16] Choosing most often to promote those passages that reinforced tenets of their new faith such as Israel's covenant relationship with God,[17] the gathering of the elect in preparation for Christ's

13. Marsden, "Everyone One's Own Interpreter," 81–84.

14. Noll, *America's God*, 376–81; Marsden, "Everyone One's Own Interpreter," 80–81.

15. Grant Underwood, "Book of Mormon Usage in Early LDS Theology," *Dialogue: A Journal of Mormon Thought* 17, no. 3 (Autumn 1984), 53.

16. Gordon Irving, "The Mormons and the Bible in the 1830s," *BYU Studies Quarterly* 13, no. 4 (1973): 479–87.

17. See, for example, Deut. 28–33; Rom. 11:19–28; Acts 3:19–25; Ezek. 37.

return,[18] the future millennial state of the earth and its worthy inhabitants,[19] gospel revelation by heavenly messengers,[20] the importance of contemporary prophets and revelation,[21] the uniformity and antiquity of the Gospel,[22] and primitive church patterns such as the possession of priesthood[23] and a focus on the doctrines of faith in Christ, repentance, baptism, and the gift of the Holy Ghost.[24]



Many of the assumptions that guided church members' understanding of the scriptures were similar to the literal, common-sense approach followed by many of their contemporaries: the Bible had direct application to modern times, the meaning of scriptures was clear and consistent, the Old Testament was to be read through a New Testament lens, historical accounts were real and accurate, and prophetic statements were the word of God and were to be fulfilled exactly as written—often in nineteenth-century America.[25] Like their Protestant contemporaries, members of the Church of Jesus Christ of Latter-day Saints also compared themselves to individuals in the Bible as a way to make sense of their experiences and to establish authority—although the extent to which they did this was greater than most.[26]

Church members' strong emphasis on acquiring knowledge through revelation in addition to empirical study, however, set them (and their biblical interpretations) apart from their religious peers.[27] For while they were highly influenced by the Enlightenment, Baconian Rationalism, and Common Sense philosophies of the time,[28] they were also influenced by currents of Romantic thought that called for a more intimate relationship with the divine and rejected full reliance on human reason. True knowledge was obtained through personal experience in combination with supernatural encounters.[29] This interesting

18. See, for example, Matt. 24; Mark 16:14–19; Joel 2:2–32; Isa. 11:11–16.

19. See, for example, Isa. 24:16–23; Rev. 20; Zeph. 3:8–20; Matt. 25:21–23.

20. See, for example, Gal. 1:6–12; Acts 1:9–11; Rev. 22:17–19.

21. See, for example, Eph. 4:11–17; 2 Pet. 1:20–21; Amos 3:7; Matt. 7:7–8.

22. See, for example, Acts 3:19–25; John 17:10–24; Rom. 15:4; 1 Cor. 14:33.

23. See, for example, 1 Cor. 12; Mal. 3:8–12.

24. See, for example, Heb. 11; Acts 2:33–39; Acts 3:19–25; Luke 24:39–50; Gal. 3:6–9.

25. Irving, "The Mormons and the Bible," 477; Barlow, *Mormons and the Bible*, 10.

26. For more on identification and performed Biblicism in early nineteenth-century America, see Perry, *Bible Culture and Authority*, 67–76, 111.

27. Steven C. Harper, "Infallible Proofs, Both Human and Divine: The Persuasiveness of Mormonism for Early Converts," *Religion and American Culture: A Journal of Interpretation* 10, no. 1 (Winter 2000): 104–6, 110–12.

28. Christopher C. Smith, "Joseph Smith in Hermeneutical Crisis," *Dialogue: A Journal of Mormon Thought* 43, no. 2 (Summer 2010): 88–91.

29. Benjamin E. Park, "'Build, Therefore, Your Own World': Ralph Waldo Emerson, Joseph Smith, and American Antebellum Thought," *Journal of Mormon History* 36, no. 1 (Winter 2010): 45, 51.

blend of revelation and reason had significant impact on church members' use and understanding of the Bible. For example, they valued both the Old and the New Testament because they found in each a record of God's divine power and interactions with humankind. In particular, they displayed a strong affinity for the Old Testament patriarchs—Adam, Enoch, Noah, Melchizedek, Abraham, Joseph, Moses, and Elijah.[30] Seeing themselves as participants in an ongoing covenantal relationship between God and his chosen people, Israel, members of the church looked to the Bible for models of how to live and how to enable direct encounters with God as well as for prophecies about their time. Church members' belief in continual revelation also contributed to them seeing the unaided Bible as an inadequate religious compass—personal and prophetic lines of revelation were also necessary.

Joseph Smith's new translation of the Bible provides significant insights into how early members of the Church of Jesus Christ of Latter-day Saints viewed the Bible. For instance, the Bible was not seen as the final authority but as a springboard to revelations from God.[31] It also was not seen as inerrant. In opposition to most individuals in early nineteenth-century America, members of the church believed that the Bible contained mistakes of translation and transmission.[32] In producing his new translation of the Bible, Smith relied on revelation to correct the errors he saw, to clear up many doctrinal teachings, and to greatly expand several passages.[33] Significantly, though, Smith "did not see himself as reading anything into the Bible but simply drawing through revelation the true meaning out of the Bible," as he presented his interpretations as though they should have been clear to any reader.[34] However, as Barlow reminds us, we must distinguish between what Smith said about the Bible (i.e., his statements suggest his agreement with a common-sense understanding of the Bible) and his biblical revisions that "reveal that he found the KJV frequently unclear, contradictory, and erroneous. He often interpreted scripture metaphorically, and he spoke of the mysterious passages of the Bible whose meanings were opened to him only by revelation."[35] The changes Joseph Smith made provide insight into the difficulties and contradictions that many

30. Irving, "The Mormons and the Bible in the 1830s," 476.

31. Kent P. Jackson, "Joseph Smith and the Bible," *Scottish Journal of Theology* 63, no. 1 (2010): 38–40; Barlow, *Mormons and the Bible*, 46–47.

32. Most significant is Smith's statement in the Wentworth Letter, "We Believe the Bible to be the word of God as far as it is translated correctly." 'Wentworth Letter' republished in *Times and Seasons* 3, no. 9 (March 1842), 706–7. See also Brigham Young, 'Temperance,' *Journal of Discourses* 14 (August 27, 1871), 226–27.

33. Barlow, *Mormons and the Bible*, 10–11, 50–51.

34. Jackson, "Joseph Smith and the Bible," 38.

35. Barlow, *Mormons and the Bible*, 35.

individuals encountered in the Bible.[36] While nineteenth-century Americans wanted to see the Bible as an inerrant, common-sense source of truth, the reality was the common-sense philosophy of the Bible did not play out in the real world.



## THE BIBLE IN ANTEBELLUM AMERICA: 1840S–1870S

Moving into the middle of the nineteenth century, the tension between the "immutable truths of the Bible" and people's ability to judge the meaning of the scripture for themselves intensified as individuals and groups increasingly cited chapter and verse to adjudicate public controversies such as states' rights, slavery, temperance, immigration, and women's rights.[37] With people from every side of every issue advancing biblical arguments it soon became clear that "a common trust in Scripture was producing anything but a common conclusion"[38]—an alarming finding given the continued faith that immutable truths could be clearly seen by employing inductive scientific reasoning in scripture and nature alike.

Baconian Science and Common Sense Realism continued to be defining influences of mid-nineteenth-century America's literal hermeneutic. Science and religion were seen as compatible, as theologians championed scientific advances and modeled their own work on that of natural scientists.[39] As Stone-Campbell Restorationist James S. Lamar writes, "The Scriptures admit of being studied and expounded upon the principles of the inductive method; and . . . when thus interpreted they speak to us in a voice as certain and unmistakable as the language of nature heard in the experiments and observations of science."[40] The aspect of the Common Sense philosophy that advanced a shared humanity throughout time was also essential to nineteenth-century Americans' understanding of the Bible as a guidebook for Christian living—applicable at all times and places. For both clergy and lay members alike, the practical uses of scripture were most important. They turned to it for everyday guidance and comfort and continued to see it as the infallible words of God, despite the great variance in interpretations of those words.[41]

36. See Grant Underwood, "Joseph Smith's 'New Translation' of the Bible," in this volume.

37. Noll, *America's God*, 370.

38. Noll, *America's God*, 369.

39. Marsden, "Everyone One's Own Interpreter," 84.

40. James S. Lamar, *Organon of Scripture; or, The Inductive Method of Biblical Interpretation* (Philadelphia, 1860), 176.

41. Marsden, 91.

## BIBLICAL CULTURE IN THE EARLY UTAH PERIOD: 1840S–1870S



Unfortunately, our knowledge of how members of the Church of Jesus Christ of Latter-day Saints interpreted the Bible in the early Utah period is incomplete, as scholars have primarily studied Joseph Smith and the early years of the formation of the church. The one study of this period, which is part of Barlow's seminal work, is well done but limited as it focuses exclusively on the writings of Brigham Young, the second prophet of the church, and Orson Pratt, one of Smith's original Twelve Apostles and a leading scripturist, theologian, and intellectual. Such a focus is advisable in an opus like Barlow's *Mormons and the Bible* since Young and Pratt were the dominant church leaders of the day and provide two distinct approaches to biblical interpretation. However, this choice does open up many reception history questions, such as whose responses are deemed important, how is the choice of material to be justified, and to what end is it being marshalled. As we look at Young's and Pratt's views of the Bible, we should remember to regard them as a starting point, as Barlow acknowledges in his work, to understanding this time—recognizing that extensive research is still warranted.[42]

Under Brigham Young's leadership the Bible remained fundamental to Latter-day Saint thought; nonetheless, the gulf expanded between nineteenth-century Protestant belief in *sola scriptura* and the inerrancy of scriptures and the Latter-day Saint belief that the unaided Bible was an inadequate religious compass that contained mistakes due to translation and transmission. For while Young regularly encouraged church members to read the Bible and maintained an enduring and fundamental belief in the Bible throughout his life, he was also vocal in his belief that the revelations he received from God superseded written scripture and made statements indicating that not all parts of the Bible were of equal value or to be taken literally. For example, "Young dismissed parts of the Genesis creation account as 'baby stories' that should naturally be outgrown" and stated that the ancient prophets at times "acted foolishly."[43]

In comparison, Orson Pratt's approach to the Bible was more in alignment with the Protestant theologians of his time. He shared their scholarly, scientific belief that the Bible may be studied empirically and saw no significant discrepancies among science, the Bible, and theology of the Church of Jesus

42. Barlow, *Mormons and the Bible*, xxii. Barlow notes in his introduction that more work is needed to fully understand each time period that he covers.

43. Barlow, *Mormons and the Bible*, 86, 99. For Barlow's complete discussion, see 84–88.

Christ of Latter-day Saints. He also shared the assumptions that biblical truths were accessible to anyone possessed of common sense, that the Bible should be taken literally, and that the Bible held the answers to contemporary social questions.[44] Pratt differed from his Protestant contemporaries in his insistence that the Bible contained translation errors and in his decision to most often use the Bible to demonstrate the scriptural legitimacy of practices and beliefs taught in the Church of Jesus Christ rather than to urge "Christian" living.[45]

To begin to address the need for further research of this period, I read through the journal entries and letters of over two dozen female members writing during this time, and what I found indicates that women's use of the Bible in their private writings was in many ways more in line with their female Protestant contemporaries than their male church leaders.[46] In these personal writings, women did not offer overt interpretations of scripture or use scripture to explain church doctrine as Pratt and Young did; instead, they wove scriptures into their depictions of the people and events that mattered to them. For instance, Caroline Barnes Crosby incorporates Matthew 6:11, "He has given us this day our daily bread," to express her appreciation to the Lord for the food given to her by the inhabitants of the Society and Austral Islands where she was a missionary with her husband during the 1850s.[47] Louisa Barnes Pratt uses Matthew 24:12 "iniquity abounded, which caused the love of many to wax old" to explain her husband and daughter's reluctance to leave San Bernardino and join her in Utah.[48] Hannah Tapfield King likens herself to both Hannah giving her son Samuel to the Lord and Abraham sacrificing his son Isaac to the Lord to express the intense sorrow she feels when she sends her only living son on a mission.[49] And both Sarah DeArmon Pea Rich and Bathsheba Wilson Bigler Smith explain that "like Sarah of old," they have given their husband multiple wives.[50] Turning to the scriptures for a language of self-understanding, women sanctified their lives, finding greater purpose and connection to God.

44. Barlow, *Mormons and the Bible*, 94–97.

45. Barlow, *Mormons and the Bible*, 88–102.

46. Amy Easton-Flake, "Mormon Women and Scripture in the Nineteenth Century," in *The Routledge Handbook of Mormonism and Gender*, edited by Taylor Petrey and Amy Hoyt (London: Routledge, 2020), 102–4.

47. E.L. Lyman, S.W. Payne, and S.G. Ellsworth, *No Place to Call Home: The 1807–1857 Life Writings of Caroline Barnes Crosby, Chronicler of Outlying Mormon Communities* (Logan: Utah State University Press, 2005), 141.

48. Louisa Barnes Pratt and George Ellsworth, *The History of Louisa Barnes Pratt: Being the Autobiography of a Mormon Missionary Widow and Pioneer* (Logan: Utah State Press, 1998), 273.

49. Hannah Tapfield King, *Hannah Tapfield King Autobiography, 1864–1872*. [manuscript] Church Archives. (Salt Lake City, UT: Church History Library), 131.

50. Sarah DeArmon Pea Rich, *Sarah DeArmon Pea Rich, 1814–1893 Autobiography* [typescript]; Bathsheba Wilson Bigler Smith, *Bathsheba W. Smith, 1822–1906 Autobiography* [typescript]. Both found in

Not surprisingly, women most often turned to the Bible for this self-understanding during times of trial. Consequently, scriptures that communicate the need for trials or suffering in order to become perfected such as Hebrews 2:10 are among the most frequently cited.[51] As are scriptures that express God's watchful care and awareness of his people: "[A] sparrow does not fall to the ground without His notice."[52] Or a belief that "God is good and will not suffer us to be tried beyond that we are able to bear."[53] Reading through these personal writings, these women's belief that the Lord was leading them individually and the church collectively is highly evidenced in the scriptures they incorporated.[54] They often envisioned themselves as the new Israel—"We go as Abraham went, not knowing whither we go, but the Lord will go before us, and be our frontward and rearward"[55]—and this self-understanding drove them and sustained them through many of the challenges they faced during this era. This preliminary research into women's personal writings during the 1840s to 1870s indicates that women were often using scriptures for different purposes than were their church leaders. A finding that reaffirms the need for more specific studies that look at differences across time, location, stewardship within the church, gender, and age.

## INTRODUCTION OF HIGHER CRITICISM TO AMERICA: 1880–1900

Americans' understanding of the Bible underwent significant changes in the last third of the nineteenth century. Before 1870, most Protestants (including academics and theologians) believed the Bible recorded the infallible words of God. Its truthfulness and commonsense clarity were a given. By 1900, however, "Christians contended with each other as to *how* the Bible was the Word

---

Writings of Early Latter-day Saints and Their Contemporaries, Special Collections, Provo, UT: Harold B. Lee Library, accessed boap.org.

51. See for instance, Nancy Naomi Alexander Tracy, *Nancy Naomi Alexander Tracy, 1816–1846, Autobiography* [typescript]. Writings of Early Latter-day Saints and Their Contemporaries, Special Collections, Provo, UT: Harold B. Lee Library, accessed boap.org.

52. Matthew 10:29. See for instance, Sarah Studevant Leavitt, *Sarah Studevant Leavitt, 1798–1847 Autobiography* [typescript], Writings of Early Latter-day Saints and Their Contemporaries, Special Collections, Provo, UT: Harold B. Lee Library, accessed at boap.org.

53. 1 Corinthians 10:13. See for instance, King, *Autobiography*, 75.

54. See for instance, Martha Spence Heywood, *Not by Bread Alone: The Journal of Martha Spence Heywood, 1850–1856, ed. by Juanita Brooks* (Logan: Utah State Press, 1998), 25.

55. See for instance, Sally Randall, June 1, 1846 letter, in Kenneth W. Godfrey, Audrey M. Godfrey, and Jill Mulvay Derr, *Women's Voices: An Untold History of the Latter-day Saints, 1830–1900* (Salt Lake City, UT: Deseret Book, 1982), 144.

of God. And the academic world at large had asked *if* it was."[56] Divisions in Americans' understanding of the Bible came in response to an array of new information and methods. New findings from historians, archaeologists, and world travelers provided access to the ancient world of the Bible and allowed the Bible to be approached in scientific, historical, and new theological terms. Likewise, the discovery of earlier New Testament manuscripts and the project of revising the King James Version of the Bible in light of new understanding of Hebrew and Greek eroded some people's belief in the Bible's infallibility as transmission and translation issues came to light. Greater acceptance of Darwin's theory of evolution and geological evidence that pointed to the earth being millions of years old also led many to question the veracity of the Bible.[57] Where the Bible and science had previously been seen as compatible, the two now seemed to many to be at odds.

The rise of critical Bible scholarship in the United States corresponded with the rise of the modern American university as many new programs embraced the German model of higher criticism.[58] The historical-critical method starts from the belief that any religious text, belief, or movement must be understood in its original context because ideas, values, and institutions are always a product of the age in which they exist.[59] From the 1880s until the 1920s, a struggle raged in the American academy over how to employ the historical-critical method. Those regarded as being in the liberal camp were committed to the historical-critical method and to science in organic, evolutionary terms. They saw the Bible as a human book, that "even if its authors were somehow inspired by God, they were writing to commend a religious position which could be explained by any number of factors quite apart from divine revelation." Many of this persuasion believed the Old Testament was largely fiction and that the New Testament was the product of competing forces within the early church.[60] Those regarded as being in the conservative camp remained committed to the Bible as the divinely inspired word of God and to inductive research. They were open to many of the new advances in history, archaeology, and higher criticism, believing that if scholarly methods were properly applied the ideas

56. Mark Noll, *Between Faith and Criticism: Evangelicals, Scholarship, and the Bible in America* (New York: Harper & Row, 1986), 11.

57. For more on developments that challenged traditional approaches to reading the Bible as God's inspired, infallible word, see Marion Ann Taylor and Heather E. Weir, *Let Her Speak for Herself: Nineteenth-Century Women Writing on the Women of Genesis* (Waco, TX: Baylor University Press, 2006), 11–12. See also Jason Combs, "Historical Criticism and Latter-day Saints," in this volume.

58. Noll, *Between Faith and Criticism*, 12.

59. For a brief overview of the historical-critical method, see Gerald Bray, *Biblical Interpretation: Past and Present* (Downers Grove, IL: IVP Academic, 1996), 221–24.

60. Bray, *Biblical Interpretation*, 272–73.

professed in the more liberal camp would be shown to be faulty. They contended that biblical authors could both reflect their historical circumstances and be inspired by God. Many were able to accept nontraditional conclusions about scriptures as long as these new conclusions could be seen as reinterpretations of the infallible Bible rather than as examples of biblical error. They often stressed that the Bible was not intended to explain human science or history and justified errors in the Bible by attributing them to transmission errors.[61]

Looking at the writings of lay individuals—both men and women—found within the popular press, we can see how insights from science, history, and geography influenced lay individuals' understanding of and approach to the Bible. While individuals at times brought in modern insights to inform their reading, the focus remained on spiritual and theological understandings of the text.[62] Some of the most common features of this noncritical approach were searching for timeless and universal truths, emphasizing connections between biblical characters' lives and the lives of the readers, drawing moral inferences, using the New Testament as a lens to interpret the Old Testament, and employing various modes of interpretation including typology, association, and proof texting. Most prominent was appropriating the message of the text and applying it to their own lives—when insights from science, history, and anthropology aided this endeavor, they were employed.[63] Through the end of the nineteenth century, this noncritical exegesis of lay individuals and the conservative Evangelical approach to scholarship that combined academic rigor with traditional reverence for the Bible dominated Americans' interpretations of the Bible.[64] The Church of Jesus Christ of Latter-day Saints' interpretation of the Bible in the late nineteenth century may best be understood within the context of these two approaches, as the more liberal view promoted by some within the academy did not make inroads into the Church of Jesus Christ of Latter-day Saints in the nineteenth century.

61. Bray, *Biblical Interpretation*, 273–74; Noll, *Between Faith and Criticism*, 16–26; Timothy P. Weber, "The Two-Edged Sword: The Fundamentalist Use of the Bible," in *Bible in American Culture*, 106.

62. Christiana de Groot and Marion Ann Taylor, *Recovering Nineteenth-Century Women Interpreters of the Bible* (Atlanta: Society of Biblical Literature, 2007), 9; Taylor and Weir, *Let Her Speak*, 14.

63. Taylor and Weir, *Let Her Speak*, 15–17.

64. Noll, *Between Faith and Criticism*, 11–12, 27–31; Bray, *Biblical Interpretation*, 306; Taylor and Weir, *Let Her Speak*, 14–15.

## LATE NINETEENTH-CENTURY BIBLICAL INTERPRETATION WITHIN THE CHURCH: 1880–1900

As we approach how members of the Church of Jesus Christ of Latter-day Saints interpreted and used the Bible at the end of the nineteenth century, we will follow the example of many biblical reception scholars who seek to include the voices of lay men and women by recognizing the theological work taking place in genres such as devotional writing, moral instruction, poetry, hymns, periodicals, biographies, and dramas.[65] While the male leadership of the Church of Jesus Christ of Latter-day Saints has produced the majority of recorded biblical interpretation, extending the discussion to lay members—both men and women—within the church has great value because it not only allows us to see how the interpretations and understandings of church leaders are being filtered, accepted, or rejected but also, more importantly, provides insight into the general membership of the Church of Jesus Christ of Latter-day Saints and greatly expands our comprehensive breadth of how members of the church interpreted and used the Bible.[66]

Looking at late nineteenth-century periodicals put out by members of the Church of Jesus Christ of Latter-day Saints is particularly useful as it provides access to both the writings of leaders and lay individuals. Here we discover that church members who wrote for and read these magazines received at least some limited exposure to ideas coming out of higher criticism from the fields of geology, anthropology, archaeology, linguistics, and others. Authors within the church may be found engaging with different sources regarding biblical interpretation as they quote from, refute, or recommend the work of scholars and Protestant theologians. More often than not, these writers refuted new ideas, but at times—similar to their Protestant contemporaries—they acknowledged insights from higher criticism that enhanced their understanding of the Bible or shored up biblical claims. Their articles display an awareness of new findings such as the Gospel According to the Hebrews (an apocryphal gospel recovered and translated in 1879) as well as information coming from various fields of biblical studies that confirm scriptural accounts, such as the

65. Groot and Taylor, *Recovering Nineteenth-Century Women*, 10; Rebecca Styler, *Literary Theology by Women Writers of the Nineteenth Century* (Farnham, UK: Ashgate, 2010), 1; Julie Melnyk, "Women, Writing, and the Creation of Theological Cultures," in *Women, Gender and Religious Cultures in Britain, 1800–1940*, edited by Sue Morgan and Jacqueline DeVries (New York: Routledge, 2010), 32–4.

66. For an excellent overview of how B.H. Roberts, Joseph Fielding Smith, and William H. Chamberlin represent the range of Mormon responses to higher criticism between 1880 and 1930, see Barlow, *Mormons and the Bible*, 112–61.

finding of giant bones to substantiate the Bible's claim of giants or scientific explanations of miracles such as Moses turning the Nile red or the sun standing still in the days of Joshua.[67] Some articles also display an awareness of scholars using insights from higher criticism to grapple with perplexing passages, such as Jephthah sacrificing his daughter.[68] Thanks to the expansive nineteenth-century print culture, interested individuals (notably this number appears to be very small) were able to stay abreast of important debates and discoveries and then share what they found most pertinent with readers of church periodicals.

A crucial point of debate within late nineteenth-century biblical criticism was the question of how science and the Bible were to be understood in relation to one another. Were they still to be seen as compatible, or had advances in science and higher criticism revealed them to be in opposition? If so, was the Bible or science to be trusted? The sentiments expressed within church periodicals are similar to and often explicitly drawn from conservative Evangelical theologians and scholars. While some simply proclaimed the superiority of the Bible and the speculative (or limited) nature of science,[69] more often these authors seemed interested in showing how science and the Bible support one another. At times, they did this by quoting scientists who backed up supposed biblical assertions[70]; other times, they departed from a literalist interpretation of the scriptures and admitted to what humankind does not know from the Bible to create a space for the Bible and science to exist harmoniously.[71] Common refrains included the declaration that the Bible does not claim to offer insights into geology or astronomy but rather to act as a record of God's dealings with humanity.[72] The statement of one author best summarizes the dominant position put forth in these periodicals: "Christianity and true science have always been and will always be true friends.... The word of God and science will not disagree except as a result of misunderstanding."[73]

While some articles do display a familiarity and concern with biblical criticism, much more prevalent in periodicals published by members of The

67. "Recovery of an Ancient Record," *Deseret News,* July 9, 1879, 6; "Moses and the Red Nile," *Millennial Star* 58, no. 24 (June 11, 1896), 381–83; "Confirmation of Scripture," *Millennial Star* 52, no. 40 (6 October 1890), 638.

68. "Jephthah's Vow," *Deseret News,* August 22, 1888, 7.

69. J.R.W. "Who Are the Idiots?" *Deseret News,* February 29, 1888, 14.

70. Pratt, "Discourse," *Deseret News,* January 10, 1877, 2; George Q. Cannon, "The Fear of God the Beginning of Wisdom," *Millennial Star* 50, no. 24 (June 11, 1888), 371–72.

71. James Talmage, "The Infidel's Book," *Millennial Star* 50, no. 24 (June 11, 1888), 369–71.

72. George Reynolds, "Are the Stars Inhabited Worlds?" *Millennial Star* 41, no. 42 (20 October 1879), 657–60.

73. J.M.S. "The Bible and the Sciences," *Millennial Star* 50, no. 40 (October 1, 1888), 628, 630.

Church of Jesus Christ of Latter-day Saints is the noncritical exegesis that dominated late nineteenth-century Protestant use of the Bible as well. Similar to Bible readers of both the nineteenth century and today, members of the church, as indicated by nineteenth-century periodicals, used the Bible to teach of Christ, explain religious doctrine, encourage desired behaviors, and argue for the correctness of certain political or social views. For instance, women within the church regularly used biblical women to provide Christian role models who spoke to their own needs, particularly in the contexts of nineteenth-century gender debates and to authorize the expansion of women's public roles. Common exegetical practices included using different translations, explaining the occasion that brought forth the scriptural passage, likening the biblical narrative to current day, expanding on narratives in order to read themselves and their ideals into the Bible, and emphasizing portions of the Bible that supported their world view while ignoring or glossing over parts with which they were uncomfortable.[74] Members of the church also followed the general Protestant trend of increasingly coming to favor the New Testament over the long nineteenth century. While Irving's study of 1830s church periodicals reports that 63 percent of the passages referenced came from the New Testament,[75] my recent study of church periodicals in the last quarter of the nineteenth century found that the New Testament accounts for 72 percent, indicating a 9 percent growth in New Testament usage.[76]

While church members' biblical interpretations and interpretive practices shared much in common with their religious contemporaries, distinct theological beliefs of the Church of Jesus Christ created significant differences as well. For instance, men writing for church periodicals regularly used the Bible to explain and support their faith practices and theology. Among the most frequently discussed topics were the nature of Christ and God (including that they had bodies), baptism, celestial marriage, polygamy, discerning spirits, preexistence, the Creation, resurrection, foreordination, priesthood, the sacrament, the truth of the Book of Mormon, and the gathering of Israel. Likely because belief in modern-day revelation, prophecy, and prophets was among the most controversial doctrines taught by the Church of Jesus Christ, men

74. Amy Easton-Flake, "Biblical Women in the *Woman's Exponent*: Nineteenth-Century Mormon Women Interpret the Bible," in *The Bible in American Life*, edited by Philip Goff, Arthur E. Farnsley II, and Peter J. Thuesen (New York: Oxford University Press, 2017), 91, 93–8.

75. Irving, "The Mormons and the Bible in the 1830s," 479.

76. Amy Easton-Flake, "The Bible in the *Millennial Star* and *Woman's Exponent*: Biblical Use and Interpretation in The Church of Jesus Christ of Latter-day Saints in the Late Nineteenth Century," *BYU Studies* 60, no. 1 (Winter 2021), 13.

repeatedly cited scriptures that addressed the reality of personal revelation, prophets and modern-day revelation, and the fulfillments of ancient prophecies. In contrast, women writing for church periodicals were most often not interested in using the Bible to distinguish themselves from their Christian contemporaries. Instead, they turned to scriptures for practical purposes—to acquire instruction for living a sanctified life, to support women's advancement, to find comfort and solace, and to inspire greater effort through learning from Christ's example. Both men and women regularly used the Bible to interpret current events, to urge one another to prepare for Christ's second coming, and to rebuttal persecution and undesirable laws.[77] From their point of view, members of the Church of Jesus Christ were the true followers of the Bible, and they regularly reproached other Christians for dismissing or misunderstanding portions of the Bible.[78] Significantly, Jesus Christ is at the center of scripture usage,[79] and the deployment of these scriptures continue to illustrate distinctions along gender lines. While scriptures about Christ cited by men most frequently expounded on Christ's nature and life or how he makes salvation possible, scriptures cited by women most frequently focused on the role Christ played in individuals' lives as a model, mentor, and enabler.[80] Such consistent discrepancies along gender lines, reinforces the need for more studies that account for gender.

## CONCLUSION

Perhaps the defining belief that separated members of The Church of Jesus Christ of Latter-day Saints from other Christians throughout the nineteenth century (and still today) was their emphasis on the necessity of revelation to understand the Bible and their belief that revelation may supersede the Bible. While they shared the common Protestant belief that scriptures speak directly to contemporary readers, they also believed, as one individual wrote in the *Millennial Star* in 1879, that "the great truths of the Bible can only be comprehended by the investigator being in possession of a portion of the spirit that inspired the speakers and writers of the divine record."[81] Likewise, revelation was essential to faith and living the gospel (and the Bible was to corroborate

77. Easton-Flake, "The Bible," 32–8

78. For primary examples, see William C. Dunbar, "Remarks to the Young," *Deseret News*, January 1, 1874, 10–1; and William M. Palmer, "Preaching and Baptizing," *Deseret News*, February 7, 1877, 10.

79. Easton-Flake, "The Bible," 24.

80. Easton-Flake, "The Bible," 37.

81. "The Gospel to the Living and the Dead," *Millennial Star* 41, no. 50 (15 December 1879), 786.

the living word of God as spoken by modern prophets). As B.F. Cummings wrote in 1879,

> While the Latter-day Saints hold the Bible, together with other ancient and modern Scripture, to be of a value altogether beyond computation, and while there is no other people in the world who walk so closely to the rules therein contained, their religion is founded upon the principle of continuous revelation, rather than upon an account of the religion which some previous generation has possessed.[82]

As illustrated in this passage, members of The Church of Jesus Christ of Latter-day Saints would express an increasing reverence for the Bible as the nineteenth century passed into the twentieth, but they would always be "Bible-believing Christians with a difference"[83] as they continued to express, as their founder Joseph Smith did, a need for personal and prophetic revelation and guidance beyond that offered within the Bible.

82. B.F. Cummings, "On What Is Your Religion Founded," *Millennial Star* 41, no. 14 (7 April 1879), 213.
83. Barlow, *Mormons and the Bible,* 111.

# 13

# Historical Criticism of the Bible among the Latter-day Saints

JASON ROBERT COMBS

Latter-day Saints care about history. As with other Christians, the faith of the Latter-day Saints is rooted in affirmations about the historical figure, Jesus of Nazareth, and in the ancient texts found in the Bible. Beyond any shared beliefs about the past, Latter-day Saints also profess faith in particular events from the life and work of the nineteenth-century American Prophet Joseph Smith Jr., as well as in the scripture Smith produced and in the work of the church he founded. In recent decades, the Church of Jesus Christ of Latter-day Saints has increasingly welcomed the work of historians trained in the field of Mormon history—suggesting the potential for similar official engagement with the work of historians trained in the field of biblical studies.[1] This chapter introduces

1. Beginning in the late twentieth century and more particularly in the early twenty-first century, the Church of Jesus Christ of Latter-day Saints adopted a new openness regarding the sources and facts of its history. See David J. Whittaker, "Mormon Studies as an Academic Discipline" in *The Oxford Handbook of Mormonism,* edited by Terryl L. Givens and Philip L. Barlow (New York: Oxford University Press, 2015), 92–105, here 98–102. See also Matthew Bowman, *The Mormon People: The Making of an American Faith* (New York: Random House, 2012), 241, 244–45. This has included academic openness—most prominently *The Joseph Smith Papers* project, which publicly shares all historical documents related to Joseph Smith Jr.; see http://www.josephsmithpapers.org, accessed April 15, 2020. The church also disseminated academic resources in a publicly accessible format in the online Gospel Topics Essays, which address difficult issues within the faith in a series of informed and well-documented essays; and in the 2017 supplementary Sunday School manual for Latter-day Saints' study of the Doctrine and Covenants, *Revelations in Context,* which summarizes the work of historians from the *Joseph Smith Papers* project; see https://www.churchofjesuschrist.org/study/manual/gospel-topics-essays/essays and https://history.churchofjesuschrist.org/landing/revelations-in-context, accessed April 15, 2020. By contrast, the 1979 publication of the LDS edition of the KJV Bible, which included a Bible Dictionary adapted from the *Cambridge Bible Dictionary*, seems to have employed no scholars who were actively publishing academic work in the field of biblical studies; see Lavina Fielding Anderson, "Church Publishes First LDS Edition of the Bible" *Ensign* 9, no. 10 (Oct 1979): 8–18, and Philip L. Barlow, *Mormons and the Bible: The Place of Latter-day Saints in American Religion*, rev. ed. (Oxford, UK: Oxford University Press, 2013), 224–33.

readers to the work of historians who study the Bible and describes the relationship of Latter-day Saints to that work. The variety of methods employed to study the Bible from a historical perspective are often grouped under the term *historical criticism.*



## "HISTORICAL CRITICISM" AND ITS METHODOLOGIES

The term *historical criticism* emerged in the seventeenth century as a biblical-studies counterpart to other forms of Enlightenment scholarship.[2] Richard Simon, a French priest and Bible scholar whose work was influenced by Baruch Spinoza (see hereinafter), coined the term *historical criticism* in relation to the study of the Bible when he published his *Histoire Critique du Vieux Testament* in 1680, followed in 1689 by his *Histoire Critique du texte du Nouveau Testament.* In these works, the term *criticism* was not used in the pejorative sense of "criticizing" or being "critical" of something. Rather, as Reinhart Koselleck explains,

> What was meant by ["criticism"] was the art of objective evaluation—particularly of ancient texts, but also of literature and art, as well as of nations and individuals. The term was initially used by the Humanists; it incorporated the meaning of judgement and learned scholarship, and when the philological approach was expanded to Holy Scripture, this process too was called "criticism."[3]

Historical criticism has also been called "higher criticism" or simply "biblical criticism." Some opponents of historical criticism have implied that the term *higher criticism* was evidence of academic arrogance: exalting the scholar's position over that of religious authorities.[4] Yet the term actually originated as a means of distinguishing between different types of academic biblical criticism: lower and higher. Lower criticism, also called textual criticism, focused on the

2. By 1781, Immanuel Kant could declare, "Our age is the genuine age of criticism, to which everything must submit"; Kant, *Critique of Pure Reason*, edited by Paul Guyer and Allen W. Wood (Cambridge, UK: Cambridge University Press, 1998), 100–1 (Preface xi, note).

3. Reinhart Koselleck, *Critique and Crisis: Enlightenment and the Pathogenesis of Modern Society* (Cambridge, MA: MIT Press, 1988), 105; trans. *Kritik und Krise: Eine Studie zur Pathogenese der bürgerlichen Welt* (Freiburg, Germany: Karl Abler, 1959). See also John Barton, *The Nature of Biblical Criticism* (Louisville, KY: Westminster John Knox Press, 2007), 120.

4. See Barlow, *Mormons and the Bible*, 136; citing Joseph Fielding Smith, *Man: His Origin and Destiny* (Salt Lake City, UT: Deseret Book, 1954), 490.

history of textual transmission—how the text of the Bible changed over time and what the original text most likely said. Higher criticism focused on the meaning of the text—its authorship, audience, original context, etc.[5] It was "higher" only in that it asked questions beyond the level of the text itself. As a collection of methodologies for studying the historical meaning of the Bible, historical criticism has also been called "biblical criticism" to distinguish it from the historical study of other literary texts.[6]

Those methods that fall under the umbrella of historical criticism include source criticism, form criticism, redaction criticism, history of events and individuals, and other methodologies that emphasize historical context.[7] Source criticism, as the name implies, attempts to identify within an individual biblical text the sources adopted to fashion that text. Form criticism asks how those source-texts functioned in the religious life of ancient Israel or early Christianity before they became part of the Bible. Redaction criticism works to understand why the sources were brought together by an editor or "redactor" in the way they now appear; that is, how the writing was shaped by political and cultural contexts or by literary trends and theological concerns. Lastly, some use the texts of the Bible in conjunction with other evidence from antiquity in order to reconstruct the history of events or individuals that lie behind the biblical narratives—investigating, for example, whether the Israelites settling in Canaan destroyed all the inhabitants of the land (Joshua) or whether many of the native inhabitants remained (Judges); whether Jesus was crucified before the beginning of Passover (John) or after (Matthew, Mark, and Luke). These examples are simpler than anything found in current historical studies. Nevertheless, they illustrate an important point: all of these methodologies grew out of attempts to understand the literal or plain meaning of the text and to reckon with challenges that the text itself presents to such a reading.[8]

5. The term *higher criticism (die höhere Kritik)* was first used in reference to biblical studies by Johann Gottfried Eichhorn in the second edition of his *Einleitung in das Alte Testament*, three vols. (1787). The term first appeared in English in the late 1800s; see the discussion in C., "The Term Higher Criticism," *The Old Testament Student* 3, no. 8 (1884): 310–11.

6. For example, Barton, *Nature of Biblical Criticism*.

7. Other historical methodologies include sociohistorical criticism, archaeology or material culture approaches, and those types of literary criticism that attempt to situate genre and style in the historical context of the period in which the text was written—i.e., forms of rhetorical criticism and certain approaches to intertextuality. For detailed descriptions and applications of all these methods, see John H. Hayes and Carl R. Holladay, *Biblical Exegesis: A Beginner's Handbook*, 3rd ed. (Louisville, KY: Westminster John Knox, 2007); and John Barton, *Reading the Old Testament: Method in Biblical Study* (Louisville, KY: Westminster John Knox, 1996).

8. See Barton, *Reading the Old Testament*, 22.

## THE HISTORY OF HISTORICAL CRITICISM AND ITS CHALLENGE TO RELIGIOUS AUTHORITY

Historical criticism has roots within both the church and the academy, within the Reformation and the Age of Enlightenment.[9] Today historical critics as well as many Latter-day Saints and other Christians share the assumption that to understand the Bible one must interpret it according to its plain sense, also called its "literal" meaning. Yet, in the early history of Christianity, this literal reading was at times the least important. For some Christian readers, allegorical interpretation, understood to reveal a text's "spiritual" meaning, mattered more.[10] The modern emphasis on literal reading can be traced, in part, to Martin Luther (d. 1546), who believed that the Catholic Church had obscured the plainness of scripture with its allegorical interpretations.[11] Luther insisted that the literal meaning of scripture, what he called its "grammatical, historical" meaning, was so plain that it could be understood without an appeal to tradition or church authorities (this is the Protestant doctrine, *Perspicuity of Scripture*).[12] If disagreements over the meaning of scripture arose, the answer again was scripture: only scripture could interpret scripture (*sola scriptura*).

Some scriptural passages become problematic if they are interpreted literally. When allegorical interpretation thrived, problematic passages could be accepted as divine hints that the reader should search for a spiritual meaning. The early third-century Christian theologian, Origen of Alexandria, called such passages "stumbling blocks":

9. For the history of Hebrew Bible (Old Testament) scholarship, see Magne Sæbø, ed., *Hebrew Bible/Old Testament: The History of Its Interpretation, vol. 2–3.2* (Göttingen, Germany: Vandenhoeck & Ruprecht, 2008–2014). For the history of New Testament scholarship, see Werner Georg Kümmel, *The New Testament: The History of the Investigation of Its Problems*, trans. S. McLean Gilmour and Howard C. Kee (Nashville, TN: Abingdon, 1972); and William Baird, *History of New Testament Research, vol. 1–3* (Minneapolis, MN: Fortress Press, 1992–2013).

10. For example, Origen, *On First Principles* 4.2.9; Cassian, *Conferences* 14.8. Others, such as Theodore of Mopsuestia, emphasized literal or historical interpretation. For allegorical interpretation in Judaism, see Folker Siegert, "Early Jewish Interpretation in a Hellenistic Style," in Sæbø, *Hebrew Bible/Old Testament*, 1/1:130–98, especially 165 and 179.

11. Martin Luther, "Answer to the Hyper-Christian, Hyperspiritual, and Hyperlearned Book by Goat Emser in Leipzig (1521)," in *Luther's Works, vol. 39*, edited by Eric W. Gritsch, trans. Eric W. Gritsch and Ruth C. Gritsch (Philadelphia: Fortress Press, 1970), 175–203; see also Kümmel, *The New Testament*, 22–23. On Luther's continued use of allegorical interpretation, see Siegfried Raeder, "The Exegetical and Hermeneutical Work of Martin Luther," in Sæbø, *Hebrew Bible/Old Testament*, 2:371–76.

12. Luther, "Answer to the Hyperchristian," *Luther's Works*, 39:181. See also Kümmel, *The New Testament*, 20–21.

> [T]he Word of God has arranged that certain *stumbling blocks*, as it were, and *obstacles and impossibilities* be inserted into the midst of the Law and the narrative... the principal aim being to announce the connection amongst spiritual events ... [That is,] the Scripture interwove in the narrative something that did not happen, sometimes what could not happen, and sometimes what could happen but did not, and occasionally a few words are inserted which are not true according to the bodily [literal] sense, and occasionally a greater number.[13]

With the Protestant shift toward literal interpretation, *sola scriptura*, and the Perspicuity of Scripture, it became theologically difficult to account for historical inaccuracies in scripture.[14] The Age of Enlightenment added to this challenge new questions about which events in scripture could or could not have happened. Readers of the Bible had to reconcile its significance with a new larger world (discovery of the Americas in 1492), with new discoveries in science and astronomy (Galileo d. 1642), and with philosophical innovations (Descartes 1650).[15]

Dutch philosopher and Sephardic Jew Baruch Spinoza (1632–1677) is often credited as being the father of modern historical criticism. Like the earlier Protestant Reformers, Spinoza affirmed that "all knowledge of scripture must be sought from scripture alone."[16] To deal with passages that appeared contradictory, either to each other or to new Enlightenment understandings of the world, Spinoza suggested distinguishing "between true meaning and truth of fact"; "the former," Spinoza wrote, "must be sought simply from linguistic usage, or from a process of reasoning that looks to no other basis than Scripture."[17] In other words, for Spinoza, scripture must first be understood on its own terms in its original language.

13. Origen, *On First Principles* 4.2.9 (Greek); trans. John Behr, *Origen: On First Principles, vol. II*; Oxford Early Christian Texts (Oxford, UK: Oxford University Press, 2017), 514–17; brackets and ellipses added.

14. This assumption resulted in curious new approaches to inconsistencies in scripture; for example, Martin Luther found Hebrews, James, Jude, and Revelation to be at odds with his reading of the rest of the New Testament, so he relegated those four books to the very end of his translation of the Bible and did not include them in the table of contents; see Kümmel, *The New Testament*, 26.

15. Travis L. Frampton, *Spinoza and the Rise of Historical Criticism of the Bible* (New York: T&T Clark, 2006), 202; see also Charlotte Methuen, "On the Threshold of a New Age: Expanding Horizons as the Broader Context of Scriptural Interpretation," in Sæbø, *Hebrew Bible/Old Testament*, 2:665–89.

16. Baruch Spinoza, *Theological-Political Treatise*, trans. Samuel Shirley, 2nd ed. (Indianapolis, IN: Hackett, 2001), 88. For more on the influence of the Reformers on Spinoza, see Frampton, *Spinoza and the Rise of Historical Criticism*.

17. Spinoza, *Theological-Political Treatise*, 89; see Frampton, *Spinoza and the Rise of Historical Criticism*, 225.

Despite Spinoza's Protestant-like approach to scripture, his careful reading of the Bible yielded results that conflicted with longstanding religious traditions. For instance, Spinoza concluded that Moses did not write the Pentateuch after identifying numerous passages that were not written from the perspective of Moses.[18] When Spinoza moved beyond the text itself—his "true meaning"—to consider what he called "truth of fact," he applied new Enlightenment understandings of the world to make sense of the biblical narratives. Miracles were explained as misperception or as the result of natural law. For instance, Spinoza argued that the miracle witnessed by Joshua at Gibeon (Joshua 10:12–13) was not actually the sun standing still. Since it is scientifically impossible for earth to alter its rotation in a way that would cause the sun to appear motionless, Spinoza concludes that some other natural event must have occurred that confused the senses of those present and appeared miraculous.[19]

The Protestant emphasis on scripture alone and on its literal historical meaning had paved the way for new Enlightenment understandings of scripture.[20] The most reasonable means of dealing with scriptural incongruities, what Origen had called "stumbling blocks," became historical context. And with every new discovery of the Enlightenment, the distance between the present and the biblical past seemed to grow. The biblical world, in which the divine was ever active, became increasingly unfamiliar.

Separated by an ocean, most Americans in the early 1800s did not confront the full force of Enlightenment scholarship.[21] This period marked the height of the Second Great Awakening and the birth of the Church of Jesus Christ of Latter-day Saints; and, for many in this period, God remained actively involved in the world. When Joseph Smith Jr. read the Bible, he did not assume a position of intellectual distance or objectivity common among the European scholars of his time. Rather, like other dispensationalist visionaries, Smith understood his

18. For example, Gen 22:14, Deut 3:14, etc. See Frampton, *Spinoza and the Rise of Historical Criticism*, 227–28; and Steven Nadler, "The Bible Hermeneutics of Baruch Spinoza," in Sæbø 2:827–36.

19. Spinoza, *Theological-Political Treatise*, 26–7; see Frampton, *Spinoza and the Rise of Historical Criticism*, 226 and note 89. For modern historical critical approaches to the miraculous, see hereinafter.

20. For more on how the Enlightenment shaped a variety of approaches to the Bible, see Jonathan Sheehan, *The Enlightenment Bible: Translation, Scholarship, Culture* (Princeton, NJ: Princeton University Press, 2005); and Michael G. Legaspi, *The Death of Scripture and the Rise of Biblical Studies*, Oxford Studies in Historical Theology (Oxford, UK: Oxford University Press, 2010).

21. Enlightenment scholarship was, however, influential on certain key figures who were responsible for the First and Second Great Awakening; cf. Robert E. Brown, *Jonathan Edwards and the Bible* (Bloomington: Indiana University Press, 2002); and Michael J. Lee, *The Erosion of Biblical Certainty: Battles Over Authority and Interpretation in America* (New York: Palgrave Macmillan, 2013), 53–85.

relation to the Bible to be one of continuity.[22] He was like the biblical Abraham or Moses, another Elijah or John the Baptist, but heralding a new dispensation and proclaiming the second coming of Christ. Yet Smith also engaged regularly with the scholarly theological work available to him. For instance, in his preaching and perhaps also in producing his "New Translation" of the KJV Bible (JST), Smith was influenced by *Buck's Theological Dictionary* and by Adam Clarke's *Commentary on the Bible*.[23] Smith also found inspiration in his study of biblical and theological languages, including Hebrew, Greek, Latin, and German.[24] At the foundations of the modern Church of Jesus Christ, therefore, one finds the prophetic impulse to seek understanding directly from God through prayer and other spiritual practices, and one also finds the intellectual impulse to learn languages, to study out of the best books, and to seek knowledge wherever it may be found.[25] The natural tension between these two impulses can be productive or divisive. And, by the beginning of the twentieth century, both of these results are manifest in the traditionalist/modernist debates that played out in churches across the United States.[26]

When historical criticism arrived in American universities, it was accompanied by a German model of academic study that focused on internal dialogue among scholars with little concern for dogma or for a denominational

22. See David F. Holland, "American Visionaries and Their Approaches to the Past," in *Approaching Antiquity: Joseph Smith and the Ancient World*, edited by Lincoln H. Blumell, Matthew J. Grey, and Andrew H. Hedges (Provo, UT: BYU Religious Studies Center, 2015), 23–60; Richard Lyman Bushman, *Joseph Smith: Rough Stone Rolling: A Cultural Biography of Mormonism's Founder* (New York: Knopf, 2005), 133–37; and Barlow, *Mormons and the Bible*, 10–45.

23. See Barlow, *Mormons and the Bible*, 49–67; Matthew Bowman and Samuel Brown, "Reverend Buck's Theological Dictionary and the Struggle to Define American Evangelicalism, 1802–1851" *Journal of the Early Republic* 29, no. 3 (2009): 441–73, 469–71; Thomas A. Wayment and Haley Wilson-Lemmon, "A Recovered Resource: The Use of Adam Clarke's Bible Commentary in Joseph Smith's Bible Translation," in *Producing Ancient Scripture: Joseph Smith's Translation Projects in the Development of Mormon Christianity*, edited by Michael Hubbard MacKay, Mark Ashurst-McGee, and Brian M. Hauglid (Salt Lake City: University of Utah Press, 2019), 262–84.

24. On Joseph Smith's study of ancient languages, see Matthew J. Grey, "'The Word of the Lord in the Original': Joseph Smith's Study of Hebrew in Kirtland," in *Approaching Antiquity*, 249–302; John W. Welch, "Joseph Smith's Awareness of Greek and Latin," in *Approaching Antiquity*, 303–28. See also Matthew J. Grey, "Approaching Egyptian Papyri Through Biblical Language: Joseph Smith's Use of Hebrew in His Translation of the Book of Abraham," in *Producing Ancient Scripture: Joseph Smith's Translation Projects in the Development of Mormon Christianity*, edited by Michael Hubbard MacKay, Mark Ashurst-McGee, and Brian M. Hauglid (Salt Lake City: University of Utah Press, 2019), 390–451.

25. These two impulses are promoted in LDS scripture as mutually beneficial, see Doctrine and Covenants 88:118; 90:15; 109:7, 14.

26. For more on the traditionalist/modernist debates, see George M. Marsden, *Fundamentalism and American Culture*, 2nd ed. (New York: Oxford University Press, 2006), 102–8, 118–23, 141–95; Mark A. Noll, *Between Faith and Criticism: Evangelicals, Scholarship, and the Bible in America* (New York: Harper & Row, 1986), 32–61.

audience.[27] In the period between 1870 and 1930, student enrollment in colleges across the United States increased twenty-ninefold, and Christians increasingly took notice of the academic approach to the Bible.[28] While some embraced this rigorous methodology for biblical study, others saw it as a threat to the Bible's divinity and authority. The response of some traditionalist Christians was fundamentalism.[29] Named for a series of pamphlets, *The Fundamentals*, produced between 1910 and 1915, fundamentalism responded to the results of historical criticism with arguments for the necessity of traditionalist Protestant theological positions.[30] One such pamphlet, while allowing that "errors and mistakes of translators, copyists and printers" could exist in the Bible today, insists that the "historicity of the Bible" is the very "basis of its authority."[31] As such, any questions regarding historicity, whether of authorial attribution or of events described in the Bible, become a direct assault on the divine inspiration of the Bible and on its authority for the church. From this fundamentalist perspective, the very questions of historical critics make them the enemies of the church.

Latter-day Saints in the first half of the twentieth century responded to historical criticism in ways that broadly parallel the trajectories observed in American Protestantism.[32] In this period, the Church of Jesus Christ's official position on historical criticism is best summarized in a First Presidency letter written in 1922 by Charles W. Penrose and Anthony W. Ivins on behalf of President Heber J. Grant. In that letter, they acknowledge problems with assuming Mosaic authorship of the entire Pentateuch, they allow for the possibility that biblical characters such as Jonah or Job are fictitious, and they emphasize the importance of the Bible's doctrinal accuracy over its historical

27. Noll, *Between Faith and Criticism*, 33; Robert W. Funk, "The Watershed of the American Biblical Tradition: The Chicago School, First Phase, 1892–1920" *Journal of Biblical Literature* 95, no. 1 (1976): 4–22. For the earliest influence of historical criticism in America, see note 21.

28. Noll, *Between Faith and Criticism*, 220, note 2; citing *Historical Statistics of the United States: Colonial Times to 1957* (Washington, DC: Bureau of the Census, 1960), 210–12.

29. David S. Katz, *God's Last Words: Reading the English Bible from the Reformation to Fundamentalism* (New Haven, CT: Yale University Press, 2004), 312–13; see also Marsden, *Fundamentalism and American Culture*, 118–23.

30. Katz, *God's Last Words*, 312–13.

31. Rev. James M. Gray (Dean of Moody Bible Institute, Chicago), "The Inspiration of the Bible—Definition, Extent and Proof," in *The Fundamentals: A Testimony to the Truth, vol. II*, edited by R.A. Torrey et al. (Grand Rapids, MI: Baker Book House, 1972 [1917]), 9-43. See also Marsden, *Fundamentalism and American Culture*, 122.

32. On American Protestant trajectories, see note 26. Philip Barlow has shown that LDS responses can be situated along a continuum spanning the modernist/traditionalist debate, with such figures as William H. Chamberlin representing the extreme modernist position, Joseph Fielding Smith the extreme traditionalist position, and figures such as B.H. Roberts and John A. Widtsoe occupying intermediate positions. See Barlow, *Mormons and the Bible*, 112–61.

accuracy. Regarding the church's preference for a traditionalist hermeneutic versus a historical-critical reading of the Bible, they wrote, "to answer yes or no … is unwise and should not be undertaken by one representing the church."[33] Philip Barlow has aptly summarized the church's position as "a guarded 'no comment.'"[34] With a cautious openness to academic methodology, Latter-day Saints began to earn advanced degrees in biblical studies and to publish on challenging issues related to the Bible. Moreover, historical criticism was originally included in the training of all Seminary and Institute teachers—professional high school and college level theological instructors in the Church of Jesus Christ.[35]

Focusing on this evidence alone could lead to the erroneous conclusion that the Church of Jesus Christ had sided with the modernists in the traditionalist/modernist debate. Yet some Latter-day Saints were concerned by modernist trends including the historical critical approach to the Bible. For instance, Apostle and later church President Joseph Fielding Smith (Apostle beginning 1910; President 1970–1972) considered historical criticism to be a serious threat to faith.[36] From the perspective of Fielding Smith, historical critics were dangerous:

> They call themselves "higher critics" of the sacred record; but in fact they are destructive critics. They proclaim that the books of the Bible are without divine inspiration and were not written at the time indicated by the record, and in many instances were written by others than those whose names they bear.[37]

Joseph Fielding Smith's understanding of the Bible in this regard reflects the fundamentalist Protestant view described previously. Barlow summarizes his perspective as follows: "Smith's most fundamental hermeneutical assumption was that the Bible … [was] essentially God's speech in print," and "[a]ll

33. Charles W. Penrose to Joseph W. McMurrin, October 31, 1922, FP, letters sent; as cited in Thomas G. Alexander, *Mormonism in Transition: A History of the Latter-day Saints, 1890–1930* (Urbana, IL: University of Chicago Press, 1986), 283 and 366, note 35; see also Barlow, *Mormons and the Bible*, 150.

34. Barlow, *Mormons and the Bible*, 113.

35. Barlow, *Mormons and the Bible*, 152–57; Casey Paul Griffiths, "The Chicago Experiment: Finding the Voice and Charting the Course of Religious Education in the Church," *BYU Studies* 49, no. 4 (2010): 93–97; Thomas W. Simpson, *American Universities and the Birth of Modern Mormonism, 1867–1940* (Chapel Hill: University of North Carolina Press, 2016), 99–101.

36. Bowman, *The Mormon People*, 180.

37. Joseph Fielding Smith, *Man: His Origin and Destiny*, 33; see also Bruce R. McConkie, *Mormon Doctrine*, 2nd ed. (Salt Lake City, UT: Bookcraft, 1979), 353–55.

internal contradictions and historical mistakes in the Bible were to be blamed on intruding copyists and translators."[38] The influence of Joseph Fielding Smith—and of his son-in-law, Apostle Bruce R. McConkie, who held similar views—cannot be overstated. Their matter-of-fact rhetoric combined with their prolificacy shaped a generation and became a mainstay in the official manuals of the Church of Jesus Christ.[39]



This brief history of historical criticism highlights key developments that have influenced how Latter-day Saints engage with biblical scholarship. Latter-day Saints today are heirs to modes of thought born of the Reformation and the Enlightenment. They have also inherited from Joseph Smith foundational commitments to both reason and revelation; and yet the consequences of the early-twentieth century traditionalist/modernist debate left some Latter-day Saints deeply suspicious of academic biblical studies. Despite the challenges that biblical studies can pose to religious beliefs, Latter-day Saints have developed meaningful ways to engage with both current academic methodology and their own religious commitments.

## THE PHILOSOPHY BEHIND HISTORICAL CRITICISM

To understand the challenges Latter-day Saints face in navigating their dual commitments to study and faith, it is necessary to review the philosophical assumptions that lie behind historical critical methodology. At the end of the nineteenth century, Protestant theologian Ernst Troeltsch wrestled with the consequences of historical criticism for traditional Christian theology and belief. Troeltsch identified three principles or foundational assumptions that lie at the basis of historical critical studies of the Bible. Van A. Harvey, in

38. Barlow, *Mormons and the Bible*, 137, 140–41; describing Joseph Fielding Smith, *Seek Ye Earnestly* (Salt Lake City, UT: Deseret Book, 1970), 364–65; and Joseph Fielding Smith, *Man: His Origin and Destiny*, 490–528, especially 491–92. Joseph Fielding Smith is responding primarily to fellow Latter-day Saint Heber Cyrus Snell, *Ancient Israel: Its Story and Meaning*, 2nd ed. (Salt Lake City: Utah Printing Co., 1957 [1948]); see *Man: His Origin and Destiny*, 515. See also Richard Sherlock, "Faith and History: The Snell Controversy," *Dialogue: A Journal of Mormon Thought* 12, no. 1 (1979): 27–41.

39. Their opinions gained popularity despite the attempts of President David O. McKay and others to manage their increasingly disproportionate influence, see Barlow, *Mormons and the Bible*, 133–41, 156–57, 203–12; see also Gregory A. Prince and Wm. Robert Wright, *David O. McKay and the Rise of Modern Mormonism* (Salt Lake City: University of Utah Press, 2005), 45–53. Consider one of the most recent textbooks for LDS college students, *New Testament Student Manual: Religion 211–212* (Salt Lake City, UT: Church of Jesus Christ of Latter-day Saints, 2014), which includes approximately two hundred references to Bruce R. McConkie. By way of contrast, the same manual includes no more than fifty references to any church president with the exception of Joseph Smith, who surpasses McConkie only when references to the "Joseph Smith Translation" (the "New Translation" of the Bible) are included in the count.

his work *The Historian and the Believer*, summarizes these "three interrelated principles" as follows:

> (1) The principle of criticism, by which [Troeltsch] meant that our judgments about the past cannot simply be classified as true or false but must be seen as claiming only a greater or lesser degree of probability and as always open to revision; (2) the principle of analogy, by which he meant that we are able to make such judgments of probability only if we presuppose that our own present experience is not radically dissimilar to the experience of past persons; and (3) the principle of correlation, by which he meant that the phenomena of man's historical life are so related and interdependent that no radical change can take place at any one point in the historical nexus without effecting a change in all that immediately surrounds it. Historical explanation, therefore, necessarily takes the form of understanding an event in terms of its antecedents and consequences, and no event can be isolated from its historically conditioned time and space.[40]

Harvey's own study is an attempt to grapple with these principles and the ostensible problems they present for "the [Protestant] believer."[41] For Latter-day Saints, some of these principles are less problematic than others. For instance, the "principle of criticism"—that our understanding of the past is based on probabilities and remains tentative—potentially destabilizes the meaning of the Bible as a foundation for faith since meaning (as historical meaning) becomes itself contingent and unfinalizable.[42] In practice, Latter-day Saints who approach their scripture with fundamentalist sensibilities may be discomfited by a historian's application of this principle, such as in questioning the historicity of biblical events. Nevertheless, Latter-day Saints, like Catholics, can appeal to ecclesiastical authority and tradition outside of the Bible. For that reason, this "principle of criticism" need not disturb the foundations of their faith in the same way it might for those who profess *sola scriptura*. In fact, with a belief in open canon and continuing revelation, the notion of

40. Van A. Harvey, *The Historian and the Believer: The Morality of Historical Knowledge and Christian Belief* (Urbana: University of Illinois Press, 1996 [1966]), 14–15. See Ernst Troeltsch, "Historical and Dogmatic Method in Theology (1898)," in *Religion in History*, trans. by J.L. Adams and W.F. Bense (Minneapolis, MN: Fortress, 1991), 11–32, here 13–15.

41. Harvey, *Historian and the Believer*, 14–15.

42. Harvey, *Historian and the Believer*, 17–19, 32–33.

unfinalizable knowledge could itself be affirmed as a foundational truth-claim for Latter-day Saints.

The second principle, the "principle of analogy"—that the world generally functioned in the past as it does today—is a necessary premise for understanding any narrative from the past. Yet how does the modern historian, who has never witnessed loaves and fishes multiply or seen a person walking on water, make sense of such phenomena?[43] Early historical critics attempted to explain the miraculous solely through the lens of post-Enlightenment rationality, at first as misperception (as we saw with Spinoza) and later as myth.[44] For some Christians, such explanations were particularly problematic when applied, for instance, to the resurrection of Jesus. A historian's study of Jesus may never completely satisfy the Christian who professes bodily resurrection to be the greatest of all miracles. Nevertheless, for such Christians, academic studies of the miraculous have become less problematic in the wake of postcolonial critiques of earlier positivist historiography.

Post-Enlightenment Western scholars once assumed, as postcolonial historian Dipesh Chakrabarty explains, "that the human is ontologically singular, that gods and spirits are in the end 'social facts,' that the social somehow exists prior to them."[45] Yet many scholars now realize that this assumption imposes on the past (and on the present) an ontology and epistemology shared only by a relative few. This critique is not a claim that the historical critic should or could attempt to inhabit the pre-Enlightenment mind. Rather, acknowledging with Chakrabarty that there is "no society in which humans have existed without gods and spirits accompanying them," it is better in practice to "take gods and spirits to be existentially coeval with the human, and think from the assumption that the question of being human involves the question of being with gods and spirits."[46] In other words, the modern Western historian is better served by allowing for experiences of the world (and of the otherworldly) that lie outside of her own culturally conditioned worldview. Consequently, it is rare today to find an academic who studies biblical miracles or divine manifestations with the intent either to discredit them or to rationalize them as Spinoza once did—even if the scholar does not personally believe in miracles.[47]

43. Harvey, *Historian and the Believer*, 31–32; and Barton, *Nature of Biblical Criticism*, 47–48.

44. See Sheehan, *Enlightenment Bible*, 223–58; Legaspi, *Death of Scripture and the Rise of Biblical Studies*, 3–51.

45. Dipesh Chakrabarty, *Provincializing Europe: Postcolonial Thought and Historical Difference* (Princeton, NJ: Princeton University Press), 16.

46. Chakrabarty, *Provincializing Europe*, 16.

47. See Barton, *Nature of Biblical Criticism*, 48–49.

Troeltsch's final principle is the principle of correlation: historical context is necessary for understanding any event in the past because any "radical change" precipitates change in the immediate "historical nexus." This is likely the most challenging of Troeltsch's three principles for Latter-day Saints. Some of Joseph Smith's revelations make claims about the past that run contrary to current historical knowledge; they disrupt the principle of correlation, normal sequences of cause and effect. For instance, the Book of Mormon and Book of Abraham as well as the Book of Moses and other texts from Joseph Smith's "New Translation" of the Bible unitedly give historical-narrative form to the Christian theological affirmation that Jesus Christ is present in the pages of the Old Testament (e.g., Luke 24:27; 1 Corinthians 10:1–4; 1 Peter 1:10–12).[48] This thoroughgoing Christianization of pre-Christian texts disrupts Troeltsch's principle of correlation by suggesting that Christian beliefs and practices existed in ancient times and places for which there is no evidence outside of the scripture revealed in the early 1800s CE through Joseph Smith. In other words, Smith's scripture implies that "radical change" did take place in the ancient "historical nexus without effecting a change in all that immediately surrounds it"—or, at least, without effecting change in ways that remain perceptible in the extant historical record today.[49]

The post-Enlightenment historian makes decisions regarding a past event based on well-reasoned analysis of evidence relevant to the time and place of that event, not based on either ecclesiastical tradition and authority or an a priori rejection of that tradition.[50] The study of history, as an academic discipline, strives to remain theologically neutral.[51] How, then, do Latter-day Saints who study the Bible using historical critical methodology negotiate the tension between the historical nexus of the Bible and the scripture revealed through

48. See Bushman, *Rough Stone Rolling*, 133–37; Barlow, *Mormons and the Bible*, 36–40, 46–79; Kathleen Flake, "Translating Time: The Nature and Function of Joseph Smith's Narrative Canon," *The Journal of Religion* 87.4 (2007): 497–527; and Terryl Givens and Brian Hauglid, *The Pearl of Greatest Price: Mormonism's Most Controversial Scripture* (Oxford, UK: Oxford University Press, 2019), 123–24.

49. Harvey, *The Historian and the Believer*, 15. See Harvey's full description of Troeltsch's "principle of correlation."

50. See Immanuel Kant, "An Answer to the Question: 'What Is Enlightenment?'" in *Political Writings*, edited by H.S. Reiss (New York: Cambridge University Press, 1991), 54–60; and Kant, *Critique of Pure Reason*, 100–1 (Preface xi, note).

51. On the challenge of theological neutrality in the practice of historical criticism, see Jon D. Levenson, *The Hebrew Bible, The Old Testament, and Historical Criticism: Jews and Christians in Biblical Studies* (Louisville, KY: Westminster/John Knox, 1993), xiii, 6–7; see also Elisabeth Schüssler-Fiorenza, *In Memory of Her: A Feminist Theological Reconstruction of Christian Origins* (New York: Crossroad, 1983), 4–6.

Joseph Smith?[52] Some Latter-day Saints have defended the historical claims of Smith's scripture. These apologetic studies accept the logic of Troeltsch's principle of correlation and work to assemble comparable evidence from antiquity to demonstrate, for instance, that the Book of Mormon or Book of Abraham fit within the ancient "historical nexus."[53] Others have theoretically bracketed questions regarding the historical claims of Smith's scripture—often still defending the theological and religious value of those texts—and studied the Bible within its ancient historical context while studying Smith's scripture within the context of early nineteenth century American Christianity.[54] This is an oversimplification of the variety of Latter-day Saint approaches to the Bible, but it serves to illustrate how thoroughly Troeltsch's principle of correlation influences Latter-day Saints who adopt historical methodology to study scripture.



## CONCLUSION

Given the historical affirmations implicated in the beliefs of Latter-day Saints, the methodology and conclusions of historical criticism will continue to be relevant as Latter-day Saints study their scripture. Yet historical criticism is a tool, one among many, for engaging with biblical texts and working to answer the various questions they pose. In matters of faith, historical criticism alone is insufficient. Theological readings, as well as post-colonial, feminist, queer,

52. The challenge of reconciling historical evidence with modern beliefs is not unique to Latter-day Saints; see Marc Zvi Brettler, Peter Enns, and Daniel J. Harrington, *The Bible and the Believer: How to Read the Bible Critically and Religiously* (Oxford, UK: Oxford University Press, 2012); and the collection of articles by Matthew J. Grey and Cory Crawford, James L. Kugel, Candida R. Moss, Peter Enns, David Rolph Seely, D. Jill Kirby, and Philip L. Barlow, in *Studies in the Bible and Antiquity* 8 (2016): 1–129. See also Martin E. Marty's address to LDS church historians, "Two Integrities: An Address to the Crisis in Mormon Historiography," *Journal of Mormon History* 10 (1983): 3–19.

53. For example, Paul Y. Hoskisson, ed., *Historicity and the Latter-day Saint Scriptures*, Religious Studies Center Monograph Series 18 (Provo, UT: BYU Religious Studies Center, 2001). For an overview of LDS apologetic work on the Book of Mormon that attempts to adopt historical methodology, see Terryl L. Givens, *By the Hand of Mormon: The American Scripture that Launched a New World Religion* (Oxford, UK: Oxford University Press, 2002), 89–154. For a review of apologetic work on the Book of Abraham, see Givens and Hauglid, *The Pearl of Greatest Price*, 159–69.

54. See Grant Hardy, *Understanding the Book of Mormon: A Reader's Guide* (Oxford, UK: Oxford University Press, 2010), xvi. For a variety methodological approaches to reading the Book of Mormon, see Elizabeth Fenton and Jared Hickman, eds., *Americanist Approaches to The Book of Mormon* (Oxford, UK: Oxford University Press, 2019). For variety of interpretative positions on the Book of Abraham that do not "forsake reasonableness," see Givens and Hauglid, *The Pearl of Greatest Price*, 193–94, 201–2. Some have gone further and rejected the historical claims of Smith's scripture, leading to rigorous debates, accusations of heresy, and even threats of legal action; for review of such debates surrounding the Book of Mormon, see Givens, *By the Hand of Mormon*, 155–84. For a review of LDS historical approaches to the Bible, see above and Barlow, *Mormons and the Bible*, 112–61.

race-critical, disability studies, and other interpretive strategies are also useful.[55] To acknowledge the insufficiency of historical criticism is not an argument for historical relativism—when asking questions about the past, some conclusions are better supported by the evidence than others. And critical thought, especially about scripture and religious beliefs, has been a cornerstone of the Church of Jesus Christ of Latter-day Saints from its foundations. Joseph Smith's critique of Christian creedalism was born, in part, out of his desire for freedom to explore the theological possibilities of scripture. While some of that originary freedom has cemented into certain creed-like affirmations today, Latter-day Saints' open canon and expectation of additional revelation holds the door open for new thought and new inspiration, even through the methodology of historical criticism.

55. Historical critics today acknowledge that the range of potential historical meanings of a text does not delimit all possible meaning for that text through time. In other words, what a text *meant* in the past may not be the same as what that text *means* today; see Krister Stendahl, "Biblical Theology, Contemporary," in *The Interpreter's Dictionary of the Bible*, four vols. (Nashville, TN: Abingdon Press, 1962), 1:418–32, here, 419; updated and reprinted in *Reading the Bible in the Global Village: Helsinki*, edited by. Heikki Räisänen et al. (Atlanta: Society of Biblical Literature, 2000), 67–106. See also Barton, *Nature of Biblical Criticism*, 3–4.

# 14

# Biblical Theology and the Latter-day Saint Tradition

JOSEPH M. SPENCER

As other essays in the present volume attest, the Latter-day Saint tradition has sustained an uneasy relationship with biblical studies as an academic discipline. It may be unsurprising, therefore, that the academic subdiscipline of biblical theology—itself at times or in ways unstable and often contested—has drawn relatively little attention from Latter-day Saint scholars. Although a self-identifying discipline called biblical theology has been in existence since before the birth of Joseph Smith, it has until recently had relatively little impact on Latter-day Saint thinking about the Bible. This essay explores reasons Latter-day Saint scholars have not engaged with biblical theology, while also making a case that this marks a missed opportunity, especially since much of twentieth-century biblical theology has served to critique (without rejecting) strictly historical-critical scholarship. Latter-day Saint critics of "higher criticism" might well have developed more sophisticated critiques by engaging with biblical theology, and they might have found a place for themselves in the larger academic conversation concerning the Bible. Arguably, however, the lack of Latter-day Saint interest in biblical theology is due in large part to the Latter-day Saint tradition's similarly uneasy relationship with academic theology. Because Latter-day Saints have often "considered the very enterprise of theology to be largely a secular enterprise, a sign of true religion's failure," biblical theology has been easily dismissed alongside other theological projects.[1] It has thus really been only in the context of a recent revitalization of



1. Terryl L. Givens, *Wrestling the Angel: The Foundations of Mormon Thought: Cosmos, God, Humanity* (New York: Oxford University Press, 2015), 6.

speculative Latter-day Saint theology that biblical theology has begun to draw the serious attention of (some) Latter-day Saint scholars.

In the following pages, I will (1) review briefly the history and current state of biblical theology, (2) outline points of potential contact between the interests of biblical theologians and Latter-day Saint readers of the Bible, and (3) sketch the recent emergence of a (still-nascent) discipline of Latter-day Saint biblical theology.

## BIBLICAL THEOLOGY

Depending on the definition of the word *theology,* it can be said that biblical theology is older than Christianity itself. Critical work on the Bible has shown how the final or canonical shape of many biblical texts is the result of complicated and often prolonged processes of editing. Careful reconstruction of these processes reveals the role played in them by theological reflection.[2] Further, critical work on the Bible has shown how often the production of biblical texts was undertaken in the first place with an eye to the theological implications of other biblical texts. Close study of relationships among biblical texts thus indicates that later texts offer implicit theological interpretations of earlier texts.[3] Thus, long before Jews and Christians began to develop an identifiable discipline of theological interpretation *of* the Bible, there was already a rich tradition of theological interpretation that takes place *within* the Bible. In certain ways, then, Jewish and Christian theological interpretation of the Bible has simply continued and developed what the Bible itself already offers to its readers: a disciplined reflection on the relevance to the present of what previous generations have received as God's word.

Although the history of theological interpretation thus stretches into the ancient world, the *discipline* of biblical theology is generally regarded as distinctly modern and largely Protestant. That is, most discussions of biblical theology focus on the discipline that began in the eighteenth century to distinguish itself deliberately from both the strict practice of textual exegesis and the heady work of systematic theology.[4] The two alternative disciplines have often

2. See, most famously, Brevard S. Childs, *Introduction to the Old Testament as Scripture* (Philadelphia: Fortress Press, 1979).

3. The foundational work in this connection is Michael Fishbane, *Biblical Interpretation in Ancient Israel* (New York: Oxford University Press, 1985).

4. See important discussions in John Sandys-Wunsch and Laurence Eldredge, "J.P. Gabler and the Distinction between Biblical and Dogmatic Theology: Translation, Commentary, and Discussion of His Originality," *Scottish Journal of Theology* 33, no. 2 (April 1980): 133–58; and John Sandys-Wunsch, "G.T. Zachariae's Contribution to Biblical Theology," *Zeitschrift für die altestamentliche Wissenschaft* 92 (1988): 1–23.

in the modern period functioned as rival opposites. Textual exegesis has generally made empirical history the determining horizon within which Christian scripture acquires a (relatively) stable meaning, while systematic theology has generally made ideal reason the guiding principle for deciding the larger doctrinal framework within which Christian scripture is to be read rightly. Biblical theology, however, has labored to loosen the strictest intellectual commitments of these rivals while nonetheless drawing inspiration and insight from both.

Biblical theology is thus historically conditioned, taking its rise in the wake of and in response especially to the development of the modern "history of religions" approach to biblical study. The latter project, as Krister Stendahl nicely puts it, "drastically widened the hiatus between our time and that of the Bible" or "between the questions self-evidently raised in modern minds and those presupposed, raised, and answered in the Scriptures." The effect of this development was that "the question of meaning was split up in two tenses: 'What *did* it mean?' and 'What *does* it mean?'"[5] Biblical theology is effectively the discipline that assigns itself the task of investigating the boundary between these two differently tensed questions. It depends on the work of critics who seek principally to establish the original meaning of biblical texts, but it asks about the relevance of those texts for the contemporary world and the church as well. It also remains conversant with the work of ecclesiastical leaders and church-committed thinkers who reflect on the nature of God and the God-led life, but it insists at the same time on tying all theological reflection to the task of interpreting the biblical canon responsibly.

From its inception, the discipline of biblical theology began to fragment. Within a decade of the discipline's formal announcement by J.P. Gabler in 1787, G.L. Bauer was drawing a distinction between Old Testament theology and New Testament theology. As Brevard Childs notes, this development responded to "the growing conviction that the historical discontinuities between the testaments defied all attempts to maintain a traditional canonical unity."[6] Despite certain conservative efforts at interpreting the whole of the Christian Bible in its unity, this conviction only grew stronger over the course of the nineteenth century. By the beginning of the twentieth century, it began to appear that biblical theology was doomed to be regarded as "largely anachronistic," an "unfortunate vestige from a past era."[7]

5. Krister Stendahl, "Biblical Theology, Contemporary," in *The Interpreter's Dictionary of the Bible: An Illustrated Encyclopedia*, ed. George Arthur Buttrick, five vols. (Nashville, TN: Abingdon Press, 1962), 1:419.

6. Brevard S. Childs, *Biblical Theology of the Old and New Testaments: Theological Reflection on the Christian Bible* (Minneapolis, MN: Fortress Press, 1992), 5.

7. Childs, *Biblical Theology of the Old and New Testaments,* 6.

Things changed drastically in the first decades of the twentieth century, beginning with the publication of a book that Walter Brueggemann calls "a *novum* without antecedent": Karl Barth's 1918 commentary on Paul's letter to the Romans.[8] Calling for a return of biblical texts to the care of the church, and identifying the theory-laden presuppositions of historical critics, Barth "interrupted the assumptions of modernity that had emptied the biblical text of any serious theological claim."[9] This seems to have enlivened theologically inclined scholars of the Old Testament, and by the mid-1920s an important debate between Otto Eissfeldt and Walter Eichrodt brought to the fore the question originally posed by the discipline of biblical theology: whether and how such a discipline could be distinguished from textual exegesis and dogmatic theology.[10] The next several decades then witnessed the appearance of the most robust and influential works in biblical theology. For the New Testament, one must point to the controversial work of Rudolf Bultmann.[11] As regards the Old Testament, the towering figure of Gerhard von Rad stands out from other interpreters.[12] These were the work of German scholars, but they had an immediate impact throughout the world of biblical studies.

One major effect of the forceful return of the discipline of biblical theology was the emergence of what Brevard Childs called "a biblical theology movement" in the United States of America following World War II—led especially by G. Ernest Wright.[13] According to Craig Bartholomew, "dates for this movement can be set with precision, from around 1945 to 1961, when publications by [Langdon] Gilkey and [James] Barr are said to have sunk" it definitively.[14] What distinguished the movement from previous efforts in twentieth-century biblical theology was its strong emphasis on the unity of the Christian Bible's two testaments and its insistence that the whole of the Bible attests to God's self-revelation through divine acts in history.[15] Even adherents to the discipline of biblical theology agree that the movement had problems as a project.

8. Walter Brueggemann, *Theology of the Old Testament: Testimony, Dispute, Advocacy* (Minneapolis, MN: Fortress Press, 2005), 16.

9. Brueggemann, *Theology of the Old Testament*, 18.

10. See the helpful summary in James K. Mead, *Biblical Theology: Issues, Methods, and Themes* (Louisville, KY: Westminster John Knox Pres, 2007), 40–41.

11. Rudolf Bultmann, *Theology of the New Testament*, two vols., trans. Kendrick Grobel (New York: Scribner's, 1951–1955).

12. Gerhard von Rad, *Old Testament Theology*, two vols., trans. D.M.G. Stalker (New York: Harper & Row, 1962–1965).

13. Brevard S. Childs, *Biblical Theology in Crisis* (Philadelphia: Westminster Press, 1970), 9.

14. Craig G. Bartholomew, "Biblical Theology," in *Dictionary for Theological Interpretation of the Bible*, edited by Kevin J. Vanhoozer (Grand Rapids, MI: Baker Academic, 2005), 86.

15. G. Ernest Wright, *God Who Acts: Biblical Theology as Recital* (London: SCM Press, 1952).

Most often noted is the fact that the movement embraced a set of historical disciplines that raise questions about the exceptionality—and therefore the authority—of the Bible even as the movement (usually implicitly) refused to question biblical authority, taking the Bible as a guide for understanding the moral place of human beings in the world.[16] Nonetheless, the movement's failures spurred a further resurgence of the discipline, beginning especially with Childs's 1970 diagnosis of the movement's failings and alternate proposal for the project of biblical theology. Consequently, the whole field in the first decades of the twenty-first century is colored by the need to resolve what the biblical theology movement left unresolved.



Today, English-speaking biblical theology is a diverse discipline that finds its unity principally in its complex genealogical relationship to the expired biblical theology movement of the mid-twentieth century and more broadly in its insistence on remaining distinct from both exegesis and dogmatics. Also shared by most working in the discipline is a conviction that the principal object of biblical theology is to reflect on the theological relationship between the Bible's two testaments, despite their origins in historically and religiously divergent contexts.[17] Despite certain commonalities, helpful surveys of contemporary work in biblical theology distinguish among a wide variety of methods that differ in how they understand the relationship between the strictly theological and the strictly historical.[18] Further, some approaches to biblical theology remain squarely within the Enlightenment project, while others use so-called "postmodern" approaches to biblical texts by way of contesting Enlightenment perspectives. Still more, certain biblical theologians argue that theological reading of scripture is primarily the purview of the confessing church, while others insist that the project should remain a strictly academic project—and practitioners can be located as much among the clergy as among those in academic posts (although the latter represent the majority). So much diversity might be suggestive of a period of confusion, but the first decades of the twenty-first century have produced careful attempts to sift the various

16. See Childs, *Biblical Theology in Crisis*, 51–90.

17. Looking for promising continuity where historians see primarily discontinuity, biblical theologians underscore ways in which God's involvement in the world suggests consistent patterns that might reveal something about the nature of God, or about what ideal relationships with God and with other human beings look like. Others emphasize the possibility of finding in historical change the basic contours of a theological story about God's involvement with the world, a story that clarifies divine intentions and ideal human responses. For a good outline of basic positions on these matters, see Mead, *Biblical Theology*, 169–239.

18. See the helpful typology worked out in Edward W. Klink III and Darian R. Lockett, *Understanding Biblical Theology: A Comparison of Theory and Practice* (Grand Rapids, MI: Zondervan, 2012). See also the discussion in Mead, *Biblical Theology*, 121–67.

proposals and to establish the meaning of the project going forward. In many ways, the future of biblical theology looks bright.



Current practitioners of biblical theology claim to see the renaissance of the past few decades "as a gift, a springtime of biblical interpretation." Precisely for that reason, though, many are asking how students of the Bible might rightly "receive this gift" and "contribute toward its maturing."[19] In many ways, it seems that these are questions that Latter-day Saints might productively ask for themselves as well.

## MISSED OPPORTUNITIES AND LIVE POSSIBILITIES

The Latter-day Saint intellectual tradition first encountered critical study of the Bible in the last years of the nineteenth century, soon after this scholarship began to arrive in the American context (see Combs in this volume).[20] In 1895, B.H. Roberts (1857–1933) published criticisms of David Strauss's and Ernest Renan's naturalistic portrayals of the life of Jesus.[21] He was unimpressed, to say the least: "To this then it comes at last, a Christianity without a Christ."[22] Significantly, however, Roberts clearly felt that higher criticism of the sort represented by Strauss and Renan, especially because of the strife it caused within European Christianity more generally, called less for human than divine response. Because "the divided state of Christendom of itself argues something wrong," along with "the existence of a broad and constantly widening stream of unbelief," Roberts concluded that the world was "in need of a new witness for God," which he of course identified with the restoration of earliest Christianity in the Church of Jesus Christ of Latter-day Saints.[23] The rise of biblical criticism was for him more a symptom than a challenge.

Roberts's response in many ways established the tone for the twentieth century. Some fifteen years after his first published statement about biblical criticism, church-owned BYU hired a few professors who introduced the new criticism to their students. The result was a difficult—if nonetheless largely local—battle over the Latter-day Saint tradition's relationship to modernism,

19. Craig G. Bartholomew and Heath A. Thomas, eds., *A Manifesto for Theological Interpretation* (Grand Rapids, MI: Baker Academic, 2016), ix.

20. Philip L. Barlow, *Mormons and the Bible: The Place of the Latter-day Saints in American Religion* (New York: Oxford University Press, 1991), 103–47.

21. B.H. Roberts, *A New Witness for God* (Salt Lake City, UT: George Q. Cannon and Sons, 1895), 25–41.

22. Roberts, *A New Witness for God*, 35.

23. Roberts, *A New Witness for God*, 41, 43.

which resulted in a general distaste for critical biblical study.[24] These events set the stage for an emerging biblical literalism of a fundamentalist sort, represented especially by the profoundly influential author and church leader Joseph Fielding Smith (1876–1972).[25] In Philip Barlow's words, Smith's "censure of [historical criticism's] methods and its conclusions . . . approached the absolute."[26] Because of his popularity with members of the Church of Jesus Christ of Latter-day Saints, and thanks to the way his work was appropriated and confirmed by his equally popular son-in-law and eventually fellow apostle, Bruce R. McConkie (1915–1985), Smith's approach to biblical interpretation largely held sway among average Latter-day Saints to the end of the twentieth century.[27] Although Smith differed from Roberts deeply on other intellectual matters (most famously on the theological implications of evolution), the two shared a suspicion that biblical criticism signaled larger systemic problems in Christianity.[28] Neither would make a serious attempt to learn from biblical criticism, and neither ever saw the virtues of the discipline of biblical theology for placing important limits on the perceived excesses of the historical critical project.

The early encounter between the Latter-day Saint tradition and the world of academic study of the Bible arguably marked a missed opportunity. Latter-day Saint intellectuals early developed understandable concerns about biblical criticism, but rather than leading them into a fuller study of biblical scholarship and therefore into an awareness of the resources of biblical theology, these concerns led them to privilege dated and secondary conservative scholarship over what might have spoken more directly to their interests.[29] By the time the most important works of twentieth-century biblical theology became available in English translation, there were unfortunately few Latter-day Saints inter-

24. Thomas W. Simpson, *American Universities and the Birth of Modern Mormonism, 1867–1940* (Chapel Hill: University of North Carolina Press, 2016), 69–91.

25. I here use "fundamentalist" in a technical sense. For some discussion, see James Barr, *Fundamentalism* (Philadelphia: Westminster Press, 1977), 1–10.

26. Barlow, *Mormons and the Bible*, 122.

27. Matthew Bowman, *The Mormon People: The Making of an American Faith* (New York: Random House, 2012), 179–83, 200–204. See also Barlow, *Mormons and the Bible*, 185–94.

28. For a good summary of the conflicts between Roberts and Smith, see Richard Sherlock and Jeffrey E. Keller, "The B.H. Roberts/Joseph Fielding Smith/James E. Talmage Affair," in *The Search for Harmony*, edited by Gene A. Sessions and Craig J. Oberg (Salt Lake City, UT: Signature Books, 1993), 93–116.

29. On the use of dated and conservative scholarship by major Latter-day Saint authors, see Malcolm R. Thorp, "James E. Talmage and the Tradition of Victorian Lives of Jesus," *Sunstone* 12 (January 1988): 8–13. See further comments by Matthew J. Grey, "Latter-day Saint Perceptions of Jewish Apostasy in the Time of Jesus," in *Standing Apart: Mormon Historical Consciousness and the Concept of Apostasy*, edited by Miranda Wilcox and John D. Young (New York: Oxford University Press, 2014), 147–73.

ested in seeing what biblical theologians might contribute to Latter-day Saint thinking about the Bible, let alone what Latter-day Saint perspectives might themselves contribute to the field of biblical studies. Even university-trained biblical scholars from within the Latter-day Saint tradition, both liberal and conservative, apparently did not draw in their research on works by major biblical theologians.[30] The sole possible exception to this trend during the mid-twentieth century would be Hugh Nibley (1910–2005), whose work can be productively interpreted as a theological project in ways akin or in response to certain strains within biblical theology.[31] Even Nibley, however, never offered a serious assessment of the discipline of biblical theology as such, drawing only occasionally on its most illustrious authors (especially Rudolf Bultmann) for his own apologetic purposes. And his genuinely theological readings of biblical texts are very few and very far between.[32]

This lack of direct engagement with biblical theology on the part of Latter-day Saint intellectuals is disappointing, especially during the twentieth century when biblical theology had its strongest and most direct impact on the world of biblical studies. What makes it so disappointing is that biblical theologians have done the most serious work in attempting to draw up the limits of biblical criticism while nonetheless recognizing the serious gains made by critical work. That is, it is within the larger discipline of biblical theology that a *non-reactionary* critique of the excesses of criticism has been successfully and compellingly offered. Biblical theology therefore represents the most serious available arguments for the need to recognize the role that the Bible has played and that it should still play in the life of faith, as well as in the life of the church. In failing to engage with biblical theology, Latter-day Saint students of the Bible run the risk of retreating into an unreflective conservatism, a Latter-day Saint form of biblical fundamentalism that has often been characteristic of the tradition, or of assimilating unreflectively into biblical liberalism,

30. The names of no established figures from the biblical theological tradition appear either in Heber C. Snell, *Ancient Israel—Its Story and Meaning*, 3rd ed. (Salt Lake City: University of Utah Press, 1963); or in Sidney B. Sperry, *The Spirit of the Old Testament*, 2nd ed. (Salt Lake City, UT: Deseret Book, 1970)—the representative liberal and conservative Latter-day Saint biblical scholars of the mid-twentieth century.

31. Stuart A.C. Parker, "History through Seer Stones: Mormon Historical Thought, 1890–2010" (PhD diss., University of Toronto, 2011), 218–66.

32. The only two biblical texts for which Nibley has given strikingly provocative theological (rather than merely historical) interpretations are Matthew 16:17–19 and 1 Corinthians 13:8–13. For his basic theological exegeses of these passages (repeated and developed elsewhere in his writings as well), see Hugh Nibley, "Baptism for the Dead in Ancient Times," in *Mormonism and Early Christianity* (Collected Works of Hugh Nibley, vol. 4), edited by Todd M. Compton and Stephen D. Ricks (Salt Lake City, UT: Deseret Book and FARMS, 1987), 100–167.

an intellectual elitism that often finds itself alienated from the life of devotion. In other words, because the Latter-day Saint intellectual tradition often finds itself, as Martin Marty has pointed out, caught between "two integrities" (faith and knowledge), it stands to learn from—and perhaps to contribute to—the subdiscipline within biblical studies that has attempted most carefully to work out its responsibilities to the same two integrities.[33]

In many ways, as has been seen, it is unsurprising that the Latter-day Saint intellectual tradition during the twentieth century missed its opportunity to interact with biblical theology. In the end, however, it may have been less important during the twentieth century than it will be during the twenty-first century for Latter-day Saint scholars to reflect, in conversation with serious biblical theologians, on the relationship between the Bible as an object of secular study and the Bible as an object of living faith. In 1991, Philip Barlow could not point to a "biblical-studies renaissance among the Mormons" parallel to that "in evangelical biblical study" after World War II.[34] Today, however, precisely such a renaissance seems to be underway, with Latter-day Saints represented in a wide variety of disciplines in biblical studies. Not only are there believing Latter-day Saint scholars writing about the Bible for strictly academic venues, but there has also been in recent years a clear uptick in publications about critical biblical studies aimed at a lay Latter-day Saint audience.[35] It seems it is therefore especially important in the present that biblical theology receive a hearing in the Latter-day Saint context.

## THE BEGINNINGS OF A DISCIPLINE

With so many Latter-day Saint academics now working in biblical studies, it would be impossible to say that biblical theology is being overlooked by the Latter-day Saint intellectual community. It is nonetheless true that most Latter-day Saints working in biblical studies have found their places somewhere within the more strictly historical subdisciplines—archaeology, Dead Sea Scrolls, papyrology, early Christian history, and so on. Curiously, the few

33. Martin E. Marty, "Two Integrities: An Address to the Crisis in Mormon Historiography," *Journal of Mormon History* 10 (1983): 3–19. Areas of potential conflict between critical biblical study and Latter-day Saint faith commitments—which are therefore areas where biblical theology might provide important avenues for academic study—include the shape of the Pentateuch, relationships among parts of Isaiah, and the orientation of apocalyptic portions of the New Testament.

34. Barlow, *Mormons and the Bible*, 225–26.

35. See especially David Bokovoy, *Authoring the Old Testament: Genesis–Deuteronomy* (Draper, UT: Greg Kofford Books, 2014); and Michael Austin, *Re-reading Job: Understanding the Ancient World's Greatest Poem* (Salt Lake City, UT: Greg Kofford Books, 2014).

Latter-day Saint scholars who have begun to draw quite directly on biblical theology in their work, even if it cannot yet be said that they have made a reciprocal impact on the field of biblical theology, have largely been trained as philosophers rather than strictly as biblical scholars. These have taken their bearings from what they regard as the present need for a renaissance in serious Latter-day Saint theological reflection, rather than from the renaissance already underway within Latter-day Saint biblical studies. But because these thinkers and theologians have insisted, for a variety of reasons, on rooting their explicitly speculative project always and indelibly in canonical scripture, they have turned their attention in a sustained way to biblical theology. (Because I am myself among these thinkers and theologians, an early contributor to a burgeoning discussion, I will speak of Latter-day Saint biblical theologians in the plural first person and, somewhat awkwardly, refer to some of my own contributions in the discussion that follows.)

Scriptural theologians are, of course, in no way the only voices in the contemporary resurgence of Latter-day Saint theological reflection. Within the "room to talk" that mid-twentieth-century Latter-day Saint philosopher Truman Madsen created,[36] a variety of distinct theological projects have established themselves. David Paulsen and Blake Ostler have initiated a Latter-day Saint theological conversation with analytic philosophers of religion.[37] Almost singlehandedly, Terryl Givens has undertaken to construct a Latter-day Saint Romanticism that presents its conception of Latter-day Saint theology to both non-Latter-day Saint academics and average Latter-day Saints.[38] But alongside these less scripturally oriented theological projects stands that of Latter-day Saint scriptural theology, as we who serve as its proponents have titled our work.[39] Spearheaded in many ways by James Faulconer, but represented also by thinkers like Adam Miller and myself (among others who have recently begun to establish a publishing track record, such as Kimberly Matheson

36. See James E. Faulconer, "Room to Talk: Reason's Need for Faith," in *Revelation, Reason, and Faith: Essays in Honor of Truman Madsen*, edited by Donald W. Parry, Daniel C. Peterson, and Stephen D. Ricks (Provo, UT: FARMS, 2002), 85–120.

37. See especially Blake T. Ostler, *Exploring Mormon Thought*, three vols. (Salt Lake City, UT: Greg Kofford Books, 2001–2008). A helpful list of Paulsen's publications through 2012 can be found in Jacob T. Baker, ed., *Mormonism at the Crossroads of Philosophy and Theology: Essays in Honor of David L. Paulsen* (Salt Lake City, UT: Greg Kofford Books, 2012), 345–48.

38. See again, Givens, *Wrestling the Angel*; as well as Terryl L. Givens and Fiona Givens, *The God who Weeps: How Mormonism Makes Sense of Life* (Salt Lake City, UT: Ensign Peak, 2012).

39. See James E. Faulconer and Joseph M. Spencer, eds., *Perspectives on Mormon Theology: Scriptural Theology* (Salt Lake City, UT: Greg Kofford Books, 2015).

and Rosalynde Welch),[40] this movement of sorts has centralized its efforts in the Latter-day Saint Theology Seminar, which organizes annual seminars dedicated to the theological investigation of Latter-day Saint scriptural texts, seminars whose proceedings it then publishes. As the introduction to the first published volume produced by the Seminar simply puts it, those involved in the Seminar "understand Mormon theology to be primarily the work of reading Mormon texts. Theology reads."[41]



The status of the Bible within the nascent project of Latter-day Saint scriptural theology is complex. All three early proponents of the new discipline (including myself) have written substantial treatments of Paul's letter to the Romans, making clear our collective interest in direct theological engagement with the Bible (or at least with the New Testament).[42] And yet we, these same three thinkers, clearly expand the scope of biblical theology by including the whole of the Latter-day Saint scriptural canon as their object of study, something signaled by our talk of *scriptural* (rather than simply *biblical*) theology. At the same time, the project clearly grants the Christian Bible a foundational place in the canon. This is perhaps clearest in my own recent writings, where uniquely Latter-day Saint scripture is consistently the primary object of investigation, but the methodology employed in studying uniquely Latter-day Saint scripture focuses on how the latter offers a set of hermeneutical principles for reading biblical texts.[43] For Latter-day Saint scriptural theology, it seems, it is increasingly the case that uniquely Latter-day Saint scripture is interpreted as itself outlining a biblical theology. To read the Book of Mormon or the Doctrine and Covenants carefully *is* to do biblical theology in a Latter-day Saint fashion.[44]

40. Particularly interesting are Latter-day Saint feminist interpreters of scripture, who tend to be influenced by biblical hermeneutics. See, most representatively, Lynn Matthews Anderson, "Toward a Feminist Interpretation of Latter-day Scripture," *Dialogue: A Journal of Mormon Thought* 27, no. 2 (1994): 185–203.

41. Adam S. Miller, ed., *An Experiment on the Word: Reading Alma 32*, 2nd ed. (Provo, UT: Neal A. Maxwell Institute Press, 2014), 2.

42. See James E. Faulconer, *The Life of Holiness: Notes and Reflections on Romans 1, 5–8* (Provo, UT: Neal A. Maxwell Institute Press, 2012); Adam S. Miller, *Badiou, Marion, and St Paul: Immanent Grace* (New York: Continuum, 2008); Adam S. Miller, *Grace Is Not God's Backup Plan: An Urgent Paraphrase of Paul's Letter to the Romans* (n.p.: Adam S. Miller, 2015); and Joseph M. Spencer, *For Zion: A Mormon Theology of Hope* (Salt Lake City, UT: Greg Kofford Books, 2014).

43. This is clearer in my most recent works. See especially Joseph M. Spencer, "The Book of Mormon as Biblical Interpretation: An Approach to LDS Biblical Studies," *Studies in the Bible and Antiquity* 8 (2016): 130–56; and Joseph M. Spencer, "Isaiah 52 in the Book of Mormon: Notes on Isaiah's Reception History," *Relegere: Studies in Religion and Reception* 6, no. 2 (2016): 1–29.

44. The methodology increasingly taking shape here might well be compared to the category of biblical theology Klink and Lockett call "biblical theology as worldview-story." See Klink and Lockett, *Understanding Biblical Theology*, 91–122.

As might be expected, Latter-day Saint scriptural theologians regularly interact in their writings with major contributors to biblical theology. At the same time, likely because we have largely had our training in philosophy, we most consistently engage with philosophers in our work of reading and thinking about scripture. Faulconer's work tends to respond to the French phenomenological tradition and its critics, while Miller and I have both interacted with what is sometimes called post-'68 thought (thinkers like Gilles Deleuze, Alain Badiou, and Giorgio Agamben).[45] It can thus be said that, from within the world of philosophy (and in particular of twentieth-century French philosophy), we Latter-day Saint scriptural theologians largely mimic the approach of Paul Ricoeur, who was by training and interest a philosopher, but who was also deeply engaged with biblical criticism and biblical theology.[46] Our project is as much philosophical as biblical-theological, but it seldom wanders from the hermeneutical task, emphatically convinced of the need to keep scripture at the heart of both Latter-day Saint religious devotion and Latter-day Saint academic research. Propositions emerging from recent Latter-day Saint biblical theology look much like those on offer in the broader discipline of biblical theology, albeit with a Latter-day Saint inflection: reflections on the divine nature but within a philosophically materialist frame; articulations of right relations among human beings but with an eye to the Latter-day Saint idea of Zion; treatises on grace but beginning from a theology of human co-eternality with God; and outlines of covenantal, divinely orchestrated history, but oriented by the distinctive perspectives of uniquely Latter-day Saint scripture.

Of course, Latter-day Saint scriptural theology, to the extent that it exists, is an extremely young subdiscipline of Mormon studies. Whether it will help to fuel a substantial academic project, whether it will assist other disciplines in revitalizing serious study of the Bible among lay Latter-day Saints, and whether it will find a way to contribute to non-Latter-day Saint biblical theology—all this, for the moment, remains to be seen. Already in its infancy, it has been confronted with some serious theoretical challenges from historicist biblical scholars from within the Latter-day Saint tradition, especially those whose

45. See James E. Faulconer, *Faith, Philosophy, Scripture* (Provo, UT: Neal A. Maxwell Institute Press, 2010); Adam S. Miller, *Rube Goldberg Machines: Essays in Mormon Theology* (Salt Lake City, UT: Greg Kofford Books, 2012); Adam S. Miller, *Future Mormon: Essays in Mormon Theology* (Salt Lake City, UT: Greg Kofford Books, 2016); Joseph M. Spencer, "The Four Discourses of Mormonism," *BYU Studies* 50, no. 1 (2011): 4–24; and Spencer, *For Zion*.

46. See, for instance, André LaCocque and Paul Ricoeur, *Thinking Biblically: Exegetical and Hermeneutical Studies*, trans. by David Pellauer (Chicago: University of Chicago Press, 1998); and Paul Ricoeur, *Figuring the Sacred: Religion, Narrative, and Imagination*, edited by Mark I. Wallace, trans. by David Pellauer (Minneapolis, MN: Fortress Press, 1995).

commitments to historicism are bound up with suspicion toward the wedding of scripture and authority. Thus, in a recent issue of *Element: The Journal of the Society for Mormon Theology and Philosophy*, Taylor Petrey has accused the Latter-day Saint school of scriptural theology of being theologically foundationalist, "stop[ping] short of the critical interrogation of the scriptural text and the interpretive process."[47] Major proponents of scriptural theology have already issued initial responses to these accusations, but the conversation has only just begun.[48]



47. Taylor G. Petrey, "Theorizing Critical Mormon Biblical Studies: Romans 1:18–32," *Element: The Journal of the Society for Mormon Philosophy and Theology* 8, no. 1 (Spring 2019): 12.

48. See responses from James Faulconer, Rosalynde Welch, Adam Miller, and myself in the same issue of *Element*, along with a response to these responses by Petrey.

15

# Textual Criticism

LINCOLN H. BLUMELL

In a famous address, Joseph Smith Jr. declared, "I believe the Bible as it read when it came from the pen of the original writers; ignorant translators, careless transcribers, or designing and corrupt priests have committed many errors."[1] This dictum, as well as the first part of the eighth Article of Faith—"We Believe the Bible to be the word of God as far as it is translated correctly . . ."—often informs Latter-day Saint (LDS) approaches to the biblical text. Though the Bible is included in the LDS scriptural canon, since the beginning of Mormonism it has never been regarded as inerrant since it is believed to contain errors and corruptions resulting directly from faulty transmission and improper translation (cf. 1 Ne. 13:26–35). It would therefore be fair to say that Smith's teaching in March 1833 concerning the Apocrypha is probably indicative of how many Latter-day Saints today treat the text of the Bible as a whole: "There are many things contained therein that are true, and it is mostly translated correctly; There are many things contained therein that are not true, which are interpolations by the hands of men. . . . Therefore, whoso readeth it, let him understand, for the Spirit manifesteth truth" (D&C 91:1–2, 4). Consequently, a feature of Joseph Smith's approach (and thus Mormonism's approach) to the biblical text has been that it is corrupted in places and needs to be understood in light of revelation, which at times even includes textual emendation, as in Smith's "New Translation" project. Therefore, LDS engagement with the Bible has a distinct "text-critical" component. With this in mind, this chapter seeks to introduce and elucidate the discipline of biblical textual criticism and to do



1. *Joseph Smith Papers, History, 1838–1856*, vol. E-1 (July 1, 1843–April 30, 1844), 1755.

so in dialogue with LDS approaches and text-critical assumptions regarding the Bible.

## WHY DO TEXTUAL CRITICISM



Despite sensational claims to the contrary, no original manuscript (called "autographs") is extant for any book of the Bible. The oldest extant witness of a biblical text, which naturally comes from the Old Testament (OT), are two small silver amulets that contain a *version* of the priestly blessing in Numbers 6:24–26 and date to the seventh or early sixth century BCE.[2] After this, the next oldest extant pieces of the Bible (OT) come from the Dead Sea Scrolls (DSS) and date between c. 200 BCE and 70 CE.[3] So, for the sake of argument, if Moses, who is traditionally believed to have lived in the latter half of the second millennium BCE,[4] authored any of the Torah, the earliest extant remains of any significant block of text occur some one thousand years later. Furthermore, up until 1947 the oldest complete manuscript of the OT (in Hebrew) was Codex Leningradensis dated to 1008 CE. While the extant manuscript evidence for the New Testament (NT) has closer temporal proximity to the time in which it was originally written in the first century CE, the earliest significant NT witnesses come from the third and subsequent centuries.[5] For example, the earliest extant Bibles that contain the NT between two covers (as well as the OT in Greek) date to the latter part of the fourth century. Thus, any printed edition of the Bible, whether it be a modern edition or an early modern edition like the King James Version (KJV), is based on manuscripts that in the best cases date to hundreds, or in some cases over one thousand years after the original text was purportedly produced.

In light of the nature of the evidence, the primary purpose of textual criticism is to determine the most reliable wording of the biblical text from the existing manuscripts given that these later copies contain numerous differences and variants. While biblical textual criticism once sought, and even claimed, the ability to recover the "original text" (*Urtext*) of the Bible, in the last few

2. Emmanuel Tov, *Textual Criticism of the Hebrew Bible*, 2nd rev. ed. (Minneapolis, MN: Fortress Press, 2001), 118.

3. Frank M. Cross, "The Oldest Manuscripts from Qumran," *Journal of Biblical Literature* 74 (1955): 147–72.

4. On the biblical chronology of Moses see J. Finegan, *Handbook of Biblical Chronology: Principles of Time Reckoning in the Ancient World and Problems of Chronology in the Bible*, rev. ed. (Peabody, MA, 1998).

5. Lincoln H. Blumell, "Scripture as Artefact," in *Oxford Handbook of the Early Christian Interpretation of Scripture*, edited by Paul M. Blowers and Peter W. Martens (New York: Oxford University Press, 2018).

decades it has backed away significantly from such unattainable aspirations. Due to the lack of early manuscript data, uncertainties about the exact process of scribal transmission, as well as the recognition of the complexities involved with oral composition and dissemination, biblical textual criticism today seeks to identify an "initial text" (*Ausgangtext*) of the Bible that can account for subsequent textual developments.[6] Accordingly, there is a general recognition among textual critics of the Bible that there are inherent limitations to what this discipline can attain in recovering the earliest text of the Bible. But notwithstanding these limits, textual criticism has greatly improved the text of the Bible overall as it has been able to identity earlier readings, later interpolations, and has successfully classified diverse manuscript families and recensions of biblical texts. In this process textual criticism has even expanded its horizon somewhat in an attempt to provide some context for certain kinds of variants that are clearly deliberate and motivated by theological concerns at different stages in the transmission of the biblical text.[7]

Unlike the modern world where a text can be written and mass-produced very easily and with a high degree of stability due to modern technologies like the printing press and computer, in the ancient world the transmission of a text was often quite laborious as it had to be hand-copied letter by letter. Not only did this make production of any substantial text in the ancient world rather difficult, but it also meant that every time a text was copied (and recopied) there was a good chance that errors and variants could be introduced, both incidental and deliberate, with the result that the textual stability was compromised. To give some rather staggering statistics, for the OT a variant reading occurs in the ancient and early medieval manuscript evidence on average at least once in every ten words;[8] so the famous Isaiah scroll from Qumran (1QIsa[a]) that dates to the first century BCE and contains all sixty-six chapters has a little over 1,300 variants from the way Isaiah is rendered in most modern editions of the Bible (including the KJV).[9] Turning to the NT, of the roughly 5,700 extant NT manuscripts that include papyri, uncials, minuscules, and lectionaries, there are hundreds of thousands of variants; as one prominent textual critic has put

6. Tommy Wasserman and Peter J. Gurry, *A New Approach to Textual Criticism: An Introduction to the Coherence-Based Genealogical Method* (Atlanta: SBL Press, 2017), 11–3.

7. Bart D. Ehrman, *The Orthodox Corruption of Scripture: The Effects of Early Christological Controversies on the Text of the New Testament*, rev. ed. (New York: Oxford University Press, 2011).

8. Paul D. Wegner, *A Student's Guide to Textual Criticism of the Bible: Its History, Methods, and Results* (Downer Grove, IL: IVP Academic, 2006), 25.

9. Martin G. Abegg Jr., Peter Flint, and Eugene Ulrich, *The Dead Sea Scrolls Bible: The Oldest Known Bible Translated for the First Time into English* (New York: HarperOne, 1999), 267–71.

it, "There are more variations among our manuscripts than there are words in the New Testament."[10]

Though initially staggering, these kinds of statistics do not imply that the copyists and scribes who transmitted both the OT and NT in the age before the printing press were negligent, unskilled, or necessarily malicious, nor that every single verse in the Bible has been subject to corruption and alteration. To be sure, some of the transmitters of the biblical text would have fit within one or all these characterizations, but the manuscript evidence for the most part suggests that the transmitters who hand-copied the biblical text for so many centuries often did their best to accurately reproduce and convey the text. This becomes more apparent when the above statistics are cast in a different light: the majority of these variants are spelling errors or phonetic shifts, the addition or omission of a particle, conjunction, definite article, or a single word. Thus, about 65 percent of biblical variants have to do with alternate spellings and another 25 percent with minor changes that do not significantly alter the overall meaning of the text; therefore, about 90 percent of biblical variants are rather insignificant and make little difference for interpretation. For example, it does not make a big difference whether Joshua 6:9 (KJV) reads "ark of the covenant" or just "ark," or, for that matter, whether Matthew 2:28 (KJV) reads "lamentation, and weeping, and great mourning" or just "weeping and great mourning."

On the other hand, a survey of the extant variants attested in biblical manuscripts reveals that some are more significant and go well beyond the omission/addition of a word or two. In the familiar story of David and Goliath (1 Sam. 17), according to one textual tradition (on which the KJV is based) Goliath towers "six cubits and a span" (17:4) or nearly ten feet in height (depending on the length of a cubit), but according to another textual tradition (which is much older and is attested in the DSS) he is "four cubits and a span" or just under seven feet.[11] Turning to the NT, in John 5:1–9 there is the story of Jesus healing a infirm person at the pool of Bethesda and in the preamble a description is given of the environs wherein it is reported that "an angel" was responsible for stirring the water so that the first person entering thereafter was healed (vv. 3b–4). In a number of ancient manuscripts the same story appears but without any mention of the angel troubling the water. To give another NT example, most ancient manuscripts end Mark's Gospel with 16:8 and women fleeing from the empty tomb "for they were afraid" and contain no post-resurrection

10. Bart D. Ehrman, *Misquoting Jesus. The Story Behind Who Changed the Bible and Why* (New York: HarperOne, 2005), 90.

11. This is the reading given in DSS 1 Samuel. See Abegg et al., *The Dead Sea Scrolls Bible*, 229.

appearances of Jesus; the ending preserved in the KJV that comprises verses 9–20 is known as the "Longer Ending" of Mark and only appears in later manuscripts. Dozens of other similar such variants, which not only affect the meaning of the text but also potentially have theological implications, could also be cited from both the OT and NT.[12]

## HISTORY OF TEXTUAL CRITICISM

Already in the ancient world perceptive readers of the biblical text noticed that there were variant readings among the different manuscripts. One early Christian, Origen of Caesarea (died ca. 253 CE), who became a renowned biblical exegete in his own day, made the following observation about the biblical manuscripts available to him:

> Now it is plainly manifest that many differences of the copies [of the scriptures] have occurred either from the laziness of certain copyists or from the wicked recklessness of some or from those neglecting improvement of the writings or also from those who either add or omit [to the text] supposing in themselves to improve it [i.e., the scriptures].[13]

Thus, Origen recognized that variants in the scriptural text had arisen both from inadvertent errors caused by negligent copyists as well as deliberately by copyists who added or omitted text as they saw fit. Picking up on the latter point, allegations of deliberate scriptural alteration are widespread in early Christian literature and appear as early as the second century.[14]

While variant readings have long been noted, biblical textual criticism has its roots in the Reformation and Enlightenment. While the Vulgate (Latin translation of the Bible) was the very first book to be published (i.e., the Gutenberg Bible in the 1450s), it took nearly seventy-five years for printed (not hand-copied) editions of the OT (in Hebrew) and New Testament (in Greek) to appear. The first printed Greek edition of the New Testament appeared in 1516 and was produced by the Dutch humanist Desiderius Erasmus (1466–1536). Due to the sway that the Vulgate held in the church, and by extension the

12. For an introductory overview of both Old Testament and New Testament biblical variants along with useful bibliography for further reading see Wegner, *A Students Guide to Textual Criticism of the Bible*, 44–57.

13. Origen, *Commentary on Matthew* 15.14. Translation is my own.

14. Origen, *Against Celsus*, 2.27 (where Celsus [second century] is cited); Eusebius, *Ecclesiastical History* 5.28.13–19 (quoting Victor the bishop of Rome ca. 190 CE).

academy, the text was printed in two parallel columns: Greek in the left and Latin in the right. Once printed it did not take long for bilingual readers to begin to notice differences between the Greek and the Latin text and debates soon thereafter emerged over variant readings.[15] One passage in particular that created no little stir when Erasmus' Greek text was published was 1 John 5:7–8. In Erasmus' first two editions (1516 and 1519) this passage read (in translation): "[7]There are three that bear record: [8]the spirit, and the water, and the blood: and these three are one." However, the Latin preserved a longer reading (in translation): "[7]There are three that bear record *in heaven, the Father, the Word, and the Holy Ghost. And these three are one.* [8]*And there are three that give testimony on earth*: the spirit, and the water, and the blood: and these three are one" (emphasis added to indicate difference). Many at the time viewed the longer reading as authentic, not only because it appeared in the Vulgate (*the* Bible of the church), but also because they felt it was an important Trinitarian proof text. In reply, Erasmus pointed out that the longer reading that included references to heaven, earth, Father, Son, and Holy Ghost, was not attested in any Greek manuscript. Under mounting political and ecclesiastical pressure, as well as the "discovery" of a Greek manuscript of 1 John that was written for the sole purpose of including this passage (Codex Montfortianus from the sixteenth century), Erasmus ultimately included this reading in his 1522 edition of the New Testament (notoriously known today as the "Johannine Comma").[16] Thus, this erroneous reading is preserved in the KJV since its NT Greek text was essentially based upon Erasmus' third edition of 1522; however, this interpolation has been dropped in all modern translations of the Bible.[17]

As the sixteenth century progressed and printed editions of Greek and Hebrew manuscripts became more widely available, this inevitably gave rise to a greater awareness of biblical variants as well as differences between the Hebrew and Greek texts of the OT and the Greek and Latin of the NT. The first systematic attempt to incorporate, but not arbitrate, the variant readings in the biblical text was in Brian Walton's six-volume Polyglot Bible published between 1655–1657 where variants were published at the foot of every page.[18] Over the

15. In anticipation of this Erasmus published a large appendix to the volume (titled *Annotationes in Novum Testamentum*) wherein he justified his Greek text and produced various text-critical arguments for specific readings.

16. Grantley McDonald, *Biblical Criticism in Early Modern Europe: Erasmus, the Johannine Comma and Trinitarian Debate* (Cambridge, UK: Cambridge University Press, 2016).

17. In the Latin Vulgate, this interpolation is first attested in manuscripts of the sixth century.

18. P.N. Miller, "The 'Antiquarianization' of Biblical Scholarship and the London Polyglot Bible (1653–57)," *Journal of the History of Ideas* 62 (2001): 463–82.

course of the next century various scholarly editions of both the OT (Hebrew) and NT (Greek) would regularly appear with textual variants printed alongside the text, which resulted in much debate in the academy and the church as debates and accusations of heresy raged over the status of the biblical text.[19] During this period even Isaac Newton entered the fray of textual criticism and vehemently argued both for and against various readings in the Bible.[20]

The birth of "modern" textual criticism of the Bible began with Jakob Griesbach (1745–1812), a professor of divinity at the University of Jena from 1775 until his death. Though primarily a scholar of the NT, Griesbach's text-critical methodology applied equally to the OT, and some of the principles he outlined are still used today. Griesbach went beyond just cataloging variants or making theological arguments for one reading or another but laid out an actual methodology for trying to reconstruct the text of the Bible when faced with a host of variant readings for one passage. Beyond arguing that more ancient manuscripts should be given greater weight than more recent ones in text-critical matters and that original language manuscripts should generally be accorded more weight than translations—thus the Greek manuscripts of the NT should be regarded with more esteem than Latin manuscripts—he also quarried the writings of early church fathers to see how they quoted disputed passages. Finally, he came up with a list of fifteen canons for textual criticism, among which were the principles of *lectio brevior* (a shorter reading is probably older than a longer reading of the same passage) and *lectio difficilior* (a more difficult reading is probably older than a reading that makes more sense). Drawing on these and other principles he set forth a number of treatises on variant readings in the Bible and remarkably in a few cases he even anticipated some readings that were later borne out with newer manuscript discoveries.[21]

When Griesbach died at the beginning of the nineteenth century, NT textual criticism was dominated by German scholarship with all the major studies being written in German (or Latin). It was not until the middle of the nineteenth century that text-critical studies of the Bible began to appear in English, the first significant one being J. Scott Porter's *Principles of Textual Criticism*

19. This period is concisely summarized in Bruce M. Metzger and Bart D. Ehrman, *The Text of the New Testament: Its Transmission, Corruption, and Restoration*, 4th ed., (New York: Oxford University Press, 2005), 152–64.

20. J.A.I. Champion, "'Acceptable to Inquisitive Men:' Some Simonian Contexts for Newton's Biblical Criticism, 1680–1692," in *Newton and Religion: Context, Nature, and Influence*, edited by J.E. Force and R.H. Popkin (Dordrecht, Netherlands: Springer, 1999), 77–96.

21. He showed, for example, that the shorter form of the Lord's Prayer in Luke 11:3–4 was likely the most ancient version and this was largely proven with the discovery of Codex Vaticanus.

*with their Application to Old and New Testaments* published in 1848. Of course, this does not mean that there was no scholarship in English available on the subject in the early nineteenth century as English Bible commentaries, dictionaries, and encyclopedias were disseminating some text-critical scholarship. For example, Reverend Charles Buck's *Theological Dictionary* (1802), Adam Clarke's *Bible Commentaries* (1810–1826), and Edward Robinson's *Dictionary of the Holy Bible* (1832)—all of which Joseph Smith read[22]—contain text-critical materials. However, aside from the "New Translation" (JST)[23] and passing comments made by Joseph Smith about the text of the Bible,[24] neither in his lifetime nor in those of his immediate successors was there any significant engagement with the text-critical studies of the day.

The second half of the nineteenth century witnessed a dramatic increase in English text-critical studies of the Bible with over a dozen different monographs appearing before the turn of the century. This flurry was prompted in part by the monumental publication in 1862 of Codex Sinaiticus, a virtually complete fourth-century CE copy of the Bible (in Greek) that was found at St. Catherine's Monastery (Sinai) by Constantin von Tischendorf (1815–1874). The culmination of these developments contributed to the publication in 1881 (NT) and 1885 (OT) of the Revised Version (RV)—a revision of the KJV that not only included an updated translation but also took into account new textual readings that had appeared since the KJV was first published in 1611 (among other things it dropped the Johannine Comma). The same year that the RV NT was published two British scholars, Brooke F. Westcott (1825–1901) and Fenton J.A. Hort (1828–1892), published a new Greek edition of the New Testament in two volumes titled *The New Testament in the Original Greek*. While the positivistic use of "original" speaks more about the times in which it was published and is not taken today to be the "original text," the NT text and principles laid out by Westcott and Hort are by and large accepted in contemporary scholarship. The

22. Christopher C. Jones, "The Complete Record of the Nauvoo Library and Literary Institute," *Mormon Historical Studies* 10, no. 1 (2009): 192–93; Matthew Bowman and Samuel Brown, "Reverend Buck's *Theological Dictionary* and the Struggle to Define American Evangelicalism, 1802–1851," *Journal of the Early Republic* 29, no. 3 (2009): 469. See also Thomas A. Wayment and Haley Wilson-Lemmon, "A Recovered Resource: The Use of Adam Clarke's Bible Commentary in Joseph Smith's Bible Translation," in *Producing Ancient Scripture: Joseph Smith's Translation Projects in the Development of Mormon Christianity*, edited by Michael Hubbard MacKay, Mark Ashurst-McGee, and Brian M. Hauglid (Salt Lake City: University of Utah Press, 2020).

23. For Robert J. Matthews, while the JST restores to some extent the intent of the ancient meaning, he does not maintain that it every case it is a text-critical restoration. Robert J. Matthews, "*A Plainer Translation:*" *Joseph Smith's Translation of the Bible: A History and Commentary* (Provo, UT: BYU Press, 1975), 234–37.

24. *Joseph Smith Papers, History, 1838–1856*, vol. A–1 (December 23, 1805–August 30, 1834), 183.

principal contribution of this work was that it effectively overthrew the *textus receptus* ("received text") underlying the KJV NT, which up until that point had been reverenced in many quarters as *the* canonical Greek text of the NT.

Not all welcomed the rapid advances in biblical textual criticism and the publication of the RV. John W. Burgon (1813–1888), dean of Chichester, in a series of lectures and publications denounced both the RV and the Greek NT text of Westcott and Hort; for him, it was seemingly incomprehensible that the *textus receptus* underlying the KJV NT could need any significant revision, viewing it as he did, to have been the inspired text of God. Though Burgon's arguments attracted much attention at the time, in part because there was a large group of KJV-only supporters who did not like the RV, his text-critical assumptions and arguments have been almost completely rejected in modern scholarship as they are often based on faulty assumptions and special pleading. Even though many of Burgon's text-critical arguments were refuted in the decades following his death, in certain quarters they persisted well into the twentieth century.[25]

## LDS APPROACHES TO TEXTUAL CRITICISM

Here one finds an intersection with what is the only LDS monograph dealing extensively with textual criticism and published by an LDS leader. In 1956, J. Reuben Clark Jr. (1871–1961), then a member of the quorum of the twelve apostles, published *Why the King James Version*.[26] While the book is not explicitly about textual criticism, textual criticism undergirds much of Clark's discussion about the differences between the KJV and other translations like the RV, American Standard Version (ASV), and the Revised Standard Version (RSV). The survey the book offers of ancient biblical manuscripts and witnesses is adequate and even somewhat useful (by 1950s standards) insofar as it is descriptive—relying as it does on the descriptions of ancient texts given by Fredrick G. Kenyon (1863–1942) who was the keeper of manuscripts at the British Library from 1889–1931. But where the book periodically has problems is in the text-critical arguments where it is regularly asserted that the KJV preserves the most accurate readings whereas more contemporary English translations are viewed with much distrust and even disdain (e.g., RV, ASV, RSV). Since Clark was not a biblical scholar and had no training with ancient languages

25. Edward F. Hills, *The King James Defended! A Christian View of the New Testament Manuscripts* (Des Moines, IA: The Christian Research Press, 1956).

26. J. Reuben Clark Jr., *Why the King James Version* (Salt Lake City, UT: Deseret Book, 1956).

or texts—a caveat that is explicitly stated at the outset of the book[27]—he relied heavily on the arguments Burgon made over half a century earlier to defend the KJV and its textual basis. Beyond the inherent problems of using Burgon's text-critical arguments, Clark ended up, perhaps unwittingly, defending passages like the Johannine Comma and others that LDS today would be more than happy to excise for purely theological reasons to say nothing of the fact that they are later interpolations.[28]

While Clark's publication is the only monograph published by an LDS leader that substantially engages with textual criticism of the Bible, the subject was occasionally broached by a few other twentieth-century LDS leaders. As president of the quorum of the twelve apostles, Joseph Fielding Smith (1876–1972) published in 1954 *Man: His Origin and Destiny* in which chapters 26 and 27 respectively deal with the authenticity of the OT and NT. In both chapters, there are brief excurses on biblical textual criticism wherein the work of Kenyon is cited, and it is acknowledged that the text of the Bible has been transmitted with alterations and corruptions.[29] Likewise, Bruce R. McConkie (1915–1985) as an apostle wrote a three-volume *Doctrinal New Testament Commentary* (1965–1973) where the subject is brought up very generally. While there is no explicit engagement with biblical textual criticism, the commentary contains a number of text-critical assertions and in a few instances McConkie discusses a New Testament passages for which there is a notable variant (of which he is seemingly unaware) and asserts that something is wrong with the text as it appears in the KJV.[30]

27. Clark, *Why the King James Version*, 21, states, "Since the author's own scholarship is wholly insufficient to enable him to do any original research in this great field of human thought (which means the author has no standing in that field—and ought to have none), and since, as a matter of fact, the original sources were not available to him even if he could have used them, he has quoted most extensively from writers who are learned and who have done the research necessary to give them a standing." Shortly before publishing the book Clark consulted David O. McKay, then president of the church, to run it by him. While McKay left the decision to publish solely with Clark, he did have some reservations with the project and appropriately warned him. See Philip L. Barlow, *Mormons and the Bible: The Place of Latter-day Saints in American Religion*, rev. ed. (New York: Oxford University Press, 2013), 185.

28. Clark, *Why the King James Version*, 247, where a defense of the Johannine Comma is implied based on a quote drawn from F.H. Scrivener (1813–1891).

29. Joseph Fielding Smith, *Man: His Origin and Destiny*, 6th ed. (Salt Lake City, UT: Deseret Book, 1965), 509–11.

30. For example, in the story of Jesus' healing at the pool of Bethesda (John 5:1–9) McConkie notes that the angel troubling the water so that first person thereafter entering was healed "was pure superstition ... If we had the account as John originally wrote it, it would probably contain an explanation that the part supposedly played by an angel was merely a superstitious legend." See Bruce R. McConkie, *Doctrinal New Testament Commentary, vol. I: The Gospels* (Salt Lake City, UT: Bookcraft, 1965), 88.

## TEXTUAL CRITICISM GIVETH AND TEXTUAL CRITICISM TAKETH AWAY

As it is practiced by trained scholars, textual criticism provides a somewhat mixed bag of evidence for LDS claims about the Bible. On one hand, it is evident that both the Old and New Testaments were susceptible to textual change and corruption over the course of their transmission history and that variants were not just inadvertent or accidental; even if such variants account for the vast majority of the changes there is clear evidence that at times the text was purposely changed for theological reasons.[31] On this front one notable case that text-critically corresponds with an underlying LDS hermeneutic of suspicion with the biblical text is Luke 22:43–44 that narrates Jesus' suffering in Gethsemane: "And there appeared an angel unto him [Jesus] from heaven, strengthening him. And being in an agony he prayed more earnestly: and his sweat was as it were great drops of blood falling down to the ground." For LDS, Jesus' salvific act of atonement was not just confined to the events on the cross but included his sufferings in Gethsemane on the night before he was crucified, which is even found in non-biblical LDS scriptures like Mosiah 3:7 and Doctrine and Covenants 19:16–19, where Jesus' "bleeding from every pore" is part of his act of atonement. Few LDS are aware, however, that this passage (Luke 22:43–44) is either altogether omitted by certain modern translations or is included and marked with asterisks or placed in brackets because it does not appear in some ancient manuscripts. Recently, I have argued that this passage was most likely a part of Luke's Gospel but that it was deliberately excised by later Christians because it posed theological problems in the aftermath of the Council of Nicaea in 325 CE[32]—in fact, this is the only passage in the Bible for which we have direct ancient evidence that "orthodox" (i.e., pro-Nicene) Christians were deliberately excising it.[33] For LDS readers, this could call to mind a paradigm in which "plain and precious" parts of the Bible would be taken away (cf. 1 Ne 13:26–35).

On the other hand, just as textual criticism might give so might it also take away in a very literal sense. The beloved story of the woman caught in adultery in John 7:53–8:11 and not being condemned to death by Jesus is clearly

31. Carmel McCarthy, *The Tiqqune Sopherim and Other Theological Corrections in the Masoretic Text of the Old Testament* (Freiburg, Germany: Universitätsverlag; Göttingen: Vandenhoeck & Ruprecht, 1981).

32. Lincoln H. Blumell, "Luke 22:43–44: An Anti-Docetic Interpolation or an Apologetic Omission?" *TC: A Journal of Biblical Textual Criticism* 19 (2014): 1–35.

33. See Epiphanius, *The Anchored One*, 31.3–5.

an interpolation; while it might have some ancient pedigree, it was certainly not originally a part of the Gospel of John. Furthermore, textual criticism can potentially cause some problems for LDS non-biblical scriptures that parallel biblical texts for which there are variants. In 3 Nephi 13:9–13 appears a version of the Lord's Prayer (cf. Matthew 6:9–13) and in v. 13 it reads: "For thine is the kingdom, and the power, and the glory, forever. Amen." While this corresponds verbatim with Matthew 6:13b in the KJV, modern translations have universally dropped this passage since it does not appear in the earliest manuscript evidence and is typically thought to be an interpolation that was added when the Lord's prayer was later read in worship services.

In summary, it is best to avoid extremes in text-critical assertions—namely, every verse of the Bible has been altered and corrupted or that non-biblical LDS scriptures always preserve the most original reading that can emend the biblical text. Along these lines, Latter-day Saints would also do well to have a little less antipathy toward modern translations of the Bible since they often have a much better textual basis than the KJV; in most places where the KJV text differs from that of a modern version (translation issues aside) the latter is likely to preserve a more ancient reading because of the underlying textual basis. Thus, when a number of modern translations do not include a verse (e.g., Matthew 23:14, Mark 15:28, Luke 17:36, Acts 15:34, Acts 28:29, and Romans 16:24), it is not because they are trying to hide something but rather because the ancient manuscript evidence is decidedly against its authenticity.

# 16

# Biblical Archaeology in Latter-day Saint Perspective

GEORGE A. PIERCE

Connections to the Near East by members of the Church of Jesus Christ of Latter-day Saints stretch from the mission of Orson Hyde to Jerusalem in 1841 to the modern construction of the Brigham Young University Jerusalem Center for Near Eastern Studies and the active participation by Latter-day Saints in current archaeological excavations in the Near East.[1] Historically, the establishment and growth of the Latter-day Saint church and engagement with the Near East by its members developed at nearly the same time as European and American scholarly interests were realized in the military campaigns, journeys for research, mapping, or leisure, and early excavations in lands either directly or tangentially connected to the Bible. The purpose of this chapter is to provide an overview of the development and aims of "biblical archaeology," or the archaeology of the Levant, from the nineteenth century through the present and discuss the employment of information gleaned from archaeological efforts as a resource of Scripture study and instruction in non-specialist academic and ecclesiastical settings and the influence of biblical archaeology on modern Latter-day Saint interpretations of biblical events and places.

The archaeology of the Near East traces its modern academic origins to the group of scientists who accompanied Napoleon's campaigns in Egypt and the Holy Land in 1799, tasked with documenting the ancient art and architecture of the ancient Egyptian ruins that they encountered. Following the decipherment of Egyptian hieroglyphs on the Rosetta Stone in 1822 by Jean-François Champollion, academic and popular interest in the ancient Near East was



1. See LaMar C. Barrett and Blair G. Van Dyke, *Holy Lands: A History of the Latter-Day Saints in the Near East* (American Fork, UT: Covenant Communications, 2005) for a thorough treatment of the subject.

piqued. During the nineteenth century, two approaches attempted to relate the material culture and physical remains of the Near East to the biblical narrative.[2] The first method has been termed "Bible lands archaeology," referring to early archaeological explorations of areas tangentially related to the Bible such as Syria, Anatolia, and Mesopotamia, which began in earnest in the 1840s with excavations at Assyrian palaces. The second approach was known as "biblical archaeology" and is currently broadly defined by Eric Cline as "a subset of the larger field of Syro-Palestinian archaeology—which is conducted throughout the region encompassed by modern Israel, Jordan, Lebanon, and Syria. Specifically, it is archaeology that sheds light on the stories, descriptions, and discussions in the Hebrew Bible and the New Testament from the early second millennium BCE, the time of Abraham and the Patriarchs, through the Roman period in the early first millennium CE."[3]

## THE RISE AND FLORUIT OF BIBLICAL ARCHAEOLOGY

With the attention given to the Near East in the early nineteenth century came interest in the exploration of the Holy Land itself. One of the observable problems encountered in Palestine was the relative lack of tells, mounds of ruins formed by successive settlement layers, clearly defined from the surrounding landscape as existed in Syria and Mesopotamia, making site discovery and identification challenging. Second, the veneration of holy sites for Christian pilgrims since the fourth century CE meant that most biblical sites, in the opinion of nineteenth-century scholars, were already well-known and marked by churches, obviating further investigation. Additionally, the European and North American image of Ottoman-era Palestine was one of poverty and violence among the tribes that live there ruled by overbearing governors. As Rachel Hallote notes, "the only redeeming features of the land were the fact that it was the locus of the core biblical narratives and that it was a good connecting byway to get to places like India or Africa—places where Europeans had colonial holdings."[4]

2. Rachel Hallote, "'Bible Lands Archaeology' and 'Biblical Archaeology' in the Nineteenth and Early Twentieth Centuries," in *The Old Testament in Archaeology and History*, edited by J. Ebeling et al. (Waco, TX: Baylor University Press, 2017), 111–12.

3. Eric. H. Cline, *Biblical Archaeology: A Very Short Introduction* (Oxford, UK: Oxford University Press, 2009), 1.

4. Hallote "'Bible Lands Archaeology' and 'Biblical Archaeology,'" 121.

When it began to emerge as a discipline, biblical archaeology traces its origins to the work of antiquarians, biblical scholars, and military engineers who operated under a colonial mindset of appropriating elements of the past that they deemed relevant or important to European and North American Jews and Christians. The earliest investigation in Palestine was that of Lady Hester Stanhope, a British aristocrat who initiated excavations at Ashkelon in 1815, under the auspices of reclaiming treasure for the Ottoman sultan. Starting in the 1830s, the journeys of Edward Robinson and other biblical geographers were also fundamental in the identification of biblical places based on the names of ruins and sites and descriptions of visible remains mostly dating from the Roman period or later. Robinson's effort to identify features of ancient Jerusalem showed that the Jerusalem of the nineteenth century looked greatly different from the city of the Second Temple period. This sparked controversies between Protestants and Catholics over the authenticity of sites. The most notable dispute concerned the Church of the Holy Sepulcher, the traditional location of the crucifixion, burial, and resurrection of Jesus. An alternative proposal by General Charles Gordon made in 1883 of the Garden Tomb located it north of the city. While the investigations of Lady Hester at Ashkelon had treasure-finding as their *raison d'être*, the labors of historical geographers and others like the French numismatist Félicien de Saulcy in Jerusalem at the so-called "Tomb of the Kings" had religious overtones and motivations.

British engineers Charles Wilson and Charles Warren in the 1860s documented Jerusalem's water systems, conducted archaeological soundings to gain a knowledge of the city's history, and introduced more precise and scientific approaches to the archaeology of the Holy Land. Similarly, Claude Conder and Horatio Kitchener accurately surveyed and mapped western Palestine and Transjordan under the auspices of the Palestine Exploration Fund in the 1880s. The Egyptologist William Matthew Flinders Petrie recognized that tells, visible artificial mounds, were composed of former occupation layers and excavated Tell el-Hesi (identified as biblical Eglon) and Tell el-'Ajjul, considered by Petrie to be ancient Gaza. Petrie introduced ceramic typology and seriation as a method for dating archaeological layers, or strata. Following Petrie's efforts and continuing through World War I, scholars from Britain, France, and Germany conducted excavations at biblical sites such as Gezer, Beth-Shemesh, Samaria, Megiddo, Taanach, Jericho, and Jerusalem.

The years following World War I through the later 1960s are considered the floruit of biblical archaeology. Many of the excavations during this period were led by scholars who were primarily theologians and had religious interest in their results. During this period, American, British, French, and German excavations resumed at the aforementioned biblical sites. Other sites included Tell en-Nasbeh (biblical Mizpah), Shiloh, Tell el-Kheleifeh (argued to be biblical Ezion-geber), and the site of et-Tell, identified as 'Ai from Joshua 7–8. The excavations of William F. Albright at Tell el-Ful (biblical Gibeah of Benjamin), Bethel, and Tell Beit Mirsim combined field work with historical geography, history, biblical studies, and wider ancient Near Eastern parallels. The efforts of Albright and his student G. Ernest Wright to integrate biblical theology and archaeology led to the rise of "biblical archaeology," defined by William G. Dever as an American construct that developed from the 1930s and ended in the late 1960s.[5]

For Albright and others, faith could be bolstered by having "proof" of the historicity biblical events resulting from archaeological endeavors. Additionally, archaeology, more specifically epigraphic discoveries, could provide an explanation or reconstruction of biblical history. Wright described biblical archaeology as

> a special 'armchair' variety of general archaeology, which studies the discoveries of the excavators and gleans from them every fact that throws a direct, indirect, or even diffused light upon the Bible . . . its chief concern is not with strata or pots or methodology. Its central and absorbing interest is the understanding and exposition of the Scriptures.[6]

The primacy of the biblical record is evident in this definition, and such importance privileged the text above material culture, reaffirming the notion of archaeology being a handmaiden to history.

## THE DEMISE AND REBIRTH OF BIBLICAL ARCHAEOLOGY

One of the problems that emerged from more archaeological knowledge of the Holy Land and its history was the disconnect between archaeology and the biblical record, which served to negate the aims of "biblical archaeology"

5. William G. Dever, "A Critique of Biblical Archaeology: History and Interpretation," in *The Old Testament in Archaeology and History*, edited by J. Ebeling et al. (Waco, TX: Baylor University Press, 2017), 141–57.

6. G. Ernest Wright quoted in William G. Dever, "Biblical Theology and Biblical Archaeology: An Appreciation of G. Ernest Wright," *Harvard Theological Review* 73, nos. 1–2 (1980): 1–15.

as conceived by Albright and Wright. For instance, the excavations of John Garstang at Jericho, once thought to prove the biblical narrative of Joshua's conquest, were redated by Kathleen Kenyon to the Early Bronze Age (3300–2000 BCE), predating Joshua by nearly two thousand years.[7] According to Kenyon's results, Jericho was not a large, walled city at the time that scholars assumed Joshua and the Israelites conquered the town. Likewise, while a thick layer of debris and ash evident at Hazor appears to confirm the biblical text (Josh 11:10–11), excavations at et-Tell/'Ai did not reveal settlement remains or destruction debris dated to the Late Bronze Age (c. 1500–1200 BCE), considered the period of the Israelite conquest. Increasingly, the model of the early Israelite settlement in Canaan arising from a near-literal reading of the biblical text as a conquest began to unravel. Further analyses into ceramic forms and architecture considered by Albright to be Israelite showed such elements of material culture to be present in Canaan predating the Israelite settlement. Similarly, finds related to David and Solomon, Israel's greatest kings according to the Bible, were also elusive with only architecture bearing proof of some of Solomon's construction programs. Later, archaeologists would also redate strata at Megiddo from the original assumed era of Solomon to that of the ninth century BCE and time of King Ahab. The United Monarchy as portrayed in the biblical text did not find support in the archaeological record. Such apparent contradictions from archaeology seemed to trump the biblical record, frustrating and confusing believing lay persons looking to archaeology as a support for their faith and forcing a reconsideration of the meaning of the text in light of archaeological results.[8]

Following World War II, and the establishment of the State of Israel and the Kingdom of Jordan, scholarly preoccupation with biblical sites continued. However, as each country developed its own nationally sponsored archaeological endeavors, the emphasis on archaeology for its own sake, rather than having a biblical agenda, emerged. The effect of European and North American trends in archaeology on the archaeology of the southern Levant resulted in an emphasis on the scientific method of hypothesis, focused research questions, and testing of theories.[9] Research excavations branched out from large major sites to smaller sites that required only limited excavation, salvage excavations

7. Kathleen M. Kenyon, "Jericho," in *The New Encyclopedia of Archaeological Excavations in the Holy Land*, vol. 1, edited by E. Stern (New York: Simon and Schuster, 1993) 674–81.

8. The archaeology of the New Testament was also problematic regarding the location of certain sites or the paucity of early Roman period remains in other places.

9. William G. Dever, "The Impact of the 'New Archaeology' on Syro-Palestinian Archaeology," *Bulletin of the American Schools of Oriental Research* 242 (1981): 15–29.

began to be conducted in advance of construction, and systematic surface surveys were conducted to record sites and inform scholars about settlement systems in lieu of excavations.

Together with the apparent conflict between the biblical text and archaeology, the shift to more professional and secular approaches to the archaeology of the Levant signaled the death of conservative, traditional "biblical archaeology" and the rebirth of the discipline to understand the cultural processes and lifeways of the region's ancient inhabitants that may not be reflected in biblical or extrabiblical texts.[10] The resulting archaeology of Syria-Palestine, or southern Levant, in the biblical period can be defined as, according to Dever, "a sub-branch of biblical studies, an interdisciplinary pursuit which seeks to utilize the pertinent results of archaeological research to elucidate the historical and cultural setting of the Bible."[11]

## LATTER-DAY SAINT INTERACTIONS WITH BIBLICAL ARCHAEOLOGY

The majority of the use of biblical archaeology and historical geography by Latter-day Saint leadership and scholars can be broadly categorized as aimed at a non-specialist Latter-day Saint audience and others interested in the Latter-day Saint perspective. These approaches may appear in either ecclesiastical or scholarly publications. Ecclesiastical literature is defined here as devotional or instructional works, including talks, sermons, books, magazines, or manuals, authored by a general authority of the Church of Jesus Christ of Latter-day Saints or by authors commissioned and sanctioned by the church. Scholarly publications are peer-reviewed works published in outlets whose principal audience is Latter-day Saints who generally do not have advanced degrees in academic fields related to biblical studies.[12] Other publications, such as visual reference guides of the Old and New Testaments, incorporate maps and images of art, artifacts, and photographs of sites intended for a popular audience of lay Latter-day Saints. These works are included within scholarly literature given the research and academic treatment of archaeology, geography, and textual

10. William G. Dever, "Archaeological Method in Israel: A Continuing Revolution." *Biblical Archaeologist* 43, no. 1 (1980): 40–8.

11. Dever, "Biblical Theology and Biblical Archaeology," 15, note 34.

12. It should be noted that Latter-day Saint scholars also publish in venues intended for academic audiences of scholars who teach and research in academic disciplines related to archaeology or biblical studies. To survey these publications is beyond the scope of this chapter.

studies employed in producing such reference volumes.[13] Latter-day Saint use of biblical archeology in both venues has reflected the conservative impulse to bolster faith, following both nineteenth century perspectives of biblical archeology and its mid-twentieth century manifestation. However, recent trends toward further expertise and professionalization have brought many Latter-day Saint archeologists into more contemporary approaches in the field.



## ECCLESIASTICAL VENUES

Leaders within the Church of Jesus Christ of Latter-day Saints have used accessible and relatable information provided by biblical archaeology to establish context, lend color, or provide an element of realism to connect their audiences to the biblical passages from which a spiritual lesson is drawn. The most widely read volume incorporating elements of historical geography and non-scientific ethnography, yet little to no biblical archaeology, is *Jesus the Christ* by James E. Talmage, published in 1915. His completed volume reflects the state of knowledge about historical geography and ancient lifeways in the nineteenth century and the colonialist attitudes of his sources toward the inhabitants of the Holy Land, interpreted as a representation of ancient practices.[14] Talmage quoted descriptions of places based on nineteenth-century travelogues and observations of life in Ottoman Palestine in his footnotes that would be better understood through later archaeological excavations.

The amount of data about the ancient world stemming from ancient texts, archaeological excavations, and scholarship has grown exponentially since the publication of *Jesus the Christ* and better informs readers of the context of Christ's life and ministry.[15] Talmage's lack of inclusion of or reliance on biblical archaeology may reflect the nascent state of the field when his sources were written. Although explorations in Jerusalem and at other sites were published decades before *Jesus the Christ*, it appears that Talmage selected conservative, established sources and did not incorporate or synthesize newly published information with older sources. Moreover, it is likely that the accessibility and

13. See Richard Neitzel Holzapfel, Dana M. Pike, and David Rolph Seely, *Jehovah and the World of the Old Testament* (Salt Lake City, UT: Deseret Book, 2010); Richard Neitzel Holzapfel, Eric D. Huntsman, and Thomas A. Wayment, *Jesus and the World of the New Testament* (Salt Lake City, UT: Deseret Book, 2014).

14. Neil Asher Silberman, "Power, Politics and the Past: The Social Construction of Antiquity in the Holy Land," in *The Archaeology of Society in the Holy Land*, edited by T.E. Levy (London: Leicester University Press, 1995), 9–23.

15. James E. Talmage, *Jesus the Christ: A Study of the Messiah and His Mission according to the Holy Scriptures both Ancient and Modern with Revised and Updated Notes*, edited by Lincoln Blumell, Gaye Strathearn, and Thomas Wayment (Springville, UT: Cedar Fort Inc., 2015), vii.

utility of archaeological information simply did not suit Talmage's goal. For example, contrary to the concern exhibited by nineteenth-century explorers and archaeologists in the environs of Jerusalem about the location of the death and burial of Jesus, Talmage stated that "the origin of the name [Golgotha/ Calvary] is of as little importance as are the many divergent suppositions concerning the exact location of the spot."[16] For Talmage, the location of certain events was of no consequence to his volume.

Lay church members as well as church leadership have at times uncritically employed archaeological results to associate a place with a biblical event in the minds of their audience. To illustrate, in the early 1970s, a group of LDS General Authorities traveled to the Holy Land and reported their experiences. Among these, Lorin F. Wheelwright, a member of the Sunday School General Board, described the area of Jericho and the wilderness of Judea: "At Jericho are ruins of ancient walls that fell to the trumpets of Joshua."[17] While this may refer solely to a summation of the narrative of Joshua 6, Wheelwright's association between ancient ruined walls present at Jericho with the activities of Joshua and the Israelites reported in the Hebrew Bible is implied without reference to excavation or conflicting interpretations of such results that either upheld or downplayed the biblical account.

A more notable example of a General Authority linking places to events is the series of statements regarding several sites made by Harold B. Lee, and then First Counselor in the First Presidency, on the same trip to Holy Land.[18] About visiting the Garden Tomb, Lee recalled, "Something seemed to impress us as we stood there that this was the holiest place of all, and we fancied we could have witnessed the dramatic scene that took place there."[19] Lee's comments about his perception of sites and their purported events, specifically the Garden Tomb and its likelihood as the place of Jesus's burial and resurrection, have been accepted as definitive by many rank-and-file Latter-day Saints and were seemingly bolstered by remarks made by Spencer W. Kimball during a visit to the Holy Land in 1979. He stated about the Garden Tomb: "We accept this as the burial place of the Savior. We realize people have different ideas about these places, but this seems to be the logical place. I feel quite sure that this is the place where his body was laid. It gives me such a sacred feeling just

16. Talmage, *Jesus the Christ*, 6th ed. (1922), 667, note 3.
17. Lorin F. Wheelwright, "Five Roads to Jericho," *Ensign* (April 1972): 8–12.
18. Harold B. Lee, "I Walked Today Where Jesus Walked," *Ensign* (April 1972): 3–7.
19. Lee, "I Walked Today Where Jesus Walked," 6.

to be here."[20] The acceptance by many Latter-day Saints of Harold B. Lee's utterance as authoritative rather than personal testimony or opinion, coupled with Kimball's later quote, provided an impetus to favor the Garden Tomb over the Holy Sepulcher as the authentic site of Jesus's death and burial.

Lee's itinerary comprised several sites associated with the life and ministry of Jesus, namely: Shepherd's Fields and the Church of the Nativity in Bethlehem, the baptismal site at Qasr el-Yehud, the Tomb of Lazarus in Bethany, the Garden of Gethsemane at the Church of the Agony, the Via Dolorosa, the Church of the Holy Sepulcher, and the Garden Tomb. Lee noted that his mindset and that of his companions: "as we left our room each time, we prayed that the Lord would deafen our ears to what the guide said about historical places but would make us keenly sensitive to the spiritual feeling so that we would know by impression, rather than by hearing, where the sacred spots were."[21] Lee sought a spiritual confirmation or a testimony of the event that occurred rather than the veracity of a site related by historical or archaeological details. Throughout his account, Lee used terms reflecting their mental visualizations and spiritual impressions, such as "in fancy," "we fancied," "we felt," "it seemed to us," or "in our mind's eye," including the negative impression they felt on the Via Dolorosa and at the Church of the Holy Sepulcher. Part of what led them not have a feeling of spiritual significance at those sites was their physical location, observing that those sites were within the city walls and did not have a garden nearby, seemingly in contrast to Hebrews 13:12 and John 19:41–42. In describing the Garden Tomb, Lee cited features that coincided with his understanding of the location of Jesus's crucifixion and burial. For instance, the rock-hewn tomb is located outside of the extant walls of the Old City of Jerusalem, it has a garden nearby, and there is a stone track that is assumed to guide the stone that would cover the entrance to the tomb. Further, the tomb is adjacent to a hill with eroded areas in it escarpment that resemble the eye sockets and nasal cavity of a skull, which has led to its identification as "Golgotha," the place of the skull.

20. For statements by Spencer W. Kimball, see Jack Marshall, "Walking Where Jesus Walked," *Deseret News,* March 19, 2011, available at https://www.deseretnews.com/article/705369028/Walking-where-Jesus-walked.html; see also John A. Tvedtnes, "The Garden Tomb" *Ensign* (April 1983), available at https://www.lds.org/ensign/1983/04/the-garden-tomb?lang=eng; Jeffrey R. Chadwick, "In Defense of the Garden Tomb," *Biblical Archaeology Review* 12, no. 4 (July/August 1986): 16–17, D. Kelly Ogden and Jeffrey R. Chadwick, *The Holy Land: A Geographical, Historical, and Archaeological Guide to the Land of the Bible* (Jerusalem: HaMakor and BYU Jerusalem Center, 1990), 340–45; and Andrew C. Skinner, *The Garden Tomb* (Salt Lake City, UT: Deseret Book, 2005). It should be noted that Chadwick later published an article accepting an Iron Age date for the Garden tomb, see note 24.

21. Lee, "I Walked Today Where Jesus Walked," 3.

Much like Talmage, the statements made by Lee and Kimball about biblical events relating to the Garden Tomb reflected the state of archaeological knowledge about that particular site at that time. While the tomb is outside the walls of Jerusalem's Old City, the walls that modern observers see are not the Herodian walls of the first century CE but rather were built in 1537–1540 at the behest of the Ottoman sultan Suleiman the Magnificent.[22] For over one hundred years from its discovery until 1975, only one report of excavation, written in 1874, was published about the Garden Tomb. Archaeologist Gabriel Barkay investigated the Garden Tomb's features, excavated material, and other nearby burial complexes immediately north and south of the tomb and concluded that the Garden Tomb was originally cut as a tomb in the eighth or seventh centuries BCE, and reused as a tomb in the Byzantine period (fifth to seventh centuries CE).[23] The track in front of the tomb was not used to guide an immense rolling stone to block the door; rather, its intended use was a watering trough for livestock during the Crusader period.[24] The preponderance of evidence suggests that the Garden Tomb was not the actual location of Jesus' burial and resurrection. In a visit to the site in 2000, President Gordon B. Hinckley said, "Just outside the walls of Jerusalem, in this place or somewhere nearby was the tomb of Joseph of Arimathea, where the body of the Lord was interred," which leaves open the possibility that the actual location of Jesus' burial might have been elsewhere, including in the Church of the Holy Sepulcher, which attests positive evidence of Roman-era burial chambers hewn into the bedrock currently within the existing church building.[25]

22. Katharina Galor and Hanswulf Bloedhorn, *The Archaeology of Jerusalem: From the Origins to the Ottomans* (New Haven, CT: Yale University Press, 2013) 234–35.

23. Gabriel Barkay, "The Garden Tomb—Was Jesus Buried Here?" *Biblical Archaeology Review* 12, no. 2 (March/April 1986): 40–57. See also Dan Bahat, "Does the Holy Sepulchre Church Mark the Burial of Jesus?" *Biblical Archaeology Review* 12, no. 3 (May/June 1986): 26–45.

24. Jeffrey R. Chadwick, "Revisiting Golgotha and the Garden Tomb," *Religious Educator* 4, no. 1 (2003): 13–48.

25. Gordon B. Hinckley, in *Special Witnesses of Christ*, videotape, Intellectual Reserve, Inc., 2000. While space does not permit a full discussion of the merits and limitations of identifying the Church of the Holy Sepulcher as the place of the death and burial of Jesus, archaeological evidence indicates that Roman era burial chambers were hewn into bedrock currently within the bounds of the extant church building. Excavations under the nearby Lutheran Church of the Redeemer also revealed that the church would have been outside the city walls at the time of Christ; see Marcel Serr and Dieter Vieweger, "Golgotha: Is the Holy Sepulchre Church Authentic?" *Biblical Archaeology Review* 42, no. 3 (May/June 2016): 28–29, 66. Tradition also lends weight to the discussion. Although no veneration of holy places is mentioned prior to Origen (c. AD 250), "in this instance it may be countered by the question whether the Christians of the Apostolic and Sub-Apostolic epochs would have been careless even of preserving the remembrance of the place where the Lord suffered death and was buried, and bequeathed it to those who came after them" [H.T.F. Duckworth, *The Church of the Holy Sepulchre* (London: Hodder and Stoughton, 1922) 42.]

## SCHOLARSHIP FOR A NON-SPECIALIST AUDIENCE

Latter-day Saint scholars have also used the results of surveys and excavations in the southern Levant for traditional academic audiences as well as non-specialist Latter-day Saint audiences reached through periodicals, edited volumes, and monographs produced by Mormon publishers. Much of the use of biblical archaeology exhibits sound academic research and has been evoked to establish geographic or historical context, illustrate ancient lifeways, and relate material culture from antiquity to the present.[26] Scholars have also used archaeological information in discussion for lay Latter-day Saints about sensationalist claims surrounding the so-called Jesus Family Tomb or James Ossuary in relation to the textual account of the death, burial, and resurrection of Jesus Christ.[27]

Beyond these uses, Latter-day Saint academics have drawn on the archaeology of the southern Levant in the Bronze and Iron Ages to establish context for discussion of events or persons within the Book of Mormon. In his lectures and writings about the Old Testament and Book of Mormon and their relationship to the ancient world in the 1950s to the 1990s, Hugh W. Nibley used such material. For example, Nibley extensively cited mid-century biblical archaeologists such as W.F. Albright, F.J. Bliss, J.L. Starkey, and H.L. Frankfort in discussing the Near Eastern archaeological record that illustrates the backgrounds to Lehi prior to and during the events of the early chapters of 1 Nephi.[28] Such comparative methodology continues to be applied widely to corroborate Book of Mormon details with Near Eastern antecedents.[29]

More recently, professional Latter-day Saint archeologists actively participate in current fieldwork in the Near East combining traditional methods of

26. For example, see Matthew J. Grey, "'Beholdest Thou . . . the Priests and the Levites,'" in *The Sermon on the Mount in Latter-day Scripture*, edited by Gaye Strathearn, Thomas A. Wayment, and Daniel L. Belnap (Provo, UT: Religious Studies Center, BYU; Salt Lake City, UT: Deseret Book, 2010), 173–201; or George A. Pierce, "Understanding Micah's Lament for Judah (Micah 1:10–16) through Text, Archaeology, and Geography," in *Prophets and Prophecies of the Old Testament*, edited by Aaron Schade, Brian M. Hauglid, and Kerry Muhlestein (Provo, UT: Religious Studies Center, 2017) 163–86.

27. Richard Neitzel Holzapfel et al., "Jesus and the Ossuaries: First-Century Jewish Burial Practices and the Lost Tomb of Jesus," in *Behold the Lamb of God: An Easter Celebration*, edited by Richard Neitzel Holzapfel, Frank F. Judd Jr., and Thomas A. Wayment (Provo, UT: Religious Studies Center, BYU, 2008), 1–16.

28. See notes throughout Hugh Nibley, *Lehi in the Desert; The World of the Jaredites; There Were Jaredites, Collected Works of Hugh Nibley* (Provo, UT: Foundation for Ancient Research and Mormon Studies and Deseret Book, 1988).

29. For example, Warren P. Aston and Michaela Knoth Aston, *In the Footsteps of Lehi: New Evidence for Lehi's Journey Across Arabia to Bountiful* (Salt Lake City, UT: Deseret Book, 1994); George Potter and Richard Wellington, *Lehi in the Wilderness: 81 New Documented Evidences That the Book of Mormon Is a True History* (Springville: Cedar Fort Publishing, 2003); and Lynn M. Hilton and Hope A. Hilton, *Discovering Lehi: New Evidence of Lehi and Nephi in Arabia* (Springville, UT: Cedar Fort Publishing, 2015).

textual analysis, survey, excavation, and analysis such as ceramic seriation and stratigraphy together with modern applications such as digital data recording, drone flights, spatial analysis, and other varied computer applications. These methods illuminate the varied peoples and places of the Near East throughout time using the best practices of archaeology in the twenty-first century rather than engaging in biblical or Book of Mormon apologetics.[30] Excavation results and careful textual analysis have been used to correct misinformation and folklore associating archaeological site(s) with events and people of the Book of Mormon, such as the so-called "Cave of Lehi" at Khirbet Beit Lei.[31] Latter-day Saint archaeologists are also involved with the National Geographic-funded excavations of a fifth century CE synagogue at Huqoq, Israel that have revealed mosaics depicting various scenes from the Hebrew Bible and intertestamental period.[32] Current and future activities by Latter-day Saint archaeologists will continue to explore the archaeology of the Near East, not as a way to prove the Bible or the Book of Mormon, but as a means of understanding the contexts of these texts and the cultural heritage of the inhabitants of these lands.

Harkening back to the academic interest in the Near East and Napoleon's campaigns, biblical archaeology originally stemmed from geographic and archaeological investigations in the Holy Land as a means to verify and enliven the Bible, strengthen faith, and reconstruct the history of ancient Israel. As the discipline of archaeology changed, so too the concept of "biblical archaeology" evolved into its current iteration. The archaeology of the southern Levant provides context and illumination of biblical people, places, and events to orient the audiences and establish a link between the present and the hallowed past. Latter-day Saint church leaders' comments about particular places like the Garden Tomb reflect the state of archaeological knowledge at the time that such statements were made and should not be always taken as normative or inerrant. Despite occasional uncritical use in ecclesiastical settings, the value of biblical archaeology lies in establishing cultural contexts for biblical narratives and production while providing a richer, fuller picture of the biblical world complementing the text of Bible with the material culture of the people of the Bible.

30. See various regional studies covering multiple time periods George A. Pierce, "GIS Studies of Tell Dothan and the Dothan Valley," in *Dothan I: Remains from the Tell (1953–1964)*, edited by Daniel M. Master et al. (Winona Lake, IN: Eisenbrauns, 2005), 17–22; or George A. Pierce and Daniel M. Master, "Ashkelon as Maritime Gateway and Central Place," in *Ashkelon 5: The Land Behind Ashkelon*, Final Reports of the Leon Levy Expedition to Ashkelon (Winona Lake, IN: Eisenbrauns, 2015), 109–23.

31. Jeffrey R. Chadwick, "Khirbet Beit Lei and the Book of Mormon: An Archaeologist's Evaluation," *Religious Educator* 10, no. 3 (2009): 17–48.

32. See Huqoq Excavations Project, available at https://www.nationalgeographic.org/news/huqoq-excavation-project/.

17

# Orality, Literacy, and the Cultural World of the Bible in Ancient Near Eastern Scholarship and Latter-day Saint Reception

ERIC A. ELIASON

Immense gulfs of time, culture, and religious practice separate us today from those who composed and first interpreted the Bible. Both Latter-day Saint understandings of Restoration and critical biblical scholarship, each in their own way, seek to recover this "lost world."[1] Investigating ancient orature's relationship to ancient literate practice, notions of authorship, the sacred drama of temple worship, as well as successive transformative technological developments can inform both enterprises. And they might also inform each other. Such an investigation reveals that the relationships between oral and written composition and transmission, as well as scripture's emergence and reception did not happen how we moderns might assume when looking myopically at these matters from our society's frame of reference.[2]

## ORAL- AND WRITING-CENTRIC WORLDS

Jesuit scholar Walter Ong famously posited fundamental psychological differences between people in oral versus literate cultures—the latter not necessarily better.[3] Many in pre- and semi-literate societies are capable of, what seem to us, astounding feats of memory—performing hours-long epic poems, ritual

1. Beginning with *The Lost World of Genesis One: Ancient Cosmology and the Origins Debate* (Downers Grove, IL: IVP Academic, 2009), John H. Walton has foregrounded the term *lost world* in his "*Lost World of . . .* " series of books that seek to recover initial understandings of Biblical content in the light of literary and cultural understanding of the time.

2. Martin S. Jaffee, *Torah in The Mouth: Writing in Ancient Palestinian Judaism 200* BCE *to 400* BCE (Oxford, UK: Oxford University Press, 2001).

3. Walter J. Ong, *Orality and Literacy: The Technologizing of the Word,* 2nd ed. (New York: Routledge, 2002).

dramas, and sacred narratives formulaically recited over and over again with minimal variation.[4] Society-wide increases in literate skillsets tend to displace such oral capabilities. This is one reason ancients did not see literacy as the unambiguous good that today's education institutions generally do. Anciently, performers could recite Homer, Greek philosophers, and/or Hebrew or Egyptian wisdom sayings to demonstrate the highest level of learning—even without being able to read or write a single word.[5] Plato argued against literacy, claiming it will "result in forgetfulness, for they will no longer need to use their memory.... They will read much, but not be taught; they will appear knowledgeable, but ... will be ignorant."[6]

Ong's hard oral/literate divide is now regarded as overly binary. When the written Bible's received text took shape, literacy had already been around for thousands of years.[7] But as a tiny minority skill, it was also still millennia away from eclipsing orality as the prestige mode of cultural transmission. Bible-era society valued scribal literacy akin to our regard for computer programming or auto mechanics—respectable and useful skillsets, usually best left to professionals. Scribal literacy was far from being any sort of baseline measure of minimal learnedness that everyone ought to have.[8]

Oral-centricity was such an unremarkable given that the Bible only rarely reveals the verbal world from which it emerged. Jesus says when referencing the law of Moses, "ye have heard it *said*," not "ye have *read*" (Matt 5:21). Romans likewise does not refer to "*readers* of the law," but explains "not the *hearers* ... but the doers of the law shall be justified" (Rom 2:13). Elsewhere, an oral-centric lens helps discern texts' most likely initial meanings. When Luke prefaces his work with an explanation of his subject matter and methods that read, "delivered ... unto us, which from the beginning were eyewitnesses, and

4. Albert Bates Lord, *Epic Singers and Oral Tradition* (Ithaca, NY: Cornell University Press, 1991); Albert Bates Lord, *The Singer of Tales* (Cambridge, MA: Harvard University Press, 1960); Jacob Neusner, *Oral Tradition in Judaism* (New York: Routledge, 1987).

5. David M. Carr, *Writing on the Tablet of the Heart: Origins of Scripture and Literature* (New York: Oxford University Press, 2008) and *The Formation of the Hebrew Bible: A New Reconstruction* (New York: Oxford University Press, 2011).

6. Plato, *Phaedrus*, 275a.

7. On the emergence and establishment of scribal training and culture and its influence on the received text of the Bible, see William M. Schniedewind, *The Finger of the Scribe: How Scribes Learned to Write the Bible* (New York: Oxford University Press, 2019) and Christopher A. Rollston, *Writing and Literacy in the World of Ancient Israel: Epigraphic Evidence from the Iron Age* (Atlanta: Society of Biblical Literature, 2010).

8. John H. Walton and D. Brent Sandy, *The Lost World of Scripture: Ancient Literary Culture and Biblical Authority* (Downers Grove, IL: Intervarsity Press, 2013), 18.

ministers of the word," oral traditions are likely among the sources he seemed to regard as more authoritative than his own writing.[9]

Getting modern Western minds around oral transmission's cultural centrality is difficult when our most familiar modern oral genres—urban legends, jokes, gossip—are widely deemed spurious and frivolous. However, examples abound of oral traditions passing on significant information with fidelity. *The Iliad* and *Odyssey*'s locations were presumed fictive until Calvert and Schliemann found Troy.[10] Icelandic epics, transcribed in the Middle Ages after hundreds of years of oral transmission, tell of a *Vinland* west of Greenland. This was not deemed evidence of Norse landfall in North America until 1958 when archeologists unearthed Viking longhouses in Newfoundland.[11] As a chaplain in Afghanistan in 2004, I worked with a *hafiz* who had memorized the whole Quran twice—once in Arabic, which he could sing but did not understand, and also a gloss for each surah in his native Pashto. My friend was considered a highly educated man but, like most Afghans, was unable to read or write in any language. He represents a recent link in an ongoing chain of Muslim oral transmission that extends back to before there was written Quran.[12]

## ORALITY, VARIATION, AND "ORIGINAL TEXTS"

While amazing fidelity of massive texts over hundreds of years can characterize oral transmission, written texts could also follow and reflect an oral tradition's developing nature. The discovery of the Dead Sea Scrolls demonstrated both an astounding thousand-year faithful transmission of Biblical materials in a mostly illiterate society, *and* variants, retellings, and expansions upon—and possible omissions of, in the case of Esther—material that came to be canon. Different genres and contexts allow for varying amounts and kinds of change. The Bible text reveals language changes, updated place names, and later

9. According to the four-document hypothesis, Luke drew from Mark, the Q Source (a deduced, but now lost, written source) and the L source, an oral tradition in the early Christian community Luke drew from that passed on many of the parables and the tradition of the virgin birth. Robert W. Funk, Roy W. Hoover, and The Jesus Seminar, "Introduction," *The Five Gospels* (San Francisco: HarperSanFrancisco, 1993), 1–30; Brice B. Jones, *Matthean and Lukan Special Material: A Brief Introduction with Texts in Greek and English* (Eugene, OR: Wipf and Stock, 2011).

10. Susan Heuck Allen, *Finding the Walls of Troy: Frank Calvert and Heinrich Sleimann at Hisarlik* (Berkeley: University of California Press, 1999); Michael Wood, *In Search of The Trojan War* (Berkeley: University of California Press, 1998).

11. Magnus Magnusson and Herman Palsson, *The Vinland Sagas: The Norse Discovery of America* (New York: Penguin, 1965).

12. Andrew G. Bannister, *An Oral-Formulaic Study of the Qur'an* (Lanham, MD: Lexington Books, 2014).

explanatory glosses. In both the Gospels and the Pentateuch, variations appear between different sources' recounting of the same stories. Added sections, not in extant older manuscripts, sometimes appear. The New Testament's woman taken in adultery pericope,[13] and Chronicles' paraphrastic retelling of Adam through Solomon, all demonstrate canon's emergence from ongoing interaction among variable and developing authoritative oral and textual traditions.

Another feature of orality is how speech produces new variants with each recitation. Writing-centric culture's extreme attention to precisely similar wording is not, and cannot be, part of a speech-centric world. Crossing the Red Sea and Deborah's war with Sisera both differ in their prose and poetic versions. (Did the sea swallow Pharaoh's army or were they flung into it? Did Jael strike Sisera before he fell, or after he lay down?) The sign placed over Jesus on the cross was presumably a single fixed written text, but each Gospel presents a different wording.

> This is Jesus, king of the Jews. (Matt. 27:37)
> The king of the Jews. (Mark 15:26)
> This is the king of the Jews. (Luke 23:38)
> Jesus of Nazareth, the king of the Jews. (John 19:19)

A writing-centric approach might see these variations as a problem to explain. Not so much for oral-centric ancients. To them, these variants could all be close-enough paraphrases reliably conveying the essential gist of what was written.

Scholars in previous decades invested immense effort into reconstructing "original texts." But considering orality reveals that, at any point in time a text might be "fixed," multiple preceding and concurrent (let alone subsequent) written and oral versions would have existed—with oral versions frustratingly less recoverable. And since, under certain circumstances, both oral and written traditions were open to additions, subtractions, modifications, and reworkings before, during, and after any canonical text might emerge, it seems dubious that earlier texts would necessarily be more authoritative.[14]

Even in the more writing-centric world since Joseph Smith, Restoration scripture displays similar "living text" features of redaction, variation, and

13. John 7:53–8:11

14. Brennan W. Breed examines many of the issues in imagining there is ever such a thing as an "original text" in his *Nomadic Text: A Theory of Biblical Reception History* (Bloomington: Indiana University 2014), 15–55.

multiple textual traditions, even though these works emerged more recently, over a shorter time, and involved fewer contributors and redactors in a more centrally organized faith tradition.[15] The church's record-keeping commitment has provided a detailed account of a scriptural emergence process scholars might look to in imagining analogous textual development landscapes for the Bible's formation.



## AUTHORSHIP, PSEUDEPIGRAPHA, AND JOSEPH SMITH

Orality helps explain why some Bible books seem not to have been written by their traditionally assumed authors. Today, when we read a poem, novel, police report, office memo, or most anything, we assume that the name affixed is the text's author. This convention is so pervasive, it is hard to imagine any other arrangement as legitimate. Stylistic, linguistic, and historical evidence for multiple Isaiah authors, as well as other, usually later, authors for "Solomon's wisdom"[16] and some of "Paul's letters," can seem to reveal pseudepigrapha or "false writing." This may seem like a kind of reverse-plagiarism whereby the work of a lesser-known person appears under a more famous name to boost its credibility and positive reception. Some believers have seen in this a scholarly attack on scriptural reliability. They may want to double down on "single authorship" for Isaiah and Pauline letters—even though accepting Biblical authority requires neither claim, and many modern notions of "authorship" are anachronistic to the times when these works emerged.

The ancient oral-centric world did not, and could not, share our writing-centric authorship conceptions. Attaching names to texts did not always

15. Royal Skousen, *The Book of Mormon: The Earliest Text* (New Haven, CT: Yale University Press, 2009). See also his Book of Mormon Critical Text Project, especially *Vol. 3: The History of the Text of the Book of Mormon* (Provo, UT: Neal A. Maxwell Institute for Religious Scholarship, forthcoming). Robin Scott Jensen, Robert J. Woodford, and Steven C. Harper, *The Joseph Smith Papers: Revelations and Translations: Manuscript Revelation Book* (Salt Lake City, UT: Church Historian's Press, 2009); Robin Scott Jensen, Richard E. Turley Jr., and Riley M. Lorimer, *The Joseph Smith Papers, Vol. 2: Revelations and Translations, Published Revelations (Joseph Smith Papers: Revelations and Translations)* (Salt Lake City, UT: Church Historian's Press, 2011). Terryl Givens and Brian Hauglid, *The Pearl of Greatest Price: Mormonism's Most Controversial Scripture* (New York: Oxford University Press, 2019).

16. Some may imagine Solomon personally composing the whole of Proverbs, but the Bible itself does not support this. Prov 25:1 indicates one section at least was transcribed by Hezekiah's court hundreds of years later. And Prov 31 begins with the cryptic "the words of King Lemuel, the prophecy that his mother taught him." Was the mother a conduit or original recipient of this prophetic material about King Lemuel? Does "him" refer to Lemuel or Solomon? Was Lemuel another name for Solomon (making Bathsheba the mother), or another traditional authority figure known only in this passage?

imply authorship as we now understand it. A quarter of Thucydides's writings are speeches he composed and attributed to ancient generals and statesmen.[17] To him this maintained "as much as possible the sense of what was spoken."[18] Thucydides was widely read and commented on anciently, but his having long-dead historical figures say what he thought they should have said was not remarked upon as problematic.[19] The relationship of David, Solomon, Isaiah, and Paul to their associated ancient writings might range from "author of" to "collector of" to "commissioner of" to "written for" to "commissioner of the collection of" to "composed in the tradition honoring" to "composed by recognized successors of" to "drawn from the oral tradition about" and to, both figuratively and literally, "inspired by."[20]



While scholars find such distinctions noteworthy, ancients likely did not so much. Literary convention allowed and may have sometimes required, authors to compose in a preceding authority's name. Both oral and written composition draw from multiple sources in ways ignored by the dubious modern notion of whole-cloth individual authorship. Bible content-producing communities saw themselves as divinely guided in following these conventions.[21] With an open canon, scribes were not only copyists and oral tradition transcribers but also, when seen as under inspiration, could legitimately compile, reword, add to, and adapt material for new purposes. Whoever may have produced new texts in the name of previous authority figures, God could well be seen as the work's more significant source. There is little reason to believe revered figures' names attached to other's canonical writings always evidences duplicity. Overreaching "Pseudepigrapha" accusations can seem like an anachronistic projection of our own conceits onto a past that had little conception of them.[22] Authors—secular and religious, ancient and modern—often refer to the writing process in terms of inspiration, losing sense of time and self, and feeling like words come from elsewhere. Should it be surprising that ancient writing sometimes took on names associated with inspiration from God? Keeping one's name off of a text could be more a sign of humble reverence than an attempt to pass off one's own work as someone else's.

17. Walton and Sandy, *Lost World of Scripture*, 101.

18. Thucydides, *The History of The Peloponnesian War*, 1.22.1

19. Michael Grant, *Greek and Roman Historians: Information and Misinformation* (New York: Routledge, 1995), 44–53.

20. Walton and Sandy, *Lost World of Scripture*, 64.

21. Walton and Sandy, *Lost World of Scripture*, 63.

22. Walton and Sandy, *Lost World of Scripture*, 73.

Biblical accounts of angelic messengers, the voice of God, Moses and Elijah's appearance at the mount of transfiguration,[23] and possibly Samuel through the witch of Endor,[24] are ways ancients recognized previous, even deceased, authority figures might inspire the writing of sacred words. These accounts are worth comparing to how Latter-day scripture emerged. Through his subjective experiences of inspiration, sometimes accompanied by angelic ancient prophet visitation, Joseph Smith felt authorized to take up the mantle of translator, redactor, and producer of canon expansions. Associates usually transcribed the Prophet's dictations, which he often presented as being more significantly associated with past Bible and Book of Mormon figures than with his own nineteenth century American context.[25] He and his followers received the texts Joseph Smith spoke as most significantly directly from God—rather than the Prophet's mind, or his scribes' pens. In this light, Joseph Smith's role in producing the Book of Mormon and his "New Translation" Bible additions more resemble, rather than break with, how the Bible came to be.

As with ancient pseudepigrapha, some have seen Joseph Smith's corpus as fraudulent unauthorized evocation of ancient authorities. However, assuming some stability in subjective prophetic experience over time, a comparison to Latter-day Saint scripture and its receptions might help put biblical pseudepigrapha claims in a fuller light. In appreciating the potentially immense ramifications of new canonicity claims, whether scholars regard any writing as legitimate or not has rarely been as important as understanding how their earliest readers experienced those writings' significance. The major divisions of the Abrahamic religion family all have to do with what Bible times evoking texts to accept as authoritative. Acceptance of rejection of Post-Pentateuch Jewish scripture (for Samaritans) and of the Talmud (for Karaites) or the New Testament (for Christians), the Quran (for Muslims), and the Book of Mormon (for Latter-day Saints) is precisely what defines new religious movements against older ones.[26]

23. Matt 17: 1–9.

24. Christopher James Blythe, "The Prophetess of Endor: Reception of 1 Samuel 28 in Nineteenth Century Mormon History," *Journal of the Bible and its Reception* 4, no. 1 (2017): 43–70.

25. The names of the Book of Mormon's constituent books also don't seem to follow modern conceptions of proper authorial attribution. Parts of them sometimes do, as with much of 1 Nephi and Jacob. But much of 2 Nephi is Nephi's lengthy quotation of a version of Isaiah. The book names Mosiah, Alma, Helaman, and Mormon each seem named after a prominent Nephite leader active within the rough time frame described in each book. Each book has words attributed to its eponymous figure but other speakers, and Mormon's redaction, are also present.

26. Each of these communities has a somewhat different collection of texts in mind when they speak of "the Bible." See Jaroslav Pelikan, *Whose Bible Is It? A History of the Scriptures Through the Ages* (New York:

## Orality's Decline and a Restoration in Latter-day Saint Temples

Despite Joseph Smith presenting his scriptural corpus as emerging from his reentry into the prophetic stream active during ancient open canon eras, his Restoration scriptures appeared only after significant historical shifts and technological developments transformed how believers experienced and conceived of scripture. Imagining a "book" as a physical object, rather than an oral tradition around a namesake figure, could not have fully emerged until after the codex's second century invention. For much of its early history, the written Bible referred not to a single volume, but to a collection of books from which a reader might select one volume to read at a time—the Book of Job or Book of Esther perhaps. Cost and technology barriers prevented all but a very few from ever hoping to own a physical copy of the whole "Bible library." So, Bibles tended to be curated by institutions on behalf of their constituent communities.

The Bible began to be seen as a single book anyone could own and study silently only after Gutenberg's invention of movable type reduced printing costs and dramatically increased printing volumes. Luther quickly fetishized this new technologically mediated way of experiencing the Bible. He insisted the church's long practice of disseminating scriptural knowledge through public liturgy, dramatic performance, and visual depictions of Bible scenes—and not giving just anyone access to their rare, fragile, and expensive written Bibles—was a conspiracy to conceal scripture rather than the time-honored best practice—indeed, previously the *only* possible way of sharing it.[27] Luther's notions seemed to many at the time as bizarre as it would be today to suggest that the only legitimate way to experience a play or a movie would be to read the script alone in one's room—theatres being a massive plot to deprive us of this authentic experience.

However, printed material's steadily increasing affordability helped propel Luther's views to transformative influence in Western culture. The lone reader, without priestly mediation, earnestly poring over the printed text for its plain meaning shorn of paraphrastic accretion and florid allegorical interpretation,

---

Viking International, 2005). Not only can differences in which stories are canonically included divide communities, but different versions of the same stories, interpreted differently can as well. Providing further evidence that written canons drew from oral traditions and their multiple variants, the Quran presents variant versions of stories Bible readers would find familiar. Sometimes, the Quran just makes allusions that seem to presume an audience familiar with the Bible. Robert C. Gregg, *Shared Stories, Rival Tellings: Early Encounters of Jews, Christians, and Muslims* (New York: Oxford University Press, 2015).

27. See Miranda Wilcox, "Medieval Bibles"; and Jason A. Kerr, "Reformation and Early Modern Biblical Interpretation," in this volume.

is a foundational trope for both rigorous Protestantism and modern Bible scholarship. In intellectual history's broader sweep, these two traditions seem more like fraternal twins than the antagonistic opposites of our present's myopic perspective.



Latter-day Saints have imbibed Luther's individual scripture study ethos to a significant degree. After all, Joseph Smith's pivotal moment has come to be seen as him reading his Bible, alone in his room, and coming upon James 1:5, "if any of you lack wisdom, let him ask of God . . . ." His reaction to this passage prompted his prayer in the Sacred Grove and the First Vision, later seen as inaugurating his prophetic calling. Yet, the Prophet's culminating role in the Restoration might be his introduction of Latter-day Saint temple rites.

Transcriptions exist for these rites, but for use only in temples and only as cribs for officiators learning speaking roles. They are unavailable for devotional or scholarly study. Purloined transcriptions can, like many things, be found on the internet. For faithful Latter-day Saints, this represents a most sacrilegious removal of the sacred into a profane context.[28] Kathleen Flake suggests that focusing temple-goers' attention on the enacted rites themselves and not on their variations through time maintains their sense of timeless authority.[29] Temple ceremonies occur only in the manner scripture was experienced anciently—orally in face-to-face community enactment. No written versions even existed from the rites' 1840s introduction in Nauvoo until Utah's first temple opened in St. George in 1877.[30] Joseph Smith tasked Brigham Young—known for his acting performances in secular theater—to memorize and pass on the rites.[31] For decades, temple rites were an entirely oral tradition. In most

28. A parallel may exist here to the *disciplina arcani*—or "rule of silence" alleged to have existed in early Christianity concerning some doctrines and practices that were to be kept secret and shared only in restricted ritual settings and only with believers more seasoned in the faith. Origen, *Contra Celsum* (1,1), *The Catholic Encyclopedia, Vol. V.* (New York: Robert Appleton Company, Nihil Obstat, May 1, 1909). Similar practices have emerged when new religious movements are subject to persecution for beliefs and practices unpopular with those around them—for example, Alawite and Druze forms of *taquiya*, Russian Orthodox Old Believer secret services, and Scientology's attempts to keep its upper-level auditing training content restricted. Latter-day Saints were in a similarly precarious situation when the rites of endowment and plural marriage were introduced in Nauvoo. Yaron Friedman, *The Nusayri Alawis: An Introduction to the Religion, History and Identity of the Leading Minority in Syria* (Leiden, Netherlands: Brill, 2010); Robert Brenton Betts, *The Druze* (New Haven, CT: Yale University Press, 1990); Robert O. Crummey, *Old Believers in a Changing World* (DeKalb: Northern Illinois University, 2011); James R. Lewis, ed., *Scientology* (New York: Oxford University Press, 2009).

29. Kathleen Flake, "'Not to Be Riten': The Mormon Temple Rite as Oral Canon," *Journal of Ritual Studies*, 9, no. 2 (Summer 1995): 1-21.

30. David J. Buerger, *The Mysteries of Godliness: A History of Mormon Temple Worship* (Salt Lake City, UT: Signature Books, 2016); Devery Scott Anderson, *Development of LDS Temple Worship, 1846–2000* (Salt Lake City, UT: Signature Books, 2011).

31. Leonard Arrington, *Brigham Young: American Moses* (Champaign: University of Illinois Press, 1985), 287–93.

Latter-day Saint temples today, dramatic performance has migrated from live actors to projection screens, but essential elements can still be shared only orally with face-to-face human contact.

Notably, printed Bibles and Restoration scripture can be found in temples—not so much for liturgical use, but for décor and reading while waiting one's turn with the tactile ordinances. Mormons tend not to think of temple rites when listing the faith community's canonical works. The temple is widely experienced by Latter-day Saints as a thing apart, perhaps even more holy and liturgically significant than the textual Latter-day Saint scriptural canon sometimes called "The Standard Works." The temple might be a higher canon, or even an institution distinct from and more important than canon. Temple-goers may think of the endowment ceremony's interactive creation narrative presentation as being drawn from Genesis's Garden of Eden narrative. Scholarship suggests it was originally the other way around; Genesis was a transcription of an ancient participatory dramatic performance to help people remember covenants.[32] But this is the case for much of the Bible.[33] Joseph Smith unlikely entertained any scholarly theories of orality, but if his desire to restore ancient religion included a return to the oral and community-ritual way scripture was formerly experienced, temple ceremonies serve this purpose quite well.

## ORALITY IN AND ALONGSIDE THE WRITTEN BIBLE

While orality's significance is often underappreciated,[34] the Bible is not simply a word-for-word written capture of oral expression.[35] Though the Song of Deborah may come close.[36] Widely seen as the oldest wording in the Bible, as evidenced by its Canaanite imagery and archaic Hebrew grammatical features. Israelite women may have sung it to celebrate deliverance from Sisera

32. Hugh Nibley, *Temple and Cosmos: Beyond This Ignorant Present* (Salt Lake City, UT: Deseret Book, 1992); Marcus Borg, *Reading the Bible Again for the First Time* (San Francisco: HarperOne, 2001), 69–70.

33. Much of the literature on this is assembled in Walton, *The Lost World of Genesis One*, and Walton and Walton and Sandy, *The Lost World of Scripture*.

34. Alan Dundes, *Holy Writ as Oral Lit: The Bible as Folklore* (Lanham, MD: Rowan and Littlefield, 1999); Susan Niditch, *Oral World and Written World: Ancient Israelite Literature* (Louisville, KY: Westminster John Knox Press, 1996); Susan Niditch, *Folklore and the Hebrew Bible* (Eugene, OR: Wipf & Stock, 2004) highlight many instances where Bible texts show signs of being drawn from oral transmission.

35. William M. Schniedewind, *How the Bible Became a Book: The Textualization of Ancient Israel* (Cambridge, UK: Cambridge University Press, 2005).

36. Serge Frolov gives an overview of the various views on the Song of Deborah's provenance. These range from it being the oldest part of the Bible (not in how long ago the scenes it describes were, but in that the specific Hebrew wording of this transcribed folksong's lyric phrases have remained essentially unchanged for over 2200 years—longer than any other received wording in Scripture, to on the other hand, that it is more substantially a much more recent product of the monarchy several hundred years later. Frolov, "How Old Is the Song of Deborah?" *Journal for the Study of the Old Testament* 36, no. 2 (2011): 163–84.

and subsequent threats, for generations, before its transcription into Judges 5. Traditional music's rhythm and structure often exerts tremendously conservative effects on language, shielding it from change. Not just older versions of still-spoken tongues, but otherwise moribund languages may yet thrive through music—as with choirboy Latin and Louisiana Zydeco's French Creole—possible analogs of Judges 5's archaic Hebrew folksong lyrics.

Much of the Gospels reads like collections of transcribed oral anecdotes lightly adapted into written form.[37] Circulating in multiple variants, and told a few at a time, little attention would have been paid to chronological ordering or to relating them all at each telling. This helps explain why each synoptic Gospel presents a different number, in a different order, of Jesus' parables, sayings, and miracles and signs.[38] This seeming inconsistency has bedeviled efforts to harmonize a chronology of Jesus' ministry and determine whether there are separate loaves-and-fishes events depicted or merely multiple transcribed versions of the same story. Such bedevilment may reveal more about our largely literate culture's peculiar expectations when reading than it does any actual New Testament "textual problems."

Job uses oral features like dramatic dialogue and Leviathan imagery but contains words whose playful ambiguity works only with ancient written Hebrew's lack of vowel markers. This, and a liberal peppering of exotic loan words, stylistic evidence of multiple textual sources woven together over many years, and an overwrought elevated tone make the received Job text read like it was composed as a written work.[39] Acrostics, where the first letter of each poetic verse spells out a word or follows alphabetic order, such as in some of Lamentations, Psalms, and Proverbs' praise of the good wife are evidence of literate hands at work—or at least the work of oral composers employing a recitational mnemonic device that relies on some minimal written spelling ability.[40]

37. Much of the vast literature on oral predecessors to the New Testament Gospels is surveyed in James D.G. Dunn, *The Oral Gospel Tradition* (Grand Rapids, MI: Eerdmans, 2013).

38. William A. Wilson notes that small groups' orally transmitted corpus of stories about their own history often takes the form of a cycle of numerous short narratives, one or a few of which are recounted when a situation arises where it is appropriate to share them, or something happens that reminds people of a past event. So as they are told through time, they do not progress chronologically through the cycle. Compiling and transcribing such stories presents an opportunity to arrange them in chronological order. But this is challenging since for many kinds of stories, this is something that never happens in the oral tradition if it is not deemed particularly important to know exactly what order Jesus' pericopes and parable tellings came in. (The parable telling likely happened numerous times to numerous audiences.) The passion narrative events form a longer sustained narrative, so the Gospels break from their "collection of anecdotes" presentation style when recounting Jesus' trial, crucifixion, burial, resurrection, and appearances. William A. Wilson, "Personal Narratives: The Family Novel," in *The Marrow of Human Experience: Essays of Folklore*, edited by Jill Terry Rudy and William A. Wilson (Logan: University of Utah Press, 2006): 261–82.

39. Robert Alter, *The Wisdom Books: Job, Proverbs, and Ecclesiastes* (New York: Norton, 2010), 3–10.

40. Lamentations 1–4; Psalms 25, 34, 37, 111, 112, 119, and 145; and Proverbs 31:10–31.

Whatever influence orality might have, meaning can be lost in transcription—especially in orthographies, like ancient Hebrew's, without vowel markers, punctuation, paragraph breaks, or word spacing. Consider the sentence, "I never said she stole my money." Speaking it seven times emphasizing a different word each time reveals seven distinct meanings. These emerge by slightly increasing each word's volume, pitch, and duration. Written English is not well-equipped to capture much of this nuance that is so easily conveyed verbally. Italicizing for emphasis is common but not universal, nor is it as clear as the spoken means. The church-published Latter-day Saint Bible italicizes words that KJV translators reluctantly added to make their translation grammatical in English, but were not there in the Hebrew and Greek for which they strove to provide a word-for-word translation. Unfortunately, for twenty-first century readers, emphasis is the opposite of the KJV translators' intention.

As readers' primary subjective experiences of the Bible experience migrated from orature to literature, companion oral traditions sometimes kept untranscribed meanings alive. The earliest Hebrew manuscripts have no vowel markings, but by around 1000 CE, the Masoretes had implemented them.[41] A rigorous oral tradition had long informed cantors on how to recite written Hebrew despite its limited orthography that led to pervasive ambiguities. Recently published Bibles go even further in ethnopoetically transcribing oral signification, marking poetic verse and diptych divisions with easy-to-see new lines.[42] Yet, for centuries, Jewish and Christian oral cantillation has expressed the received rhythms of Biblical poetry—even when "reading" from texts where poetic lines and stanzas all run together undifferentiated. As orthographies over time have trended toward fuller written representation of speech features, written Bibles have become less-and-less cribs for oral performance, and more-and-more the primary means of scriptural transmission.

Authoritative traditions outside the Bible text exist for many Abrahamic faith communities. Central to rabbinic Judaism is the notion of an Oral Torah (passed on face-to-face since Sinai, and later transcribed into the Talmud) of different content, but of equal or even greater authority, than the Written Torah. Catholic, Anglican, as well as Eastern and Oriental Orthodox communions

41. A long running, but much contested, notion holds that the Masoretes were Karaites who rejected the Oral Law's legitimacy, and saw only the written Tanakh as authoritative. A Karaite connection might explain the Masoretes' interest in developing a text easier to read without reference to orally transmitted versions of, and understandings of, the text. Elvira Martín-Contreras and Lorena Miralles-Maciá, eds., *The Text of the Hebrew Bible: From the Rabbis to Masoretes (Journal of Ancient Judaism. Supplements)* (Göttingen, Germany: Vandenhoeck & Ruprecht, 2013).

42. On ethnopoetics, or methods of conveying oral language features in written texts see Jan Blommaert, "Applied Ethnopoetics," *Narrative Inquiry* 16, no. 1 (Jan 2006): 181–90.

hold that "Sacred Tradition" has perpetuated true Christian practices and beliefs since apostolic times. For these faiths, the Bible emerges from Sacred Tradition, not the other way around, as Luther imagined. A Latter-day Saint theology of anything like Sacred Tradition has remained underdeveloped despite temple rites' importance. Belief in continuing revelation can perhaps make tradition seem a redundant or even inappropriate authority source. One of the few attempts by General Authorities of the Church of Jesus Christ of Latter-day Saints to articulate something along these lines is apostle Boyd K. Packer's "The Unwritten Order of Things."[43]

Appropriately authorized or not, extra-Biblical tradition's significance can be seen in over half the world's population belonging to Abrahamic faith traditions that identify the Garden of Eden's serpent as Satan. This identification has no textual justification anywhere in the Bible, which shows how powerful Bible-adjacent interpretive traditions can be in understanding the Bible—even for Protestants.[44] Latter-day Saints accept several varying accounts of the in Eden serpent's identity—including the temple's endowment rite; the KJV Bible's Genesis account; and the account in the Book of Moses in the restoration Scripture, the Pearl of Great Price, which is an excerpt from Joseph Smith's "new translation/inspired version" emendations now known as the "Joseph Smith Translation" (JST).[45] These sources differ on whether Satan is mentioned at all; the Serpent is a separate being influenced by Satan; or the names "Satan," "Lucifer," and "the Serpent" are essentially interchangeable. The latter understanding is the most common. Curiously, among Mormons, there seems to be no well-developed discussion about, or even much of a recognition *that*, there may be any potentially problematic "contradictions" to resolve between these distinct authoritative accounts officially accepted by the Church of Jesus Christ of Latter-day Saints.[46]

43. BYU devotional address, October 15, 1996.

44. As a Mormon missionary in the 1980s, a lapsed member of one of the Netherlands' many much-subdivided Protestant denominations told me a story he said partly explained why he chose not to take organized religion too seriously anymore. A history buff, he read of a local congregation that had argued over whether it was right to refer to Eden's "Serpent" as "Satan." Unable to agree, they schismed and formed two denominations from one. Each one was the one true church; and the other was all hellbound heretics. This example of Protestantism taken to its logical extremes seemed, to this Dutchman, too trivial a matter to warrant enough contention to cause a rupture in the Body of Christ—however well it might serve as a metonym for Protestantism's long history of, and current state of, fractiousness, seemingly much fueled by *sola scriptura*'s collision into people's tendency to have a great variety of reactions to the Bible.

45. Moses 4:5–6.

46. The Quran explicitly identifies Eve's tempter as Satan, Surah Al-A'raf (7:22). This gives Muslims and Mormons both extra-Biblical scriptural justification for this identification. Catholics have the Magisterium,

## WHITHER BIBLE WORDS AND WORLDS INTO THE FUTURE?

Caution is prudent for any scholarly proposition about the Bible. Compared to other fields, Bible scholarship's impressively voluminous yearly publication output unfortunately emerges from a woefully meager number of available relevant data points. Remaining indefinite may be especially apropos when such data points are often only comparative, ancillary, reconstructed, and/or emergent from societies experiencing rapid technological and cultural change that may have entertained many points of view, only a few if any of which, have survived to the present. So some reticence is advisable before proffering any bold claims about issues of "pseudepigraphic" authorship, original texts in the light of ancient oral-centric cultures, or the "most authentic" or "best" way to experience the Bible.

We might even be in the last years of Luther's "one reader and the Bible's printed text" as the privileged paradigm. A great shift may be happening, of similar magnitude to the shift from an oral to a written world. Pixels on screens are pushing out ink on pages. Many young Bible readers do not even own printed versions.[47] A child's smart phone can access almost as many commentaries, translations, images of ancient manuscripts, and interpretive notes as could Bible scholars at top universities just a few decades ago. Since the printed page and bepixeled screens both rely on essentially the same sets of representational visual symbols, an ink-to-phosphors shift may not be quite so significant as the oral to written culture transition has been. But the growth of digital audio scriptures listened to while driving, exercising, or winding down at night portent to bring the Bible full-circle back to a kind of orality. Spreading cell phone technology is making high levels of literacy less essential to Bible access by bringing Bible audio, video, and even dramatic visual presentation to even the poorest corners of the world.[48] The scope and speed of all this taken together may well yet come to be regarded as inaugurating a set of shifts as momentous as orality to literacy has been.

leaving Protestants as the main faith tradition without a solid basis for this belief according to their own traditional authoritative sources.

47. First day of class show-of-hands polls of my Bible as Literature students, at overwhelmingly Latter-day Saint BYU, demonstrate that they invariably *all* have Bibles. In recent years, the fraction who own a paper-and-ink version as well as an electronic version has dipped to only about one half.

48. Worldwide cell phone usage in 2016 was 62.9 percent. Smart phone usage alone grew from 11% of the world's population in 2011 to 36 percent in 2018. "Number of smartphone users worldwide from 2014 to 2020," *Statistica*, available at https://www.statista.com/statistics/330695/number-of-smartphone-users-worldwide/.

How will believers and scholars adapt to these fast-moving changes compared to past technological and cultural transformations? How long before some reformer or new religious movement founder discovers the sure-to-come massive multiplayer immersive virtual reality haptic glove and verisimilitudinous goat smell-enhanced interactive Bible world metaverse simulation? "You haven't yet tried both the nine- and six-foot Goliath skins for your avatar and felt David's rock sink into your forehead? You haven't 3D-printed replica pottery shards from the palace archeological dig and used The Museum of the Bible's free sonic resonance imprint recovery app to listen to his Psalms as they were originally sung? Well then, you haven't experienced the Bible as it was meant to be by its earliest composers and readers!"

The speculative scenario above almost certainly won't happen with these particular details. But if history is any guide, future feasters on the Word will do so in some equally novel, transformative tech-mediated ways that will seem to them a natural restorative return to how things were meant to be. But to others, this may seem an unwarranted innovative deviation from "the good old religion." And they will remain blind to their own innovations that make their own practices also quite different from earlier modes. From this difference, multiple distinctive traditions may emerge, each one claiming to be the legitimate inheritor of the original message from God.

# 18

# Feminist Biblical Criticism

DEIDRE NICOLE GREEN[1]

Feminist biblical scholars share the common purpose of interpreting scripture in the service of women with an awareness that *all* interpretations, including those that are historical, sociological, and theological, are influenced by both the conscious and unconscious interests of the interpreters.[2] Placing women and their lived experience at the center of religion and interpretation of scripture, feminist biblical criticism takes as its task the examination of the Hebrew and Christian Bibles to unpack their notions of gender, sexuality, and relationships of power while considering the texts' historical connections to patriarchy,[3] a complex system of practices, beliefs, and attitudes that deny women's full agency and humanity. Acknowledging that the "patriarchal stamp of scripture is permanent," Phyllis Trible holds that it is simultaneously true that the "interpretation of its content is forever changing."[4] This iterability of interpretation allows for the possibility of more egalitarian and liberatory readings, which work to expand women's agency. Therefore, rather than simply jettisoning a text that many women consider a source of authority for their lives, feminist biblical criticism strives to preempt readings of biblical texts that legitimate unjust relationships of domination and focuses on the biblical vision of love

1. I acknowledge here the significant contributions to this article made by my undergraduate research assistants at BYU: Britta Adams, Niquelle Cassador, Savannah Clawson, Rachel Huntsman, and Robert Tensmeyer.

2. Katheryn Pfisterer Darr, *Far More Precious than Jewels: Perspectives on Biblical Women* (Louisville, KY: Westminster John Knox Press, 1991), 35.

3. Nyasha Junior, *An Introduction to Womanist Biblical Criticism* (Louisville, KY: Westminster John Knox Press, 2015), xxiii.

4. Phyllis Trible, *God and the Rhetoric of Sexuality* (Philadelphia: Fortress Press, 1978), 202.

and justice to inspire women in their struggle for wholeness and dignity.[5] This essay explores the principles that have informed scholars engaged in feminist biblical criticism, the LDS interaction with this scholarly movement, and LDS traditions that favor women's interpretation.



## FEMINIST BIBLICAL CRITICISM

Averring that feminist biblical interpretation is not meant to dispense with biblical texts, Musa Dube emphasizes the fact that it focuses on "restoring the canonicity of the Bible by insisting that what is normative, what is the authoritative Word of God, is only that which embraces the liberation of women and, indeed, all the marginalized people of God." That is to say that the authority is not within the texts themselves, but rather "measured by the liberation of women and all God's oppressed people of the world." Canonicity is the justice and righteousness of God enacted in and through God's living creation.[6] In other words, feminist biblical criticism goes beyond exegesis to concern itself with analyzing the way biblical teachings are internalized and contextualized in women's lives through structures of domination.[7] For example, the ambiguity between love and rape in the story of David and Bathsheba in 1 Samuel 11 can work to condone sexual violence against women both within the text and in the lives of its readers.[8] Readings of the text that decry the violation of women's bodily integrity work to resist attitudes and practices that condone women's victimization both within the world of the text and the world beyond it. While some feminist scholars construct feminist readings based primarily on the text, others maintain that problems for women remain so deeply embedded in western culture that a broader analysis beyond the text is needed.

Focusing largely on the text itself, Carolyn Osiek categorizes feminist hermeneutics of the Bible according to five basic types, namely rejectionist, loyalist, revisionist, sublimationist, and liberationist.[9] The rejectionist position holds that the Bible, as well as the Judeo-Christian traditions associated with it, are irremediably corrupt, patriarchal, and oppressive. From this perspec-

5. Elisabeth Schüssler Fiorenza, *Wisdom Ways: Introducing Feminist Biblical Interpretation* (Maryknoll, NY: Orbis, 2001), 1.

6. Musa W. Dube Shomanah, "Scripture, Feminism, and Post-Colonial Contexts," in *Women's Sacred Scriptures*, edited by Kwok Pui-Lan and Elisabeth Schüssler Fiorenza (Maryknoll, NY: Orbis, 1998), 47.

7. Schüssler Fiorenza, *Wisdom Ways*, 2.

8. Mieke Bal, *Lethal Love: Feminist Literary Readings of Biblical Love Stories* (Bloomington: Indiana University Press, 1987), 11.

9. Carolyn Osiek, "The Feminist and the Bible: Hermeneutical Alternatives," in *Feminist Perspectives on Biblical Scholarship*, edited by Adela Yarbro Collins, (Chico, CA: Scholars Press, 1985), 98–103.

tive, the only appropriate response to the Bible is to sever ties with it. On the opposite end of the spectrum, the loyalist hermeneutic maintains that because the Bible is the word of God, it cannot be oppressive; this means that apparent endorsements of oppression reveal a mistake in the interpreter and her interpretive tradition rather than with the text.[10] The revisionist approach views the tradition as worth saving and, in seeking to rehabilitate the tradition through reform, takes the tactic of highlighting the importance of women within religious history, "portraying their dignity within patriarchy."[11] The sublimationist hermeneutic lifts up feminine imagery and symbolism, operating on an assumption of the otherness of the feminine. Examples of this include conceiving of Israel as the bride of God, the church as the bride of Christ, particular perspectives on Mary, identifying Christ with Sophia, and feminine imagery for the Holy Spirit. Liberation feminism, inspired by liberation theology, takes as a starting point an orientation toward the realization of an eschatological order that includes equality.[12] These varied interpretive strategies reveal a range of views about both the Bible and women, including those that uphold the authority of the Bible and acknowledge that not all women experience the Bible as oppressive; yet those that do not see it as oppressive still experience benefits from employing feminist tools.



A basic element of the various approaches of feminist biblical criticism is a hermeneutic of suspicion, which entails investigating ideological claims of biblical texts rather than accepting traditionally normative readings of potentially oppressive texts as authoritative.[13] This approach assumes that biblical authors do something other than simply recount events just as they transpired from a disinterested and objective standpoint, maintaining that patriarchal contexts shaped the crafting of the Bible just as it shapes modern interpretation of it.[14] Schüssler Fiorenza specifies that this suspicion must include assessment of sociological and anthropological models for the kyriarchal implications and limitations they contain.[15] Schüssler Fiorenza opts for the term *kyriarchy* over against *patriarchy* because it encompasses a broader view of the types of oppression religious life confronts one with; *kyriarchy* refers to multiple forms

10. Pfisterer Darr, *Far More Precious Than Jewels*, 36.

11. Osiek, "The Feminist and the Bible," 101.

12. Osiek, 101–3.

13. Rosa Cursach Salas, "A Christian Feminist Hermeneutics of the Bible," in *Feminist Biblical Studies in the Twentieth Century*, edited by Elisabeth Schüssler Fiorenza (Atlanta: Society of Biblical Literature, 2014), 167.

14. Pfisterer Darr, *Far More Precious Than Jewels*, 40.

15. Schüssler Fiorenza, *Wisdom Ways*, 147.

of domination that result from structural power and accounts for the fact that a person can be dominated in one social setting and privileged in another.[16] Insofar as kyriarchy is structured around the property rights of elite males and relies on the "exploitation, dependency, inferiority, and obedience" of women,[17] feminist criticism must expose this ideology or else it will reinforce rather than decenter the marginalizing dynamics of problematic texts.[18] Moreover, this hermeneutic of suspicion must be multifaceted because aspects of identity are "multiplex" and "shaped by intersecting structures of dominations"—race, gender, class, and imperialism must be addressed as disparate forms of dominating power that converge in various ways, creating multiple kinds of subordination.[19] Diverse configurations of domination call for liberating interpretive strategies that reflect this diversity.

Another major tool of feminist biblical criticism is historical reconstruction, which attempts to reconstruct the lives of early women within their societies.[20] Schüssler Fiorenza adapted this hermeneutical approach in the hope that women would use the Bible for their "well-being and not in order to internalize their subordination and second class citizenship."[21] On her view, feminist historical reconstruction should be contrasted with historical studies in that the latter works to distance contemporary readers from the time of the text while, conversely, the former seeks to bridge the chasm that historical positivism constructs between those readers and the biblical text.[22] Feminist historical reconstruction seeks to displace kyriocentric dynamics in the text by recontextualizing the text in a different "socio-political-religious historical context to make the subordinated and marginalized 'others' visible, and their repressed arguments and silences 'audible' again." It thereby attempts to recover women's religious historical agency and the memory of their struggles, achievements, and victimization.[23] Beyond demonstrating men's oppression and domination over women, feminist methods of historical reconstruction conceptualize women's historical agency and struggles against kyriarchal subordination and

16. See Elisabeth Schüssler Fiorenza, "Introduction," in *Feminist Biblical Studies in the Twentieth Century: Scholarship and Movement*, edited by Elisabeth Schüssler Fiorenza (Atlanta: Society of Biblical Literature, 2014), 11–3 (electronic version).

17. Schüssler Fiorenza, *Wisdom Ways*, 118.

18. Schüssler Fiorenza, 147.

19. Schüssler Fiorenza, "Between Movement and Academy," 10, 11.

20. Junior, *Womanist Biblical Criticism*, 82.

21. Salas, "A Christian Feminist Hermeneutics of the Bible," 177.

22. Schüssler Fiorenza, *Wisdom Ways*, 40, 95. NB: Historical positivism assumes a true meaning of the text that can be established objectively through disinterested observation and analysis.

23. Schüssler Fiorenza, *Wisdom Ways*, 143.

oppression,[24] to undermine the univocal discourse of all types of suppression, including colonialism, racism, and cultural imperialism.[25]

Another text-centered approach advocates for a practice of labeling as unauthoritative passages that denigrate women and using modern methods that write women back into texts where they are all but invisible, as well as strongly emphasizing those passages that empower women.[26] Elucidating that lifting up female figures is not tantamount to offering a feminist perspective on the Bible, she explains that female biblical characters cannot serve unambiguously as role models for contemporary women because they are "enmeshed in patriarchy and are presented and behave in androcentric ways."[27] Instead, feminist scholars seek texts and interpretations that are disruptive and transgressive to a patriarchal framework that reifies and sacralizes relationships of domination and subordination and are simultaneously emancipatory to those on the underside of power.

Some scholars substantiate such concerns by exposing the misogynous ways in which female figures are presented and interpreted within the biblical text. Famously, Trible popularized the term *texts of terror* to describe problematic periscopes such as the stories of Hagar (Genesis 16–17, 21), the daughter of Jephthah (Judges 12), the Levite's Concubine (Judges 19), and Tamar (2 Samuel 13). Outlining three types of feminist engagement with these texts, she describes documenting the cases against women in ancient Israel and the early church; developing a remnant theology that challenges the sexism of scripture.[28] The remnant interpretive strategy attempts to recover overlooked and neglected texts and characters and find anti-patriarchal texts to counter patriarchal texts.[29] Trible's method searches for the remnant in unlikely places,

24. Schüssler Fiorenza's approach comprises four hermeneutical strategies, including suspicion, proclamation, remembrance, and creative actualization. Elisabeth Schüssler Fiorenza, *Bread Not Stone: The Challenge of Feminist Biblical Interpretation* (Boston: Beacon Press, 1984).

25. Postcolonial feminist criticism of scripture holds forth a promising potential yet to be developed within Mormon Studies. Some relevant readings of postcolonial feminist biblical criticism include Laura E. Donaldson, "The Sign of Orpah: Reading Ruth Through Native Eyes," in *Ruth and Esther: A Feminist Companion to the Bible,* 2nd series, edited by Athalya Brenner (Sheffield, UK: Sheffield Academic Press, 1999); Musa W. Dube, *Postcolonial Feminist Interpretation of the Bible* (Atlanta: Chalice Press, 2000); Kwok Pui-lan, *Discovering the Bible in the Non-Biblical World* (Maryknoll, NY: Orbis Books, 1995).

26. Elisabeth Schüssler Fiorenza, *In Memory of Her: A Feminist Theological Reconstruction of Christian Origins* (New York: Crossroad, 1983); quoted in Adela Yarbro Collins, *Feminist Perspectives on Biblical Scholarship* (Chico, CA: Scholars Press, 1985)

27. Yarbro Collins, "Introduction," 5.

28. Phyllis Trible, *Texts of Terror: Literary-Feminist Readings of Biblical Narratives* (Philadelphia: Fortress Press, 1984), 3.

29. Mary Ann Tolbert, "Defining the Problem: The Bible and Feminist Hermeneutics," *Semeia* 28 (1983b): 115.

interpreting "stories of outrage" so as to advocate for female victims to recover an overlooked history, to remember a past that is embodied by the present, and to hope that such terrors will not be recreated.[30] By uncovering the injustice in the text, rather than leaving it unquestioned, readers can reimagine women's future within the Jewish and Christian traditions.



Whereas some feminist scholars engage these "texts of terror" mainly as descriptive, others take a stronger stance that assumes authorial intention in conveying misogynistic messages. For example, Esther Fuchs adopts a hermeneutic of resistance against the Bible, claiming that biblical writers deliberately marginalize women to advance male superiority.[31] She maintains that the Hebrew Bible not only presents women as marginal but further endorses that marginal status; the text is not only authored by men, but it further "fosters a politics of male domination."[32] For these reasons, Fuchs holds that there can be no middle ground that accepts both the worldview of the Bible and feminism. Rejecting any claim that the patriarchy in the Bible is reducible to historical context, she asserts that in terms of sexual politics, the Bible most often functions prescriptively, effectively invoking scriptural authority to leverage power over those who are already disempowered in society.[33]

Fuchs' hermeneutic points toward a more expansive strategy in feminist biblical criticism that reaches beyond the text's approach to women to more broadly offer a "critique of culture in light of misogyny."[34] This more systemic approach acknowledges that structures of domination determine both men and women's readings of the Bible.[35] For this reason, it calls for the replacement of unidimensional perspectives with a "radical democratic form of thinking" that fosters diverse perspectives and imaginative creativity, with the goal to go beyond conveying information to contribute to conscientization,[36] a process characterized by praxis that insists on women's full humanity and agency and then goes further toward the critical exploration of systemic oppression and liberatory paths.[37] Essential to this process are both theoretical and practical

30. Trible, *Texts of Terror,* 3.

31. Esther Fuchs, *Sexual Politics in the Biblical Narrative: Reading the Hebrew Bible as a Woman* (Sheffield, UK: Sheffield Academic Press, 2000), 11–12, 17.

32. Fuchs, 11.

33. Fuchs, 13–14.

34. Trible, *God and the Rhetoric of Sexuality,* 7.

35. Elisabeth Schüssler Fiorenza, "Between Movement and Academy: Feminist Biblical Studies in the Twentieth Century," in *Feminist Biblical Studies in the Twentieth Century,* edited by Elisabeth Schüssler Fiorenza (Atlanta: Society of Biblical Literature, 2014), 3.

36. Schüssler Fiorenza, *Wisdom Ways,* 16, 18.

37. Schüssler Fiorenza, 97, 93, 15.

goals because conscientization aims to transform academic and ecclesial biblical interpretation.[38] The practical objective is fitting given that movements for social change have significantly impacted feminist biblical criticism, in some regards even more than has the academy due to the fact that many early critics were not academic theologians but women involved with and informed by secular women's movements and that the academy often discriminates against those marginalized groups that are seeking emancipation, effectively withholding from those groups the critical tools necessary for efficacious emancipatory efforts.[39]

The use of critical tools intended to emancipate women from androcentric texts and interpretations is complicated by the fact that the concept "woman" is considered by many scholars to be an unstable category that is constantly shifting. At the same time that women are primarily defined by their gender, rather than according to other individual qualities, within patriarchal cultures, which consider the female/male division to be the basic and essential difference of humanity, women are rendered invisible by androcentric language. Because language and patriarchal structures precede individual's subjectivity and remain unfixed, people's sense of who they are is in perpetual flux so that women's identities are "always the site of conflicting discourses."[40] Yet, patriarchy and kyriarchy—the myriad, intersecting forms of oppression that go beyond gender as a result of the power of political leaders, masters, fathers and husbands over subordinates—function at the level of language, symbols, culture, ideology, and social institutions, and makes these identities appear natural and static.[41] To engage in emancipatory interpretations of scripture, feminist readers must first become aware of the mechanisms of oppression and alienation and then critique them in a way that encourages global justice and communal flourishing.

A case in point is the myriad interpretations of Genesis 1–3 that have kept women in subordinate positions. Schüngel-Straumann claims that women-denying interpretations of these chapters so fundamental for the establishment of a definitive theological anthropology within numerous traditions are ubiquitous. These chapters, she asseverates, serve as the "crux of all considerations of the role of women and the start of all discrimination against women."

38. Schüssler Fiorenza, 97.

39. Schüssler Fiorenza, 6.

40. Schüssler Fiorenza, 116, 110–16.

41. Elisabeth Schüssler Fiorenza, *Jesus: Miriam's Child, Sophia's Prophet: Critical Issues in Feminist Christology* (New York: Continuum, 1995), 14, 124.

Reinterpreting these texts requires a knowledge of their reception history and their embeddedness in western culture.[42] Some of the major values that have been inculcated through the deployment of the inceptive pericopes of the Hebrew and Christian Bibles include woman's value solely as mother, woman as subordinate to man, woman's fall from grace and susceptibility to temptation, and woman as less than human.[43] Yet the nineteenth-century feminist and suffragist Elizabeth Cady Stanton, who like Fuchs read the Bible as prescribing gender roles, had made strides in this direction with the publication of her *Woman's Bible.* Claiming that Genesis 1:27 demonstrates that the simultaneous creation of man and woman suggests their equal importance in humanity's development, Cady Stanton maintains that every theory that assumes that man was prior in creation has "no foundation in Scripture" and that women's subordination is unsupported by the text given that "equal dominion is given to woman over every living thing, but not one word is said giving man dominion over woman."[44] Her radical reading reveals the multivalence of biblical texts and multiple possibilities for more egalitarian interpretations that work to expand women's agency both within the text and beyond.

Strikingly, Dube suggests that women's silence and absence make multivalence possible. The paucity of women's voices in the biblical text bears a single advantage in that it provides a "space of speaking new life-affirming words."[45] Similarly, Elsa Tamez argues that the sacred text must be related to women's lives *as* sacred text, explaining that feminist scholars must go beyond objecting to oppressive biblical texts and highlighting texts favorable to women by seeking for the "Spirit of God made manifest in other texts, living or written."[46] This is not to say that all of women's lives amount to sacred text: just as the revelation of God is absent from texts that discriminate against women, the revelation of God is likewise absent from women's lives that manifest "hatred, envy, violence, disrespect and subjection of one to another."[47] Tamez concludes that God's revelation through sacred texts provides women with authority to recognize the sanctity of their own lives, as "something to be cared for and defended." Women's life stories disclose God as one who "challenges the whole

42. Helen Schüngel-Straumann, "From Androcentric to Christian Feminist Exegesis: Genesis 1–3" in *Feminist Biblical Studies in the 20th Century: Scholarship and Movement,* edited by Elisabeth Schüssler Fiorenza (Atlanta: Society of Biblical Literature, 2014), 142.

43. Schüngel-Straumann, 125–7.

44. Cady Stanton, *The Woman's Bible,* 15.

45. Dube, "Scripture, Feminism, and Post-Colonial Contexts," 53.

46. Elsa Tamez, "Women's Lives as Sacred Texts," in *Women's Sacred Scriptures,* edited by Kwok Pui-Lan and Elisabeth Schüssler Fiorenza (Maryknoll, NY: Orbis, 1998), 62.

47. Tamez, "Women's Lives as Sacred Texts," 63.

of society, men and women, to live as creatures made in the divine image and likeness."[48] In this way, women's lives can become a new sacred text, a sort of midrash incarnate of the creation story and its attendant theological anthropology that transcends the limits of the interpretive tradition.

## LDS SCHOLARSHIP ON FEMINIST BIBLICAL CRITICISM

One avenue that LDS feminist approaches to the canon might pursue is a form of midrash on the biblical accounts of creation, particularly a feminist midrash that tends toward egalitarian interpretations resistant to denigrating women due to culpability for original sin. In its more traditional usage, midrash refers to an imaginative interpretation of biblical text that involves enhancing the story as the interpreter sees fit. While the biblical text provides stories, language, metaphors, covenant promises, and prophecies, these need to be extended, elaborated, and applied to make meaning of them in one's contemporary context.[49] Midrash is primarily a way of interpreting scripture in the "context of one's life and interpreting life in the context of [s]cripture," relying on a view of scripture as something dynamic instead of static—a living word addressed to a community living in the present.[50] This mode of interpretation is one by which feminist conscientization shifts attention away from kyriocentric texts and toward women as reading subjects. Resisting the subject position the Bible offers them, women can go beyond identifying with dissident voices in the Bible to provide their own dissident voices.[51]

Writing within the context of Mormonism, Robert Rees has called for LDS women to use the tradition of midrash as a model for feminist interpretation of scripture. Rees encourages women to expand their limited sphere of religious authority within Mormonism by using not only their scholarly and expressive skills, but also "their imaginations, their personal experience, their presence, and their point of view in approaching our scriptural literature" to create "new elaborations, extensions, and imaginings of scriptural narratives." Midrash, he explains, contains "interesting, provocative, and inspirational literature about women." More than rabbinic expansions of scriptural narratives, midrash also

48. Tamez, "Women's Lives as Sacred Texts," 63.

49. Schüssler Fiorenza, *Wisdom Ways*, 149–50.

50. Mary Calloway, *Sing, O Barren One: A Study in Comparative Midrash* (Atlanta: Scholars Press, 1986), 5; quoted in Katheryn Pfisterer Darr, *Far More Precious than Jewels: Perspectives on Biblical Women* (Louisville, KY: Westminster/John Knox Press, 1991), 30.

51. Schüssler Fiorenza, *Wisdom Ways*, 152, 155.

include "fictive inventions that greatly enlarge and expand stories and characters," sometimes out of only a modicum of information. Within midrashic narratives on the female figures of the Bible, women "come alive, perform interesting and sometimes heroic deeds, manifest great faith, and at times even challenge their husbands and other male leaders, turning the original texts on their heads." Rees encourages LDS women to create their own "Mormon Midrash" that would encompass transformed scriptural narratives through retellings, imaginative elaboration, poetry, drama, and stories.[52] It is notable that *Exponent II,* a Latter-day Saint feminist quarterly magazine started in 1974 and inspired by the *Woman's Exponent* of the previous century, has held competitions for feminist midrash and published some of these essays in recent years.[53]

As one example of this midrashic approach, LDS scholar Julie M. Smith identifies feminist archetypes in the Hebrew biblical figure Huldah,[54] who prophesied after reading the Book of the Law, validating its authority at the request of King Josiah. Smith suggests that what it means to translate within this context is to use texts as "source material from which to proclaim the word of the Lord anew."[55] She asserts that the "pattern is simple: receive a divine book, read the book, and engage the book with your world through the prophetic voice. Huldah sets a pattern followed by Lehi, by Alma, by Joseph Smith, and, ideally, by every modern reader of the Book of Mormon."[56] I would extend her argument here to claim that one might read texts like 2 Nephi 2; Moses 5:1, 11; and passages from the Joseph Smith Translation of the Old and New Testaments as a sort of feminist midrash on the biblical creation account and prescriptive passages concerning women and marriage as working to mitigate misogynistic tendencies in the extant texts. For example, in 2 Nephi 2 and Moses 5, Eve is depicted as laboring alongside Adam and as a hero who acts judiciously and efficaciously in partaking of the forbidden fruit.

Following in the vein of liberationist hermeneutics, Lynn Matthews Anderson promotes the use of feminist theology as an interpretive lens for canonical texts unique to the LDS tradition. Noting the paucity of female figures within the Book of Mormon, Doctrine and Covenants, and the Pearl of Great

52. Robert A. Rees, "Toward a Feminist Mormon Midrash," *Sunstone* 166 (2012), 55, 56, 57.

53. See, for example, "Eve and her Mother—a Midrash," accessed September 12, 2021, at https://www.the-exponent.com/eve-and-her-mother-a-midrash/.

54. See 2 Kings 22:14 and 2 Chronicles 34:22.

55. Julie M. Smith, "Huldah's Long Shadow," *A Dream, a Rock, and a Pillar of Fire: Reading 1 Nephi 1,* edited by Adam S. Miller (Provo, UT: Neal A. Maxwell Institute for Religious Scholarship, 2017), 9.

56. Smith, "Huldah's Long Shadow," 9.

Price, which cumulatively name only fourteen women,[57] she asserts a hope that the tools of religious scholarship can lead to positive change. She opines that although the canon is "steeped in patriarchal language and imagery," the tools of feminist theology make it possible to use scripture to "overcome the sin of patriarchy in three ways: contextually, interpretively, and thematically."[58] Such engagement with the tools of religious feminism are a necessary corrective for the basic contemporary approach which has been to "ignore the facts of women's historical exclusion in all walks of life" and assume that "scriptures abounding in masculine language [ . . . ] were meant to be universal in application."[59] Rather than placing the onus on individuals to do the work of extrapolating to women scriptures directed at men, women can be spared an added burden given their already marginalized status through engagement with feminist biblical scholarship at a higher level.

Margaret Toscano has argued that the Book of Mormon can be considered a text of liberation in a way that nicely complements Anderson's argument and highlights the promising compatibility of feminist theology and LDS scripture. Toscano maintains that Mormon scriptural texts support the most salient biblical texts on equality. For example, Paul's assertion in the New Testament that there is "neither Jew nor Greek, there is neither bond nor free, there is neither male nor female" in Christ (Galatians 3:28) is buttressed by Nephi's assertion in the Book of Mormon, which itself reads like a midrash or extension of Galatians 3:27–28, that Christ "denieth none that come unto him, Black and white, bond and free, male and female; and he remembereth the heathen; and all are alike unto God, both Jew and Gentile" (2 Nephi 26:33). Affirming that the Book of Mormon can "easily be read as a text of liberation" due to its continual theme of combining spiritual liberation with political and social liberation, she further argues that this theme continues into the Doctrine and Covenants (see D&C 1:19, 20, 35).[60] Given that from an LDS perspective the Doctrine and Covenants and the Book of Mormon offer an interpretive lens through which to read the Bible, Toscano's arguments strengthen the case for allowing feminist scholarship to inform LDS readings of the Old and New Testaments.

57. Lynn Matthews Anderson, "Toward a Feminist Interpretation of Latter-day Scripture," *Dialogue: A Journal of Mormon Thought* 27, no. 2 (1994): 186.

58. Matthews Anderson, "Toward a Feminist Interpretation of Latter-day Scripture," 198.

59. Matthews Anderson, "Toward a Feminist Interpretation of Latter-day Scripture," 191.

60. Margaret Toscano, "Is There a Place for Heavenly Mother in Mormon Theology? An Investigation into Discourse of Power," in *Discourses in Mormon Theology: Philosophical and Theological Possibilities*, edited by James M. McLachlan and Loyd Ericson (Salt Lake City, UT: Greg Kofford Books, 2007), 212.

This lens ought to include an emphasis on individual agency exercised by women as it is by men; this would lift up women's place in the canon in a way that resonates with a basic LDS religious value. Cory Crawford has worked to show that recognizing women's agency operative within the biblical text need not undermine or contradict much of what Mormonism values in terms of women's gender roles. Crawford has argued that engaging the Bible using contemporary scholarly methods and tools reveals a "remarkable and often overlooked tradition of female authority." According to him, critically analyzing the history of biblical interpretation uncovers "two and a half *millennia* of repeated efforts to suppress traditions of female authority and to present misogynistic readings as normative."[61] Analyzing Hannah's role in 1 Samuel, for example, he asserts that Hannah held "authoritative agency," demonstrated through her actions of "naming, vowing, sacrificing, dedicating, composing. Rather than circumscribing Hannah's power, maternity leads her to exercise authority in reference to her existence as a woman." According to Crawford, Hannah's example provides a "foundation for imagining female priesthood power in a way that does not collapse gender difference."[62] These strategies suggest that LDS values of the equal partnership between women and men and the agency shared by all human beings should engender feminist readings of scripture.

## LDS TRADITION AND WOMEN'S INTERPRETATION

Contemporary Mormon feminists continue a tradition well-established by Latter-day Saint women in the nineteenth century. In an exegetical piece published in the *Woman's Exponent*,[63] editor Emmeline B. Wells deftly interprets the Old Testament story of Ruth in an effort to empower women while simultaneously claiming her own authority in relation to scripture—she didactically proclaims the methods for reaching scripture found within post-Enlightenment Protestantism to be misguided. Building on common ground by rhetorically asking what Christian has not admired the character of Ruth, Wells proceeds to show how traditional readings of the Book of Ruth prove unsatisfactory for speaking

61. Cory D. Crawford, "The Struggle for Female Authority in Biblical and and Mormon Theology," *Dialogue* 48, no. 2 (2015): 3–4.

62. Cory D. Crawford, "The Struggle for Female Authority in Biblical and Mormon Theology," *Dialogue* 48, no. 2 (2015): 19–20.

63. The *Woman's Exponent* was a bimonthly newspaper published by Relief Society members. The newspaper was published from 1872 to 1914; accessed September 12, 2021, at https://history.churchofjesuschrist.org/training/library/eliza-r-snow-research-guide/womans-exponent.

to modern women. Noting that Christian women "all over the civilized world" look to Ruth as an example of beauty, sweetness, grace, and strong affections,[64] Wells invites her readers to see this figure anew as a woman so brave and heroic that, if she were alive in the nineteenth century, would be rejected by contemporary women who would not dare to imitate her. Wells denigrates post-Enlightenment readings of biblical stories as encouraging less-than-literal readings of the Bible, which from her perspective, disempowers women who could otherwise be seen as agents negotiating their (sinful, patriarchal) world as skillfully as did female biblical figures. Wells calls for more literal readings of the Bible that highlight the centrality of women's agency and engender women's appropriation of the texts to perform them in their everyday lives. Note the degree of agency she ascribes to Ruth: "How very indiscreet was the widow Ruth, young and fair and full of grace, and abounding in affection as she was, to wash and anoint herself, and put on her raiment, and go and lie down at the feet of a man and actually propose to him that he take her to wife." Immediately following her robust reading of Ruth, Wells asks, "Would not modern society be shocked by the conduct of any young woman who did the works of Ruth?" Women who read scripture properly, Wells implies, reduplicate it with their lives.

While Wells uses feminist tools to construct her argument, namely drawing on a woman's experience as a source of authority, making a woman the central focus of the narrative, and highlighting her agency, one cannot overlook the fact that she employs these tools to justify the nineteenth-century Mormon practice of polygyny. In this effort, Wells invokes the names of Rachel, Leah, Sarah, and Hannah in addition to Ruth. While "all good Christians reverence the character of Ruth" and render her artistically through art, poetry, and prose, Latter-day Saint women must go further and *become* her. In the case of Ruth, God "blessed this peculiar marriage, and through this lineage came the Christ"; similarly, modern Mormon women ought employ their agency to negotiate familial relationships that would proliferate into an elect posterity. Rather than making Ruth's loyalty in passively following Naomi and bearing her progenitors the main theme, Wells emphasizes Ruth's initiative. That contemporary women are no longer willing to "enact the part of Ruth literally" by insisting on receiving what is theirs by right of kinship, is to their shame rather than to their credit.[65] What is most significant here is Wells' self-assumed

64. Emmeline B. Wells, "The Integrity of Ruth," *Woman's Exponent* 7, no. 12 (November 15, 1878): 1.
65. Wells, "The Integrity of Ruth," 1.

authority to interpret the Bible not only for herself, but also for others, while not relying on ecclesiastical authorities or biblical scholarship. Further, she views the Bible as authorizing women to employ their agency, viewing Ruth as a vital actor in the book named for her and further using Ruth's narrative to leverage women's power to act as agents in the world. The agency and innovation she highlights within the text ought to be reflected by its readers not only in their lives but also in their engagements with the text.

The *Woman's Exponent* further highlighted women's agency in the biblical text by reprinting entire sections of Cady Stanton's *Woman's Bible*.[66] There were salient points of similarity between her project and the LDS tradition, such as the suggestion that it would only be rational that Heavenly Mother would have been a participant in the consultation of the Godhead described in Genesis 1:26, 28.[67] Helpfully, Cady Stanton concludes from Genesis 1:27, which states that "God created man in his own image, male and female," that scripture "declares the eternity and equality of sex."[68] Although Stanton's reading of Genesis 1 clearly resonated with the LDS women of the nineteenth century, her reading is not straightforward and could thereby effectively encourage LDS women not to passively accept traditional readings of the text. Explaining that the intellectual tradition that began with Stanton's *Woman's Bible* centers around the "conviction that biblical texts about women need to be interrupted rather than continued," Schüssler Fiorenza argues against allowing an essentialist notion of woman to shape readings of scripture. Instead, this notion must be "critically analyzed rather than taken up as an analytic lens."[69] Scholars facilitate egalitarian readings of scripture by not limiting themselves to essentialist notions of the self—it is critical to consider how such readings could enhance contemporary LDS interpretations of the canon.

One way to do this is to claim women's experience as an authoritative source. Modeling this view, nineteenth-century LDS women overtly asserted that women's experience shared the same authority as scripture. Hannah Tapfield King pens sentiments similar to Tamez and Dube's suggestions that women's lives could be interpreted as scripture:

66. For example, the first chapter of Stanton's *Woman's Bible* appears in the *Woman's Exponent* 23, no. 17 (1895): 248.

67. Elizabeth Cady Stanton, *The Woman's Bible* (Amherst, NY: Prometheus Books, 1999), 14; reprinted as Elizabeth Cady Stanton, "The Woman's Bible," *Woman's Exponent* 23, no. 17 (1895): 248.

68. Stanton, *The Woman's Bible,* 15.

69. Schüssler Fiorenza, "Between Movement and Academy," 15.

> Woman know thyself—study thy divine mechanism; leave the science of mathematics if you must give up one; but read yourself like an open book. Walk through the length and breadth of your heart and brain, and you will find the hand of God has been busy there; see that you render back some return to the Divine Architect. The Scriptures say no more on the Sisters of Bethany, but it is all written in that book which has yet to be opened.[70]



The authority that Wells assumes in her reading of Ruth, which requires no buttressing by male scholarship or ecclesiastical leadership, is here declared to be universally available to LDS women.

This authority was to some extent validated by LDS apostle James E. Talmage, who published the seminal extracanonical LDS treatment of Jesus Christ in 1915. He claims there that the "world's greatest champion of woman and womanhood is Jesus the Christ."[71] Seeking to elevate the status of women within the text, Talmage emphasizes that Christ was born of a woman and that Genesis 3:15 prognosticates that redemption from the Fall comes through the "seed of the woman." Focusing on biblical figures such as Mary Magdalene, he argues that Jesus viewed women as on par with (or greater than) men. Jesus's estimation of women legitimized women's ability to be divinely inspired, recognize Christ and the veracity of his teachings, and women's authority to testify of spiritual truths.[72] This egalitarian impulse appears in more recent writings as well. Camille Fronk Olson, former department chair of Ancient Scripture at Brigham Young University, argues that Jesus neither placed women on pedestals nor denigrated them. Rather than lauding women as men's moral superiors, Jesus showed his "female disciples" the same love and care that he showed to his apostles and other male disciples.[73] For this and other reasons, Chieko N. Okazaki, when acting as counselor in the General Relief Society Presidency, encouraged women to search the canon for themselves to know Christ, rather than to learn secondhand from others. When asked how women in the church could become as God wants them to be, she responded, "I think women should continue really immersing themselves in the scriptures and

70. Hannah T. King, "Scripture Women," *Woman's Exponent* (1878), 185.

71. James E. Talmage, *Jesus the Christ* (Lexington, KY: Valde Books, 2009), 475.

72. Talmage, *Jesus the Christ,* 43, 82, and 97.

73. Camille Fronk Olson, *Mary, Martha, and Me: Seeking the One Thing that Is Needful* (Salt Lake City, UT: Deseret Book, 2006), 129–30.

praying so that they know what Christ really thinks."[74] Although there are limitations on coming to know "what Christ really thinks" by appealing to scripture, the clear injunction is for LDS women in the twenty-first century to be no less active than their ancient or nineteenth-century forebears in adopting an authoritative role in scriptural interpretation or in relationship to the divine.

Assuming this authority and employing agency in interpretation is nowhere better demonstrated than in the life of nineteenth-century pioneer Jane Manning James. She relies on scripture to make a claim on white male LDS leaders to receive her temple blessings, which had been denied her due to her race. Although she granted, in keeping with the contemporary view that Black people were descendants of Ham, the son of Noah, that her racial identity had been "handed down through the flood," she refused to let such an interpretation of the Bible permanently obstruct her access to a desired blessing that would signify her equal status with other church members. In an 1884 letter addressed to church President John Taylor, she turned limiting readings of her identity on their head by proclaiming that her relation to Ham notwithstanding, "God promised Abraham that in his seed 'all the nations of the earth should be blest' and as this is the fullness of all dispensations is there no blessing for me [?]'"[75] Refusing to accept racist interpretations of the Bible that would bar her from making claims on the institutional church, James employs a literal reading of scripture applied directly to herself to move herself from the margins of Latter-day Saint society toward its center and does so without needlessly constructing others that would be marginalized in her stead. In this way, she exemplifies not only women's authority to interpret scripture but the practice of doing so with an eye to justice on a global scale that bears the potential to liberate herself and others. James and other LDS women of the nineteenth century offer a model of how Latter-day Saints ought to engage scripture today: their boldness and innovation in asserting and appropriating the meaning of canonical text, combined with the insights of contemporary feminist biblical criticism, can capacitate the contemporary LDS community toward more inclusive and liberating readings of scripture.

74. "'There is Always a Struggle': An Interview with Chieko N. Okazaki," *Dialogue: A Journal of Mormon Thought* 45, no. 1 (Spring 2012): 138.

75. MSS SC 1069, "A Test of Faith: Jane Elizabeth James and the Origins of the Utah Black Community," *Twentieth Century Western and Mormon Manuscripts,* L. Tom Perry Special Collections, Harold B. Lee Library, BYU.

PART IV

# Inheritance and Divergence

*Latter-day Saints Read Others Reading the Bible*

# 19

# The Use of Jewish Scripture in the New Testament

JARED W. LUDLOW

Before the New Testament was canonized, early Christians relied on existing Jewish scripture for guidance and instruction. This reliance on Jewish scripture should not be too surprising since many of the New Testament's notable early figures (Jesus, John the Baptist, Paul, the authors of the Gospel of Matthew, John, etc.) were themselves Jews raised in Jewish tradition. Not only did Christians incorporate hundreds of quotations from the Old Testament in the production of the New Testament, but they also mined these Jewish writings for relevant prophecies for their day.[1] With time, the rift grew between Jews and Christians and their writings took on more unique characteristics. The later name of the Christian scripture, the *New* Testament, both shows its connection to another, older, testament as well as its distinction from it.[2] Jewish scripture thus provided a valuable foundation upon which Jesus's early followers built and expanded, considering their new movement the continuation and fulfillment of many earlier scriptural promises. This expanded view of God's word and work mirrors the Latter-day Saint understanding of its place amongst God's promises found in both Jewish and Christian scripture. Rather than ignoring or rejecting Jewish scripture, unique Latter-day Saint scripture

1. "Of the approximately 8,000 verses in the New Testament, more than 250 quote the Tanakh [Old Testament], and perhaps twice as many directly allude to it; if verses with more distant allusions are included, the number is far greater." From Amy-Jill Levine and Marc Zvi Brettler, eds., *The Jewish Annotated New Testament* (New York: Oxford University Press, 2011), 504.

2. "A critical element in determining the character and content of NT theology is the fact that the writings which provide its subject-matter are described as the *New* Testament. That is, they are defined by their relation to the writings known as the *Old* Testament. NT theology, in other words, is determined in part at least by its character as *new*, over against the theology which is characterized as *old*." From James D.G. Dunn, "New Testament Theology," in *The Oxford Handbook of Biblical Studies*, edited by J.W. Rogerson and Judith M. Lieu (New York: Oxford University Press, 2006), 700.

and biblical interpretation incorporates this material within its self-understanding. This chapter will examine how early Christians interacted with earlier Jewish scripture in the New Testament, which was subsequently adopted by Latter-day Saint tradition, and then discuss how some of these Christian features foreshadowed ways Latter-day Saints adapted Jewish scripture after the Restoration.

Authors of the New Testament texts relied on the authority of earlier Jewish scripture, especially when their audience was fellow Jews. The canonical Gospels, for instance, had the intention of quoting Jewish prophecy and explaining its fulfilment by Jesus, John the Baptist, or some other figure or practice. For instance, David Jasper argues,

> The evangelist's [Matthew's] concern is to show that Jesus is the fulfillment of all the prophecies of the Hebrew Bible, and insofar as he is this, he is confirmed as the expected Messiah. Everything happens "according to Scripture." In short, the evangelist reads the Hebrew Bible in the light of later events, and he reads later events in the light of the Hebrew Bible—a perfectly good hermeneutic circle![3]

Early Christian writers like the author of Matthew found religious meaning and presented new teachings by using Jewish scripture. Those texts were a source of ideas and shared history demonstrating how God had interacted with his covenant people in the past and how he now interacted in their day.

These examples show a process of what one scholar, Leslie Allen, terms reverse exegesis.

> Instead of providing exegesis of the OT text as a commentary does, with hindsight the NT often used the OT to provide exegesis for the phenomenon of Jesus. . . . At times NT writers show their awareness of the difference between straight exegesis and reverse exegesis. They know that the first kind takes its interpretation from the OT context, while the second derives its interpretation from an aspect of Christ or the Christian message and understands the OT text in this way.[4]

3. David Jasper, *A Short Introduction to Hermeneutics* (Louisville, KY: Westminster John Knox Press, 2004), 30.

4. Leslie C. Allen, *A Theological Approach to the Old Testament: Major Themes and New Testament Connections* (Eugene, OR: Cascade Books, an Imprint of Wipf and Stock Publishers, 2014), 159–160.

Paul exemplifies this exegetical method by applying a very specific law about muzzling an ox (Deut 25:4) "to the right of Christian workers to receive material recompense. He is quite aware of a literal exegesis, even while he brushes it away for present purposes."[5]



At the beginning of the first century, Jewish scripture was still in flux. Although later Jewish leaders closed their canon, this was certainly not the end of Jewish texts. Besides books later canonized in the Hebrew Bible (Old Testament), other religious texts were produced and/or copied in the few centuries before Jesus's birth. Some notable examples are the Dead Sea Scrolls, which not only provided significant early manuscript copies of biblical books but also included other sectarian and para-biblical scriptural texts, and the Pseudepigrapha, a modern collection of dozens of early Jewish texts written about Old Testament figures but "falsely ascribed" to the authority of these earlier figures (see Dana Pike and Jared Ludlow's essays, in this volume).

Another important collection of early Jewish scriptural texts is the Septuagint, the Greek translation of the Hebrew Bible. One of the challenges for New Testament scholars is determining whether the Hebrew Bible, the Septuagint, or other scriptural texts such as the Aramaic translations (*targumim*) were sources for the authors of New Testament texts. Overall, it seems for most early Christians, when they read or quoted from "scripture," they used the Septuagint, though there are some exceptions when they used the Hebrew version or brief quotations or allusions to non-canonical texts from the Pseudepigrapha.

When examining Paul's use of scripture, for example, there is not a clear-cut answer, as he seems to quote passages similar to the Hebrew Bible, Greek Septuagint, or a version slightly different than both. In this last category, he could be relying on a version that is not part of the mainstream transmission or doing his own translation to strengthen his argument or to fit a new situation. For example, in Romans 9:33, Paul quotes Isaiah 28:16 but adds the words "stumblingstone and rock of offence," rather than a "precious corner stone." In Paul's teachings, the crucified Messiah became a "stumblingstone" to belief for many, so perhaps he added these words here to emphasize that fact.

Orality may provide another explanation for the differences between the quotations and the original versions in Greek or Hebrew (e.g., Rom 9:33 quoting Isa 28:16; 1 Cor 15:54 quoting Isa 25:8; and 1 Cor 15:55 quoting Hos 13:14). Early Christian apostles and teachers spread the new word in preaching before they began to fix their teachings in writing. In such an oral context, it could

5. Allen, *A Theological Approach to the Old Testament*, 160.

have been commonplace to recite Jewish scripture loosely without exact reference to a written manuscript. The form of the citation eventually found in New Testament writings then may not be precisely from the Hebrew Bible, Greek Septuagint, or other textual traditions, but a loose paraphrase. This process created a more fluid, dynamic text than would have existed with simply copying directly from a manuscript.

Direct quotation is the easiest example of the use of Jewish scripture to recognize and agree on because it so closely matches earlier manuscripts.[6] A common pattern in this regard included *formulae quotationis*, or standard introductions to Jewish scripture citations, which usually drew from the past to show its present fulfillment. By paying attention to the many stereotypical *formulae quotationis* scattered throughout the New Testament, such as "as it is written," "for the scripture says," "for [prophet] says," and "according to the law," we begin to see how much the New Testament authors used Jewish scripture in their writing. The Gospel of Matthew is the most notable for this type of usage as it repeatedly, some sixty times, introduces a passage of Jewish scripture with a phrase such as "this was done, that it might be fulfilled which was spoken by the prophet, saying [quotation of scripture]" (see Matt 1:22–23; 2:17–18, 23; 27:9). In the Sermon on the Mount, Jesus quotes existing scriptures to reinterpret their meaning in a new "higher-law" setting: "Ye have heard that it was said by them of old time, ... [quotation of scripture or tradition], but I say unto you, ... [reinterpretation or giving the higher law]" (see Matt 5:21–22, 27–28, 33–34, 38–39, 43–44).

Quotations from scripture are also prevalent in the dialogues between Jesus and opponents. For example, Jesus quotes three different passages from the Hebrew Bible in his response to Satan (Matt 4:4, 7, 10). In Mark 7, he quotes from Isaiah (verse six) and Moses (verse ten) as part of his argument against the Pharisees. The Gospels also quote the Psalms and Proverbs to explain events. Sometimes the Psalms were treated as prophecies of Jesus' crucifixion (especially Psalm 22). John's Gospel (1:1–18) draws on the concept of personified wisdom presented at the beginning of Proverbs (see Prov 1:19–20; 8:22–31).

6. These two categories are simplifications of more technical terminology that biblical scholars have developed to categorize the way a New Testament writer may have used Jewish scripture: "citation, direct quotation, formal quotation, indirect quotation, allusive quotation, allusion (whether conscious or unconscious), intertextuality, influence (either direct or indirect), and even tradition." From Stanley E. Porter, "The Use of the Old Testament in the New Testament: A Brief Comment on Method and Terminology," in *Early Christian Interpretation of the Scriptures of Israel*, edited by Craig A. Evans and James A. Sanders (Sheffield, UK: Sheffield Academic Press, 1997), 80. As Porter points out, however, the exact meaning of these terms and how to distinguish one from another are elusive and can vary from scholar to scholar.

Some scholars working on this phenomenon see the New Testament usage of earlier scripture as a response to Jesus' "failed" Messiahship where he did not come in the form and with the success of the messianic expectations of many Jews in the first century. Therefore Jesus' suffering and death were explained in the New Testament through citations and fulfillments of passages from scriptures like Psalms (especially 22, 35, and 69) and Isaiah (the Songs of the Suffering Servant, especially 52:13–53:12) that attempted to explain why he had to suffer and die.[7] Other scholars argue that from an early Christian perspective, quoting from Jewish scripture brought out the text's true meaning, not only fulfilling the prophecy, but fully preaching or executing what the original text meant to say.

Some ancient Jewish writers had similar ways of quoting earlier scripture and then elaborating on it. *Pesharim* were prevalent among the Dead Sea Scrolls where the authors quoted passages from prophets like Isaiah or Habakkuk and then gave the "true" interpretation for their community. This contemporizing application of earlier scripture is similar to how early Christian authors commented on Jewish scripture, such as Messianic prophecies that took on new life in the Christian community, thereby transmitting the belief that these were the predicted meanings centuries earlier. As discussed later, this phenomenon is also present in Latter-day Saint restoration scripture where earlier passages were likened to later situations. Through introductory formulae like "For our sakes, no doubt, this is written" (1 Cor 9:10), Paul and others emphasized that there was only one intended meaning for these passages and it belonged to the later Christian community.

Besides quoting and performing exegesis of Jewish scripture, many authors of the texts in the New Testament cite by allusion. Allusion is more plentiful than direct quotation, but it can be harder to determine definitively. Some may claim a word or two alludes to a Jewish scripture passage where others may disagree. On one hand, ancient listeners and readers were likely well versed in Jewish scripture and thus could make the necessary associations and connections between the stories easier than those not immersed in that culture. However, sometimes alleged allusions owe more to the creativity of modern interpreters than to the original intentions of the New Testament author. The number of identified allusions is usually around two thousand, but modern scholarly counts can vary dramatically in their criteria for evaluating allusions.

7. See summary in Bart D. Ehrman, *The New Testament: A Historical Introduction to the Early Christian Writings*, 4th ed. (New York: Oxford University Press, 2008), 285–87. See also additional suggested readings on 290.

For example, the book of Revelation seems to make hundreds of allusions to the Old Testament, particularly Daniel and Ezekiel, while it does not contain any direct quotations. The Gospel of John also is full of allusions to Old Testament events, like the brazen serpent, which it interprets as foreshadowing Christ, and argues that Abraham knew the preexistent Christ (see John 8:40, 56). Thus, many New Testament writings are meant to be read in light of Jewish scripture and would be incomplete without an understanding of them.

Another tactic was to allegorize scripture or use typological interpretation to find its true intended meaning. This approach was common among ancient Jews, demonstrated by the example of Philo, the Jewish philosopher from Alexandria. The authors of the New Testament texts used this tool as well. In Galatians 4:22–31, Paul allegorizes the story of Abraham, Sarah, and Hagar to give it a completely new meaning. In a related vein, typology is another way the New Testament used Jewish scripture. Different from prophecy or exegesis, typology is a prefiguration of something similar in the Jewish past to the Christian present. Because early Christians believed that God had always and would continue to work with his covenant people, earlier events, persons, or institutions became examples and patterns for later Christians. One Old Testament theologian noted,

> The parallels came to be regarded as anticipatory pointers to the phenomenon of Jesus, which stimulated the taking up of the parallels and bringing them together in a new synthesis.... From a NT perspective, OT types are preliminary prototypes that give way to fully developed versions. The element of transcendence introduces a note of discontinuity into the overall message of continuity.[8]

The *type* thus shows higher fulfillment in the Christian experience such as the comparison between Adam and Christ—old, natural man and new, spiritual man—or Noah's flood and baptism (see 1 Pet 3:20–21). What becomes clear from these varied techniques for using scripture is that in the creation of what would become new or additional scripture, the writers of the New Testament texts drew on earlier Jewish scriptures as their chief resource. It also becomes evident that these Jewish scriptures were read, recited, and known well enough by the listeners and readers to use as support and authority for their Christian teachings.

8. Allen, *A Theological Approach to the Old Testament*, 164.

Throughout the process of interacting with Jewish scripture, early Christians were recomposing or reevaluating their cultural past. Rather than promoting a clean break with their Jewish ancestors, early Christians saw themselves as continuing many traditions and aspirations of their forefathers. The early prophets provided source material for understanding their place in God's plan. However, early Christians developed unique interpretations and perceived fulfillments that distinguished them from fellow Jews who had not accepted Jesus as the Messiah. Some early Christians further distinguished themselves from other Jews in regard to the interpretation of the Law. Some may have believed that the law was necessary to prepare and lead to Christ, but no longer necessary for salvation (see Gal 3:23–25; Rom 3:20–22, 10:4–10; Matt 5:17–18). Yet others repurposed the principles of expiation and redemption prevalent in Jewish sacrifice and scripture to understand Jesus' death and resurrection. The expiatory nature of Jesus' sacrifice hearkened back to the Law's atonement (see Mark 10:45; cf. Heb 9:11–28). As A.T. Hanson has shown, "The writer of Hebrews strings one Old Testament citation after another with the purpose of interpreting Christ in terms of the Jewish cultus."[9]



Early Christian writers also drew on messianic prophecies scattered throughout Jewish scripture in their efforts to convince their Jewish compatriots that Jesus was indeed the promised Messiah. Some would argue that the view of Jesus as a divine Messiah who brought redemption for sin through his death is actually a combination of several separate ideas found scattered throughout Jewish scripture. Jesus was linked to the lineage of David, Son of Man traditions in Ezekiel and Daniel, suffering servant descriptions in Isaiah, high priestly roles, and many other concepts. In addition to messianic concepts, early Christian texts draw one of the most developed parallels between Moses and Jesus as lawgivers. In Matthew, even before giving the Sermon on the Mount, several events portray Jesus like Moses: deliverance from slaughter when an infant, descent to Egypt, and preparation and endurance against temptation in the wilderness. Matthew then symbolically shows Jesus ascending on a mountain to give a new law to his disciples. The relationship between Jesus and the Law continues throughout the Gospels as Jesus spars with Jewish opponents over the true interpretation or importance of the law especially over the less authoritative traditions of the elders (see Mark 7:1–13). Jesus' miracles also hearkened back to the prophetic ministries of Elijah and Elisha in the

9. A.T. Hanson, "Hebrews," in *It Is Written: Scripture Citing Scripture*, edited by D.A. Carson and H.G.M. Williamson (Cambridge, UK: Cambridge University Press, 1988), 292–302.

raising of the dead, healing lepers, and multiplying food thus showing that Jesus was similar to the Hebrew prophets.

Some authors of New Testament texts adopted and amplified apocalyptic thought found in Jewish scripture. Angelic figures, who begin playing roles in late Jewish texts, such as Daniel, Tobit from the Apocrypha, and throughout pseudepigraphic texts, also play roles in the New Testament. Beginning with annunciations and revelations in the Gospels to the predominant roles of angels in the book of Revelation, apocalypticism looking toward the end times plays a role in early Christian thought. Richly symbolic, divine revelations about history and the heavenly realm contain concepts that can often be traced back to Jewish roots through the related scriptures. The book of Jude, for example, contains one of the clearest quotations from these kinds of texts; an eschatological event found in 1 Enoch (see Jude 1:14–15; 1 Enoch 1:9). One prominent scholar from last century went so far as to state that "the influence of Enoch in the New Testament has been greater than that of all the other apocryphal and pseudepigraphical books taken together."[10]

One important point to note is that even after the canonization of the texts of the New Testament, Christians continued the adaptation of Jewish scripture in the text. In the transmission of the manuscripts of the New Testament, later scribes would sometimes correct their copies to match the biblical text currently in circulation. Thus certain versions of Jewish scripture continued to influence the development of the NT.

## RELEVANCE TO LATTER-DAY SAINT READERS

What is the relevance of Jewish scripture in the New Testament to Latter-day Saint approaches to biblical interpretation? First, as with other readers of the New Testament, understanding the Jewish roots and foundation of many teachings within the New Testament helps them make sense as they are read as part of the canon (both OT and NT). But also, the variety of interpretive methods used by early Christians might also illuminate how many "unique" Latter-day Saint doctrines are also rooted in Jewish scripture. For example, the expanded role of Enoch (and other figures like Melchizedek) and additional accounts

10. R.H. Charles, *The Apocrypha and Pseudepigrapha of the Old Testament*, two vols. (Oxford, UK: Clarendon Press, 1966), 2:180. For discussions of how Enochic writings impact NT texts, see David A. deSilva, *The Jewish Teachers of Jesus, James and Jude. What Earliest Christianity Learned from the Apocrypha and Pseudepigrapha* (New York: Oxford University Press, 2012), 101–40; and Larry R. Helyer, *Exploring Jewish Literature of the Second Temple Period: A Guide for New Testament Students* (Downers Grove, IL: IVP Academic, 2002), 77–92, 136–39, 379–88.

about him are common in Latter-day Saint teachings. Such expansions, independent of their source, resemble a similar development of Enochic traditions from the Old Testament to Second Temple Jewish literature and the New Testament. Latter-day Saint teachings about the "translation" of peoples into God's presence, ancient priesthood keys passed on to Joseph Smith, or the eternal role of the Abrahamic covenant are fleshed out in Latter-day Saint scripture and biblical interpretation. The Joseph Smith "New Translation," also called the Joseph Smith Translation (JST), is often similar to "rewritten Bible" texts found among the Dead Sea Scrolls and Pseudepigrapha (and arguably within the Old Testament itself, for example Chronicles' adaptation of Kings). Smith makes changes "in at least 3,410 verses and consists of additions, deletions, rearrangements, and other alterations that cause it to vary not only from the KJV but from other biblical texts."[11] These many differences may point to similar processes as "rewritten Bible" texts to explain or update a text's meanings.



Another way the presence of Jewish scripture in the New Testament is relevant to Latter-day Saint readers is to show an example of scripture quoting earlier scripture. Latter-day Saint scriptures such as the Book of Mormon and the Doctrine and Covenants are full of OT scripture allusions and quotations because these accounts situate their people as a continuation of the Jewish covenant community, albeit in a radically different form.[12] Notable features of the narratives include genealogical connections to Ephraim and Manasseh, coming from the land of Jerusalem, and being descendants of the house of Israel. Particularly noteworthy are references to the books of Moses and lengthy quotations from the book of Isaiah found in the Book of Mormon that Nephi explains are shared "that they might know concerning the doings of the Lord in other lands, among people of old. And I did read many things unto them which were written in the books of Moses; but that I might more fully persuade them to believe in the Lord their Redeemer I did read unto them that which was written by the prophet Isaiah" (1 Ne 19:22–23). The narrators in the Book of Mormon often clearly state a belief in these earlier texts even as they show how they apply to their own situation.

References to other texts from figures such as Zenos and Neum in the Book of Mormon suggest a wider pool of scripture than the biblical texts. Even

11. Robert J. Matthews, "Joseph Smith Translation of the Bible (JST)," in *Encyclopedia of Mormonism*, edited by Daniel H. Ludlow (New York: Macmillan, 1992), 763–4.

12. For useful charts of Book of Mormon references that reflect historical information in the Old Testament and Isaiah passages in the Book of Mormon see Dennis L. Largey, ed., *Book of Mormon Reference Companion* (Salt Lake City, UT: Deseret Book, 2003), 344, 617.

the original source of these texts, called the plates of brass, varies from the Hebrew Bible that became part of the Masoretic tradition in that it has some recognizable quotations but goes beyond them (and omitted others) similar to how canonical and non-canonical texts show up among the Dead Sea Scrolls and Pseudepigrapha. The primary narrator of the Book of Mormon, Mormon, gave as part of his concluding testimony "*this* [the Book of Mormon] is written for the intent that ye may believe *that* [the Bible]; and if ye believe *that* ye will believe *this* also; and if ye believe *this* ye will know concerning your fathers, and also the marvelous works which were wrought by the power of God among them" (Mormon 7:9, emphasis added). The notion presented is that the two books of scripture—the Bible and the Book of Mormon—should complement one another, with both the New Testament and the Book of Mormon having similar strategies such as applying the prophecies to one's own situation, explicating Messianic prophecies, and placing one's history into God's greater salvation history through the house of Israel.

## CONCLUSION

One of the most significant recent scholarly works on the Jewish context to the New Testament, *The Jewish Annotated New Testament*, was written by Jewish scholars with expertise in relevant fields with the hope that non-Jewish readers could "learn to appreciate that significant sections of the New Testament derive from the heart of Judaism."[13] Christian scripture is built upon the essential foundation of Jewish scriptures, a collection of teachings and prophecies that early Christian writers tapped into and from which developed a Christocentric hermeneutic to show the fulfillment of God's eternal covenant with his children. Building on this understanding, Latter-day Saint biblical interpretation and scripture also draw on these Jewish texts to present a new stage of development in God's salvation history connecting themselves to the house of Israel and the Abrahamic covenant.

13. Levine and Brettler, *The Jewish Annotated New Testament*, xiii.

# 20

# Early Christian Biblical Interpretation

CARL GRIFFIN AND KRISTIAN S. HEAL

The florescence of recent interest in patristic exegesis among American Protestants has been motivated by a dissatisfaction with post-Enlightenment forms of biblical criticism.[1] What is the nature of this dissatisfaction? "Could it not be," responds Frances Young, "that the dissatisfaction with biblical criticism is not really dissatisfaction with its methods, but with its apparent results? And could not its apparent results be the outcome of limiting the questions to concrete realities we think we can call 'facts'?"[2] What Frances Young and others have advocated for instead is an exegetical practice that is concerned not only with the facts of scripture, the primary concerns of the contemporary biblical criticism, but also with the fact that these ancient literary texts are Holy Scripture and the "the Word of God."[3] Developing an authentic biblical hermeneutic is a pressing problem for Latter-day Saint readers. Resistance to modern critical approaches largely turns on concerns like those articulated by Frances Young. The results of such critical approaches can challenge the holiness and authenticity of scripture in ways that are disturbing not only to the hierarchy, but also to rank and file Latter-day Saints. The purpose of this essay is to highlight methods and practices of early Christian interpretation that have potential to respond to this pressing hermeneutical question and aid in the development of a richer hermeneutic for Latter-day Saint readers of the Bible.

1. See, e.g., David Dockery, *Biblical Interpretation Then and Now: Contemporary Hermeneutics in the Light of the Early Church* (Grand Rapids, MI: Baker, 1992); and John L. Thompson, *Reading the Bible with the Dead: What You Can Learn from the History of Exegesis that You Can't Learn from Exegesis* (Grand Rapids, MI: Eerdmans, 2007).

2. Frances Young, *The Art of Performance: Towards a Theology of Holy Scripture* (London: Darton, Longman and Todd, 1990), 19.

3. *Articles of Faith* 1:8.

## THE BEGINNINGS OF CHRISTIAN BIBLICAL INTERPRETATION



When followers of Jesus first emerged as a distinct Jewish sect following his death, the earliest adherents continued to accept Jewish scripture as inspired and normative. They differed from other Jews not in scripture but in their exegesis of it. They interpreted the significance of Jesus' life and ministry through a messianic reading of key texts from the Jewish Bible (the Christian Old Testament). The first church historian, Luke, represents this exegetical practice as central in the earliest Christian preaching.[4] Some other Jews accepted such biblical texts as prophesying of a messiah but rejected their application to Jesus of Nazareth. Such scriptures were understood by these Jews to prophesy of a conquering hero who would vanquish Israel's enemies and reign over it as king. How could they possibly apply to the humiliated and crucified criminal whose followers called him the Christ? In response, the Christians established a broader base of scriptural proofs that showed Jesus to be Israel's promised Lord and King, but also a suffering servant. He was subject to scorn and condemned to crucifixion because his true nature and salvific mission had been hidden from the "wise" and "the rulers of this age" (1 Cor 2:8).

This innovative, Christological exegesis was a vital parturitive act that differentiated the Christians from other Jews. It also made their distinctive "gospel" about Jesus attractive not only to Jews, but to the many gentiles who were either affiliated with diaspora Jewish congregations or at least intrigued by Jewish teachings and scripture. Luke illustrates this with the story of Philip and the Ethiopian eunuch (Acts 8:26–39). The Spirit leads Philip to the eunuch as he happens to be reading a key scripture on the suffering servant, Isaiah 53:7–8 ("Like a sheep he was led to the slaughter"). Perplexed at its application, the eunuch asks Philip if the prophet is speaking "about himself or about someone else." Philip took full advantage of this missionary moment, "and starting with this scripture, he proclaimed to him the good news about Jesus" (Acts 8:35). Won instantly by the power of this exegesis, the eunuch, says Luke, demanded to be baptized a Christian.

Luke and other New Testament authors give abundant evidence for the centrality of exegetical proofs to early Christian evangelism. But the authors of the New Testament also show significant diversity in how Christians understood

4. See, e.g., Peter's Christological use of passages from Psalms in the first missionary sermon, Acts 2:14–36.

the Old. Crucially, some conservative Jewish Christians maintained the authority of the prescriptions of the Law as well as the election of Israel—the plain teaching of Jewish scripture. This was an acute hindrance for the gentile mission and was resisted by Paul. He argued that scripture certainly had this outer meaning, the object of human wisdom, but also an inner, spiritual meaning that was "secret and hidden" (1 Cor 2:7). This hidden "meat" was only for "the mature," but it was revealed by the Spirit of God to inspired interpreters like Paul himself: "And we speak of these things in words not taught by human wisdom but taught by the Spirit, interpreting spiritual things to the spiritual" (1 Cor 2:13; cf. 2:6; 3:1–4). This spiritual meaning was hidden by God in Jewish scripture at its writing, but it could be made manifest only through the Christ-event, a "mystery that was kept secret for long ages but is now disclosed, and through the prophetic writings is made known to the Gentiles" (Rom 16:25). Explicit in Paul's language is a hierarchy of biblical truth. Scripture's outward, literal meaning was good, but also merely preparatory for the reception of its higher, hidden, spiritual meaning. Scripture's highest truth was esoteric.

Though different in origin, the trajectory of Latter-day Saint engagement with the Bible points to a similar convergence with early Christian exegetical practices. Joseph Smith responded to rising doubts in his day about the perspicuity of the Bible, not with recourse to more technical and modern hermeneutics, but with the production of both a revised Bible and supplementary scripture, which aimed to reveal the plain meaning of the Bible.[5] However, as a result of interpreting the Bible through new scripture rather than through other hermeneutical strategies, Mormons did not develop a "theory or doctrine of scripture that is adequate for the modern world," instead dwelling in "a hermeneutical Eden, innocent of a conscious philosophy of interpretation."[6] They are untroubled in their reading of the Bible as a (Mormon) Christian witness. No less than early Christians, Mormons find the gospel of Jesus Christ present in the Old and New Testaments alike. Though not deliberate continuators, they are in this sense clear inheritors of the early Christian interpretation of the Bible.[7]

5. See Christopher C. Smith, "Joseph Smith in Hermeneutical Crisis," *Dialogue: A Journal of Mormon Thought* 43, no. 2 (Summer 2010): 86–108; Lydia Willsky-Ciollo, "The (Un) Plain Bible: New Religious Movements and Alternative Scriptures in Nineteenth-Century America," *Nova Religio* 17, no. 4 (2014): 13–36, who examines Smith together with Mary Baker Eddy and Henry David Thoreau as analogous respondents to the "plain Bible" crisis.

6. Philip L. Barlow, *Mormons and the Bible: The Place of the Latter-day Saints in American Religion*, updated ed. (New York: Oxford University Press, 2013), 246–47.

7. While recognizing this inheritance from Christian tradition, certainly the more proximate and important source of Mormon hermeneutics is the Book of Mormon's own biblical exegesis and its

## DEVELOPING METHODS OF BIBLICAL INTERPRETATION

From the second century onward, Christian exegesis might appear a linear progression of the Christological typology we find in New Testament authors like Paul. The reality is more complex. While authentically primitive, the New Testament itself represents a certain curated view of earliest Christianity. It contains only scriptural writings acceptable to the official "orthodox" Christianity adopted as the imperial religion by the Roman emperor Constantine (d. 337) and to the traditions preceding it. But in the pre-Constantinian era, Christianity was a welter of divergent and competing sects, sometimes with competing scriptural texts. Even where scripture was more or less shared, Christians battled over the form and authority of these texts and how they should be interpreted.

Some early Christians continued to accept Jewish scripture as Christian revelation, as we find in New Testament authors. Some gentile Christian communities and schools, with negligible or hostile relationships to Jews, considered it suspect or rejected it completely. Antipathy ran high for its "Jewish" law and doctrine of Israel's election. Some "Gnostic" Christians rejected the Old Testament as inspired by a malignant, or at least ignorant, creator god who was also author of the Mosaic Law. Other Gnostics, like the Valentinian Ptolemy (mid-second century), could discriminate some partial value in it. Even the most disparaging Gnostic Christians might draw upon select Old Testament figures and narratives in elaborating their complex, hybridic cosmologies.[8]

This ambivalence about the Old Testament and how to interpret it is evident in early Christian writers. While journeying to Rome under arrest, the martyr-bishop Ignatius of Antioch (d. ca. 110) wrote seven epistles to various communities in Asia Minor and Greece, and to Rome itself. To them all he exhorts and expounds the Christian faith. But perhaps with regard for his

---

description of "pre-Christian Christianity" within an Old Testament context. See Terryl L. Givens, *By the Hand of Mormon: The American Scripture that Launched a New World Religion* (New York: Oxford University Press, 2002), 45–51.

8. Scholars have increasingly recognized that Gnostic rejection of Jewish scripture has been often overstated. A survey by Robert McL. Wilson illustrates both the variety and perhaps surprising extent of the Gnostic use of Jewish scripture; surviving Gnostic writings quote from seventeen different OT books and make significant use of Genesis ("The Gnostics and the Old Testament," in *Proceedings of the International Colloquium on Gnosticism, Stockholm, August 20–25, 1973*, edited by Geo Widengren [Stockholm, Sweden: Almqvist & Wiksell, 1977], 164–68). It might even be said that the central myth of Gnosticism, in both its classical and Valentinian form, "expressed a massive revision of the cosmogony and history taught in the books of Moses" (Bentley Layton, *The Gnostic Scriptures* [New York: Doubleday, 1987], 306).

gentile Christian audience, he references the Old Testament just a handful of times and never cites from the books of the Law. In contrast we see First Clement (ca. 96), an early Roman epistle to the church in Corinth, ranging across the entire the Old Testament—but nevertheless avoiding Christian typology. Its author prefers traditional Jewish moral exegesis, which invoked Old Testament figures as examples of virtue.[9]



But in the pseudonymous *Epistle of Barnabas* (ca. 130) we find a next-order Christian exegesis that both inherits and moves beyond the Pauline tradition. The author employs Jewish modalities of figurative reading (midrash) to fundamentally reinterpret the Law of Moses as Christian allegory and typology. Ps.-Barnabas insists that the Jews lost their covenantal status as God's people due to sinfulness; Moses showed this on Sinai by smashing the tablets of the Law, which was never meant to be literally observed.[10] All the Law and the words of the prophets looked forward to Christ and the Christian people, who were the true Israel. Scripture needed to be read spiritually in the light of that truth. As would a long succession of Christian interpreters to follow, Ps.-Barnabas blames Jewish literalism on spiritual blindness, invoking scripture itself against any literal understanding of the Law: "For [God] has made perfectly clear to us through all the prophets that he needs no sacrifices or burnt-offerings or consecrated gifts, saying, 'What to me is the multitude of your sacrifices?' "[11]

The bishop Irenaeus of Lyons (d. ca. 200) forcefully opposed Gnostic Christians. He wrote a long polemic against them titled *The Examination and Refutation of So-Called "Knowledge" (Gnosis).* Irenaeus' adversaries fully agreed that scripture must be read in the light of the gospel—however different their gospels or opposed their conclusions. Their conflict was less over interpretive method than interpretive authority. In response, Irenaeus founds orthodox authority on a threefold "canon of truth." Scripture was itself the first canon or "pillar," but interpretation required two others. One was plain reason, believed by itself to thoroughly debunk the Gnostics. Irenaeus develops extensive arguments to expose the perceived contradiction and folly of Gnostic theology and exegesis. But as a second witness he affirms that rational interpretation accords fully with the apostolic tradition, that deposit of truth passed down

9. One exception is 1 Clement 12.7–8, where Rahab is invoked as an example of "both faith and prophecy" since her scarlet thread "reveals that through the blood of the Lord all who believe and hope in God will win redemption."

10. *Barnabas* 4.6–8; 14.1–5.

11. *Barnabas* 2.4–5, citing Isa 1:11.

to Christians from Christ through orthodox bishops.[12] Early Christians did not believe the Bible was self-interpreting. Its full and correct meaning was revealed only in the twofold light of reason and tradition.

Their way of reading the Bible both permitted orthodox Christians to fully claim Jewish scripture as a Christian revelation and armed them in contests with religious competitors. Against Jews and Jewish Christians, such exegesis delegitimized the traditional and "literal" legal reading of the Old Testament and provided evidence for the Christian supersession of the Jewish people. This made orthodox (gentile) Christians the "true Israel" and the authoritative interpreters of Israel's scripture. Against Gnostics, the Old Testament was defended by faith and reason as both fully inspired and a "perfect gnosis."[13]

Biblical exegesis would continue to be shaped, throughout the patristic era, by continuous conflicts between "orthodoxy" and "heresy." There evolved a variety of interpretive interests and practices. Authors and "schools" could exhibit their own distinctive styles, though their methods were not rigid. Very common was the free admixture of literal, typological, and allegorical interpretation. One reading was often layered upon another without any essential consideration of their relationship or an explication of interpretive method. Their hermeneutic did not require it. Yet throughout this diversity we encounter three constants inherent to patristic biblical interpretation.

### *The Unicity of Scripture*

We might describe early Christians as holding a dual conception of prophecy. A kind of "direct inspiration" was attributed to biblical prophets and writers, whereby the Holy Spirit "made use of them as a flute player breathes into a flute."[14] But more important was "the indirect inspiration of the prophet, that is, inspiration as mediated through the sacred text," as David Aune explains.[15] We have seen that this empowered "spiritual" interpreters from Paul onward to discern in Jewish scripture the mystery of Christ that the Christian gospel made plain. They therefore made no effective distinction between the Old

12. Later authors would call this inherited tradition the "rule of faith." Irenaeus famously summarizes this tradition in credal form (*Against Heresies* 1.10.1; cf. 4.33.7), just as later authors might reference the Nicene creed as the rule of faith. In either case these formulas were understood as a distillation. Tradition was seen to encompass the totality of orthodox doctrine.

13. See *Barnabas* 1.5; 6.9; 18.1.

14. Athenagoras, *Plea for the Christians,* 9.

15. David E. Aune, "Charismatic Exegesis in Early Judaism and Early Christianity," in *The Pseudepigrapha and Early Biblical Interpretation,* edited by James H. Charlesworth and Craig A. Evans (Sheffield, UK: JSOT Press, 1993), 129; cf. 143–48.

and New Testaments as Christian revelation. The fundamental message of all scripture equally was that Christ is the fulfillment of all things.

This belief in the Bible's unicity had a certain conventional basis. It was a commonplace of ancient literary theory that every book had a central *hypothesis*, a comprehensive meaning or "gist" that the reader must rightly apprehend to interpret the meaning of its various parts and details. In arguing against Gnostics, Irenaeus claimed their interpretation of the Bible was consistently wrong because they failed to understand its governing hypothesis: "There is only one God, the Father, and one Jesus Christ our Lord, who came according to the economy and who recapitulated all things in himself."[16] This permitted early Christians to build an "integrated reading of the entire Old Testament in and through connections to Jesus Christ."[17] They certainly recognized that constituent parts of the Bible were separated by circumstance of history and composition, even if, by modern comparison, their critical tools and methods for investigating this were modest. But they did not believe that the meaning of the Bible was historically constrained or determined or that the collective message of its various voices was anything other than God's revelation in and through Christ Jesus.



### *The Richness of Scripture*

For early Christians a natural corollary of biblical unity was, according to Wiles, "the significance of detail, since God can neither be inconsistent with himself nor do anything without a purpose."[18] Since every particular was significant to the whole, they worked to reveal the abundant Christian meaning of every verse and word. They believed the Bible revealed not just a single truth, but manifold truths that were fully commensurate with the reader's diligence. In John Chrysostom's words:

> For, just as with grains of incense, the more they are moved about with your fingers, the greater fragrance they give out, so it is with the Scriptures in our experience: the more you devote yourself to studying them,

16. Irenaeus, *Against Heresies* 3.16.6. Translation and full discussion in John J. O'Keefe and R.R. Reno, *Sanctified Vision: An Introduction to Early Christian Interpretation of the Bible* (Baltimore: Johns Hopkins University Press, 2005), 33–44, to which we are indebted here.

17. O'Keefe and Reno, *Sanctified Vision*, 76.

18. Maurice Wiles, *The Making of Christian Doctrine: A Study in the Principles of Doctrinal Development* (Cambridge, UK: Cambridge University Press, 1967), 47.

> the more you are able to discover the hidden treasure in them, and thereby gain great and unspeakable wealth.[19]



Since scripture was infinitely rich, it could never contain anything impoverished or defective. Obscurity was only apparent and marked the presence of mysterious truths, everywhere and always. The more contradictory or irrelevant scripture might seem, the more interpreters felt compelled to uncover its true but hidden meaning. For example, Origen of Alexandria (d. ca. 253) dedicated a long sermon to Numbers 33, a prosaic account of the stages of Israel's exodus from Egypt. He believed the very dullness of this chapter, so great it "seems unnecessary to read," instead "turns the eyes of our mind toward Him who ordered this to be written and to ask of Him its meaning."[20] Doing this we find it filled with "mysterious descriptions of the ascent of the soul to heaven and the mystery of the resurrection of the dead."[21] Origen discovers lessons that train the soul in virtue in the etymologies of the names of the stations at which the Israelites encamped—all forty-two of them. So we should not "be surprised if toils [Halus/Alush] follows health [Raphaca/Dophkah]. For the soul acquires health from the Lord in order to accept toils with delight and not unwillingly."[22] As a more general example, the erotic qualities of the Song of Solomon that might for some raise questions of inspiration made it an early object of exegetical fascination. It was the serious subject of homily and commentary from the third century forward, from Origen to Gregory the Great. This patristic fascination would be impressively continued in Bernard of Clairvaux (d. 1153), who wrote eighty-six sermons (for monks) on just its first two chapters.

### *The Inexhaustibility of Scripture*

The abundant creativity of patristic interpreters might be thought to draw far more from the Bible than it contains, but for them that was not possible. Expositors like Ephrem the Syrian continually marveled, "Who is capable of comprehending the extent of what is to be discovered in a single utterance

19. *Homilies on Genesis* 13.3; trans. by Robert C. Hill, *John Chrysostom: Homilies on Genesis 1–17* (FOC 74; Washington, DC: Catholic University of America Press, 1999), 170.

20. *Homilies on Numbers XXVII* 1; trans. by Rowan A. Greer, *Origen: An Exhortation to Martyrdom, Prayer, and Selected Works* (New York: Paulist Press, 1979), 247, slightly altered.

21. *Homilies on Numbers XXVII* 4; trans. by Greer, *Origen*, 252.

22. *Homilies on Numbers XXVII* 12; trans. by Greer, *Origen*, 262. See Num 33:13: "They set out from Dophkah and camped at Alush."

of Yours? For we leave behind in it far more than we take from it, like thirsty people drinking from a fountain."[23] This inexhaustibility became the basis for an ethics of reading that stressed the virtue of humility. For them, as even a modern interpreter might recommend, "humility represents the stance of standing 'under' the definite meaning and force of the text rather than 'over' it: understanding rather than overstanding."[24] But inexhaustibility did not imply that the meaning of scripture was indeterminate or in any way incoherent. The Bible's contents and organization were seen as an extension of the divine economy ("plan of salvation") that ordered both the cosmos and history. But discerning that order was much more a work of ceaseless exploration than any modernist project of mastery through conquest. While scripture was the self-disclosure of God, the Word clothed in words, human language is not capable of circumscribing God. As Blowers dichotomizes, "Negatively, this implies an unbridgeable chasm (*diastēma*) between scriptural words and the divine reality; positively, it prompts a never-ending search for the meaning of Scripture, or, more precisely, for the divine Logos ever disguised within it."[25]



Where does the church fit in this tripartite view of scripture? This is a vital question for Latter-day Saints, since a fundamental of Mormon theology is that God's "only true and living church" is predicated on divine revelation to "living prophets" (presiding general leaders) whose word is the same as God's "own voice" (scripture).[26] Thus, the truth and meaning of scripture is regarded as co-identical with "continuing revelation" and modern prophetic teaching. Mormons often speak of scripture "reading," "study" or "use," but only infrequently of scriptural "interpretation," because, as one influential LDS leader has put it, "the practice of the church constitutes the interpretation of the scripture."[27] All this would seem to obscure for Mormons the historical Christian function of scriptural exegesis as a primary medium of divine revelation. However, the unicity, richness, and inexhaustibility of scripture was not self-sustaining for early Christians. Rather, "the Bible was a book of the church and it was understood and interpreted within the context of the

23. *Commentary on the Diatessaron* 1.18; trans. by Sebastian P. Brock, "St Ephrem the Syrian on Reading Scripture," *The Downside Review* 125 (2007): 49.

24. Richard S. Briggs, *The Virtuous Reader: Old Testament Narrative and Interpretive Virtue* (Grand Rapids: Baker, 2010), 20.

25. Paul M. Blowers, "Eastern Orthodox Biblical Interpretation," in *A History of Biblical Interpretation, vol. 2: The Medieval through the Reformation Periods,* edited by Alan J. Hauser and Duane F. Watson (Grand Rapids, MI: Eerdmans, 2009), 176.

26. See D&C 1:30, 37–38; cf. D&C 68:4.

27. Bruce R. McConkie, "Our Relationship with the Lord," *Brigham Young University 1981–82 Speeches,* 8, available at https://speeches.byu.edu/talks/bruce-r-mcconkie_relationship-lord/

church's faith and life, its creeds, its liturgy, its practices and beliefs."[28] Thus, unlike other contemporary approaches to the Bible, whether theological or historical-critical, the model of early Christian exegesis does not set the Bible against the church, but within the church.

## PERFORMING BIBLICAL INTERPRETATION

The Bible became universal in early Christian writing and art, imprinting every facet of Christian culture. Contemporary appreciation of this fact has created a growing interest in "reception history," the broad study of the Bible's historical use and effects. Formal acts of exegesis were just one part of the early Christian biblical matrix. The increasing practice has been to describe and bring into dialogue a wider range of examples of biblical influence and enactments, moving beyond the traditional study of history of interpretation. But this expanded work on biblical reception is contextualizing rather than diminishing the importance of those discrete "settings of interpretation in literature and life" to which the Bible was most central.[29] And foremost among these interpretive settings are two exegetical genres still central to Christian biblical interpretation today, homily and commentary. Both offer rich opportunities for the Latter-day Saint interpretation of the Bible.

### *Homily*

The preached homily or sermon was a regular part of Christian worship from the very beginning. It was adopted by Jewish Christians from the synagogue service, and as in Jewish worship, Christian preaching was based on the exposition of a scriptural lection (see Luke 4:14–21). Justin Martyr (mid-second century) provides an early description of preaching in weekly worship: "And on the day called Sunday all who live in cities or in the country gather together to one place, and the memoirs of the apostles or the writings of the prophets are read, as long as time permits. Then when the reader has finished, the leader (of the congregation) in a discourse instructs and exhorts to the imitation of these

28. Robert Louis Wilkin, "*In Dominico Eloquio*: Learning the Lord's Style of Language," *Communio* 24.4 (1997): 846–66, cit. 863.

29. See William Horbury, "Old Testament Interpretation in the Writings of the Church Fathers," in *Mikra: Text, Translation, Reading and Interpretation of the Hebrew Bible in Ancient Judaism and Early Christianity*, edited by Martin Jan Mulder (Philadelphia: Fortress, 1988), 731–58, cit. 731. In addition to homily and commentary, discussed here, Horbury describes as other key settings catechesis, apologetic, ecclesiastical law, liturgy, poetry, and art.

good things."[30] These twin elements of the exposition of a scriptural lection (instruction) and its application to the life of the congregation (exhortation) have continued to form the foundation of homiletics down to the present. Homilies were also preached in a variety of liturgical settings beyond the Sunday service and at rituals like baptismal services. Its fixed presence in Christian worship made homiletic a principal medium for Christian scriptural teaching.



Early Christian homilists worked within few conventions or formal constraints. Homilies were highly individual to the homilist, who might choose to treat the entire biblical reading or focus on just a verse or two, who might offer a close exegesis of the lection or largely ignore it in pursuit of other interests. The practical constraint of endurance (the preacher's or the audience's) might foreshorten an exposition, but in that case the preacher might choose to address his topic over successive homilies. Festal seasons such as Lent and Holy Week gave natural scope to the preaching of series of homilies on relevant topics and biblical texts. Many homilies survive that were occasional to these feast days, due to their ongoing usage in festal homiliaries, part of a great diversity of sermon collections covering the lectionary and liturgical year. Patristic homilies became authoritative and saw a variety of uses deep into the Middle Ages and would even be preached verbatim rather than preachers composing afresh. Today, scholars naturally turn to them as a principal resource for the study of early Christian biblical interpretation.

## *Commentary*

Early Christian commentaries undertook a more systematic exegesis of either entire biblical books or significant sections, such as the Genesis account of the six days of creation. Christians drew primarily on Hellenistic literary and philosophical commentaries as models. Literary commentaries were important to classical education. They explained the texts central to the school curriculum, such as Homer and Virgil, focusing heavily on grammatical, rhetorical, and historical questions. The commentator worked systematically, first citing a short section of the text (*lemma*) and then offering a comment. That comment might do as little as gloss a word while at other times indulge in lengthy

30. Justin Martyr, *1 Apology* 67; trans. by Leslie W. Barnard, *St. Justin Martyr: The First and Second Apologies* (ACW 56; Mahwah, NJ: Paulist Press, 1997), 71, slightly altered. Justin's description is of the Roman Church in his day, but there was substantial regional variety in liturgical reading practices. On this and forms of liturgical scriptural use beyond homily, see Gerard A. M. Rouwhorst, "The Reading of Scripture in Early Christian Liturgy," in *What Athens Has to Do with Jerusalem*, edited by Leonard V. Rutgers (Leuven, Belgium: Peeters, 2002), 307–31.

discursus. Christians readily adapted this style of commentary to the Bible and it remains the most common format for commentary yet today.

Philosophical commentaries exchanged the lemma/comment form for a looser, lengthier, and more contemplative meditation on a given philosophical work. Some Christian philosophers would have known the Aristotelian and Platonic commentaries of teachers like Proclus and Iamblichus. More directly influential was a Jewish scholar, Philo of Alexandria, who wrote commentaries on Jewish scripture. Philo exemplified for the first generation of Christian commentators, also at Alexandria, a compelling form of mystical and philosophical commentary based on allegorical methods of interpretation.

While influenced by these historical forms, Christian commentary became highly individual to author, context, and function. The distinction between homily and commentary was itself quite permeable. Homilists drew on commentaries for scriptural exposition while commentaries might themselves be strongly homiletic. Some early commentaries were in fact revised collections of homilies, adapted from preaching into publishable form. Other commentaries originated in classroom teaching. Yet others were written for friends or patrons, or so authors said, even if inevitably their work was intended for publication.

From our perspective today, these early commentaries can sometimes appear to be theology or polemics by other means. They were often produced in controversial contexts and their theological objectives were explicit. The earliest known Christian commentary was written in the mid-second century, on the Gospel of John, by the Valentinian author Heracleon.[31] We know it primarily from citations in the first orthodox commentary on John, by Origen of Alexandria (d. ca. 254), who intended his own work to be a refutation of Heracleon. Origen was the most important early Christian biblical scholar and wrote extensively on most of the Bible. Later condemned as a heretic, his works were proscribed; many were either lost or survive only in adulterated translations. Regardless, the work of Origen and other patristic commentators became highly authoritative, important deep into the Middle Ages and of enduring interest today.

31. A commentary on just the prologue to the Gospel of John was also apparently written, slightly early, by another Valentinian Gnostic, Ptolemy (see Irenaeus, *Against Heresies* 1.8.5).

## MORMONS AND EARLY CHRISTIAN EXEGESIS

The Bible has provided to all Christians, Mormon and other, everywhere and throughout their entire history, grounding language and narratives from which they have constructed discursive identity. The Bible is also, and always has been, the paradoxical interstice from which grows both Christian unity and diversity. It is both an establishing and precipitating document, a deposit of fixed Christian truth and engine of perpetual Christian change. Reading the Bible makes Mormons, too, the subjects of biblical change through the call and response of exegesis. Exegesis draws Mormons into dialogue, not only with the text, but with its historical interpreters—wittingly or not. Modern Mormons must also still negotiate the meaning of the Bible, for their religion and for their lives, just as did the first Christian readers. In this way, too, reading the Bible connects Mormons to ancient Christians, just as certainly as it bound those Christians to one another.

## 21

# Early Christian Literature

GRANT ADAMSON

Mormonism's belief in a cycle of apostasy and restoration shapes LDS understandings of the primitive church and the patristic period. God is said to reveal gospel truth intermittently, which is then corrupted and lost before being revealed again or restored. According to this dispensationalist tenet, the worst corruption and loss happened after the death of Jesus and the apostles. Hardly an agentless occurrence, the "great apostasy" is supposed to have been perpetrated by a "great and abominable church," the "whore of all the earth" seated "upon many waters," to quote the Book of Mormon and in keeping with contemporary anti-Catholic interpretation of John's Apocalypse in Protestant England and post-revolutionary America.[1] When and how the truth was corrupted and lost have never been pinned down in Mormon thought, and some Latter-day Saints do explore early Christian writings into the second, third, and fourth centuries, looking for vestiges.[2] But most would be unfamiliar with anything outside the New Testament. Mormons are not Trinitarian, they do not recite the Niceno-Constantinopolitan Creed or the Apostles' Creed, and they have no professionally trained clergy versed in patristics. As taught in LDS Sunday Schools, youth seminaries, and college institutes of religion, ancient church history effectively terminates with the Bible and the first century. The dual argument of this chapter is that study of canonical and non-canonical early Christian literature must go hand-in-hand, and that the Mormon prophet of the restoration, Joseph Smith, and his collaborators were not so uninformed;

1. 1 Nephi 13:1–9, 20–29; 14:1–17; 22:13–14; 2 Nephi 6:12; 10:16; 28:18.

2. Further, some scholars in the LDS tradition are rethinking the narrative altogether; see Miranda Wilcox and John D. Young, eds., *Standing Apart: Mormon Historical Consciousness and the Concept of Apostasy* (New York: Oxford University Press, 2014).

they owned copies of some best-selling titles in the 1800s on the history of Christianity, theology, and even a number of apocryphal gospels.

## POTENTIAL CATEGORIES



In addition to the twenty-seven books that were eventually canonized in the New Testament, early Christians wrote a mass of literature that is much more challenging to classify than the canonical texts. The most common arrangements are groupings by chronology, region and language, theological orientation, and genre, but none are without problems. Take chronology, as a jumping-off point. Where does the early Christian period and thus early Christian literature begin and end? In determining answers to this seemingly simple question, a straightforward timeline would be helpful to have, but it is lacking since much of the literature was written anonymously or under a pseudonym. And in cases where the author is known, the possible dates for the author's life may vary a sizable amount. This means that within the early Christian period, however defined, the literature cannot readily be arranged chronologically by century let alone by decade. Other groupings are also of limited use.

### *Region and Language*

Whether in Greek, Latin, Syriac, Coptic, etc., often this or that text survives in later, maybe much later, versions, not the tongue in which it was composed. Moreover the ancient Mediterranean and Near Eastern world of early Christianity was multilingual and multicultural. Travel, though more difficult then, was not rare. Mobility and communication throughout the western and eastern halves of the Roman Empire and beyond defy any organization of early Christian literature around geographical schools or sees. Although there were important centers, such as Antioch in Syria, Alexandria in Egypt, and the city of Rome proper, these were quite cosmopolitan hubs. People came and went, and with them, information flowed freely.

### *Theological Orientation*

Early Christians labeled some concepts as right or wrong, orthodox or heretical. But the representation of the correctness of thought, opinion, belief, and practice is not a reliable gauge for categorizing early Christian texts, in light of the fact that orthodoxy and orthopraxy are in the eye of the beholder. The earliest writings by any believer in Jesus, namely Paul's undisputed letters, attest to the diversity and the internal and external hostility of Christian literature from the beginning. Whether Paul himself was a pious convert or a wicked apostate depended in the first century, as is does today, on the judgments of social hierarchies, not some standard of original unmixed truth.

### *Genre*

In the second to fourth centuries, Christians developed an entire kind of writing known as heresiology. Intended to expose and denounce other Christians as heretics along with the Jews and pagans that supposedly overinfluenced them, the genre did just as much to invent 'correct' Christianity. Other types of writing in early Christian literature are the apologia, a reasoned defense of the faith against pagan and/or Jewish critics; and the martyrology, an account of the torture and suffering of the Christian hero, whether male and/or female, who refuses to compromise with the human and daemonic powers of the world. But not even genre holds the master key to categorization. For instance, Eusebius of Caesarea's landmark *History of the Church*, from the preexistence of Jesus, to the ostensible triumph of proto-Catholic Christianity under the watchful care of the Emperor Constantine in the 310s and 320s, is part heresiology, part apologia, and part martyrology, not to mention other literary components of the text.

## INSIDE AND OUT OF THE CANON

Classifying this extensive literature has been a main focus of modern scholarly study—and a cause for disagreement. The determination of boundaries is freighted with religious truth claims about which texts are more authoritative and why the New Testament should be treated differently/separately from other early Christian writings. A summary of some academic reference volumes and the chosen periodization of each will illustrate. In their *Storia della letteratura cristiana antica greca e latina* (1995–1996), in two volumes, translated into English as *Early Christian Greek and Latin Literature* (2005), Moreschini and Norelli start with Paul and the rest of the books of the New Testament, interlaced with other texts from the first and second centuries.[3]

3. Claudio Moreschini and Enrico Norelli, *Early Christian Greek and Latin Literature*, trans. by M.J. O'Connell (Peabody, MA: Hendrickson, 2005), 1: Ch. 1–13.

They stop with the transition to the medieval period, which they define in the west as "the age of Gregory the Great, Gregory of Tours, and Isidore of Seville," who wrote during the 500s and 600s. In the eastern half of the Roman Empire, Moreschini and Norelli admit that they have arbitrarily stopped with "the last descendants of the Fifth Ecumenical Council of Constantinople," which was held in 553 and was the second one in that city—the previous ecumenical or universal councils being the Council of Nicaea in 325, the First Council of Constantinople in 381, the Council of Ephesus in 431, and the Council of Chalcedon in 451.[4]



Döpp and Geerlings begin and end later. In their edited *Lexicon der antiken christlichen Literatur* (1998), translated into English as *Dictionary of Early Christian Literature* (2000), they do not include any entries on the books of the New Testament at all. They end with Isidore of Seville in the west but go even further in the east, finishing not with the Second Council of Constantinople but with the oeuvre of John of Damascus who was writing into the mid 700s.[5]

Volume editors Young, Ayres, and Louth start with Paul, dedicating ten initial chapters in *The Cambridge History of Early Christian Literature* (2004) to "The Beginnings: The New Testament to Irenaeus"; that is, Irenaeus of Lyon who wrote, among other things, the oldest surviving heresiology in the 180s.[6] The cut-off for Young, Ayres, and Louth is the fifth century, more than a hundred years sooner than Moreschini and Norelli in the west and more than two hundred years sooner than Döpp and Geerlings in the east.

Depending on the reference volumes consulted, then, early Christian literature may or may not include the New Testament, and it can encompass the 400s, the 500s, the 600s or more. There are disciplinary reasons for this. The study of early Christianity has often but not always been treated as a distinct academic field lying between New Testament studies here and medieval studies there. The overlap with the biblical canon is of particular concern.

*The Oxford Handbook* series puts the New Testament alongside the "Old Testament" in the volume on biblical studies, which is appropriate for that handbook.[7] But the series keeps the New Testament apart from the study of early Christianity, as though the canonical texts could not benefit from being

4. Moreschini and Norelli, *Early Christian Greek and Latin Literature*, 2: xvii.

5. Siegmar Döpp and Wilhelm Geerlings, eds., *Dictionary of Early Christian Literature*, trans. by M. O'Connell (New York: Crossroad, 2000), viii.

6. Frances M. Young, Lewis Ayres, and Andrew Louth, eds., *The Cambridge History of Early Christian Literature* (Cambridge, UK: Cambridge University Press, 2004), Ch. 1–10.

7. J.W. Rogerson and Judith M. Lieu, eds., *The Oxford Handbook of Biblical Studies* (New York: Oxford University Press, 2006).

treated more than once in more than one volume and within more than one cognate discipline. If that was a publishing decision out of their control, still the editors of *The Oxford Handbook of Early Christian Studies* (2008), Harvey and Hunter, attempt to solidify the parameters of the field as well as the limits of their volume when they matter-of-factly state, "Early Christian studies examines the history, literature, thought, practices, and material culture of the Christian religion in late antiquity (c. 100–600 CE)."[8] Harvey and Hunter justify the compartmentalization of canonical and non-canonical texts as follows. "This volume takes as its chronological duration . . . the period roughly stretching from the end of the New Testament era to the eve of Islam's appearance on the historical horizon. New Testament studies is itself a field of massive scholarly enterprise, and its work is handled in a separate volume of the Oxford Handbook series."[9] To be sure, not only does the series feature a separate volume on biblical studies as a whole, but the series also features a volume of over four hundred pages on the study of the Gospel and Letters of John alone.[10] No one disagrees that scholars have traditionally paid far more attention to the canonical texts. The issue is whether that imbalance should be supported any longer as an insular academic pursuit. Arguably, the compartmentalization of canonical and non-canonical early Christian literature has little to do with chronology and periodization. Rather, it has to do with the legacy of the Christian Church's claims that the inspired books of the New Testament were written by Jesus' eyewitness apostles and their close companions, a view accepted by few modern scholars.

Canonical texts do not necessarily reflect an earlier time than non-canonical early Christian literature. Few of the books in the New Testament were written before the year 50. Most were written between 50 and 150, the same time that a number of non-canonical texts were also composed, such as the letters of Ignatius of Antioch, one of the "apostolic fathers" of the church, so called because of his purported spiritual and ecclesiological proximity to the apostles in the line of succession. From an academic standpoint, despite the sacred status of the Bible in the Christian faith, the books of the New Testament are human products of the same culture and society as the rest of early Christian literature and accordingly should be grouped together and studied together

8. Susan Ashbrook Harvey and David G. Hunter, eds., *The Oxford Handbook of Early Christian Studies* (New York: Oxford University Press, 2008), 1.

9. Harvey and Hunter, eds., *Oxford Handbook of Early Christian Studies*, 3.

10. Judith M. Lieu and Martinus C. de Boer, eds., *The Oxford Handbook of Johannine Studies* (New York: Oxford University Press, 2018).

with the non-canonical texts. Hence, in the introduction to volume one of their *Early Christian Greek and Latin Literature*, Moreschini and Norelli state,

> It goes almost without saying that we ourselves have completely given up the idea of dealing in separate chapters with the New Testament writings, the "Apostolic Fathers," the apocrypha, heretical literature, and so on. These are corpora that were established a posteriori and were dictated by theological and not historical or literary considerations.[11]



Young, Ayres, and Louth do not completely give up the idea of canonical priority in *The Cambridge History of Early Christian Literature*. But in her introduction to the initial chapters on "The Beginnings: The New Testament to Irenaeus," Young explains and endorses how modern critical scholarship has left behind pre-critical evaluations of what is canonical and non-canonical, orthodox and heretical.[12] And while the next chapter in the volume is titled "The Apostolic and Sub-apostolic Writings: The New Testament and the Apostolic Fathers," it swiftly proceeds to dismiss any such distinctions.[13] So even when the terminology of the traditional boundaries is preserved, out of some necessity, the boundaries themselves do not have to be assumed; in fact, they should not be.

## CURRENT EDITIONS AND TRANSLATIONS

This business of categories and arrangements and groupings and classifications and distinctions may feel tedious to those who would prefer to get on with reading the literature itself. But these items at the top of the agenda are important because they frame how that reading will be done. And there are yet other categories well worth being aware of. Even as the foregoing sections dealt with classificatory problems, from chronology to the canon, this section briefly complicates the very term *Christian* in the process of outlining where the texts can be read. Most of the earliest Christian texts also ought to be viewed as Second Temple and early Jewish literature because most of the earliest Christians such as Paul were Jews who happened to believe in Jesus. Furthermore, Jesus was a Jew. Of course, Jews and Christians, themselves multicultural, were not the sole inhabitants of the ancient Mediterranean and Near

11. Moreschini and Norelli, *Early Christian Greek and Latin Literature*, 1: xiii.
12. Young, Ayres, and Louth, eds., *Cambridge History*, 5–10.
13. Young, Ayres, and Louth, eds., *Cambridge History*, 11–19.

East, and consequently, early Christian writings ultimately ought to be seen as a comparatively small wavelength on the full color spectrum of literature from long-late antiquity: Greco-Roman, Jewish, Christian, Persian, Manichaean, etc., up to and potentially including the rise of Islam.[14]



Non-canonical, parabiblical texts can be read in one of the designated collections of what are called New Testament apocrypha, the most famous of which are specifically Gnostic and have resurfaced—or to be frank, have often been looted—from the sands of Egypt to grab media headlines in the 1900s and 2000s.[15] The study of Gnosticism is a contested subfield within early Christian studies. Some experts think the first Gnostics were a non-Christian and even pre-Christian phenomenon in Second Temple Judaism and the Greco-Roman world. Besides the New Testament apocrypha, Gnostic or not, the other corresponding parabiblical texts need to be mentioned, namely the Old Testament pseudepigrapha, so called. They need to be mentioned because several of them were composed and many of them were revised by early Christians who sought to capitalize on and exploit the Jewish pedigree of Christianity. They can be read in their own designated collections.[16] Last but in no way least, the writings of the church fathers and the occasional church mother, female martyr, or nun can be read in one of the propriety translation series; some English translations are available in broader literature series too.[17] The patristic texts are generally understood to be proto-Catholic or proto-orthodox, as opposed to the heterodox and Gnostic literature. But once again, those divisions, like the divisions between the canonical and non-canonical texts, are not hard and fast. Neither was proto-orthodox Christianity a monolith, as the fierce debates of Nicaea and the other ecumenical councils attest.[18]

14. See, for example, Gillian Clark, *Late Antiquity: A Very Short Introduction* (New York: Oxford University Press, 2011); Gillian Clark, *Christianity and Roman Society* (Cambridge, UK: Cambridge University Press, 2004).

15. For example, James K. Elliott, ed., *The Apocryphal New Testament* (New York: Oxford University Press, 1993, repr., 2009); Marvin W. Meyer, ed., *The Nag Hammadi Scriptures* (New York: HarperOne, 2008); Tony Burke and Brent Landau, eds., *New Testament Apocrypha: More Noncanonical Scriptures* (Grand Rapids, MI: Eerdmans, 2016).

16. For example, James H. Charlesworth, ed., *The Old Testament Pseudepigrapha,* two vols. (New York: Doubleday, 1983, repr., Peabody, MA: Hendrickson, 2015); Richard Bauckham, James R. Davila, and Alexander Panayotov, eds., *Old Testament Pseudepigrapha: More Noncanonical Scriptures* (Grand Rapids, MI: Eerdmans, 2013).

17. Such as Ancient Christian Writers and the Fathers of the Church; Oxford World's Classics; and Penguin Classics. For more, see Clark, *Christianity*, 118; Harvey and Hunter, eds., *Oxford Handbook of Early Christianity*, 968–69.

18. See e.g. Bart D. Ehrman, *Lost Christianities: The Battles for Scripture and the Faiths We Never Knew* (New York: Oxford University Press, 2003).

## PUBLICATIONS AVAILABLE IN AMERICA AT THE TIME OF JOSEPH SMITH



Due to the apostasy-and-restoration narrative in the Book of Mormon, and its theme of hidden records to come forth, there has always been a certain Latter-day Saint fascination with the "lost books" of the Bible.[19] The reasons behind the allure are not only that these missing scriptures might contain old echoes of the truth restored by Joseph Smith, but also that they might vindicate him as a prophet since he could not possibly have been familiar with them, so it has been argued by some more or less self-appointed defenders of the LDS faith.[20] Many of the largest manuscript discoveries of parabiblical writings from the early Christian period were indeed made after Smith founded his new religious movement as a restoration of the primitive church. Likewise, no English-language translation series of patristic texts was done in Smith's lifetime; they were done afterward.[21] Nevertheless, he and his collaborators had plenty of access to information about early Christianity and early Christian literature even outside the canon. Some of the best-selling titles of the day were Foxe's *Book of Martyrs*, Mosheim's *Ecclesiastical History*, Buck's *Theological Dictionary*, and Hone's *Apocryphal New Testament*.

John Foxe was an outspoken English Protestant. Building on Latin foundations, he published his *Book of Martyrs* in 1563 then revised it in 1570, 1576, and 1583.[22] For the immensely expanded 1570 edition, he adopted a thoroughgoing apocalyptic framework. The church suffers persecution until the Emperor Constantine converts in the 300s. Then, on Foxe's reading of the Book of Revelation, Satan is bound for a thousand years as the church enters a period of decline and as persecution is renewed, this time against English proto-reformer John Wycliffe in the 1300s; one and the same Devil is thought to be lurking behind persecution by the Roman Empire and persecution by the Roman Catholic

19. Theme of hidden records: 1 Nephi 13:38–41; 14:26; 2 Nephi 29; and D&C 6:25–27; 7; 8:1; 9:2. For the roots of LDS interest in lost books of the Bible but not so much the Old Testament Apocrypha of the Catholic canon, see Gerrit Dirkmaat, "Lost Scripture and 'the Interpolations of Men': Joseph Smith's Revelation on the Apocrypha," in *Producing Ancient Scripture: Joseph Smith's Translation Projects in the Development of Mormon Christianity,* edited by Michael Hubbard MacKay, Mark Ashurst-McGee, and Brian M. Hauglid (Salt Lake City: University of Utah Press, 2020), 285–303.

20. For example, Hugh Nibley, "Baptism for the Dead in Ancient Times," *Mormonism and Early Christianity* (Provo, UT: FARMS, 1987), 100–167, esp. 148–49.

21. One series, the Oxford Library of the Fathers, did commence in the 1830s, but it was not done until the 1880s; see Harvey and Hunter, eds., *Oxford Handbook of Early Christianity*, 12–13.

22. See Mark Rankin, "Foxe, John," in *Wiley-Blackwell Encyclopedia of Literature: The Encyclopedia of English Renaissance Literature,* edited by G.A. Sullivan and A. Stewart (Hoboken, NJ: Wiley-Blackwell, 2012), Credo Reference online.

Church, with the pope and the Catholics being identified as the Antichrist and the "whore sitting vpō [upon] many waters," mentioned in the Apocalypse, Chapter 17.[23] Foxe's expansion resulted in twelve books. He assigned the bulk of book one, at 144 pages, to coverage of the early Christian martyrs.[24]

The 1576 and 1583 editions also ran to twelve books, and in the coming centuries, the magnum opus was abridged and updated. In the United States, Foxe's *Book of Martyrs* was printed in New York (1794, 1828, 1829, 1842), Philadelphia (1807, c.1813, 1830, 1832, 1836, 1842), Cincinnati (1831, 1832, 1834, 1835), and Boston (1837, 1840). There were no less than four versions: one revised by Paul Wright, another by John Malham, another by Amos Blanchard, and a fourth by Henry Wightman.[25] The Malham version, printed most, was a rearrangement of Foxe, although it maintained the Protestant essentials of Foxe's apocalyptic framework, with "the declining state of the church and of true religion" in the thousand years after Constantine, and "the time of Antichrist reigning and raging in the church, since the loosing of Satan," as the Reformation dawns; according to Malham, that framework "may well deserve a place in the memory of every sincere Christian," every non-Catholic, that is.[26]

Johann Lorenz von Mosheim, a Lutheran minister, was on the faculty of the University of Kiel and the University of Helmstedt before becoming university chancellor and head of theology at Gottingen. Between 1726 and 1755, he published and revised the four books of his *Ecclesiastical History* in Latin under the short title *Institutiones historiae christianae*. The four books were translated into English by Archibald Maclaine in Holland in 1764 and then again by James Murdock in the United States in 1832.[27] Maclaine's translation was printed in Philadelphia (1797–1798, 1812), Charlestown/Boston (1810–1811),

23. John Foxe, *The Unabridged Acts and Monuments Online* or *TAMO* (1570 ed.), book 1, 62 [49], 157 [144]; book 2, 158 [158], 192 [192]; book 4, 237 [237]; book 5, 514 [514], 590 [590], 595 [595]; book 6, 801 [801] (Sheffield, UK: HRI Online Publications, 2011), available at http//www.johnfoxe.org.

24. Foxe, *TAMO* (1570 ed.), book 1, 26–157 [26–144], esp. 62–157 [49–144].

25. I have examined digital copies of the Malham version printed in Philadelphia, c. 1813; New York, 1829; Philadelphia, 1830; and a digital copy of the Wightman version printed in Boston, 1837. Available at https://www.hathitrust.org. For the other printings, including those of the Wright version and the Blanchard version, I have relied on the bibliographic entries at https://www.worldcat.org.

26. *Fox's Book of Martyrs; or The Acts and Monuments of the Christian Church,* rev. by J. Malham (Philadelphia: Leary, c. 1813), 19.

27. See John Lawrence Mosheim, *An Ecclesiastical History, Ancient and Modern,* trans. by A. Maclaine (Charlestown, MA: Etheridge, 1810), 1: iii–vi, ix–xv; John Lawrence Mosheim, *An Ecclesiastical History, Ancient and Modern,* trans. by A. Maclaine, continued by C. Coote (Baltimore: Harrod, 1832), 1: iv–v; John Lawrence von Mosheim, *Institutes of Ecclesiastical History, Ancient and Modern,* trans. by J. Murdock (New Haven, CT: Maltby, 1832), 1:3–8.

New York (1821, 1824), and Baltimore (1832, 1833, 1834, 1837, 1840, 1842), while Murdock's was printed in New Haven (1832) and New York (1839, 1841, 1842).[28]

In either translation, Mosheim's *Ecclesiastical History* opens with his methodological introduction that divides the history of the church into the "external" context and the "internal" Christian beliefs, practices, and "heresies" of each century. The scare-quotation-marks on the word heresies are essentially Mosheim's and reflect his theoretical desire to avoid bias.[29] But in the implementation of his method, his treatments of heterodox Christians and the host of non-Protestants—pagans, Jews, Catholics, "Mahometans," and others—do not qualify as objective. Following the introduction, the four books of the history advance systematically through externals and internals, century by century. On top of this, the four books are organized into four periods of note: book one, from Jesus to Constantine; book two, from Constantine to Charlemagne; book three, from Charlemagne to "the memorable period when Luther arose in Germany to oppose the tyranny of Rome, and to deliver divine truth from the darkness that covered it;" and book four, from Luther to the time of publishing.[30] In US printings of the Maclaine and Murdock translations, book one, from Jesus to Constantine, could extend a full 400 pages all by itself. There was virtually no aspect of early Christianity and early Christian literature that Americans were unable to find at least something about within the comprehensive scope of Mosheim.

Charles Buck was an English evangelical preacher whose *Theological Dictionary* was published in 1802 and numerously reprinted.[31] Three main editions competed on the US bookselling market, all printed in Philadelphia (1807, 1810, 1814, 1815, 1818, 1820, 1821, 1823, 1824, 1825, 1826, 1829, 1830, 1831, 1833, 1835, 1836, 1837, 1838, 1841). The William Woodward edition, later inherited by Woodward's son Joseph, was the first to appear, in 1807, and the one most printed. The Edwin Scott edition appeared in 1820 and was short lived. George Bush's revised edition made its appearance in 1830 and beat out the Woodward edition by 1833; after an unsuccessful ad campaign in 1830 and 1831, Joseph

28. I have examined digital copies of the Maclaine translation printed in Charlestown/Boston, 1810–1811; New York, 1821, 1824; Baltimore, 1832, 1834, 1840, 1842; and of the Murdock translation printed in New Haven, 1832; New York, 1839, 1841, 1842. Available at https://www.hathitrust.org. For the other printings, I have relied on the bibliographic entries at https://www.worldcat.org.

29. Mosheim, *Ecclesiastical History* [1810 ed], 1: 1–8.

30. Mosheim, *Ecclesiastical History* [1810 ed], 1: 16–7.

31. See Matthew Bowman and Samuel Brown, "Reverend Buck's *Theological Dictionary* and the Struggle to Define American Evangelicalism, 1802–1851," *Journal of the Early Republic* 29, no. 3 (2009): 441–73.

Woodward himself ceased printing the Woodward edition and went with the Bush edition instead.[32]

The format of Buck's publication made it more user-friendly than the chronological narratives of Foxe and Mosheim, particularly when those publications were printed sans table of contents or index. In Buck's dictionary, Americans had easy access to information on the apostolic fathers and later patristic authors, the canon and canonical texts, early Christian councils and creeds, as well as persecution and martyrdom, the development of monasticism, plus apocryphal texts and "heretics," including many of the Gnostic variety. There were also descriptions of the pagan religions and philosophies of ancient Greece and Rome, of Judaism and Islam, their origins, history, religious writings, and more. This is to say nothing of topics in contemporary Christian theology that would come to have characteristic relevance in Mormonism.[33] For an example of information about early Christianity, under "Bible, rejected books of the," Buck has a list: "The apocryphal books of the New Testament are the epistle of St. Barnabas, the pretended epistle of St. Paul to the Laodiceans, several spurious gospels, Acts of the Apostles, and Revelations; the book of Hermas, entitled the Shepherd; Jesus Christ's letter to Abgarus; the epistles of St. Paul to Seneca, and several other pieces of the like nature."[34] But even as user friendly and information rich as Buck's *Theological Dictionary* was, it did not feature the actual texts of, say, any of the New Testament apocrypha, which were, however, accessible in another best-selling publication of the nineteenth century.



William Hone was a British pamphleteer, bookseller, political satirist, and antiquarian. He published his *Apocryphal New Testament* in 1820.[35] It was reprinted in the United States in Boston (c. 1821, 1832), Buffalo (1824), Philadelphia (1825), and Ravenna (1832) and Chillicothe (1835), Ohio.[36] The very

32. I have examined digital copies of the Woodward edition printed in 1810, 1815, 1818, 1821, 1825, 1826, 1829, 1830, 1831; of the Scott edition printed in 1823; and of the Bush edition printed in 1830, 1833, 1835, 1838, 1841, available at https://www.hathitrust.org. For the other printings, I have relied on the bibliographic entries at https://www.worldcat.org.

33. Charles Buck, *A Theological Dictionary, Containing Definitions of All Religious Terms* (Philadelphia: Woodward, 1815), esp. 19–20 ("Angels"), 104–5 ("Creation") 127–8 ("Dispensation"), 178 ("degrees of glory in heaven"), 180–81 (nature and duration of punishment in hell), 246 ("Keys"), 319–20 ("Millennium"), 413–15 ("Pre-existence of Jesus Christ"), 469 ("Satan"). I cite this printing for convenience: it seems to be the first to combine both volumes of the dictionary into one.

34. Buck, *Theological Dictionary*, 47.

35. See Kyle Grimes, "Hone, William," *Wiley-Blackwell Encyclopedia of Literature: The Encyclopedia of English Renaissance Literature,* Credo Reference online.

36. I have examined digital copies of the printings in Boston, c. 1821, 1832, and in Buffalo, 1824, available at https://www.hathitrust.org. For the other printings, I have relied on the bibliographic entries at https://www.worldcat.org.

title was provocative: "The apocryphal New Testament, being all the Gospels, Epistles, and other pieces now extant attributed in the first four centuries to Jesus Christ, his apostles, and their companions and not included in the New Testament, by its compilers. Translated from the original tongues and now first collected into one volume." And turning to the first page, Hone scandalously asked, "After the writings contained in the New Testament were selected from the numerous Gospels and Epistles then in existence, whai [sic] became of the Books that were rejected by the compilers?" Hone told his readers they held those books in their hands, informing them that such texts were "historical records" akin to the New Testament and "considered sacred" by early Christians. Several of Hone's readers were outraged. In the preface to the second edition he defended himself by challenging not only the boundaries of the canon and the accuracy of New Testament manuscripts, as he had in the first edition; Hone also said that the Council of Nicaea was a sham, "presided over by this Barbarian Founder of the church militant," that is, Constantine. He went on to add that if they would return to primitive Christianity and the inspiration of the Jerusalem Council of apostles in the 40s, then "every man [will] become a priest unto himself."[37]



Hone's introduction and preface were heavily indebted to the learning of others, and he could not claim the translations in *Apocryphal New Testament* to be his—he pirated them. Still he played a major role. Hone made many non-canonical and parabiblical writings from the early Christian period available to English-speaking audiences at a low price. Although the title was not equally fitting of them all, his collection featured: infancy gospels, such as the Proto-Gospel of James and the Infancy Gospel of Thomas; the letters between King Abgar of Edessa and Jesus; the Gospel of Nicodemus; the Apostles' Creed; Paul's letter to the Laodiceans; the letters between the Roman philosopher Seneca and Paul; the Acts of Paul and Thecla, a female ascetic and martyr; the letters of Clement of Rome addressed to the Corinthians; the letter of Barnabas; the letters of Ignatius of Antioch addressed to the Ephesians, Magnesians, Trallians, Romans, Philadelphians, Smyrnaeans, and to Polycarp, bishop of Smyrna; the letter of Polycarp to the Philippians; and the Shepherd of Hermas. Capping off the collection, Hone appended a catalogue of dozens and dozens of lost apocrypha "mentioned by Writers in the first four Centuries of Christ, with the several Works wherein they are cited or noticed."[38] It was as if he were leaving

37. William Hone, *The Apocryphal New Testament* (Boston: Bazin & Ellsworth, c. 1821), iii (title page), v, viii, xvi–xix.

38. Hone, *Apocryphal New Testament*, 283–86.

his readers eager for more, perhaps prompting them to a discovery in some way, be it by research, physical excavation, and/or communiqué from the divine.

Joseph Smith and his collaborators owned and used copies of Foxe's *Book of Martyrs*, Mosheim's *Ecclesiastical History*, Buck's *Theological Dictionary*, and Hone's *Apocryphal New Testament*. In terms of ownership, one copy of "Book of Martyrs by Fox," one copy of "Mosheims Church History 1 vol.," two copies of "Buck's Theological Dictionary," and one copy of "Apochryphal Testament" were contributed to the Nauvoo Library and Literary Institute in 1844. Joseph Smith himself was the owner and contributor of the copies of Mosheim and Hone.[39] In terms of usage, briefly, I am not aware of any published scholarship that looks at Mormonism and Foxe, Mosheim, Buck, or Hone in depth, but some connections have certainly been made. For instance, Buck is plainly cited in the Lectures on Faith, and Buck was used in an editorial on "Baptism for the Dead," with specifics of early Christian Marcionite practice, in the *Times & Seasons* during Smith's editorship.[40] While correlation is not causation, the Anglophone historical context cannot be denied and needs no special pleading, unlike claims of ancient truth restored in the 1800s.

These best-sellers by Foxe, Mosheim, Buck, and Hone do not explain away Smith's restoration scriptures and latter-day revelations. But they do show how much information was widely available—a lot more than we might imagine. Instead of jumping to the conclusion that Smith was unfamiliar with some detail of early Christianity, a safer bet would be to check these and other representative publications for what was accessible and understood then, such as the apocalyptic and anti-Catholic framework of church decline and reformation in Foxe, or the disregard for the constraints of the canon and Nicaea in Hone. Although Smith positioned himself as a prophet, seer, and revelator, in the interest of sustainability and ecumenicalism today Mormons may want to settle for preacher, exegete, and creative theologian. Another benefit of the compromise would be an increased LDS appreciation of Christian writings from the "great apostasy."

39. See Christopher C. Jones, "The Complete Record of the Nauvoo Library and Literary Institute," *Mormon Historical Studies* 10, no. 1 (2009): 192, 194–95, 202; discussion: Kenneth W. Godfrey, "A Note on the Nauvoo Library and Literary Institute," *BYU Studies* 14, no. 3 (1974): 386–89; Richard Lloyd Anderson, *Understanding Paul* (Salt Lake City, UT: Deseret Book, 1983), 399–402; D. Michael Quinn, *Early Mormonism and the Magic World View*, rev. ed. (Salt Lake City, UT: Signature, 1998), 188–90, 496–97 note 78.

40. See John Henry Evans, *Joseph Smith, an American Prophet* (New York: Macmillan, 1933), 95–96; Bowman and Brown, "Reverend," 469; Samuel M. Brown, "Early Mormon Adoption Theology and the Mechanics of Salvation," *Journal of Mormon History* 37, no. 2 (2011): 35–36. More connections as well as earlier ones could be made, such as the possible use of Buck in 1832 in Joseph Smith and Sidney Rigdon's vision of the heavenly degrees of glory (D&C 76), and in 1830 in Smith's revelation on eternal punishment (D&C 19); see note 33.

22

# Medieval Bibles

MIRANDA WILCOX

Latter-day Saints believe that Christ's original church fell into a spiritual darkness that persisted until Joseph Smith restored Christ's gospel and priesthood authority on the earth. At the turn of the twentieth century, influential leaders borrowed paradigms and biases from eighteenth- and nineteenth-century Protestant historians to articulate a Latter-day Saint identity distinct from other Christian denominations.[1] One evidence of apostasy that Latter-day Saints focused on during the medieval period was clerical control of scripture. For example, Apostle and church historian Joseph Fielding Smith summed up his perception of restricted access to scriptures during the "Dark Ages" in his *Essentials in Church History* (1922) as follows:

> The few copies of the Bible extant were guarded by the clergy, and the scriptures were not accessible to the common people, and since they could neither read nor write, and in very few instances understood Latin, they would have been helpless even with the Bible in their hands. Under these conditions it is not to be wondered at that the poor people of those benighted countries of Europe, credulous and filled with superstitious fear, were ready to accept almost anything that was made known to them, in doctrine or deed, by unscrupulous priests.[2]

1. Eric Dursteler, "Historical Periodization in the LDS Great Apostasy Narrative," in *Standing Apart: Mormon Historical Consciousness and the Concept of Apostasy,* edited by Miranda Wilcox and John D. Young (New York: Oxford University Press, 2014), 23–54; and Matthew Bowman, "James Talmage, B.H. Roberts, and Confessional History in a Secular Age," in *Standing Apart*, 77–92.

2. Joseph Fielding Smith, *Essentials in Church History* (Salt Lake City, UT: The Church of Jesus Christ of Latter-day Saints, 1922), 15. Compare with B.H. Roberts, *Outlines of Ecclesiastical History*, 3rd ed. (Salt Lake City, UT: Deseret News, 1902), 65–67, and *The Gospel: An Exposition on Its First Principles: and Man's*

Smith cited the popular textbook *An Introduction to the History of Western Europe* (1902) by American Progressive historian James Harvey Robinson and the *Era of the Protestant Revolution* (1874) by English economic historian Frederic Seebohm. These sources promoted the paradigm of the Middle Ages typical in their day, a paradigm Eric Dursteler has identified as "infused with post-Reformation polemics" that judged the Middle Ages "as a period of ignorance (synonymous with illiteracy) and barbarism; these were the 'Dark Ages' awaiting the enlightenment of the Renaissance, the Reformation, and the progressive reforms of the nineteenth century."[3] Smith and other leaders wedded the historical paradigm of the Dark Ages with the Latter-day Saint binary of a Great Apostasy and Restoration to create a powerful narrative of Latter-day Saint self-definition. Though academic historians have challenged and largely rejected previous assumptions about the profound alterity of the medieval Dark Ages, this narrative has been repeated and distilled in Latter-day Saint curricular and evangelical material for over a century.[4]

This essay complicates three assumptions (and generalizations) made in Latter-day Saint discourse about the Bible and its use in the Middle Ages.[5] First, "the Bible," as it is known today, as a standardized text of a canonized set of books published in a single volume was still emerging in the medieval period. Second, technological, social, and linguistic challenges impacted who had access to medieval biblical texts. Third, primary evidence must be examined closely when determining who mediated access to biblical texts. While few generalizations can be made about the approximately thousand-year period in Europe and the Mediterranean typically called the Middle Ages, it is clear that the Bible was central to medieval life. Indeed, the medieval period can be bookmarked between Jerome's completion of his Latin translation of the Bible circa 405 and Gutenberg's first printing of the Bible in 1455. Beryl Smalley, a pioneer in the study of the Bible in the Middle Ages, attests to the ubiquity of the Bible in medieval life: "The Bible was the most studied book of the middle

---

*Relationship with Deity* (Salt Lake City, UT: Deseret News, 1901), 69–71. Compare with James E. Talmage, *The Great Apostasy: Considered in Light of Scriptural and Secular History* (Independence, MO: Press of Zion's Printing, 1909), 102–3.

3. Dursteler, "Historical Periodization," 33; Michael T. Clanchy, *From Memory to Written Record: England 1066–1307*, 3rd ed. (Chichester, UK: Wiley-Blackwell, 2012), 11.

4. Gabrielle M. Spiegel, "In the Mirror's Eye: The Writing of Medieval History in America," in *Imagined Histories: American Historians Interpret the Past*, edited by Anthony Molho and Gordon S. Wood (Princeton, NJ: Princeton University Press, 1998), 238–62; Lee Patterson, "On the Margin: Postmodernism, Ironic History, and Medieval Studies," *Speculum* 65, no. 1 (1990): 87–108, at 92–97.

5. Miranda Wilcox, "Narrating Apostasy and the LDS Quest for Identity," in *Standing Apart*, edited by Wilcox and Young, 93–125, at 111–12.

ages.... Such knowledge was not confined to the specialist: both the language and the content of Scripture permeate medieval thought."[6]

## WHAT WAS "THE BIBLE" IN THE MIDDLE AGES?



English-speaking Latter-day Saints typically conceive of "the Bible" based on their experience using their church's edition of the King James Version of the Bible published in a uniform style and format. Medieval Christians did not expect the same level of standardization in bibles. While they were united in their belief in the sanctity of a holy written corpus, there was significant variation in the physical manifestations of the *sacra biblia* (sacred books) and disagreement about which books should be canonized as scripture.[7] Most medieval biblical manuscripts contained only part of the sacred corpus, because making codices was time intensive and expensive. In addition, each bible was uniquely crafted for use in a community, and its function would determine the size of the manuscript, the layout of the text on the pages, and even the wording and language of the text.

Two biblical manuscripts produced at the twin monasteries of Wearmouth-Jarrow in northeast England in the early eighth century illustrate this variety. Although founded in 674, less than fifty years after the Christianization of the kingdom of Northumbria, Wearmouth-Jarrow became a center of learning and an outstanding scriptorium at the edge of Christendom.

In 716, Abbot Ceolfrith and a group of his monks departed for Rome with a massive bible, now called the Codex Amiatinus, as a gift for St. Peter's Basilica in Rome.[8] Scholars estimate that the monks slaughtered over 515 calves and then stretched and scraped their hides to make enough vellum for a team of scribes to copy the entire Old Testament and New Testament onto the codex's 1,030 folios (2,060 pages) weighing more than seventy-five pounds.[9] Manuscripts containing both the Old and New Testaments in a single volume were called pandects and were rare due to their size and expense. Astoundingly, the Codex Amiatinus was the third of three pandects produced over approximately

6. Beryl Smalley, *The Study of the Bible in the Middle Ages* (South Bend, IN: University of Notre Dame Press, 1998), xxvii.

7. Frans van Liere, *An Introduction to the Medieval Bible* (Cambridge, UK: Cambridge University Press, 2014), 20–52.

8. Florence, Biblioteca Medicea Laurenziana, Amiatino 1. Christopher de Hamel, *Meetings with Remarkable Manuscripts: Twelve Journeys in the Medieval World* (New York: Penguin Random House, 2016), 54–95.

9. de Hamel, *Meetings with Remarkable Manuscripts,* 68, 82.

a quarter of a century at Wearmouth-Jarrow. Not until the rise of universities in the thirteenth century and the development of minuscule scripts and thinner parchment would both testaments regularly be bound together in a single portable volume for students.



Most medieval biblical codices contained only part of the biblical corpus. Biblical books commonly circulated in small groups (as the Pentateuch or the Gospels) or individually (as the Psalter or the Apocalypse). Perhaps a decade after gifting the Codex Amiatinus, the monks of Wearmouth-Jarrow produced a small pocket-sized codex, now called the St Cuthbert Gospel, containing ninety-four folios with the Gospel of John.[10] At some point they gave it to the monastery located about sixty miles north on the island of Lindisfarne. This codex was discovered with an intricate leather-tooled cover in the tomb of St. Cuthbert, a revered early English saint and former bishop of Lindisfarne, after his community fled south from Viking invaders.[11]

Because people encountered biblical texts in multiple volumes, they conceived of them as a *biblioteca scripturarum*, a "library of sacred writings," rather than reified as "the Bible." An illustration at the beginning of the Codex Amiatinus depicts this sacred library. On folio 5r, a haloed scribe sits in front of an open cabinet of books surrounded by bookmaking instruments. The inscription identifies this scribe as the prophet Ezra and refers to the apocryphal legend that Ezra restored and corrected the Hebrew scriptures after they were burned by Chaldeans.[12] In the cupboard behind Ezra lay nine volumes. The inscriptions on their spines identify them as the five books of the Law and the four Gospels; together they signal the harmony of the Old and New Testaments and visually represent one way of organizing the contents of the Codex Amiatinus.[13]

The canon of biblical books was fluid through the medieval period.[14] There were books that definitely revealed the Word of God (e.g., the Pentateuch and Gospels). There were also books that were considered edifying and possibly having sacred origins (e.g., 4 Ezra and Judith), and books whose authorship

10. London, British Library, additional MS 89000.

11. Claire Breary and Bernard Meehan, eds., *The St Cuthbert Gospel: Studies on the Insular Manuscript of the Gospel of John (BL, additional MS 89000)* (London: The British Library, 2015).

12. Scott DeGregorio, trans., *Bede On Ezra and Nehemiah* (Liverpool, UK: Liverpool University Press, 2006), 231; and 4 Ezra 14:22–44.

13. Jennifer O'Reilly, "The Library of Scripture: Views from Vivarium and Wearmouth-Jarrow," in *New Offerings, Ancient Treasures: Studies in Medieval Art for George Henderson*, edited by Paul Binski and William Noel (Stroud, UK: Sutton Publishing, 2001), 3–39, at 8, 14–18.

14. van Liere, *Introduction*, 53–79.

and authority were uncertain (e.g., Gospel of Nicodemus).[15] The order of the biblical books also varied. The seventy-two books in the Codex Amiatinus follow the same order in the New Testament as today's Bible, but the order differs in the Old Testament. The Codex Amiatinus sets out the Old Testament in these categories: Law, History, Wisdom books, Prophets, and Narratives (including the books of Tobit, Judith, Wisdom, Ecclesiasticus, and 1 and 2 Maccabees), while Protestant bibles—used also by Latter-day Saints—put a much smaller group of narrative books after the history books. Not until after the invention of printing would ecclesiastical councils regulate the scriptural canon.[16] In addition, every biblical manuscript contained some textual variation due to scribal errors, which medieval scholars, such as Alcuin and Stephen Harding, periodically attempted to correct.[17]

As the Codex Amiatinus and St Cuthbert Gospel highlight, medieval bibles differ in many ways from modern bibles, and their variety should be acknowledged when characterizing their use in the Middle Ages.

## HOW ACCESSIBLE WERE BIBLES IN THE MIDDLE AGES?

Latter-day Saints often repeat the narrative generated during the Reformation that medieval clergy intentionally restricted access to the Bible.[18] For example, Apostle M. Russell Ballard preached in 2007, "The Dark Ages were dark because the light of the gospel was hidden from the people. They did not have the apostles or prophets, nor did they have access to the Bible. The clergy kept the scriptures secret and unavailable to the people."[19] Overwhelming evidence suggests otherwise. As Christianity expanded beyond the Judeo-Greco-Roman milieu of its origin, missionaries encountered technological, social, and linguistic obstacles in conveying divine revelation transmitted in sacred scripture to new converts. Producing texts was time-consuming and expensive. Many

15. van Liere, *Introduction*, 77–78.

16. van Liere, *Introduction*, 265–68. The Council of Trent declared the Catholic biblical canon in 1546, and the Calvinist *Belgic Confession* determined the Protestant canon in 1561.

17. van Liere, *Introduction*, 80–109; Richard Marsden and E. Ann Matter, eds., *New Cambridge History of the Bible: From 600 to 1450*, vol. 2 (Cambridge, UK: Cambridge University Press, 2012), 69–109.

18. For example, B.H. Roberts, *Outlines of Ecclesiastical History*, 3rd ed. (Salt Lake City, UT: Deseret News, 1902), 65–67, and *The Gospel: An Exposition on Its First Principles: and Man's Relationship with Deity* (Salt Lake City, UT: Deseret News, 1901), 69–71; James E. Talmage, *The Great Apostasy: Considered in Light of Scriptural and Secular History* (Independence, MO: Press of Zion's Printing, 1909), 102–3.

19. M. Russell Ballard, "The Miracle of the Holy Bible," General Conference, April 2007, https://www.churchofjesuschrist.org/study/general-conference/2007/04/the-miracle-of-the-holy-bible?lang=eng.

cultures transmitted knowledge orally rather than textually and had limited need for social institutions devoted to teaching textual skills, such as reading and writing. Communities spoke different languages unrelated to Greek or Latin, the languages bridging peoples across the Mediterranean through late antiquity.



In response to these challenges, the clerical class assumed responsibility and pioneered strategies for preserving, transmitting, and teaching scripture as well as promoting textual literacy. In doing so, they fostered textual communities centered on biblical texts. They established educational institutions that, over time, yielded wider access to sacred texts beyond the ranks of the professed religious. They also translated biblical texts into vernacular languages to make the Word of God accessible to people with limited knowledge of a prestige language: Latin, Greek, and Arabic. These strategies attest to the ecclesiastical impulse to make scripture widely accessible throughout the Middle Ages.

Medieval people understood literacy as a communal practice, while modern people typically measure literacy in terms of individual skill.[20] In the (early) Middle Ages, few individuals had the resources or skills to make or buy a book. Most books were produced by communities for communal use, and certain individuals were delegated the responsibility to transmit the text to the whole community, often via public reading; so not every individual in the community needed to learn how to read and write to learn textual content. Sharing technologies, skills, and knowledge formed textual communities.[21]

Medieval textual communities entwined "faith, language, and literacy" in complementary ways.[22] Early textual communities grew out of monasteries; monasteries focused on preserving and transmitting biblical texts, because laity needed to learn about Christianity and clergy needed to learn how to perform scriptures in liturgical worship. Subsequent clerical schools and universities continued to study biblical texts, systemizing methods for interpreting them and preparing clergy to preach them. Much of the instruction was oral, since bibles, until the late Middle Ages, were generally communal possessions shelved in monastic libraries, chained to church lecterns, or treasured in royal courts. A teacher would read passages from the shared biblical manuscript; students would copy the passages onto wax tablets and memorize them. Teach-

20. Clanchy, *From Memory to Written Word*, 7–16. See also Eliason's chapter in this volume.

21. Brian Stock, *The Implications of Literacy: Written Language and Models of Interpretation in the Eleventh and Twelfth Centuries* (Princeton, NJ: Princeton University Press, 1983), 90–91.

22. Andrey Rosowsky, "Faith Literacies," in *The Routledge Handbook of Literacy Studies*, edited by Jennifer Rowsell and Kate Pahl (London: Routledge, 2015), 180.

ers also trained clerical students to interpret biblical texts. Their exegetical methods resuscitated ancient scriptural texts within contemporary religious contexts by celebrating their multivalency. Early examinations of allegorical and typological senses gradually shifted to privilege the literal sense as Christians encountered Jewish and Arabic scriptural exegesis.[23]



As the cultural capital of textual literacy increased, lay aristocracy and later the bourgeois sought opportunities to function more actively in their textual communities by learning to read and write. Ambitious laity learned a prestige language. Latin was the prestige language of learning, administration, and religion in the medieval West. The title *literatus*, "literate or educated," was reserved for those who demonstrated fluency in Latin, not competency in reading or writing.[24] By 1300 in England, kings and princes might learn Latin at court schools, nobility and baronage from household clerics, gentry and bourgeois at home and at town schools, and peasantry at parish churches.[25]

The Blackburn family illustrates the expansion of textual literacy and domestication of bible reading in the late Middle Ages. The Blackburn family were wealthy merchants living in York in the early fifteenth century.[26] They endowed their parish church All Saints, North Street with stained glass windows in the 1420s that reflect their family's engagement with biblical texts.[27] One window depicts almost life-size figures of St Anne teaching her daughter the Virgin Mary to read a penitential psalm from an open book. Below them, two generations of Blackburn couples kneel in prayer. The older and younger women, both named Margaret, also hold open books with penitential psalms. The image of St Anne and the sequence of penitential psalms in the All Saint's glass link the Blackburn family with a small, richly illustrated book of hours made in the early fifteenth century in York, perhaps at the Dominican priory near the Blackburn home.[28] Books of hours were the laity's devotional manual, containing an abbreviated cycle of daily prayers modeled after the ecclesiastical

23. John Whitman, "The Literal Sense of Christian Scripture: Redefinition and Revolution," in *Interpreting Scriptures in Judaism, Christianity, and Islam*, edited by Mordechai Z. Cohen and Adele Berlin (Cambridge, UK: Cambridge University Press, 2016), 133–58.

24. Rosamund McKitterick, ed., *The Uses of Literacy in Early Medieval Europe* (Cambridge, UK: Cambridge University Press, 1990), 4.

25. Clanchy, *From Memory to Written Word*, 233–54.

26. Nicola McDonald, "A York Primer and its Alphabet: Reading Women in a Lay Household," in *Oxford Handbook of Medieval Literature in English*, edited by Elaine Treharne and Greg Walker (New York: Oxford University Press, 2010), 181–99, at 183.

27. E.A. Gee, "The Painted Glass of All Saints' Church, North Street, York," *Archaeologia or Miscellaneous Tracts Relating to Antiquity* 102 (1969): 151–202.

28. York, Minster Library, add. MS 2.

Divine Office and excerpts from the Latin Gospels and Psalms, including the seven penitential psalms.[29]

Alice Bolton, one of the daughters of Nicholas and Margaret Blackburn senior, owned this book of hours, now known as the Bolton Hours. Scholars argue that it may have been commissioned by or for her mother Margaret.[30] On folio 35v of the Bolton Hours is a full-page illustration of St. Anne teaching the Virgin Mary along with her half-sisters Mary Cleophas and Mary Salome.[31] This unusual configuration of figures may have been designed to represent Margaret Blackburn teaching her three daughters to read.[32] Books of hours functioned as religious and educational primers. Over the course of the Middle Ages, basic reading skills gradually moved out of the cloister and into lay households. Books of hours often included alphabets, for "learning to read was the first step in the formation of a good Christian, and throughout the Middle Ages elementary education, facilitated by the use of the primer, was first and foremost a function of piety."[33] In the Bolton Hours, the alphabet "starts with a crucifix, illuminated with the bloodied body of Christ, and ends with an amen," so even learning the letters of the alphabet generated affective devotion.[34]

The Bolton Hours was not the only book the Blackburn and Bolton families owned; "they had a sizeable collection of books in both Latin and English, including another primer, . . . and a large Latin roll that had an illustrated treatise on the Bible on one side and an exposition on the Lord's prayer on the other."[35] In 1437, Nicolas Blackburn junior was bequeathed an English translation of the scriptures by his uncle.[36] Documentary evidence attest that their family's book ownership was not unusual; other local merchants, gentry, clergy, and aristocrats owned religious and secular books. Their piety and engagement with biblical stories was also typical.

29. McDonald, "York Primer," 181; Eamon Duffy, *Marking the Hours: English People and Their Prayers 1240–1570* (New Haven, CT: Yale University Press, 2006), 3–22.

30. Patricia Cullum and Jeremy Goldberg, "How Margaret Blackburn Taught Her Daughters: Reading Devotional Instruction in a Book of Hours," in *Medieval Women: Texts and Contexts in Late Medieval Britain: Essays for Felicity Riddy*, edited by Jocelyn Wogan-Browne et al. (Turnhout, Belgium: Brepols, 2000), 217–36.

31. Michael Clanchy, "Did Mothers Teach Their Children to Read?" in *Motherhood, Religion, and Society in Medieval Europe, 400–1400: Essays Presented to Henrietta Leyser*, edited by Conrad Leyser and Lesley Smith (Farnham, UK: Ashgate, 2011), 148–49.

32. Clanchy, "Did Mothers?" 144–45.

33. McDonald, "York Primer," 186.

34. McDonald, "York Primer," 187.

35. McDonald, "York Primer," 188.

36. Jo Ann Hoeppner Moran, *The Growth of English Schooling, 1340–1548: Learning, Literacy, and Laicization in Pre-Reformation York Diocese* (Princeton, NJ: Princeton University Press, 1985), 185–220, at 190.

Even though the cultural prestige of Latin conferred special authority to Latin biblical translations, medieval Christians did not forget that they were encountering scripture via translation. The seventh-century encyclopedist, Isidore of Seville, traced the history of translating scripture, beginning with the Greek Septuagint translated by seventy legendary scholars from the Torah for the library in Alexandria as early as the third century BCE and ending with Jerome's Latin Vulgate. In 382, Pope Damasus invited Jerome to make a new Latin translation of the Bible to replace the locally produced translations often collectively called the *Vetus Latina*. Jerome completed this project, partly a revision and partly a new Latin translation from the Greek and Hebrew in 405. Over several centuries, Jerome's version (now called the Vulgate) became the preferred biblical text in Western Christendom. Isidore said that Jerome's "translation is deservedly preferred over the others, for it is closer in its wording, and brighter in the clarity of its thought."[37] The monks at Wearmouth-Jarrow agreed; they believed Jerome's "new translation" to be the superior biblical text even though their model pandect contained a version of the *Vetus Latina*. The Codex Amiatinus is the oldest extant complete Vulgate Bible.

Vernacular biblical translations were an effort to make the word of God more accessible but not supplant the authority of the Latin Vulgate or Greek Septuagint. Wherever Christianity took root, from Iran to the British Isles, vernacular versions of the Bible appeared. Vernacular translations proliferated from the third century in Syriac and thereafter in Coptic, Gothic, Armenian, Ethiopic, Arabic, Georgian, Sogdian, Slavonic, Germanic, English, Scandinavian, and Romance languages.[38] The dissemination of vernacular Bible translations varied according to region and period. The degree to which the vernacular translations attempted to reproduce the Latinate or Greek wording and style varied; some were bilingual interlinear glosses, and others were standalone translations. Richard Marsden explains, "Most of the languages of the modern Christian world that are distinguishable by the end of the medieval period had found their literary feet, and often their alphabetic form, through activities of Christian missionaries and monks."[39] While ecclesiastical leaders occasionally expressed reservations about translating the Bible into vernacular languages and about facilitating public access to scriptures, wholehearted

37. Isidore, *The Etymologies of Isidore of Seville*, trans. by Stephen A. Barney et al. (Cambridge, UK: Cambridge University Press, 2006), 139.

38. Mardsen and Matter, *New Cambridge History*, 110–306.

39. Mardsen and Matter, *New Cambridge History*, 2.

opposition was rare and generally ineffective.[40] These isolated incidents have been overgeneralized and emphasized in Latter-day Saint narratives. Scholars now argue, "The flourishing culture of lay biblical literacy in the vernacular helped created the milieu that made Luther's achievement possible."[41]

When evaluating the accessibility of biblical texts during the Middle Ages, the ecclesiastical impulses to make biblical texts widely available via textual communities, education, and vernacular translations needs to be acknowledged. The complexity of medieval literacy also needs to be addressed.

## WHO MEDIATED ACCESS TO THE BIBLE IN THE MIDDLE AGES?

From the previous discussion, it is clear that clergy played a significant, but not exclusive, role in transmitting, teaching, and preaching biblical texts in the Middle Ages. Did they monopolize control of the Bible for their own ends as typically asserted in Latter-day Saint narratives? Considering the pastoral responsibilities of clergy provides context for their periodic anxiety about regulating access to biblical translations.

Medieval clergy felt a pastoral duty to teach people the Bible, but many wanted to maintain control over how biblical texts were taught and interpreted. For example, Ælfric, a monk at Cerne Abbas at the end of the tenth century, articulated his concerns about "trying to capture the precise sense and form of the Bible in English, and the perils of misinterpretation by untutored readers" in the preface to his Old English translation of the book of Genesis.[42] In his preface, Ælfric cautions Ealdorman Æthelweard, a powerful nobleman who requested the translation, that unlearned readers (religious or lay) may be confused by the apparent simplicity of the "naked narrative" without guidance about how to interpret the spiritual meaning of the Old Testament in light of the New. Ælfric was particularly concerned about the polygamy and incest found in Genesis. Ælfric suggested that preaching was a better alternative than translating for teaching people the Bible: "Priests are established as teachers for lay people. Now it behooved them that they know the old law with spiritual

40. van Liere, *Introduction*, 177–207.

41. Andrew Gow, "Challenging the Protestant Paradigm: Bible Reading in Lay and Urban Contexts of the Later Middle Ages," in *Scripture and Pluralism: Reading the Bible in the Religiously Plural Worlds of the Middle Ages and Renaissance*, edited by Thomas J. Heffernan and Thomas E. Burman (Leiden, Netherlands: Brill, 2005), 161–91.

42. Malcolm Godden, "Ælfric and the Alfredian Precedents," in *A Companion to Ælfric*, edited by Hugh Magennis and Mary Swan (Leiden, Netherlands: Brill, 2009), 139–63, at 144.

understanding, and what Christ himself and his apostles taught in the new testament, so that they could properly guide the people to God's faith and set an example in good works."[43] In spite of Ælfric's anxiety, he was a mere monk in a peripheral monastery "in no position to control or censor what was in circulation," and he produced the most extensive body of English scripture before the fourteenth century.[44]

Some of Ælfric's concerns about unmediated biblical translation were addressed in the thirteenth century when Guyart Desmoulins, a canon in northern France, produced "a good 'beginner's Bible,' well suited for the untrained layperson." [45] His *Bible historiale* [History Bible] included a French translation of the historical books of the Bible augmented with a sanctioned biblical commentary by Peter Comestor. Similar history bibles appeared in Dutch, German, Castilian, Czech, and Old Norse.[46]

Isolated clerical antagonism toward vernacular biblical translations often involved more rhetorical threat than centralized control since there were few mechanisms for enforcing widespread censorship in medieval manuscript culture.[47] For example, the ecclesiastical legislation promulgated in 1409 by Thomas Arundel, archbishop of Canterbury, prohibiting the ownership and use of biblical translations after the time of John Wycliffe has often been interpreted as evidence for widespread censorship of vernacular translations.[48] However, more than 250 copies of Wycliffite Bibles survive, and many were decorated and even commercially produced.[49] Given that "hundreds, if not thousands of Middle English works survive in fewer than ten copies," the impact of Arundel's legislation on the circulation of vernacular Bible translations was limited.[50]

43. My translation of Jonathan Wilcox, ed., Ælfric's *Prefaces* (Durham, UK: Durham Medieval Texts, 1994), 117, lines 36–40.

44. Godden, "Ælfric and the Alfredian Precedents," 145.

45. van Liere, *Introduction*, 195.

46. van Liere, *Introduction*, 195–8; Christopher de Hamel, *The Book: A History of the Bible* (London: Phaidon Press, 2001), 140–65.

47. Kathryn Kerby-Fulton, *Books Under Suspicion: Censorship and Tolerance of Revelatory Writing in Late Medieval England* (Notre Dame, IN: University of Notre Dame, 2006), 15–20, 397–401.

48. See Nicholas Watson, "Censorship and Cultural Change in Late-Medieval England: Vernacular Theology, the Oxford Translation Debate, and Arundel's Constitutions of 1409," *Speculum* 70, no. 4 (1995): 822–64.

49. de Hamel, *The Book*, 166–89; Mary Dove, *The First English Bible: The Text and Context of the Wycliffite Versions* (Cambridge, UK: Cambridge University Press, 2007), 37–67.

50. A.R. Bennett, "What Do the Numbers Mean? The Case for Corpus Studies," in *Manuscript Culture and Medieval Devotional Traditions: Essays in Honour of Michael G. Sargent*, edited by Jennifer N. Brown and Nicole R. Rice (York, UK: York Medieval Press, 2021), 58; Ralph Hanna, "English Biblical Texts Before Lollardy and Their Fate," in *Lollards and Their Influence in Late Medieval England*, edited by Fiona Somerset, Jill C. Havens, and Derrick G. Pitard (Woodbridge, UK: Boydell, 2003), 141–53, at 151.

Many families cherished their English Bibles without fear of censorship as private devotional aids to understand the Latin Bible.[51] Elizabeth Schirmer argues that the Lollard controversy was a struggle between two groups for the authority "to teach a particular model of biblical reading" in English, and that these competing textual programs were "designed to enact opposing models of the church." She concludes that the Lollards and their institutional opponents were thus "equally concerned to contain and control, as well as to educate, lay readers" via direct scripture translation as well as supplementary texts, such as glosses, sermons, narrative paraphrases, and devotional meditations.[52]



As the center of medieval textual communities for a thousand years, biblical texts generated magnificent art. Biblical engagement profoundly transformed medieval culture as Christians narrated and illustrated bible stories in light of their particular circumstances. Mary Carruthers describes how a text can function as the source of communal memory.

The Latin word *textus* comes from the verb meaning "to weave" and it is in the institutionalizing of a story through *memoria* that textualizing occurs. Literary works become institutionalized as they weave a community together by providing it with shared experience and a certain kind of language, the language of stories that can be experienced over and over again through time and as occasion suggests. Their meaning is thought to be implicit, hidden, polysemous, and complex requiring continuous interpretation and adaptation. *Textus* also means "texture," the layers of meaning that attach as a text is woven into and through the historical and institutional fabric of a society.[53]

In this fashion, the Bible wove medieval Christianity together and textured its cultural development.

Bede, a monk at Wearmouth-Jarrow and the greatest biblical scholar of his age, illustrates how biblical imagination interwove medieval textual, visual, and oral culture. In addition to composing dozens of biblical commentaries in Latin, Bede was reported to have been translating the Gospel of John into Old English at his death in 735. He described paintings of scriptural scenes displayed in his monastery's chapels: "Thus all who entered the church, even those who could not read, were able, whichever way they looked, to contemplate the dear face of Christ and His saints, even if only in a picture, . . . and . . .

51. de Hamel, *The Book*, 187; Kerby-Fulton, *Books under Suspicion*, 16.

52. Elizabeth Schirmer, "Canon Wars and Outlier Manuscripts: Gospel Harmony in the Lollard Controversy," *Huntington Library Quarterly* 73, no. 1 (2010): 1–36, at 1–4.

53. Mary Carruthers, *The Book of Memory: A Study of Memory in Medieval Culture* (Cambridge, UK: Cambridge University Press, 1990), 12.

be brought to examine their conscience."[54] Bede also preserved the story of the origin of Old English biblical poetry in his *Ecclesiastical History of the English People.* According to Bede, an illiterate cowherd named Cædmon living at a monastery near Whitby in the late seventh century received the gift of turning Christian scripture into Old English poetry from an angelic visitor. When hearing of this miracle, Hild, the abbess of the monastery invited Cædmon to leave the stables and join the monastic brothers who retold him stories about the Creation, Fall, Exodus, life of Christ, apostles, and Last Judgment to render into poetry.[55] While only one of Cædmon's compositions survives, other Old English epic poems adapted these scriptural episodes in socially familiar and theologically accessible ways.



The Blackburn family of York also illustrates how biblical imagination flourished in medieval communities. As one of the wealthiest merchants in York, Nicholas Blackburn was a prominent member of the Mercers guild. It was from the Mercers' guild church, Holy Trinity Mickelgate, that the pageant wagons embarked at dawn on a twenty-hour procession through the city of York on the feast of Corpus Christi. The wagons "functioned as portable theaters, on which the guilds of the town staged consecutive plays, aiming to depict the entire biblical narrative of creation, fall, and redemption."[56] Each guild was responsible for performing one of the forty-seven plays in the cycle. The public watched the plays performed at twelve designated points along the parade route. Often guilds performed plays associated with their craft; for example, the bakers performed the Last Supper. The Mercers performed the Doomsday play, the final pageant in the cycle enacting the end of the world and Last Judgment. At the climax of this pageant, an actor playing Christ descends and judges those who have and have not performed Works of Mercy:

> When I was hungry, ye me fed;
> To slake my thirst your heart was free . . .
> To least or most when ye it did,
> To me ye did the self and same.[57]

54. Bede, *Lives of the Abbots of Wearmouth and Jarrow,* in *Age of Bede*, trans. by D.H. Farmer (London: Penguin, 1998), 192–93.

55. Bede, *The Ecclesiastical History of the English People,* edited by Judith McClure and Roger Collins (New York: Oxford University Press, 2008), 215–18.

56. van Liere, *Introduction*, 256.

57. Richard Beadle and Pamela M. King, eds., "The Last Judgement," in *York Mystery Plays: A Selection in Modern Spelling* (Oxford, UK: Oxford University Press, 1999), 285–86, 363–64.

Staging the biblical drama of salvation history through the York Mystery Plays provided the city's inhabitants the opportunity to display their piety, to personalize biblical stories, and to enrich their Christian belief.[58]

Throughout the Middle Ages, most people had access to biblical texts by participating in their local textual communities. These communities included people with a range of reading and writing abilities who mediated biblical texts via ecclesiastical transmission and artistic transformation. In many respects, medieval communities were more biblically literate than contemporary communities, communities that might have a higher percentage of members who know how to read but who choose not to read the Bible.

Although this chapter only briefly sketched the complexity of medieval bibles, perhaps it might invite Latter-day Saints to reassess their traditional assumptions about the Middle Ages. Instead of treating the Middle Ages in terms of crude binaries that condemn them "to the role of all-purpose alternative," perhaps Latter-day Saints could look to the Middle Ages as a mirror of self-awareness about their contemporary concerns about scriptural accessibility.[59] Studying medieval biblical manuscripts may engender gratitude for the generations of medieval scribes who devoted their lives to preserve biblical texts for widespread, personal, and inexpensive access today. Studying the tension between prestige and vernacular languages in medieval biblical transmission may prompt Latter-day Saints to think more deeply about the challenges of scriptural access for global membership even as church administration primarily occurs in English. Studying how medieval textual communities wove scripture into their cultural imagination invites parallels with Latter-day Saints' emphasis on making scripture relevant to their own lives and might inspire new ways of personally and communally engaging with scripture. Such methods of studying the Middle Ages would stress continuity rather than otherness.

58. Lynette R. Muir, "Staging the Bible," in *New Cambridge History*, 860–73.

59. Patterson, "On the Margin," 93. I thank Don Chapman and Eowyn McComb for their feedback on this essay.

23

# Reformation and Early Modern Biblical Interpretation

JASON A. KERR

Arguments about how to read the Bible lie near the heart of the Reformation that unfolded in Europe during the sixteenth and seventeenth centuries. Print technology and increasing literacy meant that more people could read the Bible for themselves, which had massive effects on nearly every imaginable sphere of life: religion, politics, social practices, art, literature, popular culture, and more. As access to the text expanded, interpretations proliferated, and the inevitable conflicts that arose out of this teeming complexity provoked questions about how to read the Bible: did proper interpretation require the guidance of the church, or was interpretation a matter of a private encounter between a person, the text, and the Holy Spirit? If the latter, as the English Nonconformist Richard Baxter (1615–1691) put it, "Is the scripture to be tried by the Spirit, or the Spirit by the scripture?"[1] What, to use a term of long duration in Christianity, is the rule of faith?[2]

This essay will focus on Reformation debates about the rule of faith, including as they bear on contemporary questions about translation and canonicity. Latter-day Saints often think about the Reformation as a necessary precursor to the Restoration, the beginning of light breaking (however inadequately) through the "dark ages" of Catholic apostasy—a narrative built largely on nineteenth-century Protestant polemical history.[3] Rather than take sides in the

1. Richard Baxter, *A Christian Directory* (London, 1673), 910.

2. The phrase originates (as *regula fidei*) with Tertullian in the second century. Augustine, borrowing from Romans 12:6, used the term *analogia fidei*. Hence, the rule of faith is sometimes also called the "analogy of faith."

3. This narrative appears in the church's current missionary manual, *Preach My Gospel* (Salt Lake City, UT: Intellectual Reserve, 2004), 34. Apostle D. Todd Christofferson recently invoked the story of William Tyndale in a similar vein: "The Blessing of Scripture," April 2010 General Conference. For context on

debates of the sixteenth and seventeenth centuries, as this narrative implicitly (and often explicitly) did, this essay aims to show the particular influences of these debates on Mormonism, as well as the way that they continue within it. Mormonism, in other words, has not resolved these debates, but continues to participate in them. The Restoration did not supersede the Reformation, whose influence remains very much alive in contemporary Mormonism.



## SCRIPTURE AS RULE OF FAITH

"The BIBLE, I say, The BIBLE only is the Religion of Protestants!" declared the English cleric William Chillingworth in 1638.[4] These words express a commonplace beneath whose surface lies a more complex reality. Many centuries earlier, St. Augustine addressed the question of how to interpret ambiguous passages by appealing to "the rule of faith, as it is perceived through the plainer passages of the scriptures and the authority of the church."[5] "The plainer passages" implies that scripture is a coherent whole with a unified meaning that can be accessed more readily through some nodes on the network than others. Difficult passages (so-called because they seem to conflict with this central meaning) thus need to be reconciled, and the means appears in passages where that meaning is clear. This approach begs the question, though, of which passages are the plain ones and which the difficult—hence Augustine's recourse to the authority of the church.

Protestants collectively challenged the Pope's authority as the final arbiter of scriptural interpretation, but what exactly that rejection entailed for the rule of faith varied. Partly, the argument hinged on when exactly the church had gone wrong, which turned the argument toward one about the church fathers, with the implication that some of them at least conveyed the true apostolic tradition. For instance, Augustine was important for both Luther (who began his career as an Augustinian friar) and Calvin (who quotes only scripture more than Augustine in the *Institutes*). In this sense, although scripture should be the final arbiter ("God's word shall establish articles of belief, and nothing else, not even an angel," wrote Luther), in practice Reformation writers remained open

the place of the Reformation in Mormon apostasy narrative, see the essays in Part One of Miranda Wilcox and John D. Young, eds., *Standing Apart: Mormon Historical Consciousness and the Concept of Apostasy* (New York: Oxford University Press, 2014). Mormonism's complex relationship to Protestantism operates in tandem with its relationship to Americanism; see Armand Mauss, *The Angel and the Beehive: The Mormon Struggle with Assimilation* (Urbana: University of Illinois Press, 1994).

4. William Chillingworth, *The Religion of Protestants* (London, 1638), 375.

5. Augustine, *De Doctrina Christiana,* edited by R.P.H. Green (Oxford, UK: Clarendon, 1995), 133.

to the use of materials that they considered consonant with scripture.[6] In other words, the Reformers departed less from Augustine's rule of faith than appears at first: they were not so much questioning the role of tradition in scriptural interpretation as they were questioning which tradition was authentic.[7] This comfort with appeal to tradition seen as in harmony with scripture appears in William Whitaker's definition of the rule of faith: 

> Now the analogy of faith is nothing else but the constant sense of the general tenour of scripture in those clear passages of scripture, where the meaning labours under no obscurity; such as the articles of faith in the Creed, and the contents of the Lord s Prayer, the Decalogue, and the whole Catechism: for every part of the Catechism may be confirmed by plain passages of scripture. Whatever exposition is repugnant to this analogy must be false.[8]

Determining precisely how the Apostles' Creed accorded with scripture, particularly in its passage about "one holy, catholic, and apostolic church," proved a matter of heated controversy. Even so, Whitaker's definition shows that the Protestant rule of faith depends more on a sense of what is scriptural than on scripture per se.[9]

Baxter's heuristic, quoted previously—asking whether the Word should be tried by the Spirit or the Spirit by the Word—adds an additional dimension to the problem by illuminating the way that private spiritual experience could bear on interpretation, to disruptive effect. Scripture has the advantage of communal acceptance (although the next sections will trouble this assertion): if people may disagree about the interpretation of a particular passage, at least the text provides some foundation for the discussion. But if what matters most is not the text but the Spirit presumed to have inspired it, scripture ceases to afford the stability it otherwise might, as it gives way to the heteronomy of revelation. The emphasis on "inner light" among the Quakers (a group that

6. Martin Luther, *Artickel so da hätten sollen aufs Conciliol zu Mantua* [Smalcald Articles] (Wittenberg, Germany, 1538), fol. C1v.

7. On the relationship between scripture and tradition in Luther, see Mark D. Thompson, *A Sure Ground on Which to Stand: The Relation of Authority and Interpretive Method in Luther's Approach to Scripture* (Carlisle, UK: Paternoster, 2004), 252–65, ch. 6 generally.

8. William Whitaker, *A Disputation of Holy Scripture* (Cambridge, 1849), 472; translating *Disputatio de Sacra Scriptura* (Cambridge, 1588), 353.

9. For a good overview of Reformed theology of scripture in conversation with medieval precedents, see Richard A. Muller, *Holy Scripture: The Cognitive Foundation of Theology*, 2nd ed., vol. 2 of *Post-Reformation Reformed Dogmatics* (Grand Rapids, MI: Baker Academic, 2003).

emerged in England during the 1650s) provides one example of this Spirit-centered practice, and the long persecution they endured attests to the way that scripturally minded people perceived the spiritual approach as a threat.

Mormonism's intervention in these debates about the rule of faith is complex. For Joseph Smith, the "war of words" and "tumult of opinions" that characterized contemporary Protestant scriptural interpretation was enough "to destroy all confidence in settling the question [of which church to join] by an appeal to the Bible."[10] Smith therefore rejected the premise of *sola scriptura* in favor of direct revelation. And yet, the church he founded did not quite follow the Quakers in fully privileging the "inner light" as experienced by individual members: the publication of the Book of Mormon in 1830 and a collection of Smith's revelations in 1835 demonstrate an ongoing commitment to written scripture, albeit with an expanded canon. Furthermore, a September 1830 revelation centralized Smith's role as the channel of new spiritual knowledge: "no one shall be appointed to receive commandments and revelations in this church excepting my servant Joseph Smith, Jun., for he receiveth them even as Moses."[11] Over time, Smith revealed an ecclesiastical structure based on prophets and apostles and grounded in priesthood authority, and this centralized authority determines, among other things, which translations of scripture Latter-day Saints are to use. In this respect, Mormonism partially resembles Catholicism: church leaders are the final arbiters of scriptural interpretation. And yet even this is too neat, for the Book of Mormon concludes, in a passage endlessly repeated by missionaries across the globe, with the invitation for readers to gain their own spiritual witness of its truth, promising that "by the power of the Holy Ghost ye may know the truth of all things."[12] The breadth of this promise points to a tension that ran through the Reformation and remains inherent in Mormonism: if the Spirit remains the ultimate ground of truth, will the Spirit reliably and universally affirm the good-faith positions established by the hierarchy? Even though Smith learned in the Sacred Grove that "all [of the other churches'] creeds were an abomination in [God's] sight," Latter-day Saints still often operate under the assumption that the profession of orthodox belief should exist in perfect harmony with the correct interpretation of scripture and personal spiritual witness, meaning that perceived disjunctions can provoke significant discomfort.

10. Joseph Smith-History 1:10, 12.
11. Doctrine and Covenants 28:2.
12. Moroni 10:3–5.

## HUMANISM AND BIBLICAL TRANSLATION



Given the Bible's centrality to the rule of faith, both Protestant and Catholic, the question remains: which Bible? Although vernacular Bible translation did not begin with the Reformation, the new translations differed from previous efforts in that they worked from the Hebrew and Greek rather than the Latin Vulgate that was the standard Catholic Bible of the time. These linguistic efforts began prior to the Reformation, arising from Renaissance humanism's impulse to trace things back to their originals. In the fifteenth century, the Florentine Giannozzo Manetti translated most of the New Testament from Greek into Latin, in addition to translating the Psalms from Hebrew into Latin (because copies of the Vulgate often included the Psalms as translated from the Greek Septuagint).[13] Also in the fifteenth century, Lorenzo Valla undertook a comparison of the Vulgate New Testament to Greek texts available to him in manuscript.[14] In 1504, the Dutch scholar Erasmus discovered a manuscript of Valla's work and had it printed; this encounter led Erasmus to undertake his own investigations into the Greek text to produce a new Latin translation of the New Testament. In 1516, Erasmus printed the *Novum Instrumentum*, which presented a Greek text of the entire New Testament in print for the first time, with his Latin translation in a parallel column.

Although the impetus for these efforts was to establish the best text of the Bible, the acknowledgment of textual variants that comes with any such editorial process did have some destabilizing influence. One response to this instability was to assert, as did the seventeenth century English divine John Owen, "that the whole Word of God, in every letter and tittle, as given from him by inspiration, is preserved without corruption," while insisting that variation only occurs in "things of less, indeed of no importance."[15] In practice, however, most people came to rely on editions that effectively became standard. Thus, when Martin Luther began translating the Bible into German, he used the 1519 edition of Erasmus's work (which came to be known as the *Textus Receptus*). Luther's New Testament appeared in 1522, and the complete Bible, with the Old

13. Henning Graf Reventlow, *Renaissance, Reformation, Humanism*, vol. 3 of *History of Biblical Interpretation*, trans. by James O. Duke (Atlanta: Society of Biblical Literature, 2010), 5–11.

14. John Monfasani, "Criticism of Biblical Humanists in Quattrocento Italy," in *Biblical Humanism and Scholasticism in the Age of Erasmus*, edited by Erika Rummel (Leiden, Netherlands: Brill, 2008), 21.

15. John Owen, *On the Divine Originall . . . of the Scriptures* (Oxford, UK, 1659), 14. Notably, the earliest manuscripts of the Hebrew scriptures do not use vowel points ("tittles").

Testament translated from Hebrew, appeared in 1534.[16] In Zurich, Huldrych Zwingli's use of Erasmus's work in his preaching, in addition to contact with Luther's ideas, provoked his own efforts at Reformation, as well as a translation of the Bible into Swiss German. Building on Erasmus's work, the French scholar Robert Estienne published in 1550 the first Greek New Testament to feature textual apparatus identifying the manuscripts used; his 1551 edition introduced the chapter and verse divisions still used in most modern Bibles. In 1579, Franciscus Junius and Immanuel Tremellius produced an influential Latin translation of the Old Testament from the Hebrew. Together with Theodore Beza's Latin/Greek New Testament, their work proved popular with scholars and divines writing in Latin for Continental audiences. Even though not all of the scholars participating in these editing and translation projects were Protestant, the Catholic Church asserted the authority of the Vulgate at the Council of Trent, and it issued new editions in 1590 and 1592.

The flurry of biblical translation in the sixteenth and seventeenth centuries has direct relevance for Latter-day Saints, because the official church Bibles in English, Spanish, and Portuguese derive from translations done in this period. The first official Bible published by the LDS Church was an edition of the King James Version in 1979. This translation, first published in 1611, emerged primarily in response to the Geneva Bible of 1560, which was the product of English Protestant exiles living in Calvin's Geneva during the reign of the Catholic Mary I. The Geneva Bible, unlike the official Great Bible (1539) that preceded it and the Bishop's Bible (1568) that soon followed it, included extensive interpretative notes.[17] King James found some of the notes doctrinally or politically distasteful: for instance, when Samuel is displeased at Israel's desire for a king in 1 Samuel 8:6, the note explains that this is, "Because they were not content with the order that God had appointed, but would be governed as were the Gentiles." Accordingly, the new translation was to have no notes except for explanations of the Hebrew or Greek, and it would take a conservative approach to the language itself, as with the decision to use "charity" (a Catholic reading, rooted in the Latin Vulgate's *caritas,* but also used in the Bishops' Bible) in 1 Corinthians 13 instead of "love" (Tyndale's reading, also used in the Great Bible).

As discussed in Wayment's essay in this volume, the LDS Church uses the King James Version for several reasons. Restoration scripture echoes the

16. Stephen Füssel, *The Luther Bible of 1534: A Cultural-Historical Introduction* (Cologne, Germany: Taschen, 2003), 36, 41.

17. For a larger treatment of English Bible translations, see David Daniell, *The Bible in English* (New Haven, CT: Yale University Press, 2003).

language of the KJV, with the effect of creating a "sacred language" distinct from ordinary speech. Thus, familiarity with the idiom of the KJV aids understanding of Restoration scripture.[18] But the ongoing politics of biblical translation also have their hand in the decision.[19] In 1956, J. Reuben Clark, then of the First Presidency, published *Why the King James Version.* His book aligned itself with (and expressly drew on) conservative Protestant concerns about the Revised Standard Version, an attempt to update the KJV in light of modern biblical scholarship. Clark and his Protestant allies felt that the new translation undermined traditional Christian belief in such matters as the Messiahship of Jesus, Christ's eternal Godhood, and the perpetual virginity of Mary.[20] His book, reinforced by the LDS edition of the Bible in 1979 and a statement from the First Presidency in 1992, cemented the KJV's status as Mormonism's official English Bible for the foreseeable future.[21]

Official LDS Bibles in Spanish and Portuguese also have their origins in the Reformation period. In 1569, Casiodoro de Reina published a translation of the Bible into Spanish from Hebrew and Greek, consulting earlier translations, like Francisco de Enzinas's 1543 New Testament. Cipriano de Valera published a revised version of Reina's "Biblia del Oso" ("Bible of the Bear," after the picture on its title page) in 1602. As Protestants hailing from an overwhelmingly Catholic country, both Reina and Valera spent much of their lives in exile, Reina in Frankfurt and Valera in Cambridge. In 2009, the LDS Church issued a Spanish Bible featuring an updated version of the 1909 Reina-Valera text.[22] Similarly, in 2015 the church issued a Portuguese Bible based on the seventeenth century Protestant translation of João Ferreira Annes d'Almeida.[23] The choice to use these translations seems to involve the intersection of tradition and copyright

18. On the complicated relationship between archaic language in the Book of Mormon and the KJV, see Roger Terry, "What Shall We Do with *Thou*? Modern Mormonism's Unruly Usage of Archaic English Pronouns," *Dialogue: A Journal of Mormon Thought* 47, no. 2 (2014): 1–35; and Roger Terry, "Archaic Pronouns and Verbs in the Book of Mormon: What Inconsistent Usage Tells Us about Translation Theories," *Dialogue: A Journal of Mormon Thought* 47, no. 3 (2014): 53–84.

19. For more on the KJV and modern translations, see Thomas A. Wayment, "The KJV and Modern Translation of the Bible," in this volume, as well as Philip Barlow, *Mormons and the Bible: The Place of the Latter-day Saints in American Religion,* rev. ed. (Oxford, UK: Oxford University Press, 2013), ch. 6.

20. J. Reuben Clark Jr., *Why the King James Version.* (Salt Lake City, UT: Deseret Book, 1956), 315–18.

21. On the KJV's transition from Mormonism's "common" to its "official" Bible, see Barlow, *Mormons and the Bible,* ch. 5. "First Presidency Statement on the King James Version of the Bible," *Ensign,* August 1992, available at https://www.lds.org/ensign/1992/08/news-of-the-church/first-presidency-statement-on-the-king-james-version-of-the-bible.

22. Joshua M. Sears, "Santa Biblia: The Latter-day Saint Bible in Spanish," *BYU Studies Quarterly* 54, no. 1 (2015): 42–75.

23. "LDS Edition of Bible in Portuguese," *Ensign,* November 2015, available at https://www.lds.org/ensign/2015/11/news-of-the-church/lds-edition-of-bible-in-portuguese.

availability.[24] Consequently, a vast majority of Latter-day Saints encounter the Bible in versions that grew out of advances in biblical scholarship during the Reformation period but have less exposure to the significant changes that have happened in subsequent centuries. Nowhere is the influence of the Reformation on Mormonism clearer than in the translations that a majority of members use to read the Bible.



## CANON WARS

Debates about the Rule of Faith turned on what constituted the authentic Christian tradition, so it was almost inevitable that these debates should take up the scriptural canon itself. Because Mormonism proceeds fundamentally from the idea that the canon needed to open to include modern scripture—the Book of Mormon, the Doctrine and Covenants, and the Pearl of Great Price—it has paid fairly little attention to the questions of canon that vexed the sixteenth and seventeenth centuries.[25]

Reformation debates about canon had roots in earlier problems. With regard to the Old Testament, the question of canon was complicated by divergences between the Greek Septuagint text (probably completed in the second century BCE) and the Hebrew Masoretic Text (standardized in the second half of the first millennium CE). New Testament writers often quote from the Septuagint, but occasionally quote passages only found in Hebrew sources. In the fourth century CE, Augustine argued successfully at the Council of Carthage that the Septuagint should be canonical for Christians, but his contemporary Jerome preferred Hebrew sources and used them as the basis for his influential Latin Vulgate translation, which nevertheless included Greek texts from the Septuagint, marking them as deuterocanonical.[26] Confusingly, some copies of the Vulgate had the Psalms translated from Greek and others had them translated from Hebrew, which numbers them differently. Broad acceptance of the Vulgate left the status of the Apocrypha (those Greek texts without Hebrew counterparts) unresolved. Similarly, New Testament canonization unfolded messily over the course of several centuries, with texts still in dispute (James,

24. Sears, "Santa Biblia," 46.

25. The exception is a revelation to Joseph Smith (D&C 91) relieving him of the need to include the Apocrypha in his new translation of the Bible.

26. Augustine, *De Doctrina Christiana,* 68–71.

Jude, 2 Peter, 2–3 John, Hebrews, Revelation) called *Antilegomena*. Revelation was the last book to be universally accepted into the canon.[27]

The Reformation reopened these debates to a certain extent. Luther's translation of the Bible included prefaces to the individual books, and some of these take up the question of canon. The prefaces to the apocryphal books find Luther often skeptical about the authenticity of the materials, which he evaluates by comparison with more securely canonical writings: of Baruch, for instance, he writes that "the book's chronology does not agree with the [accepted] histories. Thus I very nearly let it go with the third and fourth books of Esdras, books which we did not wish to translate into German because they contain nothing that one could not find better in Aesop or in still slighter works."[28] Other books, like Judith and Tobit, he finds historically suspect but devotionally useful. With the New Testament, Luther found much good in the Epistle of James, but rejected it as apostolic because its author "wanted to guard against those who relied on faith without works, but was unequal to the task."[29] He worried about the origins of Jude. Of Revelation, he wrote, "My spirit cannot accommodate itself to this book. For me this is reason enough not to think highly of it: Christ is neither taught nor known in it."[30] In this way, Luther invited others to question the authenticity of scripture itself.



The Catholic Council of Trent pushed back in 1546, listing the previously deuterocanonical books as canonical. Whereas both Luther and Calvin argued that the authority of scripture did not depend on any human witness, including that of the church, but instead depended solely on the witness of the Spirit, Cardinal Bellarmine argued that the question of canon—what counts as scripture—depended inescapably on the church, as manifest in the ancient Council of Carthage and the recent Council of Trent, because scripture itself does not address the issue, even though individual books witness to their own origins from the Spirit.[31] Thomas Hobbes takes up a version of this argument in his *Leviathan* (1651), where he assigns the authority for determining canon to civil sovereigns before mounting an assault on the ability of scripture itself

27. For the larger history, see F. F. Bruce, *The Canon of Scripture* (Downers Grove, IL: Intervarsity, 1988), and Bruce Metzger, *The Canon of the New Testament* (New York: Oxford University Press, 1987).

28. E. Theodore Bachman, ed., *Word and Sacrament I*, vol. 35 in *Luther's Works* (Philadelphia: Muhlenberg, 1960), 349–50.

29. Bachman, *Word and Sacrament I*, 397.

30. Bachman, *Word and Sacrament I*, 399. This quotes his 1522 preface; his 1530 preface took a more favorable view.

31. See, for example, John Calvin, *Institutio Christianae Religionis* (Geneva, 1559), 14 (I.vii.1). Roberto Bellarmino, *Disputationum Roberti Bellarmini . . . de Controversiis Christianae Fidei*, vol. 1 (Ingolstadt, 1601), 1–7, 12–13. This book is paginated by column.

to resolve the question, arguing from internal evidence that Moses could not have written the Pentateuch, nor Joshua the book that bears his name. Two decades later, Benedict de Spinoza carried these arguments further in his *Tractatus Theologico-Politicus* (1670), with the end of wresting the Word of God ("the divine mind as revealed to the prophets") free from "a certain number of books" that inevitably adapted the Word to their time and circumstances.[32] In effect, Spinoza was arguing that biblical texts needed to be read as historical artifacts, not authoritative documents. Another important early advocate of the historical method was the Catholic Oratorian Priest Richard Simon, who published his *Histoire Critique du Vieux Testament* in 1678. These works helped to inaugurate modern historical biblical criticism.

Mormonism complexly takes several sides in these controversies about canon, siding with Protestants over the Apocrypha and with Catholics by putting questions of canon under church control (albeit to an effect that would suit neither Protestants nor Catholics). For better or worse, Mormonism's reliance on translations from the Reformation period, combined with a relative lack of interest in the question of the biblical canon, has insulated the tradition from the shock waves that biblical scholarship sent through much of the Christian world in the nineteenth and twentieth centuries.[33]

## PREACHING AND THE WORD

Mormonism departs from Reformation approaches to the rule of faith in one major way: preaching. In 1519, Erasmus famously changed the Latin translation of the Greek *logos* in John 1:1 from *verbum* to *sermo,* shifting the emphasis from a static Word to a lively speaking. Some churches that emerged from the Reformation (e.g., Lutherans, Anglicans, some Methodists) continue to follow a lectionary, reading out passages of scripture as part of the worship service, augmenting these readings with a sermon based on them, while others (typically more evangelically minded, like Baptists) abandoned the lectionary altogether in favor of preaching. Such preaching aims to carry the biblical message into the hearts of its hearers and, accordingly, typically takes its theme from a given passage, either from the lectionary or selected for the occasion. Accordingly, sermons generally build on a foundation of biblical exegesis, the implications of which may subsequently be applied to the particular circumstances of the congregation.

32. Benedict de Spinoza, *Tractatus Theologico-Politicus* (Hamburg, Germany, 1670), fol. *5v. Spinoza, *Complete Works,* trans. by Samuel Shirley (Indianapolis, IN: Hackett, 2002), 392.

33. See Jason Combs, "Historical Criticism and Latter-day Saints," in this volume.

The practical need for ministers to perform such exegesis produced a brisk trade in biblical commentaries. Luther's 1535 *Commentary on Galatians* is widely acknowledged (including by Luther himself) as one of his most important theological works. After an introductory summary of Paul's argument in the epistle as Luther sees it, the commentary proceeds through the epistle phrase by phrase, following each phrase with commentary that often runs to several pages.[34] Thus, Luther's commentary on an epistle that filled seven pages in his 1522 New Testament occupies over seven hundred (admittedly smaller) pages in the 1538 edition. As might be expected, the comments range widely. With regard to the epistle's first phrase—"Paul the Apostle, neither by humans nor through human [authority], but through Jesus Christ and God the Father, who raised him from the dead"—the commentary addresses the way that it summarizes the theological argument of the epistle by showing the primacy of divine over human works, thus thwarting the doctrine promulgated by Satan and false teachers in his control. It goes on to discuss at length the topic of vocation, both Paul's own calling as an apostle and the way that calling in general serves to glorify God rather than the humans called. Luther then uses these doctrines to inveigh against "false teachers" and "fanatics" who claim mistakenly to be followers of the apostolic way. He discusses the vocations of princes and magistrates before taking up the question of gospel ministry.[35] All this—more than ten pages of commentary—from what appears in modern Bibles as one verse!



Luther's example shows that commentary is never neutral, but always controversial, in conversation with other interpreters. Unsurprisingly, commentaries proliferated, with John Calvin, the major exponent of the Reformed alternative to Lutheran Protestantism, contributing voluminously to the genre, as did many others. Because commentary goes beyond simply explaining the meaning of the text to considering its theological and cultural ramifications—Luther referred to commentary on Galatians as *ennarratio*, which "takes the theology out of the text and applies it in public"—commentaries feed naturally into the work of writing sermons.[36]

34. Luther's practice had a complex relationship to its medieval precedents; see Erik Herrmann, "Luther's Absorption of Medieval Biblical Interpretation and His Use of the Church Fathers," in *The Oxford Handbook of Martin Luther's Theology*, edited by Robert Kolb, Irene Dingel, and Ľubomir Batka (New York: Oxford University Press, 2016), ch. 5.

35. Martin Luther, *In Epistolam S. Pavli ad Galatas Commentarius ex Praelectione D. Mart. Luth. Collectus* (Wittenberg, Germany: 1538), fol. B2v–C3v, my trans.

36. Kenneth Hagen, *Luther's Approach to Scripture* (Tübingen, Germany: Mohr Siebeck, 1993), 50.

Mormon commentaries on scripture certainly exist, but they are generally geared either to personal study or preparation for teaching Sunday School.[37] Even in that latter case, the name of the adult Sunday School course—"Gospel Doctrine"—indicates a privileging of topical dogmatics over exegesis (an approach that also has Reformation precedent, beginning with Phillipp Melanchthon's 1521 *Loci Communes Theologici*). The aim is for scripture to support and illuminate doctrinal teaching, and, in case of conflict, doctrine wins. Similarly, modern Mormon preaching tends to be topical, rather than scriptural, and only rarely do Mormon sermons engage in extended scriptural exegesis. In part, this difference owes to Mormonism's tradition of lay preaching. Professional clergy might reasonably be expected to amass a collection of commentaries, theological texts, and works of biblical scholarship over the course of their seminary education and subsequent careers. In the Reformation period universities were still primarily training grounds for future clergymen, and although the results of such training were variable as ever, universities produced a vast output of learned writing on scripture, along with a group of people eager to read it, digest it, and convey it to parishioners.[38] These structures do not exist in Mormonism in the same way, and accordingly, even the church's highest leaders (who are professional clergy, even though they have come up through the ranks as laypersons) tend to preach thematically on doctrinal subjects, engaging in scriptural interpretation as it proves useful (and occasionally citing commentaries in the process). Lay members, after all, by definition have secular vocations that tend not to require sustained scriptural study.

Mormonism's rule of faith thus seems, again, to privilege the hierarchical structure of the church, what Latter-day Saints call priesthood authority. Even though much of Mormonism's scriptural inheritance owes to the Reformation, in this respect it partially resembles Catholicism, as noted previously. Far from being an abstract theological point, this difference is manifest in weekly worship through the manner of preaching and instruction. Thus, even as Mormonism continues to participate in debates fomented by the Reformation, these engagements tend to happen in tacit and generally unrecognized ways.

37. Examples include David J. Ridges's Made Easier series (Springville, UT: Cedar Fort, 2011) and James Faulconer's Made Harder series (Proto, UT: Neal A. Maxwell Institute for Religious Study, 2014). BYU Studies is also in the process of publishing a New Testament commentary series, which has thus far received mixed reviews.

38. If any evidence is needed that this ideal was too rarely met, even as it was earnestly desired, see Richard Baxter, *Gildas Salvianus: The Reformed Pastor* (London, 1656). Abridged versions of this work are still in print.

PART V

# Latter-day Saint Approaches to the Bible's Major Genres and Divisions

24

# The Pentateuch

DAVID BOKOVOY

The Christian Old Testament begins with a collection of five books that establishes the religious and literary foundation for the entire Hebrew Bible—the books of Genesis, Exodus, Leviticus, Numbers, and Deuteronomy. Known in Greek as the Pentateuch or *pentáteuchos*, meaning "five books," the collection is traditionally referred to in Judaism as the Torah or the "Law." The Pentateuch holds a meaningful place of prominence in Mormonism and its scriptures. Latter-day Saints view the Pentateuch as an inspired collection, and the books (especially Genesis) appear cited and reformulated in Restoration scripture, including the Book of Mormon, the Book of Moses, the Book of Abraham, and Joseph Smith's Inspired Translation of the Bible.

While in terms of quantity of words, most of the Pentateuch is comprised of narrative, some scholars see the literal and figurative climax of the story as the legal material given on Sinai, the majority of its substance presents a single continuous narrative. The story commences with a depiction of creation and then moves through the adventures of Israel's ancestors, to an account of the Israelite exodus out of Egypt, and eventually concludes with the death of Moses outside the promised land of Canaan. Hence, as a collection, the Pentateuch features six major thematic sections:[1]

| | | |
|---|---|---|
| 1. | The Primeval History | Genesis 1–11 |
| 2. | The Patriarchs | Genesis 12–50 |
| 3. | The Liberation from Egypt | Exodus 1:1–15:21 |
| | (interim: 15:22–16:36) | |



1. Richard Elliot Freedman, "Torah (Pentateuch)," *AB* VI 605.

| | |
|---|---|
| 4. The Stay at Sinai/Horeb | Exodus 17–40; Leviticus |
| 5. The Journey | Numbers |
| 6. Moses' Farewell | Deuteronomy |



Though the Pentateuch features a unified chronological narrative, the collection itself draws on assorted historical material, redacted into its present form by Judean editors. In contrast to modern forms of editing, which attempt to create a unified consistent authorial perspective, the redaction of the Pentateuch did not create a singular viewpoint. Instead, the editing process preserved a variety of distinct perspectives and contradictory traditions found in each of the books. Contemporary scholars recognize that the first proto-Pentateuchal narrative telling the story from creation to Moses dates to the exilic period at the earliest.[2]

These six narrative turning points are spread unevenly through each of the five books in their present form. The first book of the Pentateuch, Genesis, receives its English name from the Greek translation of the Hebrew word *toledot* that appears thirteen times in Genesis (2:4; 5:1; 6:9; 10:1,32; 11:10,27; 25:12,13,19; 36:1,9; 37:2). *Toledot* is typically translated as "generations" in the King James Version of the Bible used by Latter-day Saints. In Hebrew, Genesis is known as *Bereshit*, a term that derives from the book's opening word, "In the beginning." The title is an appropriate one. Genesis depicts the beginning of the world, the beginning of the first humans, and then focuses its attention on the origin stories of Jacob/Israel's ancestors.

The second book in the Pentateuch, the book of Exodus, continues the narrative of Genesis by depicting the prosperity of Israel's family in Egypt. Exodus depicts how that success led to Egyptian persecution and extermination attempts. The name "Exodus" stems from the Greek title given the book in the Septuagint, *Exodos Aigyptou*, "Departure from Egypt." In Hebrew, Exodus is known as *Shemot*, meaning "Names," a reference to the second Hebrew word featured in the account. Exodus contains legal compositions of Israelite laws and concludes with an account of the construction of the tabernacle, a portable shrine that the Israelites reportedly carried with them in their desert wanderings toward the Promised Land.

The third book of the Pentateuch is the book of Leviticus. Its English name stems from the Latin *Leviticus*, which in turn derives from the Greek, *Leuitikon*, referring to "Levi," the priestly tribe of the Israelites. The name, however,

2. David Carr, *The Formation of the Hebrew Bible* (New York: Oxford University Press, 2011), 359.

is somewhat of a misnomer, since the book itself is not about the Levites who are mentioned only in 25:32–33. The Hebrew name of the text is *(wa)yyiqra*, meaning "(and) he [the LORD] called." Leviticus consists of holiness and ritual instructions given by God to Moses and his brother Aaron. In terms of its narrative, Leviticus constitutes a portion of a lengthy account that extends from Exodus 25 to Numbers 10 sometimes called, "When the Tabernacle Stood at Sinai."[3]

The fourth book in the Pentateuch, the book of Numbers, follows Leviticus. The English name derives from the Greek Septuagint, which titled the work after the censuses presented in the book's first four chapters. The Hebrew title stems from the fifth word in the book, *Bemidbar*, meaning "in the wilderness [of Sinai]. Numbers recounts the Israelite desert wanderings from Sinai to the plains of Moab. It therefore resumes the story beginning in Exodus and continued in the book of Leviticus.

The final book of the Pentateuch is the book of Deuteronomy. The English name is again based on the Greek name meaning "Second Law." The title reflects the view that Deuteronomy presents a retelling of the earlier laws given by God to Moses presented in the previous books. In Hebrew, Deuteronomy is known as *Devarim*, meaning "Words," a term that derives from the second word in the book. The account begins where Numbers concludes with the Israelite community on the plains of Moab ready to enter the Promised Land. Deuteronomy, therefore, presents the climax to the story commencing in Genesis where God promises the land of Canaan to the Israelites through their ancestral patriarch Abraham.

The lengthy continuous narrative featured in these five books is the reason they have traditionally been seen as a collection. The Pentateuch's major themes include the early development of Israel as a people, the covenant between God and the community, and the promise of sacred land. None of these themes, however, are attested throughout every segment of the Pentateuch, and they all continue into the Bible's subsequent books, including the book of Joshua, which depicts a fulfillment of the Pentateuchal promises. This fact has led some scholars to speak of a Hexateuch collection that includes Joshua rather than a Pentateuch ending at Deuteronomy, or even the Enneateuch up through 2 Kings (minus Ruth).[4]

3. Adele Berlin and Marc Zvi Brettler, *Jewish Study Bible* (New York: Oxford University Press, 2004), 203.

4. This issue is addressed in Thomas B. Dozeman et al., eds., *Pentatuech, Hexateuch, or Enneatuch: Identifying Literary Works in Genesis through Kings* (Atlanta: Society of Biblical Literature, 2011); see also

## MESOPOTAMIAN CONTEXT

The disparate Judean sources that appear in the Pentateuch exhibit a strong Mesopotamian influence. Historically, the rise of the Assyrian empire led to the development of scribalization in the ancient Near East, and this movement greatly affected the Southern kingdom of Judah.[5] The Assyrians used writing to record detailed information as a political tool to govern conquered territories. In addition to scribalization and the increased development of written texts, the Assyrian empire had another significant impact on Judea and the eventual creation of the Pentateuch: the rise of the Assyrian empire transformed the political landscape of the ancient world by creating urbanization (meaning the physical growth of urban population centers).[6] This process can be seen in terms of the Judean King Hezekiah, whom the Bible presents as responsible for several government building projects, including fortifications (the broad wall of Jerusalem), water projects (his famous tunnel), and even a new government center (Ramat Rahel). Urbanization served as a means for the development of even greater scribal skills in ancient cities such as Jerusalem. All this provided an important context for the creation of the Pentateuchal material. From a historical perspective, rather than Moses, Israelite scribes trained and influenced by their Assyrian conquerors were the authors who produced the written sources that appear in the Pentateuch.

In terms of the creation story of the Pentateuch, it is difficult to overstate the significance of Mesopotamian influence on the material. The first few chapters of Genesis provide a clear "breadcrumb-like" trail documenting this imprint. The story of creation in Genesis 1 reads somewhat like a traditional Mesopotamian creation narrative, similar to the classic Babylonian epic Enūma Elish.[7] The story of Eden shares many motifs in common with the famous

Thomas Römer and Marc Zvi Brettler, "Deuteronomy 34 and the Case for a Persian Hexateuch," *Journal of Biblical Literature* 119 (2000), 401–19, and Baruch J. Schwartz, "The Pentateuchal Sources and the Former Prophets—A Neo-Documentarian's Perspective," in *The Formation of the Pentateuch: Bridging the Academic Cultures of Europe, Israel, and North America,* edited by Jan C. Gertz, Bernard M. Levinson, Dalit Rom-Shiloni, and Konrad Schmid (Tübingen, Germany: Mohr Siebeck, 2016), 783–94; Cynthia EdenBurg, "Do the Pentateuchal Sources Extend into the Former Prophets?—Joshua 1 and the Relation of the Former Prophets to the Pentateuch," 795–812; Thomas Römer, "The Problem of the Hexateuch," 813–30.

5. See David P. Wright, "The Covenant Code Appendix (Exodus 23:20–33, Neo-Assyrian Sources, and Implications for Pentateuchal Study," *The Formation of the Pentateuch*, 47–86.

6. Michael L. Satlow, *How the Bible Became Holy* (New Haven, CT: Yale University Press, 2014), 33–119.

7. For a recent analysis of conceptual parallelisms between Enūma Elish and a variety of biblical texts, including Job, Psalms, and Genesis 1, see Luciano Zanovello, "Enuma Elish e Bibbia Ebraica, *BibOr* 48 (2006): 205–22; for an argument for direct dependence, see Victor Hurowitz, "The Genesis of Genesis: Is the Creation Story Babylonian?" *BR* 21 (2005): 36–48.

Mesopotamian *Epic of Gilgamesh*, including references to sexuality as a type of pathway to becoming human and a serpent that robs a person of a plant that would provide everlasting life.[8] According to the Genesis account, the garden itself was located to the land "east" of Israel, and the Pentateuch specifically identifies Eden as a land connected with the Tigris and Euphrates rivers in Mesopotamia (Gen. 2:14). Genesis then features an amalgamated flood narrative that borrows heavily from a traditional Mesopotamian flood story. Before the Pentateuchal narrative enters into what its authors would have considered the "historical" era, readers encounter the story of Babel, an account concerning the construction of a Mesopotamian ziggurat that directly critiques Babylonian culture and religion.

The literary pattern in the Pentateuch, with creation accounts followed by individual stories that depict a mythic time period before the great flood, reflects the structure found in one of the Sumerian King Lists.[9] In addition to the basic structure, a specific connection appears to exist between Genesis 5 and the King List. Beginning with Adam, Genesis 5 features a list of ten patriarchs that bridges the gap between creation and the flood. The ages attributed to all of these men are unusually high. Cainan, for example, lives 910 years (v. 14), Mahalaleel 893 (v. 16), Jared 962 (v. 20), and Methuselah 969 (v. 27). In the Bible, the flood, therefore, signifies the transition into the historical era. From that point, biblical narratives no longer present "mythic" type stories about the past. Instead, Genesis depicts human ages as much more reflective of a natural lifespan. This pattern is derivative. In the Sumerian King List, the Sumerian king Alulim is claimed to have ruled for 28,800 years, Alaingar for 36,000, En-men-lu-ana for 43,200, En-men-gal-ana for 28,800 years, etc. The lengthy lifespans that humans enjoyed in both the Sumerian King List and in Genesis reflects a common perspective of a type of idyllic age in the distant past followed by successive generations of increasingly worse and worse eras. This same theme is then adopted in the genealogy list that appears in Genesis 5. Noah is described as having lived 950 years (Gen. 9:29). Then, after Noah and the flood, the number of years quickly becomes more reflective of the actual human condition.

8. For a basic introduction to these parallels, see Alexander Heidel, *The Gilgamesh Epic and Old Testament Parallels* (Chicago: University of Chicago Press, 1963); Harold Victor Matthews and Don C. Benjamin, *Old Testament Parallels: Laws and Stories from the Ancient Near East* (Mahwah, NJ: Paulist Press, 2007), 21–32.

9. See John A. Walton, *Ancient Israelite Literature in Its Cultural Context* (Grand Rapids, MI: Zondervan, 1994).

Following these introductory chapters of prehistory, the Pentateuch transitions to the "historical" era where readers witness a type of reversal of the Babylonian exile of the Jewish community, as Abraham, the great biblical patriarch, leaves the city-state of Ur in southern Mesopotamia and enters the promised land of Canaan.[10] The connections between the Pentateuch and Mesopotamian sources continue in the Bible's legal material. The so-called Covenant Code in Exodus 20–23 has been shown to have been directly influenced by the Babylonian Laws of Hammurabi, the oldest complete law collection in the world dating from approximately 1772 BCE.[11] Moreover, the final book of the Pentateuch, the book of Deuteronomy, has been directly influenced by Assyrian Vassal treaties.[12] The authors of these biblical accounts thematically replaced Israel's God for the Mesopotamian kings attested in these sources.

Even the Pentateuchal story of Moses draws on Mesopotamian traditions concerning the great King Sargon of Akkad, who created the first world empire in the Near East around 2300 BCE. The beginnings of Moses's life are recounted in Exodus 1:22–2:10, where Moses has a secret birth to a Levite (and therefore priestly) mother (2:1–2), his life is saved by placing him in the Nile River in a reed basket sealed with pitch (v. 3), and he is found and adopted by the daughter of Pharaoh and raised as her son (vv. 5–10). The Mesopotamian legend of Sargon is similar. Sargon was the founder of the Dynasty of Akkad (also translated as Agade), which appears listed in the biblical "Table of Nations" in Genesis 10 and is connected with Nimrod, the mighty hunter (whose name

10. Because of a desire to connect Ur with Egyptian influences suggested in the Book of Abraham, some LDS scholars have tried to argue for a Northern location for Ur, but these problematic arguments have failed to impact the mainstream consensus locating Abraham's Ur in southern Mesopotamia; see for example, Paul Y. Hoskisson, "Where Was Ur of the Chaldees?," *The Pearl of Great Price: Revelations from God*, edited by H. Donl Peterson and Charles D. Tate Jr. (Provo, UT: Religious Studies Center, 1989), 119–36; John Gee and Stephen D. Ricks, "Historical Plausibility: The Historicity of the Book of Abraham as a Case Study," *Historicity and the Latter-day Saint Scriptures*, edited by Paul Y. Hoskisson (Provo, UT: Religious Studies Center, 2001), 69–72. The following statement by Jean-Cl. Margueron regarding Ur in the *Anchor Bible Dictionary* illustrates the general academic view: "A very important Sumerian city that played an active role in the third millennium and in the beginning of the second millennium BC. Its modern name is Tell Muqqayyar. . . . After Babylon, it is without a doubt the best known Mesopotamian site in the Bible because it is mentioned in connection with Abraham. According to Gen. 11:31 it is from the city of Ur in Chaldea that Terah and his clan left to go to Haran, a great caravan site located in the belt of the Euphrates in n. Syria." Jean-Cl. Margueron, "Ur," 766.

11. See David P. Wright, *Inventing God's Law: How the Covenant Code of the Bible Used and Revised the Laws of Hammurabi* (New York: Oxford University Press, 2009).

12. See Jeffrey H. Tigay, *JPS Torah Commentary: Deuteronomy* (Philadelphia: Jewish Publication Society, 2003) 497.

may reflect the Mesopotamian king Naram-Sin, the grandson of Sargon).[13] The Akkadian story of his birth reads:

> I am Sargon the great king, the king of Agade.
> My mother was a high priestess, I did not know my father ...
> My mother, the high priestess, conceived me, she bore me in secret.
> She placed me in a reed basket, she sealed my hatch with pitch.
> She left me to the river, whence I could not come up.
> The river carried me off, it brought me to Aqqi, drawer of water.
>
> Aqqi, drawer of water, brought me up as he dipped his bucket.
> Aqqi, drawer of water, raised me as his adopted son.[14]



The parallels to Moses in the Pentateuch are obvious. Both were born to "priestly" mothers who bore their sons in secret, both were was placed in a river in a reed basket sealed with pitch, and both were then discovered and raised as adopted sons.

As the namesake of the earlier Akkadian king, the Assyrian king Sargon II (721–705 BCE) took special interest in the legend of Sargon of Akkad, which may have even been written during the reign of Sargon II to provide support for his own royal claims.[15] Israelites and Judeans would have been familiar with Sargon II, as he appears to have responded to their rebellions after Shalmaneser V's conquest of Israel. Moreover, Sargon II was the grandfather of Esarhaddon, whose Vassal Treaties influenced Deuteronomy. Understood in historical context, the Pentateuch is part of a broader Ancient Near Eastern religious, political, and territorial conversation.

## AUTHORSHIP AND SOURCES

The view of Mosaic authorship of the Pentateuch reflects traditional Jewish and Christian assumptions, and not from anything explicit in the text itself. Exodus states that Moses stayed on Mount Sinai in the presence of God for forty days and forty nights (Exod. 24:18, 34:28; Deut. 9:9, 10:10). Later Jewish interpreters concluded that this constituted too long of a period of time for Moses to have

13. See Eckart Otto, "Political Theology in Judah and Assyria: The Beginning of the Hebrew Bible as Literature," *SEÅ* 65 (2000): 72–75.

14. As translated by Benjamin R. Foster in *COS* 1: 461.

15. See Wright, *Inventing God's Law*, 243.

only received the laws that the Bible itself identifies as a Mosaic revelation.[16] Traditions, therefore, developed that Moses received the entire written Pentateuch, Genesis through Deuteronomy, at this time. Eventually, Jewish rabbis even expanded this view to include the entire oral tradition that provided an authoritative interpretation of the written Torah. This view, however, does not reflect the way most contemporary scholars understand the Pentateuch.

In terms of the books themselves, only Deuteronomy contains a possible allusion to Mosaic authorship. The book appears introduced as "the words which Moses spake unto all Israel beyond the Jordan" (Deut. 1:1). Moses is also attributed as a source for later sections of Deuteronomy (4:44; 31:24; 32:45). However, in the subsequent biblical books of Joshua and Kings, the expression "the torah of Moses" should be taken as a reference to the laws of Deuteronomy rather than the Pentateuchal collection (Josh. 8:31–32; 23:6; 1 Kgs. 2:3; 14:6; 23:5).[17] The legal material of Deuteronomy is the basis for the adjudication of leadership in Joshua through 2 Kings.

The concept of a Pentateuch or Torah that appears in Judaism and in later biblical books such as Ezra and Nehemiah began with Deuteronomy and the Josianic writers.[18] In terms of its initial sources, most scholars believe that the Pentateuch took its preliminary shape in Jerusalem during the late eighth century BCE.[19] This was the historical period of the prophet Isaiah and the Judean king Hezekiah. However, this observation does not mean that scholars assume that absolutely no form of these texts existed prior to this point. Instead, it suggests that with the emergence of Jerusalem as an important political center, together with the rise of the Assyrian empire, Judean scribes began at this time to collect and record Israelite oral traditions, as well as compose new religious literature that would eventually make their way into the pages of the Pentateuch.

The problematic attribution of the Pentateuch to Moses was recognized as early as the Middle Ages via the medieval Jewish scholar Abraham ibn Ezra (twelfth century). Ibn Ezra noted that texts such as Genesis 12:6, which refers to the Canaanites as a people who "were then in the land," must have been

16. Marc Zvi Brettler, "Torah," in *Jewish Study Bible* (Oxford, UK: Oxford University Press, 2004), 2.

17. John J. Collins, *Introduction to the Hebrew Bible and Deutero-Canonical Books* (Minneapolis, MN: Fortress Press, 2014), 50.

18. Collins, *Introduction to the Hebrew Bible*, 50.

19. William Schniedewind, *How the Bible Became a Book: The Textualization of Ancient Israel* (Cambridge, UK: Cambridge University Press, 2004), 5.

written after the time period of Moses and the Israelite entry into Canaan.[20] Similar observations and challenges to traditional assumptions emerged with the rise of European Rationalism. During this era, scholars began to question the long held assumption that Moses wrote the Pentateuch and that the collection represents a unified, consistent whole. Questions initially raised by European rationalists, such as Thomas Hobbes (1588–1779) and Benedict (Baruch) Spinoza (1632–1677), eventually led to the development of European biblical criticism and eventually the Documentary Hypothesis near the end of the nineteenth century. According to the view first synthesized by German scholar Julius Wellhausen, the Pentateuch represents an amalgamation of four main sources edited together: J, E, P, and D.[21] Each source or "document" appears embedded in the Pentateuch as a consistent literary whole.

The existence of these sources explains the conflicting historical claims found throughout the Moses story. For example, is it Moses who strikes the Nile River to enact the blood plague in Egypt (Exod. 7:20, second half of the verse), or does he simply stand by as his brother, Aaron, holds out his hand over Egypt's waters (Exod. 7:19 and the first half of verse 20)? Does Moses turn his rod into a serpent before the Israelites (Exod. 4:3–4, Exod. 4:30), or is it Aaron who performs this wonder before the Egyptian king, Pharaoh, not the Israelites (Exod. 7:10)? Does Moses lead the Israelites out of Egypt in the middle of the night (Exod. 12:29–34), or do they wait until morning to go (Exod. 12:22)? Upon descending from Mount Horeb, does Moses immediately deliver to the Israelites the laws that Yahweh gave him there (Exod. 24:3–8), or does he wait until the end of the wilderness period to deliver Yahweh's laws (Deut. 1:5, Deut. 5:1, Deut. 6:1)? Does Moses teach the Israelites that they may eat meat from animals found dead (Lev. 17:15), or does he insist that they may not (Deut. 14:21)?

These inconsistencies became comprehensible once scholars recognized that various authors preserved distinct traditions and told different stories about Moses. These disparate accounts now appear combined and arranged as a single story in the Pentateuch. This arrangement could be accomplished in part because the individual sources had significant similarities in addition to their marked differences from other sources. Because the compiler of these

20. For an English translation of Ibn Ezra's collection of these references, see Jay F. Schachter, trans., *The Commentary of Abraham Ibn Ezra on the Pentateuch: Vol. 5, Deuteronomy* (New York: KTAV Publishing House, 2003).

21. Julius Wellhausen, *Prolegomena zur Geschichte Israels* (Berlin, 1882; 3rd ed., 1886; English trans., Edinburgh, 1883, 1891; 5th German ed., 1899; first published in 1878 as *Geschichte Israels*) English translation *Prolegomena to the History of Israel* (Atlanta: Scholars Press, Reprints and Translation Series, 1994).

sources was conservative, saving as much of his sources as possible and making changes to them infrequently, the Documentary Hypothesis maintains that it is possible for scholars to reverse the process of compilation and differentiate the sources from each other. The compilation of the Pentateuch demonstrates that there were many distinct traditions about Moses in ancient Israel and Judah. It is likely that only a fraction of them are preserved in the Hebrew Bible.

In recent years, scholars have questioned many of the traditional assumptions of the Documentary Hypothesis as synthesized by Wellhausen. Many continental scholars have abandoned the traditional theory of documentary sources in the Pentateuch as a relevant model for explaining its development, and in its place adopted a "Fragmentary" or "Supplementary" Hypothesis.[22] These theories have called into question many previously held assumptions by biblical source critics. This assessment does not mean to suggest that continental studies have *entirely* rejected the basic premise of separate sources within the Pentateuch, nor that they have returned at all to precritical assumptions of Mosiac singular authorship. "The newer contributions to Pentateuchal research from Europe do not aim at overthrowing the Documentary Hypothesis," writes Konrad Schmid, "rather, they strive to understand the composition of the Pentateuch in the most appropriate terms, which ... includes 'documentary' elements as well."[23] Although in continental Europe and Great Britain most scholars have turned toward alternative approaches to understanding the composition of the Pentateuch, the documentary approach still has a strong following amongst both Israeli and American scholars, and new arguments have been put forward recently reaffirming its validity.[24] In reality, these academic debates often share more in common than they do differences. Presently, virtually all mainstream scholars recognize the fact that the Pentateuch is an

22. The so-called Fragmentary Hypothesis was inaugurated by Johann Severin Vater in his work *Commentar über den Pentateuch: Mit Einleitungen zu den einzelnen Abschnitten, der eingeschalteten Übersetzung von Dr. Alexander Geddes's merkwurdigeren critischen und exegetischen Anmerkungen, und einer Abhandlung über Moses und Verfasser des Pentateuchs* (Halle, Germany: Waisenhaus-Buchhandlung, 1802–1805), 393–94.

23. Konrad Schmid, "Has European Scholarship Abandoned the Documentary Hypothesis?," *The Pentateuch: International Perspectives on its Current Status,* edited by Thomas B. Dozeman, Konrad Schmid, and Baruch J. Schwartz, FAT 78 (Tübingen, Germany: Mohr Siebeck, 2011), 17–18.

24. See, for example, Joel S. Baden, *J, E, and the Redaction of the Pentateuch,* FAT 68 (Tübingen, Germany: Mohr Siebeck, 2009); Baruch J. Schwartz, "The Priestly Account of the Theophany and Lawgiving at Sinai," in *Texts, Temples, and Traditions: A Tribute to Menachem haran,* edited by Michael Fox (Winona Lake, IN: Eisenbrauns, 1996), 103–34; Jeffrey Stackert, *Rewriting the Torah: Literary Revision in Deuteronomy and the Holiness Legislation,* FAT 52 (Tübingen, Germany: Mohr Siebeck, 2007); Richard Elliot Friedman, *The Bible with Sources Revealed: A New View into the Five Books of Moses* (San Francisco: HarperSanFrancisco, 2003), 160–61; Ronald S. Hendel, "Leitwort Style and Literary Structure in the J Primeval Narrative," in *Sacred History, Sacred Literature: Essays on Ancient Israel, the Bible, and Religion in Honor of R.E. Friedman on His Sixtieth Birthday,* edited by Shawna Dolansky (Winona Lake, IN: Eisenbrauns, 2008), 93–109.

amalgamation of separate documentary strands. Debate, however, continues as to which sources are best understood as literary wholes and how each source relates to each other historically.[25]



## PENTATEUCHAL SOURCE CRITICISM AND LDS SCRIPTURE

For Latter-day Saints, the Pentateuch constitutes sacred scripture. Within Mormonism, the collection has traditionally been understood as the Five Books of Moses, in part because the Book of Mormon refers to them as such (1 Nephi 5:11; cf. 19:23).[26] This perspective reflects the view featured in the LDS canonized scripture now known as the Book of Moses. As a segment of Smith's "New Translation" of the King James Bible, the Book of Moses represents a highly modified version of the opening chapters of Genesis. The Book of Moses constitutes a new revelatory introduction to the Pentateuch that provides an innovative *Sitz im Leben* or "setting in life" for the biblical material. The Pentateuchal stories of human prehistory featured in Genesis, including creation, Adam and Eve, and the flood are identified in Smith's scriptural work as narratives literally written by Moses himself as part of a vision the prophet experienced on an "exceedingly high mountain" (1:1). This unique Latter-day Saint scriptural work elevates the sacred status of the Pentateuch within Mormonism by attributing the books to Mosaic, and therefore, prophetic authorship, and, like ancient forms of "rewritten scripture" such as Jubilees, solves interpretative and theological problems by reimagining foundational works. The Book of Moses changes the way Latter-day Saints read the Genesis material as revelation given in connection with a mountain and therefore symbolic "temple" setting.[27]

The Book of Moses is not the only Mormon scripture that affects the way Latter-day Saints have traditionally understood the Pentateuch. The term "Five Books of Moses" appears as a reference to the collection in the Book of Mormon. According to the account presented in the Book of Mormon, the Pentateuch was recorded on "brass plates" (1 Ne. 3:3) and written in the "language

25. See the summary presented by Reinhard Kratz, "The Pentateuch in Current Research: Consensus and Debate," in *The Pentateuch: International Perspectives on Current Research*, 36. Kratz argues that more than half of the Pentateuch is identified and agreed upon within Pentateuchal scholarship.

26. "Pentateuch" in *Bible Dictionary* (Salt Lake City, UT: Church of Jesus Christ of Latter-day Saints, 1981).

27. Carla Sulzbach, "The Function of the Sacred Geography in the Book of Jubilees," *Journal for Semitics* 14 (2005): 290.

of the Egyptians" (Mosiah 1:4). 1 Nephi 5 provides a glimpse of the contents of that scriptural material. The text states that once the prophet Lehi obtained the Brass Plates, he "did search them from the beginning" (v. 11). This phrase appears to function as a type of wordplay on the opening line of the Pentateuch, "in the beginning God created the heaven and the earth" (Gen. 1:1), as well as the traditional name of the book of Genesis in Hebrew, *Bereshit* or "Beginnings." The Book of Mormon suggests that the prophet Lehi began his study of the material in the sixth century BCE with what scholars refer to as the Priestly account of creation (Gen. 1–2:4a). The description continues, suggesting that in addition to an account of "the beginning," Lehi and the Book of Mormon people had access to "the five books of Moses, which gave an account of the creation of the world, and also of Adam and Eve." This perspective, however, is historically anachronistic, since the notion that Moses wrote five books of Torah dates to the Persian period in Jewish history, and subsequent Jewish writings reveal that the Torah was commonly understood as the Book of Moses only in the Hellenistic era.[28]

Modern source critical readings of the Pentateuch present challenges for traditional interpretations of another scriptural text produced by Smith, the Book of Abraham. Smith produced the Book of Abraham between 1835 and the early 1840s as part of his effort to translate Egyptian funerary texts purchased from a traveling mummy exhibition. The Church of Jesus Christ of Latter-day Saints canonized the work in 1880.[29] Smith's Book of Abraham tells the story of the ancient patriarch's life and travels to Canaan and Egypt. It purports to be a first-hand account written by Abraham himself. Smith's text, however, relies heavily on the King James Bible, and it blends disparate Pentateuchal sources into a single harmonious record. For example, the biblical story of Abraham begins in Genesis 11 through a source that critical scholars attribute to the Priestly writer.[30] In the Priestly version, Genesis 11:31–32 states that Abram (later Abraham) began his trek toward Canaan together with his father. This contradicts the subsequent Genesis assertion that scholars have traditionally attributed to the J or Yahwistic source: "The LORD said to Abram, 'Go forth from your native land and from your father's house to the land that I will show you'" (Gen 12:1; JPS). The Book of Abraham takes these two contradictory

28. Brettler, "Torah," 6.

29. Terryl Givens with Brian M. Hauglid, *The Pearl of Greatest Price: Mormonism's Most Controversial Scripture* (New York: Oxford University Press, 2020), 109–222.

30. See Friedman, *The Bible with Sources Revealed.*

Pentateuchal sources and presents them as a unified account written by Abraham himself (2:1–4).

Smith's scriptural work also presents a revised version of the Priestly story of creation (Gen. 1–2:4a), and the Yahwistic account of creation and the story of Eden (Gen. 2:4b–3). These disparate historical documents appear blended together in chapters four and five of the Book of Abraham, depicting Abraham as the author. When read carefully, this passage presents some challenges for how it adapts the Genesis sources:

> "These are the generations of the heavens and of the earth when they were created, in the day that the Lord God made the earth and the heavens" (Gen. 2:4).
>
> P: "These are the generations of the heavens and of the earth when they were created."
>
> J: "In the day that the LORD God made the earth and the heavens"

The Book of Abraham includes both accounts while transitioning from a revision of P directly into the J narrative: "And the Gods came down and formed these the generations of the heavens and of the earth, when they were formed in the day that the Gods formed the earth and the heavens" (Abraham 5:4).

The first line in the Book of Abraham stems from P: "these are the generations of the heavens and of the earth when they were created" (Gen. 2:4a). This statement served as the original conclusion to the Priestly narrative. This portion of the verse links with Genesis 1:1 to create an *inclusio* that marks the text's definitive ending. This combination of separate Pentateuchal sources in the Book of Abraham results in the awkward transition, "when they were formed in the day that the Gods formed the earth and heavens." It shows that the Book of Abraham is reliant on the Judean documentary sources rather than the other way around. In light of these types of critical observations, many Latter-day Saint scholars who accept the mainstream observations concerning Pentateuchal sources see the Book of Abraham as a type of inspired pseudepigraphic work that actualizes the Abrahamic story for a Mormon audience.[31] Notably, Smith's own various editions in the Book of Moses and Book

31. David Bokovoy, *Authoring the Old Testament: Genesis Through Deuteronomy* (Draper, UT: Kofford Books 2014).

of Abraham creation stories do not line up with one another, adding to the complexity of competing sources.

In recent years, Latter-day Saints have begun to address some of these observations in terms of their religious convictions and extra-biblical scriptural texts. Rather than a historical presentation of the past written by Moses, the Pentateuch is being increasingly seen as a religious work that presents a story about the past, which reflects Israelite traditions and scribal interactions with Mesopotamian sources. For many Latter-day Saints, this view does not contradict the Pentateuch's religious status as sacred scripture. Historical criticism, however, does indeed present challenges to a traditional Latter-day Saint understanding of specifically Mormon scripture, including the Book of Mormon, the Book of Moses, and the Book of Abraham. A possible reconciliation between historical criticism of the Pentateuch and Mormon scripture might be made by reinterpreting Smith's scriptural productions as an inspired effort to actualize Pentateuchal material for a Latter-day Saint audience by reformulating the biblical sources into scriptural texts that reflect Smith's own doctrinal and theological insights. This would make Smith's work similar to other religious efforts in both Jewish and Christian traditions. From this angle, Smith might be seen as similar to the Judean scribes themselves who appropriated and reformulated Israelite traditions and Mesopotamian sources into the creation of the Pentateuch.

25

# From Exodus to Exile

DAVID ROLPH SEELY

The biblical narratives from Exodus through 2 Kings, 1 and 2 Chronicles relate a history of Israel that, in its own chronological understanding, includes the period under discussion in this essay, the thirteenth century to 586 BCE. It includes the exodus from Egypt, the lawgiving at Sinai, the wilderness wanderings, settlement in Canaan, establishment of Israel as a united and then divided monarchy and, ultimately, the demise of both kingdoms. Alongside the monarchy, we find during this period the establishment and growth of institutions of priesthood and prophecy. According to the historians who compiled this narrative, because of Israel's apostasy from the covenant with Yahweh it was conquered and exiled by its enemies: the northern kingdom by the Assyrians in 722, and later the kingdom of Judah by the Babylonians in 586.

This essay surveys distinctive LDS readings of historical and textual issues in the period covered by the narratives outlined previously. Particular emphasis is given to instances where LDS scholarship has intersected and interacted with critical biblical theory and methods. While traditional LDS scholarship remains conservative, many LDS biblical scholars now are conversant with and trained in modern biblical criticism and methodologies and who use it in varying degrees in their work.[1]

1. Philip Barlow, *Mormons and the Bible: The Place of the Latter-day Saints in the American Religion* (New York: Oxford University Press, 2013), 112–61; David Rolph Seely, "'We Believe the Bible to Be the Word of God, as Far as It Is Translated Correctly': Latter-day Saints and Historical Biblical Criticism," *Studies in the Bible and Antiquity* 7 (2016): 64–88.

## EXODUS NARRATIVES: EXODUS, LEVITICUS, NUMBERS AND DEUTERONOMY



Israel's escape from Egypt is a central and defining event in the biblical narratives. The lack of specific historical correlation between the biblical account and non-biblical sources or archaeological evidence has led to much scholarly discussion about the historicity and chronology of this event. Many who defend historicity suggest an early Iron Age date in the late thirteenth century BCE that correlates with archaeological evidence of the emergence of Israelites in Canaan.[2]

Latter-day Saint readings of the Exodus narratives are heavily influenced by other books of LDS scripture. In particular, Latter-day Saint readings are enhanced by the fact that the Book of Mormon contains a story structurally similar to that of the exodus. Book of Mormon authors beginning with Nephi narrate their experience of deliverance in terms of the Exodus typology including deliverance from bondage, divine guidance through the wilderness, miracles of food and protection, and finally arrival at the promised land. LDS biblical and literary scholars have explored these as typological narratives deployed in the Book of Mormon.[3]

Like many religious groups, early Latter-day Saints identified the events of the exodus as a typological foretelling of their own religious history.[4] They describe their expulsion from Nauvoo as a driving into the wilderness, crossing the frozen Mississippi as crossing dry-shod through the Red Sea, and Brigham Young as a latter-day Moses leading his people through the wilderness to the Promised Land—identified with the Salt Lake basin and its environs. Upon arrival in Utah the Mormon pioneers even named the river connecting the Great Salt Lake with the freshwater lake to the south as the River Jordan and labeled their landscape with biblical place names, including Canaan Creek, Hebron, Little Egypt, Moab, and Mounts Nebo and Pisgah.[5] The association

2. For a summary of the historical issues connected with the Exodus, see C.A. Redmount, "Bitter Lives: Israel In and Out of Egypt," in *The Oxford History of the Biblical World*, edited by Michael D. Coogan (New York: Oxford University Press, 1998), ch. 2.

3. George S. Tate, "The Typology of the Exodus Pattern in the Book of Mormon," in *Literature of Belief: Sacred Scripture and Religious Experience,* edited by Neal E. Lambert (Provo, UT: Religious Studies Center, BYU, 1981), 245–62; Joseph Spencer, *An Other Testament: On Typology*, 2nd ed. (Provo, UT: Neal A. Maxwell Institute for Religious Scholarship, 2016).

4. For a short study on how Latter-day Saints identified themselves with the Exodus narratives, see Joel S. Baden, *The Book of Exodus: A Biography* (Princeton, NJ: Princeton University Press, 2019), 149–53.

5. See Richard Jackson, "The Mormon Experience: The Plains as Sinai, the Great Salt Lake as the Dead Sea, and the Great Basin as Desert-cum-Promised Land," *Journal of Historical Geography* 18, no. 1 (January 1992): 41–58.

of the Mormon pioneers with the biblical exodus was explicitly expressed by Brigham Young in 1862:

> [T]he miracles wrought in the days of Moses for the deliverance of the children of Israel from Egyptian bondage as recorded in the Old Testament appear to be wonderful displays of the power of God. . . . The children of Israel, it is written, were brought out of Egypt to inherit a land flowing with milk and honey. . . . The distance to their land of promise was but a few miles from the country of their bondage, while a great number of this people have traversed across over one-half the globe to reach the valleys of Utah.[6]



The figure of Moses in LDS scripture and theology acquires several dimensions beyond the Moses of the biblical text. Moses in the Bible is presented as a deliverer, a lawgiver, and a prophet, and at the end of his life, Moses died and was "buried by the hand of the Lord" (Deut. 34:5–7). According to modern LDS revelation, Moses did not die at Mount Nebo, but rather was translated like the later prophet Elijah who ascended to heaven without dying (Alma 45:19). LDS tradition teaches Moses and Elijah did not experience death to appear later on the Mount of Transfiguration to deliver priesthood authority to Peter, James and John (Matt. 17:1–4; D&C 138:45). Latter-day Saints see Moses as having returned with Elijah in a similar fashion to deliver priesthood authority to Joseph Smith and Oliver Cowdery in the Kirtland Temple on April 3, 1836 (D&C 110:11).

## BIBLICAL COVENANT AND LAW

Biblical scholars have long noted the similarities between Hittite and Neo-Assyrian treaties to covenants and covenant rituals in the Hebrew Bible.[7] Latter-day Saints have applied the results of this scholarship to studies of Book of Mormon texts. For example, writers have identified the elements of the ancient

6. *Journal of Discourses* 10:25–26.

7. George E. Mendenhall, *Law and Covenant in Israel and the Ancient Near East* (Pittsburgh: Biblical Colloquium, Presbyterian Board of Colportage of Western Pennsylvania, 1955); Moshe Weinfeld, *Deuteronomy and the Deuteronomic School* (Oxford: Oxford University Press, 1972), 59–157. For a more recent discussion, see Bernard M. Levinson and Jeffrey Stackert, "Between the Covenant Code and Esarhaddon's Succession Treaty: Deuteronomy 13 and the Composition of Deuteronomy," *Journal of Ancient Judaism* 3 (2012): 123–40; and Joshua A. Berman, "Histories Twice Told: Deuteronomy 1–3 and the Hittite Treaty Prologue Tradition," *Journal of Biblical Literature* 132 (2013): 229–50.

Near Eastern treaty/covenant pattern in King Benjamin's covenantal sermon in Mosiah 1–6 as well in the sermon of Limhi in Mosiah 7.[8] Some LDS scholars have even argued the same pattern of structural elements of biblical covenant can be seen in the "new and everlasting covenant" of the Mormon Restoration.[9]

Like other Christians, Latter-day Saints read the ritual and ethical laws in the law codes of the Pentateuch as part of the "Law of Moses" that was implemented to prepare ancient Israel for the coming of Jesus Christ (Rom. 10:4; Gal. 3:24; Heb. 9:12). However, based on Latter-day Saint scripture and teachings of Joseph Smith, Latter-day Saints believe that a highly Christological form of the Gospel was taught from the beginning—from Adam and Eve—and the Hebrew prophets had a fully Christian understanding of biblical doctrine and history. Some scholars both in and out of the church argue that this Christianization of the Old Testament in LDS scripture and tradition is highly anachronistic and reflects nineteenth century ideas. Some have postulated that these readings resemble midrashic interpretations.[10]

For example, Exodus 34:1–2 states that the second set of tablets contained the same law given on the first set of tablets. Joseph Smith, however, revised this passage indicating that the Law of Moses on the second set of tablets given to Moses represented a different and lesser form of the law than on the first set of tablets. Cory Crawford explains, "This scriptural revision is one that also enabled Joseph Smith and his followers to see such institutions as temple, priesthood, prophecy, patriarchy, and polygamy not as bound to outmoded revelation, but, rather, as the residue of once pristine doctrine."[11]

LDS scholars are also particularly interested in Pentateuchal legislation as it plays a role in the Book of Mormon. According to the text, the ancient Book of Mormon people had a copy of the "Law of Moses" on the Brass Plates that

8. Stephen D. Ricks, "The Treaty/Covenant Pattern in King Benjamin's Address (Mosiah 1–6)," *BYU Studies* 24 (Spring 1984): 151–62; Blake T. Ostler, "The Covenant Tradition in the Book of Mormon," in *Rediscovering the Book of Mormon,* edited by John Sorenson and Melvin J. Thorne (Provo, UT: FARMS, 1991), 230–40.

9. David J. Whittaker, "A Covenant People: Old Testament Light on Modern Covenants," *Ensign* 10 (August 1980): 36–40; David Rolph Seely, "The Restoration as Covenant Renewal," in *Sperry Symposium Classics: The Old Testament,* edited by Paul Y. Hoskisson (Provo, UT: Religious Studies Center, BYU, and Deseret Book, 2005), 311–36.

10. Anthony A. Hutchinson, "A Mormon Midrash? LDS Creation Narratives Reconsidered," *Dialogue: A Journal of Mormon Thought* 21, no. 4 (1988): 11–72; Melodie Moench Charles. "The Mormon Christianizing of the Old Testament," in *The Word of God: Essays on Mormon Scripture*, edited by Dan Vogel (Salt Lake City, UT: Signature Books, 1990), 131–42.

11. See the discussion in Cory D. Crawford, "Competing Histories in the Hebrew Bible and in LDS Tradition," in *Standing Apart: Mormon Historical Consciousness and the Concept of Apostasy,* edited by Miranda Wilcox and John D. Young (New York: Oxford University Press, 2014), 132.

they brought with them from Jerusalem, which they lived by throughout the Book of Mormon (2 Ne. 5:10; Alma 30:3; Hel. 13:1), until Christ came to the New World to fulfill it (3 Ne. 9:17–21; 15:5). While the Book of Mormon does not contain specific law codes like the Bible there are ample allusions to Pentateuchal legislation throughout. For example, the Ten Commandments are quoted from Exodus 20 by the prophet Abinadi (Mosiah 12:34–35; 13:12–24) and also quoted by the resurrected Jesus in his sermon at the temple that parallels the Sermon on the Mount in the New Testament (3 Ne. 12:21–37; Matt. 5:21–37). Additionally, throughout the Book of Mormon, there are allusions to sacred gatherings and celebrations that LDS scholars have interpreted as various biblical festivals.[12] And there are a host of legal and judicial cases in the Book of Mormon that LDS writers have attempted to connect to legal procedure in the Bible and ancient Near East. These have been examined at length by an LDS legal scholar John W. Welch in his book *The Legal Cases in the Book of Mormon.*[13]

## DEUTERONOMY AND THE DEUTERONOMISTIC HISTORY

For most scholars, the book of Deuteronomy is a developed form of the book found in Josiah's renovation of the Jerusalem temple and represents a revolution that reshaped Israel's state-sanctioned religion around its precepts. The Deuteronomistic History is the narrative from Joshua through 2 Kings postulated to have been created by editing together many ancient sources by a school that retold the history of Israel emphasizing the Deuteronomic themes including, the centralization of cult, the struggle against idolatry, and the covenant with YHWH.[14] Latter-day Saint scholars have a particular interest in Deuteronomy because its theology of blessings and curses appears to be the governing theology throughout the Book of Mormon. For example, the words of Lehi, "And inasmuch as ye shall keep my commandments, ye shall prosper" (1 Ne. 2:20–21; Alma 9:13) and "If iniquity shall abound cursed shall be the land for their sakes, but unto the righteous it shall be blessed forever" (2 Ne. 1:7),

12. Terrence L. Szink and John W. Welch, "King Benjamin's Speech in the Context of Ancient Israelite Festivals," in *King Benjamin's Speech: "That Ye May Learn Wisdom,"* edited by John W. Welch and Stephen D. Ricks (Provo, UT: FARMS, 1998), 147–224.

13. John W. Welch, *The Legal Cases in the Book of Mormon* (Provo, UT: BYU Press and the Neal A. Maxwell Institute for Religious Scholarship, 2008).

14. See Gary N. Knoppers and J. Gordon McConville, eds. *Reconsidering Israel and Judah: Recent Studies on the Deuteronomistic History* (Winona Lake, IN: Eisenbrauns, 2000); and Thomas Römer, *The So-Called Deuteronomistic History: A Sociological, Historical, and Literary Introduction* (London: T & T Clark, 2005).

echo the same theology familiar from Deuteronomy in passages like "Keep therefore the words of this covenant, and do them, that ye may prosper in all that ye do" (Deut. 29:9 KJV) and in the lists of blessings and curses in Deuteronomy 27–28. Similarly, as pointed out by LDS scholar Mack Stirling, the way of life and way of death language in Deuteronomy (30:15–20) appears to have influenced several narratives in the Book of Mormon.[15]

Furthermore, Latter-day Saints are comfortable with the idea of an edited narrative like the Deuteronomistic history as proposed by biblical scholars. This is because the text of the Book of Mormon presents itself as largely the work of the final editor Mormon who abridged, edited, and incorporated other ancient records, shaping them into a finished product emphasizing several overarching themes like blessings and curses, the way of life and the way of death, the deadly results of pride and wealth, secret combinations, the scattering and gathering of Israel, and the coming of a Messiah. The literary construct of Mormon's work as an editor is described and analyzed by Grant Hardy who points out how Mormon, much like the authors of the Deuteronomistic History, skillfully dealt with competing agendas and parallel narratives in his sources and created a unified work that employed three patterns: prophecy/fulfilment—both the prophecies fulfilled in the Book of Mormon narrative itself and those projected for the future, the theme that obedience brings prosperity and disobedience destruction, and the cycle of prosperity to pride, to political problems, and to humility, repentance, and deliverance.[16]

## THE CONQUEST: JOSHUA AND JUDGES

The books of Joshua and Judges portray the events of the Israelite conquest and settlement in Canaan usually dated between 1250 and 1000 BCE. Biblical scholars attempting to correlate the textual and archaeological evidence have developed several different models to account for the arrival and presence of Israelites in Canaan including military conquest, gradual infiltration, peasant revolt and nomadism.[17] The Deuteronomistic editors of these two books have apparently drawn from various sources and fused them together to form a continuous narrative.

15. Mack C. Stirling, "The Way of Life and the Way of Death in the Book of Mormon," *Journal of Book of Mormon Studies* 6, no. 2 (1997): 152–204.

16. Grant Hardy, Under*standing the Book of Mormon: A Reader's Guide* (New York: Oxford University Press, 2010): 89–213.

17. See Israel Finkelstein and Amihai Mazar, *The Quest for the Historical Israel: Debating Archaeology and the History of Early Israel* (Atlanta: Society of Biblical Literature, 2007).

The book of Joshua begins after the death of Moses and describes Joshua leading the Israelites in a lightning military operation, facilitated by the miraculous intervention of Yahweh, that systematically conquered the whole of Canaan (Josh 1–12). The text then describes the division of the land between the twelve tribes (13–22) and concludes with an account of the covenant renewal ceremony at Shechem (23–24) where Joshua, in accordance with Deuteronomy 27, gathered Israel together for a renewal of the covenant (Joshua 24).

Judges begins after the death of Joshua and presents a different and more complex account where the land is never fully conquered, and because of the reluctance of Israel to completely destroy the Canaanites they survive and are left to live alongside the Israelites (Judg. 2:3). The history of Israel in Judges is patterned on a cycle beginning with the apostasy of Israel in forsaking the worship of Yahweh to worship the Canaanite gods Baal and Ashtaroth. Yahweh punishes their apostasy by subjugating them to their enemies, and when Israel cries to the Lord he raises judges—charismatic military leaders including Deborah, Gideon, and Samson—to deliver them from their enemies. The judges restore the Israelites to peace and plenty—at which point the cycle begins anew (see, e.g., Judg. 2:11–19). The Book of Mormon is edited in such a way as to view history in a cycle similar to that in Judges. LDS readers call this the "the pride cycle" consisting of a period of prosperity followed by pride and divisiveness, subjugation by the enemy, calling on the Lord, and repentance and eventual deliverance. This is especially apparent in Helaman 3–4, 5–12 and 3 Nephi 5–9 and in a general way throughout the Book of Mormon.[18]

The book of Judges ends with the terse editorial note, "In those days there was no king in Israel: every man did that which was right in his own eyes" (Judg. 21:25), suggesting the solution to the problem of chaos in ancient Israel was to be found in a king. This refrain sets up the need for monarchy that will play out in the Samuel narratives, where the judge-prophet Samuel will orchestrate the transition to monarchic governance under Saul and then David.

## THE RISE OF KINGSHIP: SAUL AND DAVID: 1, 2 SAMUEL

The book of Samuel also appears to be a work collated from various ancient sources that narrates the shift from the rule of judges to the rise of the monarchy in the tenth century. The narrative in Samuel begins with the story of

18. Grant Hardy, *Understanding the Book of Mormon*, 114.

Samuel, who is called to be a priest, judge, and prophet (1 Sam. 1–7) and who would anoint the first two kings of Israel: Saul and David. 1 Samuel 8 narrates Israel demanding of Samuel "a king to judge us like all the nations" (1 Sam. 8:5). The rise and fall of king Saul (1 Sam. 9–31) is juxtaposed with the dramatic rise of King David who would overshadow and eventually replace Saul. The narrative, likely composed in the court of a Davidic dynast, shows David successfully uniting the twelve tribes, defeating their surrounding enemies, and conquering the Jebusite city of Jerusalem that would become Israel's capital. Although David's house would see tragedy in the form of rape, murder, and civil war, the Deuteronomistic historian marks David's house as one that would become an enduring dynasty.

While the narratives in Samuel describe the shift from the system of judges to the monarchy, the Book of Mormon narratives describe the Nephite shift from monarchy to judges with many echoes of biblical traditions.[19] For example, just as in Samuel kingship in the Book of Mormon is established by the will of the people who asked Nephi to be king (2 Nephi 5:18; 6:2), made Zeniff king "by the voice of the people" (Mosiah 7:9), and desired Alma to be king (Mosiah 23:6). While it is not clear if Nephi was actually anointed as king in his lifetime or not, he was a ruler like a king, and upon his death, he anointed a man to be king thus initiating the rule of kings (Jacob 1:9). Ben McGuire has argued, based on a series of literary allusions, that the Book of Mormon account of Nephi killing Laban is patterned after the story of David and Goliath (1 Samuel 17) and is part of the attempt to establish Nephi as the rightful king over the Nephites.[20] Warnings about kingship were given by Mosiah and Alma (Mosiah 29) similar to those given by Samuel and Deuteronomy (1 Sam. 8:1–22; 10:18–25; Deut. 17:14). And the narratives in the book of Mosiah of King Benjamin (Mosiah 1–6) and King Noah (Mosiah 11–19), just like the stories of Saul and David in Samuel and Kings, demonstrate the advantages and disadvantages of having a king.

Following centuries of kingship the Nephites under the direction of king Mosiah decide that while it is good to have a king if he were a just man like king Benjamin (Mosiah 29:13) because of the iniquity caused by unjust kings like king Noah (Mosiah 29:16–24), it would be better to shift governance to a

19. See Richard L. Bushman, "The Book of Mormon and the Revolutionary War," *BYU Studies* 17, no. 1 (1976): 3–6; Noel B. Reynolds, "Nephite Kingship Reconsidered," in *Mormons, Scripture, and the Ancient World: Studies in Honor of John L. Sorenson,* edited by Davis Bitton (Provo, UT: FARMS, 1998), 151–89.

20. Ben McGuire, "Nephi and Goliath: A Case Study of Literary Allusion in the Book of Mormon," *Journal of Book of Mormon Studies* 18, no. 1 (2009): 16–31.

rule by a system of judges who would be chosen by the voice of the people and who would provide a series of checks and balances within a hierarchy of judges. Judges in the Book of Mormon are similar to the biblical judges in that they do exercise some responsibilities in terms of raising and outfitting armies (Alma 46:34; 60:12–19), and they exercise authority in judicial situations, perhaps similar to Deborah and Samuel (Judg. 4:4–5; 1 Sam. 7:16–17). But they are very different from the charismatic biblical judges who were called from various tribes to deliver the people from specific military threats in that they are part of an organized system that continues through most of the Book of Mormon.



## THE UNITED AND DIVIDED MONARCHIES: 1–2 KINGS; 1, 2 CHRONICLES

The book of Kings begins with the death of David (ca. 961 BCE) and recounts the history of the monarchy in Israel until the Babylonian exile in 586 BCE.[21] Kings is a continuation of the Deuteronomistic History's theological treatise describing the failure of both kingdoms of Israel and Judah to remain loyal to Yahweh that resulted in the curses promised in Deuteronomy 28 of destruction and scattering. The narrative in Kings is divided into three units: the reign of Solomon over the united kingdom including an account of his wealth and wisdom and building of the temple (1 Kings 1–11); the divided monarchy recounting the circumstances of the division of the kingdoms between the north and the south (922 BCE), and a synchronistic telling of both the histories of Israel and Judah including the activities of the prophets Elijah and Elisha, ending with the fall of Israel to the Assyrians in 722 BCE (1 Kings 12–2 Kings 17), and finally the destruction and exile of Judah by the Babylonians in 586 BCE (2 Kings 18–25).

Three specific issues in the book of Kings are of interest to LDS readers and scholars: Solomon's Temple, Josiah's reforms, and the fact that the last days of Judah provide the historical setting for the beginning of the Book of Mormon.

## SOLOMON'S TEMPLE

The Hebrew Bible is dominated by two main sanctuaries, the wilderness tabernacle and the Jerusalem temple—to house the divine presence and to be the

21. The book of Chronicles is another history of Israel beginning with Adam and ending with the Babylonian exile. This history blended and edited the Deuteronomistic History and the priestly literature.

center of ancient Israelite worship (Exodus 25–40; 1 Kings 6–8). When Joseph Smith dedicated the Kirtland (Ohio) Temple in 1836 he intended a renewed temple tradition as a continuation of ancient temple traditions.[22] He prayed at the dedication "that the holy presence may be in this house continually" (D&C 109:12). Many LDS believe that their temple rituals are at some level the restoration of various forms of rituals attested in the Old Testament, including washings and anointings, and sacred vestments, and being officiated by priesthood authority. LDS temples all bear the inscription "Holiness to the Lord" reminiscent of the headpiece on the high priest (Exod. 28:36).

While the architecture of LDS temples often owes more to European forms than to biblical description, some elements draw on Exodus and Kings narratives, such as the bovine-supported font (1 Kgs. 7:23–26) and the curtains or "veils" separating zones of holiness (Exod. 36:8–19). Early LDS rituals loosely resembled biblical rituals of washings and anointings in the Kirtland temple, but in Nauvoo the temple ceremonies, perhaps influenced by Freemasonry which also claimed ancient origins, became more elaborate.[23] Ritual dramas adapted and reenacted biblical narratives of creation and Eden, but in keeping with the assertion of pre-Christian Christology, Joseph Smith also incorporated New Testament concepts and personas. Drawing on 1 Cor 15:29, Smith also instituted a means by which the necessary rituals could be done by proxy for deceased ancestors. Although these rites have changed somewhat since Smith's day, they retain their basic reliance on biblical forms and texts to this day.

LDS temple studies were instigated by Hugh Nibley, trained at Berkeley in ancient history, who began to explore ancient texts using the comparative method that was popular at the time to find evidence that defended the church from attacks against the antiquity of the Book of Mormon, the books of Moses and Abraham and Latter-day Saint temple worship and theology. Nibley scoured ancient literatures of the world where he found and published a wealth of ancient parallels to LDS scripture and to Mormon temples and temple worship.[24] Following Nibley's comparative model many LDS scholars continue the tradition of studying ancient temples producing volumes of studies that explore various biblical and ancient Near Eastern aspects of temples.[25] One of

22. Richard Lyman Bushman, *Joseph Smith: Rough Stone Rolling* (New York: Alfred Knopf, 2006), 215–9.

23. Michael W. Homer, *Joseph's Temples: The Dynamic Relationship between Freemasonry and Mormonism* (Salt Lake City: University of Utah Press, 2014).

24. Hugh W. Nibley, "Temple and Cosmos: Beyond This Ignorant Present," *The Collected Works of Hugh Nibley,* vol. 12 (Salt Lake City, UT: Deseret Book, 1992).

25. See, for example, Donald W. Parry, ed., *Temples of the Ancient World: Ritual and Symbolism* (Salt Lake City, UT: Deseret Book, 1994); and Jeffrey R. Chadwick, Matthew J. Grey, and David Rolph Seely,

Nibley's students, John Lundquist, produced a study addressed to the broader academic community articulating a typology of ancient temples common to many ancient Near Eastern temples, including the Israelite tabernacle and temple.[26] Lundquist's typology gained some attention in non-LDS academic studies, but seems to have declined in influence with the skepticism of the value of such typologies in general.[27]

Scholarship employing the comparative method, including the myth-ritual school, has been critiqued in terms of methodology. While the comparative method successfully identifies many apparent parallels, the non-critical use of this method has led to excesses that have been called "parallelomania"[28] where parallels between various cultures are non-critically assigned significance. Shemaryahu Talmon has described the perils of this method when specific parallels in different cultures from different time periods and contexts are assigned significance without a cautious analysis of contextual material.[29] Comparative studies continue to be an important part of ancient Near Eastern and biblical studies, but its results are more carefully monitored by methodological considerations, including proper analysis of textual and cultural contexts and temporal and geographical propinquity. Hopefully future LDS scholarship employing comparative methods will be characterized by more attention to these methodological concerns.

## JOSIAH'S REFORM

According to the account in 2 Kings 22–23, king Josiah in conjunction with the renovation of the Jerusalem Temple discovered a "book [scroll] of the law

eds., *Ascending the Mountain of the Lord: Temple, Praise, and Worship in the Old Testament,* 2013 Sperry Symposium (Provo, UT: Religious Studies Center, BYU/Deseret Book, 2013).

26. John M. Lundquist, "What Is a Temple: A Preliminary Typology," in *The Quest for the Kingdom of God: Studies in Honor of George E. Mendenhall,* edited by H.B. Huffmon, F.A. Spina, and A.R.W. Green (Winona Lake, IN: Eisenbrauns, 1983), 205–19.

27. Scholars who cite Lundquist in their work include John H. Walton, *Ancient Near Eastern Thought and the Old Testament* (Grand Rapids, MI: Baker Book, 2006) and Steven W. Holloway, "What Ship Goes There: The Flood Narratives in the Gilgamesh Epic and Genesis Considered in Light of Ancient Near Eastern Temple Ideology," *ZAW* 103:3 (1991), 321. Important scholars who do not cite Lundquist's typology include Victor Hurowitz, *I Have Built You and Exalted House: Temple Building in the Bible in Light of Mesopotamian and Northwest Semitic Writings* (Sheffield, UK: Sheffield Academic Press, 1992); and Michael B. Hundley, *Gods in Dwellings: Temples and Divine Presence in the Ancient Near East* (Atlanta: Society of Biblical Literature, 2013).

28. Samuel Sandmel, "Parallelomania," *JBL* 81/1 (1962): 1–13.

29. Shemaryahu Talmon, "'The Comparative Method' in Biblical Interpretation—Principles and Problems," *Supplements to Vetus* Testamentum 29 (1977): 320–56.

[*torah*]" (2 Kgs. 22:8), later designated "book of the covenant" (2 Kgs. 23:2). When the book was read to Josiah it became apparent, at least in the framework of the narrative, that Israel had not been living the law of the covenant. The book contained the curses that would come upon the kingdom of Judah if they did not repent, and because of its theology and language most scholars believe this book was an early version of the book of Deuteronomy. Consequently, Josiah determined to reform the national religion according to the laws in the book. A central commandment recorded in this book (found in Deuteronomy 12), was to centralize all worship and sacrifice to Yahweh only in the temple in Jerusalem and to destroy all the other places of sacrifice to Yahweh and Baal and Asherah. The narrative in 2 Kings 22–23 records how Josiah fulfilled the injunctions found in this book by cleansing the Jerusalem temple of non-Yahwistic worship, destroying the Judean high places and by centralizing the Israelite cult to the Jerusalem temple. Some scholars refer to these reforms that implemented the laws found in the book of Deuteronomy as the Deuteronomic Revolution.[30] Most scholars are confident that the core of Deuteronomy was written around the time of Josiah to form the basis of his reforms that consolidated his power in Jerusalem in the context of renewed Assyrian expansion.

While the Deuteronomistic history records that Josiah in his reform destroyed apostate idolatrous objects and practices from Judahite religion, scholars, based on archaeological and epigraphic evidence, note that Josiah in his enforcement of the centralization of the cult and the rejection of the high places, and various so called "apostate practices" was actually removing institutions that had become normalized in Yahwistic popular religion.[31] Until the time of Hezekiah and Josiah, for example, the biblical and archaeological evidence agree that the Israelites did not follow the Deuteronomic idea of centralization after the construction of the temple. Margaret Barker argues that Josiah also purged many ancient and authentic Israelite beliefs with origins in patriarchal religion and beyond. Using her comparative methodology she identifies some of these elements that were purged, such as the tree of life, visions of the divine council, associations between stars and angels, and El Elyon as the High God and Yahweh as his son. Barker argues that these elements of the purged ancient religion can be identified since remnants (as she surmises)

30. Moshe Weinfeld, "Deuteronomy's Theological Revolution," *Bible Review* 12, no. 1 (1996): 38–41, 44–5.

31. For a discussion, see Ziony Zevit, *The Religions of Ancient Israel: A Synthesis of Parallactic Approaches* (London: Continuum, 2001), especially pages 658–64.

of these beliefs are preserved in later Jewish and Christian apocryphal and pseudepigraphical literature.[32] A group of LDS writers—some untrained in biblical studies—note that this perspective resonates with phenomena in the Book of Mormon and LDS temple traditions.[33] For these LDS scholars there are some significant finds that resonate with LDS traditions that see Christology in pre-Christian writings: a Father and a Son in biblical texts, a rich historical tradition of Melchizedek Priesthood, and that Yahweh had a consort signifying the importance of the feminine in biblical religion.[34] The methodology of this movement has been critiqued by both LDS and non-LDS scholars because much of the evidence for the old religion is culled from sources that date from later periods and later historical contexts.[35] It does, however, represent perhaps the widest LDS acceptance of at least some results of critical biblical scholarship, even while it takes those results to extreme ends.

## THE LAST DAYS OF JUDAH AND THE SETTING OF THE BOOK OF MORMON (2 KINGS 22–25)

The reforms of King Josiah (627–622 BCE) as recorded in 2 Kings and Jeremiah led to the resurgence of Judahite nationalism during a period of dramatic change in the international scene in the ancient Near East. The Neo-Babylonian empire destroyed and replaced the Neo-Assyrian empire: Nineveh was destroyed in 612, Josiah was killed in battle at Megiddo in 609, and Nebuchadnezzar, victorious at the Battle of Carchemish in 605, eventually consolidated the west into his territory. A series of prophets in Jerusalem, including Jeremiah, warned the Judahites that unless they repented from their apostasy they would be destroyed (Ezekiel, Habakkuk, Zephaniah). Babylon invaded Judah in 598 and took many into exile and placed king Zedekiah on the throne. Zedekiah would eventually submit to Judahite nationalism and rebel against Babylon, leading to Nebuchadnezzar's second invasion of Judah resulting in

32. Margaret Barker, "What Did King Josiah Reform?," in *Glimpses of Lehi's Jerusalem*, edited by John W. Welch, David Rolph Seely, and Jo Ann H. Seely (Provo, UT: FARMS, 2004), 521–42. See also Margaret Barker, *The Great Angel: A Study of Israel's Second God* (London: SPCK, 1992), and Margaret Barker, *The Older Testament: The Survival of Themes from the Ancient Royal Cult in Sectarian Judaism and Early Christianity* (London: SPCK, 1987).

33. Kevin Christensen, *"Paradigms Regained:" A Survey of Margaret Barker's Scholarship and its Significance for Mormon Studies*, FARMS Occasional Papers (Provo, UT: FARMS, 2001).

34. See, for example, Daniel C. Peterson, "Nephi and His Asherah," *Journal of Book of Mormon Studies* 9, no. 2 (2000): 16–25, 80–81.

35. William J. Hamblin, "Vindicating Josiah," *Interpreter: A Journal of Mormon Scripture* 4 (2013): 165–76.

the destruction of Jerusalem and the temple and another exile of Judahites to Babylon.

For Latter-day Saints this historical period provides the setting for the opening of the Book of Mormon account that begins in "the first year in the reign of Zedekiah (1 Ne. 1:4). LDS scholars take very seriously the data in the Book of Mormon and have worked to elucidate the historical, cultural, and geographical connections with the narratives in the Bible. Hugh Nibley and others produced a significant corpus of work on the relationship of the Bible to the Book of Mormon including studies on the history and politics of Judah in the seventh century.[36] A recent collection of studies by LDS scholars entitled *Glimpses of Lehi's Jerusalem*, contains studies that examine history, geography, archaeology, agriculture, Israelite inscriptions, prophecy, customs, and legal traditions related to Jerusalem so as to provide context for the opening setting of the Book of Mormon.[37] LDS scholars and archaeologists continue to publish scholarly work interfacing with biblical scholarship exploring the biblical background of the Book of Mormon.

For the Book of Mormon this impending destruction was the beginning of the journey of Lehi's family to a new promised land. In the Bible efforts to make sense of the destruction are frequently accompanied by hope for the future. Jeremiah (29:10), Deuteronomy (30:1–5) and Book of Mormon (2 Ne. 25:11) all foresaw the return and restoration of the Judeans in their land.

From the beginning Latter-day Saint scripture, tradition and practice has demonstrated a dynamic relationship with biblical texts and traditions. The Book of Mormon and the Pearl of Great Price as well as the Doctrine and Covenants are infused with Old Testament characters, quotations, and allusions. While many LDS readings of the Hebrew Bible follow traditional Jewish and Christian interpretations, Latter-day Saints often read and interpret the Bible in a distinctive way. Several examples of distinctive readings include the LDS belief of a developed Christology in Old Testament times, LDS temple theology, and the idea of a developing of biblical traditions in the New World represented by the Book of Mormon. As LDS scholars become more conversant with critical biblical scholarship it is likely that there will be a continued exploration of these issues from various perspectives.

36. See, for example, Hugh W. Nibley, *An Approach to the Book of Mormon*, 3rd ed., in *The Collected Works of Hugh Nibley: Volume Six: The Book of Mormon* (Salt Lake City, UT: Deseret Book and Foundation for Ancient Research and Mormon Studies, 1988).

37. Welch, Seely, and Seely, *Glimpses of Lehi's Jerusalem.*

26

# Prophets and Prophetic Literature

DAVID BOKOVOY

Prophets fulfill a pivotal role within Mormonism. The Latter-day Saint traditions are founded upon a belief that Joseph Smith Jr. was a prophet of God in line with those of the Hebrew Bible.[1] Today, Latter-day Saints refer to the president of the church by the honorific title *the* Prophet (a twentieth-century development), and they sustain members of the Quorum of the Twelve Apostles as "prophets, seers, and revelators."[2] In the LDS tradition, prophets oversee the rights to administer sacred priesthood ordinances. They provide church members with spiritual guidance that Latter-day Saints accept as the inspired word of God. While some contemporary LDS views of prophets certainly correlate with aspects of biblical traditions, important distinctions exist between Latter-day Saint prophets and the prophetic traditions in the Bible. The same observation also proves true for traditional Mormon readings of prophetic literature. Latter-day Saints interpret the prophetic books in the Bible as inspired scripture. Yet this material is frequently contextually and historically misunderstood.

1. For LDS scholarly treatments of prophets and prophetic literature, see Richard Neitzel Holzapfel, Dana M. Pike, and David Rolph Seely, *Jehovah and the World of the Old Testament* (Salt Lake City, UT: Deseret Book, 2009); Ralph A. Britsch and Todd A. Britch, "Prophet," in *Encyclopedia of Mormonism*, vol. 3, edited by Daniel H. Ludlow (New York: Macmillan Publishing Company), 1164–67; see also David Bokovoy, "The Calling of Isaiah," in *Covenants, Prophecies, and Hymns of the Old Testament: The Thirtieth Annual Sidney B. Sperry Symposium* (Salt Lake City, UT: Deseret Book, 2001); David Bokovoy, "On Christ and Covenants: An LDS Reading of Isaiah's Prophetic Call," *Studies in the Bible and Antiquity* 3 (2011): 29–49; David Bokovoy, "Thou Knowest That I Believe": Invoking the Spirit of the Lord as Council Witness in 1 Nephi 11," *Interpreter: A Journal of Mormon Scripture* 1 (2012): 1–23.

2. For the historical evolution of these titles in Mormonism, see D. Michael Quinn, *The Mormon Hierarchy: Origins of Power* (Salt Lake City, UT: Signature Books, 1994), 8–9; Quinn, *The Mormon Hierarchy: Extensions of Power* (Salt Lake City, UT: Signature Books, 1997), 40–41, 355–65.

## PROPHECY IN ANCIENT NEAR EASTERN CONTEXT



In its origin, the English word *prophecy* stems from the Greek term *prophētēs*, meaning "proclaimer."[3] It refers to one who speaks on behalf of a god or goddess. In the Old Testament, the English word "prophet" most frequently translates the Hebrew noun *nābī'* (the singular form of *Nevi'im*). Some scholars have suggested that this Hebrew term is a loanword originally borrowed from a foreign language without translation. The closest parallel is perhaps the Akkadian word *nabītu*. This would connect the Hebrew noun with the Akkadian verb *nabū* meaning "to call" or "to proclaim."[4] It seems likely, however, that Hebrew *nābī'* simply derives from the general Semitic root *n-b-'*, that would have denoted "'the one called/named' by a god."[5] The related term *nabû* is attested as a Northwest Semitic noun, meaning "diviner."[6] Over time, Hebrew *nābī'* came to be used in Israelite and Judean societies as a type of catchall expression covering a wide range of religious figures. Despite the frequent attestation of the term *nābī'*, it is not the only word used for "prophet" in the Bible (or in any other Near Eastern source). 1 Samuel 9:9 states that a person called a *nābī'* was anciently known in Israel as a *rō'eh* or "seer" (cf. Amos 7). Two other expressions that appear in the Hebrew Bible as terms for "prophets" include *'îš [hā]'elōhîm* "man of God" and *hōzeh* "visionary."

Biblical prophecy traces its origins to general Near Eastern traditions. As a phenomenon, it evolved out of the common Near Eastern perspective that a human mediator could ascertain the will of deity—that supernatural oracle was then directly relevant to the proper course an individual or a community should follow. Since divinities controlled the world and their will could be discerned by human beings, prophecy became a venerable profession throughout the ancient Near East. In royal courts, prophets served as professional diviners who helped define a proper moral, social, or political direction. As professional

3. John J. Collins, *Introduction to the Hebrew Bible* (Minneapolis, MN: Fortress Press, 2014), 305.

4. Martha T. Roth, ed., *The Assyrian Dictionary of the Oriental Institute of the University of Chicago* (Chicago: Oriental Institute of Chicago, 1980), 11:32.

5. John Huehnergard, "On the Etymology and Meaning of Hebrew *nābî'*," *Eretz-Israel* 26 (1991): 91.

6. John J. Schmitt, "Pre-Exilic Hebrew Prophecy," in *Anchor Yale Bible Dictionary,* edited by David Noel Freedman (New Haven, CT: Yale University Press, 1992) 5:482–89.

diviners, Near Eastern prophets were often highly educated men and women,[7] well-versed in the arts of poetic and musical expression.[8]

To be taken seriously, a prophet needed to first capture his or her audience's attention. This was often accomplished through strange or erratic behavior. The Bible preserves a variety of stories that illustrate the notion that in ancient Israel, prophets were strange people who did odd things. Hosea was commanded to marry "a wife of whoredom" and name their children symbolic names (Hos. 1–3). Isaiah untied his sackcloth from his loins, removed his sandals from his feet, and went about "naked and barefoot" for three years (Isa. 20:3–4). The Judean prophet Jeremiah wore a yoke around his neck to represent captivity (Jer. 27–28). And Ezekiel reports he was commanded to lie on his left side for 390 days next to a miniature model of Jerusalem while eating food cooked over human dung (Ezek. 4:12–15).

Artistic expression and erratic behavior would sometimes create such an intense response on the part of an audience that scribes would capture the prophet's words and put them to writing. This perhaps explains why some of the prophetic oracles in the Bible were preserved. Many biblical prophets were also poets, employing striking literary images and elegant phrasing. Yet, critical studies have shown that many of the writings attributed to biblical prophets were most likely produced by scribal schools writing under the name of a prophetic figure rather than the prophet himself.[9]

The prophetic literature in the Bible is divided into two sections—the Major and the Minor prophets. The names reflect both the size of the material and the fact that twelve minor prophets could originally fit onto a single scroll, hence the Aramaic name for this material, "[The scroll] of the Twelve." The Major prophetic books include Isaiah, Jeremiah, and Ezekiel. The Minor books are the twelve that follow in the biblical canon—Hosea, Joel, Amos, Obadiah, Jonah, Micah, Nahum, Habakkuk, Zephaniah, Haggai, Zachariah, and Malachi. In the traditional Jewish canon, the prophetic books appear in the second division of the Bible, known simply as "the prophets." The historical books

7. Jonathan Stökl and Corinne L. Carvalho, eds., *Prophets Male and Female: Gender and Prophecy in the Hebrew Bible, the Eastern Mediterranean, and the Ancient Near East* (Atlanta: Society of Biblical Literature, 2013).

8. On ancient Near Eastern prophecy in general, see Jonathan Stökl, *Prophecy in the Ancient Near East: A Philological and Sociological Comparison* (Leiden, Netherlands: Brill, 2012); see also Martti Nissinen, *Prophets and Prophecy in the Ancient Near East* (Atlanta: Society of Biblical Literature, 2003).

9. James D. Nogalski, *Interpreting Prophetic Literature: Historical and Exegetical Tools for Reading the Prophets* (Louisville, KY: Westminster John Knox Press, 2015), 7–10.

such as Joshua, Judges, Samuel, and Kings are known as the "Former Prophets," whereas the Major and Minor works are called the "Latter."

The Bible does not contain a consistent prerequisite concerning the qualifications that define a prophet. Moses functioned as a political and judicial leader, as well as a lawgiver (Deut. 34:10). Deborah served as a warrior chieftain and judge (Judg. 4:4). Nathan assumed the role of a moral advisor to king David (2 Sam. 7:2). Amos insists that he did not belong to the guild of prophets (Amos 7:14). This brief list illustrates the challenge in defining the qualifications that define the status "prophet" in the Bible. Though biblical sources label figures such as Moses, Miriam, Deborah, and Samuel as "prophets," important distinctions exist between the way they functioned as prophets versus traditional prophetic roles. People like Moses and Deborah exercised direct political and religious authority over their community. In this sense, their prophetic role can be conceptually linked with the general LDS tradition, in which prophets serve as leaders of the religious community.[10] In the traditional meaning of the term, biblical prophets such as Elijah, Elisha, and Jeremiah did not assume this role. Instead they functioned as outsiders and critics of authority. They were individuals who censured both the religious and social system of ancient Israel. Rather than administrating *over* the people (in either a religious or a political sense), the way prophets traditionally function in Mormon traditions, the biblical prophet was typically a figure who instructed leaders concerning the way they should properly exercise their authority in terms of military, cultic, and moral activities. In ancient Israel, prophets provided a check on the power of the king, the upper class, and the religious leaders who controlled the system. This historical fact may account for the decline of prophecy in Judean society after the waning of the monarchy following the Babylonian captivity.

Scholars typically divide biblical prophets into two categories: pre-classical and classical.[11] These two types of biblical prophets existed at the same time historically. The terminology does not imply that pre-classical prophets operated prior to the classical tradition. Classical prophets are those who spoke and wrote to the general population. This would include figures such as Isaiah, Jeremiah, Amos, and Micah. Each of these prophets has a book connected with him as "author." In contrast, pre-classical prophets spoke primarily to the king. Their messages were brief and appear in the context of biblical narrative.

10. Cory Crawford, "The Struggle for Female Authority in Biblical and Mormon Theology," *Dialogue: A Journal of Mormon Thought* 48, no. 2 (Summer 2015): 1–66.

11. See the analysis provided by Marc Zvi Brettler, *How to Read the Bible* (Philadelphia: Jewish Publication Society, 2005), 142–48.

This would include biblical prophets such as Nathan and Gad from the tenth century BCE, and Elijah and Elisha from the ninth century. Many of these figures appear nameless in the Bible and the evidence is quite clear that some were female.[12] The contrasting streams of information regarding the pre-classical prophets may derive from the legendary sources incorporated into the Deuteronomistic history, a fact that might account for the various distinct religious views.[13]



Many of the pre-classical prophets worked and lived together as a group in what is sometimes called a "guild," who were referred to in the books of Kings as the *benei-ha-nevi'im* or "sons of the prophets" (1 Kgs. 20:35; 2 Kgs. 2:3, 5, 7, 15; 4:1, 38; 5:22; 6:1). This group was also mentioned in 1 Samuel 10:10. Pre-classical prophets sometimes apparently used music as a way to enter a prophetic state of mind (2 Kgs. 3:15) and instruct their audience. Unlike the classical prophets, these figures often performed miracles as a sign that established the authenticity of their religious commission.

The pre-classical prophets functioned as a type of professional freelance consultant for individuals who needed to ascertain the divine will. This practice makes pre-classical prophecy quite similar to other Near Eastern prophetic traditions. For example, the book of Kings includes a story of a Shunammite woman who attempted to converse with the Israelite prophet Elisha. Her husband asked the question, "why go to him today? It is neither new moon nor Sabbath" (2 Kgs. 4:23). The question suggests that Elisha would serve as a professional consultant determining the divine will on specific occasions. According to the story concerning Saul and the "man of God" in 1 Samuel, it seems that Israelite prophets were traditionally paid in exchange for their skills (9:6–8). However, as witnessed in the case of Elijah and Ahab, the primary role fulfilled by the pre-classical prophet was to prophesy either good news or judgment to the king. This role was perhaps assumed, since the pre-classical prophets were generally thought to be able to determine what was happening in distant places where the king could not physically see (2 Kgs. 6:12).

In contrast, the classical prophets, such as Isaiah, Jeremiah, Ezekiel, and Amos speak to a much larger class of people (such as Israel or Judah as a whole). Their speeches often appear in long poetic discourse. Generally speaking, the classical prophets do not claim to know secret or hidden information,

12. Biblical references to female prophets include Exod. 15:20–21; Judg. 4:4; 2 Kgs. 22:14–20; Neh. 6:14; Isa. 8:3; Luke 2:36.

13. Alexander Rofé, *The Prophetic Stories: The Narratives About the Prophets in the Hebrew Bible, Their Literary Types and History* (Jerusalem: Magnes Press, 1988).

nor do they appear consulted on fixed occasions as part of a professional guild in all cases. Instead, Yahweh called them (often described as against their own will), to deliver his divine message. This explains, for example, Amos' famous response to Amaziah's assertion that he should go practice his profession in Judah (since his prophetic services were not wanted in Israel):



> I am no prophet, nor a prophet's son; but I am a herdsman, and a dresser of sycamore trees, and the LORD took me from following the flock and the LORD said to me, 'Go, prophesy to my people Israel.' (Amos 7:14–15)

Amos, in other words, was not a member of the professional prophetic guild discussed in the book of Kings, that is, the "sons of the prophets" (*benei-ha-nevi'im*). Amos was a laborer that for some reason, Yahweh called to deliver a message of judgment that the Israelite leadership did not wish to receive.

Differences certainly exist between the way Joseph Smith, the first prophet in the LDS tradition, received and delivered the prophetic word versus later church presidents sustained as prophets. Smith often delivered his revelations as direct first-person speech, recorded by a scribe taking dictation. Many of these revelations were then compiled into canonized scripture. The introduction to the LDS Doctrine and Covenants, for example, presents Smith's revelation as the direct word of God:

> Wherefore, I the Lord, knowing the calamity which should come upon the inhabitants of the earth, called upon my servant Joseph Smith, Jun., and spake unto him from heaven, and gave him commandments. (D&C 1:17)

In contrast, later LDS prophets have adopted a significantly different approach to convey the prophetic word. Prophetic messages are typically given in General Conference meetings. Usually, these messages are not dictated as first person "thus saith the Lord" statements from divinity, nor are they typically added to the LDS canons of scripture. Instead, LDS prophets after Joseph Smith have generally presented their revelations of God's word in the form of sermons that instruct church members concerning the application of religious principles in their lives. Both types of activities are accepted by Latter-day Saints as inspired prophetic oracles. However, they clearly represent two distinct categories of prophetic traditions.

## PROPHETIC MESSAGES

Even though classical prophets primarily spoke to their own people concerning contemporary concerns, the books associated with these figures are often viewed by Latter-day Saints—as heirs of a long Christian tradition of interpretation—as predictive of future events. This is especially true for the prophet Isaiah. Anciently, a prophet was a person who received inspiration from divinity that caused him or her to speak out. Prophets were practitioners of the art of prophecy, and prophecy was the means of transmitting divine messages by a human mediator to a third party. Ancient Israelite and Judean prophets were not predominantly predictors of future events. Instead, they often assumed a critical role in trying to alter their society to bring it into harmony with the will of deity (though there were prophets such as Jeremiah who taught that society had gone too far in its sinning and simply needed to be punished).

Biblical prophets held a variety of concerns, but they appear highly vested in what is often today referred to as "social justice." Speaking generally, classical prophets believed that the establishment of "justice and righteousness" was the purpose of Israel's existence (see also Isa. 5:7; Jer. 4:2; 7:5–6; 22:3–4; Ezek. 18:5–9; Mic. 6:8; Zech. 7:9–10).[14] The prophetic literature illustrates that prophets felt deeply concerned with the distribution of wealth in the covenant community, and the moral imperative to take care of the poor and needy. The call to liberate the financially enslaved is therefore characteristic of the prophetic call for social reform. This theme, for example, appears articulated in the oracles of Micah who condemned the government of his day for failing to properly care for the poor in Israel:

> Hear this, you rulers of the house of Jacob and the chiefs of the house of Israel who abhor justice and pervert all equity.... Therefore, because of you Zion shall become a heap of ruins, and the mountain of the house a wooded height. (Mic 3:9–12)

For Micah, the rulers of the house of Israel had perverted the way of God by failing to create an environment conducive to maintaining financial and social equity. As a result of this perversion, Jerusalem, Micah prophesied, would be destroyed.

14. Moshe Weinfeld, *Social Justice in Ancient Israel and the Ancient Near East* (Jerusalem: Hebrew University Magnes Press, 2000), 7.

This same message that the covenant community needed to eradicate financial inequality and debt-slavery appears time and again throughout the Hebrew Bible, but especially in the prophetic books. The call for economic justice is perhaps best illustrated through the oracles attributed to the prophet Amos. His initial oracle against Israel articulates Yahweh's anger with the covenant community:

> Thus said the LORD: For three transgressions of Israel, and for four, I will not revoke the punishment; because they sell the righteous for silver, and the needy for a pair of sandals—they trample the head of the poor into the dust of the earth, and push the afflicted out of the way. (Amos 2:6–7)

During Amos' time, the northern kingdom of Israel had grown exceedingly prosperous. But from Amos' perspective, they had done so by pushing the heads of the poor and needy into the dust and neglecting their wants. For this sin, Israel would face the wrath of a deity who felt compelled, according to the biblical prophets, to champion the cause of those in financial bondage. The existence of the covenant community, from Amos' perspective, was to establish social justice by eradicating economic oppression. Israel was called to "let justice roll down like water, and righteousness like an ever-flowing stream" (Amos 5:24). And God, the champion of the poor, did not take their failing to do so lightly. This creates an interesting thematic connection with Joseph Smith's prophecies canonized in the LDS tradition. Many of Smith's revelations address the community's responsibility to alleviate poverty. It appears as one of the primary prophetic concerns in Smith's revelatory works.[15] Many of these prophetic utterances read similarly to biblical oracles including D&C 56:16:

> Wo unto you rich men, that will not give your substance to the poor, for your riches will canker your souls; and this shall be your lamentation in the day of visitation, and of judgment, and of indignation: The harvest is past, the summer is ended, and my soul is not saved!

In the biblical tradition, classical prophets addressed very specific social, political, and economic situations pertaining to their own time. Modern readers,

15. See, for example, D&C 38:16, 35; 42:30–71; 44:6; 51:5; 52:40; 58:8, 11, 47; 72:12; 78:3; 82:12; 83:6; 84:105, 112; 104:16–18; 105:3; 124:21, 75, 89.

therefore, cannot properly understand prophetic messages without taking into consideration the historical context of each source. The biblical view that prophets were primarily forthtellers rather than foretellers stands in contrast to what most Latter-day Saints assume, having inherited a long Christian tradition of reading these historically context-specific prophecies as predictions for a distant future. For many, "prophet" brings to mind an individual with the ability to look into the far distant future and predict very specific events. Within Mormonism, many of these predictions are linked with aspects of the Latter-day Saint Restoration movement. For example, Ezekiel's prophecy of "two sticks" written for the tribes of Joseph and Judah is often taken as a prediction of the Book of Mormon and the Bible (Ezek. 37:16–17; D&C 27:5). Isaiah's prophecy that a "book" would be given to someone who was "unlearned" is understood as a prediction of Joseph Smith and the translation of the Book of Mormon (Isa. 29:11–12; JS-H 1:65; 2 Ne. 27:7–26). Malachi's oracle concerning the messenger who would prepare the world for the way of the Lord is often read as a prediction of Joseph Smith (Mal. 3:1; D&C 35:4). The Book of Mormon itself takes the Isaianic oracle concerning a voice that speaks from the ground with a familiar spirit as a prophetic prediction of the work (see 2 Ne. 26:16; Morm. 8:23). This appropriation of biblical prophetic material is common within LDS scripture and discourse.

## PROPHETIC MATERIAL IN THE SCRIPTURAL TRADITION

Within the Book of Mormon, this technique of applying the biblical prophets to modern-day situations is referred to as the process of "likening." The character Nephi, for example, quotes heavily from the biblical Isaiah, prefacing the citations with the statement, "I, Nephi, write more of the words of Isaiah, for my soul delighteth in his words. For I will liken his words unto my people" (2 Ne. 11:2). This "likening" process continues throughout the entire work. One of the most significant prophetic texts appropriated into the Book of Mormon is Isaiah 52:1–2:

> Awake, awake; put on thy strength, O Zion; put on thy beautiful garments, O Jerusalem, the holy city: for henceforth there shall no more come into thee the uncircumcised and the unclean. Shake thyself from the dust; arise, and sit down, O Jerusalem: loose thyself from the bands of thy neck, O captive daughter of Zion.

The first Book of Mormon allusion to this passage (written for the exilic Judean community) appears in 2 Nephi 1 where the Book of Mormon prophet Lehi delivers a series of final sermons. Facing the prospect of his own mortality, Lehi encourages his sons to wake up and avoid spiritual death with an allusion to Isaiah 52: "O that ye would awake; awake from a deep sleep ... Awake! and arise from the dust ... Awake, my sons; put on the armor of righteousness. Shake off the chains with which ye are bound, and come forth out of obscurity, and arise from the dust" (2 Ne. 1:13–14, 23). The same Isaianic passage then provides the focus of Lehi's son Jacob's first inaugural sermon for the Nephite people (2 Ne. 8:24–25). A resurrected Jesus also appears toward the middle of the book appropriating Isaiah 52:1–2 as a representation of the Book of Mormon people (3 Ne. 30:36–37). Finally, the book concludes with an appropriation of Isaiah 52:1–2 as a symbol of the entire literary work (Moro. 10:31).

Another way of looking at the appropriation of biblical prophecy in the LDS tradition is that LDS sources actualize prophetic material for the religious community. This reflects the general use of prophetic texts both within Judaism and within the larger Christian tradition. Within these traditions, prophetic material is often used creatively to link the past with the present. This process occurs within the Hebrew Bible and the Christian New Testament. For example, both the authors of Matthew and Luke present narratives concerning Jesus' birth to a virgin mother. According to these authors, Jesus was not the son of Joseph, the carpenter; Jesus was the son of God. The author of Matthew connects the virgin birth story with a prophecy from the book of Isaiah (Matt. 1:22–23). Historically, however, the original Isaianic passage had nothing to do with Jesus' birth. The Hebrew text is addressed to the Judean king Ahaz telling him, "Look, the young woman is with child and shall bear a son, and shall name him Immanuel. He shall eat curds and honey by the time he knows how to refuse the evil and choose the good" (Isa. 7:13–14).[16]

Despite the way the verse appears quoted in the book of Matthew, all modern scholars agree that the Hebrew word *'almah* in Isaiah's passage means a young woman of marriageable age, not a "virgin" (the "virgin" imagery stems from the later translation in the Greek Septuagint). Contextually, the child that would be born to this woman would serve as a sign to Ahaz. Clearly, Jesus' miraculous birth some seven hundred years later would not have accomplished this purpose. The child signifies that Yahweh was with the kingdom of Judah at

16. On this passage, see, among the many treatments, Joseph Blenkinsopp, *Isaiah 1–39* (AB 19; New York: Doubleday, 2000); see also Peter Dubovsky, "Tiglath-pileser III's Campaigns in 734–732 BC: Historical Background of Isa. 7; 2 Kgs. 15–16 and 2 Chr. 27–28," *Biblica* 87 (2006) 153–70.

this specific moment of national crisis. This child would grow to be a man, but before he reached the age of accountability, that is, "learned to reject the bad and choose the good," the kings who threatened Ahaz would fall. The entire point of the prophecy, therefore, was that there was no reason for Ahaz to accept a political alliance with these men. Today, most biblical scholars believe that the child Isaiah referred to was king Hezekiah who ascended to the Judean throne in 715 BCE. Rather than a prophecy concerning a future Messiah, Isaiah was giving a very specific oracle to a Judean king that pertained directly to political events in Isaiah' own day.

For Isaiah, Hezekiah was a chosen child—a king who would be a righteous leader, a sign that "God was with" the kingdom of Judah. Years later, Hezekiah did engage in a series of significant religious reforms with Isaiah's help. The birth of this Judean king was the sign God gave Ahaz that he should take Isaiah's counsel seriously. Instead of providing a historical reading of this passage, the author of Matthew used Isaiah 7:13–14 as a creative springboard to understand Jesus. In so doing, the author offers a theological reinterpretation. This reinterpretation makes the passage directly relevant for the author's current religious community. This does not mean that the author of Matthew believed he was offering a creative reinterpretation. He very well might have assumed Jesus was a literal fulfillment of the prediction.

In the Hebrew Bible, authors used religious texts in a similar way. This process occurs in the book of Isaiah itself. Scholars typically divide the book of Isaiah into three historical sections—First Isaiah written mainly in the eighth century BCE (more or less the initial thirty-nine chapters), Deutero-Isaiah written during the mid-sixth century BCE (Chapters 40–55), and Third Isaiah written during the late sixth or early fifth century BCE (Chapters 56–66). The later contributors to the Isaiah corpus intentionally adapted the words and themes that appear in First Isaiah, thereby manifesting a similar approach to prophetic texts as the author of Matthew. Thus, like Matthew, the book of Isaiah adopts and reconfigures earlier prophetic texts, often taking those sources out of historical context. The interpretive method was simply part of a long, venerable tradition, witnessed in the book of Isaiah itself.

Like New Testament authors, other Jewish theologians continued this tradition through the production of later texts that adapted and added onto preexisting "biblical" sources. For example, the Dead Sea Scroll community at Qumran produced a type of biblical commentary known as *pesharim* that interpreted earlier material in light of the community's history. Their *pesharim* illustrate that Jews living at the time of Jesus were not concerned with identifying the literal, historical meaning of scripture. Instead, they were more interested in producing creative reinterpretation that explained contemporary religious views. Developing out of this same religious environment, early Christian authors adopted and recontextualized prophetic material as messianic prophecies pointing to Jesus.



Another parallel to this process appears in the writings of the first century Jewish historian Josephus. In his twenty volumes of history titled *Jewish Antiquities*, Josephus created a new rewritten Bible of sorts by quoting portions of the Septuagint verbatim and then adding both new material and his own commentary directly to the account. This same time period saw Philo of Alexandria, a Hellenistic Jewish philosopher, combine Jewish texts with Platonic philosophy. Through this effort, Philo created new religious material based on biblical sources.

This method of using biblical literature (including the prophets) can be seen as similar to the work Joseph Smith performed in creating a new expanded canon based upon the Bible—texts such as the Book of Moses and the Book of Abraham. As theological expansions upon biblical material, Joseph Smith's scriptural works parallel an ancient literary pattern for revelatory text. This same type of genre is seen in later Jewish pseudepigrapha and Rabbinic midrash, as well as within the Bible itself. The term *midrash* refers to a method of interpreting biblical material that fills in literary and legal gaps featured in the biblical sources. Joseph Smith's work fits in well with the way earlier authors used prophetic texts as a springboard to create new religious literature, independent of original authorial intent and historical setting. For Latter-day Saints, a text such as the Book of Abraham, therefore, can be defined as inspired prophetic midrash.

## ISAIAH AND THE BOOK OF MORMON

One of the most significant challenges for traditional LDS readings of prophetic material is the fact that this literature grew over time and was most likely not produced by the men whose names are connected with the biblical books. This is especially true for the composition of Isaiah. Since the twentieth century, virtually all mainstream scholars have held the position that Isaiah chapters 40–66 were written after the Jewish exile into Babylon (c. 586 BCE). This means that the historical Isaiah, a prophet who lived in Jerusalem during the eighth century BCE, did not write the second half of the book of Isaiah. For Latter-day Saints, this presents a direct challenge for traditionally held paradigms concerning the Book of Mormon, since some of its material attributes these later chapters to Isaiah himself. If scholars are correct, then this material would not have been available to the Book of Mormon people because it was not written until after they had arrived in the New World. Its attestation in the Book of Mormon is therefore anachronistic.



There are several compelling reasons scholars argue that Isaiah 40–66 is not a prophecy given by the historical Isaiah. Amongst other points, these factors include the following: (1) First Isaiah mentions Isaiah son of Amoz and provides biographical material regarding him and others of his time whereas the material in Second and Third Isaiah makes no mention of his name; (2) Deutero-Isaiah provides a polemical response to the Cyrus Cylinder and mentions the Persian ruler by name; (3) the historical Isaiah of the eighth century believed in the inviolability of Jerusalem and the authors of 40–66 present a message of comfort to the Judean exiles that directly counters Isaiah's theological conviction; (4) the authors of 40–55 know the alter-prophetic work of Jeremiah, but Jeremiah shows no signs of knowing the Deutero-Isaiah prophecies; (5) the authors of 40–66 knew exilic and postexilic material including Lamentations; (6) Deutero-Isaiah shows signs of Aramaic and Post-Exilic Hebrew influence (but this same linguistic trace does not appear in the oracles of the historical Isaiah). [17]

Any one of these issues would be enough to convince biblical scholars that Isaiah 40–66 is postexilic material added to Isaiah proper. All of them together provide undeniable evidence for the scholarly consensus. Exactly how and why later scribes attached these oracles to those of an earlier prophet is unknown. Yet contemporary scholars are certain that 40–66 does not reflect the work of the eighth century Isaiah son of Amoz. LDS apologetic responses to this challenge typically approach the topic by focusing on the Book of Mormon as a revelatory work given through Joseph Smith.[18] In creating the Book of Mormon, Smith did not simply work his way line upon line through an ancient script carved into golden plates. The translation of the Book of Mormon was more likely a revelatory, creative experience similar to the adapta-

17. On issues of dating see, for example, discussion and bibliography in Joseph Blenkinsopp, *Isaiah 40–55* (AB 19A; New York: Doubleday, 2002); for a summary of the evidence for Deutero-Isaiah and its relationship to Mormonism, see David Bokovoy, "The Truthfulness of Deutero-Isaiah: A Response to Kent Jackson," Pt. 1 and 2; Rational Faiths, accessed November 12, 2021 at https://rationalfaiths.com/truthfulness-deutero-isaiah-response-kent-jackson/ and https://rationalfaiths.com/truthfulness-deutero-isaiah-response-kent-jackson-part-2/.

18. See, for one example, Daniel T. Ellsworth, "Their Imperfect Best: Isaianic Authorship from an LDS Perspective," *Interpreter: A Journal of Latter-day Saint Faith and Scholarship* 27 (2017): 1–27.

tion of scriptural sources seen in earlier biblical and post biblical traditions. Mormon scholars argue that Latter-day Saints should expect that the book would contain inspired prophetic, midrashic use of material known to Smith, including the material in Isaiah 40–66.[19]



Latter-day Saints hold in high regard the prophetic tradition in the Bible—indeed, it is written into the foundations of the tradition. They believe that Joseph Smith and the church leaders who followed after him continue that same institution. There are certainly some general correspondences between these two traditions. These would include a belief in an ability for a human messenger to ascertain the will of deity, and then to offer an inspired oracle to help guide their respective communities. But unlike the LDS tradition, biblical prophets did not "hold priesthood" (to use LDS parlance) as a rule. They were not exclusively male, and typically speaking, biblical prophets were critics of those in authority, rather than individuals who held that authority themselves. These differences illustrate the importance of reading both biblical and LDS prophetic literature in its historical and social context.

19. David Bokovoy, "'The Book Which Thou Shalt Write': The Book of Moses as Prophetic Midrash," in *The Expanded Canon: Perspectives on Mormonism and Scripture,* edited by Blair G. Van Dyke, Brian D. Birch, and Boyd J. Petersen (Salt Lake City, UT: Greg Kofford Books, 2018), 121–42; and David Bokovoy, *Authoring the Old Testament: Genesis-Deuteronomy* (Draper, UT: Greg Kofford Books, 2014).

27

# Wisdom Literature and the Psalms

RYAN CONRAD DAVIS

Proverbs, Job, Ecclesiastes, and the Psalms provide a rare view into the rich culture of ancient Israel. Proverbs, Job, and Ecclesiastes are often categorized as "Wisdom Literature" by modern scholars because these books share a common interest in wisdom (Heb. *ḥōkmâ*) and its opposite, folly. Proverbs contains instructions and maxims designed to achieve life through wisdom and avoid folly that leads to death. The books of Job and Ecclesiastes, however, problematize the idea that the cosmos operates within such a consistent paradigm and see different ways forward. The Book of Psalms is a diverse collection of poetic compositions, many of which were performed in the Jerusalem temple, but many of these psalms share the theme of escaping death and securing life. While a full description of each of these rich and diverse books is not possible in this essay, their common interest in securing life while avoiding death allows us to discuss these books together and compare their sometimes conflicting viewpoints.

In this essay, the description of each biblical book will be primarily informed by modern academic approaches to the Hebrew Bible, but throughout I will reflect on some LDS approaches reflected in church curriculum with occasional nods to more academically oriented LDS works. This essay can only briefly note some ways that Latter-day Saints have engaged with these books, with full realization that Latter-day Saints fall across a wide spectrum of peoples and cultures with diverse backgrounds and reading strategies.

## LIFE AND DEATH

In ancient Israel, life was more than just being physically alive, it meant being a part of a community; a community that included both Yahweh and mortals.[1] Death, however, comes as these bonds to Yahweh and one's community are severed and broken, and the individual is left isolated and vulnerable.[2] In the



1. Bernd Janowski, *Arguing with God: A Theological Anthropology of the Psalms*, trans. Armin Siedlecki (Louisville, KY: Westminster John Knox, 2013), 49.

2. Janowski, *Arguing with God*, 50–51; Christopher B. Hays, *A Covenant with Death: Death in the Iron Age II and Its Rhetorical Uses in Proto-Isaiah* (Grand Rapids, MI: Eerdmans, 2015), 185–86.

Psalms, one's connection to the social sphere is intimately connected with one's own physical and emotional health; any rupture in one is thought to manifest in the other. In Proverbs, wisdom is not only rooted in a relationship with Yahweh, or "fear of the Lord" (Prov. 9:10), but it is meant to maintain proper social connections with one's community (e.g., Prov. 6:1–3; Prov. 23). The fact that death disconnects the individual from Yahweh and one's community is a common theme in both the Wisdom books and the Psalms. For example, in Ps. 88:4–5, the psalmist laments that "I am counted among those who go down to the Pit; I am like those who have no help, like those forsaken among the dead, like the slain that lie in the grave, like those whom you remember no more, for they are cut off from your hand."

In previous scholarship it has been common to take passages like the one cited as a lack of a belief in an afterlife, since Sheol is often considered to be the final resting place of all humankind. More recently some scholars have questioned this monolithic understanding of Sheol in light of repeated emphasis on Yahweh's power over Sheol (Amos 9:1–2; Ps. 6:5–6; 16:10; 49:16; Jonah 2:3),[3] and the generally positive view of death found elsewhere in the Hebrew Bible.[4] In the Pentateuch, when the patriarchs died, they were "gathered to [their] people" (see Gen. 25:8, 17; 35:29; 49:29). Matthew Suriano has claimed that Sheol, in certain contexts, is a liminal area where the dead undergo a transition from the deceased to ancestors.[5] Thus, those that have passed on are able to avoid the disconnection and isolation of Sheol by maintaining connections to their community even after death.[6] This connection was maintained by being buried on one's ancestral land, and through being honored by one's living descendants, which took the form of food offerings.[7] Those that lacked this connection faced the grim isolation of Sheol.

Although some scholars are able to accept that Israelites believed in an afterlife of some kind, most agree that a widespread belief in bodily resurrection did not occur until the Second Temple period. Throughout the Hebrew Bible, judgment is expected to take place in mortality, a judgment that may

3. Matthew Suriano, "Sheol, the Tomb, and the Problem of Postmortem Existence," *Journal of Hebrew Scriptures* 16 (2016): 21.

4. Jon D. Levenson, *Resurrection and the Restoration of Israel: The Ultimate Victory of the God of Life* (New Haven, CT: Yale University Press, 2006), 67–81; Stephen L. Cook, "Funerary Practices and Afterlife Expectations in Ancient Israel," *Religion Compass* 1, no. 6 (2007): 660–83; Suriano, "Postmortem Existence."

5. Suriano, "Postmortem Existence."

6. Cook, "Funerary Practices and Afterlife Expectations in Ancient Israel."

7. Herbert Chanan Brichto, "Kin, Cult, Land and Afterlife: A Biblical Complex," *Hebrew Union College Annual* 44 (1973): 1–54. For a summary of the archaeological evidence, see Hays, *A Covenant with Death*, 147–53.

very well have afterlife implications. Because life in its fullest sense is found in maintaining connections to one's community, the Wisdom Books and many of the psalms focus on preserving, maintaining, and mending these connections; but they do so in opposing ways and with different assumptions.



Latter-day Saints generally expect to find their conceptions of life, death, and the afterlife in the Hebrew Bible, even though LDS scripture itself attests to developments in afterlife expectations. The Book of Mormon shares a simple heaven/hell dichotomy, similar to the New Testament, but Doctrine and Covenants 76, known as the "Vision," significantly changed LDS beliefs from a dichotomy to a continuum. Despite this development, Latter-day Saints have not fully engaged with ideas of death and afterlife in the Hebrew Bible. Full engagement would yield interesting results. Latter-day Saints have cited passages from the Hebrew Bible in support of their distinctive beliefs about connecting and interacting with ancestors beyond the grave. For example, Ecclesiastes 9:10, "for there is no work, nor device, nor knowledge, nor wisdom, in the grave" (KJV), has been used to explain why proxy work for the dead in temples must be done in mortality; after Joseph Young quotes this verse, "there is no device there [i.e., grave], for so says brother Brigham, the Prophet. He says that all the endowments have to be given on this side of the veil."[8] Although some rituals done for deceased ancestors, such as setting food out for them, might feel foreign to many North American Latter-day Saints,[9] performing rituals to secure for them a better afterlife is an important tenant of faith (D&C 128:18).

## PROVERBS

With Israelite views of the importance of social embeddedness to life and death serving as the backdrop, the Book of Proverbs offers the most empowering and positive assessment of humankind's ability to secure life and avoid death. For Proverbs, wisdom is the solution to death. The application of wisdom will lead to the correct course of action in any given situation. Wisdom is hailed as the key to "long life" and "riches and honor" (Prov. 3:16), and the means by which Yahweh himself "founded the earth" and "established the heavens" (Prov. 3:19). Within Proverbs, Wisdom is often personified as a woman who readers are encouraged to love and be faithful to (Prov. 4). The assumption

8. *Journal of Discourses* 6:242
9. Latter-day Saints in South Korea, for example, would be comfortable with such a practice.

that underlies this book is that humans, empowered by the divine guidance afforded by wisdom, have enormous power over their own destinies. Proverbs implicitly claims that humankind can prevent the severing of one's connection with Yahweh and community through wisdom. In fact, wisdom is described as a "tree of life" (Prov. 3:18).



The Book of Proverbs mainly participates in two ancient Near Eastern genres, instructions, and proverbs. Proverbs 1–9 is framed as the instructions of a royal father to his son on choosing life and avoiding death. These types of compositions are found in both Mesopotamia and Egypt, where the father is usually a famous figure of the cultural past. Scholars generally view the attribution of these texts to these famous figures to be an attempt by ancient scribes to garner authority, and give them little historical credibility. Additionally, proverbs collections are common in both Egypt and Mesopotamia, and it is clear that Israel is participating in a common enterprise since passages from the Book of Proverbs bear a close resemblance to those in the earlier Egyptian text *The Instruction of Amenemope*.[10]

Latter-day Saints generally quote from the Book of Proverbs in piecemeal fashion, something that is natural, considering its anthological nature. Although there is very little systematic engagement with the book itself, the paradigm that it enshrines finds widespread support in LDS scripture. One of the fundamental themes of the Book of Mormon narrative is the divine promise, "Inasmuch as ye shall keep my commandments ye shall prosper in the land; but inasmuch as ye will not keep my commandments ye shall be cut off from my presence" (2 Nephi 1:20). Prosperity is connected with obedience, and a rupture in one's connection to God comes through disobedience. The Book of Mormon takes an empowering view toward human agency and teaches that it is ultimately up to human choice how one's life will fare (2 Nephi 2:27). Despite the paradigm echoing throughout LDS scripture, there is much left to explore about the book itself that Latter-day Saints would uniquely appreciate. The optimistic outlook of Proverbs is the closest that Latter-day Saints might come to seeing the doctrine of eternal progression in the Hebrew Bible. For example, one could read Prov. 8:22–23 as saying Yahweh "acquired" (Heb. root: *qānâ*) wisdom "at the beginning of his way," and the reader is invited to "acquire (Heb. root: *qānâ*) wisdom" as well (Prov. 4:5; KJV). Thus, Proverbs could be read as an invitation to follow Yahweh's own acquisition of wisdom.[11]

10. See Miriam Lichtheim, *Ancient Egyptian Literature*, three vols. (Berkeley: University of California Press, 2006), 2:146–163.

11. Alan Lenzi notes, "Yahweh, therefore, is the prototype of what a human is supposed to do: acquire wisdom," in "Proverbs 8:22–31: Three Perspectives on Its Composition" *JBL* 125 (2006): 696, note 38.

## ECCLESIASTES

The idea that one can find certainty in maintaining connections to Yahweh and one's community sounded hollow to the author of Ecclesiastes. Ecclesiastes, also translated as "the Preacher" (Heb: *qōhɛlɛt*), writes as a king in a way that resembles both monumental inscriptions and royal autobiographies. In tone, however, Ecclesiastes resembles a group of Egyptian and Mesopotamian texts that emphasize humanity's limited capacity. Each of these texts are themselves reacting to the positive and optimistic assertions of the paradigm found in Proverbs. As Christopher Hays notes, even for cultures like Egypt where belief in a good afterlife is robust and well-described, "to say that a happy afterlife was the natural state of death to an Egyptian would be like saying that a rose garden is the natural state of the field."[12] Expectations for the afterlife were not always certain, so that even in Egypt there was skepticism about one's final state. In one song inscribed on an Egyptian tomb wall, the singer questions the state of those who have passed on, "those who built tombs, their places are gone, what has become of them? . . . None comes from there, to tell of their state, to tell of their needs, to calm our hearts, until we go where they have gone!"[13] This lack of knowledge about the future leads the singer to exhort the listener to find joy in the journey and to seize the day, "Hence rejoice in your heart! Forgetfulness profits you, follow your heart as long as you live! Put myrrh on your head, dress in fine linen, anoint yourself with oils fit for a god."[14] The uncertainty of one's state in the afterlife is coupled with this advice in Mesopotamian compositions such as the *Ballad of the Early Ruler* and the *Epic of Gilgamesh*. Ecclesiastes appears to be writing with these traditions in view. Not only is Ecclesiastes skeptical about what might happen in the afterlife, but he is skeptical that one can know the results of one's own efforts in mortality (Eccl. 3:1–11).

One of the purposes of the book is to answer the question, "what is of lasting value?" Ecclesiastes goes through different tests of experience, only to conclude that "all is vanity [or futile] and a chasing after wind" (Eccl. 1:14). If we read Ecclesiastes as making a positive argument, we may say that life is not in the destination, it is in the journey.[15] Ecclesiastes tests the common "destinations," such as wisdom, mirth, wealth, and finds that these are "vanity" and provide no lasting value. Indeed, the final destination for all, death, creates a host of injustices itself (Eccl. 9:1–3). Ecclesiastes, however, exhorts readers to

12. Hays, *A Covenant with Death*, 88.
13. Lichtheim, *Ancient Egyptian Literature*, 1:196.
14. Lichtheim, *Ancient Egyptian Literature*, 1:196–197.
15. John J. Collins, *Introduction to the Hebrew Bible* (Minneapolis, MN: Fortress, 2009), 521.

stop worrying about the destination and find joy in the journey. He argues that we should "[g]o, eat your bread with enjoyment, and drink your wine with a merry heart; for God has long ago approved what you do. Let your garments always be white; do not let oil be lacking on your head. Enjoy life with the wife whom you love" (Eccl. 9:1). As noted previously, Ecclesiastes' argument has an ancient pedigree.

Again, Latter-day Saints typically do not engage Ecclesiastes as a whole, yet some interesting reading strategies have developed in some church curricula. A current seminary manual states that "although the Preacher is a believer, he often poses questions and makes statements as if he were not."[16] Such an approach is unsurprising since Ecclesiastes' tone was alarming even to early rabbis who debated whether Ecclesiastes should be in the canon at all.[17] Such a skeptical view may be behind an earlier manual's call for students to engage in dialogue with "the preacher."[18] Students are asked to agree or disagree with his assertion that "much wisdom is much vexation and those who increase knowledge increase sorrow" (Eccl. 1:18). An invitation to disagree with scripture is not typical in LDS tradition. Also interesting is that the current seminary manual takes the last few verses, which many scholars see as later additions to soften his alarming teachings, as the reading guide for the entire book. Thus the injunction to "fear God, and keep his commandments" (12:13) and that "God shall bring every work into judgment (12:14) become a way to disengage with most of the book's message.[19] Adam S. Miller, an LDS philosopher, has published a fine paraphrase of Ecclesiastes, and leaves out these verses entirely. Miller interprets Ecclesiastes message in light of Christian teachings of grace; arguing that "before we find Christ, we must give up hope in everything else."[20] Although Latter-day Saint curricula do not engage with the core message of the book, finding joy in the journey, this uncontextualized teaching has been shared as commendable in general conference.[21] Nephi, however, finds such a teaching—one that neglects the importance of destination—to be alarming

16. *Old Testament Seminary Teacher Manual* (Salt Lake City, UT: Church of Jesus Christ of Latter-day Saints, 2015), 418.

17. See Mishnah Yadayim 3:5

18. *Old Testament Student Study Guide* (Salt Lake City, UT: Church of Jesus Christ of Latter-day Saints, 2002), 136.

19. *Old Testament Seminary Teacher Manual*, 418. This sentiment is also echoed in the LDS Bible Dictionary where Ecclesiastes 11 and 12 are called "the most spiritual part of the book" (s.v. Ecclesiastes; 631).

20. Adam S. Miller, *Nothing New Under the Sun: A Blunt Paraphrase of Ecclesiastes* (self-published, 2016).

21. See Thomas S. Monson, "In Search of Treasure," *Ensign* (May 2003), 121.

and warns, "there shall be many which shall say: Eat, drink, and be merry, for tomorrow we die; and it shall be well with us" (2 Ne. 28:7; cf. Eccl. 8:15).

## JOB

The Book of Job shares the skepticism of Ecclesiastes, but challenges the paradigm of Proverbs in a different way. Similar to Ecclesiastes, the main themes of Job have ancient Near Eastern precedents. In the Babylonian poem, "I Will Praise the Lord of Wisdom" (*ludlul bēl nēmeqi*), the issue of undeserved suffering is addressed in two ways; Thorkild Jaocobsen describes these as an answer for the mind and another for the heart.[22] The answer to the mind is that human standards cannot be applied to divine conduct; in the poem, the protagonist complains,

> I wish I knew that these things were pleasing to a god!
> What seems good to one's self could be an offense to a god,
> What in one's own heart seems abominable could be good to one's god!
> Who could learn the reasoning of the gods in heaven?[23]

The answer to the heart is that not only do the gods have power to wound, but we can trust in their mercy to heal. In a related composition, the healed sufferer triumphantly declares,

> He dashed me down, then grabbed me (as I fell),
> He scattered me wide, then garnered me,
> He thrust me away, then gathered me in,
> He threw me down, then lifted me high.[24]

One can find these same themes in the Book of Job; there is acknowledgment that human notions of justice are not easily applied to God, and in one reading, Job takes comfort and submits to a God who has complete power to destroy and make alive. These are not the only ways of reading Job, and the book lends itself to a number of readings.

22. Thorkild Jacobsen, "Mesopotamia: The Good Life," in *The Intellectual Adventure of Ancient Man: An Essay on Speculative Thought in the Ancient Near East,* edited by H. Frankfort et al. (Chicago: University of Chicago Press, 1946), 215–16.

23. Benjamin R. Foster, *Before the Muses: An Anthology of Akkadian Literature*, 3rd ed. (Bethesda, MD: CDL Press, 2005), 399.

24. Foster, *Before the Muses*, 411.

The book of Job includes a narrative written in prose (Job 1–2; 42:7–17) that frames a long conversation in poetry between Job and his friends (Eliphaz, Bildad, and Zophar; Job 3–31), and rebuttals by Elihu and Yahweh, the latter of which are often known as the "whirlwind speeches" (Job 32–42). Near the beginning of the book God holds court with the divine council, and one of the council's members who is in charge of prosecuting evil, challenges God's approval of Job saying, "Does not Job have good reason to fear God?" (Job 1:9; JPS). The accuser challenges God, asserting that Job's righteous is merely self-interest, and the prologue sets up an important question for the book. Is disinterested righteousness possible? Can one be righteous without expecting a reward?

This question, however, is not the issue for the character of Job throughout the book. Initially, Job himself trusts God unfailingly even as he is afflicted "without cause" with God's permission (Job 2:10). Yet, in the poetic dialogue with his friends, Job begins to question whether God's conduct is just. Job accuses God of violating the very standard to which he holds Job (Job 30:16–26). Job wishes to bring God to court so that he can prove his own innocence and God's injustice (Job 13:3). Job himself holds to the retribution paradigm, but since his personal experience has shown that God still afflicts the righteous (Job 9:22), he questions God's justice. Job's friends also hold to the paradigm, yet they cannot accept Job's innocence, and instead hold God guiltless and Job at fault.

Yahweh finally does respond to Job, but his answer has long remained a puzzle. Rather than explain his debate about disinterested righteousness with the accuser, Yahweh points to Job's lack of both knowledge and power by describing his own role as creator (Job 38–41). Some scholars read Yahweh's response as vicious and uncompassionate, putting Job in his place and confirming that power rather than justice is the more important operating principle in the cosmos. But others still read this as a response by Yahweh meant to teach Job that Yahweh is an involved creator, one who tames destruction and sets boundaries, and inform Job that there is more going on in the cosmos than his own problems.[25] Either way, it is clear that Yahweh does not offer any defense for his treatment of Job, but rather shows that he is in charge.

When the prose narrative begins again, God tells Job that he (Job) has spoken that which is right but the friends have not (42:7). Yahweh may be referring to all of Job's words accusing Yahweh of injustice, or he may be referring to Job's submission (42:6). If the former, it says something about the importance

25. Michael V. Fox, "God's Answer and Job's Response," *Biblica* 94, no. 1 (2013): 1–23.

of honest theological discourse over received tradition,[26] and if the latter, it still explicitly condemns the friends for justifying God at Job's expense (cf. Job 13:7–8). However, even after the story basically confirms that Yahweh's actions cannot be held to human standards, God then blesses and rewards Job for his good behavior. Yahweh's reward of Job seems to confirm the very paradigm that the book seems to challenge. The accuser does not reappear nor does his conversation with God resume. Did Job prove God right by submitting to him even without the promise of blessing? Or did the accuser win, because God put another hedge around Job?



Latter-day Saints typically limit their engagement to the narrative framing of the book. They know of a Job who remained faithful despite tests and trials and who is ultimately recompensed twofold for his trouble. This is the Job mentioned in James who talks of "the patience of Job" (5:11). Church President John Taylor frequently referred to the prose narrative of Job, but also engaged with the character of Job during the dialogues. He once commented that "we read about the patience of Job; but I do not think he was a very patient man."[27] Latter-day Saints typically take the story as proof that sin does not always correlate to suffering.[28] More recently, there have been more sustained engagements with the book of Job, including one book-length treatment.[29] This book on Job written by Michael Austin, a Latter-day Saint who is a trained literary critic, is rare instance of a study that fully embraces academic approaches the Bible while still being directed at a general Latter-day Saint audience.

Latter-day Saints typically approach Job as an account about a historical individual and find this confirmed by his mention in a revelation to Joseph Smith, which reads, "Thou art not yet as Job; thy friends do not contend against thee, neither charge thee with transgression, as they did Job" (D&C 121:10). Despite this general historical approach to Job, the current seminary manual reads portions of Job as fiction to ease theological tension. Latter-day Saint readers are often uncomfortable with the dialogue between Satan and God, and the current seminary manual deals with this by saying that "Job 1:6–12 contains a poetic version of an imagined conversation" and that "[i]t is likely

26. Greenstein's interpretation in Adele Berlin and Marc Zvi Brettler, eds., *Jewish Study Bible*, 2nd ed. (New York: Oxford University Press, 2015), 1494.

27. John Taylor, *Journal of Discourses*, 7:197–98

28. See LDS Bible Dictionary, s.v., Job

29. See Michael Austin, *Re-Reading Job: Understanding the Ancient World's Greatest Poem* (Salt Lake City, UT: Greg Kofford Books, 2014); John S. Tanner, "Hast Thou Considered My Servant Job?," in *Sperry Symposium Classics: The Old Testament*, edited by Paul Y. Hoskisson (Provo, UT: Religious Studies Center, BYU, 1990).

such a conversation . . . never took place."[30] Most scholars argue that the concept of Satan developed over time, so at this time, he was considered a member of God's court in charge of prosecuting injustice—a role indicated by the use of the definite article in Hebrew, thus, "the satan" or "the prosecutor."[31] Although the seminary manual is open to assuming parts of the book are fiction, it does not carry this idea any further. Austin, however, makes the case that it is important to dissociate worry about the historical Job from the genre of the book itself, and he finds support for approaching Job as literature in a letter written by Charles W. Penrose with Anthony W. Ivins on behalf of the First Presidency in 1922.[32] In summarizing this letter, historian Thomas Alexander notes that

> While they thought Jonah was a real person, they said it was possible the story as told in the Bible was a parable common at the time. The purpose was to teach a lesson, and it "is of little significance as to whether Jonah was a real individual, or one chosen by the writer of the book" to illustrate "what is set forth therein." They took a similar position on Job.[33]

This letter was written to an individual and not widely circulated, and most Latter-day Saints would be surprised by this position.

Job 38:7 is frequently cited as demonstration of the Latter-day Saint belief in the premortal life. It occurs in the whirlwind speech when the Lord asks Job where he was "[w]hen the morning stars sang together, and all the sons of God shouted for joy?" (Job 38:7; KJV). Latter-day Saint understanding of the phrase "sons of God" is not entirely congruous with the Hebrew Bible's use of the term. In the Hebrew Bible, this phrase depicts divine beings who were members of God's divine council and were often associated with the stars or "host of heaven" (1 Kgs. 22:19). This imagery is used in the New Testament when, in Revelation, the dragon takes a third of the stars as his followers (Rev. 12:4, 9). In Job, Latter-day Saints understand the phrase "sons of God" to refer to premortal spirits who will yet come to earth. The Book of Mormon does provide a bridge between the Hebrew Bible's use of the phrase "sons of God" and Latter-day Saint understanding when it describes Jesus and his apostles as

30. *Old Testament Study Guide for Home-Study Seminary Students* (Salt Lake City, UT: Church of Jesus Christ of Latter-day Saints, 2015), 234.

31. See Ronan Head's contribution in Julie M. Smith, ed., *As Iron Sharpens Iron: Listening to the Various Voices of Scripture* (Salt Lake City, UT: Greg Kofford Books, 2016).

32. Austin, *Re-Reading Job*, 15–18.

33. Thomas G. Alexander, *Mormonism in Transition: A History of the Latter-day Saints, 1890–1930* (Urbana: University of Illinois Press, 1996), 283.

members of the divine council descending from the sky with brightness similar to the sun and stars before their mortal births (1 Nephi 1:8–10).

## THE BOOK OF PSALMS

As noted previously, the Book of Psalms can be put into conversation with the Wisdom Books in their varied approaches to securing life and avoiding death. The Book of Psalms has a variety of perspectives. Among its poetic compositions, one can find compositions that express optimism in the power of human agency to secure life, and one can also find compositions that seek comfort as they wrestle with the prosperity of the wicked (see Ps. 1, 37, 73). However, more of the book itself agrees with Job that, regardless of why we suffer, a relationship with Yahweh is the only way back to life, and it also agrees with Job that the sufferers should be able to speak their mind.

The book itself is an anthology of poetic compositions, many of which are attributed to named individuals, such as Moses, David, Solomon, and various temple personnel. This attribution is often assumed to indicate authorship, but the Hebrew is ambiguous enough to offer a range of possibilities.[34] Regardless of what this attribution originally meant, scholars generally assume that the psalms were written by anonymous scribes.[35] The headings also indicate that many of these psalms were expected to be set to music and performed by Levites. One of the most important advances in our reading of the book of Psalms came when the early twentieth century scholar Hermann Gunkel grouped and analyzed the psalms by genre or type.[36] His pioneering endeavor has allowed us to better understand individual psalms by understanding the genres they participate in. Many different ways to group the psalms have emerged, but one may group many psalms into laments (prayers for help), praises (praise and thanksgiving), royal psalms, liturgies, and wisdom psalms.[37] Sigmund Mowinckel, a Norwegian biblical scholar, built off of the work of Gunkel and argued that there was a ritual background to many of the psalms.[38] Mowinckel

34. For a discussion on attribution, see Nancy L. deClaissé-Walford, Rolf A. Jacobson, and Beth LaNeel Tanner, *The Book of Psalms* (Grand Rapids, MI: Eerdmans, 2014), 9–11.

35. For example, because Rolf Jacobson does not see these attributions as indications of authorship, he assumes that "for practical purposes, all of the psalms are anonymous" (deClaissé-Walford, Jacobson, and Tanner, *The Book of Psalms*, 11).

36. Hermann Gunkel, *Introduction to Psalms: The Genres of the Religious Lyric of Israel*, trans. by James D. Nogalski (Eugene, OR: Wipf & Stock, 2020).

37. This list is slightly adapted from deClaissé-Walford, Jacobson, and Tanner, *The Book of Psalms*, 19–21.

38. Sigmund Mowinckel, *The Psalms in Israel's Worship*, two vols. (Oxford, UK: Blackwell, 1962).

argued that many of them were performed as part of an annual enthronement festival that celebrated Yahweh's kingship. Although few scholars today would follow Mowinckel this far,[39] many scholars do agree that many psalms could find a plausible background in the first or second Jerusalem temple. More recently, however, focus has turned away from the ritual context of the psalms and focused on their textual setting within the Book of Psalms itself.[40] This approach hopes to read the Book of Psalms as a unity and look for the message intended by its editors. Scholars can use evidence of editorial activity to interpret the book as a whole and interpret individual psalms in light of the whole. One well known mark of editing can be seen in the organization of the Book of Psalms into five books or sections (Psalm 1–41; 42–72; 73–89; 90–106; 107–50), each marked by a doxology or praise to God (41:13; 72:18–19; 89:52; 106:48; 150:6).[41]

The practice of grouping psalms by category remains an important way of reading the psalms, and the most important categories, for our purposes, are the two largest, lament and praise, and the two stand at the heart of Israel's relationship with Yahweh.[42] Laments, or rather "prayers for help," are prayers to Yahweh by individuals and the entire community when their links to Yahweh and those around them are rupturing; in other words, they are facing death and Sheol. These psalms typically include a "lament" section, where the crisis is described, and the problem usually comes down to three issues: self, enemies, or Yahweh.[43] The individual faces disconnection from Yahweh and his or her community, and this is manifest in death beginning to take hold on the person. Psalm 13, often considered the model "prayer for help," includes all three, "How long, O LORD? Will you forget me forever? How long will you hide your face from me? (Yahweh) How long must I bear pain in my soul, and have sorrow in my heart all day long? (Self) How long shall my enemy be exalted over me? (Enemy)" (Ps. 13:1–2). These laments can be blunt, wondering "my God, my

39. For a scholar who still supports a "modified version of Mowinckel's theory," see J.J.M. Roberts, "Mowinckel's Enthronement Festival: A Review," in *The Book of Psalms: Composition and Reception*, edited by Peter W. Flint and Patrick D. Miller Jr. (Leiden, Netherlands: Brill, 2005), 97–115.

40. Gerald Henry Wilson, *The Editing of the Hebrew Psalter* (Chico, CA: Scholars Press, 1985); Nancy L. deClaissé-Walford, ed., *The Shape and Shaping of the Book of Psalms: The Current State of Scholarship*, Ancient Israel and Its Literature 20 (Atlanta: SBL Press, 2014).

41. deClaissé-Walford, Jacobson, and Tanner, *The Book of Psalms*, 25–26.

42. Claus Westermann is well known for arguing the centrality of lament and praise in the Book of Psalms; see Claus Westermann, *Praise and Lament in the Psalms*, trans. by Keith R. Crim and Richard N. Soulen (Edinburgh, UK: T & T Clark, 1981); Claus Westermann, *The Psalms: Structure, Content, and Message* (Minneapolis, MN: Augsburg Fortress, 1980).

43. See Westermann, *The Psalms*, 37–39.

God, why have you forsaken me?" (Ps. 22:1), but these demands are supported by a deep and abiding trust in Yahweh, who is expected to rescue, or save, those who trust in him. Despite the accusation that Yahweh has forgotten the supplicant, the psalmist in Psalm 13 still expresses trust, "But I trusted in your steadfast love; my heart shall rejoice in your salvation" (v. 5). Prayers for help often end in a vow to praise Yahweh when their prayer is answered (Ps. 13:6).

Under the category of praise, thanksgiving psalms are the praise that are promised in the "prayers for help." When a prayer was answered, individuals came to the temple to offer a sacrifice and to praise Yahweh; not only Yahweh but friends, family, and priests would participate in the feast and listen to the words of the rescued worshipper (see Ps. 22:22–31). The praise of thanksgiving psalms is the inverse of the "prayers for help," "I will extol you, O LORD, for you have drawn me up, and did not let my foes rejoice over me. O LORD my God, I cried to you for help, and you have healed me. O LORD, you brought up my soul from Sheol, restored me to life from among those gone down to the Pit." Although Sheol was the epitome of disconnection from Yahweh and community, the corollary location in the Psalms was not heaven, but Yahweh's earthly residence, the temple. As Jon Levenson notes, the temple is "paradise, the place rendered inviolable by the pervasive presence of God" and while "death is the norm outside of Zion … [t]o journey to the temple is to move toward redemption."[44]

The Book of Psalms is commonly said to be the most read book of the Old Testament among Christians, but among Latter-day Saints this book of scripture just does not hold the same pride of place.[45] Despite less frequent engagement with Psalms compared to other Christians, in many ways Latter-day Saint approaches mirror traditional protestant interpretation of the text. In church curriculum, focus is placed on reading the psalms as prophecies of Jesus Christ, reading them as illuminating a biographical moment in David's life, and reading them as sources of praise and thanksgiving to God.[46] These reading strategies are not distinctive to Latter-day Saints. The entry for "Psalms" in the LDS Bible Dictionary also demonstrates a lack of distinctive

44. Jon D. Levenson, *Resurrection and the Restoration of Israel: The Ultimate Victory of the God of Life* (New Haven, CT: Yale University Press, 2006), 92.

45. For example, W.H. Bellinger Jr. states, "The book of Psalms is the most read, the most used, of all the Old Testament books" (*Psalms: A Guide to Studying the Psalter* [Grand Rapids, MI: Baker Academic, 2012], 1). Although Latter-day Saints do not engage the Book of Psalms with the same frequency, Elder Jeffrey R. Holland of the Quorum of the Twelve has recently written a selective commentary on Psalms in Jeffrey R. Holland, *For Times of Trouble: Spiritual Solace from the Psalms* (Salt Lake City, UT: Deseret Book, 2012).

46. *Old Testament: Gospel Doctrine Teacher's Manual* (Salt Lake City, UT: Church of Jesus Christ of Latter-day Saints, 2001), 111–22.

reading strategies. The LDS Bible Dictionary was based on an older *Cambridge Companion to the Bible*, and the entry for "Psalms" repeats the same entry in the 1905 edition almost word for word.[47] Similar to other Christians, Latter-day Saint worship also includes hymns that are influenced and based on individual psalms.[48] However, the psalms that heavily use or are based on the psalms that are included in the current Latter-day Saint hymnbook are mostly drawn from the broader Christian tradition.[49]

Despite the fact that Latter-day Saints read and use the hymns in traditional ways, they do have some approaches to the text that are influenced by their distinctive theology. For example, because the temple is a living institution for Latter-day Saints, the frequent mention of the temple in the Psalms allows Latter-day Saints to read their own experiences more easily into the psalms. In a Sunday School manual, the lesson invites class members to read a selection of psalms and invites the instructor to ask, "What can we learn about the temple from these psalms?"[50] Rather than using the text to understand ancient Israelite temples, a follow up question makes it clear that these verses are expected to be directly applicable to modern LDS temples, "What can we learn about preparing ourselves to go the temple?"[51] The temple as an ideal is expected to transcend time and place, so little time is spent on its ancient context.

However, if the present relevance of temples allows a reader to pass over the ancient context, it has also encouraged Latter-day Saint scholars to spend more time uncovering the ancient temple context through the text of the psalms. Latter-day Saint scholars LeGrand Baker and Stephen Ricks have coauthored a volume where, taking inspiration from Sigmund Mowinckel, they argue that the Book of Psalms contains a sacred drama that was performed as part of

47. Some material is deleted or rearranged, but there is only one instance of a minor grammatical change in one sentence; see *The Cambridge Companion to the Bible* (Cambridge, UK: University Press, 1905), 127–32.

48. Shon Hopkin and J. Arden Hopkin take a brief look at the how the psalms have been set to music and sung among Jews, Latter-day Saints, and other Christians in J. Arden Hopkin and Shon D. Hopkin, "The Psalms Sung: The Power of Music in Sacred Worship," in *Ascending the Mountain of the Lord: Temple, Praise, and Worship in the Old Testament*, ed. David Rolph Seely, Jeffrey R. Chadwick, and Matthew J. Grey (Provo, UT: Religious Studies Center, BYU, 2013), 329–48.

49. For example, the hymns used to exemplify the use of psalms in Latter-day Saint hymn singing are "We Love Thy House, O God, "For the Beauty of the Earth, "Rejoice, the Lord is King, "Precious Savior, Dear Redeemer," "The Lord is My Shepherd", "The Lord is My Light," "How Great Thou Art", and "Praise to the Lord, the Almighty"; see *Old Testament: Gospel Doctrine Teacher's Manual*, 121; Hopkin and Hopkin, "The Psalms Sung: The Power of Music in Sacred Worship," 344. These hymns are all drawn from the broader Christian tradition.

50. *Old Testament: Gospel Doctrine Teacher's Manual*, 120.

51. *Old Testament: Gospel Doctrine Teacher's Manual*, 120.

ancient Israelite temple worship.[52] For Latter-day Saints, the idea that individual psalms might reflect the remnants of sacred drama that centered around the temple is certainly influenced by their own experience in modern LDS temples.[53] Donald Parry has also read Psalm 15 and 24 as temple entrance hymns to explore the moral qualities expected of those who enter the temple and the possible ritual context for the psalms.[54] Although Latter-day Saint scholars have reflected on and contributed to understanding Psalms in terms of genre and ritual setting,[55] few, if any, have engaged the more recent interest in the editorial shape and shaping of the book itself.



Aside from promoting an interest in the ancient ritual setting of Psalms, distinctive Latter-day Saint doctrines have caused focused interest on isolated passages. For example, the statement in Ps 82:6 that "You are gods" has received attention, especially since it is quoted by Jesus in John 10:34. This passage has been read as affirmation of humanity's divine potential and parentage as well as hinting at the plurality of gods.[56] There are many interpretive cruxes to Psalm 82, but most scholars accept that it describes a divine council where its disobedient members are sentenced to die like men.[57] Some Latter-day Saint scholars have also interacted with contemporary academic approaches, such as Daniel Peterson who sees echoes of the premortal divine council described in Abraham 3.[58]

52. LeGrand L. Baker and Stephen D. Ricks, *Who Shall Ascend Into the Hill of the Lord?: The Psalms in Israel's Temple Worship in the Old Testament and in the Book of Mormon* (Salt Lake City, UT: Eborn Books, 2009).

53. For another example of an LDS scholar that sees a much more limited selection of Psalms involved in a temple-centered drama, see Janet Ewell, "Seeing Psalms as the Libretti of a Holy Drama," *Interpreter: A Journal of Latter-Day Saint Faith and Scholarship* 31 (2019): 259–76. Janet Ewell builds on the work of Jeffrey M. Bradshaw from "KnoWhy OTL25A—Is There More to Psalm 23 Than Words of Solace and Comfort?," *The Interpreter Foundation*, July 4, 2018, available at https://interpreterfoundation.org/knowhy-otl25a-is-there-more-to-psalm-23-than-words-of-solace-and-comfort/.

54. Donald W. Parry, "'Who Shall Ascend into the Mountain of the Lord?': Three Temple Entrance Hymns," in *Revelation, Reason, and Faith: Essays in Honor of Truman G. Madsen*, edited by Donald W. Parry, Daniel C. Peterson, and Stephen D. Ricks (Provo, UT: FARMS, 2002), 729–42.

55. The generic categories of the psalms are touched on in Hopkin and Hopkin, "The Psalms Sung: The Power of Music in Sacred Worship."

56. For an excellent article that reviews devotional and academically oriented LDS approaches, see Daniel O. McClellan, "Psalm 82 in Contemporary Latter-Day Saint Tradition," *Interpreter: A Journal of Latter-Day Saint Faith and Scholarship* 15 (2015): 79–96.

57. For a thorough examination of Psalm 82; see Peter Machinist, "How Gods Die, Biblically and Otherwise: A Problem of Cosmic Restructuring," in *Reconsidering the Concept of Revolutionary Monotheism*, edited by Beate Pongratz-Leisten (Winona Lake, IN: Eisenbrauns, 2011), 189–240.

58. Daniel McClellan offers a nice summary of Peterson ("Ye Are Gods: Psalm 82 and John 10 as Witnesses to the Divine Nature of Humankind," in *The Disciple as Scholar: Essays on Scripture and the Ancient World in Honor of Richard Lloyd Anderson*, edited by Stephen D. Ricks, Donald W. Parry, and Andrew H. Hedges [Provo, UT: FARMS, 2000], 471–594) and others while offering his own approach in "Psalm 82 in Contemporary Latter-Day Saint Tradition."

## REFLECTION

Biblical scholarship paints a picture of Israelite literature as part of its ancient Near Eastern cultural setting. The disagreement and debate that is found within the Hebrew canon is reflected in similar texts in the ancient Near East. Each of these compositions has a different strategy for securing life, some of which are at odds with each other. Latter-day Saint approaches, which we have only briefly touched on, tend to assume that these texts share a theology that is both internally consistent and similar to their own. This generally prevents them from fully engaging the conflicting viewpoints in Wisdom Literature and fully reading the Psalms in their ancient setting. This general approach is showing signs of change as more Latter-day Saints become comfortable with the many voices of scripture, and the recent volume of Julie M. Smith, *As Iron Sharpens Iron*, is a testament to this.[59] Latter-day Saints' more widespread acceptance that even nineteenth century Latter-day Saints had beliefs and customs that are at variance from their own is also laying the groundwork for different ways of reading scripture, ways that might point toward new vistas in examining the texts treated here.

59. Smith, *As Iron Sharpens Iron*.

# 28

# Jesus and the Gospels

ERIC D. HUNTSMAN

In June 1829, Joseph Smith and Oliver Cowdery began to lay out the central beliefs of the religious movement that would later become The Church of Jesus Christ of Latter-day Saints. Eventually canonized as Doctrine and Covenants 20, this document stressed the central role of Jesus Christ as follows:

> [T]he Almighty God gave his Only Begotten Son, *as it is written in those scriptures which have been given of him*. He suffered temptations but gave no heed unto them. He was crucified, died, and rose again the third day; And ascended into heaven, to sit down on the right hand of the Father, to reign with almighty power according to the will of the Father; That as many as would believe and be baptized in his holy name, and endure in faith to the end, should be saved—. (D&C 20:21–25, emphasis added)

In the context of section 20, the scriptures "which have been given of him" were the Bible, especially the New Testament Gospels, and the Book of Mormon, which was said to contain "the fullness of the gospel of Jesus Christ" and prove "that the holy scriptures are true" (D&C 20:9, 11). Thus, from the beginning of the Latter-day Saint movement, Mormon understanding of Christology—the person and work of Jesus as the Christ—has been rooted in the received biblical record, confirmed, and subsequently expanded by the Book of Mormon and other Restoration scripture and teaching.

Such a doctrinal reaffirmation predisposed early Mormons to favor a theological interpretation of scripture at the very time that developing historical-critical approaches to the Bible were beginning to ask important questions about the nature of the portraits of Jesus in the New Testament Gospels.[1] While the earliest Latter-day Saints do not seem to have questioned the Gospels, their authorship, or their basic historicity, some Book of Mormon passages began to bring into question the reliability of the received biblical record (e.g., 1 Nephi 13:20–29). Then shortly after the founding of the church, Joseph Smith quickly began his "New Translation" project to clarify, correct, and at times expand the King James Bible. Since Smith's time, Latter-day Saint interpretation of the biblical Jesus material has come to be more and more informed by unique Restoration scripture and teaching. In addition, this interpretation is often shaped by the assumption that Latter-day Saint leaders—especially those sustained as prophets, seers, and revelators—are uniquely qualified to interpret scripture generally and the doctrine of Christ in particular. This has produced tension as Latter-day Saints have increasingly engaged the conclusions of biblical scholarship, as can be seen in differing Latter-day Saint approaches to the compositional history and historicity of the New Testament Gospels, a tendency towards harmonizing them in teaching, and the continued privileging of Latter-day Saint doctrine and insights.

## BIBLICAL CRITICISM OF THE GOSPELS

Even as the Latter-day Saint movement was gaining momentum in America in the nineteenth century, a new approach to the Bible, the historical-critical method, arose in the universities of Germany. Undergirded by earlier Enlightenment assumptions, this critical approach employed rationalistic assumptions as well as linguistic, historical, cultural, and literary analysis of the texts.[2] When applied to the Gospels and their portraits of Jesus, the historical-critical method resulted in what has been dubbed "The Quest for the Historical Jesus." In its first phase, beginning with the work of David Friedrich Strauss (1808–1874) and ending with Albert Schweitzer (1875–1965), this quest tried to separate a few basic historical facts about the man Jesus of Nazareth from claims of divinity and miracles, which were seen as largely non-historical projections

1. While the new, developing modes of biblical criticism attempted to identify the original meaning of texts to their original audiences, early Latter-day Saints, like many of their contemporaries, often seem to have allowed the lens of their own doctrinal assumptions to govern interpretation of scripture. For the perils of what even noted evangelical scholars describe as "Theological Interpretation of Scripture (TIS)" when it is not controlled by arguably more objective historical-literary biblical criticism, see William Klein, Craig Blomberg, and Robert L. Hubbard, *Introduction to Biblical Interpretation*, 3rd ed. (Grand Rapids, MI: Zondervan, 2017), 50–53.

2. See David Jasper, *A Short Introduction to Hermeneutics* (Louisville, KY: Westminster Press, 2004), 89–98; Klein, Blomberg, and Hubbard, *Introduction to Biblical Interpretation*, 99–102.

of the early Christian faith into the texts of the Gospels.[3] This early phase of historical Jesus studies—sometimes described as "the First Quest" to differentiate it from later historical, literary, and theoretical developments—sought to distinguish the historical Jesus from the traditional "Christ of Faith," opening it to criticism from conservative Christians that it reduced Jesus to a mere mortal teacher at the cost of his divinity. Nevertheless, important lessons from the First Quest, even for believers, included the need for reading the Gospels—and all scripture—critically, together with the recognition that religious tradition could give rise to misreadings of the texts.

Largely abandoning the idea that the historical Jesus could actually be found, the works of such scholars as Karl Barth (1886–1968) and Rudolf Bultmann (1884–1976) led to the next phase of Historical Jesus Studies, what is sometimes termed "the Second Quest," which saw the significance of the Gospels as being primarily theological. The Second Quest maintained that what was important was the meaning *behind* the text, and efforts to "demythologize" the Gospels did not, as some might think, undercut the message of Jesus. Instead, it sought to get to the heart of the fact that somehow Jesus' appearance in history had been God's way of changing the world.[4] From the 1980s until today, advances in our knowledge of the ancient world, many of them arising from the contributions of archaeology, anthropology, and the discovery of new texts, have led to renewed confidence in the ability of scholars to historically and culturally contextualize the Gospels. Including a full spectrum of conservative to liberal scholars, the current Third Quest takes the Gospel portraits and interprets them according to various models, seeing Jesus as everything from an apocalyptic prophet, a charismatic healer, and a cynic philosopher to a more traditionally Jewish social prophet or messianic figure.[5]

## THE LATTER-DAY SAINT HERMENEUTIC OF AUTHORITY

The historical-critical method had reached America by the mid nineteenth century, but it had little impact on Latter-day Saint approaches to the Bible.[6]

3. N.T. Wright, "Jesus, Quest for the Historical," *Anchor Yale Bible Dictionary* (New Haven, CT: Yale University Press, 1992), 3:796–98; Jasper, *Short Introduction to Hermeneutics*, 91–95.

4. Wright, "Jesus, Quest for the Historical," 3:798; Jasper, *Short Introduction to Hermeneutics*, 100–3; Klein, Blomberg, and Hubbard, *Introduction to Biblical Interpretation*, 104–6.

5. Wright, "Jesus, Quest for the Historical," 3:798–801; Ben Witherington, *The Jesus Quest: The Third Search for the Jew of Nazareth* (Downers Grove, IL: InterVarsity Press, 1997); Klein, Blomberg, and Hubbard, *Introduction to Biblical Interpretation*, 107–8, 110.

6. Even through the early twentieth century, leading Latter-day Saint commentators who were church authorities but did not have any training in biblical languages or studies either had little exposure to biblical

Perhaps the best known Latter-day Saint writer on Jesus in the Gospels was James E. Talmage (1862–1933), who completed his *Jesus the Christ* while a member of the Quorum of the Twelve Apostles. In it he took a largely uncritical approach to the question of the historical Jesus. Published in 1915 by the church itself[7] and framed more as a Victorian biography of Jesus than an analysis of the Gospel texts, Talmage's *Jesus the Christ* was dependent on others for historical, linguistic, textual, cultural, and archaeological evidence, and his secondary sources were conservative even for that period. Some of these were already dated when it was written.[8]

Given Talmage's ecclesiastical authority and the repute that *Jesus the Christ* obtained, many Mormon readers were, and some still are, disposed to accept Talmage's conclusions and interpretations over the suggestions of biblical scholarship. Although *Jesus the Christ* remains a rather singular example, some writings of subsequent authorities—such as later apostle Bruce R. McConkie's Mortal Messiah or Doctrinal New Testament Commentary series[9]—have received similar deference. Although none of McConkie's works gained the "classic" status that Talmage's did, his extensive writing and speaking, forceful style, and clear sense of mission combined to give him a reputation as an expert on the mission of Christ. McConkie often positioned the authoritative hermeneutic that he espoused over and against critical New Testament scholarship.[10]

Latter-day Saint scholars of the Bible, on the other hand, have taken different approaches. One example is the University of Chicago educated Russel B. Swensen (1902–1987). A professor of Religious Education and Medieval History at BYU from 1933 to 1973, Swensen wrote important church Sunday School manuals on New Testament Literature, the Synoptic Gospels, and the

---

criticism, especially in Historical Jesus Studies, or actively resisted it. B.H. Roberts (1857–1933) was conversant with it only through the medium of Bible commentaries, and Joseph Fielding Smith (1876–1972), an apostle and later church president, was openly hostile to such scholarship. See Anthony Hutchinson, "LDS Approaches to the Holy Bible" *Dialogue* 15, no. 1 (Spring 1982): 100–105, and Philip L. Barlow, *Mormons and the Bible: The Place of Latter-day Saints in American Religion*, updated ed. (Oxford, UK: Oxford University Press, 2013), 112–61.

7. James E. Talmage, *Jesus the Christ* (Salt Lake City, UT: The Church of Jesus Christ of Latter-day Saints, 1915; repr. 1982).

8. Some, for instance, were resistant to the developing historical and textual criticism of the time, but Talmage was attracted to these authors, many of them Anglican divines, because of their patent belief in the divinity of Christ and his mission. See Malcolm R. Thorp, "James E. Talmage and the Tradition of Victorian Lives of Jesus," *Sunstone* (January 1988): 8–13.

9. Bruce R. McConkie, *The Mortal Messiah*, four vols. (Salt Lake City, UT: Deseret Book, 1979–81), and *Doctrinal New Testament Commentary*, three vols. (Salt Lake City, UT: Bookcraft, 1965–1973).

10. See esp. his "The Bible, A Sealed Book," A Symposium on the New Testament, (1984), 1–7, reprinted in *Teaching Seminary Preservice Readings Religion 370, 471, and 475* (Salt Lake City, UT: Church of Jesus Christ of Latter-day Saints, 2004), 123–32.

Gospel of John that incorporated important elements of the biblical scholarship of the day.[11] These short volumes presented mainstream mid-twentieth century church members with significant background on the composition of the Gospels, what was known about their authors, and their individual intents, themes, and styles. They often included far more critical material than what is found in any current manual or even some scholarly monographs written by current writers publishing with Latter-day Saint presses.



## ISSUES OF COMPOSITION AND HISTORICITY

Traditional and authoritative hermeneutics combined to lead early and many current Latter-day Saints to uncritically accept conventional assumptions regarding the composition of the New Testament Gospels. For instance, traditional authorship of the four canonical Gospels was assumed with little question, and the only formal input Joseph Smith gave on this question was to change the titles of Matthew and John from "Gospel" to "Testimony" in his New Translation, perhaps to underscore what he felt was the apostolic authority behind the First and Fourth Gospels.[12] Still, the fact that Joseph Smith and other leaders, past and current, have often referred to the evangelists by name when citing the Gospels might imply inspired confirmation of their authorship to some Latter-day Saints. Further, many Latter-day Saint readers, accustomed to the clear self-identification of authors in Book of Mormon texts, may simply have not thought to question how authorship attributions in the Gospels had come about.

Critical scholarship, on the other hand, usually begins the study of the Gospels by trying to identify their provenance and situate them in their *Sitz im Leben*, or authorial context. The Gospels are all formally anonymous, and the titles that claim to identify their authors only began to appear in the second century.[13]

11. Russel Swensen, *New Testament Literature: A Study for College Students* (Salt Lake City, UT: LDS Department of Education, 1940); *The Synoptic Gospels* (Salt Lake City, UT: Deseret Sunday School Union, 1945); *The Gospel of John* (Salt Lake City, UT: Deseret Sunday School Union, 1946); *New Testament: Acts and Epistles* (Salt Lake City, UT: Deseret Sunday School Union, 1947).

12. Kevin L. Barney, "The Joseph Smith Translation and Ancient Texts of the Bible," *Dialogue: A Journal of Mormon Thought* 19, no. 3 (1987): 88; Scott H. Faulring, Kent P. Jackson, and Robert J. Matthews, eds., *Joseph Smith's New Translation of the Bible: Original Manuscripts* (Provo, UT: Religious Studies Center, 2004), 235, 314, 359, 442. As Barney notes, Joseph Smith was not original in this but may have been following the lead of Alexander Campbell, who had changed the titles to "Testimony" for all four Gospels in his 1828 translation.

13. Raymond E. Brown, *Introduction to the New Testament* (New Haven, CT: Yale University Press, 1997), 100–101, 109. For the earliest manuscript attestations for the attributed authorship of each Gospel, see the critical apparatus for their respective titles in *Nestle-Aland Novum Testamentum Graece*, edited by Barbara Aland et al., 28th ed. (Stuttgart, Germany: Deutsche Bibelgesellschaft, 2012), 1 (for Matthew), 102 (for Mark), 177 (for Luke), and 292 (for John).

As a result, scholarly efforts to determine original authorship must consider indirect evidence about the author and original audiences from the texts themselves while critically judging early claims made by postapostolic sources. The consensus of these efforts judges that Mark, written sometime in the 60s by an unknown Jewish author to a group of early Christians in Rome, was the first of the Gospels and was the basic narrative source for Matthew and Luke.[14]

These two Gospels, written in the 70s or 80s, wove into the basic Marcan storyline sayings of Jesus unknown to the author of Mark. Many scholars postulate a common source for these sayings, perhaps written but probably oral, which they have called Q (from the German *Quelle* for "source").[15] To the Marcan narrative and the Q material, the author of Matthew added an infancy narrative and some of his own unique material, fashioning it into a Gospel for both Jewish and Gentile Christians that portrayed Jesus as the Son of David who fulfilled many Jewish expectations while also suffering, dying, and rising again for all humankind.[16] Luke, on the other hand, wrote for a largely Gentile audience, combining the Marcan and Q sources (or perhaps Mark and a revision of Matthew's sayings material) with a considerable amount of his own material and adding a very different infancy narrative. The Jesus in Luke, in turn, was a more divine but also loving Savior figure, one who drew on both Jewish and Greco-Roman models.[17]

Because of their dependences upon the same base Marcan narrative, these three Gospels are usually called the Synoptic Gospels, because they *look* at the ministry, death, and resurrection of Jesus from largely the same point of view. Nonetheless, different emphases, different Christologies, and sometimes different material often make it difficult to harmonize the three. This difficulty is even more pronounced with the Gospel of John, which is considerably different than the other three, coming close to them only in its passion narrative. Presenting a much more elevated, divine Jesus, this Gospel seems to have arisen from a very different tradition—one that was based on the witness and memories of the figure of the Beloved Disciple, who may or may not have been the apostle John.[18]

14. Brown, *Introduction to the New Testament*, 158–64.

15. Brown, *Introduction to the New Testament*, 111–23; Stanley E. Porter and Bryan R. Dyer, eds., *The Synoptic Problem: Four Views* (Grand Rapids, MI: Baker Academic, 2016), 1–26.

16. Brown, *Introduction to the New Testament*, 203–16; Tyler J. Griffin, "Matthew's Portrayal of Jesus," in *Thou Art the Christ: The Son of the Living God: The Person and Work of Jesus in the New Testament*, edited by Eric D. Huntsman, Lincoln H. Blumell, and Tyler J. Griffin (Provo, UT: Religious Studies Center, 2018), 67–91.

17. Brown, *Introduction to the New Testament*, 262–73; Eric D. Huntsman, "Luke's Jesus," in *Thou Art the Christ*, 112–35.

18. Brown, *Introduction to the New Testament*, 364–76; Eric D. Huntsman, "The Gospel of John" in *New Testament History, Culture, and Society*, edited by Lincoln H. Blumell (Provo, UT: Religious Studies

Some Latter-day Saints, like other conservative Christians, have resisted these proposals, perhaps fearing that they weaken the authority of the texts as scripture. Swensen's introductions to the Gospels, while not discounting the traditional authorship, considered the matter thoughtfully and from an informed perspective, looking at evidence as well as tradition,[19] and more recent introductions to the Gospels by Latter-day Saint religious educators have considered authorship and compositional issues even more with the aid of recent scholarship.[20] In a similar fashion, some Latter-day Saint approaches to the Gospel of John still acknowledge apostolic authority behind the original author or at least the source while still recognizing that the text as we have it might have had a complex compositional history.[21]

The historicity of the content of the Gospels, especially when it comes to the divine identity and role of Jesus Christ, however, is a more significant issue. Accordingly, Robert L. Millet, emeritus professor of Ancient Scripture and a former Dean of Religious Education at BYU, wrote, "We have every reason to believe that the four Gospels are true and accurate and that the essential message of historical Christianity—that Christ lived, taught, lifted, strengthened, renewed, healed, prophesied, communed with Deity, suffered, rose from the dead, appeared thereafter to hundreds, and will come again in glory—is to be taken seriously."[22]

Because many of the proponents of the First Quest for the Historical Jesus seemed to reject *a priori* the possibility of anything miraculous or supernatural, such a critical approach could be seen as undercutting not only the reality of Jesus's works but even his divine identity. This suspicion was not only limited to conservative church leaders such as Joseph Fielding Smith or Bruce R. McConkie but has also extended to some Latter-day Saint scholars. For many of them, historicity is not limited just to Jesus's divine identity and to his saving mission; instead it includes most other aspects of his earthly ministry, namely his words, deeds, and miracles.[23] Paul Y. Hoskisson, another emeritus professor of

---

Center, 2019), 304–21.

19. Swensen, *New Testament Literature*, 39–64; *The Synoptic Gospels*, 11–15, 37–44, 61–67; and *The Gospel of John*, 1–7.

20. See for instance, Richard Neitzel Holzapfel, Eric D. Huntsman, and Thomas A. Wayment, *Jesus Christ and the World of the New Testament* (Salt Lake City, UT: Deseret Book, 2006) 62–145, and Gaye Strathearn and Frank F. Judd Jr., "The Distinctive Testimony of the Four Gospels," *Religious Educator* 8, no. 2 (2007): 59–85.

21. Huntsman, "The Gospel of John," 305–9.

22. Robert Millet, "The Historical Jesus: A Latter-day Saint Perspective," in *Historicity and the Latter-day Saint Scriptures*, edited by Paul Y. Hoskisson (Provo, UT: Religious Studies Center, 2001), 186.

23. Although writers of ancient historiography regularly wrote speeches for their subjects (nevertheless keeping them, as Thucydides wrote, as close as possible to what was actually said), Latter-day Saint

ancient scripture, has maintained, "Without the historicity of the central events, scripture becomes little more than a manual for ethical living, illustrated with quaint, sometimes strange, and often implausible stories, stories that have no more value than any other form of literature."[24] Nevertheless, as Jonathan Brown has observed, biblical texts can preserve historical truths even if they are not word-for-word transcriptions of what was said or perfectly accurate descriptions of what was said.[25] There is a growing awareness among some Latter-day Saint scholars that the Gospels, like other scripture, are primarily theology, not history, and that individual authors had literary liberty in their organization and portrayal of the events they recorded. For instance, without questioning the historicity of Jesus' miracles, Huntsman has argued that it is possible to see the miracles of Jesus as teaching additional truths, showing how the symbolism of these miracles reflected Jesus' atonement and wider healing work.[26] What is essential for such a view is that Jesus "was crucified, died, and rose again the third day, and ascended into heaven," according to the proclamation of D&C 20, not necessarily the exact details of all the stories related in the Gospels.

## HARMONIZING VERSUS INDIVIDUAL APPROACHES TO THE GOSPELS

Much contemporary Latter-day Saint study of the New Testament Gospels continues to be characterized by a tendency to harmonize the texts, which in this context means attempting to resolve the differences between the Gospels on the premise that such differences are impossible or only apparent. At the most basic level, the impulse to read the four Gospels as a single story is an ancient one, of which the earliest documented example is that of the second century Tatian the Syrian, who labored to synthesize the four narratives into a single text known as the *Diatessaron*. Joseph Smith himself engaged in

---

authorities and many members have generally assumed that the recorded parables and speeches are effectively what Jesus said. This is a particularly complex issue when the wording of the King James Bible appears in the Book of Mormon, as is the case with much of Matthew's Sermon on the Mount appearing in the Sermon in the Temple of 3 Nephi, to say nothing of the growing awareness among Latter-day Saint scholars that many smaller and less noticeable phrases from the KJV NT permeate the entirety of the Book of Mormon text.

24. Paul Y. Hoskisson, "The Need for Historicity: Why Banishing God from History Removes Historical Obligation," in *Historicity and the Latter-day Saint Scriptures*, 116.

25. Jonathan A.C. Brown, "Did the Prophet Say It or Not? The Literal, Historical, and Effective Truth of Hadiths in Early Sunnism," *Journal of the American Oriental Society* 129, no. 2 (2009): 264–65.

26. See, for instance, Eric D. Huntsman, *The Miracles of Jesus* (Salt Lake City, UT: Deseret Book, 2014), esp. 7–11, 123–25, 136–37.

harmonization of biblical texts that went beyond simply trying to synthesize four Gospel accounts into either one chronology or a single flowing narrative.[27] Indeed, in his New Translation, Smith felt authorized to emend the received texts themselves, making outright changes or at least very strong interpretations. The nature of and reasons for his changes and additions were varied.[28] As Philip Barlow has observed, "Because scripture was truth from God and therefore could not be self-contradictory, Smith reconciled passages that seemed to conflict with other passages. In addition to harmonizing the Bible internally, Smith rendered it compatible with his own experience and revelations."[29]

Barlow's prime example of this latter type of harmonization is John 1:18, which maintains that "no man hath seen God at any time," which Joseph changed to read, "And no man hath seen God at any time, except he hath borne record of the Son; for except it is through him no man can be saved" (JST John 1:19). Julie Smith, an independent Latter-day Saint scholar, has noted that while Joseph Smith could have followed the harmonizing efforts of earlier Christian history in trying to produce one synthetic Gospel, his drive to revise each separately resulted in changes that "suggest that preserving and enhancing the unique voice of the writers was an important impulse of the JST ... he not only preserved all four but also enhanced some of the distinct aspects of each writer."[30]

While church leaders since Joseph Smith have not continued to change the text itself, Latter-day Saint hermeneutics have still tended to harmonize both the portraits of Jesus and the interpretation of his teachings in view of wider Mormon theology and expectations. Such efforts have generally been aimed at producing a working chronology of Jesus' ministry and then using that chronology to structure study and teaching that draws on all the Gospels at once.[31] Talmage followed this approach in *Jesus the Christ*, and J. Reuben Clark took this a step further by producing an actual collation of the King James Gospel texts published in 1957 as *Our Lord of the Gospels*.[32] The success of these works, and no doubt the standing of these two figures as important Latter-day Saint leaders, may help account for the fact that the curriculum of

27. Brown, *Introduction to the New Testament*, 13–14, 839.

28. *Joseph Smith's New Translation of the Bible: Original Manuscripts*, 8–11, argues that some of these changes "consisted of new revelation" while others represented grammatical corrections or clarification of the meanings of the King James base text, inspired commentary, or harmonization.

29. Barlow, *Mormons and the Bible*, 56.

30. Julie M. Smith, "Five Impulses of the Joseph Smith Translation of Mark and Their Implications for LDS Hermeneutics," *Studies in the Bible and Antiquity* 7 (January 2015): 6.

31. Strathearn and Judd, "The Distinctive Testimony of the Four Gospels," 59.

32. J. Reuben Clark, *Our Lord of the Gospels* (Salt Lake City, UT: Deseret Book, 1957).

the LDS Sunday School, seminary, and institute program continue to follow this approach, and it is even used by many BYU religion courses and even some commentaries.[33] Such harmonization, however, obscures the unique emphases and messages of each Gospel and obscures the often insurmountable differences between the Synoptic Gospels and John.

Perhaps uniquely, the Latter-day Saint impulse to revise the Gospel portraits of Jesus has not been limited to only the text of the New Testament but has even extended to producing *doctrinal* harmony. Indeed, the degree to which Latter-day Saint harmonization efforts of this kind occurs often correlates directly with the degree to which speakers and writers have rejected, accepted, or chosen to engage with critical scholarship and methods. As Anthony Hutchinson noted in his 1982 survey of Latter-day Saint expositors of the Bible, conservative Latter-day Saint commentators such as Joseph Fielding Smith and Bruce R. McConkie have been disposed to a "harmonizing hermeneutic," meaning that overriding doctrinal and pastoral concerns dictate their interpretation, and even corrective emendation, of authoritative texts. Authors such as Talmage, Clark, and Sidney B. Sperry have employed a "critically modified hermeneutic," meaning that they were willing to accept some of the insights of critical scholarship while continuing to allow Latter-day Saint theology and insights to shape their overall interpretation. While William Chamberlin and Russell Swenson employed what was largely a "critical hermeneutic," many Latter-day Saint New Testament scholars today use what Hutchinson called a "critical hermeneutic with harmonizing."[34]

More recently, however, Latter-day Saint scholars and other teachers have begun to treat the Gospels individually to better discern and appreciate their individual portraits of Jesus, noting their different Christologies, themes, and emphases.[35] Several recent commentary volumes have been produced that incorporate at least some of the latest biblical scholarship as well as Latter-day Saint readings of the texts.[36] With such a strong authoritative hermeneu-

33. For instance, D. Kelly Ogden and Andrew C. Skinner, *Verse by Verse, The Four Gospels* (Salt Lake City, UT: Deseret Book, 2006) follows a harmonizing approach for the Gospels even though other books in this commentary series always move sequentially through individual books.

34. Anthony A. Hutchinson, "LDS Approaches to the Holy Bible," *Dialogue: A Journal of Mormon Thought* 15, no. 1 (Spring 1982), 100–101, 104.

35. Roger R. Keller, "Mark and Luke: Two Facets of a Diamond," in *Sperry Symposium Classics: The New Testament*, edited by Frank F. Judd Jr. and Gaye Strathearn (Provo, UT: Religious Studies Center, BYU and Deseret Book, 2006), 92–107; Richard Holzapfel, *A Lively Hope* (Salt Lake City, UT: Bookcraft, 1999), 1–8.

36. S. Kent Brown, *The Testimony of Luke, Brigham Young University New Testament Commentary* (Provo, UT: BYU Studies, 2015); Julie M. Smith, *The Gospel of Mark, Brigham Young University New Testament Commentary* (Provo, UT: BYU Studies, 2019).

tic, together with a pattern of interpreting the Gospels through the lens of Restoration scriptural theology, Latter-day Saint biblical scholars often find constructive, and sometimes creative, ways to continue to engage with critical scholarship to bring the insights of biblical studies to their faith community. Many Mormon biblical scholars have opted to employ Hutchinson's third category, that of a "critical hermeneutic with harmonizing." Regarding the Gospels, this approach employs the basics of historical-critical scholarship, seeking to establish their provenance by carefully considering the evidence for authorship and audience and better setting the texts within their cultural context. While current Latter-day Saint scholarship varies in the degree to which it employs source, form, narrative, and other forms of criticism, there seems to be a growing acceptance of the work that must precede close readings and then applications of the text. In modern applications, most Latter-day Saint readings still harmonize by considering Latter-day Saint theology and Restoration scripture.[37] These approaches, however, are just beginning and probably still represent a minority.

## THE INFLUENCE OF RESTORATION SCRIPTURE AND TEACHING

Instead, doctrinal harmonization continues to reflect the overarching role that Restoration scripture and authoritative teaching have had on Latter-day Saint understanding of the Bible, especially of the Gospels and their portrayal of Jesus. As Barlow has observed, "even when Mormons' attention is explicitly focused on a biblical text, the text is generally interpreted through awareness of the Book of Mormon, other Latter-day Saint scriptures, and Latter-day Saint theology."[38] In regard to the Book of Mormon, John Turner, associate professor of religious studies at George Mason University, has noted that it presented ideas about Jesus that "were a mixture of the familiar and novel" to its first readers. Using almost Trinitarian language, it portrays a Jesus who, though clearly distinct from the God the Father, nonetheless is proclaimed "the God of Israel, and the God of the whole earth" (3 Nephi 11:14). While the full impact

37. Examples of the spectrum of combinations of biblical scholarship and different degrees of harmonization can be found in various contributions in the three volumes of *The Life and Teachings of Jesus Christ,* edited by Richard Neitzel Holzapfel and Thomas A. Wayment (Salt Lake City, UT: Deseret Book, 2003–6).

38. Barlow, *Mormons and the Bible*, xxxix.

that this new portrait had on the first Latter-day Saints is still unclear,[39] it may be that many Latter-day Saints since have had the Book of Mormon's Jesus in mind as they read his four different New Testament depictions.[40] Perhaps even more clearly influential have been Joseph Smith's own experiences with the Risen Lord, beginning with his later retellings of his First Vision and the subsequent encounters that he had such as that which occurred in the Kirtland Temple in 1836.[41]

In fact, Joseph Smith's descriptions of the resurrected, deified Jesus, together with the high Christology of the Book of Mormon, may be factors that have led to a Latter-day Saint propensity to favor the Gospel of John, which Bruce R. McConkie once called "pure gold."[42] This may be because the portrayal of Jesus in the Fourth Gospel is the most divine, according more fully with the understanding many Latter-day Saints have of Jesus. Many Johannine scholars maintain that the more theologically advanced conception of Jesus at the time of the Fourth Gospel's composition led to the more divine portrayal of Jesus in John; perhaps Joseph Smith's starting point, reinforced by his experiences and revelations, moved him in a similar direction as he increasingly embraced a more Johannine lens. Blake Ostler, for instance, has observed a shift from Pauline categories about grace to more Johannine conceptions of Jesus and his saving work in the revelations now contained in the Doctrine and Covenants.[43] Indeed, Nicholas Frederick has shown a ubiquitous use of Johannine language throughout Restoration scripture.[44]

In turn, the way the Book of Mormon and the Doctrine and Covenants describe Jesus informs the way many contemporary Latter-day Saints describe him. For instance, though the Gospels regularly refer to Jesus simply by his given name, Mormons tend to refer to Jesus by his titles instead. While this impulse might partially reflect the injunction "to avoid too frequent repetition of his name" (D&C 107:4), it may also reflect the usage of Restoration Scripture. The title "Savior," for example, only occurs three times in the New Testament Gospels (Luke 1:47; 2:11; John 4:42), but it appears twelve times in the Book of

39. Terryl L. Givens, *By the Hand of Mormon* (New York: Oxford University Press, 2003), 62–88, esp. 69–71, notes that for the earliest Latter-day Saints the Book of Mormon functioned more as a sign than it did a hermeneutical lens through which to understand other scripture.

40. John G. Turner, *The Mormon Jesus: A Biography* (Cambridge, MA: Belknap Press, 2016), 28–37.

41. Turner, *The Mormon Jesus*, 66–80.

42. McConkie, "The Bible, A Sealed Book," 127.

43. Blake T. Ostler, "The Development of the Mormon Concept of Grace," *Dialogue: A Journal of Mormon Thought* 24, no. 1 (1991): 68–74, 81.

44. Nicholas J. Frederick, *The Bible, Mormon Scripture, and the Rhetoric of Allusivity* (Madison, NJ: Farleigh Dickinson University Press, 2016)

Mormon and twenty-one times in the Doctrine and Covenants. "Christ," either alone or with "Jesus," occurs sixty times in the New Testament Gospels but 388 times in the Book of Mormon and 132 times in the Doctrine and Covenants, perhaps explaining why Latter-day Saints often speak of "Christ" more than "Jesus." "Redeemer," a term found eighteen times in the Hebrew Bible, appears forty-one times in the Book of Mormon and twenty-two times in the Doctrine and Covenants but not at all in the New Testament. This usage is made more powerful because it is frequently put in the mouth of the Risen Jesus himself, as when he said, "listen to the words of Jesus Christ, your Lord and your Redeemer" (D&C 15:1 and parallels).[45]

This Latter-day Saint scriptural usage is reflected in the writings and sermons of Latter-day Saint leaders, which naturally reinforces their use among Latter-day Saints generally. Talmage's influential *Jesus the Christ*, for instance, repeatedly refers to Jesus as simply "Christ" throughout the text, and the titles "Redeemer" and "Savior" appear frequently throughout, often together in formulations such as "Redeemer and Savior of the human race."[46] But the influence of Latter-day Saint scripture and theological understanding are seen most clearly in how they lead Latter-day Saints to understand and expand select passages differently than other Christians might. The prime example of this, perhaps, was Talmage's reading of Jesus' "sweat was as it were great drops of blood falling to the ground" in Luke 22:42. Taken in isolation, this passage, which is missing in many Greek manuscripts,[47] has generally been read as referring to the agony of Jesus' *anticipation* of his coming suffering, and the Greek phrase "as it were great drops of blood" has been read both adjectivally, to describe Jesus' sweat emerging as beads of actual blood, or adverbially regarding how the sweat fell. In view of Mosiah 3:7 and especially D&C 19:15–19, however, it was clear to Talmage not only that Jesus sweat blood but that this experience was also a fundamental part of his atoning experience.[48] While fundamentals of

45. For these figures and an analysis of these and other important Christological titles, see "Appendix: Principal Christological Titles in the New Testament," in *Thou Art the Christ*, 392–408.

46. Three times, in fact, in just the introduction. See Talmage, *Jesus the Christ*, 1–5.

47. Bruce M. Metzger, *Textual Commentary on the Greek New Testament*, 2nd ed. (Stuttgart, Germany: Deutsche Bibelgesellschaft, 2002), 151. For a study of how and why this passage may have been omitted, see Lincoln H. Blumell, "Luke 22:43–44: An Anti-Docetic Interpolation or an Apologetic Omission?" *TC: A Journal of Biblical Textual Criticism* 19 (2014): 1–35. See also the analysis of Michael Pope, "A Closer Look: Luke 22:43–44 and Questions of Interpretation," *Studies in the Bible and Antiquity* 6 (2014): 127–33, and "The Downward Motion of Jesus' Sweat and the Authenticity of Luke 22:43–44," *Catholic Biblical Quarterly* 79 (2017): 262–81.

48. Talmage, *Jesus the Christ*, 568–69, 575.

this reading can be traced back to the time of Joseph Smith,[49] the authority of Talmage and the influence of *Jesus the Christ* made it a basic part of Latter-day Saint atonement theology. Taken up by Latter-day Saint leaders and teachers since, particularly by Joseph Fielding Smith and Bruce R. McConkie,[50] this reading was almost normative until recently,[51] when more attention has been given to Jesus' salvific death on the cross.[52]



## THE WAY FORWARD: HOLDING MULTIPLE READINGS IN CONSTRUCTIVE TENSION

Contemporary Latter-day Saint scholars seeking to hold faith and critical scholarship together have looked to other models than the harmonizing interpretations of the past. For those who take this view, recognizing that a passage might have had one meaning to its original audience and yet might have another to a contemporary reader need not be an either/or proposition. Jill Kirby, for instance, argues that Latter-day Saint exegetes can learn much from the experience of Roman Catholicism's engagement with historical-critical scholarship. She suggests,

> The ultimate step in combining the Latter-day Saint tradition with modern biblical scholarship is a theological meditation. The purpose of this reflection is to discern, unify, and enlarge upon the identified transcendent truths in both readings. In the broadest perspective, those truths that are held in common represent continuity between first-century Christianity and the Latter-day Saint tradition, while differences call attention to the work of the Holy Spirit in preparing and guiding the community.[53]

49. See, for instance, "A Sketch of the Travels and Ministry of Elder Orson Hyde," *Times and Seasons* 3.18 (July 15, 1842), 851: "The garden of Gethsemane ... the place where the Son of the Virgin bore our sins and carried our sorrows."

50. Joseph Fielding Smith, *Doctrines of Salvation*, five vols. (Salt Lake City, UT: Bookcraft, 1954), 129–30; Bruce R. McConkie, *Doctrinal New Testament Commentary*, 1:774–75.

51. See Jeffrey R. Holland, "Atonement of Jesus Christ," *Encyclopedia of Mormonism* 1:82–86, *n.b.* 85; S. Kent Brown, "Gethsemane," *Encyclopedia of Mormonism* 2:542–43.

52. Robert L. Millet, *What Happened to the Cross?* (Salt Lake City, UT: Deseret Book, 2007), 105; Gaye Strathearn, "Christ's Crucifixion: Reclamation of the Cross," *Religious Educator* 14, no. 1 (2013): 45–57; Eric D. Huntsman, "Preaching Jesus and Him Crucified," in *His Majesty and Mission,* edited by Nicholas J. Frederick and Keith J. Wilson (Provo, UT: Religious Studies Center and Deseret Book, 2017), 55–76.

53. Kirby, "Fractured Reality of LDS Biblical Studies," 116.

For others too, this approach accords with the potential of the Latter-day Saint tradition, which champions ongoing revelation and personal spiritual experience. For these scholars, the Historical Jesus that emerges from critical study of the Gospels need not always diverge from the traditional Christ of Faith when that Jesus is in fact the saving figure that the believers, scholars, or laypeople encounter as they experience him through both study and faith.

# 29

# Paul's Letters and Acts of the Apostles

TAYLOR G. PETREY

Paul is not only the most voluminous author in the New Testament, but his writings occupy a central position in shaping Christianity at various historical moments. Known simply as "the Apostle" by the second and third centuries, and the primary character in the Acts of the Apostles, Paul's fame and influence was widespread. Some have even gone so far as to credit him as the "founder of Christianity."[1] Though this may be an overstatement of his singular influence and a misnomer about what he was founding, the vision Paul offered about the meaning of the Christ-event substantially altered the course of the early movement of Jesus followers. But his influence did not stop there. Throughout Christian history, Pauline thought has been a driving force for both revolutionary challenges to, and also affirmations of, traditional authority. Part of the reason for this conflicted legacy is the fractured nature of Pauline thought itself, offering resources for a variety of interpretations.

The scholarly approach to Paul generally divides the relevant sources into four broad categories. First, there are the undisputed letters of Paul. Second, there are the disputed letters attributed to Paul, which many argue were written in his name by someone else after his death. Third, there is the canonical biographical information about Paul in the Acts of the Apostles, written by the same person who wrote the Gospel of Luke. Finally, there are a variety of non-canonical letters, apocalypses, and Acts of Paul that purport to offer more information about the famous apostle. Among this division of sources, scholars



1. This claim has a long legacy in biblical scholarship, but is captured in Gerd Lüdemann, *Paul: The Founder of Christianity* (Amherst, NY: Prometheus Books, 2002).

have sought to make sense not only of Paul, but of the conflicted legacy of Pauline thought and its relevance in modern contexts.[2]

Pauline ideas have also had important influences on uniquely Mormon scriptures and teachings. Joseph Smith, for instance, saw in Paul a dramatically different understanding of salvation than his Lutheran and Calvinist peers. In the twentieth century, Mormon engagement with Paul largely avoided the historical-critical scholarship about the search for the "real" Paul and mostly downplayed interests in Pauline theology. Few books in the LDS tradition focus on Paul, and fewer among those engage modern scholarship. LDS writers have focused much more on Jesus, by contrast. Yet, there has emerged some recent interest in Paul in LDS thought that offers potential for repositioning Paul as a resource for new theological investigations. LDS critical interest in the historical Paul remains tenuous.



## PAUL'S LIFE AND LETTERS

### *Authentic Pauline Texts*

With the rise of historical-critical scholarship in the Enlightenment, Friedrich Schleiermacher (1807) and F.C. Baur's (1845) studies on Paul pared down the list of texts believed to be written by the "real" Paul. The quest for the historical Paul proved to be an alluring solution to the problem of the contradictions, changes in tone and vocabulary, and variation in topic and scene in the received Pauline texts. Some have questioned the Lutheran theological presuppositions and positivist historiography that motivated these original classifications.[3] But there is little support in over two centuries to seriously challenge the thesis that the canonical texts are a mixture of authentic and pseudepigraphal.

Today, of the thirteen letters attributed to Paul in the New Testament (excluding Hebrews), most scholars believe that only seven are definitely written by him.[4] These, Romans, 1–2 Corinthians, 1 Thessalonians, Galatians, Philippians, and Philemon, are an assortment of correspondence between himself and small communities of followers (1–2 Cor., 1 Thess., Gal., Phil.), personal correspondence (Phlm.), and letters of introduction (Rom.). All are occasional letters, meaning that they are written about specific circumstances

2. Richard I. Pervo, *The Making of Paul: Constructions of the Apostle in Early Christianity* (Minneapolis, MN: Fortress Press, 2010).

3. Benjamin L. White, *Remembering Paul: Ancient and Modern Contests Over the Image of the Apostle* (New York: Oxford University Press, 2014).

4. E.P. Sanders, *Paul: The Apostle's Life, Letters, and Thought* (Minneapolis, MN: Fortress Press, 2015).

or occasions that had arisen between Paul and his audience, rather than treatises or sermons.

Because scholars consider these letters to be authentic, they are often treated as providing the most reliable information about Paul's life and thought. In them, Paul represents himself as a former persecutor of the church who was transformed after the risen Lord appeared to him (Phil. 3:6; Gal. 1:13–23; 1 Cor. 15:9). He makes frequent references to Jewish scripture in his letters, indicating a deep familiarity with them. He wrote in educated Greek using the rhetorical training of his day, and gives no reliable indication that he knew Hebrew, Aramaic, or Latin. At least at a certain point, Paul was unmarried by choice and recommends the single life (1 Cor. 7:7–8). He never speaks of any children and does not call any place home. Paul never met the mortal Jesus and indicates that he spent only minimal time with Jesus's most famous disciples (Gal. 1:18–19; 2:11). He identifies himself as a Hebrew of the tribe of Benjamin and a Pharisee, both in the present tense (Phil. 3:5). Apart from his ancestry, Paul's continued identification as a Pharisee troubles our modern assumption that Jewish and Christian religious identity must have been mutually exclusive, a claim that is not supported by the record (see also, Acts 15:5). Paul never once uses the term *Christian* to describe himself or anyone else.

None of the canonical Gospels was written before Paul's own letters. He never mentions narrative or biographical details from those texts, including the claim that Jesus was born from a virgin. The teachings and miraculous deeds of Jesus are similarly absent in Paul's writings. He has only a few passing references to the sayings of Jesus, including Jesus's prohibition on divorce (1 Cor. 7:10–11) and the words of the last supper (1 Cor. 11:23–25). Paul identified himself as an apostle based on having seen the risen Lord and was ordained by God directly, not by the laying on of hands of other authorities. He placed the resurrection of Jesus at the center of his message and expected the Lord's return in his own lifetime (1 Cor. 7:29–31; 1 Thess. 4:14–18).

Paul considered himself "the apostle to the Gentiles" and Peter/Cephas the apostle to the Jews (Gal. 2:7–8; Rom. 11:13). Paul's mission to Gentiles was controversial in its time—in rivalry with other early missionaries who taught that Gentiles who followed Christ must be circumcised and observe food laws and the Sabbath. Paul vigorously objected to all these claims (Gal. 4:10; 6:15). Paul's zeal brought him into repeated clashes with rivals. His relationship with Peter was poor and he fell out of favor with some of his other partners in Antioch (Gal. 2:11–14). Paul reports that some "false brothers" had tried to thwart his mission in Antioch though he ultimately prevailed (Gal. 2:3–5). In Galatia, the same pattern occurred with rivals challenging his teachings on the place of uncircumcised Gentiles in the community.

Paul also competed with charismatic miracle workers in Corinth. He claimed to have performed "signs and wonders" and "mighty works" himself, but that rival "super apostles" emphasized their own miraculous powers as more substantial (2 Cor. 11:5; 12:11–12). In his travels, Paul also reports that he was imprisoned, shipwrecked, and beaten several times for his message (2 Cor. 12:23–29). Despite these rivalries and tribulations, his letters reveal a close relationship of care with others (1 Thess., Phil., Phlm.). They included personal greetings, gratitude, and persuasive charm, as well as his sometimes-harsh rhetoric. He was assisted in his labors by a coterie of companions whom he often sent in his stead, especially Titus, Timothy, and Silvanus. He also praised other missionary couples, such as Prisca and Aquila (Rom. 16:3; 1 Cor. 16:19) and other apostles like Andronicus and Junia (Rom. 16:7).[5]



### *Deutero-Pauline Letters*

As a historical matter, most scholars dispute that any of the remaining letters attributed to Paul in the New Testament were actually written by him.[6] No one knows for certain who the authors may be, or even if the same author wrote more than one. The so-called Pastoral Epistles (1–2 Tim; Tit.) share numerous features that perhaps suggest a shared author, but Ephesians, Colossians, and 2 Thessalonians all differ from one another as much as they differ from the authentic Pauline corpus. Significant literary, linguistic, historical, thematic, and doctrinal differences in these texts make it difficult to reconcile with the seven authentic letters.

Written between the end of the first century and the middle of the second, the Deutero-Pauline epistles, so-called because of their secondary Pauline status, attest to an early tradition of collecting Paul's letters and considering them authoritative, perhaps motivating the imitators to write in his name. They also attest to the confusing heritage that he left, prompting many to write in an effort to clarify his teachings. Paul was subject to rival interpretations and many were struggling to define his legacy (2 Pet. 3:15–16). Those who

5. Eldon Jay Epp, *Junia: The First Woman Apostle* (Minneapolis, MN: Fortress Press, 2005).
6. David G. Horrell, *An Introduction to the Study of Paul,* 3rd ed. (New York: Bloomsbury T&T Clark, 2015).

saw themselves as disciples may have given themselves license to engage in pseudepigraphy, a phenomenon in ancient philosophical and religious circles.[7]

These letters tend to put forward conservative social teachings, imitating the conventions of Roman society. The "household codes," for instance, are a common feature of many of the Deutero-Pauline letters (Eph. 5:21–6:9; Col. 3:18–4:1; see also 1 Pet. 2:13–3:12; 1 Tim. 2:9–15; Tit. 2:1–10). These codes reflect broader Greco-Roman advice to householders about how to structure their family and slave relationships. In the NT examples of this genre, the hierarchy descends from God to Christ, to the husband/father, to the wife, children, and slaves of the household. The ethics of these codes were influential in American Christian justifications of slavery, and similarly remain influential in justifications for patriarchal leadership of the home.



The Deutero-Pauline letters also revise Paul's eschatology. Paul expected an imminent return of Jesus that would bring judgment and salvation (1 Cor. 7:29–31; 1 Thess. 4:14–18). These other letters offered clarifications when the expected return was delayed. For instance, 2 Thessalonians updates the message of 1 Thessalonians by explaining that a number of signs must occur before the Lord's return (2 Thess. 2:1–12). 1 Timothy similarly condemns those who hold onto a realized eschatology, the belief that believers are already living in the new age (2 Tim. 2:18). Yet, Colossians and Ephesians indicate that salvation and resurrection have already occurred for those who believe (Col. 2:12; 3:1; Eph. 2:1–10).

There are other anachronisms in the disputed letters. For instance, Paul himself says very little about church structure, citing only apostles, prophets, teachers, and miracle workers (1 Cor. 12:28). In Philippians 1:1, he mentions bishops (overseers) and deacons (servants), but it is not clear that these refer to official positions. Later, he describes various men and women as apostles, deacons, siblings, and coworkers (Rom. 16:1–21), but these do not seem to be formalized offices either. In contrast, Ephesians mentions apostles and prophets (Eph. 2:20). The Pastoral Epistles expand the list of titles and describe new offices, such as a single bishop, many male and female deacons, widows, and presbyters (elders; 1 Tim. 3:1–16; 5:3–6:2).

The Epistle to the Hebrews is sometimes included as a Pauline letter in certain traditions. However, it is the most doubtful of any of the disputed Pauline

7. This has become a matter of debate in recent scholarship. Bart D. Ehrman, *Forgery and Counterforgery: The Use of Literary Deceit in Early Christian Polemics* (New York: Oxford University Press, 2012). For an influential response, see David Brakke, "Early Christian Lies and the Lying Liars Who Wrote Them: Bart Ehrman's *Forgery and Counterforgery*," *The Journal of Religion* 96, no. 3 (July 2016): 378–90.

letters, most notably because it does not itself say that Paul is the author. Even many in antiquity questioned its authenticity as a Pauline text. In this text, Jesus is framed as both priest and sacrifice, offering himself in the tradition of a Day of Atonement ritual. Because Jesus was not actually a priest, the author of Hebrews invokes the priesthood of Melchizedek, the enigmatic figure in Genesis 14:18–20 who inspired mystical and apocalyptic thinking in Second Temple Judaism and early Christianity.[8]



## *Acts of the Apostles and Paul*

The second volume written by the anonymous author of the Gospel of Luke, the Acts of the Apostles, is not strictly about Paul, but he is the central character for most of the narrative. Dating to the late first or early second century, Acts is a representation of the Pauline mission long removed from the original context. Paul is the main focus in part because it is through Paul that the story of Acts may be told, "you will be my witness in Jerusalem…and to the ends of the earth" (Acts 1:8). The account then concludes, "this salvation of God has been sent to the Gentiles" (Acts 28:28). Paul is the vehicle for this message and the hero of the story.

How much Acts' narrative may be harmonized with the authentic letters of Paul remains a point of scholarly disagreement. Despite this broadly shared outline, several biographical details that Acts supplies cannot be confirmed in Paul's own writings. The Paul presented in Acts was a student of Gamaliel in Jerusalem, was known as "Saul" for a period, hailed from Tarsus in Asia Minor, and was granted authority by the high priest of Jerusalem to arrest followers of Jesus in far-away cities. After his vision and subsequent missionizing, Acts reports that Paul was arrested in Jerusalem and appealed his case to Rome as a citizen. Then, the text mysteriously ends. None of these reports, however, can be verified in Paul's own writings, and there are reasons to doubt the plausibility of some or all of them.

There are also irreconcilable tensions between the narrative of Acts and the authentic Pauline letters. For instance, Acts reports that Paul returned to Jerusalem after his visionary experience in Damascus, but Paul says that he did not go to Jerusalem until many years later (Acts 22:12–21; Gal. 1:22). Acts has Paul first preaching in the synagogues of each city (Acts 13:5, 14; 14:1; 17:1–5,

8. The Melchizedek document in the Dead Sea Scrolls (11QMelch) and the *Melchizedek* text in the Nag Hammadi library are just two of the numerous non-canonical references to this figure in this period.

etc.), but there is no evidence in Paul's writings that this was the case. He was, as he described, the "apostle to the Gentiles" and prioritized them (Rom 11:13). Further, Acts' report of the council of Jerusalem is quite different from Paul's, calling into question Acts' reliability on other matters as well (Acts 15:1–29; Gal. 2:1–10). Somewhat surprisingly, Acts rarely gives Paul the title "apostle" because in this account there are only twelve (Acts 14:4, 14; "the apostles" in Acts 1:15–26; 9:27; 15:2, 4, 6, 22; 16:4). This is in stark contrast to Paul's understanding of himself as a worthy holder of this title (Rom. 1:1; 11:13; Gal. 1:1; 1 Cor. 1:1; 9:2; 2 Cor. 1:1; 12:12–13). The literary interests of Acts may also shape the way that it constructs Paul's speeches to philosophers, depicts the reception of Paul and his companions, and celebrates Paul's oratorical skills among Roman authorities.

### *Non-Canonical Pauline Texts*

There are numerous non-canonical texts attributed to Paul or about him, including Acts, apocalypses, and additional letters. Among the most famous, in antiquity and in modern scholarship, are the *Acts of Paul*. These numerous stories include accounts of Paul as celibate, a miracle worker, and a teacher of important female charismatic leaders, such as Thecla. In contrast to the image of Paul in the Pastoral Epistles, the Paul in these texts supported women's leadership and opposed marriage, the household, and reproduction. In the Acts of Paul, we get the only physical description of apostle: "a man small in stature, bald, bow-legged, well-built, uni-browed, hook-nose, full of grace, sometimes appearing as a man, at other times having the face of an angel" (*Acts of Paul* 2.3). Joseph Smith likely had access to a copy of this text in William Hone's *Apocryphal New Testament* (1820), and it may have informed his own 1841 description of Paul's appearance.[9]

## PAUL'S PROJECT

There is no single theme that spans across Paul's letters.[10] He dealt with diverse topics such as food, sex, spiritual gifts, ritual, and the collection of funds. However, Galatians and Romans share similar themes that reveal some of his most

9. Thomas Wayment, "Joseph Smith's Description of Paul the Apostle," *Mormon Historical Studies* 13, no. 1/2 (2012): 39–53.

10. James D.G. Dunn, ed., *The Cambridge Companion to St. Paul* (Cambridge, UK: Cambridge University Press, 2003).

impactful theological ideas. In these letters, Paul evaluates the place of the Mosaic Law in his thinking. Paul's radical teaching was that "he is not a real Jew who is one outwardly ... but he is a Jew who is one inwardly" (Rom. 2:28–29). As Paul saw it, a new era had been inaugurated by Christ's resurrection, transforming the old ways. The inner condition of the spirit supplanted the outer condition of the flesh.[11] He sees the death and resurrection of Christ as the beginning of a new Messianic age. However, the ideas presented on this topic seem inconsistent between these two letters and even within these letters. Did Paul believe that "Christ redeemed us from the curse of the Law" (Gal. 3:13) or that "the Law is holy and the commandment is holy and just and good" (Rom. 7:12)?



The history of interpretation of Paul has been fought over what he meant, trying to reconcile all his teachings or selectively prioritizing one set over another. Even early Christians wrestled over what to make of his dramatic claims against the Law. Marcion (d. *circa* 160 CE), for instance, reportedly latched onto Galatians to demonstrate a conflict between the Law and the Gospel, or as he interpreted Paul, between the wicked creator God in the Hebrew Bible and the good God who sent Jesus to save humanity from the creator and lawgiver. Others read Paul to reconcile his teachings with an acceptance of the God of Jewish scripture in continuity with the Law, often through allegorical interpretation.

Martin Luther (1483–1586 CE) focused on Paul's break with Judaism and the doctrines of justification. Among the most influential interpreters of Paul, Luther began with Romans and Galatians as the foundation for his own thought. In Luther's view, Paul taught that the believer was justified before God by faith alone. Paul converted from a legalistic Judaism to a Christianity that taught that one was saved through grace. The Law was mutually exclusive with the Gospel. The contrast between the Law and the Gospel drew on stereotypes of Judaism as being concerned with works-righteousness. For Luther, Catholics shared these negative traits.

For much of the history of Pauline studies in Europe and America, the Lutheran interpretation was not only judged to be the correct interpretation, but pre-Lutheran interpreters of Paul were judged by that standard. Those who got Paul "right" focused on Lutheran questions of salvation, and those who got Paul "wrong" emphasized some other teaching in Pauline literature or failed

11. Daniel Boyarin, *A Radical Jew: Paul and the Politics of Identity* (Berkeley: University of California Press, 1994).

to grasp the importance of faith and grace. This assumption has been widely criticized, as scholars have recognized that the fragmentation of traditions interpreting Paul may all trace back to the apostle himself.



When nineteenth century historical critics approached Paul, they largely took the same view as Luther. The Hegelian acolyte F.C. Baur (1792–1860 CE) depicted Christianity as divided by the Pauline and Petrine factions. The Pauline Gentile factions were concerned about interior experience while the Petrine Judaizers were focused on external legalism. The anti-Judaism of these views hinged on a constructed view of ancient Judaism as the imagined target of Paul's critique.

After the horrific crimes against Jews in World War II, many Christians began to question the tropes in Christian theology that had long supported anti-Judaism. In biblical studies, scholars began to reevaluate Paul's supposed opposition to Jewish teachings. Krister Stendahl, in *Paul Among Jews and Gentiles* (1976), anticipated these moves, but E.P. Sanders, in *Paul and Palestinian Judaism* (1977), most fully explored the question. They discovered that rather than seeing Paul as rejecting Judaism, he actually saw himself as fully within the tradition, offering a new interpretation of ancient Judaism itself. The so-called New Perspective on Paul, in contrast to the Old Perspective put forward by Luther, began to situate him within Judaism, rather than in conflict with it.[12] Paul was thoroughly Jewish. The Radical New Perspective, a branch of this revisionist approach, holds that Paul envisioned "two covenants," one for Jews and one for Gentiles.[13]

The scholarship on Paul also has been intensely focused on his place within a broadly Hellenistic intellectual milieu and the landscape of the Roman Empire. What kinds of philosophical, medical, literary, and political trends influenced his teachings? In this context, Paul shared an intellectual setting with Cynics and Stoics as much as a supposedly distinctively Jewish context. These movements not only shaped Paul's rhetorical styles, but his ethics and politics.[14] Further, Paul's teachings often appropriate and subvert Roman political ideology.[15] Modern scholarship on Paul sees him as an active participant in a wide variety of cultural forces in his era.

12. James D.G. Dunn, *The New Perspective on Paul,* rev. ed. (Grand Rapids, MI: Eerdmans, 2008).

13. John G. Gager, *Reinventing Paul* (New York: Oxford University Press, 2002). See also a revision of the New Perspective and Radical New Perspective in Matthew Thiessen, *Paul and the Gentile Problem* (New York: Oxford University Press, 2016).

14. Dale B. Martin, *The Corinthian Body* (New Haven, CT: Yale University Press, 1999).

15. Richard Horsley, *Paul and Empire: Religion and Power in Roman Imperial Society* (Harrisburg, PA: Trinity Press International, 1997).

Feminist biblical scholarship has also been very interested in Paul.[16] In Galatians 3:28, Paul references a baptismal formula, or liturgical speech, that has been a central text in this analysis. In it, Paul affirms that "there is no longer Jew nor Greek; there is no longer slave nor free; there is no longer male nor female; for you are all one in Christ Jesus." Just as ethnic and social distinctions melt away "in Christ," so also is sexual difference irrelevant. Many have argued that this text then supports female ordination, and its status as a pre-Pauline formula gives it added authority. (Many early Christians who appointed women as prophets, bishops, and elders cited this passage as justification. See Epiphanius, *Panarion*, 49.2.) But Paul himself is not always consistent. In 1 Cor. 11:3,9, he teaches that there is mutuality between male and female, but that the man is the "head" of the woman. The even more severe sayings commanding women's silence in church (e.g., 1 Cor. 14:33–35) contradict the moderate passages, including Paul's praise for several women leaders and Junia the apostle. These exhortations to silence may be later insertions that represent one branch of the Pauline legacy that emphasized gendered hierarchy. The Deutero-Pauline texts similarly advocate for women's subordination (1 Tim. 2:11–15). One is left with a range of "Pauline" views on the topic. The overall utility of conscripting Paul into liberal re-readings remains controversial.[17]

## PAUL AND MORMONISM

No single study has yet exhausted the question of the presence of Pauline texts and intertexts in uniquely Mormon scripture. In the Book of Mormon, there are numerous quotations and allusions from nearly every one of the Pauline letters. There are substantial direct quotations of Paul, including passages on the gifts of the Spirit (1 Cor. 12:5–11=Mormon 10:8–17) and on charity (1 Cor. 13=Ether 12:35/Mormon 7:1, 44–46). Among the minor quotations are a series of Paulinisms (e.g., "By the law no flesh is justified," 2 Ne. 2:5=Rom. 3:20) and well-known sayings (e.g., "O, wretched man that I am," 2 Ne. 4:17= Rom. 7:24; "to be carnally minded, is death, and to be spiritually minded, is life eternal," 2 Ne. 9:39=Rom. 8:6). Other instances are repeated quotations about the resurrection (Mosiah 16:7–10/Alma 22:24/Alma 40:2/Mormon 6:21=1 Cor. 15:54–56), Paul's metaphor of the wild and cultivated olive trees as a description of the Gentiles (1 Ne. 15:12-18; Jacob 5=Rom. 11:17–24), and the egalitarian vision of

16. Amy Jill-Levine, *Feminist Companion to Paul: Authentic Pauline Writings* (Sheffield, UK: Sheffield Academic Press, 2004).

17. Cavan W. Concannon, *Profaning Paul* (Chicago: University of Chicago Press, 2021).

membership in Christ (2 Ne. 26:33=Gal. 3:28). Paul's own life story as a rebellious persecutor of the church who has a dramatic vision in which the Lord asks, "why are you persecuting me?" is also the story of Alma the Younger (Mos. 27; Alma 36, 38=Acts 9, 22, 26). In another passage about priesthood, the book of Alma draws heavily on sections of Hebrews (Alma 13=Heb. 3, 4, 7).



Book of Mormon quotations of Paul are often an occasion for commentary on Paul's meaning. 2 Nephi 25:23 interprets Ephesians 2:5: "by grace ye are saved" (KJV): "it is by grace that we are saved, after all we can do." The main thrust of Nephi's point is to reconcile the present-oriented understanding of salvation in the Deutero-Pauline epistles with the future-oriented Pauline theology that focuses on good works. Nephi's theological intervention is similar to post-Reformation debates about the role of good works in a soteriology of grace.[18] A fuller study of these patterns is needed.[19]

In Joseph Smith's revelations, Pauline formulations are deeply influential. Like many Christians of his day, Smith saw Paul's teachings on salvation as particularly pressing issues. Interested in more than exegesis, Smith produced important revisions of Paul in his "New Translation" (Joseph Smith Translation/JST). In the authentic Pauline letters, Smith makes significant changes to Romans, Galatians, and 1 Corinthians. Most of the revisions to Romans address the doctrine of justification, often with the view to reconcile it with the epistle of James's claim that both faith and works are necessary (James 2:14–26). As one example, in Romans 4:16 ("Therefore it is of faith, that it might be by grace; to the end the promise might be sure to all the seed; not to that only which is of the law, but to that also which is of the faith of Abraham" KJV), Smith changes it to, "Therefore *ye are justified* of faith *and works, through* grace, to the end the promise might be sure to all the seed; not to *them* only *who are* of the law, but to *them* also *who are* of the faith of Abraham" (JST Rom. 4:16). Smith's emendation makes it clear that one is justified by both faith and works.

The importance of good works is an important theme in Smith's rearticulation of Paul. In a lengthy revision of Romans 7:5–27, Smith's version makes it clear that Paul is both obedient to the Law and that he is no longer conflicted by the commandment as he once was before Christ. For instance, Romans 7:23–24 states, "I see another law in my members, warring against the law of my mind,

18. Terryl L. Givens, *Wrestling the Angel: The Foundations of Mormon Thought: God, Cosmos, Humanity* (New York: Oxford University Press, 2015), 236–40. For a contrary view, see Daniel McClellan, "2 Nephi 25:23 in Literary and Rhetorical Context," *Journal of Book of Mormon Studies* 29 (2020): 1–19.

19. I am thankful to Colby Townsend for sharing a preliminary list of biblical quotations and allusions in the Book of Mormon.

and bringing me into captivity to the law of sin which is in my members. O wretched man that I am!" Smith may have seen too much pessimism in the human condition in this passage. In Smith's version, just before the exclamation "O wretched man," Paul is said to state: "*And if I subdue not the sin which is in me, but with the flesh serve the law of sin*; O wretched man that I am" (JST Rom. 7:26). In Smith's translation, Paul is worried with the consequences of the *choice* to sin, rather than the *condition* of sin.

Smith also rejected many of the teachings of his religious peers about the fate of souls after death. In two cases, 1 Corinthians 15 was the basis for a reconsideration of what Pauline teachings on salvation and divine judgment might be. In the first instance, Smith came across John 5:29, which describes an eschatological scene where the good receive the resurrection of life and the evil the resurrection of condemnation. Concerned at this binary, Smith then receives a vision (along with his assistant Sidney Rigdon) challenging this dualistic view of the fate of humans. Their vision drew on Pauline terminology for evidence of a more just and nuanced afterlife. In this vision, there are three "degrees of glory," the celestial, terrestrial, and telestial—the latter a neologism—that correspond to the glory of the sun, the moon, and the stars (1 Cor. 15:40; see also JST 1 Cor. 15:40). Smith sees the description of these "bodies" as descriptions of the state of those in different kingdoms after the final judgment (D&C 76:50–113).

In the second major innovation about divine judgment, Smith worried about the fate of those who did not have a chance to learn fully about Christ and perform saving rites. If Jesus was correct that "no one can enter the Kingdom of God without being born of water and spirit" (John 3:5), then many would be locked out through no fault of their own. Smith looked to Paul's peculiar passage about "those who are baptized for the dead" (1 Cor. 15:29) as a solution to this problem. Citing this passage, Smith's revelations taught that baptisms for the dead are proxy rituals that have effect in the heavens (D&C 127; 128:13–16). Besides the passage in 1 Corinthians, Smith had likely learned more about baptism for the dead from other ancient sources like the Shepherd of Hermas, also included in Smith's copy of William Hone's *Apocryphal New Testament* (1820). Rather than focusing on justification, Smith expanded Paul's relevance to find what he understood as more benevolent accounts of salvation, the afterlife, and the efficacy of ritual.

In the twentieth century, Mormon scholarship on Paul has tended to follow very conservative trends. LDS biblical scholars Russel B. Swensen's Sunday School manual *The New Testament: The Acts and the Epistles* (1947) and Sidney

B. Sperry's *Paul's Life and Letters* (1955) were the first LDS introductions to Pauline studies and set the paradigm for future treatments. Swensen's manual laid out a chronology, quoted modern scholarship and archeology, and discounted the attribution of Hebrews to Paul. He made almost no mention of Joseph Smith, the Book of Mormon, or the Doctrine and Covenants as interpretive keys. However, arguing for the traditional authorship of all of the letters (including Hebrews), Sperry's volume was organized primarily as a biography and chronology of Paul's life and missions. Sperry relied heavily on Joseph Smith's "New Translation" as a guide to establishing the historicity of texts, reasoning that since no revelation to Smith questioned the authenticity of the accounts that they were therefore authentic. Sperry connected some LDS scripture to Pauline antecedents, addressed some important theological challenges (such as Paul's opposition to marriage), and buttressed LDS interpretation of proof texts (such as baptism for the dead). Despite these distinctive LDS analyses, his scholarship represented conservative Anglo-American Catholic and Protestant approaches that likewise focused on authenticity and harmonization. Sperry's scholarship avoided historical-critical issues, but included in his annotated bibliography notes such as "liberal," "liberal viewpoint," "liberal critical views," and "conservative" to describe reference works. He indicated that he relied primarily on early scholarship by Conybeare and Howson (1856), F.W. Farrar (1879), W.M. Ramsey (1895), David Smith (1920), C.J. Callan (1922), and J.E. Steinmueller (1943).

Sperry's approach has often been repeated by LDS successors, who continue to emphasize traditional authorship and harmony with Acts and highlight a few distinctive LDS teachings. Recent examples include William Victor Blacoe, *From Saul to Paul: The Road to Apostleship* (2016), which draws heavily from conservative nineteenth century Pauline scholarship; and Thomas Wayment, *From Persecutor to Apostle* (2006), which makes few LDS references but follows conservative scholarship. The BYU New Testament Commentary series has produced to date only one full-length scholarly LDS commentary on a particular epistle. Richard D. Draper and Michael D. Rhodes's *Paul's First Epistle to the Corinthians* (2015) emphasizes its importance to many LDS teachings. The commentary treats all of the Pauline epistles as genuine, privileges quotes from church leaders as more authoritative than scholars, and emphasizes harmony between Paul and contemporary LDS teachings.

Also recently, LDS scholars have attempted to engage Paul through the lens of LDS thought rather than biography and doctrine, seeking to find more points of connection between LDS beliefs and practices and these epistles. The

Pauline concept of grace has been especially important in this regard. In one version, LDS scholars Robert Millet and Stephen Robinson, among others, have attempted to locate LDS theology within Evangelical notions of grace. Robinson published with Evangelical interlocutor Craig L. Blomberg, *How Wide the Divide? A Mormon and Evangelical in Conversation* (1997), in which he made the case that LDS notions of salvation are held "*in common with Arminian Evangelicals*" rather than Calvinist Evangelicals.[20] Arminianism is the interpretation that believers are saved by grace, but must also resist sin. This approach buttressed Mormonism's affinity with other conservative Christians by citing Pauline ideas. Others LDS scholars have been attracted to the New Perspective on Paul because of its more moderate theological acceptance of works alongside grace.[21]



In the last decade or so, LDS philosophers have begun to draw on secular European reflections on Paul, including those of Georgio Agamben, Alain Badiou, and Slavoj Zizek. LDS philosophers have found Agamben and Badiou especially influential on their recent work. Adam Miller and Joseph M. Spencer are important voices in this perspective, seeing salvation not as future oriented but as participationist in a new outlook toward the world.[22] The only monograph detailing Mormon implications of this movement, Joseph M. Spencer, *For Zion: A Mormon Theology of Hope* (2014), offers a reading of Romans through the Book of Mormon.

Overall, Paul and the Pauline tradition remain understudied in LDS scholarship and are typically ignored or seen through a conservative lens. Latter-day Saints have rarely engaged the new political, theological, and historical readings of Paul, and none of these engagements has yet become mainstream. However, the new directions in Pauline studies in Mormonism show some promise for new engagement on theological matters.

20. Craig L. Blomberg and Stephen E. Robinson, *How Wide the Divide? A Mormon and Evangelical in Conversation* (Downers Grove, IL: IVP Academic, 1997), 147, emphasis in original.

21. Blake T. Ostler, *The Problems of Theism and the Love of God: Exploring Mormon Thought, Vol. 2* (Salt Lake City, UT: Greg Kofford Books, 2006), 309–85.

22. Joseph M. Spencer, *For Zion: A Mormon Theology of Hope* (Draper, UT: Greg Kofford Books, 2014); Adam Miller, *Badiou, Marion, and St. Paul: Immanent Grace* (London: Continuum, 2008).

# 30

# The Universal Epistles

## *James, 1 and 2 Peter, 1–3 John, Jude*

LUKE DRAKE

This essay discusses the divide between critical biblical scholarship and institutional Latter-day Saint readings of the Universal Epistles,[1] as well as considers a few of the opportunities and tensions that might emerge if Latter-day Saint readers were to engage earnestly with contemporary scholarship on these biblical texts. To illustrate the gulf between these two interpretive fields, I will discuss each in turn, beginning with a brief overview of the concerns, methods, and conclusions of critical biblical scholarship. The rest of the essay will examine a few of the ways in which the Universal Epistles function within institutional Latter-day Saint discourse. For practical purposes, I will limit this latter discussion to 2 Peter, though I will periodically refer to analogous material in and interpretations of the other Universal Epistles. I will then offer some thoughts on potential opportunities for future contact, and their various implications.

### CRITICAL BIBLICAL SCHOLARSHIP AND THE UNIVERSAL EPISTLES

By as early as the fourth century, the books of James, 1 and 2 Peter, 1–3 John, and Jude were collectively known by some early Christians as "Universal" (or "Catholic" from the Greek, *katholikē*), an appellation that derived partly from

1. I define "institutional Latter-day Saint" engagement as the treatment of biblical literature within Latter-day Saint scripture, official church curricula, General Conference addresses, and the writings of select Latter-day Saint authorities, especially as distributed by the church-owned Deseret Book Company. While this approach does not account for the full complexity of Latter-day Saint biblical reception and interpretation, it recognizes the powerful mechanism of church correlation (which authorizes and delivers the aforementioned materials to local units globally) and takes advantage of a broad set of searchable resources.

the belief that each letter was written for the Christian community at large (hence their universality). While this ancient terminology is still used today, biblical scholars generally agree that it is not an accurate description of the seven texts at hand; rather, each letter is thought to have been originally written for a particular situation, under a particular set of circumstances. Indeed, the efforts of critical biblical scholarship have largely been directed at answering a set of interrelated questions to elicit each text's historical context. Who wrote the text? When? To whom? Why?



In the case of the Universal Epistles, the answers to such questions may seem self-evident since several of the texts in question make an explicit authorial claim (ostensibly making it easier to situate and interpret them). In practice, however, identifying the historical context of these ancient writings is hardly straightforward. After all, within both ancient Christian and non-Christian literary circles we find a significant amount of pseudepigraphic literature in which unknown ancient authors penned political, philosophical, and theological texts *in the names of* other, more famous ancient cultural figures for a variety of economic, polemical, apologetic, pastoral, and theological reasons.[2] The extent to which ancient Christians engaged in this practice is but one of several factors that complicate contemporary efforts to establish basic information about individual texts; once a text's authorship is in question, so then are other details related to its history (its date, provenance, audience, purpose, etc.).

The question of pseudepigraphic authorship is particularly relevant here because a significant number of biblical scholars view many (if not all) of the Universal Epistles as the literary products of Greek-speaking Christians of the late first or early second centuries and not as the writings of the original Galilean disciples (Peter, John) and relatives (James, Jude) of Jesus of Nazareth. The authorial claims of some books within the corpus are more heavily contested than others. 1 Peter, for instance, is thought by some to have the best chance of tracing (in)directly back to Peter;[3] 2 Peter, on the other hand, is almost universally considered by critical scholars to be pseudepigraphic, despite its unequivocal claim to have been written by the apostle (1:1,16; 3:1,15).[4] As such,

2. For a discussion of the widespread nature of the phenomenon, as well as a comprehensive bibliography, see Bart D. Ehrman, *Forgery and Counterforgery: The Use of Literary Deceit in Early Christian Polemics* (New York: Oxford University Press, 2013), 1–27, 549–74.

3. See Raymond Brown, *Introduction to the New Testament* (New Haven, CT: Yale University Press, 1997), 718. See also Eugene Boring, "1 Peter in Recent Study," *Word & World* 24, no. 4 (2004): 359–60.

4. The evidences against apostolic authorship are compelling and can be found in any number of introductions or commentaries, e.g., George Kümmel, *Introduction to the New Testament* (Nashville, TN: Abdingdon Press, 1989), 421–24. They include the style and quality of the text's Greek, which scholars have long noted exhibits the sort of extravagance that one does not expect to find in a non-native speaker; the

for most biblical scholars, the letter likely represents the literary efforts of a late first- or early second-century Christian who wanted to exhort his contemporaries to develop the knowledge and virtues (1:5–9) that would "confirm [their] call and election" (1:10) and provide entrance into the kingdom of God (1:11). He further warns against false prophets and teachers that promote what he sees as corrupting ideas and practices (2:1–3, 12–22) and that deny an imminent parousia (3:1–4). He does all this pseudonymously, writing in the name of a revered apostolic authority.

For centuries, critical biblical scholars have sought to make a plausible case for the original historical context of each of the Universal Epistles. And while there is no shortage of differences of scholarly opinion concerning their historical particularities, a general consensus tends to emerge regarding the basic context and features of each text. The Epistle of James, then, is often understood to be a letter of exhortation written in response to later misinterpretations of Paul, inviting the reader to live a "Christian" life of virtuous works (with many scholars concluding it is pseudepigraphic). 1 Peter is generally thought to be a pseudonymous product of the late first century: filled with admonitions, warnings, and exhortations, it addresses a group of Christians who are suffering "for the name of Christ" (4:15–16). Jude is frequently described as a late-first-century attack on a set of false teachers, written in the name of Jude, the brother of Jesus. 1–3 John are commonly characterized as the literary products of the same community from which the Gospel of John emerged, albeit at a later period in the group's history (probably the turn of the second century); hence, whereas the Gospel of John plausibly reflects the Johannine community's struggle within and expulsion from the Jewish synagogue, the Johannine Epistles mark a subsequent schism within the Johannine community itself, motivated by questions regarding Christ's bodily nature and the moral standards required of Jesus' followers.[5]

---

letter's rhetorical structure—complete with *exordium, probatio,* and *peroratio*—indicative of an author that has received formal training in Greek rhetoric; the disparity between the vocabulary, style, and themes of 2 Peter and those of 1 Peter (i.e., if one accepts 1 Peter as authentic, it is difficult to maintain that the same apostolic author wrote 2 Peter); the content of the text itself consistently betrays the concerns and worldview of a revise to "late-first-/early-second-century" century Christian, not those of a mid-first century Galilean Jew; and the relative scarcity of references to 2 Peter in first- and second-century Christian literature. Hence, most biblical scholars think that 2 Peter is one of a handful of other second century texts that were written in the name of Peter (*Gospel of Peter, Acts of Peter*, *Apocalypse of Peter*, etc.). Unlike these other pseudepigraphic works, however, 2 Peter secured a position within the canon in later centuries.

5. The bibliography for each of the Universal Epistles is vast. The *Anchor Bible Dictionary* entries and Anchor Bible commentaries for each text are a good place to start when looking for peer-reviewed scholarship.

## INSTITUTIONAL LATTER-DAY SAINT READINGS OF THE UNIVERSAL EPISTLES



Institutional Latter-day Saint readings of the Universal Epistles tend to pass over the questions and conclusions of critical scholarship and emphasize instead those particular verses that can most easily be used for devotional, pastoral, doctrinal, and apologetic purposes. Bluntly stated, Latter-day Saints "prooftext." This can be readily seen in Sunday School manuals which rarely mention—let alone discuss—the text's author, provenance, genre, audience, or theological tendencies, and instead highlight exclusively the verses that the editors view as most edifying and/or relevant to contemporary Latter-day Saint concerns, irrespective, at times, of these verses' immediate literary surroundings.[6] Furthermore, when institutional materials—such as those prepared by the Church Educational System—do address historical or literary questions, they almost invariably adopt traditional positions and exhibit limited engagement with modern scholarship.[7]

Within the Universal Epistles—especially 1 and 2 Peter, and James—we encounter several verses that have proven to be particularly serviceable in institutional Latter-day Saint discourse, by means of a variety of interpretive practices. Three passages in the Universal Epistles deserve special mention on account of their significant influence on Latter-day Saint history and thought: James 1:5–6, James 2:14–26, and 1 Peter 3:18–20, 4:6. James 1:5–6 contains an ancient Christian exhortation to seek wisdom (Greek: *sophia*) through prayer and is almost universally understood to be the passage that prompted Joseph Smith's 1820 inquiry that led to a vision of God the Father and Jesus Christ.

6. For instance, prior to the curriculum revisions of 2019, the New Testament Sunday School manual dedicated one chapter to the Letter of James, and recommended that the teacher prepare to teach by studying a selection of verses (1:1–4; 1:5–7; 1:19–20, 26; 1:22–25, 27; 2:14–26; 3:2–18; 4:8; 4:17; and 5:10–11). See *New Testament: Gospel Doctrine Teacher's Manual* (Salt Lake City, UT: Church of Jesus Christ of Latter-day Saints, 2002), 174. This lesson was taught once every four years. While the revised curriculum (*Come, Follow Me—For Sunday School: New Testament 2019*) invites Sunday School teachers to read the entire letter before preparing to teach, neither manual addresses questions of authorship, date, addressees, or purpose (though see note 32 hereinafter).

7. The *New Testament Teacher Manual*—written in 2014 for Latter-day Saint college students—largely maintains a traditional view of authorship for all of the Universal Epistles. In its introduction to 2 Peter it allots two sentences to the question, gesturing to one of the difficulties of apostolic authorship and then offering two somewhat cursory solutions: "Some modern scholars … have questioned whether the epistle was truly written by Peter because the style and language differ from 1 Peter, which was written with the scribal aid of Silvanus (Silas). It may be that 2 Peter was written with the help of a different scribe, or that the epistle was put into its current form by others but contains authentic material from Peter himself," *New Testament Teacher Manual* (2014), 507. Within the same introduction we find the uncritical, and misleading, assertion that "scholars believe that [2 Peter] was written sometime between AD 64 and 68" (*ibid.*).

This passage in James is referenced in all but the earliest (1832) of Joseph's accounts of the vision and is central to Latter-day Saint retellings of the origins of their religious tradition. Its pride of place in Mormon history and culture is typified in the New Testament commentary of Latter-day Saint apostle Bruce R. McConkie (apostleship: 1972–1985):

> This single verse of scripture [James 1:5] has had a greater impact and a more far reaching effect upon mankind than any other single sentence ever recorded by any prophet in any age . . . every investigator of revealed truth stands, at some time in the course of his search, in the place where Joseph Smith stood. He must turn to the Almighty and gain wisdom from God by revelation if he is to gain a place on that strait and narrow path which leads to eternal life.[8]

In James 2:14–26, the ancient author states that believers in Jesus must manifest their faith through good works (e.g., love of neighbor) to be justified before God—an argument that appears to be aimed at later (mis)interpretations of Pauline thought, for example, Romans 3:28, "A person is justified by faith, apart from works of the Law." And while it is unlikely that Paul would have disagreed with the position in James, these two strands of ancient discourse have been central to more recent Catholic/Protestant debates on faith, works, and salvation. On this issue, Latter-day Saint theology tends to be more "Jacobian" than "Pauline" (or, perhaps, more "Catholic" than "Protestant") in that it emphasizes the importance of charitable works and ritual ordinances for salvation. James 2:17–18, for instance, is one of the twenty-five New Testament "Doctrinal Mastery Passages" studied by Latter-day Saint youth ages 14 through 18 in the *Doctrinal Mastery Core Document* (2016); no verses from Galatians or Romans are Doctrinal Mastery Passages.[9]

Finally, Doctrine and Covenants 138 contains the revelatory experience of the prophet Joseph F. Smith (prophet: 1901–1918). Smith's vision of Christ's post-mortal ministry was precipitated by—and serves as a commentary on—his reading of 1 Peter 3:18–20, 4:6 and is fundamental to contemporary

8. Bruce R. McConkie, *Doctrinal New Testament Commentary,* three vols. (Salt Lake City, UT: Bookcraft, 1971), 3:246–47.

9. For more on sacraments essential to salvation in Latter-day Saint theology, see Terryl Givens, *Feeding the Flock: The Foundations of Mormon Thought—Church and Praxis* (New York: Oxford University Press, 2017), 144–95. Mormon emphasis on good works and ordinances is a common point of tension in Latter-day Saint/Protestant relations. See Craig L. Blomberg and Stephen E. Robinson, *How Wide the Divide?: A Mormon and an Evangelical in Conversation* (Downers Grove, IL: IVP Academic, 1997), 143–88.

Latter-day Saint understandings of afterlife and the redemption of the dead. The vision was first published in 1918 and was sustained as scripture by the general membership of the church in April 1976.

Setting these more well-known passages aside, I want to focus on some other ways that institutional Latter-day Saint discourse has engaged with the Universal Epistles. In this section, I will mention only three of these practices in conjunction with a handful of verses within 2 Peter that have been consistently put to use for uniquely Latter-day Saint purposes.



### *Biblical Verses as Sites of Theological Resonance (2 Peter 1:4)*

2 Peter tells his readers at the outset that they have the opportunity to "be partakers of the divine nature, having escaped the corruption that is in the world through lust" (1:4, KJV). While this is the only place that the term *divine nature* appears in the biblical record, it now plays a prominent role in Latter-day Saint understandings of morality and the self. For whereas biblical exegetes typically see this passage as originally referring to the future reception of immortality and incorruption,[10] institutional Latter-day Saint readings of 2 Peter almost always interpret this passage in immediate terms: with regard to *immediate* access to priesthood power[11] and communion with the Holy Spirit,[12] or, more commonly, in terms of (re)integration with one's true, *eternal* self[13]—something that can happen in the here and now. The biblical phrase "be partakers of the divine nature" is frequently used to encourage moral living (one partakes of the divine nature by living according to the manner that divine figures choose to live) and/or to attest to Latter-day Saint understandings of the self (the divine nature is an essential part of the eternal human makeup).[14] In this

10. See especially Richard J. Bauckham, *Jude, 2 Peter* (Word Biblical Commentary v. 50; Waco, TX: Word Books, 1983), 179–82.

11. Russell M. Nelson, "The Price of Priesthood Power," General Conference Address (April 2016); David O. McKay, *Conference Report* (April 1957), 129–31.

12. Carol F. McConkie, "The Beauty of Holiness," General Conference Address (April 2017); Loren C. Dunn, "The Spirit Giveth Life," General Conference Address (April 1970).

13. The distinctive Latter-day Saint doctrine of premortal life is seen at the outset of the 1995 statement, "The Family: A Proclamation to the World": "All human beings—male and female—are created in the image of God. Each is a beloved spirit son or daughter of heavenly parents, and, as such, each has a divine nature and destiny." The Proclamation was written and signed by the fifteen presiding authorities of the church: The First Presidency and the Quorum of the Twelve Apostles.

14. See the Gospel Topics Essay, "Becoming Like God," available at https://www.lds.org/topics/becoming-like-god?lang=eng. The term *divine nature* is particularly common in contemporary discussions regarding Latter-day Saint women—particularly adolescent women who participate in the Personal Progress Program, which celebrates eight "values," including the "divine nature" of every female (though it is always understood that males also possess divine nature). In this context, "divine nature" is presented as the set of

latter application, "divine nature" aligns somewhat closely with ancient Greek traditions that postulated a divine element within the self that could reattain its place in the divine realm by means of a particular set of practices—be it by means of ritual within certain mystery cults, or by means of contemplation and moral purification within certain philosophical traditions. In sum, at the outset of 2 Peter, we encounter a term that Latter-day Saints have found to be resonant with and representative of a larger set of distinctive theological concerns and that is therefore cited frequently in institutional settings.[15]

## *Biblical Verses as Sources for Latter-day Scripture (2 Peter 1:5–7)*

Having assured his readers that God has provided the gifts necessary to bring them life, 2 Peter calls upon them to lead righteous lives by means of a "virtue list."[16] On two occasions, Joseph Smith adapted this ancient catalogue when composing contemporary revelations.[17] In February 1829, Smith was visited by his father, Joseph Smith Sr., who "desired to know what the Lord had for him to do" within the budding religious movement.[18] Smith sought a revelation, and wrote what would come to be known as D&C 4. The language of this short revelation brims with biblical allusions, with almost every verse echoing passages from the King James Bible. D&C 4:6 comprises a list of virtues that has been adapted from 2 Peter: "Remember faith, virtue, knowledge, temperance, patience, brotherly kindness, godliness, charity, humility, diligence." Smith's appropriation of 2 Peter abandons the Greek original's rhetorical form of sorites—by which the virtues are understood to build on one another to

---

inherent qualities and characteristics possessed by divine beings—such as God the Father, Heavenly Mother, and Jesus Christ—which lie at least partially dormant within every human soul, and which all people are invited to develop. See, for instance, *Young Women Personal Progress*, s.v. "Divine Nature," Required Value Experience 1.

15. Other verses within the Universal Epistles play a similar role in institutional Latter-day Saint readings of scripture. For instance, the term *peculiar people* from 1 Peter 2:9 has been used since the church's inception to defend a number of cultural and theological idiosyncrasies (nineteenth century: polygamy, smallness of Latter-day Saint numbers, the church's place in the Rocky Mountains, golden plates; twentieth and twenty-first centuries: adherence to the Word of Wisdom, sexual ethics, etc.). It also shores up in the same breath Latter-day Saint claims to ancient priesthood power with its allusion to the "kingdom of priests" of Exod 19:6. I thank Cory Crawford for alerting me to this last reference.

16. On the function of virtue lists in the ancient world, see Hans Dieter Betz, *Galatians* (Philadelphia: Fortress Press, 1979), 278–90.

17. Other examples of verses from the Universal Epistles that have been repurposed for Latter-day Saint scripture include James 1:5 (D&C 42:68) and Jude 1:23 (D&C 36:6).

18. "History, 1838–1856, volume A-1," 15, available at josephsmithpapers.org.

a sort of climax ("add to your faith virtue," etc.)—and instead presents them as a list of attributes to be remembered by those who "have desires to serve God" (D&C 4:3). "Humility" is added to the group, and the difficult participial phrase, rendered by King James translators as "giving all diligence," is resolved by converting "diligence" into a tenth virtue. Six years later, Smith prescribed the manner in which the presiding quorums (Presidency of the Church, Twelve Apostles, Seventy) were to enact their decisions. He once more repurposes the virtue list of 2 Peter, this time leaving the eight virtues unchanged, but appending them to a set of additional virtues that echo Ephesians 4:2,24: "The decisions of these quorums, or either of them, are to be made in all righteousness, in holiness, and lowliness of heart, meekness and long-suffering, and in faith, and virtue, and knowledge, temperance, patience, godliness, brotherly kindness and charity" (D&C 107:30).

For Latter-day Saints, these virtue lists are typically seen as both descriptive and prescriptive: they describe the attributes of all divine beings as well as all true disciples and serve as models to those who seek to become such.[19] D&C 4 and 107:30 are often applied specifically to full time missionaries[20] and priesthood holders.[21]

## *Biblical Verses as Sites of Theological Speculation and Exposition (2 Peter 1:10–19)*

In some cases, institutional readings of particular passages have been shaped by the revelatory exposition of the biblical text by Latter-day Saint prophets. For instance, in the same passage of 2 Peter, the author warns that if one lacks the qualities mentioned in 1:5–7 (faith, virtue, knowledge, etc.) then he is "nearsighted and blind" (1:9); the author therefore encourages his readers to "be all the more eager to confirm your call and election" (or, in King James parlance, "make your calling and election sure," 1:10) to gain "entry into the kingdom of our Lord and Savior." The most prominent contemporary institutional reading of this passage can be traced back to the interpretive activity of

19. Robert D. Hales, "Becoming a Disciple of Our Lord Jesus Christ," General Conference Address (April 2017).

20. The *Missionary Preparation Student Manual* (2005), 114–19, organizes its discussion of Christ-like attributes around the ten virtues listed in D&C 4.

21. See Ezra Taft Benson, "Godly Characteristics of the Master," General Conference Address (October 1986).

Joseph Smith, who saw hidden in these otherwise straightforward verses what may be described as a democratized mystical experience.[22]

On Sunday May 14, 1843, Smith gave a discourse in Tioga, Illinois, in which he discussed at length the first chapter of 2 Peter. Of particular interest to Smith was 2 Peter 1:16–19 (cited hereafter in the language of the KJV), in which the author claims to be an "eyewitness" to Jesus Christ's glory (1:16), having heard the voice of God the Father declare "this is my beloved Son" (1:17) while accompanying Jesus "in the holy mount" (1:18). These verses refer to what came to be known as the "Transfiguration," as recorded in the Synoptic Gospels (Mark 9:2–8 // Matt. 17:1–8 // Luke 9:28–36). The problem, according to Smith, is found in the placement of verse 19 ("We have also a more sure word of prophecy") *after* the reference to the Transfiguration. What, asks Smith, could be *more sure* than the voice of God declaring to someone that Jesus is the Son of God? He answers his own question by splicing the content of 1:19 ("We have also a more sure word of prophecy") with that of 1:10 ("give diligence to make your calling and election sure: for if ye do these things, ye shall never fall"). From this amalgamation, he discloses an event by which mortal men and women may have the sealing voice of Jesus declare to them that their exaltation is assured:

> Now for the secret and grand key. Though they might hear the voice of God and know that Jesus was the Son of God, this would be no evidence that their election and calling was made sure, that they had part with Christ, and were joint heirs with him. They then would want that more sure word of prophecy, that they were sealed in the heavens and had the promise of eternal life in the kingdom of God.[23]

Smith's synthesis of 2 Peter 1:10 and 1:19, then, became an injunction for all Latter-day Saints: "I would exhort you to go on and continue to call upon God until you make your calling and election sure for yourselves, by obtaining this more sure word of prophecy, and wait patiently for the promise until you

22. That Smith saw his interpretive work as an unveiling of hidden truth is indicated by multiple witnesses to his discourse. See, for instance, Willard Richards' report of Smith's words: "3 grand secrets lying in this chapter which no man can dig out. which unlocks the whole chapter. what is written are only hints of things which ex[is]ted in the prophts mind. which are not written. concer[n]ing eternal glory. I am going to take up this subj[e]ct by virtue of the knowledge of God in me.—which I have received fr[o]m heaven" ("Journal, December 1842–June 1844; Book 2, March 10, 1843–July 14, 1843," 213, available at josephsmithpapers.org).

23. *Teachings of the Prophet Joseph Smith* (Salt Lake City, UT: Deseret Book, 2009), 298. For a table that links the citations from the *TPJS* to the earliest known primary sources, see http://www.josephsmithpapers.org/articles/sources-for-teachings-of-js-by-joseph-fielding-smith.

obtain it."[24] Later that week, Smith penned what would come to be known as D&C 131:5 ("The more sure word of prophecy means knowing that one is sealed up unto eternal life"), and the following Sunday gave a two-hour sermon that dealt with the subject at length.[25]

While Smith's mystical reading of 2 Peter 1:10 was of great interest to the saints of his day, it is not clear that it was the prevalent interpretation of the biblical text for subsequent generations.[26] In 1965, however, Latter-day Saint apostle Marion G. Romney (apostleship: 1951–1988) delivered a worldwide address ("Making Our Calling and Election Sure") in which he taught Smith's interpretation and testified of the validity of the experience that Smith described.[27] More significantly, Bruce R. McConkie popularized Smith's interpretation in his worldwide addresses and published works,[28] which have been heavily cited in church manuals and curricula for decades.[29] Smith's reading of 2 Peter 1:10–19 is now standard in most church publications.[30]

## LATTER-DAY SAINT READINGS AND CRITICAL BIBLICAL SCHOLARSHIP AT THE CROSSROADS

This chapter has only briefly examined the extent of the divide between institutional Latter-day Saint interpretations of the Universal Epistles and the

24. *TPJS*, 299.

25. Years earlier, on June 27, 1839, Smith likewise described having one's calling and election made sure in these terms and included a discussion of the "Second Comforter": the literal visitation of the resurrected Christ to the person of faith. See *TPJS*, 150–51. It should be noted that there is some degree of ambiguity in Smith's usage. See Terryl Givens, *Feeding the Flock*, 192ff.

26. See, for instance, George Q. Cannon, *Journal of Discourses* 25:280. Referring to a group of church elders that had been murdered near Nashville, he stated, "To my mind there is nothing here to be sorry about, save to mourn with the relatives and friends of the martyred ones. Their calling and election has been made sure, and it will be said unto them—'enter thou into my rest.'" Cannon's understanding of having one's calling and election made sure aligns more with the surface reading of 2 Peter than with the experience described by Smith.

27. *Conference Report*, October 1965, 20–3. See also his April 1977 discourse, "The Light of Christ."

28. *Conference Report,* October 1969, 79–84 and Bruce R. McConkie, *Doctrinal New Testament Commentary* (Salt Lake City, UT: Bookcraft, 1973) 3:330–31.

29. See, for instance, *The Life and Teachings of Jesus and His Apostles: Course Manual (Religion 211–212),* (1978), 377, 416, 421–26; *Eternal Marriage Student Manual (Religion 234 and Religion 235),* (2001), 136, 168; *Doctrines of the Gospel Student Manual: (Religion 430 and 431),* (2004), 52; *New Testament Student Manual: (Religion 211 and 212),* (2014), 247, 425, 509–10. Broadly speaking, McConkie's influence on institutional readings of the New Testament is enormous: Philip Barlow notes that he is the most frequently referenced authority in the 1978 New Testament Institute Manual, cited almost three times as often (251 times) as the next closest figure, Joseph Smith (eighty-seven times), in *Mormons and the Bible: The Place of the Latter-day Saints in American Religion* (New York: Oxford University Press, 1991), 204.

30. See *New Testament: Gospel Doctrine Teacher's Manual,* (2002), 178–81; and *New Testament Student Manual,* (2014), 509–10. Also note that in the 1985 hymnal, a fourth verse was added to "Come Listen to a Prophet's Voice" (*Hymns*, 21): "Yea, keep His law with all thy might / Till thine election's sure, / Till thou shalt hear the holy voice / Assure eternal reign, / While joy and cheer attend thy choice, / As one who shall obtain." The verse was written by Bruce R. McConkie.

conclusions of critical biblical scholarship. Certainly some distance is to be expected, since the two ventures approach the literature with disparate objectives, assumptions, and methods. On the other hand, the immensity of the divide was by no means inevitable, in light of both the Latter-day Saint scriptural imperative to seek wisdom "out of the best books" (D&C 88:118) as well as the reality that much of critical biblical scholarship is amenable to Latter-day Saint thought.[31] Indeed, a more sophisticated relationship with the methods and concerns of higher criticism could arguably provide additional resources for Latter-day Saint pastoral and apologetic needs.[32]

For instance, 1 Peter 2:11 refers to his audience as "aliens" (KJV: "strangers"), a term that many biblical scholars interpret as metaphorical, that is, converts to Christianity become "resident aliens" on this earth, awaiting an eventual return to their heavenly home.[33] John Elliott's work, however, makes the case that the letter's addressees were, in fact, literal "resident aliens," a diverse set of socially and politically vulnerable people who had been marginalized on account of differences in language, ethnicity, religious practices, etc.[34] Regardless of which side of the academic debate one favors as historically accurate, both interpretations could productively contribute to Latter-day Saint devotional settings. According to one, 1 Peter offers hope to those believers who experience the painful effects of alienation; according to the other, it speaks to the Christian imperative to offer relief to "resident aliens"/"strangers" in need of refuge and allies.

Or take the scholarship on the Universal Epistles, which largely demonstrates that one or more of these seven letters are pseudepigraphic, written by a later figure in the name of an ancient authority. For some Latter-day Saints, these texts and the scholarship on them might serve as an effective, low-stakes entry into a set of conversations that are exceedingly relevant to contemporary concerns. After all, for over 1,700 years the Universal Epistles, to varying degrees, have occupied a place in the canonical, liturgical, and devotional practices of Christians throughout the world. Meanwhile, for centuries

31. For a discussion on past strains of Latter-day Saint anti-intellectualism, see Barlow, *Mormons and the Bible,* 103–47, 185–94.

32. An increased degree of engagement would not be completely without precedent in the institutional church. See the mid-twentieth century New Testament curricula published by the Deseret Sunday School Union Board, e.g., Russel B. Swensen, *The New Testament: The Acts and the Epistles* (Salt Lake City, UT: Deseret Sunday School Union Board, 1955).

33. Francis Wright Beare, *The First Epistle of Peter: The Greek Text with Introduction and Notes,* 3rd ed. (Oxford, UK: Blackwell, 1970), 135, among others.

34. John H. Elliott, *A Home for the Homeless: A Social-Scientific Criticism of 1 Peter, Its Situation and Strategy* (Eugene, OR: Wipf and Stock, 2005).

critical biblical scholarship has persuaded many Christians to reconsider basic assumptions regarding the nature of scripture, revelation, authority, and canon. Can, for instance, God's inspired word reside in the efforts of a late first or early second century Christian who placed the name of Peter on his writings—what some today might polemically call a forgery?[35]



For many Christians this line of questioning is wrenching since it disturbs particular notions of the nature and composition of the Bible. Latter-day Saints, in large measure, have little cause for such existential pain regarding the authorship of 2 Peter, whether because of the nature of traditional Latter-day Saint *understandings of* the biblical text (as something in need of literary supplementation, subordinated to living oracles), or because of the nature of traditional Latter-day Saint *engagement with* the biblical text (Latter-day Saints very rarely read it). Few Christian groups seem as culturally and theologically poised to embrace the likely reality that a handful of books of the New Testament—revered by billions as the word of God—were not written by who they say they were, thereby establishing a normative religious category of inspired and authoritative pseudepigrapha. For some Latter-day Saints, such a category could ease the tensions associated with the claims of ancient authorship made by texts unique to the Latter-day Saint tradition, most especially the Book of Abraham; analogous to, say, the somewhat divided discourse of believing biblical scholars on 1 Peter,[36] one can imagine a variety positions held by practicing Latter-day Saints regarding authorial origins (authentic, pseudepigraphic, authentic with later redactions, etc.), while maintaining a shared sense of the text's role as the word of God.[37] Whether such a category would ease more tensions than it would create—due to what many might perceive as a critique of the integrity and inspiration of Joseph Smith—remains to be seen.[38]

35. Bruce M. Metzger, "Literary Forgeries and Canonical Pseudepigrapha," *Journal of Biblical Literature* 91, no. 1 (1972): 3–24, and Brown, *Introduction*, 668.

36. See p. 439n3 above.

37. Arguably, the semblance of such a discussion is already underway, as seen in the Gospel Topics Essay, "Translation and Historicity of the Book of Abraham" (2014), available at https://www.lds.org/topics/translation-and-historicity-of-the-book-of-abraham?lang=eng, which entertains the idea that "Joseph's translation was not a literal rendering of the papyri as a conventional translation would be," but rather that the ancient papyri acquired by Smith "catalyzed" a revelatory process.

38. I am deeply grateful to Grant Hardy, Heather Hardy, and Terryl Givens for their generous feedback on the early drafts of this chapter.

# 31

# Apocalyptic Literature

JILL KIRBY

In 1838, Joseph Smith Jr. wrote a brief document outlining LDS beliefs that included this statement:

> We believe in the literal gathering of Israel and in the restoration of the Ten Tribes. That Zion will be built upon this continent. That Christ will reign personally upon the earth and that the earth will be renewed and receive its paradisiacal glory.[1]

These apocalyptic themes were remarked on more often by earlier LDS leaders and members than is now the case. Only two of the events mentioned here, the gathering of Israel and the Second Coming of Christ, remain active in LDS discourse, and the former has been spiritualized. Still, apocalyptic literature and apocalypticism are foundational to the beliefs of many Latter-day Saints and have still been part of several significant debates.

What is "apocalyptic" as a category? The classification of certain texts as apocalyptic literature was developed by Friedrich Lücke in his 1832 introduction to Revelation.[2] Although the word *apocalypse* appears in ancient literature,

1. This is the original reading of the Tenth Article of Faith. It now reads "We believe in the literal gathering of Israel and in the restoration of the Ten Tribes; that Zion (the New Jerusalem) will be built upon the American continent; that Christ will reign personally upon the earth; and, that the earth will be renewed and receive its paradisiacal glory." The first two changes are clarifying, that is, Zion is further explained as "the New Jerusalem," which must also be understood in its LDS context of a future city located in Missouri, and "this continent" becomes "the American continent." The third change updates the diction; thus "paradasaic" becomes "paradisiacal." "Church History," *The Joseph Smith Papers,* March 1, 1842, 710, accessed July 11, 2020, at https://www.josephsmithpapers.org/paper-summary/church-history-1-march-1842/5.

2. Frederick J. Murphy, *Apocalypticism in the Bible and Its World: A Comprehensive Introduction* (Grand Rapids, MI: Baker Academic, 2012), 5.

the generic description of an apocalypse is modern. As Yale Divinity School professor of Old Testament John J. Collins defines it, apocalypse is, "a genre of revelatory literature with a narrative framework, in which a revelation is mediated by an otherworldly being to a human recipient, disclosing a transcendent reality which is both temporal, insofar as it envisages eschatological salvation, and spatial, insofar as it involves another, supernatural world.[3] Texts considered apocalypses have most of these features. Adela Yarbro Collins, professor of New Testament at Yale Divinity School, adjusted the definition with a purpose statement for apocalyptic literature such as to "interpret the present, earthly circumstances in light of the supernatural world and of the future, and to influence both the understanding and behavior of the audience by means of divine authority."[4] Apocalypses were written to be understood by their earliest audiences in addition to whatever other readings might be generated.



Apocalypses may be divided into two groups: those concerned with the resolution of history and those that describe visionary experiences of heaven or hell.[5] Both types are found within the wider LDS tradition. Daniel 7–12 is concerned with history, while Paul's visionary experience in 2 Corinthians 12:2–4, Joseph Smith's Visions of the Three Degrees of Glory in Doctrine and Covenants 76, and Abraham's vision in Abraham 3 all describe supernatural worlds. John's Revelation is mixed, as it has a heavenly ascent that permits John to understand the culmination of history (Rev. 4:1). The only sustained vision of hell in the LDS tradition is found in Doctrine and Covenants 76:25–49. In addition, the LDS canon uses apocalyptic to provide an expanded version of the Hebrew Bible's primeval history through two pseudepigraphal texts, the Book of Moses and Book of Abraham, as well passages in the Doctrine and Covenants (e.g., D&C 107:53–57). In these narratives Adam, Enoch, Abraham, and Moses are all reimagined as apocalyptic seers. Visions of creation and the Christ-event serve as the basis for their preaching roles which effectively Christianize the Bible's primeval history.[6]

In addition to generic apocalypses, the wider LDS canon is shot through with apocalyptic motifs and themes including resurrection, final judgment, supernatural beings (angels), the messiah, an idealized afterlife, eschatological conflict or tribulation, the periodization of history (dispensations), the spatial

3. John J. Collins, *The Apocalyptic Imagination: An Introduction to Jewish Apocalyptic Literature,* 2nd ed. (Grand Rapids, MI: Eerdmans Publishing, 1998), 5.

4. Adela Yarbro Collins, "Introduction: Early Christian Apocalypticism," *Semeia* 36 (1986): 7.

5. Collins, *Apocalyptic Imagination*, 6–7.

6. Courtney J. Lassetter, "Dispensations of the Gospel," *Encyclopedia of Mormonism* (New York: Macmillan Publishing Company, 1992), 388–90.

organization of the supernatural world, and the culminating establishment of the sovereignty of God.[7] This apocalyptic discourse is deeply embedded within the functional LDS canon. Expressions such as "the dispensation of the fulness of times" (Eph. 1:10 KJV), the notice that God would send Elijah to "turn the heart of the fathers to the children, and the heart of the children to their fathers" (Mal. 4:6 KJV), and the prophecy that the "mountain of the Lord's House would be established in the tops of the mountains (Isa. 2:2 KJV) can evoke the entire complex of LDS apocalyptic eschatology.

In general, LDS reception of the Bible involves figural, literal, and allusive appropriation, which early Latter-day Saints brought to bear on those passages they thought spoke of the "Last Days" or indicated a pre-millennial return of Christ (D&C 84:96–107). Although they sometimes acknowledged ancient historical context, they inevitably saw themselves in these passages, typically formalized in the Doctrine and Covenants as revelation.[8] In his interaction with apocalyptic texts Smith resembles ancient seers: he recorded original experiences, reworked older biblical texts to suit his modern purposes and combined both to create entirely new narratives (e.g., D&C 88:87–116). He and his successors have used apocalyptic literature to fix the temporal, geographical, and spiritual position of the community and to comfort, correct, and inform modern believers. This is best illustrated by considering how Smith used several key biblical texts, and how some of his successors have extended or altered his contributions to meet later needs of the LDS community.

## HEBREW BIBLE

*Isaiah.* Although neither Isaiah nor any other Hebrew prophetic text is apocalyptic, their significance in the development of apocalyptic works is uncontested. Apocalyptic authors, including Joseph Smith, drew from the prophets who contributed to this work for structure, color, and tone in creating their own texts.[9] Isaiah 11, a bedrock text for the gathering of Israel, will serve as an entry point.

In context, Isaiah 11 probably comes from the era of the Syro-Ephraimite war (735–732 BCE). The return of the exiles in vv. 11–16 is a response to eight

7. Murphy, *Apocalypticism,* 8–14. For LDS usage of these terms, see the *Encyclopedia of Mormonism* (http://eom.byu.edu). See also Gerald N. Lund's *The Coming of the Lord* (Salt Lake City, UT: Bookcraft, 1971), for significant citations.

8. Grant Underwood, *The Millenarian World of Early Mormonism* (Urbana: University of Illinois, 1999), 74–75. See D&C 29, 43, 86–88, 101 and 133.

9. Murphy, *Apocalypticism,* 27–65.

century deportations from both kingdoms following the Assyrian invasion. To early members of the LDS community, however, the prophecy refers to an eschatological gathering of Israel including those who are biological descendants of Israelites (Rom. 11:25–27; 2 Ne. 30:5–6) and gentiles who are adopted into Israel through baptism (Gal. 3:26–29). Those who were deported from the Northern Kingdom are referred to as the Ten Tribes; they are thought to be an intact community and their current whereabouts is "the north country" (2 Kings 17:23; Isa. 43:6; D&C 133:26–34; 3 Ne. 15:15).[10] In preparation for their pre-millennial return, Joseph Smith indicated that Jesus's disciple John was then preaching the gospel among them, citing Revelation 10:11 as a proof-text (D&C 77:14).[11] This John is conflated with the author of Revelation (1 Ne. 14:18–27).[12] According to Smith, he was translated; that is, he remained alive to prepare for the Second Coming (D&C 7:1–3).[13]



Perhaps the most unique aspect of the gathering of Israel among Latter-day Saints is the location. The key passage is Isaiah 2:3, in which "the law" is said to "go forth from Zion and the word of Lord from Jerusalem." Read as Hebrew poetry, the expressions "Zion" and "Jerusalem" refer to the same place, the capital of ancient Israel, but in LDS reception, they are distinct. Zion was initially to be in and around Independence, Jackson County, Missouri (D&C 57:1–3) but would eventually fill the entire American continent, while Jerusalem was to be the renewed capital city of a restored Jewish nation.[14] The city associated with Zion, on the American continent, is called the New Jerusalem and was planned by Joseph Smith and first communicated to his representatives in Missouri in 1833. At the center of the city Smith pictured twenty-four temples to be used for administering the church and governing the earth during the Millennium (Rev. 20:1–6).[15] Smith also anticipated the return of the translated City of Enoch, which was to be united with his efforts (Moses 7: 25, 62–63, 69), as well as the initial return of the Ten Tribes, who would thereafter move on to

10. David L. Bollinger, "Israel: Lost Tribes of Israel," *Encyclopedia of Mormonism*, 709. For insight from LDS authorities, see Lund, *Coming of the Lord*, 159–66.

11. *History of the Church* 1:176. In the words of John Whitmer, recording events of the June 3–6, 1831 conference in Kirtland, Joseph Smith "prophesied that John the Revelator was then among the Ten Tribes of Israel ... to prepare them for their return from their long dispersion ..."

12. John D. Claybaugh, "What the Latter-day Scriptures Teach About John the Beloved," in *The Testimony of John the Beloved: The 27th Annual Sperry Symposium*, edited by Daniel K. Judd, Craig J. Ostler, and Richard D. Draper (Salt Lake City, UT: Deseret Book, 1998), 16–35.

13. Mark L. McConkie, "Translated Beings," *Encyclopedia of Mormonism*, 1485–86. See also David B. Marsh, "Give Me Power Over Death" in *Testimony of John the Beloved*, 141–54.

14. James E. Talmage, *Articles of Faith* (Salt Lake City, UT: Deseret Book, 1922), Kindle ed., Lecture XIX.1.

15. Alma P. Burton, *Toward the New Jerusalem* (Salt Lake City, UT: Deseret Book, 1985), 33–36.

Palestine. However, the Latter-day Saints were expelled from Missouri before much work was completed (D&C 105: 1–14). Some of the land purchased by Smith's representatives for this city remains in the possession of Community of Christ and the Church of Jesus Christ of Latter-day Saints. In addition, the location dedicated for the first temple is owned by the Church of Christ (Temple Lot).[16]

Eventually, the command to gather in the present was spiritualized so that conversion and baptism as a member of the church in one's own land fulfilled the gathering of Israel to Zion.[17] Although a return to Missouri is rarely part of an active discourse among modern members, it remains among the unfulfilled promises of the early era.[18] Some aspects of it rank among the darkest visualizations of LDS apocalypticism, including Brigham Young's "Yellow-Dog Prophecy" and the "White Horse Prophecy," the provenance of which is disputed.[19] Both prophecies suggest that the return to Missouri will be accompanied by civil and natural devastation. According to the White Horse Prophecy, there will be such extraordinary civil disorder that safety will be found only by living among church members in the "Rocky Mountains." In addition, the Constitution will "hang by a thread" and be saved by two groups identified as the "White Horse" and the "Red Horse." The identity of the "Red Horse" is disputed but the "White Horse" is generally understood to be church members.[20] Although LDS leaders have occasionally echoed some elements of the White Horse Prophecy, LDS scripture forbids bloodshed in establishing Zion (D&C 63:29–31) and the White Horse Prophecy itself is rejected because it cannot be linked to Joseph Smith.[21]

16. Aaron L. West, "Questions and Answers about the Temple Lot in Independence, Missouri," in *Church History*, the Church of Jesus Christ of Latter-day Saints, accessed December 23, 2015, at https://history.lds.org/article/historic-sites/missouri/questions-and-answers-about-the-temple-lot-in-independence-missouri?lang=eng.

17. Russell M. Nelson, "The Gathering of Scattered Israel," *Ensign* (November 2014): 74–7. Also, Bruce R. McConkie, *Mormon Doctrine* (Salt Lake City, UT: Bookcraft, 1966), 305–7.

18. Lund, *Coming of the Lord,* 100–139.

19. See Lund, *Coming of the Lord,* 109–12 for the Yellow Dog Prophecy, attributed to Brigham Young by Heber C. Kimball, and similar statements by LDS leaders. For a copy of the text of the White Horse Prophecy and a relatively favorable reading, see Duane S. Crowther, *Prophecy: Key to the Future* (Salt Lake City, UT: Bookcraft, 1962), 301–22. For attribution to Edwin Rushton rather than Joseph Smith, see Don L. Penrod, "Edwin Rushton as the Source of the White Horse Prophecy," *BYU Studies* 49, no. 3 (2010): 75–131. Reception of the White Horse Prophecy, whose title is taken from Revelation 6:1–2, is a social and political marker among Latter-day Saints and enjoyed some popularity during the Cold War as Crowther's comments indicate.

20. Crowther, *Prophecy,* 308; 313–14.

21. "Church Statement on 'White Horse Prophecy' and Political Neutrality," Public Affairs Department, LDS Church, January 6, 2010. McConkie, *Mormon Doctrine,* 835–36.

## Ezekiel

Like Isaiah, Ezekiel's oracles of a renewed, powerful Israel, although conveyed in distinctly priestly terms, have contributed fundamental themes and color to later apocalyptic works. In context, Ezekiel hoped to lead a renewed and restored Israel. To recover from the devastation of the Exile, his people must focus on returning to the covenant with YHWH (Ezek. 33–39) before returning to the land and reinhabiting it, this time properly ordered around a rebuilt Jerusalem temple that reflected YHWH's sanctity (Ezek. 40–48). Significant oracles are those of the restoration of Israel (Ezek. 33–37), the invasion of Gog (Ezek. 38–39), the restored Jerusalem temple (Ezek. 43–44), and the rejuvenating river that flows from under its altar (Ezek. 47).



While Ezekiel's visons are firmly anchored in his own times, Joseph Smith wove Ezekiel's prophecies into his own apocalyptic eschatology.[22] However, many aspects of Smith's apocalyptic discourse originally drawn from Ezekiel have been downplayed by his successors since the last decades of the twentieth century.[23] Some have simply dropped out of current discussion; others are no longer discussed as events but have become guidelines by which the righteous live. This may be illustrated by the reception of Ezekiel's prophecy of a renewed Israelite nation, city, and temple (Ezek. 40–48).

Early LDS readers understood that their own eschatological capital in Missouri would have a sister city: a millennial, Christianized Jerusalem functioning as the capital of a renewed Israel with a temple from which Christ would reign.[24] According to Joseph Smith, "Judah must return, Jerusalem must be rebuilt, and the temple, and water come out from under the temple, and the waters of the Dead Sea be healed. It will take some time to rebuild the walls of the city and the temple, etc.; and all this must be done before the Son of Man will make his appearance."[25] In April of 1840, Smith sent Orson Hyde

22. For example, Ezekiel's vision of the executioners of the city in Ezekiel 9 is universalized by John in the sealing angels of Revelation 7:1–8 who exercise authority over the whole earth.

23. The most stable imagery is that of the "Two Sticks" of Ezekiel 37:15–20. In context, Ezekiel is describing the reunion of Judah and Israel into one kingdom. However, most Latter-day Saints would understand this to be a prophecy of the union of the Book of Mormon and the Bible in the LDS canon (D&C 27:5; 1 Ne. 13:41) and consider the event to be a sign of the community's position on an apocalyptic timeline (3 Ne. 20:46; 21:1–7, 29). By way of contrast, discussion of events such Armageddon (created by conflation of, primarily, Rev. 16:14–16 and Ezek. 38–39) or entities such as Gog and Magog (Ezek. 38–39 and Rev. 20:7–9) in public venues has practically ceased.

24. Joseph Fielding Smith, "Zion and Jerusalem," *Improvement Era* 22, no, 9 (1919): 814–16.

25. *History of the Church*, 5:337.

to dedicate Palestine for the return of the Jews, which he did on October 24, 1841.[26] Smith's successors have indicated that the temple itself is to be built for both modern temple work (D&C 124:36–37) and ancient temple sacrificial rituals (Mal. 3:3),[27] as well a place from which Christ rules during the Millennium.[28] Finally, LDS readings of eschatological wars indicate that Jerusalem will be the target of invading armies (e.g., Ezekiel 38–39). Their defeat will be accomplished by the appearance of Christ on the Mount of Olives (Zech. 14:1–11; in context, YHWH) and after the invaders are defeated, the Jews will recognize Christ as their Messiah (Zech. 12:1–10; D&C 45:48–53).[29]



More recent use of these chapters in Ezekiel is subdued and pedagogical. The emphasis is on the significance of YHWH's return to his temple for modern temple worship rather than eschatological renewal (Ezek. 43:1–12; 44:6–9). Latter-day Saints are encouraged to read Ezekiel's description as paradigmatic of all temples so no attempt is made to bridge gaps between ancient and modern worship in terms of ritual, cultic purity, or the temple's unique status in Deuteronomistic theology. The restoration provided by the river and trees of Ezekiel 47:6–12 remains vaguely literal, but the focus of contemporary Latter-day Saint interpretation is modern temple worship as a source of individual spiritual health and healing. In the end, the temple, river, and trees all become metaphors for spiritual regeneration to be accessed by worthy church members.[30]

### *Daniel 2; 7–12*

Although Daniel presents itself as written during the Persian period, it reached final form in the second century BCE. The first six chapters are court tales, that is, stories told to illustrate Jewish success in foreign courts through faithfulness, and may have originated earlier. The final six chapters are apocalyptic narratives, built on *vaticinium ex eventu* (prophecy after the fact) to describe the destruction of God's enemies and Judah's triumph in the second century BCE.

26. *History of the Church,* 4:337.

27. Joseph Fielding Smith, *Doctrines of Salvation* (Salt Lake City, UT: Bookcraft, 1956), 3:93–94.

28. Daniel H. Ludlow, "Future of the Holy Land," *Ensign* (May 1972).

29. However, given the complexity of tensions in the Middle East and the potential for anti-Semitic readings, attempts to negotiate the import of Smith's prophecies and Hyde's prayer have proven difficult for many modern Latter-day Saints. See David B. Galbraith, "Orson Hyde's 1841 Mission to Palestine," *Ensign* (October 1991).

30. "Every Living Thing Shall Live Whither the River Cometh," *Old Testament Gospel Doctrine Teachers Manual,* Lesson 44 (2001): 207–10. While Ezekiel and early LDS leaders were interested in the river's literal renewal of the Dead Sea, Latter-day Saints are encouraged to "wade into the 'river' again and again—or, in other words, attend the temple as often as possible."

Among most Latter-day Saints, however, Daniel is considered a sixth century BCE prophet serving in the Babylonian court and his visions are read Christologically and eschatologically. Application to events of the second century BCE is affirmed, but most events and persons are read as multiple fulfillment prophecy or types. Daniel 2 and 7, both historical apocalypses, are by far the most prominent chapters but Daniel 7 has a unique reading among LDS interpreters that shifts the scenario from a judgment scene in the divine throne room to an eschatological gathering to welcome and receive Christ at his Second Coming.

Daniel 7 opens as Daniel sees a succession of grotesque beasts coming out of the sea. The fourth beast is distinguished from the others by ten horns, three of which are pulled up to allow a particularly offensive "little horn" (v8) to grow. The scene then abruptly shifts from earth to the heavenly court room for judgment. God (the Ancient of days; Dan. 7:9 KJV) takes his place on the heavenly throne, destroys the beast and its horn, then renders judgment in favor of a human figure ("one like the Son of man; Dan. 7:12 KJV). In context, the beasts are the ancient kingdoms of Babylon, Media, Persia, and Greece. The "little horn" is Antiochus Epiphanes IV, whom the Jews had to serve for three and a half years. When God renders judgment, Antiochus Epiphanes IV is destroyed while the Jews prevail over their enemies to receive the lasting kingdom.

Readings of this passage among most LDS leaders follow the common Christological interpretation in some details: the "one like a Son of man" is Christ and the "little horn" is one of many anti-Christ figures in LDS reception (the beast from the sea [Rev. 13:1], Gog [Ezek. 38:14–23], Sherem [Jacob 7:1–24], Korihor [Alma 30:6–60], and possibly the "great and abominable church" [1 Ne. 22:13–18]).[31] However, Smith's identification of the "Ancient of days" as Adam, rather than God, sets up a radically different scenario in which the heavenly court becomes a culminating reunion.

Smith's reading of Daniel 7:9–14 draws on two other texts. The first is Daniel 12:1–3, in which Michael, identified with Adam in the LDS tradition,[32] stands with Israel as its protector. The second is the expanded LDS version of the primeval history (Gen. 1–11) in Moses 3–7, which establishes that Adam presided over a dispensation. In Doctrine and Covenants 107:53–56, Joseph Smith reported that just before Adam's death he summoned his righteous descendants to the "valley of Adam-ondi-Ahman," during which he blessed them and reported his own apocalyptic vision. At the climax of this event, Christ

31. Sidney B. Sperry, *The Voice of Israel's Prophets: A Latter-day Interpretation of the Major and Minor Prophets of the Old Testament* (Salt Lake City, UT: Deseret Book, 1961), 260–61.

32. Arthur A. Bailey, "Adam: LDS Sources" *Encyclopedia of Mormonism*, 15–17.

appeared and validated Adam's royal and priestly status. According to Joseph Smith, this family gathering is to be reprised as Adam's righteous descendants, both living and dead, will return to the same location, identified as Spring Hill, near Gallatin, MO.[33] In this reading, Adam (Michael), who is the oldest man (Ancient of days, Dan. 7:9 KJV) functions as a royal priest: seated on a fiery throne, his sons will return their priesthood keys to him, and he will return them to Christ (one like a Son of man; Dan. 7:12 KJV), who holds them by right and will personally rule during the Millennium.[34]

## NEW TESTAMENT

*The Gospels.* Although the Gospels have their own essay in this volume, two points should be made within this chapter. First, modern scholars remain divided over how Jesus understood the future because of difficulties in assessing whether the present- or future-oriented sayings in the Gospels go back to Jesus himself. Of the various possibilities, the one that most closely coheres with what many members of the LDS community believe asserts that the historical Jesus had an apocalyptic eschatology. However, to scholars this means that Jesus expected God to intervene in the rather near future, while many Latter-day Saints would indicate that Jesus understood that his return was to be preceded by a delay in which the authentic understanding of Jesus' teachings and his church were to be lost through apostasy (e.g., 2 Thess. 2:3).

Second, although this understanding of Jesus goes back to Joseph Smith, the preeminent source of interpretation of the Gospels for many of his followers is James E. Talmage's *Jesus the Christ,* published in 1915.[35] Talmage's work is like a "life of Jesus," prominent in Victorian England, and his reading of the so-called "little apocalypses" in the synoptic Gospels reflects similar harmonizing sensibilities: Matthew's version as given in the Authorized Version (KJV) is the base of his reading while information in Mark and Luke and some use of the Joseph Smith Translation (JST) supplements it. In the end, Talmage's reading makes Jesus' eschatological chronology coherent with that of the LDS tradition as he understood it.

33. Jacob W. Olmstead, "Far West and Adam-ondi-Ahman," available at https://history.lds.org/article/doctrine-and-covenants-far-west?lang=eng. See the footnotes with this article for detailed citations. Rendered in Hebrew, Spring Hill is Tel Aviv.

34. Smith, *Doctrines of Salvation,* 3:13–14.

35. See James E. Talmage, *Jesus the Christ: A Study of the Messiah and His Mission According to Holy Scriptures Both Ancient and Modern* (Salt Lake City, UT: The Church of Jesus Christ of Latter-day Saints, 1915), Kindle ed., 450–65.

## Revelation

Modern scholars attribute Revelation to a single Christian leader known only as John, writing from Patmos to seven churches in Asia Minor, likely in the last decade of the first century CE. Internal evidence indicates that he knew the Old Testament well, wrote Greek poorly, and conveyed his vision as an apocalypse, which indicates he may have been a refugee from Palestine. His messages to the seven churches, as well as his interaction with the angel in Revelation 22:6–10, suggest a link with early Christian prophecy. In the wider Christian tradition, this figure was identified as John, son of Zebedee, brother of James and disciple of Jesus, or sometimes with an otherwise unknown figure called John the Elder, but this cannot be sustained.[36] According to the Book of Mormon, the author of Revelation is identified as John the disciple of Jesus, and conflated with the author of the Fourth Gospel (1 Ne. 14:18–27, Ether. 4:16, and D&C 77:1–2), an understanding that was common in the early nineteenth century.

Few texts have had a more dramatic influence on LDS thinking than Revelation.[37] It was a source of hope to early Latter-day Saints who suffered persecution at the hands of the state, gave insight into modern discipleship and church-state relationships and undergirded the community's apocalypticism—purposes that may be aligned in large part with the original audience of the text. Several sections of the Doctrine and Covenants refer to, or expand on Revelation, but Section 77 is probably the most well-known. In it, Joseph Smith recorded answers to questions that had arisen as part of his translation of the Bible or that were under debate by his followers, some of which differed from those in common circulation during his time.[38]

Although much of the apocalyptic intensity that characterized the earliest LDS leaders has not been sustained, Revelation still provides the community with salvation history in several ways. Modern scholars read Rev. 4:1–8:5 as a unit that introduces the Creator God who works through the Lamb to redeem the world. The seals themselves indicate that humans who seek the destruction of God's creation cannot find refuge, while those who die for their testimonies

36. Craig R. Koester, *Revelation: A New Translation with Introduction and Commentary* AB 38A (New Haven, CT: Yale University Press, 2014), 65–85.

37. In addition to its narrative power, Revelation is also the source of significant LDS proof texts such as the eschatological priesthood ("kings and priests," Rev. 1:5–6 KJV), the Great Apostasy (Rev. 2–3; 12) and the premortal War in Heaven (Rev. 12:7–12).

38. Andrew H. Hedges, "John's Revelation and the Restoration of the Gospel," in *Testimony of John the Beloved*, 84.

are safe under the heavenly altar.[39] Following Joseph Smith, however, many Latter-day Saints read the seals as a distinct section that illustrates thousand-year periods of the earth's history dating from Adam's expulsion from Eden (D&C 77:7). Thus, there remain many within the LDS community who identify themselves with the end of the sixth seal or the opening years of the seventh. This, however, is fraught because of the link between a reading of the seals as one thousand-year periods and creationism and has engendered a warm, and yet unresolved, debate among Latter-day Saints and their senior leaders.[40]

Second, Latter-day Saint readers also envision themselves within Revelation's plot line. They may understand themselves to have been participants in a protological battle with evil (Rev. 12:7–9; Isa. 14: 12–14; Moses 4:1–4), the War in Heaven, that continues until the Second Coming and gives context to their spiritual lives as the dragon turns against them once again (Rev. 12:17). Many also read themselves personally rather than corporately into the warnings and promises made to the seven churches, finding the motifs shared with LDS temple worship to be particularly significant (e.g., Rev 2:17; 3:12). Early LDS leaders identified the 144,000 of Revelation 7:3–4 with selected LDS males who will administer the gospel and "bring as many as will come to the church of the Firstborn," which is the designation of all who will be saved (D&C 77:11; Heb. 12:23; D&C 93:20–22). Joseph Smith indicated that the selection of these men was in progress and Wilford Woodruff suggested immanence by noting that the four angels associated with the winds had left heaven (Rev. 7:1).[41] Finally, the two olive trees and lampstands, which act as witnesses in Revelation 11:3–12, are often read by modern scholars as symbols of the corporate witnessing church.[42] Smith, however, understood them to be "two prophets that are to be raised up to the Jewish nation in the last days" (D&C 77:15). Following an approach taken by many interpreters of identifying these witnesses with one's own religious tradition or proclivities,[43] Bruce R. McConkie indicated that the two would be senior LDS leaders.[44]

39. Koester, *Revelation,* 350–435. The culmination of the destructive cycle is the question in Rev. 6:17, "who is able to stand" when God judges. This question is answered in Revelation 7 by the indication that it is those who "have washed their robes and made them white in the blood of the Lamb" (Rev. 7:14).

40. Dan Erickson, "Mormon Millennialism: The Literalist Legacy and Implications for the Year 2000," *Dialogue: A Journal of Mormon Thought* 30, no. 2 (1997): 1–32.

41. *History of the Church,* 6:196.

42. Koester, *Revelation,* 496–98.

43. Judith Kovacs and Christopher Rowland, *Revelation: The Apocalypse of Jesus Christ* (Malden, MA: Blackwell, 2004), 126–30.

44. Bruce R. McConkie, *Doctrinal New Testament Commentary* (Salt Lake City, UT: Bookcraft, 1973): 3:509.

Finally, most Latter-day Saints remain oriented toward a pre-millennial return of Christ, although ideas such as the Law of Consecration and the nature of Zion and the New Jerusalem, among which there are no poor (Moses 7:18), pull the worldview closer to post-millennialism. The Millennium is a literal, one-thousand-year period during which Christ rules a world free of evil.[45] Conditions during this period are described in utopian terms: no war (Isa. 2:4; 11:6–7), no untimely death (Isa. 65:20; D&C 101:31), and no temptation (Rev. 20:1–3; D&C 45:58). Those who enjoy this period are the righteous associated with the first resurrection (Rev. 20:5) and the righteous who are mortal at the Second Coming, although these may not all be LDS. Two efforts join the living and the resurrected: missionary work to convert non-LDS survivors of the destruction attending the Second Coming (Jer. 31:34),[46] and temple work, to identify and seal together families.[47] Daniel's notice that the kingdom would be given to the saints is interpreted literally (Dan. 7:22), so the governing role is assigned to a body known as the Council of Fifty,[48] a group that was organized for a number of years in Nauvoo and Utah.[49] Finally, the earth itself is to be "renewed and receive its paradisiacal glory," by which is meant a return to its status before the fall (AoF 1:10; Gen. 3:17–19). A second change, this time a new creation, follows the Millennium and the final destruction of evil (Rev. 20:7–10), yielding a world on which God dwells (Rev. 21:3; D&C 29:22–29; 88:19). While the Millennial reign with Christ was the goal of early Latter-day Saints, most modern members of the community are now focused on the life in the new heaven and earth,[50] a shift which probably follows from temple worship.

The LDS reception of apocalyptic literature is theologically rich and historically fascinating, providing as it does a window into nineteenth century American interest in the culmination of history. The motivations of the earliest LDS leaders were founded on their expectation that they and those they led were preparing for an immanent Second Coming. Their readings of apocalyptic literature took shape first in their hearts and minds and then in stone and timber as they built cities, temples, and families to welcome Israel's God for a literal Millennium. Now, at the end of the second century since Joseph

45. However, Brigham Young took a decidedly metaphorical stance, indicating that the Millennium would come when human hearts were united (Brigham Young, *Journal of Discourses,* 1:203).

46. McConkie, *Mormon Doctrine,* 498–99.

47. Lund, *Coming of the Lord,* 208–11.

48. Kenneth W. Godfrey, "Council of Fifty" in *Encyclopedia of Mormonism,* 326–27.

49. Matthew J. Grow and R. Eric Smith, eds., *The Council of Fifty: What the Records Reveal About Mormon History* (Provo, UT: Religious Studies Center, 2017).

50. Underwood, *Millenarian World,* 37–38.

Smith first announced that the eschaton was near, this rhetoric has been toned down. The focus is on personal righteousness, church service, and a spiritual gathering of Israel, a trend Latter-day Saints share with many other Christian communities. What a third century will bring remains hidden, as it perhaps should in a community with such deep spiritual roots in the great unveiling of God's plans and purposes.

# Contributors

Grant Adamson is senior lecturer in the Department of Religious Studies & Classics at the University of Arizona. He specializes in early Christianity and the ancient Mediterranean. His research on the Bible and Mormonism has been published in *Dialogue: A Journal of Mormon Thought* and *Journal of the Bible and Its Reception.*

Philip Barlow is a scholar at the Neal A. Maxwell Institute for Religious Scholarship at Brigham Young University. As author and editor on religion he has contemplated belief (*A Thoughtful Faith*), space and place (the *New Historical Atlas of Religion in America*, with Edwin Scott Gaustad), scripture (*Mormons and the Bible*; *Brief Theological Introductions to the Book of Mormon* (general editor, 12 volumes, with Spencer Fluhman), and the broader movement inaugurated by Joseph Smith (*Oxford Handbook of Mormonism*, co-edited with Terryl Givens).

Daniel Becerra is assistant professor of ancient scripture at Brigham Young University and is a scholar of early Christianity. His publications primarily concern moral formation in late ancient Christian ascetic contexts as well as topics relating to the theology and ethics in the Book of Mormon.

Stephen T. Betts is a PhD student in the Department of Religious Studies at the University of Virginia. His research interests include religion in modernity, religious experience, theories and methods in the study of religion, and early Mormonism.

Lincoln H. Blumell is professor of ancient scripture at Brigham Young University. He specializes in early Christianity and Greek and Coptic papyrology and epigraphy. He has published three books and more than seventy articles.

David Bokovoy holds a PhD in Hebrew Bible and the Ancient Near East. In addition to his work in Mormon studies, David has published articles on the Hebrew Bible in a variety of academic venues including the *Journal of Biblical Literature, Vetus Testamentum, Studies in the Bible and Antiquity*, and the *FARMS Review*. He is author of *Authoring the Old Testament: Genesis–Deuteronomy*.

David Calabro is visiting assistant professor of ancient scripture at Brigham Young University. His published work deals with the long-range cultural history of the Near East, including topics such as nonverbal communication, narrative, and sacred space. He also has an interest in Restoration scripture and the history of revealed pasts.

Jason Robert Combs is assistant professor of ancient scripture at Brigham Young University. Combs has published several academic articles on the literary and cultural contexts of canonical and apocryphal gospels, as well as the textual transmission of gospels. He is currently finishing his monograph on the development of Christian discourse surrounding dreams and visions in the second and third centuries CE.

Cory Crawford is associate professor in the Department of Classics and Religious Studies at Ohio University. His published work centers on the intersections of text, space, and visual culture in the Hebrew Bible and in the ancient Near East more broadly. He also has published on gender and history in the Bible and Mormonism. In 2014–2015, he held a Volkswagen Foundation Fellowship in Biblical Archaeology at the University of Tübingen, Germany.

Ryan Conrad Davis has a PhD in the Hebrew Bible and the Ancient Near East from the University of Texas at Austin. Ryan regularly teaches as Adjunct Instructor in the Ancient Scripture Department at Brigham Young University.

Luke Drake is assistant professor of classics in the Department of Comparative Arts and Letters at Brigham Young University. His research spans the New Testament and early Christian literature, with an interest in Jewish/Christian relations in Late Antiquity.

Amy Easton-Flake is associate professor of ancient scripture at Brigham Young University. Her current research focuses on nineteenth-century women's poetry and biblical hermeneutics, as well as how Latter-day Saints in the nineteenth century interpreted and used scripture. Her work may be found in the *New England Quarterly, Women's History Review, Symbiosis: A Journal of*

*Transatlantic Literary and Cultural Relations*, *American Journalism*, *BYU Studies Quarterly*, *Journal of Book of Mormon Studies*, and multiple edited volumes.

Eric A. Eliason is professor of English at Brigham Young University, where he teaches folklore and the Bible as literature. His publications include *Yet to Be Revealed: Open Questions in Latter-day Saint Theology* (with Terryl Givens); *Latter-day Lore: Mormon Folklore Studies* (with Tom Mould); *Mormons and Mormonism: An Introduction to an American World Religion*; and "Latter-day Saints (Mormons)" in de Gruyter's *Handbook of Biblical Reception in the Folklores of Africa, Asia, Oceania, and the Americas*. His Special Forces chaplain work in Afghanistan is featured in *Hammerhead Six*.



Deidre Nicole Green is assistant professor of Latter-day Saint/Mormon studies at the Graduate Theological Union. She is the author of *Works of Love in a World of Violence* and *Jacob: A Brief Theological Introduction*. She is also co-editor of *Latter-day Saint Perspectives on Atonement*, forthcoming from University of Illinois Press.

Matthew J. Grey is associate professor of ancient scripture and an affiliate faculty member of the Ancient Near Eastern Studies Program at Brigham Young University. Since 2011, he has been an excavation supervisor of the late Roman synagogue at Huqoq—an ancient Jewish village in Israel's Galilee region.

Carl Griffin has researched and published on early Christianity for over twenty years. He is a secondary educator and independent scholar. He is the author of *The Works of Cyrillona* and *Cyrillona: A Critical Study and Commentary*, both with Gorgias Press.

Grant Hardy is professor of history and religious studies at the University of North Carolina at Asheville. He is the author of several books, including *Understanding the Book of Mormon: A Reader's Guide*. He is the editor of *The Book of Mormon: A Reader's Edition* and *The Book of Mormon: Maxwell Institute Study Edition*. He is also the coeditor of the first volume of the *Oxford History of Historical Writing*.

Brian M. Hauglid is an emeritus professor of ancient scripture at Brigham Young University. He is co-editor, with Robin Scott Jensen, of *The Joseph Smith Papers, Revelations and Translations, Volume 4: The Book of Abraham and Related Manuscripts.* He has published in other scholarly venues, such as *Producing Ancient Scripture: Joseph Smith's Translation Projects in the Development of Mormon Christianity; Mormon Historical Studies;* and *Bible and Qur'an: Essays in Scriptural Intertextuality.*

Kristian S. Heal is a scholar specializing in early Syriac literature and the reception of the Old Testament in the early Syriac tradition. He is currently a Research Fellow at the Neal A. Maxwell Institute for Religious Scholarship at Brigham Young University.

Eric D. Huntsman is professor of ancient scripture specializing in New Testament Studies at Brigham Young University. He taught at the Brigham Young University Jerusalem Center from 2011 to 2012, coordinated the program in Ancient Near Eastern Studies from 2012 to 2020, and began a two-year appointment as the academic director of the Jerusalem program in 2022. His research and publications have focused on the New Testament passion and resurrection narratives and the Gospel of John.

Jason A. Kerr is associate professor of English at Brigham Young University, where he teaches early modern British literature. His scholarship attends to the intersections of literature, theology, and religious history in the later seventeenth century. He has written extensively about Milton's *De Doctrina Christiana,* and recent articles attend to women's preaching in 1640s London, kindness in *King Lear,* and Eve's church in *Paradise Lost.* He is currently working on a book about the political theology of consent in Richard Baxter's writings.

Jill Kirby is professor of religious studies and teaches biblical studies courses at Edgewood College in Madison, Wisconsin.

Jared W. Ludlow is professor of ancient scripture and ancient near eastern studies at Brigham Young University, where he has taught since 2006. Previously, he spent six years teaching religion and history at Brigham Young University—Hawaii. He also taught for two years at the Brigham Young University Jerusalem Center for Near Eastern Studies.

Taylor G. Petrey is associate professor of religion at Kalamazoo College. He is the author of *Resurrecting Parts: Early Christians on Desire, Reproduction, and Sexuality Difference* and *Tabernacles of Clay: Sexuality and Gender in Modern Mormonism*. He is the current editor of *Dialogue: A Journal of Mormon Thought.*

George A. Pierce is associate professor of ancient scripture at Brigham Young University. His research interests include cultural landscapes and historical geography, computer applications and spatial analysis in archeology, and the archeology of Israelite cult. He has excavated at several sites in Israel, the West Bank, the United Kingdom, and Florida, and is currently the Geographic Information Systems Architect for the excavations at Tel Shimron (Israel).

Dana M. Pike is professor emeritus of ancient scripture and ancient near eastern studies at Brigham Young University. He has worked as one of the international editors of the Dead Sea Scrolls.

David Rolph Seely is professor of ancient scripture at Brigham Young University where he teaches courses on Book of Mormon, Old and New Testament and ancient Near Eastern studies. He has published on the Dead Sea Scrolls, Solomon's Temple, and biblical and Book of Mormon studies.

Joseph M. Spencer is a philosopher and assistant professor of ancient scripture at Brigham Young University. He is the author of several books, the editor of the *Journal of Book of Mormon Studies*, and the associate director of the Latter-day Saint Theology Seminar.

Grant Underwood is professor of history and Richard L. Evans Chair of Religious Understanding at Brigham Young University. He is the author or editor of a number of books and articles pertaining to the Church of Jesus Christ of Latter-day Saints, including the first three volumes in *The Joseph Smith Papers: Documents Series*. His current book project is *Mormonism Among Christian Theologies*. He was founding co-director of the American Academy of Religion's "Mormon Studies" Group.

Thomas Wayment is professor of classics in the Department of Comparative Arts and Letters at Brigham Young University.

Miranda Wilcox is associate professor of English at Brigham Young University, where she teaches medieval literature. Her research focuses on intersections of religious and textual culture in early medieval Europe, especially England. She also writes about Latter-day Saint historical consciousness.

# INDEX